DEEPENING REFORM
FOR CHINA'S LONG-TERM
GROWTH AND DEVELOPMENT

Other titles in the China Update Book Series include:

DEEPENING REFORM
FOR CHINA'S LONG-TERM
GROWTH AND DEVELOPMENT

LIGANG SONG
ROSS GARNAUT
CAI FANG (eds)

Australian
National
University

PRESS

社 会 科 学 文 献 出 版 社
SOCIAL SCIENCES ACADEMIC PRESS(CHINA)

ANU PRESS

Published by ANU Press
The Australian National University
Canberra ACT 0200, Australia
Email: anuepress@anu.edu.au
This title is also available online at http://press.anu.edu.au

Title:	Deepening reform for China's long-term growth and development, Ligang Song, Ross Garnaut, Cai Fang.
ISBN:	9781925021769 (paperback)
Series:	China update series; 2014
Subjects:	International economic relations.
	Economic development--China.
	Australia--Foreign relations--China
	China--Foreign relations--Australia.
	China--Economic conditions.
	China--Commerce.
	China--Economic policy.

Other Authors/Contributors:
    Song, Ligang, editor.
    Garnaut, Ross, editor.
    Cai, Fang, editor.
Dewey Number: 337.951094

Book design and layout by Teresa Prowse, http://www.madebyfruitcup.com

Contents

Tables

Figures

Acknowledgments

The China Economy Program (CEP) at the Crawford School of Public Policy of The Australian National University (ANU) gratefully acknowledges the financial support for the *China Update 2014* provided by Rio Tinto through the Rio Tinto–ANU China Partnership. We thank Tim Lane for his support of and contributions to the Partnership activities. We also acknowledge the support and assistance provided by Elizabeth Buchanan, Yixiao Zhou, and our colleagues from the East Asia Forum at The Australian National University. The *China Update 2014* book is the fourteenth edition in the China Update book series. We sincerely thank our contributors around the world for their valuable contributions to the book series and the update events throughout these years. Thanks also go to ANU Press, especially Lorena Kanellopoulos, Beth Battrick, David Gardiner and the copyeditor, Jan Borrie, for their expeditious publication of the book series, and to Social Sciences Academic Press (China) in Beijing for translating and publishing the Chinese versions of the update book series to make the research work available to a wider readership in China.

Contributors

Alexander Ballantyne
International and Economic Research Departments, Reserve Bank of Australia, Sydney.

Robin Bordie
Rio Tinto Research, Rio Tinto, Shanghai.

Cai Fang
Institute of Population and Labor Economics, Chinese Academy of Social Sciences, Beijing.

Chunlai Chen
Crawford School of Public Policy, The Australian National University, Canberra.

Son Ngoc Chu
Crawford School of Public Policy, The Australian National University, Canberra.

Owen Freestone
International Economy Division of the Australian Treasury, Canberra.

Yingjie Feng
National School of Development, Peking University, Beijing.

Ross Garnaut
Professorial Research Fellow in Economics, University of Melbourne, Melbourne.

Xiang Gao
College of Comparative Law, China University of Political Science and Law, Beijing.

Xiumei Guo
Economics Department, School of Business, University of Western Australia, Perth.

Jonathan Hambur
International and Economic Research Departments, Reserve Bank of Australia, Sydney.

Dougal Horton
International Economy Division of the Australian Treasury, Canberra.

Yiping Huang
National School of Development, Peking University, Beijing.

Frank Jotzo
Crawford School of Public Policy, The Australian National University, Canberra.

Jane Kuang
Rio Tinto Energy, Rio Tinto, Brisbane.

Huiqin Jiang
College of Comparative Law, China University of Political Science and Law, Beijing.

Li Ran
National School of Development, Peking University, Beijing.

Lu Yang
Institute of Population and Labor
Economics, Chinese Academy of
Social Sciences, Beijing.

Guonan Ma
Monetary and Economic Department,
Bank for International Settlements
(BIS) Representative Office for Asia
and the Pacific, Hong Kong.

Ning Ma
Economics Department, School of
Business, University of Western
Australia, Perth.

Robert McCauley
Monetary and Economic Department,
Bank for International Settlements
(BIS), Hong Kong.

Xin Meng
Research School of Economics,
College of Business and Economics,
The Australian National University,
Canberra.

Ivan Roberts
International and Economic Research
Departments, Reserve Bank of
Australia, Sydney.

Ligang Song
Crawford School of Public Policy,
The Australian National University,
Canberra.

Tao Ran
School of Economics, Renmin
University, Beijing.

Fei Teng
Institute of Energy, Environment
and Economy, Tsinghua University,
Beijing.

Rod Tyers
Economics Department, School of
Business, University of Western
Australia, Perth.

Bijun Wang
Institute of World Economics and
Politics, Chinese Academy of Social
Science, Beijing.

Xiaolu Wang
National Economic Research
Institute, China Reform Foundation,
Beijing.

Stephen Wilson
Rio Tinto Energy, Rio Tinto,
Brisbane.

Woo Thye Woo
University of California, Davis;
Fudan University, Shanghai; Central
University of Finance and Economics,
Beijing; President, Jeffrey Cheah
Institute on Southeast Asia, Kuala
Lumpur.

Michelle Wright
International and Economic Research
Departments, Reserve Bank of
Australia, Sydney.

Harry X. Wu
Institute of Economic Research,
Hitotsubashi University, Tokyo.

Yanrui Wu
Economics Department, School of
Business, University of Western
Australia, Perth.

Yang Yao
National School of Development,
Peking University, Beijing.

Haiyang Zhang
Crawford School of Public Policy,
The Australian National University,
Canberra.

Ying Zhang
Economics Department, School of
Business, University of Western
Australia, Perth.

Yongsheng Zhang
Development Research Centre of the
State Council, Beijing.

Yixiao Zhou
Crawford School of Public Policy,
The Australian National University,
Canberra.

Abbreviations

ADB	Asian Development Bank
BBC	'basket, band and crawl'
CCP	Chinese Communist Party
CDs	certificates of deposit
CES	constant elasticity of substitution
CFETS	China Foreign Exchange Trade System
CFPS	Chinese Family Panel Studies
CGE	computable general equilibrium
CPI	consumer price index
CRC	China Railways Corporation
CSC	coefficient of structural change
CUI	catch-up index
ERC	Economic Research Centre
EU	European Union
EU NMS	EU new member states
FDI	foreign direct investment
GFC	Global Financial Crisis
GNI	gross national income
GNP	gross national product
GTEM	Global Trade and Environment Model
HREs	high-risk enterprises
HRS	Household Responsibility System
ICT	information and communications technology
IDIS	index of dissimilarity of industrial structures
IEA	International Energy Agency
IFC	international financial centre
1-IFC	first-tier international financial centre
IMF	International Monetary Fund
IP	intellectual property
IPC	International Patent Classification
IPRs	intellectual property rights
IVC	international vehicle currency
LAL	Land Administration Law
LCH	life-cycle hypothesis
LGIVs	local government investment vehicles
LP	labour productivity
LREs	low-risk enterprises
MEG	modern economic growth
MEPV	major episodes of political violence
MNEs	multinational enterprises

MOF	Ministry of Finance
MOFCOM	Ministry of Commerce
MOFTEC	Ministry of Foreign Trade and Economic Cooperation
MOOC	massive online open courses
MOR	Ministry of Railways
NBFIs	non-bank financial institutions
NBS	National Bureau of Statistics
NDF	non-deliverable forward
NDRC	National Development and Reform Commission
NPL	non-performing loan
OECD	Organisation for Economic Cooperation and Development
OLI	ownership-location-internalisation
PBC	People's Bank of China
PCT	Patent Cooperation Treaty
PGE	productivity growth effect
PM	particulate matter
PPF	production possibility frontier
PPP	purchasing power parity
QDII	Qualified Domestic Institutional Investor
QFII	Qualified Foreign Institutional Investor
QHD	Qinghuangdao
R&D	research and development
RBA	Reserve Bank of Australia
RCA	revealed comparative advantage
RCCs	rural credit cooperatives
repos	repurchase agreements
RMB	renminbi
ROA	returns on assets
RQFII	renminbi Qualified Foreign Institutional Investor
RRR	required rate of return
RUMiC	Rural Urban Migration in China survey
S&L	savings and loan
SAS	shadow-minus-actual spread
SASAC	State Asset Supervision and Administration Commission
SCE	standard coal equivalent
SCEs	state-controlled enterprises
SDR	special drawing rights
SE	share effect
SEZ	special economic zone
SFTZ	Shanghai Free Trade Zone
Shibor	Shanghai Interbank Offered Rate
SIPO	State Intellectual Property Office of the People's Republic of China
SMEs	small and medium enterprises

SOCBs	state-owned commercial banks
SOE	state-owned enterprise
SPC	State Planning Commission
SRA	State Railway Administration
TFP	total factor productivity
TFR	total fertility rate
TRIPS	Agreement on Trade-Related Aspects of Intellectual Property Rights
TVEs	township and village enterprises
TWI	trade weighted index
USPTO	US Patent and Trademark Office
VAT	value-added tax
VC	villagers' committee
VDR	variable deposit requirement
WIPO	World Intellectual Property Organisation
WTO	World Trade Organisation

Part I: New Model for Economic Growth

1. Reform and China's Long-Term Growth and Development

Ross Garnaut, Ligang Song and Cai Fang

Introduction

Reforms to build China's new model of economic growth have gained momentum since our mid 2013 book, *China: A New Model for Growth and Development*. This year's China Update book explores more deeply the new model of growth, through which China seeks to achieve the transition from a middle-income to an advanced economy. This book defines and discusses the reforms that are necessary to bring the new model into reality and to make it work. It describes many barriers that stand in the path to success, and the damaging consequences of failing to cross the barriers smoothly. It identifies opportunities for China to reconcile structural change with maintenance of strong growth in living standards.

In late 2013, a plenary meeting of the Chinese Communist Party's Central Committee authorised far-reaching extension of market-oriented reform. Premier Li Keqiang's *Work Report* to the National People's Congress in early 2014 outlined policies to deepen markets for capital, labour, goods and services and to accelerate progress towards the ultimate objectives of the new model: increasing the consumption and services shares of the economy; raising the relative incomes of poorer Chinese and especially rural residents and unskilled urban workers; and reducing the damage to the local and global natural environments from Chinese economic growth.

The old uninhibited investment expansion of the mid 1980s to 2011 moved China swiftly from a low-income country into the ranks of the middle-income economies. Whereas most Chinese in 1978 experienced material deprivation—living standards that placed most people in the poorer half of humanity—by 2011 a large majority was comfortably separated from shortages of the basic necessities of life and was enjoying more and more of the higher fruits of modern economic growth.

At the same time, a high proportion of the increase in incomes from rapid expansion of output within the old growth model was reinvested in new increments of investment-led growth. Large movements of workers from the countryside allowed sustained rapid expansion of the industrial and urban economies without commensurate increases in real wages. Increased incomes accrued disproportionately to state and private owners of capital, skewing the distribution of income away from ordinary people. The exceptionally investment-intensive character of growth and its concentration after the Asian financial crisis of 1997–98 on infrastructure and heavy industry made it unusually intensive in its use of energy and metals, and therefore a source of great pressure on the natural environment in China and the world.

Our introductory chapter to last year's book noted the considerable questioning of the old growth model from before the Global Financial Crisis (GFC) of 2008. Demographic transition interacted with continued strong growth in demand to make labour increasingly scarce and valuable from about 2005. China entered its turning period of economic growth, with increasing pressure for structural change—broken for a year or so by the contractionary impulse from the GFC of 2008. Preoccupation with overcoming the effects of the global economic slump on Chinese output, incomes and employment postponed the deepening of reform, and the fiscal and monetary stimulus of late 2008 through 2009 temporarily reinforced the old pattern of growth. The restoration of confidence in growth from 2010 established conditions for extending the discussion of reform and the early articulation of the new model of economic growth. Elements of the new model of growth were embodied in the Twelfth Five-Year Plan (2011–15).

The deepening of reform has proceeded more purposefully since 2012. New leaders of party and state have set out to accelerate, deepen and widen reform. Changes are evident in reforms of financial and labour markets, integration into the international economy, policy on the environmental effect of economic activity, fiscal interventions to reduce inequality in income distribution and action against corrupt high officials.

Some of the policy changes are already evident in the statistical record of economic performance. But in a big and diverse economy, some changes take much longer to leave clear marks. Economic growth has slowed as expected, from around 10 per cent per annum through the long floodtide of uninhibited investment expansion from 1992 to 2011, to a new normal of 7–8 per cent from 2012. The labour force has commenced what will be a long decline, but as yet there is little moderation of the high investment share of expenditure. Maintenance of high investment with lower growth in output suggests a considerable decline in the rate of increase in productivity. The decline in productivity has to be reversed through reform if the intended 7–8 per cent growth rate is to be sustained and Chinese expectations met. Domestic demand has increased as it was meant to do, but relatively little of that has come from expanded consumption. Wages and rural incomes have been rising rapidly, with some but so far only a small effect on the general measures of inequality. The growth in environmentally damaging emissions has slowed markedly, with targets for reductions in energy intensity and emissions intensity being met. The daunting scale of the remaining environmental challenge and early success have led to articulation in 2014 of more ambitious goals for raising the contributions of low-emissions sources of energy and reducing coal use.

Now that China has made the transition from a poor to an upper-middle-income country, major reform and structural change are necessary for it to sustain growth and enter the ranks of the developed countries. Reform is required in financial, labour and land markets, in systems of public finance and in China's relations with the international economy. This book takes the reader through recent progress in reform and structural change and associated modifications to performance in the economy as a whole and many of its sectors. It draws attention to the detail of the great challenges facing China as the Government seeks to give substance to the new model of economic growth. The reforms are technically complex and make huge demands on the knowledge and judgment of advisers to government and the skill and political capacities of leaders. They carry risks to economic stability—which, if crystallised in poor economic performance, would introduce risks to political stability.

Many other countries have stumbled at the transition from middle-income to developed-country status. Chinese reform and modern economic growth over the past three and a half decades have been brilliantly successful and China has many advantages in negotiating the next steps, but the task is so large that it would be unwise to presume a smooth transition to the status of an advanced economy.

This volume presents the challenges with unique insights from recent research by economists and some analysts from other disciplines who are following closely progress in the new era of Chinese reform. The following chapters describe advantages that China brings to this difficult stage of reform and growth, and some weaknesses that introduce risks of stumbles and falls. The reader will find indications both of early success and of emerging problems.

But first let us see how the reform era and the new challenge of transition to a developed economy fit into longer Chinese economic history.

The reform era in longer perspective

We only understand the significance of the past three and a half decades of market-oriented reform, deepening integration into the world economy and economic expansion if we compare it with the decades and centuries that went before it.

Ancient China was one of the early centres of world civilisation. Two thousand years ago, Han China, with its capital at Chang'an (now the city of Xian), was about as extensive, populous, technologically advanced and economically productive as its contemporary at the other end of Eurasia, the Roman Empire. The Han Dynasty, which lasted more than four centuries, turned out to be more successful politically than Rome, coming back together more completely after internal and external shocks broke it apart from time to time. Peace and political coherence were conducive to gradual and slow technological advancement, with population expansion absorbing the periodic episodes of increased production so that incomes per person did not increase much on a sustainable basis. This was the way of the traditional world—of global civilisation until the late eighteenth century. Ancient China contributed more than its share of technological, commercial and managerial innovation to what became the foundations of modern economic growth, but did not itself break through into sustained growth in productivity.

From 1700 to 1820, China's growth in output increased by an average of 0.85 per cent per annum. Any tendency for output and consumption per person to rise was overwhelmed by population growth. Population increased at the same average rate as output and production per person increased not at all.

What happened in China in these years was usual in the ancient world during periods of peace and prosperity. The unusual development in the late eighteenth century was in an offshore island at the western extremity of Eurasia. Sustained increases in output were established in Britain, at a pace that allowed increases in output per person as well as an increase in population. To the surprise of the early economists, higher living standards of ordinary people led eventually to a decline in fertility and population growth, so that the increase in living standards could be maintained and continuously extended. We can now recognise these developments as the beginnings of modern economic growth.

From 1820, revolution in France and the uprooting of the established order in continental Europe through the revolutionary and Napoleonic wars allowed modern economic growth to extend its presence through much of Western Europe. From 1820 to 1952—a period encompassing mostly peaceful expansion to 1914 and then the long period of war and dislocation until 1945—Europe's output grew by 1.71 per cent per annum, and output per person by 1.03

per cent. China, like most of the rest of the world at this time, stayed outside modern economic growth, with output increasing at an annual average rate of only 0.22 per cent, and output per person declining by 0.08 per cent per annum.

Small differences in growth rates compounded over more than a century add up to huge differences in economic size and strategic weight. China's share in global economic output fell from one-third to less than 5 per cent between 1820 and 1952.

China met many of the preconditions for participating in modern economic growth from the time it took root in Western Europe. There is a sense in which China was a latecomer to modern economic growth because its pre-modern system of political, social and economic organisation had been so successful. To embrace modern economic growth was to embrace disruptive change. China and other successful, established polities of East Asia embraced this disruption only when it was clear that the alternative was disruption through harassment and perhaps through conquest by others whose strategic weight had been enhanced by economic growth. Japan's political elite came to a coherent and lasting view that the disruption of modern economic growth was less damaging than the disruption of foreign interference in the third quarter of the nineteenth century—three-quarters of a century before China's political elite settled at a similar point.

China unambiguously embraced the change that was a necessary companion of modern economic growth with the establishment of the People's Republic of China in 1949. The historical circumstances of the Chinese Communist Party's accession to power caused it to take a path into modern economic growth that turned out to be a dead end. China adopted central planning on the Soviet model. The rate of increase in output as conventionally measured increased sharply, mainly as a result of a huge increase in the share of output allocated to investment—growth in output of about 6 per cent per annum by some measures from 1949 to 1978, although the nature of the growth made this statistic an unhelpful measure of economic progress. The increase in output was focused overwhelmingly in capital investment in the industrial sector, especially heavy industry. The absence of market discipline in allocation of resources and the tiny scale of international exchange meant there was little increase in productivity or in the standard of living of the Chinese people. The gaps in technology and standards of living between China and the most successful countries continued to grow wider.

All of that changed with market-oriented reform and opening to the outside world in 1978. Garnaut et al. (2013) describe the early concentration of economic dynamism in the rural economy until 1984; the awkward but in the end decisive reform of the urban economy including the central planning system from 1985; and the long period of uninhibited investment expansion from 1992. The massive fiscal and monetary expansions through state-related entities to sustain growth in the aftermaths of the Asian financial crisis (1997–98) and the GFC of 2008 made growth even more investment intensive and oriented even more strongly towards heavy industry and infrastructure from early in the twenty-first century.

The reforms transformed China's economic life. The transformation of rural China was swift, with the household responsibility system replacing the people's communes, and with a dynamic rural economy based on township and village enterprises (TVEs) emerging from the ruins of the people's communes. Decentralisation gave local governments a decisive role in economic life. Integration into the international economy gathered pace from the mid 1980s, making China in the early twenty-first century by far the largest manufacturer, exporter, trading economy, source of savings and creditor at the same time as it was a massive destination for foreign direct investment (FDI). The World Bank estimates that China will be the world's largest economy by 2015 on a purchasing power parity (PPP) basis (Cai 2014; Financial Times 2014).

Diverse patterns of business ownership emerged, requiring complex institutional innovation to ensure effective regulation with the expansion of the market economy. Living standards rose rapidly, with most Chinese coming to enjoy considerable material comfort. The largest migration in human history from the Chinese countryside swelled the resident populations of the cities.

The reforming economy grew rapidly—with increases in the labour supply, increased proportions in the urban economy and high and rising investment shares, but also rapid productivity growth. The pace of economic growth in China over an extended period was unprecedented. By 1995, China had achieved per capita output of $2000 on a PPP basis (1990 Geary Khamis dollars). Over the next 16 years, it increased output fourfold to $8000 (same 1990 dollars)—crossing the ground between these two landmark production levels in less time than any other country had ever done (Table 1.1). It had taken the old developed countries about a century to move from $2000 to $8000. The only near comparators to China were its neighbours in East Asia, Korea (20 years) and Japan (17 years).

Table 1.1 Quadrupling Living Standards from a Base of $2000 PPP GDP Per Capita

Modern country	Year achieved $2000 GDP per capita	Year achieved $8000 GDP per capita	Number of years to quadruple GDP per capita	Compound annual growth rate in period
Netherlands	1827	1960	133	1.0
United Kingdom	1839	1957	118	1.2
Australia	1848	1955	107	1.3
United States	1860	1941	81	1.7
France	1869	1962	93	1.5
Germany	1874	1962	88	1.6
Mexico	1950	2008	58	2.4
Hong Kong	1950	1977	27	5.3
Singapore	1950	1979	29	4.9
Japan	1951	1968	17	8.5
Turkey	1955	2007	52	2.7
Taiwan	1965	1985	20	7.2
South Korea	1969	1989	20	7.2
Malaysia	1969	2002	33	4.3
Thailand	1976	2005	29	4.9
China	1995	2011	16	9.1
Memo item				
World	1950	2004	54	2.6

Source: Table 5.1 from McKay and Song (2013).

Slowdown of the economy and new sources of future growth

The period of uninhibited investment-led growth within the reform era to 2011 brought great benefits to China and its people. As discussed by Garnaut et al. (2013), some elements of the old model of growth were gradually undermined by its own success—for example, the growing labour scarcity and increases in real wages from about 2005 (Garnaut 2010; Cai 2014). The old model had side effects that became less acceptable to the Chinese people as their incomes rose—especially growing inequality in income distribution, unnecessarily slow increases in consumption and unnecessarily limited consumption choices, the increasing scale of official corruption and a decline in local and global environmental amenity. Other side effects threatened economic instability: the tendency towards export surpluses, real estate bubbles and unregulated growth of debt including amongst local governments.

Many of the problems that accumulated in the course of reform are not inherently associated with market-oriented development. Rather, they reflect the underdeveloped state of market institutions and regulation, especially in relation to factor markets and the environment.

The deepening of reform within the new model of economic growth is directed towards the maturation of the market economy, through transition to a modern economy. The urgency of this reform is heightened by the movement from increase to decline in the labour force, as a share of the population absolutely. This loss of a 'demographic dividend' makes increases in productivity through more efficient allocation of resources critical to maintaining growth in living standards.

The new model of economic growth envisages a slower rate of capital accumulation. This also increases the importance of an increase in total factor productivity (TFP)—and makes it more difficult, as more productive technology tends to be embodied in a newer capital stock.

Some slowing of economic growth is inevitable. The question is whether the slowing is a moderate 2–3 per cent per annum, reflecting declining labour and more slowly growing capital stocks partially offset by higher productivity, or something much larger, reflecting a decline in productivity growth as well. At the extreme, the latter would threaten entanglement in the 'middle-income trap'.

Wang et al. (2010) note that average rates of growth in GDP per capita are considerably lower in the decade after than the decade before a country reaches US$7000 (PPP on 1990 Geary Khamis dollars). Maddison's (2006) data show that 31 of 40 economies that reached US$7000 experienced such a deceleration. The average growth rate was 2.8 percentage points less in the following decade.

China reached this inflexion point in 2008—the year of the GFC—which saw a permanently slower rate of increase in demand for China's exports in the developed countries, and added to downward pressures on Chinese growth potential. The massive fiscal and monetary expansion in China after the GFC was successful in sustaining employment and income growth, but for a while obscured the need for more fundamental productivity-raising reform (Cai 2012). Acceptance of slower growth must now be part of the implementation of the new model of growth.

The content of reform for the new model of growth

A kind of consensus has been established across a powerful part of the Chinese leadership on a wide range of reforms to implement the new model of economic growth. The accepted directions of reform embrace readjustment of the role of government in resource allocation.

The reform agenda is comprehensive as the Chinese leadership seeks to sustain growth following the disappearance of the demographic dividend and the expected decline in the rate of growth of the capital stock.

A number of measures focus on augmentation and improvement in quality of the labour supply. The Government has announced its intention to ease the one-child policy. Policies are directed at turning migrants from rural areas into permanent residents of the cities, so as to increase their number and to allow more complete use of the skills they accumulate in their early years in town (Song et al. 2010). Improved education, especially for children of rural residents and migrants, would increase the quality of the labour force.

Labour market reforms are closely linked to reforms of social security and provision of health and education services. These are important in reducing inequality in income distribution.

Other reforms focus on improved regulation of financial markets, with a view to achieving more efficient allocation of capital and to reduce risks of financial crisis. These are closely related to institutional reforms to facilitate expansion of the private sector and more productive use of resources by state-owned enterprises (SOEs). Local government finances need to be subject to more stringent fiscal discipline to avoid excessive credit expansion and rising debt leading to financial instability. The development of effective land markets is necessary for economic efficiency and to ease tensions in relations between peasants and the state.

There is an extensive agenda related to improving the legal system and market regulation of all kinds underlying the reform of factor markets. This is a subtle process of institutional change and development that in its nature must proceed at a measured pace (Perkins 2013).

One of the guiding ideas of Chinese reform is that the transformation from a centrally planned to a market economy can't be achieved in one leap. The caution embodied in that idea has been important to China's economic success in the reform area and will continue to be influential. The Chinese Government continues to see China as in transition to a market economy, with government continuing to have an important role in filling gaps left by the underdevelopment or imperfection of markets. More fundamentally, there is no retreat from established views on the continuing roles of SOEs in the provision of a wide range of infrastructure services, heavy industry and financial services.

The continued large role of the state in business and the use of administrative in place of market regulation are problems for the efficient operation of some markets. In the new phase of economic development, the continued large role of the state hampers the emergence of the higher productivity that is necessary to sustain reasonably strong growth. Naturally there is resistance to far-reaching reduction of the role of the state, arising from private gains for private agents exercising state power. This is currently the source of tension around reform efforts.

Whether China is successful in its drive from $8000 per capita (1990 PPP) towards the global frontiers of productivity and income depends on the deepening of reform within the new model of economic growth. China's success in building a modern economy is at stake. The current leadership has demonstrated commitment to strong action in many areas. Inevitably, reform challenges powerful private interests, which are inevitably damaged by new systems of resource allocation. The associated political tensions are considerable, and one cannot be certain of the outcome in advance of success.

The deepening of reform in the financial sector carries the possibility of a temporary disruption of growth, as risky practices are brought within the ambit of prudential supervision. Disruption leading to markedly slower growth of output, employment and incomes even for a short period would give rise to pressures to move more slowly with reform, and to resume the expansion of funding through the old state channels. Acceding to these pressures would cut across the reform program and reduce the chances of China emerging in a decade or so as a successful modern economy.

Other chapters of the book describe in detail various aspects of China's deepening of reform within the new model of economic growth.

Structure of the book

The book has five parts with 21 chapters. Part I discusses the way in which the big forces determining the rate of economic growth will interact to determine whether China continues to grow towards the status of an advanced economy. Part II looks at how the higher priority for domestic and global environmental amenity is affecting some important dimensions of development. Part III looks closely at various dimensions of financial sector reform—the most consequential, complex and risky of the reforms that are necessary to implement the new model of growth. Part IV focuses on factor market reform beyond the financial sector: land and labour markets and the role of FDI. Part V concludes with five chapters examining important determinants of productivity growth.

The seven chapters in Part I of the book fill out our understanding of various dimensions of China's new model of economic growth. They range over the relationships between output growth and changes in the labour force, income distribution, business ownership and investment; and the traps in the path of short-term and long-term growth that can only be avoided with reform.

Lu Yang and Cai Fang in Chapter 2 explain how China enjoyed a 'demographic dividend' in the early decades of reform, which has now disappeared and has begun to operate in reverse as the labour force shrinks. Continued strong growth requires replacement of the demographic dividend with a 'reform dividend'. The authors use simulations of various policy-induced demographic changes within a growth accounting framework to show that changes in population and labour market policies can make a significant difference. Increased TFP derived from reform is essential for maintaining reasonably strong growth. Increasing the labour force participation rate helps short-term but not long-term growth. Lifting TFP is critical to long-term growth. That means China's economic growth will increasingly depend on improvement of TFP rather than increasing inputs of factors of production.

Lu and Cai show formally how improving human capital through training of people who are already in the labour force can have powerfully positive effects on growth. Combinations of policies to increase the quantity and quality of the labour force and lift productivity can be important. Major policy implications from the chapter include the following: the transition from the 'selective two-child policy' to a 'two-child policy' should be made as soon as possible to increase the total fertility rate; reform to improve the operation of markets including through the creation of a more equal and competitive environment is essential to achieving the necessary lift in the productivity growth rate; there would be a large growth pay-off from expanding the urban residence rights of migrant workers through reforming the household registration system; and priority should be given to training programs for employees as instruments for lifting rates of innovation and productivity growth.

Xiaolu Wang and Yixiao Zhou in Chapter 3 examine the imbalances in the Chinese economy associated with an exceptionally low and until recently falling consumption share of expenditure. Massive investment has caused the rapid expansion of production capacity, while consumption growth cannot keep up with the expansion of capital investment and production capacity, resulting in a sustained lack of domestic demand and excess capacity in many areas of production. They see the weak consumer demand coming from highly and until recently increasingly inequitable distribution of income. The unbalanced distribution of income has many causes, including the underdeveloped nature of labour protection, social security and public welfare systems; the strength of business monopolies with privileged access to resources and control of markets; the competitive disadvantages suffered by labour-intensive small and medium-sized enterprises; and the large and increasing scale of improper use of public funds and corruption, made possible by the loopholes in the Government's financial and resources management systems and by weaknesses in regulatory and legal institutions and pervasive low transparency and lack of supervision in financial transactions.

The authors link the declining consumption rate until recently and the continuing low rate with over-reliance on foreign markets before the GFC in 2008–09 and on heavily expansionary fiscal and monetary policies since then. They argue that neither the over-reliance on export nor the over-reliance on fiscal and monetary expansion is sustainable in the long run. The necessary raising of consumption requires measures to improve income distribution and fairness in society. The relationship between equity and sustained economic growth is not contradictory but complementary.

Son Ngoc Chu and Ligang Song in Chapter 4 discuss the relationship between state control, entrepreneurship and resource allocation. The authors examine changes in institutions governing the availability of capital, land, energy and utilities across different ownership types. State control of capital, land and resources has created substantial rents that have been used to promote infrastructure projects and provision of public good. This has sometimes contributed to rapid economic growth. It has also supported rent-seeking activities by governments and enterprises. Competition for rents has encouraged the emergence of overcapacity in some sectors, and has set back the development of private entrepreneurship. In the most recent period, with more competitive product markets, the negative effects of state intervention in factor markets on the performance of the private sector have been larger. Nevertheless, there has been robust development of private entrepreneurship over the reform period as a whole. Reducing state control of key resources would further expand that development, with beneficial effects on productivity and economic growth.

China's investment share of GDP is exceptionally high, even compared with other East Asian economies at a similar stage of development. Owen Freestone and Dougal Horton in Chapter 5 document the likely causes of China's high rates of investment and discuss how the deepening of market-oriented reforms might reduce investment and boost household consumption. They argue that government policies have contributed substantially to excessive investment in recent years. Asian economies that preceded China's movement from middle-income towards advanced status experienced a fall of about 10 percentage points in the investment share of GDP through the transition. Using that as a guide, the authors apply a computable general equilibrium model of the world and Chinese economies to examine the effects of a 10 percentage point reduction in China's investment share of GDP (and a commensurate rise in household consumption) over a 10-year period. They conclude that this could be achieved without disruption of growth in the context of simultaneous reforms to lift the rate of growth in TFP. The rebalancing from investment to private consumption with a productivity boost would lead to reduced demand for the output of industries producing inputs into investment and increased spending on services, and to a small decrease in exports and increase in imports.

There has been much discussion in China over the past few years of countries reaching middle-income status and failing to move into the ranks of developed countries—the phenomenon of the 'middle-income trap'. Yingjie Feng and Yang Yao in Chapter 6 confirm the existence of a middle-income trap by analysing the experience of many countries which have attained middle-income status. The analysis shows that the middle-income countries which have succeeded in the transition to high-income status generally share high saving rates, large and dynamic manufacturing sectors, high levels of education, favourable demographic structures (high ratios of working-age people to dependants), political stability and relatively equal income distribution. China has most of these characteristics—but not equity in income distribution. They conclude that China still has great potential for growth, but requires effective policies to achieve more equitable income distribution. China should pay particular attention to increasing education for rural youth and training for migrant workers. The financing of education is currently principally a local responsibility. Greater benefits flow from investment in human capital than in physical infrastructure, so China's Central Government should shift its financial support for local government from infrastructure construction to education.

China's size and the slow growth of its trading partners now limit its capacity to grow rapidly through increasing exports of labour-intensive manufactures. Growth must rely more heavily on increases in domestic demand. Rod Tyers and Ying Zhang in Chapter 7 point out that domestic demand has increased since the GFC through fiscal expansion and public investment. Provincial indebtedness will constrain these sources of demand expansion in future. China's Government has sought inward-oriented growth through reform of industrial policy, trade policy, landownership laws, the one-child policy, fiscal federalism and taxation, financial market regulation, urbanisation (*hukou*) and capital account liberalisation. Change can be expected to have slight effects on short-term growth performance for most of these reforms. The exceptions are changes in industrial structure and liberalisation of the capital account.

To analyse the effects of reforms on short-term performance, Tyers and Zhang apply an economy-wide model that takes explicit account of oligopolistic behaviour in 17 industrial and service sectors. The model makes it possible to examine the interactions between industrial reform, regulatory policy and liberalisation of the capital account. The results suggest that further fiscal expansion could not contribute the major share of growth in future, even with large public investment components. Industrial reform in heavy manufacturing and services has considerable potential, reducing costs and fostering growth in output, private consumption and modern-sector employment. The effects of capital and financial account liberalisation are less certain and could be negative depending on whether demand for foreign assets is currently constrained by controls on outward movement of capital.

Part II focuses on aspects of the new objective of reconciling economic growth with conservation of the natural environment.

Yongsheng Zhang in Chapter 8 investigates how a focus on environmental amenity can accelerate development in poor areas. He first discusses the issue in a Chinese context, and then comments on its significance for poorer developing countries. Traditional development views saw poor regions encountering large obstacles to development in geographic remoteness, inaccessibility, small markets and weak endowments of resources, capital, talents and technology. Two big changes have greatly diminished these disadvantages. First, poor regions, thanks to the disadvantage of underdevelopment, retained beautiful natural and cultural characteristics, which today are rare and are an asset for development. Second, technological change has reduced the cost of transport and communications to distant places, the Internet has reduced many educational and business disadvantages of distance from the main centres of activity, and has reduced the cost of decentralised power using renewable energy. Zhang suggests that poor regions which take a different path to development will find that industries based on the high quality of the environment have considerable value.

Frank Jotzo and Fei Teng in Chapter 9 provide an update on China's greenhouse gas emissions and progress towards its 2020 emissions intensity target. The authors point out that the relatively high share of economic activity in investment and heavy industries, the rapid expansion of domestic infrastructure as well as exports and the relatively low energy efficiency in many (though not all) industries and processes have lifted Chinese energy intensity and emissions intensity to unusual heights. At the same time, they provide great potential for further reduction of China's emissions intensity. The relatively high emissions intensity of China's energy supply—around 20 per cent above US and global levels, and 36 per cent above the average EU level—is primarily due to the dominance of coal. It is a Chinese policy objective to reduce the share of coal in energy supply. There has been early progress, but a big task lies ahead.

The policy impetus to clean up the energy sector in China derives not only from climate change objectives, but also increasingly—and perhaps largely—from the desire to reduce urban air pollution. This means stemming the increase in coal use through continued improvements in energy efficiency and substitution away from coal in the energy mix. The Chinese Government has stated its intention to place greater emphasis on market mechanisms in climate change policy as well as other areas. Pilot emissions trading schemes are under way, though the real test is whether they lead to a national scheme of carbon pricing—and, if so, whether it will be effective. For pricing mechanisms to work effectively in creating incentives to cut energy use and emissions, China's energy markets need more market-oriented reform.

Part III digs deeply into the urgent, important but complex and potentially destabilising area of financial reform. The four chapters focus on widely disparate questions that together provide a strong sense of the challenge ahead.

Yiping Huang, Li Ran and Bijun Wang in Chapter 10 examine how the Chinese financial sector evolved in the reform era to where it is today, assess its achievements and then explain the reasons the authorities have now decided to accelerate financial reforms. There are three reasons the status quo is no longer an option: 1) whereas financial repression once had positive effects on growth, these are now negative; 2) financial repression is contributing increasingly to risks of financial and macro-economic instability; and 3) many of the policy restrictions are being corroded by the evolution of the economy, and a new regulatory framework is required for the emerging financial system. The authorities' reform program has 11 elements, including: opening to foreign and private financial institutions; developing multi-layered capital markets; building inclusive financial institutions; establishing market-based interest rates, exchange rates and risk-free yield curves; achieving capital account convertibility; and improving financial regulations. The central motivation of these reforms is to complete the transition to a market system in the financial sector. There are two broad emphases: in the near term, interest rate liberalisation; and over time, currency internationalisation, including capital account convertibility.

The authors caution that financial liberalisation is tricky: it improves the efficiency of capital allocation but also raises financial volatility. The key to avoiding major financial instability in the wake of liberalisation is to make sure the preconditions for reform are in place, and to undertake reforms in the right sequence. Financial crisis is a virtual certainty if the capital account is opened up before the strengthening through reform of commercial banks and other financial institutions and before elimination of misalignment of interest rates. It is important to accelerate financial liberalisation, but essential to go about it in the right way.

Alexander Ballantyne, Jonathan Hambur, Ivan Roberts and Michelle Wright in Chapter 11 point out that the financial architecture currently in place in China shares some characteristics with Australia's financial system prior to deregulation in the late 1970s and early 1980s. This chapter goes through the Australian story in great detail, not to prescribe Australian choices for China, but for Chinese economists and policymakers to have available to them lessons from the experience of a country whose financial system has much in common with China's at this stage of development. It notes aspects of the sequencing of Australia's financial reform that depart from the prescriptions in the economics literature. The chapter stresses the interdependence between financial reform and financial deepening. The authors' discussion of Australia's historical experience with financial reform extends to the contribution of financial deregulation to the inflationary boom of the late 1980s and the subsequent deep recession of 1990–91. The authors then turn to the case of China, covering banking system and interest rate reform in the 1980s, capital controls and the exchange rate in the 1980s, growth of financial markets and banking sector fragility in the 1990s, steps towards interest rate deregulation in the late 1990s and early 2000s and the currency regime and capital controls in the 1990s. The chapter then discusses China's evolving financial reform agenda.

The authors conclude that the sequencing of Australian deregulation might not be optimal for China. In some ways, China is now more advanced in institutional development than Australia was in the late 1970s—for example, with its hedging markets and prudential framework. Broadly speaking, the Australian experience suggests that reform creates its own momentum. Domestic financial deregulation creates additional channels for capital flows, making capital controls less effective and creating pressure for their removal. Capital account liberalisation may increase the need for broader financial sector reforms to manage the increased capital flows. Reform has risks and the stakes are undoubtedly higher for China today than they were for Australia in the early 1980s.

Guonan Ma and Robert McCauley in Chapter 12 compare the financial sectors and reform needs and programs of China and India. Their comparisons show the Indian financial sector is more open than China's; that opening of the capital accounts in both countries has a long way to go; and that both countries would experience pressure from large inward capital flows in the event of full capital opening. The authors caution that Chinese policymakers need to take into account the risks of such dynamics and volatility on the journey to capital account liberalisation.

The authors note the possibility that short-term net inflows could be followed by medium-term net outflows. Initially large inward portfolio and banking flows could interact in unpredictable ways with and exacerbate existing imbalances in the domestic financial system. Financial imbalances and vulnerability may then trigger capital outflows in a more liberal environment. Policymakers need to be concerned not only about the immediate money-market yield differential, and its relation to exchange rate volatility, but also the unpredictable outcome of the contemporary surge of credit in China. These considerations do not argue against incremental capital opening, but rather for keeping a strong measurement system in place so that the authorities do not find themselves flying blind.

In Chapter 13, Wing Thye Woo points out that China has now reached the stage of development at which fundamental financial sector changes are necessary to avoid falling into the middle-income trap. Woo discusses at length the profound and deeply damaging financial sector problems of the developed countries, which China has an opportunity to learn from and to avoid. Lessons from the unhappy experience of the developed countries should be applied taking China's circumstances into account. It is important not only to prevent financial failures with effective monitoring and appropriate regulation, but also to possess financial firefighting ability to put out inevitable financial sector fires. Risk management and supervision are central to successful financial deregulation.

Part IV covers reform in the land, labour and FDI markets in three chapters.

Since the early 2000s, land-related issues have been prominent sources of social tension as rapid urbanisation and industrialisation increase demand for changes in land use without mechanisms being made available to smoothly transfer land from less to more valuable uses. Chapter 14 by Tao Ran discusses the land question in relation to China's urbanisation and growth. Under the current land requisition system, rapid urban growth has led to tens of millions of farmers being dispossessed with inadequate compensation. Under the current rural land management system, farmers are not allowed by law to develop their own land for non-agricultural purposes. Tao discusses the economic and social distortions resulting from China's land management system, including the imbalance between urbanisation of population and availability of land, wasteful use of industrial land and real estate bubbles, and the role of real estate investment in the accumulation of local debt after 2008. He notes that current arrangements make the provision of affordable housing with decent living conditions extremely difficult.

Tao proposes a new model of urbanisation with coordinated reforms focusing on land. To remove the distortions in urbanisation and help China to complete its great economic transformation, the Government must carry out fundamental land reforms, which, among other things, set up a rental property market focusing on the requirements of the 200 million rural migrants who already choose to live and work in cities. This could be done by redeveloping urban/suburban villages so local farmers in these villages can legally build rental housing for migrants. Government can also levy rental income tax and, in the long run, a property tax to finance urban public services such as education for the children of migrants. To make up for the potential revenue shortfall from these measures, local government could also convert some industrial land for residential and commercial construction and levy a tax on land value appreciation from such conversion. Only by implementing real land reform and coordinating the land reform with reforms to *hukou* and local public finance can the unsustainable model of urbanisation be rectified. Tao argues that the proposed land reform package may offer some hope of a successful transition to a more healthy urbanisation model.

Chinese economic development in the reform period involved high levels of movement of rural residents to urban employment while preventing most migrants from becoming full citizens of the cities to which they have come. Understanding the restrictions facing migrants helps policymakers to avoid future mistakes. Xin Meng in Chapter 15 discusses the effects of these restrictions, and how they now pose potential challenges to the continued progress of China's urbanisation and economic development. Meng argues that institutional restrictions, explicit or implicit, on rural–urban migration make a large contribution to the shortage of unskilled labour in cities, which has been driving up wages at a rate faster than productivity. Meng discusses the implications of the newly published *National New Urbanisation Plan 2014–2020*, the recent industrial upgrading policy for migrant workers, the potential for removal of restrictions on migrants' rights, to increase urban labour supply in quality as well as quantity, and the relationship of these labour market developments to China's future urbanisation and economic development. Meng concludes that the *National New Urbanisation Plan 2014–2020* is built on inadequate understanding of labour market realities. Current industrial upgrading policy may not provide favourable labour market conditions for those currently engaged in agricultural work and soon to be redundant in the agricultural sector.

Chunlai Chen in Chapter 16 presents the results of research on the impact of FDI on China's regional growth and development. By the end of 2013, China had attracted a total of US$1.4 trillion in FDI inflows, making it by far the largest FDI recipient in the developing world. This chapter investigates and identifies empirically how FDI has contributed to China's regional economic growth. The chapter finds that FDI has contributed to China's economic growth directly through capital augmentation and technological progress and indirectly through knowledge spillovers on the local economy. The contribution of FDI to economic growth is influenced by local economic and technological conditions. FDI has a stronger impact on economic growth through capital augmentation and technological progress in the developed provinces than in the less-developed provinces. While FDI has a positive and significant impact on economic growth through knowledge spillovers in the developed provinces, the positive knowledge spillovers of FDI on economic growth are absent in the less-developed provinces.

The differences in the contribution of FDI to economic growth across provinces deserve the attention of both policymakers and academic research. The problem is not that FDI causes a widening of the gap between the developed provinces and the less-developed provinces, but that FDI has played a much less significant role in the latter than it might have done. Policy should encourage FDI flows into the less-developed provinces. The achievement of the full potential of FDI requires investment in education and infrastructure. Policies on inter-regional migration and cross-regional investments are also important in reducing regional disparity in income and production. More generally, China should encourage contact, information exchange, production and technological cooperation, joint research and development (R&D) activities, industrial linkages and competition between domestic firms and FDI firms in order to enhance and accelerate technological progress and the diffusion of positive spillovers from FDI to its economy.

Part V has five chapters discussing various matters related to productivity growth and its contribution to China's transition to an advanced economy.

Harry X. Wu in Chapter 17 measures the industry-level productivity of the Chinese economy and relates it to the reform debate—specifically reform to reduce the role of the Government in business. Since the mid 2000s, there has been a resurgence of consolidated and enlarged SOEs in so-called 'strategic industries'. Increasing government intervention in resource allocation, especially following the GFC in 2008, has been a main focus of policy debate. Since government interventions are often made through industry-specific policies and related institutional arrangements, it is necessary to examine industry-level TFP performance of the Chinese economy. This study applies the Jorgenson–Griliches framework in growth accounting to a newly constructed industry-level data set for China, to examine the sources of growth in Chinese industry from 1980 to 2010.

The estimation results show that the TFP growth of China's industrial sector as a whole for the entire period is only 0.5 per cent per annum. Although semifinished and finished goods industries have maintained slow TFP growth in the past three decades, there has been persistent TFP decline in industries that produce material inputs including energy. Wu also shows that China's World

Trade Organisation (WTO) entry was not accompanied by a continuous TFP improvement as one might have expected. Annual TFP growth for all industry fell to 1.2 per cent in 2002–07 although Chinese industry experienced its fastest output growth in history—that is, 18.8 per cent compared with 12.5 per cent in 1992–2001. The declining productivity performance in this period could be caused by the resurgence of large state corporations and the greater involvement of local governments in resource allocation. This finding highlights the urgency and importance of the Government's new strategy for growth by lifting China's industrial TFP through deepened reforms.

Yanrui Wu, Ning Ma and Xiumei Guo in Chapter 18 examine the considerable regional variations in industrial development. Their study applies a shift-share analysis of productivity gaps in industrial sectors across Chinese regions and examines issues associated with growth and structural change in China's manufacturing sector. They find that while manufacturing output has grown much more rapidly in the coastal zone than the central and western zones over the longer term, the last two started to catch up in the second half of the new century's first decade under the influence of various government policies supporting economic development in these areas. About one-third of the country's 30 regions recorded a positive productivity gap (relative to the national average). Most of these are coastal regions. Regions with relatively large negative productivity gaps are mainly in western China. The findings confirm the importance of development policies specific to each province and region. There are gains to be reaped from focusing on productivity improvement in the central and western zones and on structural rationalisation and allocative efficiency in the coastal region. Over the past decade, the official focus on western development, the rise of the middle regions and the north-eastern reinvigoration programs made significant contributions to the reduction of inter-zone disparity. The experience of the past decade demonstrates the importance of the central and local governments working together to deal with inter-zone productivity inequality.

China's railway system is the third most extensive and the busiest (million traffic units per route-km) in the world, with by far the longest and most rapidly growing high-speed passenger capacity. Robin Bordie, Stephen Wilson and Jane Kuang in Chapter 19 describe the history, current challenges and discussion of reform of China's rail system. Recent institutional changes are momentous, with the dissolution of the Ministry of Railways in 2013 and the establishment of the China Railways Corporation (CRC). The reform of the rail sector is challenging, as it must balance demands for national security, economic efficiency, primary energy transport and social stability. The natural monopoly characteristics of the rail sector create vested interests in the large 'benefit and profit' chain that become centres of resistance to reform. The CRC must pay down debt while continuing to pursue an aggressive expansion of services. Private investment is sought, but discouraged by social obligations and related subsidies. Commercial stability requires increases in freight rates, but adjustments have to take account of competition from trucking fleets offering more flexible, including door-to-door, service. Service efficiency and quality must improve while the system remains the lowest-cost and most environmentally sustainable transport option over long distances. China is clearly in the early stages of the railway reform process. The authors compare China's railway system with other countries'. China, Russia and France, but not India, have moved away from the full ministry model. The tendency is towards private or mixed state and private ownership, and towards light regulation. As the authors point out, however, no two countries are exactly alike with respect to ownership and regulatory arrangements. The industry structure and regulation in each country reflect history, the stage of development and the general approach to public policy.

Haiyang Zhang in Chapter 20 provides some insights into whether and how Chinese patent laws and related institutions have stimulated research and development, and influenced technology transfer from advanced economies to China. The Chinese Patent Law has been strengthened step by step over time. The central and local governments as well as universities and companies have introduced strong incentives for the acquisition of intellectual property rights (IPRs). The number of patent applications and grants has increased rapidly in recent years. Zhang identifies a number of differences between domestic and foreign companies in taking up patents in China. At the international level, China has also increased its international patent applications under the Patent Cooperation Treaty (PCT), especially since the mid 2000s. China has surpassed Germany and ranked third in the world in the number of PCT applications at the end of 2013. Against the background of rising numbers of patent applications in China, Zhang cautions against seeing patents as equivalent to innovation, since innovation can occur outside patented technology and many patents are never used in industry—some are taken out to obtain government subsidies or intimidate competitors. Patents also vary greatly in technical and economic significance.

Xiang Gao and Huiqin Jiang in Chapter 21 provide a comprehensive overview of China's foreign investment laws. They cover the basic framework of China's foreign investment laws and policies, historical developments and current issues and challenges. Foreign investment laws in China have been gradually improved along with the progressive deepening of reform and internationalisation of the economy. There has been progressive widening of the areas, industries and corporate structures in which foreign investment is welcome. There has been progressive improvement of the approvals process and movement towards national treatment. China's joining of the WTO played a significant role in the development of China's foreign investment legislation; however, as pointed out by the authors, problems with China's foreign investment laws remain and they include too complex and uncoordinated foreign investment laws and regulations; the complicated and ambiguous foreign investment approval process; and lack of transparency. Thus, China has some distance to travel in order to make its foreign investment laws an integral part of a system of rule of law, which China is endeavouring to establish.

References

Cai, F. (2012), *Avoid 'the Middle Income Trap'*, Beijing: Social Sciences Academic Press.

Cai, F. (2014), *Demystifying the Economic Growth in Transitional China*, Beijing: Social Sciences Academic Press.

Financial Times (2014), 'China to overtake US as top economic power this year', *Financial Times*, 30 April.

Garnaut, R. (2010), 'The turning period in China's economic development: a conceptual framework and new empirical evidence', in R. Garnaut, J. Golley and L. Song (eds), *China: The Next Twenty Years of Reform and Development*, pp. 19–38, Canberra: ANU E Press, and Washington, DC: The Brookings Institution Press.

Garnaut, R., Cai, F. and Song, L. (2013), 'China's new strategy for long-term growth and development: imperatives and implications', in R. Garnaut, F. Cai and L. Song (eds), *China: A New Model for Growth and Development*, pp. 1–16, Canberra: ANU E Press.

McKay, H. and Song, L. (2013), 'China's industrialisation: path dependence and the transition to a new model', in R. Garnaut, F. Cai and L. Song (eds), *China: A New Model for Growth and Development*, pp. 75–96, Canberra: ANU E Press.

Maddison, A. (2006), *The World Economy: A Millennial Perspective*, Paris: Organisation for Economic Cooperation and Development.

Perkins, D. H. (2013), 'New institutions for a new development model', in R. Garnaut, F. Cai and L. Song (eds), *China: A New Model for Growth and Development*, pp. 17–34, Canberra: ANU E Press, and Beijing: China Social Sciences Academic Press.

Song, L., Wu, J. and Zhang, Y. (2010), 'Urbanisation of migrant workers and expansion of domestic demand', *Social Sciences in China* 31(3): 194–216.

Wang, Q., Zhang, S. and Ho, E. (2010), *The Chinese economy before 2020: not whether but how growth will decelerate*, 20 September, Morgan Stanley Research (Asia/Pacific).

2. China's Shift from the Demographic Dividend to the Reform Dividend

Lu Yang and Cai Fang

Introduction

'Demographic dividend' refers to the positive impact on economic growth that is generated by a relatively low and falling ratio of dependants to working-age population. The supply factors required for the economic growth of a country increase when the dependency ratio falls and the working-age population rises. The so-called demographic dividend is delivered through rapid increases in the labour force, a high rate of return on capital and more efficiency in labour force reallocations, which are all conducive to economic growth.

Population growth goes through three stages in economic development: 1) the 'high fertility rate, high mortality rate and low growth rate' phase; 2) the 'high birth rate, low mortality rate and high growth rate' phase; and 3) the 'low birth rate, low death rate and low growth rate' stage. The demographic dividend often appears at the end of the second stage or the start of the third stage. The demographic dividend often appears in a specific stage of a country's economic development, which has been confirmed by the historical experiences of many countries (Williamson 1997).

The demographic transition begins with the advent of the era of a low rate of fertility. After a while, the size of the working-age population falls and the population dependency ratio increases, leading to the fall and eventual disappearance of the demographic dividend. The main characteristics of the end of the demographic dividend are a reduction in the supply of labour, which reduces in absolute number, which leads to diminishing marginal returns to other factors of production. The total factor productivity (TFP) growth rate tends to decline when rural-to-urban migration ends. Therefore, the potential growth rate declines when the demographic dividend ends.

China's working-age population, aged between fifteen and fifty-nine years, peaked in 2010 (and the population between fifteen and sixty-four years peaked in 2013). The population dependency ratio increased from 2011. Cai and Lu (2013a) and Lu and Cai (2014) estimate China's potential growth rate will slow to 6–7 per cent over the next 10 years, from the 10 per cent observed in the past 10 years. The falling potential growth rate is not a phenomenon unique to China. In a recent multi-country analysis, Eichengreen et al. (2011) construct a sample of cases where fast-growing economies slow significantly, in the sense that the growth rate downshifts by at least 2 percentage points, when their per capita incomes reach around US$17 000 (in 2005 constant international prices)—a level China should achieve by or soon after 2015.

The study also points out many other economic factors that influence the point at which the growth slowdown occurs. A higher old-age dependency rate is one such factor, which appears to increase the likelihood of an economic slowdown due to its association with lower savings rates and lower labour force participation rates. A characteristic in China—'getting old before getting rich'—will undoubtedly lead to an economic slowdown ahead of our expectation. At the same time, Eichengreen et al. (2011) emphasise that there is no mechanical relationship between per capita incomes and growth slowdowns, and that how long rapid growth continues depends also on economic policy. For some countries, after an extended period of slower growth, the responsive economic reforms adopted by governments led to a period of faster growth, but this momentum soon eased, leading to a new round of economic slowdown. Examples include the experiences of Argentina, Hong Kong, Ireland, Israel, Norway, Portugal and Singapore.

The supply of factors of production and the improvement of TFP face institutional barriers. Therefore, removing these barriers raises the potential growth rate. In this sense, the greater the presence of institutional barriers, the more radical reforms are needed, and the more significant will be the impact on the improvement of the potential growth rate, should reforms be implemented to overcome those institutional barriers. This outcome can be called the reform dividend. The chapter provides a simulation of the growth effects resulting from various possible reform measures. The short-term and long-term growth effects generated by reform measures are estimated by applying the growth accounting equation, with the goal of identifying the most efficient reform measures. It then provides some policy suggestions with respect to the ways by which the transition from China's demographic dividend to the reform dividend can take place in order to maintain long-term sustainable economic development after the end of the demographic dividend.

The theoretical logic of the reform dividend

A country's potential growth rate, determined by the growth of factors of both production and productivity, slows when the demographic dividend starts to disappear. For example, Kuijs (2010) projects that China's potential growth rate will slow from 9.9 per cent during 1978–94, to 9.6 per cent during 1995–2009, and further to 8.4 per cent during 2010–15. Kuijs places no particular emphasis on the role of demographic factors in the study. Taking into account the changing demographic structure, Cai and Lu (2013a) argue that as the end of China's demographic dividend approaches, the potential growth rate will slow from more than 10 per cent per year on average in the past 30 years to 7.3 per cent during the period of China's Twelfth Five-Year Plan (2011–15). If we take into account the role of human capital, the impacts of the population dependency ratio on capital formation and the impacts of demographics on the labour participation and natural unemployment rates in the model, China's potential growth rate will slow to 7.75 per cent during the Twelfth Five-Year Plan (Lu and Cai 2014).

Such a result is based on two hypotheses: 1) there is a continual slowdown in the labour supply; and 2) the TFP growth rate remains constant. In other words, the net effect of the demographic dividend on the potential growth rate has been estimated under the assumption that the institutional barriers that block the supply of production factors and the increase of productivity have not yet been removed. Increasing labour supply and human capital through reforms can also increase the potential growth rate from the supply factors. Furthermore, by eliminating the barriers to full competition so as to increase TFP, it is possible to further improve China's future potential growth rate.

In discussing the issue of China's reform, many express the view that there will be a trade-off between reform and economic growth. That means in order to implement the proposed reforms, the Chinese Government needs to sacrifice the economic growth rate; however, one may also argue that reforms could be conducive to economic growth. The theory of institutional change, which says that change occurs only at the point at which the benefits from reform outweigh the costs, refers only to the political benefits and costs that are considered by decision-makers—that is, whether the political support (benefits) brought by a reform exceeds its opposition (costs). But, in general, when the gains surpass the losses in economic terms, there is sufficient reason to convince policymakers to implement reform. China's reforms in many areas aim at improving the efficiency of resource allocation and income distribution. Reform programs have also been implemented to enhance the equalisation of the level of basic public services across different regions in China. These reform measures are consistent with the Government's goals of achieving a more equitable society. Therefore, in implementing these reforms, China can benefit from both the direct and the indirect reform dividends. One would need to identify the sources of economic slowdown in order to implement the relevant reforms that can bring direct effects on improving the potential growth rate, as well as other indirect effects that are conductive to economic growth.

A correct understanding of the reform benefits or reform dividend is important for the formation and cohesion of the reform consensus, helping with the provision of more options, and strengthening the impetus, for reform. Although the reforms can bring about net benefits, the costs and benefits are often asymmetrically apportioned among different parties. Two different methods can be adopted in reform decisions. First, the 'Pareto improvement' says that reforms can be promoted on the premise of not making parties, including vested interests, worse off. Second, the 'Kaldor improvement' says that although some interest groups may be negatively affected by the reforms, the net benefits the reforms bring allow a portion of these to be used to compensate the losers. The current reform task has rarely followed a Pareto improvement. There are, however, opportunities for China to recognise and grasp the benefits of reform, and use the Kaldor improvement to reduce resistance to reform. The estimation reported in this chapter has shown that reforms do bring net benefits to the economy by directly increasing China's potential growth rate. The relationship between China's reform and its economic growth rate is 'mutual promotion' rather than 'substitution'. The findings are supporting the reform agenda as promulgated at the third plenary of the Eighteenth Party Congress, calling for deepened economic and institutional reforms to promote economic growth in China.

'Reform dividend' simulation

Model specifications[1]

We use a standard Cobb–Douglas production function, adding the variable human capital, to project the potential GDP growth rate (Equation 2.1).

Equation 2.1
$$Y = AK^{\alpha}(hL)^{1-\alpha}$$

In Equation 2.1, Y is real GDP, A is total factor productivity (TFP), L is employment, K stands for capital stock (in constant prices), and h stands for human capital. We deduce labour productivity by dividing hL on both sides of Equation 2.1 (Equation 2.2).

Equation 2.2
$$Y/hL = A(K/hL)^{\alpha}$$

---

1   This method was applied by Lu and Cai (2014).

In Equation 2.2, labour productivity, Y/hL (represented by y), is a function of the *TFP* and capital–labour ratio, K/hL (represented by k). That is, $y = Ak^{\alpha}$. The labour productivity growth rate can then be rewritten and estimated from Equation 2.3.

Based on Equation 2.3, we can calculate the estimated value of return to capital, $\hat{\alpha}$, and return to labour, $(1 - \hat{\alpha})$, by using $\Delta y_t / y_{t-1}$ as the dependant variable and $\Delta k_t / k_{t-1}$ as the independent variable.

Equation 2.3

$$\Delta y_t / y_{t-1} = \Delta A_t / A_{t-1} + \hat{\alpha} \Delta k_t / k_{t-1} + \varepsilon_t$$

From the time series of $\Delta y_t / y_{t-1}$, $\hat{\alpha}$, $\Delta k_t / k_{t-1}$, the growth rate of TFP, $\Delta \hat{A}_t / A_{t-1} + \varepsilon_t = \Delta y_t / y_{t-1} - \hat{\alpha} \Delta k_t / k_{t-1}$, could be estimated by using Equation 3.3. Then $\Delta \hat{A}_t / A_{t-1}$ can be calculated by applying the Hodrick–Prescott filter method to diminish error term ε_t.

All steps above are identical with the method that calculates the growth rate of TFP. It is necessary to use potential employment, L_t^*, to calculate the potential GDP growth rate. Where $L_t^* = population_{15+,t} \times Tr_{15+,t} \times (1 - NAIRU_{15+,t})$, $population_{15+,t}$ is the population aged fifteen years and above; $Tr_{15+,t}$ is the trend of the labour participation rate, which can be estimated by the Hodrick–Prescott filter method; and $NAIRU_{15+,t}$ is the natural rate of unemployment. China's time-varying NAIRU is estimated by Du and Lu (2011).

Building on $\Delta \hat{A}_t / A_{t-1}, h_t L_t^*, \hat{\alpha}$ and $\Delta k_t^* / k_{t-1}^*$, the potential labour productivity growth rate, $\Delta y_t^* / y_{t-1}^*$, could be estimated, where $\Delta y_t^* / y_{t-1}^* = \Delta \hat{A}_t / A_{t-1} + \hat{\alpha} \Delta k_t^* / k_{t-1}^*$, which stands for the growth rate of potential labour productivity; $k_t^* = K_t / h_t L_t^*$; $y_t^* = Y_t^* / h_t L_t^*$, and Y_t^* is the potential GDP in year t. Building on $\Delta y_t^* / y_{t-1}^*$ and $h_t L_t^*$, Equation 2.4 can be deduced.

Equation 2.4

$$\Delta Y_t^* / Y_{t-1}^* = (\Delta y_t^* / y_{t-1}^* + 1) \times (h_t L_t^* / h_{t-1} L_{t-1}^*) - 1$$

$\Delta Y_t^* / Y_{t-1}^*$ is the potential growth rate in year t. In Equation 2.4, four factors influence the potential growth rate—that is, the potential growth rate of the capital–labour ratio, the potential growth rate of employment, the growth rate of human capital and the TFP growth rate. Demographics affect the first three factors directly or indirectly. The TFP growth rate is, however, related more to institutional factors—for example, migration, the *hukou* system, technical progress, and so on. If the demographic contribution to a country's economic growth can be called the 'demographic dividend' then the contribution of TFP to economic growth can be called an 'institutional dividend'.

Data

1) Y and K

The data for real GDP (at constant 2005 national prices) and real capital stock (at constant 2005 national prices) were obtained from the Penn World Table (*PWT 8.0*). China's capital stock during the period 2011–30, however, was unknown. It was necessary to estimate the missing data for capital stock by the well-known 'perpetual inventory method'—that is, $K_t = I_t + (1 - \delta_t)K_{t-1}$, where K_t and K_{t-1} are the measures of real capital stock at year t and t–1; I_t is the real capital formation of GDP in year t; and δ_t (= 5 per cent) is the rate of depreciation, noting that K_t is a weighted sum of all past levels of investment and depreciated value of the initial real capital stock.

The capital formation rate of GDP varies across countries with the stage of development, demographic structure, customs and other factors. In this chapter, we assume that the capital formation rate of GDP is a function of the population dependency ratio. Specifically, in economics, the life-cycle hypothesis (LCH) is a concept addressing individual consumption patterns—that is, members of the working-age population may save less or consume more in order to support their children and elderly members when the dependency ratio increases. It is easy to recognise, by using the expenditure approach to calculate GDP: with the rise of the population dependency ratio, the capital formation rate of GDP will decline. Thus, the basic relationship between the above two variables is obtained by the historical dataset during the period 1980–2010, Ct = 62.733 – 0.399Dt–1, where Ct stands for the ratio of current capital stock to one lag of GDP, and Dt–1 stands for one lag of the population dependency ratio. The capital formation rate of GDP was obtained from the World Development Indicators database (World Bank n.d.). Remarkably, building on the forecast data for population by age and sex, it's not difficult to predict the data value of capital formation and capital stock during the period 2011–50. The population forecast data were obtained from Guo's (2013) estimation.

2) Potential employment

The data for population and employment were obtained from the *China Statistical Yearbook* (NBS various years); the forecast data for population by age and sex were provided by Guo (2013). The potential employment is determined by demographic structure, the labour force participation rate and the natural rate of unemployment—that is, $L_t^* = population_{15+,t} \times Tr_{15+,t} \times (1 - NAIRU_{15+,t})$. The labour force participation rate is, however, a function of the population's age and sex. Building on the labour force participation rate by age and sex, which is calculated from the Sixth National Census data (2010), the labour force participation rate can be obtained by consideration of the changing demographic structure of China during the period 2011–50. The forecast data for China's economically active population were estimated as Equation 2.5.

Equation 2.5

$$ACT_{i,t}^* = \sum_{n=16}^{n=95} population_{n,i,t} \times Part_{n,i,t} \quad (i = 1, 2; \; 16 \leq n \leq 95)$$

$$ACT_t^* = \sum_{i=1}^{i=2} ACT_{i,t}^*$$

In Equation 2.5, n stands for age ($16 \leq n \leq 95$); i stands for sex ($i = 1$ male, 2 female), $population_{n,i,t}$ is the population by age and sex in year t; $Part_{n,i,t}$ is the labour force participation rate by age and sex in year t; ACT_t^* stands for the total economically active population in year t.

The natural rate of unemployment is also a function of population age and sex. That means potential employment could be estimated by Equation 2.6.

Equation 2.6

$$L_{i,t}^* = \sum_{n=16}^{n=95} ACT_{n,i,t}^* \times (1 - NAIRU_{n,i,t}) \quad (i = 1, 2; \; 16 \leq n \leq 95)$$

$$L_t^* = \sum_{i=1}^{i=2} L_{i,t}^*$$

In Equation 2.6, n stands for age ($16 \leq n \leq 95$); i stands for sex ($i = 1$ male, 2 female); $ACT_{n,i,t}^*$ is the economically active population by sex and age in year t; $NAIRU_{n,i,t}$ is the natural rate of unemployment by sex and age in year t. L_t^* stands for the potential employment in year t.

3) Human capital

The data for human capital were drawn from the index of hc in the Penn World Table (*PWT 8.0*). The hc index, in fact, is a re-estimated dataset built on the education returns estimated by Psacharopoulos (1994), and the average years of schooling provided by Barro and Lee (forthcoming). Forecast data for the average years of schooling, by each five years, were estimated by the similar method provided by Barro and Lee (forthcoming). The data for other years were filled in by a smoothing method, and the index of *hc* during 2011–50, ultimately, could be obtained.

The simulation results

1) The 'short-term' and 'long-term' effects of relaxing fertility policy

When projecting China's potential growth rate, we assumed the TFP remained unchanged, while the other factors in production, including capital, labour and human capital, change with the changes in China's demographic structure. That is, the predicted population by age and sex could influence the potential growth rate directly and indirectly. The population prediction depends on the value of the total fertility rate (TFR). In the existing 'selective two-child policy', however, the TFR will theoretically not be more than two. That means the fertility rate could not reach the replacement level. Therefore, the present study projects the trends of the potential growth rate in China by using the respective values of TFR (1.6, 1.7 and 1.94) on which Guo (2013) has forecast Chinese population by age and sex. The estimation results, which accord with Lu and Cai (2014), are shown in the first three lines of Table 2.1.

Table 2.1 Policy Simulations of China's Potential Growth Rate, 2011–50 (per cent)

Potential growth rate (%)	2011–15	2016–20	2021–25	2026–30	2031–35	2036–40	2041–45	2046–50
I The impact of a relaxation of the population fertility policy on China's potential growth rate: 2011–50 (%)								
TFR = 1.6	7.73	6.64	5.87	5.40	5.05	4.60	4.17	3.84
TFR = 1.77	7.72	6.58	5.78	5.34	5.16	4.80	4.39	4.04
TFR = 1.94	7.71	6.50	5.66	5.23	5.29	5.08	4.65	4.25
II.1 The impact of increasing the labour force participation rate on China's potential growth rate, TFR = 1.6: 2011–50 (%)								
Add 1 percentage point	7.92	6.68	5.90	5.43	5.07	4.61	4.19	3.85
Add 2 percentage points	8.11	6.71	5.93	5.45	5.09	4.63	4.20	3.86
Add 5 percentage points	8.68	6.82	6.01	5.52	5.15	4.68	4.24	3.90

Potential growth rate (%)	2011–15	2016–20	2021–25	2026–30	2031–35	2036–40	2041–45	2046–50
II.2 The impact of increasing the labour force participation rate on China's potential growth rate, TFR = 1.77: 2011–50 (%)								
Add 1 percentage point	7.91	6.62	5.81	5.36	5.18	4.82	4.40	4.05
Add 2 percentage points	8.10	6.65	5.84	5.39	5.20	4.83	4.42	4.07
Add 5 percentage points	8.67	6.76	5.92	5.46	5.26	4.88	4.45	4.10
III.1 The impact of increasing TFP on China's potential growth rate, TFR = 1.60: 2011–50 (%)								
Add 0.5 percentage points	8.30	7.32	6.62	6.20	5.88	5.44	5.03	4.71
Add 1 percentage point	8.87	8.01	7.37	7.00	6.72	6.30	5.90	5.59
III.2 The impact of increasing TFP on China's potential growth rate, TFR = 1.77: 2011–50 (%)								
Add 0.5 percentage points	8.28	7.26	6.52	6.13	5.99	5.65	5.25	4.92
Add 1 percentage point	8.85	7.94	7.27	6.93	6.83	6.52	6.13	5.80
IV The impact of increasing the enrolment rate on China's potential growth rate: 2011–50 (%)								
TFR = 1.60	7.84	6.73	5.94	5.47	5.11	4.64	4.20	3.86
TFR = 1.77	7.83	6.66	5.85	5.40	5.22	4.85	4.42	4.06
V The impact of increasing training on China's potential growth rate: 2011–50 (%)								
TFR = 1.60	8.14	7.02	6.28	5.80	5.45	4.98	4.49	4.18
TFR = 1.77	8.12	6.96	6.18	5.73	5.54	5.17	4.70	4.37
VI Multi-level simulation: adding 1 percentage point to LFPR, 1 percentage point to TFP, and increasing the enrolment rate								
TFR = 1.60	9.18	8.13	7.48	7.10	6.80	6.36	5.95	5.62
TFR = 1.77	9.16	8.06	7.38	7.03	6.91	6.58	6.18	5.83
TFR = 1.94	9.15	7.98	7.26	6.92	7.05	6.88	6.46	6.05
VII Multi-level simulation: adding 1 percentage point to LFPR, 0.5 percentage points to TFP, and increasing the enrolment rate								
TFR = 1.60	8.60	7.45	6.72	6.29	5.96	5.51	5.08	4.74
TFR = 1.77	8.59	7.38	6.63	6.23	6.07	5.72	5.30	4.95
TFR = 1.94	8.58	7.30	6.51	6.12	6.21	6.01	5.57	5.16

Potential growth rate (%)	2011– 15	2016– 20	2021– 25	2026– 30	2031– 35	2036– 40	2041– 45	2046– 50
VIII Multi-level simulation: adding 1 percentage point to LFPR, 1 percentage point to TFP, and increasing training								
TFR = 1.60	9.48	8.44	7.82	7.45	7.16	6.72	6.25	5.96
TFR = 1.77	9.46	8.37	7.73	7.37	7.25	6.92	6.47	6.17
TFR = 1.94	9.45	8.29	7.60	7.25	7.37	7.20	6.74	6.38
IX Multi-level simulation: adding 1 percentage point to LFPR, 0.5 percentage points to TFP, and increasing training								
TFR = 1.60	8.90	7.75	7.06	6.63	6.31	5.85	5.37	5.07
TFR = 1.77	8.89	7.68	6.97	6.56	6.40	6.05	5.58	5.27
TFR = 1.94	8.88	7.60	6.85	6.44	6.52	6.32	5.84	5.47

LFPR = labour force participation rate

Source: Authors' estimations.

The impact on the potential growth rate of relaxing fertility policy has different short-term and long-term effects. Newborn babies only increase the population dependency ratio; they cannot increase the working-age population in the short term. Therefore, the saving rate decreases, the consumption rate increases and the capital formation rate then declines. In the long term, however, babies grow into adults (needing at least 15 years to reach working age), and then enter the labour market, so they then decrease the population dependency ratio and increase the supply of labour, and then help increase the potential growth rate. This mechanism describes the impact of the 'baby boom' on the potential growth rate. The trends of the potential growth rates under different assumed TFRs are shown in Figure 2.1. The results accord with the economic theory.

Let us now examine additional scenarios for China's potential growth rate on the basis of different assumptions of the TFP, by increasing the labour force participation rate, human capital and TFP. In addition, the multi-level simulation has also been shown in Table 2.1, and the detailed comparison of results based on each simulation is presented in Table 2.2.

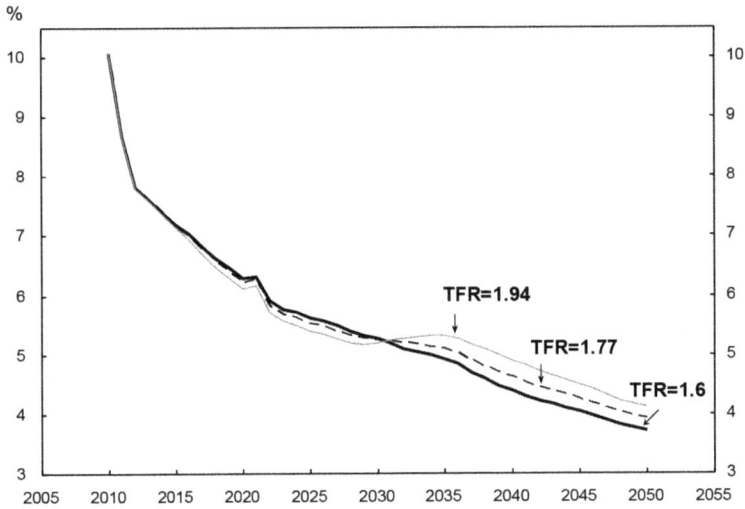

Figure 2.1 China's Long-Term Potential Growth Rate under Different Assumptions (TFR)

Source: Authors' simulations.

Table 2.2 Forecasting the Effects of Policy Measures on China's Potential Growth Rate, 2011–50 (per cent)

Potential growth rate (%)	2011–15	2016–20	2021–25	2026–30	2031–35	2036–40	2041–45	2046–50
I The influence of increasing the TFR to 1.94 on the potential growth rate: 2011–50 (%)								
Baseline (TFR = 1.60)	−0.024	−0.140	−0.204	−0.168	0.241	0.485	0.477	0.413
Baseline (TFR = 1.77)	−0.009	−0.076	−0.114	−0.103	0.135	0.279	0.259	0.209
II.1 The influence of increasing the labour force participation rate on China's potential growth rate (baseline TFR = 1.60)								
Add 1 percentage point	0.190	0.036	0.029	0.025	0.021	0.017	0.015	0.014
Add 2 percentage points	0.381	0.072	0.058	0.050	0.042	0.033	0.029	0.027
Add 5 percentage points	0.952	0.177	0.142	0.123	0.101	0.080	0.071	0.064

Potential growth rate (%)	2011– 15	2016– 20	2021– 25	2026– 30	2031– 35	2036– 40	2041– 45	2046– 50
II.2 The influence of increasing the labour force participation rate on China's potential growth rate (baseline TFR = 1.77)								
Add 1 percentage point	0.190	0.036	0.029	0.026	0.021	0.016	0.014	0.012
Add 2 percentage points	0.381	0.071	0.057	0.052	0.042	0.031	0.027	0.024
Add 5 percentage points	0.951	0.176	0.140	0.126	0.101	0.076	0.065	0.059
III.1 The influence of increasing the TFP on China's potential growth rate (baseline TFR = 1.60)								
Add 0.5 percentage points	0.568	0.680	0.748	0.797	0.828	0.844	0.858	0.869
Add 1 percentage point	1.136	1.364	1.502	1.602	1.666	1.700	1.728	1.751
III.2 The influence of increasing the TFP on China's potential growth rate (baseline TFR = 1.77)								
Add 0.5 percentage points	0.567	0.679	0.745	0.794	0.830	0.851	0.865	0.875
Add 1 percentage point	1.135	1.360	1.496	1.597	1.672	1.714	1.743	1.764
IV The influence of increasing the enrolment rate on China's potential growth rate								
TFR = 1.60	0.111	0.084	0.077	0.069	0.059	0.047	0.032	0.019
TFR = 1.77	0.111	0.084	0.077	0.067	0.060	0.047	0.031	0.017
V The influence of increasing training on China's potential growth rate								
TFR = 1.60	0.404	0.381	0.408	0.402	0.400	0.383	0.319	0.344
TFR = 1.77	0.404	0.380	0.406	0.393	0.385	0.370	0.309	0.333
VI Multi-level simulation: adding 1 percentage point to LFPR, 1 percentage point to TFP and increasing the enrolment rate, TFR increased to 1.94								
Baseline (TFR = 1.60)	1.419	1.340	1.394	1.518	2.006	2.285	2.284	2.216
Baseline (TFR = 1.77)	1.433	1.403	1.483	1.582	1.899	2.079	2.066	2.012
VII Multi-level simulation: adding 1 percentage point to LFPR, 0.5 percentage points to TFP and increasing the enrolment rate, TFR increased to 1.94								
Baseline (TFR = 1.60)	0.848	0.658	0.644	0.717	1.159	1.410	1.395	1.321

Potential growth rate (%)	2011–15	2016–20	2021–25	2026–30	2031–35	2036–40	2041–45	2046–50
Baseline (TFR = 1.77)	0.863	0.721	0.734	0.781	1.052	1.205	1.178	1.117
VIII Multi-level simulation: adding 1 percentage point to LFPR, 1 percentage point to TFP and increasing training, TFR increased to 1.94								
Baseline (TFR = 1.60)	1.72	1.64	1.73	1.85	2.33	2.61	2.57	2.54
Baseline (TFR = 1.77)	1.73	1.71	1.82	1.91	2.22	2.40	2.35	2.33
IX Multi-level simulation: adding 1 percentage point to LFPR, 0.5 percentage points to TFP and increasing training, TFR increased to 1.94								
Baseline (TFR = 1.60)	1.15	0.96	0.98	1.04	1.47	1.72	1.67	1.64
Baseline (TFR = 1.77)	1.16	1.02	1.07	1.11	1.36	1.52	1.45	1.43

Source: Authors' simulations.

Note: The baseline hypothesis for human capital accords with Lu and Cai (2014). The present study assumes that, in 2050, the rate for school-age children's enrolment remains unchanged at 99 per cent, with the graduation rates being: primary school (unchanged at 99 per cent), middle school (increased from 95 to 98 per cent) and high school (increased from 90 to 95 per cent), with other conditions unchanged.

2) Diminishing effect of the labour force participation rate

The corresponding simulation results were shown in Table 2.1 (II). The baseline scenario was keeping TFR at a constant 1.60 in II.1 and 1.77 in II.2. It is necessary to estimate the net effect of the potential growth rate by assuming the labour force participation rate increased 1 percentage point, 2 percentage points and 5 percentage points, respectively. The simulation evidence has shown that an increase in the labour force participation rate boosts the potential growth rate, whatever the TFR assumption: TFR = 1.60 or TFR = 1.70. For example, on the basis of the TFR maintaining a constant value of 1.60, China's average potential growth rate increases 0.2 percentage points during the Twelfth Five-Year Plan period if the labour force participation rate can be increased by 1 percentage point each year. The potential growth rate is increased by 1 percentage point during that period if labour force participation rate (LFPR) can be increased by 5 percentage points; however, the net effect declines (see Table 2.2). For example, the average net effect of the potential growth rate decreases from 0.18 during 2016–20 to 0.06 percentage points in 2045–50, by assuming that the labour force participation rate increases 5 percentage points every year in 2011–50. It can be said that reform focusing only on the labour force participation rate is far from a so-called 'institutional dividend' or 'reform dividend'. That means the Chinese Government cannot rely on such a policy in the long term. We can intuitively understand this conclusion from Figure 2.2.

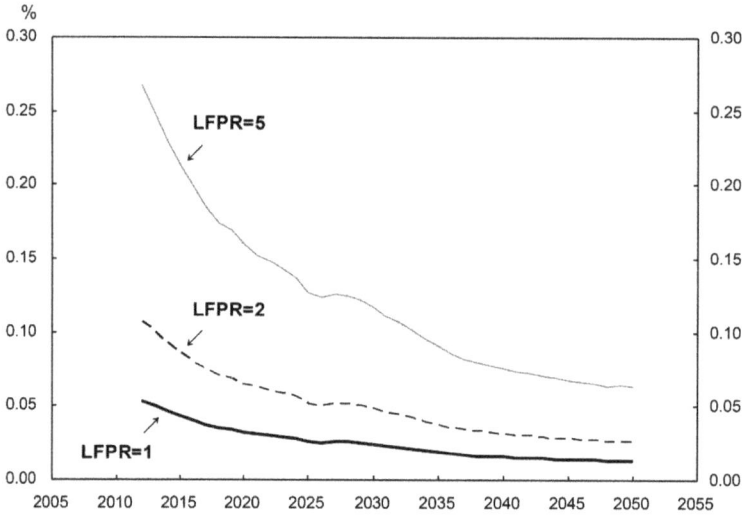

Figure 2.2 The Net Effects on the Potential Growth Rate from Increasing the Labour Force Participation Rate (baseline TFR = 1.60)

Source: Authors' simulations.

3) Ascending effect of total factor productivity

The corresponding simulation results were shown in Table 2.1 (III). The baseline scenario was keeping TFR at a constant level of 1.60 in III.1 and 1.77 in III.2. It is necessary to estimate the net effect of the potential growth rate by assuming TFP increased 0.5 percentage points and 1 percentage point, respectively. As is clearly shown in Figure 2.3, the net effects of the potential growth rate produced by TFP are obvious—for example, China's average potential growth rate will rise to 0.568 percentage points during the Twelfth Five-Year Plan period if TFP can be increased by 0.5 percentage points every year, and the average potential growth rate will rise 1.136 percentage points during that period if TFP can be increased by 1 percentage point. Notably, the 'growth effect' generated by TFP is an incremental curve—for example, China's potential growth rate, on the basis of the same scenario, rises from 0.869 in 2045 to 1.751 in 2050. Figure 2.4 clearly illustrates the 'growth effect' generated by TFP.

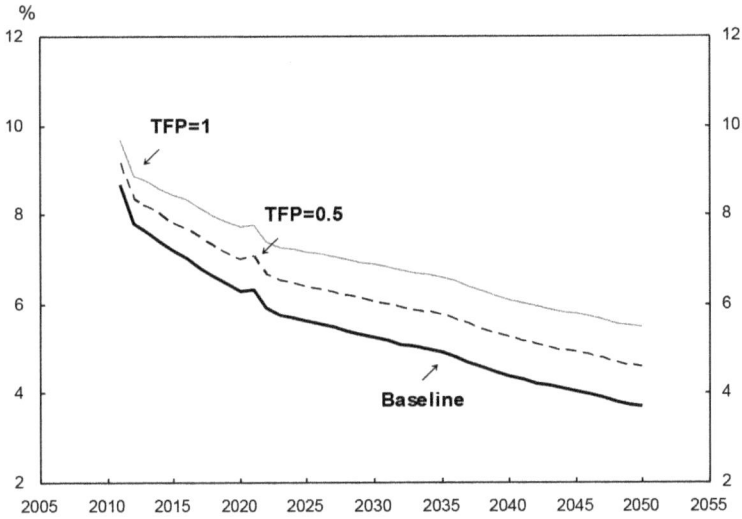

Figure 2.3 The Influence of Increasing TFP on China's Long-Term Potential Growth Rate (baseline TFR = 1.60)

Source: Authors' simulations.

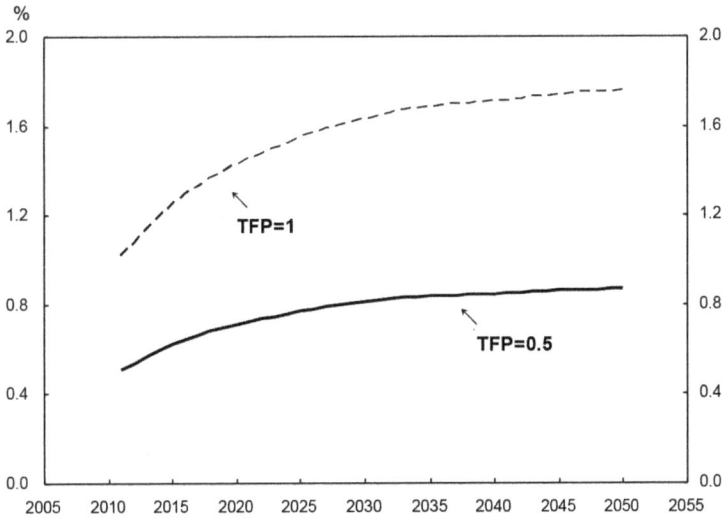

Figure 2.4 The 'Growth Effect' Generated by TFP (baseline TFR = 1.60)

Source: Authors' simulations.

4) The 'growth effect' generated by human capital: enrolment rate versus training

Improving human capital by increasing the enrolment rate is a relatively long-term effect. Our simulations assume that the average years of schooling remain unchanged for those aged over twenty-five. Human capital is estimated by years of schooling. Here we do not consider the scenario of training or further education. The change in human capital can only be affected by the enrolment rate/graduation rate at each stage of education. Specifically, this chapter assumes that, in 2050, the rate for school-age children's enrolment remains unchanged at 99 per cent, with the graduation rates being: primary school (unchanged at 99 per cent), middle school (increased from 95 to 98 per cent) and high school (increased from 90 to 95 per cent), with other conditions remaining unchanged. Overall, the growth rate of the human capital index, hc, shows a monotonically increasing trend, but its marginal growth gradually declines. Human capital also generates a positive effect on China's potential growth rate, but the marginal growth effect declines with the increase of human capital (see Figure 2.5).

In this scenario, increased education has a limited effect on the increase in the potential growth rate, if we consider human capital accumulation. If, however, the quality of human capital can be improved by training or further education in the labour market then an increase in human capital is more significant. If the Government and enterprises can provide regular training or further education opportunities for employees, this is likely to significantly increase the potential growth rate through sharply improved human capital. In order to verify this claim, we make a simplified assumption. We assume, as a baseline, that a typical worker in the labour market can access training opportunities of 1.2 months every year. That means in each year 10 workers increase their education by one school year. In other words, each typical worker's schooling rises by one year due to training programs every 10 years. This assumption implies that each employee has similar opportunities to access training programs. The probability distribution of training by ages, however, is unequal. This assumption is used to simplify our hypothesis, which is that the time for training equals the years of schooling. Based on this hypothesis, we have deduced China's average years of schooling during 2011–50.

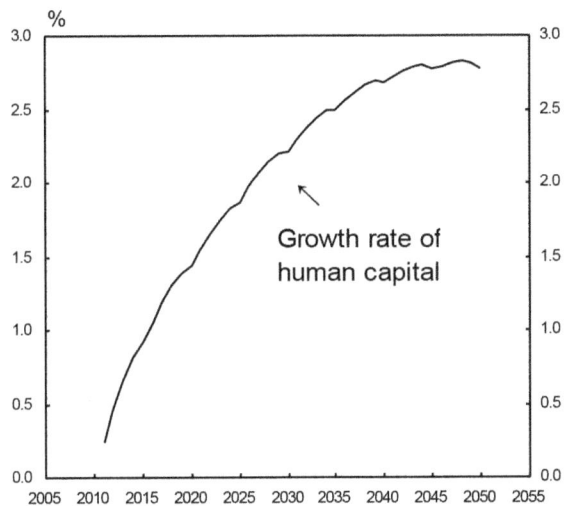

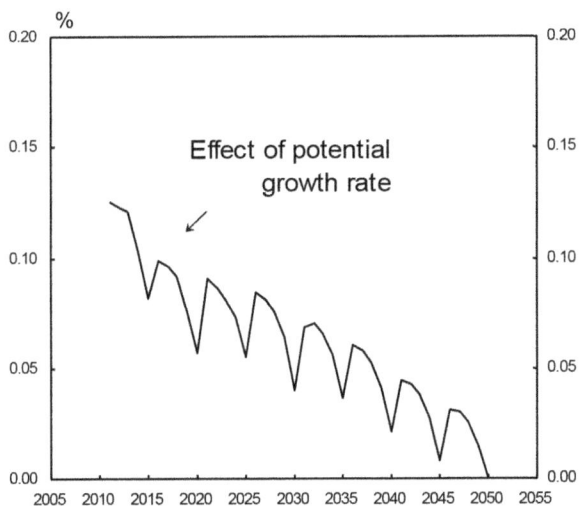

Figure 2.5 The Long-Term 'Growth Effect' Generated by Raising the Enrolment Rate/Graduation Rate (baseline TFR = 1.60)

Source: Authors' simulations.

The simulation results show that increasing the amount of training has a more significant effect in promoting the potential growth rate than increasing the enrolment rate. In the case of the Twelfth Five-Year Plan period, China's potential growth rate could be increased by 0.404 percentage points if a typical worker in the labour market can access training opportunities of an additional 1.2 months every year (from a baseline of zero). Remarkably, for a typical employee, the training has improved the human capital in year t, assuming the time of training equals the years of schooling, and therefore the new human capital in year t (which is calculated based on the amount of training) can be added into the next year, t + 1, and also in later periods. Improving human capital by increasing the enrolment rate is a very slow process. That means even if the enrolment rate could be raised dramatically, the average human capital in a country would only rise a little in the short term. Focusing on training, however, covers all the labour force. Improving the potential growth rate by training shows a significant effect if training can be treated as another way of increasing the years of schooling. According to the simulation results, the growth effect generated by increasing the amount of training does not appear to produce a significant decreasing trend. If the training programs could be started in 2011, the growth effect generated by training can still be maintained as 0.344 percentage points until the year 2045–50 (see Figure 2.6). If the Government and enterprises provide more training opportunities for their employees or the jobless, then increasing the amount of training produces a more significant impact on the potential growth rate.

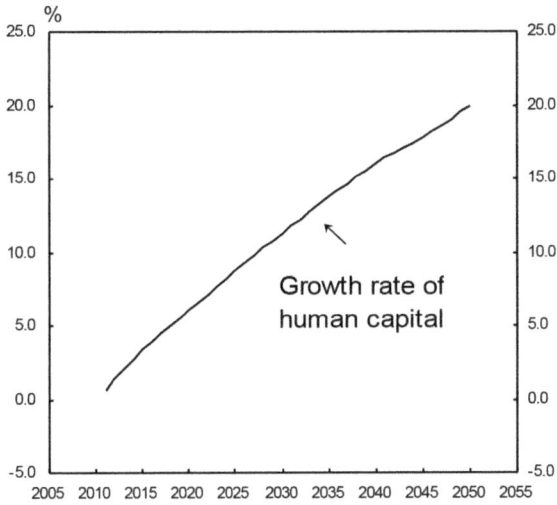

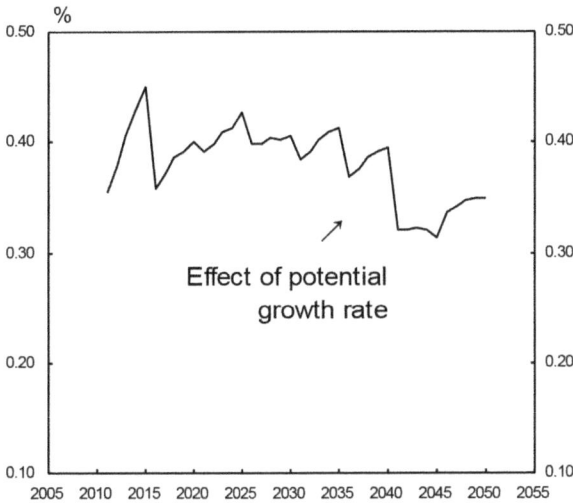

Figure 2.6 The Long-Term 'Growth Effect' Generated by Increasing the Amount of Training (baseline TFR = 1.60)

Source: Authors' simulations.

5) The 'growth effect' generated by combinations of policies

The previous section discussed the short-term and long-term effects on the potential growth rate of improving the TFR, TFP, human capital and the labour force participation rate (enrolment rate versus training). We noted that a single factor may have a limited effect on increasing the potential growth rate; however, choosing a combination of policies to expand the 'growth effect' will work well. Tables 2.1 and 2.2, respectively, have shown the influence of combinations of policies on China's potential growth rate. Our basis is a combination policy simulation whose hypothesis is that the TFR could be raised from 1.6 to 1.94, the labour force participation rate could be increased by 1 percentage point, TFP could be raised 0.5 percentage points and the graduation rates of middle school and high school students could be increased by 3 percentage points and 5 percentage points respectively in 2050; according to the growth accounting equation, the potential growth rate could be increased by 0.85 percentage points during the Twelfth Five-Year Plan period, and could be further increased to 1.32 percentage points in 2045–50. The combination policies should have a clearer effect on the potential growth rate if we take into account the effect of training on human capital. For example, keeping our other hypothesis unchanged (TFR rising from 1.6 to 1.94, the labour force participation rate increasing by 1 percentage point, and TFP by 0.5 percentage points), if the Chinese Government adopts a policy to increase the amount of training (averaging 1.2 months per year for an employee) instead of increasing the enrolment rate to improve the human capital stock, the potential growth rate could be increased from 3.84 per cent to 5.47 per cent in 2045–50—an increase of 1.64 percentage points.

The simulation results of several combination policies are shown in Figure 2.7, where the baseline scenario assumes the TFR can be kept at the level of 1.6, and we forecast China's potential growth rate. Scenario A shows the trends of China's potential future growth rate on the basis of TFR = 1.60, and by assuming that the labour force participation rate can be increased by 1 percentage point, TFP by 0.5 percentage points and the graduation rates of middle school and high school by 3 percentage points and 5 percentage points respectively in 2050. Scenario B also forecasts the trends of China's potential future growth rate on the basis of TFR remaining at 1.60, and by assuming that the labour force participation rate can be increased by 1 percentage point, TFP by 0.5 percentage points, and the Government adopts an increase in the amount of training instead of increasing the enrolment rate to improve the human capital stock. On the basis of Simulation B, Scenario C shows the trends of China's potential growth rate by assuming that China's TFR could be raised from 1.60 to 1.94 in the future. In the short term, this increases the population dependency ratio, which decreases the capital formation rate of GDP and then the capital stock. This produces a negative impact on China's potential growth rate. However, in the long term, newborns grow to enter the labour market, increasing the supply of labour, which produces a positive impact on the potential growth rate. Therefore, the short-term effect is negative while the long-term effect is positive.

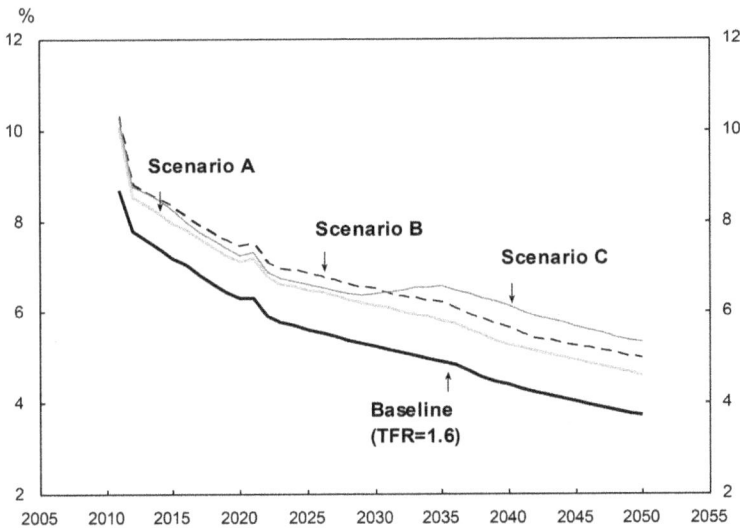

Figure 2.7 The Long-Term 'Growth Effect' Generated by Combination Policies (baseline TFR = 1.60)

Source: Authors' simulations.

Reform priorities and approach

With the reduction of the working-age population and the increase of the population dependency ratio as the main characteristics of the 'demographic dividend' having disappeared, China's potential growth rate decreases; however, this does not mean the Chinese Government is powerless to change the growth rate. A series of reform measures is conducive to clearing the institutional barriers to the supply of factors and productivity, thereby slowing the declining trend of the potential growth rate, which is the key to China's sustainable economic development. It is beneficial for the Chinese Government to choose reform priorities and a reform path based on the simulation results.

First, the Chinese Government should continue to stick to and improve its current family-planning policy. Although relaxation of the family-planning policy does not have an immediate growth effect, compared with the one-child policy, the 'selective two-child policy' produces a weak but negative impact on the potential growth rate in the first 15 years. In the long term, however, relaxing the family-planning policy is conducive to a reasonable demographic structure and an increase in the working-age population, thus generating a positive impact on China's potential growth rate. We need to recognise that while the family-planning policy affects the TFR, the declining TFR is one of the results of economic and social development. A continuing decrease in the fertility rate will, in fact, generally accompany economic development. We cannot expect a remarkable reversal in this trend in the future. Adjusting the family-planning policy sooner rather than later generates obvious effects. Therefore, the Chinese Government should make the transition from the 'selective two-child policy' to a 'two-child policy' as soon as possible, and further adjust the family-planning policy according to the reality of population development.

Second, improving the market mechanism that plays an essential role in the allocation of resources creates an equal, competitive environment for the entry and exit of firms. There is still important potential to improve productivity— that is, given the large disparities in productivity among firms within the same sector, the mobility of factors of production from low-productivity firms to high-productivity firms, which allows for more efficient enterprises to survive, expand and develop, while inefficient enterprises are eliminated, improves industry as well as national productivity. As is well documented in the economics literature, in a mature market economy like the United States, a 'creative destruction' mechanism creates allocative efficiency relating to the entry, expansion, contraction and exit of firms within narrowly defined sectors that contribute one-third to one-half of national productivity growth (for example, Foster et al. 2001, 2008). In addition, a more recent work (Hsieh and Klenow 2009) has demonstrated that by reallocating capital and labour to equalise marginal products among manufacturers to the extent observed in the United States, China's manufacturing sector could gain a 30–50 per cent increase in its TFP. The meaning of the coincidence in the two figures given by Foster et al. and Hsieh and Klenow illustrates that, so far, China has not yet obtained such a source of TFP. Therefore, associated reform in such economic spheres also could generate obvious benefits.

In fact, mixed ownership reform can give more opportunities for the private economy to enter into competitive industries, and breaking the monopoly of state-owned enterprises (SOEs) through competition could generate a reform dividend. In other words, improving the flow of factors through competition promotes the growth of TFP, and ultimately improves the potential growth rate. Further, allocative efficiency could be improved by financial system reform, which should focus on the promotion of interest rate liberalisation. It is clear that only market-based interest rates can achieve efficiency in the allocation of capital. It is not possible for the interest rate to float, reflecting the rate of return to capital, under the conditions of non-market or controlled interest rates. As a result, production and allocative efficiencies are below the optimal levels, resulting in an unnecessarily low TFP.

Third, the Chinese Government should help migrant workers by reforming the household registration system. The task can be achieved through public policy reforms, which eliminate institutional obstacles to labour mobility and continue to create resource reallocation efficiency, and help to maintain the increasing rate of TFP. Moreover, this reform can also relieve the pressure for wage hikes, and gain time for enterprises needing to upgrade their industrial structure. Reform of the household registration system could become part of the reform dividend if the Government follows three parallel paths: 1) absorb migrant workers by allowing them to be registered as urban residents; 2) provide equal basic public services to those migrants who cannot become urban residents in the short term; and 3) provide urban and rural residents with full coverage from the social security system. China should address the issue of sharing the cost of reform between the Central Government and local governments, which is conducive to the formation of the incentive compatibility mechanism for different levels of government.

Fourth, the Chinese Government and enterprises should provide a variety of training programs for employees. Taking into account the mobility of employees, companies hesitate to provide training. However, China's future economic development needs high-quality human capital. Similarly, enterprises need to improve their productivity and technological innovation, which also rely on the input of human capital. Therefore, from the point of view of enterprises, well-trained employees are much needed, while from the point of view of employees, moving between enterprises in order to achieve their own utility maximisation is inevitable. Thus, in addition to corporate training programs, the Government needs to provide more training programs to increase human capital, which could significantly improve the potential growth rate. According to this study, China's potential growth rate will increase by 0.3 to 0.4 percentage points if each employee can access one year of training opportunities in every 10 working years.

Finally, the Chinese Government, when facing a package of reforms, should pay more attention to the best order for these reforms. At present, reforms are ordered 'from easy to difficult', 'consensus first' and 'minimum package of reforms'. In fact, the Chinese Government should select reform measures that have the most obvious growth effects—for example, reforms relating to the registration of migrant workers, to transition from a 'selective two-child policy' to a 'two-child policy', reforms of the financial system and SOEs, and to increase the efficiency of the allocation of resources. In addition, increasing the quality of human capital through more training programs is conducive to enhancing productivity and innovation ability. This is also consistent with the views of Premier Li Keqiang, who says that 'reform should start from areas where the most prominent problems exist restricting China's economic and social development'.

References

Barro, R. J. and Lee, J.-W. (forthcoming), 'A new data set of educational attainment in the world, 1950–2010', *Journal of Development Economics*.

Cai, F. and Lu, Y. (2013a), 'Population change and resulting slowdown in potential GDP growth in China', *China & World Economy* 21(2): 1–14.

Cai, F. and Lu, Y. (2013b), 'Promoting reform and improving the potential growth rate', *Comparative Studies* 64(1): 29–36.

Du, Y. and Lu, Y. (2011), 'The natural rate of unemployment in China and its implications', *The Journal of World Economy* 34(4): 3–21.

Eichengreen, B., Park, D. and Shin, K. (2011), *When fast growing economies slow down: international evidence and implications for China*, NBER Working Paper No. 16919, National Bureau of Economic Research, Cambridge, Mass.

Foster, L., Haltiwanger, J. and Krizan, C. J. (2001), 'Aggregate productivity growth: lessons from microeconomic evidence', in *New Developments in Productivity Analysis*, Chicago: NBER/University of Chicago Press.

Foster, L., Haltiwanger, J. and Syverson, C. (2008), 'Reallocation, firm turnover, and efficiency: selection on productivity or profitability?', *American Economic Review* 98: 394–425.

Guo, Z. (2013), *China's population projections 2011–2050*, Working Paper.

Hsieh, C.-T. and Klenow, P. J. (2009), 'Misallocation and manufacturing TFP in China and India', *The Quarterly Journal of Economics* CXXIV(4): 1403–48.

Kuijs, L. (2010), *China through 2020—a macroeconomic scenario*, World Bank China Research Working Paper No. 9, The World Bank, Washington, DC.

Lu, Y. and Cai, F. (2014), 'Population change and resulting slowdown in potential GDP growth in China', *The Journal of World Economy* (1): 3–29.

National Bureau of Statistics (NBS) (various years), *China Statistical Yearbook*, Beijing: China Statistics Press.

Psacharopoulos, G. (1994), 'Returns to investment in education: a global update', *World Development* 22(9): 1325–43.

Williamson, J. (1997), *Growth, distribution and demography: some lessons from history*, NBER Working Paper Series No. 6244, National Bureau of Economic Research, Cambridge, Mass.

World Bank (n.d.), *World Development Indicators*, Washington, DC: The World Bank.

3. Structural Imbalance, Inequality and Economic Growth

Xiaolu Wang and Yixiao Zhou

Introduction

A series of structural imbalances has persisted in the Chinese economy. The consumption rate has been declining for years and has been significantly lower than the international average, while the savings rate and the capital formation rate have been too high and continue to rise. Massive investment has caused the rapid expansion of production capacity, while consumption growth cannot keep up with the expansion of capital investment and production capacity, resulting in a sustained excess capacity. Without structural change, the Chinese economy will gradually lose momentum due to the deficiency of domestic demand.

Since the 2008 Global Financial Crisis (GFC), there has been a deceleration in China's economic growth rate. In the 1980s, China's economic growth was accelerated from the pre-reform period, reaching an average of 9.3 per cent per year. In the 1990s, China maintained an average growth rate of 10.4 per cent. During 2001–07, the average growth rate increased slightly to 10.8 per cent. Since then, however, the growth rate has been slowing. Between 2008 and 2011, the average growth rate dropped to 9.6 per cent per year. In both 2012 and 2013, the growth rate was 7.7 per cent. In the first quarter of 2014, the growth rate was only 7.4 per cent (NBS various years). The external reason for the slowdown in growth is weak demand from the international market; and the internal reason is the lack of domestic demand caused by the structural imbalances of the economy.

Insufficient domestic consumer demand results mainly from the imbalanced income distribution. This imbalance mainly results from an excessively large income gap and the imbalance of income distribution between the government, business and consumers. These are closely related to a series of institutional problems. Currently, the new Chinese leadership is promoting institutional reforms to address these issues. If these reforms can be successfully implemented, we can expect the downward trend in economic growth will gradually reverse in the next few years and growth is likely to be restored to 8 per cent. In the next 10 to 20 years, the Chinese economy will still have huge potential to remain in the fast lane. Of course, whether this optimistic scenario occurs will depend on how the reforms progress.

Section one of this chapter analyses the declining trend of the final consumption rate and its causes, and especially how it is affected by income distribution. Section two discusses the impact of structural imbalance on economic development and the potential for China to fall into the 'middle-income trap'. Section three discusses the effect of lowering savings and raising consumption to achieve the 'golden-rule savings rate' and what adjustments in income distribution are needed to make this happen.

The impact of income distribution on consumption and saving

According to official statistics, during the planned economy period from 1952 to 1978, there was a gradual increase in China's savings rate and a decrease in the consumption rate, which fell from 78.9 per cent to 62.1 per cent. At the beginning of the reform period, the consumption rate grew and reached 65–66 per cent in the mid 1980s, but then fell again, to 62.3 per cent, in 2000.

The consumption rate dropped significantly to 48.2 per cent during the next 10 years (2000–10), which was a reduction of 14.1 per cent; in the meantime, the share of household consumption in GDP fell from 46.4 per cent to 34.9 per cent. These were the lowest points of these two series since the 1950s. The savings rate rose to 51.8 per cent of GDP in 2010, which was a rare situation globally (NBS various years; World Bank 2014). It is only in the past couple of years that the consumption rate has rebounded slightly. Figure 3.1 shows the changes in the consumption rate, the savings rate and the capital formation rate in China in the past six decades.

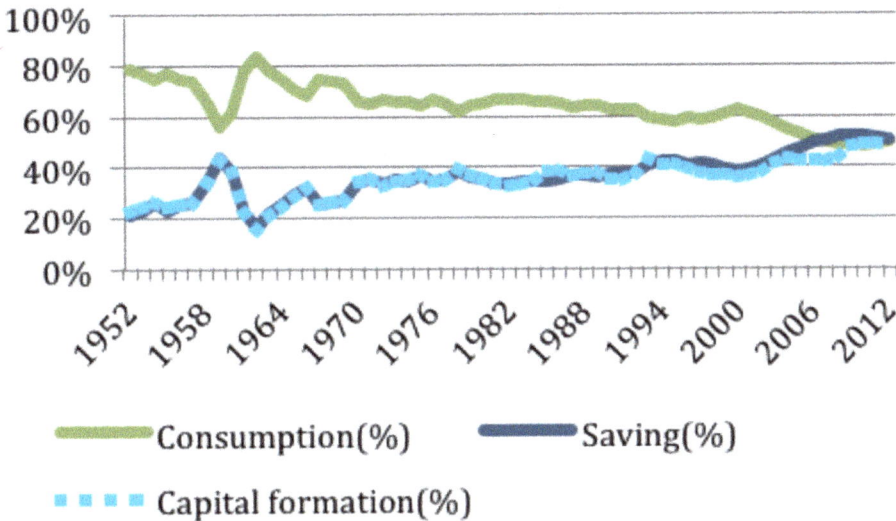

Figure 3.1 The Change in China's Consumption Rate and Savings Rate
(share of GDP) in the Past Six Decades
Source: NBS (2014).

Figure 3.1 also shows that the capital formation rate tended to rise in tandem with the savings rate, and basically coincided with the savings rate most of the time; however, after the savings rate climbed to more than 40 per cent, the two began to separate, with the capital formation rate falling short of the savings rate. The difference between the two was made up for by net exports. The overcapacity problem in China's manufacturing industry was becoming more and more serious precisely during this period. This shows that a main reason for the continuous expansion of China's trade surplus in the previous period was insufficient domestic consumer demand. The continued reliance on investment stimulation couldn't fundamentally solve the problem of insufficient aggregate demand, and has instead led to overcapacity.

It is true that, during most of the past three decades, high savings provided sufficient funds for investment becoming a powerful impetus to economic growth. High saving and high investment were undoubtedly among the main driving forces behind China's rapid economic growth in this period; however, it is not true that the higher the savings and capital formation rates, the more beneficial they are to the economy. After 2000, the declining trend of the consumption rate became stronger and the growth of the savings and capital formation rates was extraordinary, which pushed the growth rate of fixed capital stock from about 10 per cent up to close to 20 per cent (calculated based on fixed assets investment data using the perpetual inventory method), but this didn't bring about an acceleration in economic growth. On the contrary, there has been a continuous slowdown of economic growth in the past five to six years. This shows that under the condition of ultra-high saving and investment rates, the intensification of insufficient domestic demand significantly reduced economic efficiency.

The decline in China's consumption rate in the centrally planned period (1952–78) was mainly caused by forced capital accumulation conducted by the Government to promote industrialisation. After the start of market-oriented economic reforms, however, the declining trend in the consumption rate since the mid 1980s has been closely related to changes in the pattern of income distribution for what follows.

First, during this period, economic growth was faster than income growth, leading to declining shares of both household income and household consumption. A major cause of this situation is the 'dual economy' state described by Lewis (1954) in which the 'unlimited supply' of surplus labour suppresses the rise in urban wages.

Currently, there are at least 160 million rural migrant workers employed in urban areas, as well as millions of rural workers continuing to enter urban areas each year. Therefore, the supply to the labour market has long been abundant and wage growth has been far below the growth rate of per capita GDP. This has led to a declining share of employee compensation in income distribution, and has further caused the growth of household consumption to lag behind economic growth. During the 25 years from 1985 to 2010, while China's per capita GDP increased by 8.4 times, the per capita income of urban and rural residents grew by only 6.3 and 3.6 times respectively, and per capita consumption in China increased by only 4.4 times (in constant prices).

In recent years, the above situation has been changing. Some scholars have noticed a slowdown of labour transfer from rural to urban areas and argued that China has passed the 'Lewis turning point' (Cai 2010). In addition to the changing relationship between labour supply and demand, improvement of the social security system and the increase of transfer payments also contributed to the acceleration of urban and rural income and consumption growth in recent years. During 2011–13, the annual growth rates of per capita income of urban and rural residents were 8.3 per cent and 10.5 per cent (in constant prices) and exceeded the corresponding growth rate of per capita GDP by 7.7 per cent. There were signs that household consumption growth was slightly lower than household income growth, but it still exceeded per capita GDP growth.

It should be noted, however, that nearly half of the Chinese population still lives in rural areas. Although a majority of young people work in urban areas, a large proportion of the middle-aged working population remains in rural areas. Furthermore, faced with institutional barriers in *hukou* or household registration, and access to social security, welfare and housing service systems, migrant workers find it difficult to settle there and therefore have to leave their children and parents in the countryside. Many of them have to return to their rural home after working in cities for many years. The current slowdown in labour transfers from rural to urban areas is, to a certain extent, caused by these institutional barriers. If these obstacles can be gradually eliminated through reforming the household registration system, the social security and public services systems, there will still be quite a large number of rural labourers to be transferred out.

Second, the share of government revenue in GDP declined rapidly in the 1980s and the first half of the 1990s, but it has been increasing constantly since the mid 1990s. Amongst government spending, investment in fixed assets grew fastest. During 2003–12, funds for fixed assets investment in the state budget grew at an annual rate of 22 per cent (in constant prices). Meanwhile, budgetary expenditure for public services, social security and transfer payments grew relatively slowly. This has contributed to the declining share of household consumption in GDP.

Third, the widening income disparity is an important cause of the decline in the share of household consumption. Due to the diminishing marginal propensity to consume, the savings rate of the rich is much higher than that of the poor. Table 3.1 shows that, according to the 2011 data from the NBS, the savings rate of the lowest-income urban households was less than 7 per cent, while the savings rate of the highest-income households reached 40 per cent.

Table 3.1 Urban Household Savings Rate (by income levels in 2011)

	Lowest income	Low income	Lower-middle income	Middle income	Upper-middle income	High income	Highest income
Share in all households (%)	10	10	20	20	20	10	10
Per capita disposable income (RMB)	6876	10 672	14 498	19 545	26 420	35 579	58 842
Savings rate (%)	6.5	20.3	25.0	28.2	31.3	32.8	40.2

Source: NBS (2014).

During the 25 years from 1985 to 2010, China's Gini coefficient for income distribution rose from 0.31 to 0.48 and China appeared in the short list of countries with huge income disparities. The widening income gap indicates faster growth of the rich than of the poor, skewing the distribution of national income towards the minority. Therefore, the widening income gap spontaneously leads to a decrease in the consumption rate and an increase in the savings rate.

Statistics show that the overall household savings rate (weighted average of urban and rural residents) rose from 23 per cent to 29 per cent in the decade from 2000 to 2010.

It should be pointed out that the actual income inequality and the decline of the consumption rate were more serious than the statistics show. This was in part because some of the high-income households received a large amount of 'grey income' from sources that were not declared and thus not reflected in the household income statistics. According to a study based on a nationwide survey of urban residents' income, the relative income ratio between the richest 10 per cent and the poorest 10 per cent of households was 20.9 in 2011, while it was only 8.6 according to official statistics. The actual savings rate of high-income households was also significantly higher than that reported in official statistics. The major cause of this situation was the existence of loopholes in the management of public funds and public resources, imperfection of the institutions, low transparency, lack of social supervision, imperfection of the tax system, poor management of the capital and land markets, and the poor management of income distribution in monopoly industries. These led to the loss of public funds, corruption and unfair distribution (see Wang 2010, 2013; Wang and Woo 2011).

Fourth, during China's reforms, the wage determination mechanism changed from government administration to market mechanisms, which resulted in flexibility in employment and efficiency gains, whereas institutions which compensate for market imperfection, such as legislation for labour protection, social security and public welfare systems, were underdeveloped. These systems were developed in Europe in the nineteenth century and then in the United States after the Great Depression of the 1930s. With the social security systems missing, the growth of labour income and the growth of consumption significantly lag behind economic growth.

According to an official survey, 359 million people from rural areas were employed in urban areas in 2011, but only 216 million workers participated in the basic pension insurance scheme for urban workers, 252 million in the basic medical insurance scheme, 143 million people in the unemployment insurance scheme, and 177 million people in the industrial injury insurance scheme. The actual coverage of the above social insurance schemes for urban employees was only 60 per cent, 70 per cent, 40 per cent and 49 per cent, respectively. Those who were not covered by these urban social security systems were mainly migrant workers in the cities (NBS 2012). Due to the lack of social security, these workers have to compress their current consumption in order to save money to cope with future risks.

Fifth, firms in a monopoly position and endowed with advantageous resources have been enjoying rapidly rising corporate income and savings, which is one reason for the decline of the household consumption rate. These industries are protected by the Government in terms of pricing, taxation and resource allocation, and so receive profit margins that are several times those in competitive industries. These industries include banking and insurance, oil and gas, telecommunications and electricity. The unreasonable allocation of the huge revenue from land development and transfer, and the insider trading and fraud in capital markets resulting from poor regulations, are also important factors.

Sixth, local governments at various administrative levels have strong incentive to promote local economic growth and often offer policy preference to large investment projects and large enterprises, while the business environment for labour-intensive small and medium-sized enterprises which create a lot of employment is relatively worse, and these firms are at a competitive disadvantage. Consequently, the income gap is further expanded and the consumption rate declines. According to the National Economic Census data, the proportion of all small industrial enterprises in total industrial output fell from 56.4 per cent to 44.2 per cent, and that in total industrial employment fell from 67 per cent to 59.4 per cent, between 1995 and 2008 (NBS various years). The atrophy of small enterprises was unfavourable to employment growth and balanced income distribution.

In recent years, wages and farmers' income have been growing relatively rapidly, which improves the situation. The final consumption rate increased from 48.2 per cent of 2010 to 49.1 per cent of 2011 and 49.5 per cent of 2012, showing a rise for the first time in more than a decade. This new phenomenon has several causes: the labour supply and demand situation has changed in recent years and wage growth has accelerated; farmers' incomes have increased due to growth in agricultural output, agricultural price increases and favourable agricultural policies; social security has been improving and government spending on public services and transfer payments to low-income residents have increased—an example being the significant rise in the minimum wage standard. In the current circumstances, however, it is still too early to regard these changes as a turning point towards structural rebalance.

Insufficient consumption demand and structural imbalance

In the past decade, the savings rate rose continuously and the consumption rate declined continuously, which significantly changed the structure of total demand, making economic growth increasingly dependent on the demand pull from foreign markets and resulting in structural imbalances. After the GFC of

2008–09, demand from the international market remained weak, which slowed export growth markedly. This in turn prompted the Government to adopt heavily expansionary fiscal and monetary policies and to stimulate economic growth by expanding government investment, thus pushing the investment rate to higher levels. Structural imbalance can be mainly observed in the following factors.

Heavy reliance on exports

With the rise in the savings rate, the contribution of domestic final consumption to economic growth decreased. In most of the years since 2000, the contribution from domestic final consumption to economic growth has remained at about 40 per cent, whereas in the period 2000–08, the average annual growth rates of China's dollar-denominated imports and exports were 22.4 per cent and 24.4 per cent, respectively. Net exports of goods and services accounted for as much as 8.8 per cent of GDP in 2007 (but dropped to 2.8 per cent in 2012).

China's exports and trade surplus expanded rapidly after 2000. One of the reasons is the rising competitiveness and the full play of China's comparative advantages after its accession to the World Trade Organisation (WTO). Another reason was that the relative lack of domestic demand coincided with the rapid expansion of domestic production capacity so that firms could not find outlets for their products in the domestic market and were forced to turn to the international market. This last factor is, in fact, a reflection of the domestic structural imbalance.

Over-reliance on investment

From 2000 to 2011, the share of capital formation in GDP increased by 13 percentage points, from 35.3 per cent to 48.3 per cent. During the GFC from 2008 to 2010, the Chinese Government launched an expansionary investment plan of RMB4 trillion, and many local governments established platforms for large-scale financing of investment funds that involved more than ten RMB10 trillion. Bank loans were greatly relaxed in 2009, which increased by RMB10 trillion or one-third of the level of the previous year. This led to extremely eased monetary supply and rapid expansion of the scale of investment. The rate of capital formation significantly increased as a result.

Indeed, investment growth lifted up rapid economic growth in the short run. However, without corresponding household consumption growth, the rapidly expanding production capacity could not be absorbed by domestic demand and thus caused overcapacity in later periods (Table 3.2).

Table 3.2 Capacity Usage Rate in Some Industries, 2009–12 (per cent)

	2009	2010	2011	2012
Electrolytic aluminium	61.2	59.6	58.6	
Photovoltaics	/	/	/	< 60.0
Shipbuilding	/	/	/	about 60.0
Cement	67.1	65.2	64.5	67.1
Coke	72.6	70.4	69.4	
Wind turbines	/	/	/	< 70.0
Plate glass	69.2	71.4	77.6	
Crude steel	81.1	82.0	80.5	72.0
Coal	91.8	89.3	87.2	/
Electricity generation	84.2	86.4	88.6	/
Automobiles	85.7	105.0	94.4	/

Source: China Economic Information Network, internet available at <http://www.cei.gov.cn/>.

In order to avoid the problem of capacity expansion, local governments developed increasing enthusiasm for infrastructure construction and real estate development. These areas do not directly relate to production capacity, although they indirectly drive up market demand for steel, cement and other inputs, and thus stimulated the expansion of production capacity in these sectors. After the expansionary policy ended, the excess capacity became prominent.

In 2012, China's crude steel production was 724 million tonnes and the capacity utilisation rate was 72 per cent (NBS 2013; State Council 2013). This in turn forced the Government to use administrative measures to eliminate excess capacity, close businesses and destroy old equipment. This was a waste of resources. It is obvious that when the savings rate and the capital formation rate have already been high, continuous use of expansionary investment policies to stimulate demand will only have a very short-term effect and the oversupply situation will be worsened later on. Such expansionary policies have reached a dead end. Meanwhile, accompanying high inputs, high costs, high emissions, high pollution and resource and environmental degradation have all become constraints to future economic growth.

Growth slowdown and decreasing returns to capital

Investment expansion leads to overcapacity, which means part of the investment is ineffective. In Table 3.3, the annual growth rates of the Chinese economy and the fixed capital stock in the period 2000–13 are calculated and compared. We can see that, in the past 10 years, due to the rapid expansion of investment, the annual growth rate of capital stock has risen from 9 per cent to about 16 per cent, whereas the economic growth rate has been slowing. This shows decreasing efficiency of capital.

Table 3.3 also calculates the capital–output ratio (GDP/capital stock) and the incremental capital–output ratio (ΔGDP/Δ capital stock). These two indicators are the reciprocals of the average capital productivity and the marginal productivity of capital, respectively. The larger their values are, the lower is the productivity of capital. During the period 2001–12, the capital–output ratio rose from 1.97 to 3.26, while the incremental capital output ratio rose from 2.19 to 6.23.

Table 3.3 Changes in Growth Rates of China's Capital Stock and Capital–Output Ratio in the Past Decade

	Growth rate of GDP (%)	Growth rate of capital stock (%)	Capital–output ratio	Incremental capital–output ratio
2000	8.4	9.1	1.95	2.09
2001	8.3	9.3	1.97	2.19
2002	9.1	10.2	1.99	2.22
2003	10.0	12.2	2.03	2.42
2004	10.1	13.1	2.08	2.63
2005	11.3	13.9	2.13	2.57
2006	12.7	14.9	2.18	2.51
2007	14.2	15.2	2.20	2.34
2008	9.6	14.8	2.30	3.38
2009	9.2	18.0	2.48	4.48
2010	10.4	17.5	2.64	4.15
2011	9.3	16.3	2.81	4.64
2012	7.7	16.0	3.03	5.87
2013	7.7	15.8	3.26	6.23

Source: NBS (2014).

The sharply rising trend of the capital–output ratio is significantly different from the path experienced by developed countries. In Figures 3.2a and 3.2b, the capital–output ratio of China in the past 60 years (1952–2011) is compared with the average capital–output ratio of the 22 developed countries in the Organisation for Economic Cooperation and Development (OECD) during the period 1960–2001 (Australia, Austria, Belgium, Canada, Denmark, Finland, France, Germany, Greece, Iceland, Ireland, Italy, Japan, Netherlands, New Zealand, Norway, Portugal, Spain, Sweden, Switzerland, the United Kingdom and the United States).

OECD

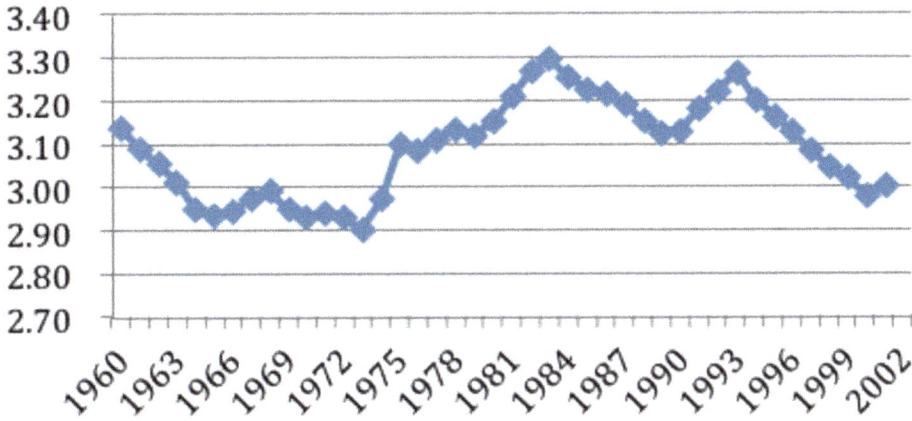

Figure 3.2a Average Trend in the Capital–Output Ratio of 22 OECD Countries

China

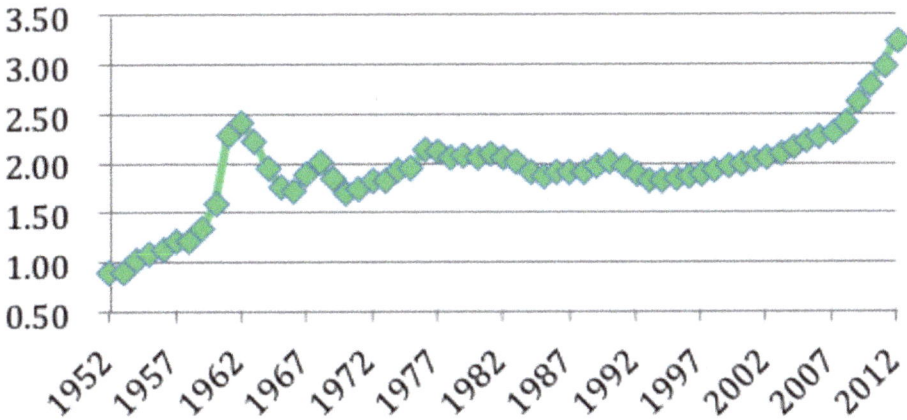

Figure 3.2b Long-Term Trend in the Capital–Output Ratio of China

Sources: Kamps (2004); and authors' calculations.

Comparison of the data shows that the capital–output ratios in China and in the OECD countries have the following differences in their long-term trends.

First, the average capital–output ratio in OECD countries fluctuated within a smaller range of 2.9–3.3 in the 42 years. For most of the countries, the bandwidths of fluctuation did not exceed one. In contrast, China's capital–output ratio increased from 1.5 to 3.3, and the range of the fluctuation is significantly larger.

Second, on average, the OECD countries' capital–output ratio did not rise continuously (or capital productivity fall continuously). During the three oil crises (1973–93), the average capital–output ratio was relatively high, with a peak at 3.3, but then dropped significantly after 1993. Until 2001, the average capital–output ratio had dropped to three. China's capital–output ratio, in contrast, has been rising continuously from the mid 1990s to the present.

Third, China's rising capital–output ratio is in some way related to its industrialisation process because the marginal productivity of capital will gradually decrease with increasing capital intensity in a capital-scarce early-stage developing country. This is reasonable in the industrialisation phase. China has not yet completed its industrialisation process, while the OECD countries have already finished theirs. Nevertheless, China's capital–output ratio was close to 3.3 in 2012, which was significantly higher than the current average level of the 22 OECD countries. For a middle-income country, this indicates that capital productivity has dropped too much. This occurred mainly in the past 10 years, reflecting the efficiency problems on China's development path in the past 10 years.

The above situation is not only related to China's expansionary fiscal and monetary policies over the period of the GFC, but also to the overenthusiasm of local governments at various levels towards pursuing GDP growth rates. Governments at various levels use various measures to attract foreign and domestic investment, such as tax reduction, cheap land prices, etc. or directly borrowing bank loans via so-called 'financing platforms' to finance various government investment projects regardless of costs. All of these practices lead to over-investment. If these conditions cannot be changed, the current structural imbalances and lack of domestic demand will be difficult to alter, and may even become more severe. Economic growth is likely to follow a downward trend into long-term weakness, and even into the middle-income trap.

On the other hand, the Chinese economy still has enormous growth potential. Currently the urbanisation rate is just more than 50 per cent and urbanisation will remain a powerful engine of growth, with another 20 years of rapid development. The process of industrial upgrading is taking place and has yet to realise its full potential. The development of the service sector is still inadequate. Both of these have great room for further development. The quality of human capital should be improved. The rate of technological progress hasn't yet reached the ideal speed, but there is great potential for catching up with technologies in developed countries. If the education and innovation systems can be improved, there is great potential for total factor productivity to grow.

For these institutional potentials to become the driving force of development, however, the obstacles need to be removed, and the economic structure needs to be rebalanced. A key to achieving these is to rebalance savings and household consumption to enable domestic demand to become a powerful engine for sustained economic growth.

Is there a 'golden-rule savings rate'?

According to Keynesian theory, a country's overall economic need comprises three parts that are substitutable with each other: consumption, investment and net exports. When there is insufficient aggregate demand (total investment < total savings) and it causes a shrinking economy, the aggregate demand can be increased by consumption expansion, the use of expansionary fiscal policy to increase government investment or easing of monetary policy to stimulate private investment. Since the household savings rate is unlikely to be determined by the Government, the fiscal and monetary policies of the Government emphasised by Keynes are basically focused on adjusting investment demand.

China twice adopted the Keynesian demand expansion policy to substantially increase investment and successfully boosted its economic growth when hit by both the Asian financial crisis in 1997-98 and the GFC in 2008; however, the inflation that occurred after the last substantial expansion, overcapacity and the steadily declining rate of economic growth prompt us to reflect on the long-term effectiveness and applicability of Keynesian policies in China.

The conditions for suitability of expansionary investment policies

Despite the fact that Keynesian theory has had many successful applications, it did not investigate the conditions under which total investment being less than total savings occurs. Macro-economic analysis shows that there is a correlation between investment and savings. If financial markets are sufficiently flexible then when the social savings rate is high enough and money supply is sufficient, interest rates will stay low, so that the scale of investment is automatically maintained at a high level. If, however, investment is still lower than savings now, this is probably due to market saturation, overcapacity and the absence of profit margins for investors. This situation is especially evident in a low-consumption, high-savings and high-investment economy like China's.

In this case, if government intervenes through fiscal policy to expand investment or through accommodative monetary policy to stimulate investment, can new demand be created? The answer is: yes, but only in the short term. New investment projects will inevitably generate new demand for investment goods, creating more purchasing power to drive short-term economic growth; however, this process doesn't end here, because once the new investment project is completed, production capacity will be expanded. So, after a short-term expansion of demand, the future supply will be further expanded. If consumer demand remains unchanged at this time, or consumption growth lags behind the growth of output, it means that the total savings rate rises rather than falls, thus creating new savings that need to be balanced by investment on an even larger scale. Thus, a larger round of expansionary fiscal or monetary policy needs to be started next round.

No sophisticated economic analyses are required for one to see clearly that without a certain balance between consumption and savings, the investment-led growth cycle is not sustainable. Thus we can easily understand why Keynesian expansionary policies are often able to achieve good results in the short run, but their effects often diminish in the medium and long runs, leading to the difficult situation of stagflation.

Is there a better alternative available to the Government? The answer is yes. It would be better for the Government to promote infrastructure investment and not productive investment. This is because investment in infrastructure does not directly create or expand production capacity. In this sense, to respond to the economic crisis caused by overcapacity, fiscal policy could be more effective than monetary policy in terms of long-term effects. Fiscal policy can be chosen to target certain directions of investment—mainly infrastructure construction. In contrast, an expansionary monetary policy stimulates economy-wide investment, resulting in a further increase in total supply.

There is, however, still a reasonable limit to fiscal policy even if it is used only in infrastructure. First, oversupply in infrastructure will lead to long-term idleness and waste of resources—a kind of overcapacity as well. Such investment drives GDP growth in statistics but does not bring about additional national welfare. Second, expanding the scale of infrastructure investment is bound to increase demand for inputs and upstream demand along the industrial chain. If a certain limit is exceeded, further increases in investment and production capacity will take place in related industries. Once the expansion ends, the newly created production capacity will become excessive.

In China in the past 20 years, the Government has promoted infrastructure construction, which indeed significantly promoted economic growth. In recent years, however, various businesses and industries have suffered from increasingly serious overcapacity, and the situation is most severe in the production of inputs such as iron, steel, cement, and so on. This is clearly the result of large-scale expansion of infrastructure investment. In the initial period of expansion, the demand for steel and other inputs is strong and prices rise, thus conveying wrong signals to these industries and prompting them to make significant investment to expand production capacity. Once expansionary policies come to an end, this newly created production capacity will become excessive.

Is there a 'golden rule' for saving and investment?

The situation described above shows that consumer demand and investment demand are not always substitutable. The higher the savings rate, the higher is the required rate of investment to maintain the balance of supply and demand, and the faster is the expansion of production capacity. The small scale and slow growth of domestic consumption are insufficient to absorb the increase of final output due to the expansion of production capacity. This will continue to generate a new supply–demand imbalance.

Therefore, for an economy to maintain structural balance and sustainable development, a reasonable savings rate is required. A very low savings rate will not be sufficient for funding investment and therefore for economic growth. On the other hand, if the savings rate is too high, production capacity will grow faster than consumption and this will continue to increase the investment rate and create new overcapacity. Consequently, economic growth will suffer as well.

Robert Barro and Xavier Sala-i-Martin (1995), both working in economic growth theories, prove that, under steady-state growth conditions, there is an optimal savings rate to ensure the maximisation of residents' long-term consumption. They call it the 'golden-rule savings rate'. The savings rate is not, however, a definite value, and it depends on the growth rates of labour and capital depreciation and other external conditions.

Here we apply a simple approach—a two-sector model—to examine the relationship between the savings rate and economic growth.

Suppose an economy consists of two basic production sectors. Sector A produces consumer goods for the whole of society and Sector B produces capital goods for both Sector A and Sector B. Each year the entire society will use 70 per cent of total output in consumption and 30 per cent of total output in investment. Therefore, the total output consists of 70 per cent consumer goods and 30 per cent capital goods. For simplicity, we assume that the marginal productivity of the two sectors is the same and equal to their average productivity; their capital intensity and labour intensity are the same; and the whole economy is initially in supply and demand equilibrium. Thus, Sector A should have 70 per cent of the capital and labour in the whole society, while Sector B owns the remaining 30 per cent.

Now assume that some external shock drives up the gross savings rate from 30 per cent to 50 per cent. Consumer demand declines correspondingly (a decline of 50 per cent/70 per cent $-1 = -28.6$ per cent). The society reduces consumption but has more money for investment. The decline in consumer demand first causes overcapacity in Sector A. In response to market signals, labour and capital flow into Sector B, causing the production capacity in Sector A to shrink and the production capacity in Sector B to expand. In the meantime, the increase in the savings rate brings more capital for investment in Sector B than in Sector A.

If, however, the actual restructuring process happens like this, the production overcapacity in Sector B will become more serious than that in Sector A. This is because with the decline in output of Sector A, the demand for capital goods from Sector A will decrease by the same proportion after a certain time lag, so that total demand for capital goods decreases by 20 per cent ($= -28.6$ per cent $\times$ 70 per cent). This will force Sector B to reduce production and further reduce the demand for capital goods from Sector B, leading to a 27.6 per cent shrinkage in the demand for capital goods. Therefore, the transfer of capital and labour from Sector A to Sector B and the new investment in Sector B are unlikely to be accomplished. Both sectors will experience overcapacity and a decline in production, leading to rising unemployment and a decline in revenue. In the first round of the fall, aggregate demand shrinks by 27.8 per cent (that is, the weighted average of the extents of declines in consumer demand and in investment demand), while the ensuing unemployment and decline in revenue, in turn, will lead to further declines in demand for consumer goods. Without other intervening factors, this vicious cycle will drag the whole economy into a downward spiral towards a state of crisis.

Now suppose that the Government implements policies to stimulate investment demand immediately after the first round of declines. To compensate for the previous 27.8 per cent of decline in total demand and to reinstate the level of aggregate demand, it is necessary that the demand for capital goods is raised by 92.7 per cent (using the level of demand for capital goods before its drop as 100 per cent). Assuming this goal can be achieved, the total output will then return to its pre-crisis level—but this is only a short-term effect. Large-scale investment will bring about the rapid expansion of the production capacity of the two sectors. After the investment cycle induced by the economic stimulus is completed, total demand is no longer expanding, while the total supply of new production capacity increases significantly. This will lead to a new round of overcapacity and the economy will again face a crisis of insufficient aggregate demand. Unless the economy-wide savings rate can be reduced to its original level or the society can export part of its output to other countries and thus maintain a long-term trade surplus, accommodative monetary policy is ineffective in the medium to long term.

Now we consider another scenario: add a public sector to the above model, and assume that the Government, instead of taking the accommodative monetary policy to stimulate investment, simply adopts an expansionary fiscal policy in the form of infrastructure investment by the public sector. In this case, the effective demand will increase due to the expansion of investment, but the new investment will not lead to further expansion of production capacity. The economy can recover from the crisis and the situation will be better than in the previous case. After the economy recovers to its pre-crisis status, however, consumer demand is still only 50 per cent of the total output, while the other 50 per cent of total output still relies on investment demand. Public investment to expand domestic demand has, however, already been completed and the demand for capital goods cannot be sustained at the level of the expansionary period. Therefore, if society cannot adjust its saving and consumption rates, the economy will again face the difficulty of insufficient aggregate demand once the expansionary public investment stops. This will force the government to continue relying on deficit financing to maintain investment expansion, which ultimately leads to stagflation.

The above analysis shows that, under certain conditions, there exist optimal consumption and saving rates. When the consumption rate is higher than the optimal level, savings, investment and capital-embodied technical progress are inadequate, leading to slow economic growth. When the consumption rate is lower than the optimal level, the demand is insufficient, which also restrains economic growth, makes the actual growth rate lower than the potential growth rate and results in loss of efficiency. In the medium to long run, very low consumption cannot be continuously compensated with investment expansion.

The policy implication of the above analysis is that when there is a lack of consumer demand, neither accommodative monetary policies nor the expansion of government-led investment can solve the fundamental problem. The key is to change the low consumption rate through institutional reforms and policy adjustments. In China, necessary and effective measures to change the consumption rate include reforming the aspects of the fiscal and taxation systems that are not entirely reasonable, rationalising government spending, reforming government management systems to improve government behaviour and to promote the rational allocation of factors, improving social security, public services and income redistribution systems, and narrowing the excessively wide income gap.

Before and after World War II, all of the developed countries improved social security, public services and income redistribution systems. These changed the situation of a polarisation of income distribution characterised in early capitalist economies and protected the basic rights of citizens for education, employment, fair compensation, access to health care, unemployment insurance and pensions, which significantly changed the large income gap and insufficient household consumption characterised in early capitalist economies. This diminished the occurring of cyclical economic crises often observed in traditional capitalist economies.

Until now, debates on the relative importance of equity and efficiency and of public welfare and free markets are continuing widely without a common conclusion. Looking back, most people would agree that the changes in income distribution and social welfare systems in the twentieth century were precisely what gave the advanced market economies new life and helped them avoid a recurrence of the Great Depression of the 1930s. The relationship between equity and efficiency is not mere substitution. This indicates there are structural imbalances due to unduly large income inequality, and improving income distribution and fairness in society will not only improve the allocation of resources, but also promote efficiency.

What are reasonable levels for the savings rate and consumption rate?

Although the existence of a 'golden-rule savings rate' can be proven, the reality differs across countries and therefore there is not a single optimal solution. Wang et al. (2009) did some preliminary econometric analyses using China's historical data for the past half-century. They use a Lucas-type growth model (Lucas 1988) and include a number of structural variables such as research and development spending, infrastructure conditions, market-oriented reforms, urbanisation, trade dependence, the final consumption rate, and so on. They found that the relationship between the final consumption rate and total factor productivity is a nonlinear function. The consumption rate being too high or too low has adverse effects on productivity and therefore on economic growth. Thus optimal band for the consumption rate is found.

The above study also finds, however, that the consumption rate is sensitive to model specifications and that its exact optimal location is not confirmed. After using the updated data, they obtain the curve shown in Figure 3.3 based on the same model. In this figure, the horizontal axis, fc, represents the consumption rate (share of final consumption in GDP); the vertical axis, f(fc), shows the effect of the consumption rate on constant price GDP value. In the figure we can find a maximum point where the impact of the consumption rate on total factor productivity and total output is largest, and therefore the consumption rate at this point can be defined as the optimal consumption rate.

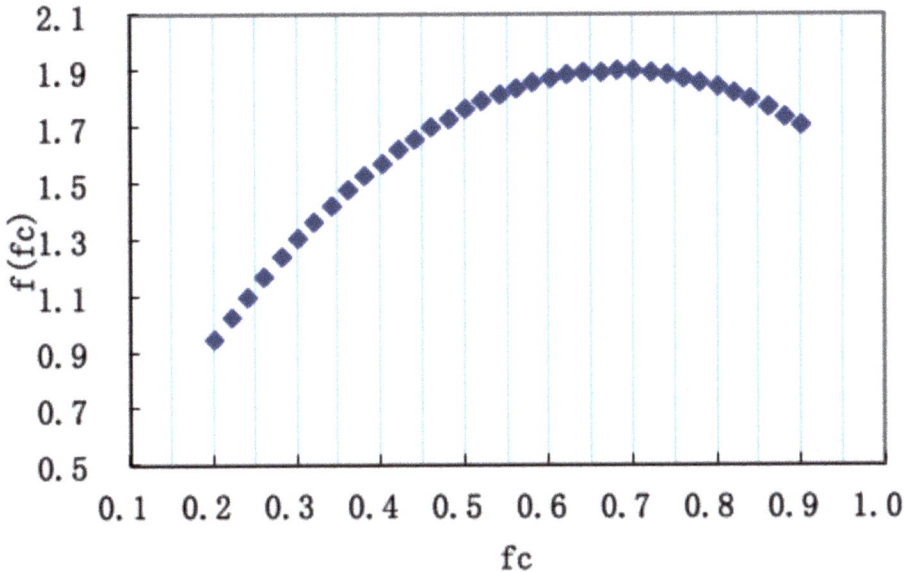

Figure 3.3 Fitted Curve of the Regression Model for the Optimal Consumption Rate

It can be seen in Figure 3.3 that the optimal consumption rate is about 60–70 per cent. Sensitivity analysis shows that the optimal point is still sensitive to model specification, changing with different model specifications. Therefore it is difficult to confirm the specific value; however, according to the analyses of empirical data from home and abroad, 60–70 per cent should be a reasonable range.

Conclusion

We may imagine economic rebalance will take place in China in the coming decade via institutional reforms and policy adjustments, to increase the final consumption rate from the current level of below 50 per cent to about 60 per cent (of GDP) and decrease the rate of capital formation from the current 48 per cent to 38 per cent and the trade surplus falls to less than 2 per cent. If these changes take place and other conditions remain unchanged, the economic growth rate will be higher than it is currently and the higher level of growth will be sustained in the longer term. Assuming these adjustments will take five years, during which the average growth rate is 7–7.5 per cent, to finish, it will not be difficult to achieve an 8 per cent growth rate for China in the following ten years.

More importantly, this growth rate will, however, be achieved with less investment, less resource and energy consumption, less pollution and environmental damage, and higher household income and consumption levels. Obviously, it will be a more sustainable, more efficient, and more welfare-enhancing state of growth.

References

Barro, R. and Sala-i-Martin, X. (1995), *Economic Growth*, New York: McGraw-Hill.

Cai, F. (2010), 'Demographic transition, demographic dividend and the Lewis turning point', *Economic Research* (4).

Chow, G. C. (1993), 'Capital formation and economic growth in China', *Quarterly Journal of Economics* (108): 809–42.

First Financial Daily (2012), 'Overcapacity being one-third, the more you invest in the iron and steel industry, the more you lose', *First Financial Daily*, 18 April 2012.

Kamps, C. (2004), *New estimates of government net capital stocks for 22 OECD countries 1960–2001*, IMF Working Paper 04/67, International Monetary Fund, Washington, DC.

Lewis, W. A. (1954), 'Economic development with unlimited supplies of labor', *Manchester School of Economic and Social Studies* (XXII) (May): 139–91.

Lucas, R. E. (1988), 'On the mechanics of economic development', *Journal of Monetary Economics* 22: 3–42.

National Bureau of Statistics (NBS) (2012), *2011 Monitoring Report of the Survey of Migrant Workers*, Beijing: National Bureau of Statistics.

National Bureau of Statistics (NBS) (2013), *2013 National Economic and Social Development Statistics Bulletin*, Beijing: National Bureau of Statistics.

National Bureau of Statistics (NBS) (various years), <http:data.stats.gov.cn/>.

State Council (2013), 'A Guideline for Defusing the Serious Overcapacity Problem', The Central Government website.

Wang, X. (2010), *Gray Income and Income Distribution: Comparison*, Beijing: CITIC Publishing House.

Wang, X. (2013), *Gray Income and Income Distribution: 2013 Report, Comparison*, Beijing: CITIC Publishing House.

Wang, X. and Woo, W. T. (2011), 'The size and distribution of hidden household income in China', *Asian Economic Papers* 10(1), Cambridge, Mass.: MIT Press.

Wang, X., Fan, G. and Liu, P. (2009), 'China's economic growth mode transformation, and sustainability of growth', *Economic Research* 1.

World Bank (2012), *World Development Indicators*, [Chinese version], Beijing: China Finance and Economics Publishing House.

Zhang, J., Wu, G. and Peng, Z. (2004), 'China's provincial capital stock estimates: 1952–2000', *Journal of Economic Research* (10).

4. State Control, Entrepreneurship and Resource Allocation

Son Ngoc Chu and Ligang Song

Introduction

State-led resource allocation has been an important part of China's economic reform strategy, having exerted substantial effects on the survival of state-owned enterprises (SOEs) and the evolution of private enterprises. Focusing on capital, land, energy and utilities as key resources, we examine how the state has changed and reformed the institutional systems governing the supply and distribution of these resources during the market reform process. At the same time, we investigate how enterprises of different ownership types have responded to access these resources. Differences in firm behaviours and responses across the sectoral and ownership patterns of investment activities, asset and output shares, and profit and productivity performance are examined. This sheds light on the puzzle of China's high economic growth with rapid expansion of the private sector in the total economy, but accompanied by the continuing predominant role of SOEs in some of the key sectors in the economy such as oil, petrochemicals, aviation, steel, coal, finance, telecommunications and railways.

In general, state control of the development of capital, land and resource markets has created substantial rents that have been directed to important infrastructure projects and provision of public goods, thereby facilitating economic transition and contributing to rapid economic growth. At the same time, such rents have also produced side effects of state control of resources including rent-seeking activities by both governments and enterprises, and distorting resource allocation. The misallocation of resources has been found to be linked with structural imbalances such as overcapacity in certain sectors, and significant negative impacts on the development of private entrepreneurship, which holds the key to increasing the productivity and growth potential of China.

Economic transition, state-controlled resources and entrepreneurship

It has been recognised that in a market economy, entrepreneurship drives economic growth through a 'creative destruction' process, a term coined by Schumpeter in the early twentieth century (Carree and Thurik 2003). Development economics views entrepreneurship as a driving force of economic growth and structural transformation (Naudé 2010; Gries and Naudé 2008). This view seems to be particularly relevant for a country in the process of economic transition from a centrally planned to a market-based economy. The connection between the market and entrepreneurship suggests that market transition is always associated with the emergence and evolution of the private sector in the economy. The progress of market reforms can be seen in the expansion and diversity of the activities of private entrepreneurs (Tanas and Audretsch 2011). While there are commonly agreed traits of entrepreneurs, such as being alert to profit opportunities, creativity and risk-taking (Lu 1994), the nature of entrepreneurship could be quite different, depending crucially on the institutional settings of an economy.

The nature and types of entrepreneurship

The Organisation for Economic Cooperation and Development (OECD) defines entrepreneurship as business activity determined mainly by entrepreneurs. Entrepreneurs are those who own and manage businesses with the purpose of value generation through creation or expansion of economic activity, by identifying and exploiting new products, processes or markets (Ahmad and Hoffman 2008).

The OECD definition of entrepreneurship is consistent with an observation made by Schumpeter in the early twentieth century. Schumpeter (1934) considered entrepreneurship to be an innovative process in which entrepreneurs, as innovators with willingness to take risks, seek profits by creating new products or new production processes with better values to replace old ones, implying higher productivity. Therefore, entrepreneurship is associated with a value-creation process, which he called 'creative destruction', which leads to true economic progress. In addition, introducing new products or processes is seen as creating disequilibrium in the existing market (Lu 1994).

The Schumpeterian view of entrepreneurship, however, which is called high-level entrepreneurship (Karlsson et al. 2004), is narrow, as it focuses only on new value created by new products or processes. Other processes that are not purely innovative can contribute to value generation too. Kirzner (1998) suggested that, being alert to market opportunities, entrepreneurs can make profits through filling the gap between supply and demand in the market, either with production or with trade. By this equilibrating role of the entrepreneur (Lu 1994), more value in terms of profit can be generated through contributing to flows of goods and services. This kind of entrepreneurship is called low-level entrepreneurship, and an example is firms in the wholesale and retail trades (Karlsson et al. 2004).

The two early views of entrepreneurship miss an important fact: not all entrepreneurial efforts bring benefits to society as a whole, despite profits brought to entrepreneurs. Baumol identified this feature of entrepreneurship in his seminal paper (1990). Baumol suggests there are different types of entrepreneurship, including productive, unproductive and destructive entrepreneurship, due to the reward structure created by a certain institutional setting with the existence of the market. Given a country's institutional structure, entrepreneurs can take market opportunities to make profit with their talent. The entrepreneur's market-based activities will create more wealth or value for society, making productive entrepreneurship. There are also profit opportunities in political and legal processes that could attract entrepreneurial efforts. The entrepreneurial efforts in political and legal arenas can accumulate personal wealth through changing government policy in taxation and subsidy; however, these efforts do not generate additional social wealth, but rather redistribute wealth, leading to so-called unproductive entrepreneurship. Moreover, in some cases, entrepreneurial efforts involve illegal activities, which may cause loss of social wealth, making entrepreneurship destructive. Whether entrepreneurial efforts become productive, unproductive or destructive depends on how profitable opportunities are in market and non-market situations. The reward outcomes depend totally on the country's institutional structure. As Sobel (2008) elaborates, productive entrepreneurship is more likely to expand in a market-supportive institutional framework that is characterised by secure property rights, a fair and balanced judicial system, effective contract enforcement, appropriate business regulation and effective control of government power.

An important implication of Baumol's theory is that entrepreneurship growth is not always translated into economic growth and the healthy expansion of entrepreneurship is determined by a sound incentive structure of institutions. Baumol's view of entrepreneurship has particularly relevant implications for the analysis of entrepreneurship development in a transitional economy like China's, in which institutional change to a market economy is central to the transition process. A transitional institutional framework may have created many non-market profit opportunities that attract those business-minded people who are able to exploit institutional loopholes and have become entrepreneurs under market transition. Moreover, transition from a centrally planned economy to a market-based one has created many rent-seeking opportunities that are conducive to unproductive entrepreneurship.

Market transition and evolution of entrepreneurship

Market transition is a long process with different stages of establishing the system with market rules and emerging private firms with different forms to those of state firms (Kolodko 2000). While it is complex to delineate the transition process and corresponding entrepreneurship, a typology of different stages of transition with different types of entrepreneurship would be useful. Estrin et al. (2008) provided such a typology by suggesting three stages of transition in which different kinds of entrepreneurship exist. The initial stage or early transition is characterised by initialising market channels of goods distribution and abandoning planned channels of resource allocation. There are frequent adjustments of relative prices and gaps between demand and supply, creating opportunities for mainly Kirznian types of entrepreneurs. There is a lot of uncertainty due to the unavailability of previous market information and macro-economic instability. In the second stage, uncertainty is reduced due to more market information, less extreme price fluctuations and a more stable macro-economic environment. The fundamentals of a market system such as property rights are established, providing incentives for Schumpeterian entrepreneurship. The third stage would follow with further development of market institutions, which becomes the main force of resource coordination and information provision for market participants. Contract enforcement becomes more dependent on courts. Entrepreneurs can have better access to resources through financial institutions and market exchange. This stage of market transition provides an institutional environment conducive for Schumpeterian entrepreneurship. As Estrin et al. (2008) noted, however, the early forms of entrepreneurship may exist in the later stage of market reform due to the inertia of institutional changes.

Determinants of entrepreneurship

In an analytical framework of entrepreneurship development, Ahmad and Hoffman (2008) suggested six factors determining the path of a country's entrepreneurship development: regulatory framework, market conditions, culture, access to finance or capital, technological capability and entrepreneurial capabilities. The first three factors could create an overall environment for the emergence and evolution of entrepreneurship. A regulatory framework comprises laws and regulations that govern the entry and operation of business activities. A regulatory framework deals with issues such as business entry and exit, product standards, taxation, social health and security, safety, health and environmental protection. Market conditions are actually market opportunities created by the establishment and evolution of a market economy. Market opportunities are driven by factors such as competition, access to domestic and foreign markets and government participation in the market (provision of public goods and procurement). A culture for entrepreneurship growth includes society's attitudes towards entrepreneurs, and desires for business ownership.

The emergence and expansion of entrepreneurship cannot happen without resource availability, which is determined by access to finance, technology and entrepreneurial capabilities. Entrepreneurial supply depends first on entrepreneurial capabilities, which can be established and accumulated by the training and experience of entrepreneurs, business and entrepreneurship education, and migration of entrepreneurs. Research and development (R&D) and technological advances create opportunities for entrepreneurs and their businesses to flourish. Technological capability contributes factors such as R&D investment, technological cooperation between firms, technology diffusion, development of information technology and a patent system; however, to take advantage of business opportunities and make a successful business, the availability of capital is the crucial factor. This factor depends on the entrepreneur's access to financial resources such as a banking system, stock markets and other financial institutions.

The above analytical framework would be useful for examining the nature, characteristics and performance of entrepreneurship in an economy with an established system of market institutions; however, there are some missing elements in the framework for a transitional economy. The analysis of the performance of entrepreneurship would need to take into account two important processes: 1) the process of setting up and building market institutions, including laws and regulations to recognise and ensure private property rights and to govern market transactions; and 2) the parallel process of ownership transformation. The next subsection will explain why it is important to incorporate these processes into analysis of entrepreneurship performance.

State control of resources and the development of entrepreneurship in transition

Market-oriented reform basically involves changing the relative role of the state and the market in the coordination of production, exchange and distribution activities with the main objective of improving efficiency and promoting economic growth. In China, like other centrally planned economies, market-oriented reform started from a point of 'only state, no market' (Zhang 2002:10).

At this starting point, the centrally planned economy is characterised by state control of all productive resources, from fixed assets such as plants, buildings, machinery and equipment to land and other natural resources. The state's control of productive resources takes the form of sole ownership and is carried out through SOEs and agricultural collectives. While financial resources in terms of savings are limited due to non-market, state-coordinated transactions of goods distribution under central planning, production surplus is captured by the state through setting inter-sectoral terms of trade, mainly between agriculture and industry or rural and urban areas. Therefore, one crucial dimension of market-oriented reform has been the transformation of the state's control of resources through ownership transformation of public assets, reducing the role of SOEs and changing the ways government intervenes in production and exchange activities based on market rules and orders. Consequently, on the one hand, market-oriented reform provides an environment for the emergence of entrepreneurship through market opportunities and the incentives of private property rights. On the other hand, market transition gives rise to entrepreneurship through reducing the extent and changing the forms of the state's control of resources—in particular, physical and financial capital, land and other natural resources.

Changing state control of resources under market conditions gives rise to the fundamental question of the interaction of the state and the market. While it is generally expected that the scope of state intervention will be reduced, an important observation is that in economic transition the state plays an indispensable and guiding role in the establishment of the market system, which provides open competition for all firms. This is particularly true of China's experience with its well-known gradual approach to market reform. The leading role of the state is needed because market reform is basically a process of institutional change. Institutional change is a long process and it takes time to build new market institutions and entrench them in an economic system (Murrel and Wang 1993; World Bank 2001). More specifically, Arrow (2001:91) explained the state's market-guiding role: 'Although the role of government in directing economic activity in a healthy economy is limited, transition does require guidance. The only source of general guidance for the economy is the state, and there is no denying that appropriate policy and leadership could considerably smooth transition.'

Given the leading role of the state in economic transition, the interaction between market liberalisation and state control of resources could affect strongly entrepreneurial activities. As discussed above, due to state-dominated ownership of all economic activities, enterprises had to rely on the state for their access not only to production factors (capital, land and other natural resources), but also to basic inputs (energy and utilities). In China as well as other transitional economies, market reform led to the development of markets for these resources, and the emergence of entrepreneurship would not be possible if the state did not reduce its control of and restriction on the access to these resources. Therefore, the dynamics and performance of the private sector would depend significantly on the extent and ways of releasing the state's control of these key resources. Moreover, state dominance through sole ownership or SOE presence means state monopoly in the markets, implying distortions and the existence of substantial rents. The literature on rent and rent-seeking suggests that the existence of rents due to state interventions during market transformation is inevitable and there are certain rents that are growth-enhancing as well as growth-destroying (Khan 2004). A crucial question here is whether the state is able to manage and utilise these rents to enhance economic development. For example, the state can promote private investment by transferring the rents to entrepreneurs through market entry and participation or the state can use the rents for financing public goods provision. In addition, the existence of rents leads to another important question of how these rents can be distributed and used in an equitable manner. We will examine these issues in the context of China's market transition and the evolution of private entrepreneurship.

State control of resources and private entrepreneurship in the initial stage of reform: 1978–1992

One key feature of the early stage of reform in China was the dual-track price system with partial market liberalisation. Following the rapid and successful transformation of agricultural cooperatives under the commune system to a household-based production system, market exchanges were gradually allowed to take a greater share along with planning channels in line with the application of a contract responsibility system in industrial enterprises later on. Liberalisation took place progressively in the product markets, from consumer goods to materials and inputs for agricultural and industrial production. Gradual marketisation created ample opportunities for the expansion of non-state private businesses through exploiting the huge gaps between demand and supply resulting from the acute shortage problems under the planning mechanism (Garnaut et al. 2001). Observing the ways private business activities emerged outside the state sector, Lu (1994) concluded that new private businesses in this period had many features of Kirznian entrepreneurship. Additional market opportunities, although limited, came from the Government's initial steps to open domestic markets to the outside world, with a focal policy to attract foreign direct investment (FDI), especially overseas Chinese FDI from Hong Kong and Taiwan to the coastal areas. Total FDI increased from US$7.4 billion in the period

1979–85 to US\$18.6 billion in the period 1986–91 (Wu 2009:34). Initial opening to FDI promoted trading activities between local entrepreneurs and their counterparts in Hong Kong, which emerged in the late 1970s (Tsai 2007:55).

China's non-state sector[1] had its rapid expansion and contribution to output and employment in the 1980s. Song (2014:190) indicates that, in the period 1978–92, the share of SOEs in gross industrial output value decreased from 78 per cent to 48 per cent while that of the non-state sector grew from more than 22 per cent to 52 per cent correspondingly. It is notable that, of the change in the share of the non-state sector, collectively owned enterprises accounted for most of the change while private enterprises expanded to nearly 10 per cent. During the first stage of reform, the institutional setting had limited formal recognition of the position private entrepreneurs and their business activities take. Their subordinate or auxiliary position resulted from the Chinese Government's experimental approach while a dominant perception of private entrepreneurs as capitalists and exploiters prevailed (Garnaut et al. 2001). Most importantly, there were no clearly defined private property rights (Huang 2008). The rapid expansion of non-state enterprises with their institutionally disadvantageous position has, however, been a big puzzle to many economists. From an institutional perspective, Huang (2008:34) suggested that in the context of property rights security was not institutionalised; what made potential entrepreneurs willing to do business was *directional liberalism*— that is, policy promises and symbolic actions made by government leaders to show the Government's reform intentions. In addition, as a way of responding to ideological and regulatory obstacles, many privately owned enterprises were registered as collectively owned enterprises, leading to a phenomenon of 'red hat' firms in the 1980s and 1990s (Garnaut et al. 2001:14).

---

1 Conceptually, the non-state sector was considered to include collectively owned enterprises, private enterprises, joint-venture enterprises, overseas Chinese enterprises and foreign enterprises (Lin et al. 1996:215). Among them, collectively owned enterprises can be urban non-state and township and village enterprises (TVEs). TVE was used for the first time in 1984 by the State Council to describe commune and brigade enterprises (Song 2014:189). TVEs constitute a major part of the non-state sector in terms of output, employment shares and the number of enterprises (Lin et al. 1996). This feature will be shown in the text. Despite the differing types, entrepreneurship is the nature of all these enterprises as they are exposed to market rules in their operation. Lu (1994) and Huang (2008) described entrepreneurs as those operating private enterprises and TVEs.

Table 4.1 Annual Average Growth Rate of Output and Total Factor
Productivity (per cent)

	1980–88	1980–84	1984–88
State sector			
Output	8.49	6.77	10.22
TFP	2.40	1.80	3.01
Collective sector			
Output	16.94	14.03	19.86
TFP	4.63	3.45	5.86

Source: World Bank (1992).

Productivity performance is both an indicator of and a contributing factor to overall performance. In this early period of transition, non-state enterprises, particularly township and village enterprises (TVEs), had better productivity performance than SOEs, as shown in Table 4.1. In the period 1980–88, and the sub-periods 1980–84 and 1984–88, the collective sector always had a growth rate of total factor productivity (TFP) nearly doubling that of the state sector. It has been widely agreed among scholars that the collective sector is in the marketised section of the economy, facing more competition and hard budget constraints; however, there would be no less important factors contributing to the high growth of output and productivity of the non-state sector in terms of the Government's role in resource allocation during this early stage of transition. This could be seen in three dimensions.

First, there was no clear focus for industrial strategy associated with SOE reform. Instead, governments at various levels aimed their reform efforts at improving the efficiency performance of all existing SOEs through creating incentives for managers and workers. The gradual and experimental approach resulted in the dual-track price system, with the planned track and the market track. Importantly, as a result, the dual-track system created channels for transferring resources, especially raw materials from the state sector, and industrial enterprises to the non-state sector through flows between planned allocation and market channels (Jefferson and Rawski 1995:141). Moreover, the secular problem of shortage under planning (Kolodko 2000) contributed to excess demand in the market for goods, especially industrial products. The excess market demand combined with improved access to materials created highly profitable opportunities for non-state firms. As suggested by Jefferson and Rawski (1995), the high price gap due to shortages implicitly generated quasi-rents that were partly captured by non-state firms. The side effect of the dual-price system, however (and also evidence of rent-seeking), was the emerging rampant corruption of SOE managers and bureaucrats, as Lu (1994) indicated.

Second, local governments played an active and significant role in promoting the TVEs, with access to land, production sites, local utility services and flexible taxation. An important impetus for local governments, especially at township and village levels, to become more involved in non-state business activities was fiscal reform. In the 1980s, fiscal reform was carried out by dividing the responsibility for and allocation of budget revenues and expenditures between the central and local governments (province, county and municipality). Local governments were given more autonomy for collecting revenues and making spending decisions. This was called the fiscal contracting system or the third contract responsibility system (World Bank 1992), or 'fiscal federalism with political centralisation' (Zhang 2002:11). Local governments were encouraged to generate revenues depending on local conditions. Therefore, the fiscal contracting system created incentives for local governments and bureaucrats to promote the development of local businesses (Bouckaert 2007). With the unfavourable institutional setting for private enterprises, the result was that local governments increased their nominal stake in local collectively owned enterprises. The involvement of local governments created favourable access for TVEs to land, production sites and local utility services and created a more equal footing for TVEs compared with SOEs. As an example, compared with TVEs, private entrepreneurs had to pay higher electricity prices and 2.5 times higher taxes in 1985 (Chang and Wang 1994:445). This fact further explains why private entrepreneurs often adopted the red-hat strategy.

Third, TVEs had favourable access to credit due to the active role of local governments in the context of limited credit and a partly commercialised banking system. In the 1980s, initial reform of the banking sector took place to establish the central bank, the People's Bank of China (PBC), and four state commercial banks, which were assigned to focus on lending to major corresponding sectors: agriculture, industry, construction and foreign trade (Riedel et al. 2007). There was also a considerable network of rural and urban credit cooperatives. With limited household savings, rural credit cooperatives had strong links with the Agricultural Bank of China for their source of funding (Huang 2008). The close connections with local governments gave TVEs a strong position from which to access capital provided by rural credit cooperatives (Huang 2008). Urban collective enterprises experienced a similar situation. Facing a hostile business environment with low status, private entrepreneurs understandably used the red-hat strategy to overcome constraints on the most important resources. Arguably, TVEs could be an important platform for private enterprises to emerge and grow in the later period of reform.

It is obvious that TVEs outperformed SOEs, due both to being exposed to market conditions with the significant involvement of private entrepreneurship and to some favourable access to resources created by local governments.

The dual-track reform had produced a latently vibrant emergence of private entrepreneurs through releasing some productive resources wholly controlled by the state sector. Importantly, non-state enterprises contributed to the adjustment of industrial structure due to their labour-intensive activities (Lin et al. 1996). The unexpected outcome in the sense of 'growing out of the plan' (Naughton 1995) created strong competition pressures on SOEs (Jefferson and Rawski 1995). That became an important factor contributing to the deteriorating performance of the state sector, with many loss-making SOEs in the late 1980s, prompting a course of comprehensive reform for SOEs after 1992.

State control of resources and private entrepreneurship in the stage of comprehensive market reform: 1993 – present

Since 1993, China has undertaken a series of market-oriented reforms and established market mechanisms in all economic activities; however, the extent of market rules and competition varies significantly across sectors of the economy. The important aspect is the extent of the role market forces play in resource allocation, which can be seen in the structure of the enterprise system with a growing share of the private sector. Under the overarching framework of institutional reforms, changes in the ways the state controls key resources have been a key determinant shaping the evolution of private entrepreneurship, in the form of private sector development.

Conducive changes in the institutional environment and market opportunities for private enterprises

Major changes in political ideology and the legal framework to recognise the private sector happened after Deng Xiaoping's tour of southern China in 1992, during which he made several important speeches signalling the supportive view of the Chinese leadership of the role of private entrepreneurs in generating the nation's prosperity (Naughton 2007). Following this event, fundamental changes in the political mind-set on private entrepreneurs took place. For example, in September 1992, the Fourteenth Chinese Communist Party (CCP) Congress officially adopted a 'socialist market economy'. The Fifteenth CCP Congress recognised private ownership as an important component of the economy. This marked a significant change in the official ideology towards being supportive of private entrepreneurs. In a related move, there were marked changes in the legal framework. The amended 1999 Constitution acknowledged the important role of private businesses in China's economy (Qian and Wu:2000). Related laws followed, enacted to govern the operation of private businesses.

The leadership's continued commitment to the market economy promoted the completion of the marketisation process of the economy in three dimensions. In the first dimension, there was further completion of liberalisation of domestic goods and product markets. Price liberalisation was implemented in 1993 and 1994 after the market-oriented reform gained momentum in 1992. In 1997, 85 per cent of agricultural output, 95 per cent of retail sales and 96 per cent of production materials were sold at market prices (Zhang 2002:12).

The second dimension is China's foreign trade liberalisation. Before accession to the World Trade Organisation (WTO) in 2001, China took major steps to reform its foreign trade regime to remove distortions and to become consistent with the international trade system. Important reform measures were unification and devaluation of the foreign exchange rate and increased access to foreign exchanges for domestic producers, removal of entry barriers to export and import activities by granting trading rights to manufacturing enterprises, expanding tariffs and gradual reduction of trade barriers as well as the application of other trade policy instruments such as import substitution and export promotion (Naughton 2007). China's WTO accession in 2001 marked another boom of market opportunities for domestic enterprises in terms of foreign market access, technology transfer and the entrance of foreign investors. While China's substantial welfare gains from WTO accession were generally acknowledged, deepening trade integration has posed a lot of competition pressure on domestic enterprises, especially SOEs. Joining the WTO has induced the Chinese Government to carry out more domestic reforms to make the country's business rules and regulations consistent with international standards. This resulted in significant reforms of the SOEs in the 2000s. Moreover, national treatment required by the WTO promoted further the status of domestic private enterprises in the Chinese economy (Song 2014).

The third dimension is the surge of FDI inflows into the Chinese economy, which was in line with the Government's clear commitment to market-oriented reform and extensive and progressive trade liberalisation. According to Chen (2009), China experienced a dramatic increase of annual FDI inflows in 1992 and 1993, while there were a slowdown and decline between 1997 and 2000 when the Asian financial crisis hit. China's accession to the WTO led to a sharp increase of annual FDI inflows, from US$33 billion in 2001 to US$80 billion in 2008. It is notable that FDI was mainly concentrated in the manufacturing sector, with 63 per cent of the total FDI inflows (Chen 2009:336). Large FDI inflows intensified domestic competition and demand for China's production factor endowments.

It appears there have been many favourable changes in the institutional setting for the development of private entrepreneurship. Marketisation and trade liberalisation have generated ample market opportunities, but significantly increased competition.

Market-based control of resources and the evolution of private entrepreneurship

It has been argued above that transformation from a centrally planned economy to a market-based one can be seen as a process of releasing productive resources from the state to be determined and directed by market rules. Restructuring SOEs is part of such a process. In addition, the progress of market reform has come about with market liberalisation in all economic sectors. China's gradual approach has, however, shown the proactive and dominant role of the state in the direction and speed of market liberalisation. It has been identified that complete liberalisation has only happened in product markets, and not factor markets (Huang and Wang 2010). The factor markets are the areas where the state exerts significant control to influence the resource flows and the pattern of economic growth.

SOE restructuring and the expansion of the private sector

In the 1990s and 2000s, SOE restructuring was implemented in tandem with promotion of private enterprises. In 1995, radical reforms of SOEs started amid their deteriorating performance (particularly profitability and output growth) since the late 1980s (Qian and Wu 2000). Reform directions were gradually developed over the years. For example, in November 1993, the CCP's *Decision on Issues Concerning the Establishment of a Socialist Market Economic Structure* set forth the direction for the SOE reform that emphasised property rights, separation of ownership and enterprise management and allowed for privatisation and diversification of ownership. In October 2003, the Third Plenum of the Sixteenth CCP Congress issued the *Decision on Issues of Perfecting the Socialist Market Economy*, which was aimed at deepening SOE reform by focusing on shareholding ownership and corporatisation of SOEs. Importantly, the SOE reform in this period was different from the previous period in terms of the ownership transformation, called *gaizhi*, and the wide scale of SOE transformation. Various measures have been adopted, ranging from bankruptcy, liquidation, listing and sales to private firms and auctioning (Song 2014). In the latter half of the 1990s, the process of transforming TVEs to private ownership took place progressively as many TVEs were facing losses due to their weak competitiveness, rigid management structure and decision-making due to collective ownership (Qian and Wu 2000). Moreover, the Government's official recognition of private property rights and support for private entrepreneurship had encouraged many privately run collective enterprises to take off their 'red hats' to become private firms (Song 2014).

Table 4.2 Number of Registered Enterprises of Different Ownership Type, 1993–2005 (all sectors)

Year	*Getihu*	Private	TVEs
1993	17 670 000	237 919	1 690 000
1995	25 280 000	654 531	1 620 000
1997	28 510 000	960 726	1 290 000
1999	31 600 000	1 508 857	940 000
2000	26 710 000	1 761 769	800 000
2001	24 330 000	2 028 548	670 000
2003	23 531 857	3 005 524	
2005	24 638 934	4 300 916	

Sources: Tsai (2007); Huang (2008).

Note: *Getihu* refers to individual businesses with less than eight employees, and private firms are private businesses with more than eight employees.

The *gaizhi* process was actually one of releasing the state's control of assets and reducing the scope of the state's direct involvement in doing business, allowing for a wider operation of the market mechanism. Notably, this process contributed significantly to the rapid expansion of the private sector in the late 1990s and 2000s. Table 4.2 shows that, in the whole economy, private enterprises had a continuous and rapid increase in number. At the same time, the number of TVEs declined at a quite rapid pace. As a result, the share of SOEs in total gross output continued to decline, giving way to the rapidly emerging private enterprises. Figure 4.1 indicates the trend of a more dramatic increase of private enterprises in the industrial sector from 1999 to 2010. The number of SOEs and TVEs had a continuous decline. At the same time, the number of foreign-funded enterprises increased quite significantly. The industrial gross output share of the private sector surpassed that of the state sector in 2010, at around 30 per cent (Song 2014).

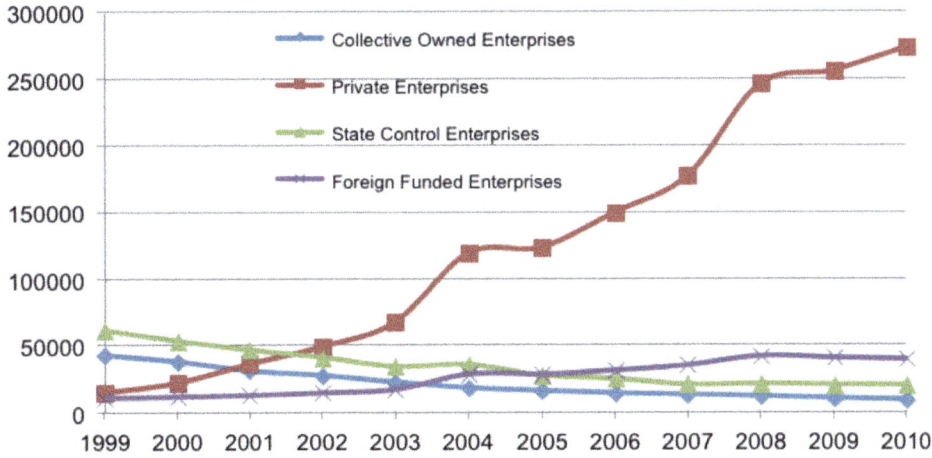

Figure 4.1 Number of Industrial Enterprises, 1999–2010
Sources: CEIC database; authors' compilation.

From the perspective of resource reallocation, SOE restructuring could be considered successful as the process led to a significant transfer of state assets to private entrepreneurs using the market mechanism, reducing the state's fiscal burden created by loss-making SOEs. The process was also successful in terms of both making room for expansion of the private sector (Xiao et al. 2009) and exploiting the dynamics and strength of private entrepreneurship in using resources (assets) more efficiently. There was also a concern about the loss of the state's assets and corruption through *gaizhi*. The problem of rent-seeking associated with unproductive entrepreneurship is unavoidable to some extent; however, there is some evidence suggesting the losses could be small in some cases due to local governments' exchange for employment protection after privatisation (Garnaut et al. 2006). Moreover, it has been found that the growing private sector contributed to reducing unemployment problems created by SOE restructuring (Song 2014).

Industrial strategy and asymmetric sectoral distribution of SOEs and non-state enterprises

An important feature of the SOE reform in the 1990s was the Government's introduction of an industrial strategy. In 1994, the State Council approved 'An Outline of the State Industrial Policies in the 1990s'. The renewed industrial policy identified machinery-electronics, petrochemicals, automobile manufacture and construction as 'pillar industries'. Later, specific policies for pillar industries were developed, such as the industrial policy for the auto industry' (Lu 2000). This policy would be one of the key factors underlying the approach of SOE reform under the slogan of 'grasping the large, letting the small go', put forward by the Fifteenth CCP Congress. Consequently, some 1000 SOEs were identified as large ones to be retained with whole state ownership when the SOE restructuring began (Song 2014). Subsequently, a group of key sectors has been identified, which includes energy, electricity, utilities, telecommunication, aviation and shipping. Since the 1990s, there have been some changes in the list of the pillar industry group, which now includes equipment, autos, electronics, information technology, construction, steel, metals, and chemicals (Baston 2014; World Bank and DRC 2013).

Table 4.3 Distribution of Private Enterprises in China, 1994–2005 (per cent)

Industry	1994	1999	2001	2005
Agriculture	4.1	4.7	5.6	6.3
Mining	1.2	1.2	1.3	2.0
Manufacturing	40.4	39.8	38.3	43.5
Power	0.9	1.1	0.7	1.1
Construction	5.5	6.4	5.9	5.4
Geology and watering	0.0	0.0	0.1	0.0
Transportation	2.4	2.3	2.5	2.5
Service and catering	27.4	20.6	21.4	26.0
Finance and insurance	0.3	0.2	0.3	0.1
Real estate	0.9	3.2	3.8	2.5
Social services	8.0	8.3	8.0	4.9
Science and technology	2.5	2.6	2.1	1.5
Others	6.5	9.6	9.9	4.2
Total	100	100	100	100

Source: Yang (2012).

Note: The data in the table were collected from repeated cross-sectional surveys of private enterprises in China, conducted by the Institute of Sociology, Chinese Academy of Social Sciences (Yang 2012:109).

Industrial policy has become one of the main tools guiding the Chinese Government's new approach to the control and allocation of key resources, especially production factors. Different policy measures have been deployed to implement the Government's industrial policy perspective. First, in line with SOE restructuring, various barriers were erected to prevent or limit the entry and competition of non-state enterprises, especially private enterprises. Apart from some industries with natural monopoly characteristics, there are several oligopolistic or monopolistic industries created by administrative measures, generating an 'administrative monopoly'. Administrative barriers include permits and business regulations such as administrative inspection, monitoring of firms' registered business activities and local governments' purchase of goods and services from targeted firms (World Bank and DRC 2013:108–9). Second, the Government controlled the financial system, especially banking, to direct credit to targeted industries, especially SOEs. Consequently, the introduction of pillar and strategic industries has a significant effect on the participation of private firms and enterprises of other kinds in different sectors of the economy. The outcome is the skewed distribution of firms by industry. Based on the data from representative sample surveys of private enterprises, Table 4.3 shows that private firms are concentrated in manufacturing and service and catering. Nevertheless, it is possible that there are not many private firms in some manufacturing industries that were designated as 'pillar' industries. In contrast, very few private enterprises operated in sectors such as power, construction, finance and insurance, and geology and watering, which are key utility sectors whose output is used by all other sectors. This situation remained unchanged from the start of SOE restructuring to the time when the deepening SOE reform was going on. The pattern of asymmetrical distribution of SOEs and private firms will be further discussed below.

Controlled financial system and private entrepreneurs' access to capital

Market liberalisation led to the retreat of the state in directing goods flows between economic sectors and regions. Price liberalisation also made it increasingly impossible for the state to distort relative prices between sectors and regions for industrialisation (Zhang 2002). With growing household and firm incomes as a result of marketisation, the allocation of financial resources has become the main form of the state's resource control. On the one hand, in line with market reform, the Chinese Government gradually promoted the financial system, including banking, stock markets and the emergence of non-bank financial firms, to mobilise and channel savings for investment demand in the growing economy. On the other hand, the Government took the monopoly position in the financial system by using state-owned commercial banks and financial corporations with strict entry barriers and regulations. In fact, in line with developing the financial system of a market economy, the Government has continued to consolidate its dominant position in the financial system since the central-planning period. Key state-controlled financial institutions are state-owned commercial banks and rural and urban cooperatives. In the 1990s, the Government started to allow the market participation of the non-state sector, including shareholding commercial banks and foreign banks (Bonin and Huang 2002; Song 2005). The participation of non-state commercial banks increased in the 2000s; however, state-owned financial institutions have been major players in the financial markets. It is clear that the controlled financial system enabled the Government to channel most savings to SOEs, particularly SOEs in pillar and strategic industries, and to undertake big infrastructure investment projects. As a result, the private sector had limited access to capital. For example, in 1999, private enterprises received only less than 0.5 per cent of loans from state-owned banks, which is in contrast with their contribution of nearly 35 per cent of industrial output in 1998 (Song 2005:117). Consequently, private enterprises had to rely much on informal financing.

The monopoly position in the financial markets allowed the Government to impose financial repression. Using its monopoly of state-owned commercial banks, the Government has been able to set a low level of interest rates for bank deposits and lending (Riedel et al. 2007). Moreover, 'the maintenance of interest rates at artificially low levels has made it difficult for domestic savers and investors to see the true price of capital' (Song 2005:115). Cheap credit has been used to keep many loss-making SOEs viable, leading to the well-known problem of non-performing loans in the banking system (Riedel et al. 2007).

By imposing low ceilings on borrowing and lending interest rates, the Government has created significant rents, which can be defined by the differences between the actual and the would-be market clearing interest rates. The rents would be much higher when taking into account the potential value of profitable projects for private entrepreneurs. There has been recognition that the extent of capital market distortions would be significant (Young 2000; Zhang and Tan 2007; Huang and Wang 2010; Brandt and Zhu 2010; Brandt et al. 2013). Huang and Wang (2010) claimed that distortions caused by government interventions are not confined to the capital markets, but are also in the labour and natural resource markets. Notably, these distortions were substantial. For example, their estimates show that the value of factor market distortions was about RMB2.1 trillion in 2008—equivalent to 7 per cent of GDP. Moreover, capital-market distortions accounted for the biggest share in the total since 2000 (Huang and Wang 2010:307). An important issue here is how to view these distortions in terms of their contribution to economic growth.

State-led development of land markets and the private sector's access

In China, land is owned and managed by local governments in urban areas and by collectives in the countryside. Due to its sole ownership of land on behalf of all the people, the Government has control of land supply and land-use rights transfer (Huang and Wang 2010).

The land market is a contrasting case with the capital market in terms of accessibility for private enterprises given a similar feature of government monopoly in the market. As a common practice, local governments have the authority to determine and collect land-use fees (Huang and Wang 2010). Many local governments have used access to land as one of the main instruments to promote industrial and economic growth. Local governments actively promoted land developments for industrial sites. To attract manufacturing enterprises, many local authorities set low land-use fees. In many cases, land-use fees were only equal to, or even lower than, the cost of land development (including compensation for existing land users, land-clearing costs and infrastructure building costs). In the past two decades, due to local competition in pursuit of rapid economic growth, many local governments have tried to reduce the cost of land development to create low land-use fees. The main method used is paying low land compensation fees to local farm households as most land transfers involve agricultural and rural land. Low land-use fees have been considered an important factor promoting rapid industrial development in many localities; however, the consequences of industrial land development are soaring land disputes and demonstrations. Land grabs are becoming a big concern for the Chinese Government. On this aspect of land market development, it appears that governments at various levels have used their monopoly position of sole ownership to release land resources with low prices for industrial enterprises, including private enterprises. Conceptually, distorted industrial land prices have implicit government subsidies, which are equivalent to implicit rents. Otherwise, industrial development would have been constrained by rising land prices due to rising demand from industrial investment.

Another aspect of land market development is urbanisation and residential land expansion. Rapid industrialisation has promoted urbanisation through attracting millions of rural migrants. Urbanisation, in combination with increasing income levels, has created huge demand for new housing and residential land. Excess demand for urban and industrial land use has caused land prices to soar due to the government-controlled supply of land. Recognising the rapid growth of demand for land, local governments have actively managed the supply of land for urban and industrial uses. Being able to control land supply has enabled local governments to determine land-use prices and collect substantial revenue for their budgets. Importantly, soaring land prices in many locations with rapid industrial and urban expansion have generated substantial rents, which can be defined here as the difference between the market price and the cost of land supply by the Government. Moreover, there could be additional rents when the actual market value of land was higher than the sale price determined by the Government. Revenues for local government budgets from residential land sales or auctions have been used mainly for building infrastructure. On this aspect of land market expansion, the Government's monopoly in land supply has generated rents that were captured by the Government for public investment.

In relation to land, the Government also has monopoly power over other natural resources such as energy and public utilities and other natural endowments. It has been argued that government control of key sectors (coal, electricity, oil and water) has distorted the markets in favour of industrial development. Huang and Wang's (2010) estimates suggest these distortions were significant during the period 2000–08, ranging from 3.6 to 6.4 per cent of GDP. Again, government control of resources has created significant economic rents, which were used to support industrialisation.

Beneficial aspects of the state control of resources during market reform

Since the SOE restructuring process started in the 1990s, the Government has made effective interventions in factor markets, which have created substantial rents. Its dominant position in these markets has helped the Government to mobilise resources, especially financial resources to build infrastructure. Large SOEs have large undertakings in public infrastructure. Government-led infrastructure investments have had both short-term and long-term effects on economic growth through long-term productivity growth. In this sense, government control of resources to generate key infrastructure has been supportive of the development of private entrepreneurship. Xiao et al. (2009:166) showed the impressive achievements of China in infrastructure building. For example, the total length of highways increased from 1.16 million km in 1995 to 3.46 million km in 2006. At the same time, the railway network expanded from 59 700 km to 77 100 km, and there was a huge increase of mobile phone subscribers, from eight million to 610 million. In terms of value, Zhang et al. (2012:9) reported that the annual amount of public expenditure increased from RMB73.2 billion in 1997 to RMB1.270 billion in 2010 at the 2005 constant price. This observation is consistent with one made by Naughton (2010:446) about China's approach: 'Public ownership can be used to exploit market power and generate revenues for investment and public goods' creation.' The active and effective role of the Chinese Government in undertaking market transition has given rise to a notion of China's development model. To some extent, Khan's (2004) observation that a state with strong capacity can generate and manage rents that are growth-enhancing seems to be relevant to China's experience.

In another dimension, the rents created by government control of resource markets, despite being a market distortion, have been used as strong incentives to attract and support investment from the non-state sector. Many studies have suggested that this has been an important factor contributing to China's investment-driven pattern of growth.

What are the inefficiency effects of resource control and when did they worsen?

Distorted investment patterns

Despite generating investment effects for growth, state-maintained low resource prices appear to have led to some overinvestment in manufacturing (Blanchard and Giavazzi 2006), resulting in lower investment returns. From the 1990s to the 2000s, the investment cost of $1 additional growth increased from $3 to $4 (Zheng et al. 2009:878). Excessive investment has gradually accumulated to generate China's structural imbalances of economic growth (Huang and Wang 2010). While there is a certain rationale for the intervention of the Government in some industries with natural monopoly characteristics, the growth of the private sector with its better performance has caused concerns about the Government's dominance in these industries. Figure 4.2 presents the share of the state sector in total assets and output in a number of industrial subsectors in 2011. It suggests there is a clear difference between the total asset share and the output share of SOEs. There are only four subsectors in which the asset share is equal to or greater than the output share: petroleum and gas, processing of nuclear and petroleum materials, tobacco, and water supply (these industries appear to be pure state monopolies). In several other subsectors, the output share is significantly smaller than the asset share held by the SOEs. This means that where there is some participation of the non-state sector, the state control of resources (capital or assets) becomes less efficient due to competition and the inherent weaknesses of some SOEs. This situation suggests that further reduction of state control in these industries would enhance their output growth.

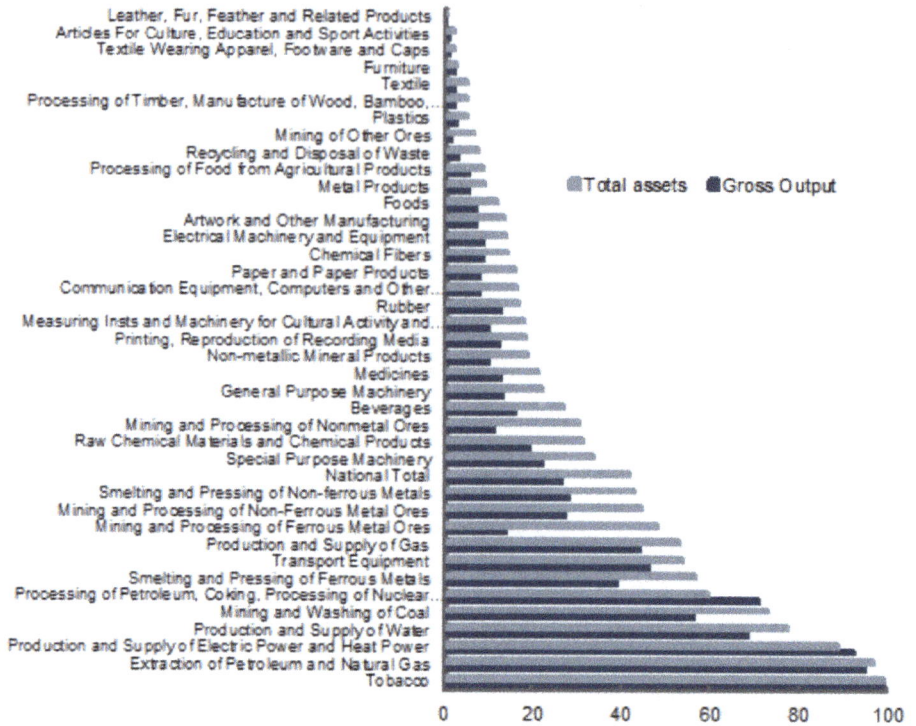

Figure 4.2 Sectoral Distribution of SOEs, 2011 (per cent of total assets and output)
Source: Zhang and Freestone (2013).

The above situation is consistent with information in Figure 4.3. From 2000 to 2013, the state's share of assets and output in the industrial sector declined steadily. Moreover, there is always a gap between the asset share and the output share, with the asset share always higher than the output share. It would therefore be growth-enhancing if there were some further reduction in the state's holding of assets in some industrial subsectors.

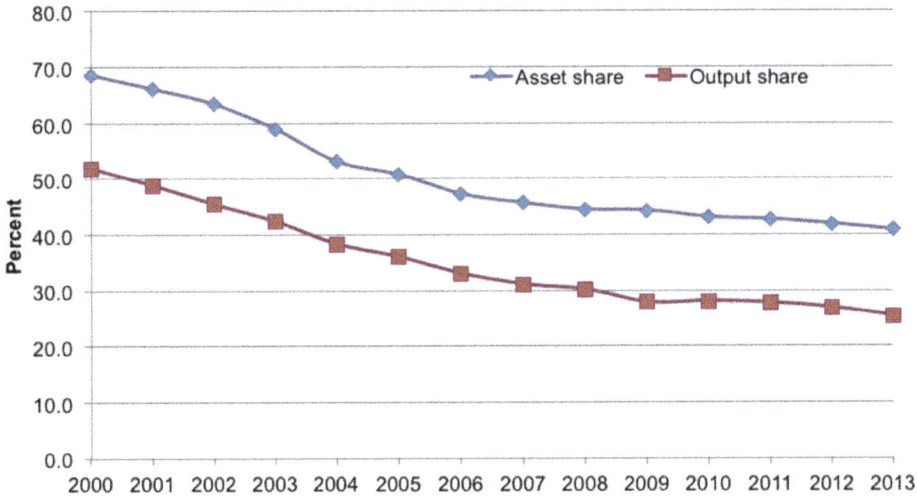

Figure 4.3 Asset and Gross Output Share of State-Controlled Enterprises (per cent)
Sources: CEIC database; authors' estimates.

Unequal access to resources, rent-seeking and unproductive entrepreneurship

Access to credit or capital is one of the most important issues for a private enterprise to succeed in the market. While there have been more and more profitable opportunities in the product markets, private firms have been constrained by the lack of capital and access to bank credit, which prevents them from taking up profitable opportunities for business start-ups or expansion. Deepening SOE reform has forced state-owned commercial banks to operate on a commercial basis and look for profitable private enterprises to which to lend (Firth et al. 2009). The tradition of favouring the SOEs has remained, however, meaning access to bank credit is a significant challenge for private enterprises, especially small and medium enterprises (SMEs), which are the main form of private entrepreneurship (Shen et al. 2009). There has long been a contradiction in the financial markets: there is always substantial excess demand on the one hand, and a limited supply of credit for entrepreneurs on the other. Therefore, there exist rents that could be significant due to the gap between the market clearing level and the regulated interest rate. The rents could be very large if we take into account the opportunity costs of forgone market opportunities identified by entrepreneurs.

To overcome credit constraints, many private enterprises have used informal channels, especially the *guanxi* network,[2] to obtain loans (Liao and Sohmen 2001). Because the state controls bank credit and other resources, government officials and people in charge of managing resources have an advantageous position from which to access capital and resources. Consequently, there has been anecdotal evidence of private firms trying to get bank loans or to gain access to government subsidies through political connections (Zhou 2009; Bai et al. 2006; Wu and Cheng 2011). Moreover, some evidence has been found showing that private enterprises with political connections perform better than those without (Choi and Zhou 2001; Faccio 2006). In a sense, there could be a concern, as suggested by Baumol (1990), that there will be some entrepreneurs who concentrate their investment in political connections for profitable opportunities. This is a kind of unproductive entrepreneurship. For other resources, especially land and property development, state control is likely to create unproductive entrepreneurship due to the speculative nature of the market in the context of the Government's controlled supply of land in localities with high demand for housing and residential land.

Financial performance of the state-controlled and non-state sectors

SOE restructuring has played an important role in promoting SOE performance, and the growth of SOEs still makes an important contribution to economic growth and government revenues. Given their large share of fixed assets in many industries, especially key and pillar industrial subsectors, an important question is how the SOEs performed compared with other non-state firms.

Figure 4.4 shows industrial enterprise performance in terms of profit rate during 2000–13. Before the Global Financial Crisis (GFC) in 2008, the SOEs had a substantially higher and faster growing profit rate than non-state enterprises. One explanation could be the SOE reform in the early 2000s—as well as their favourable access to cheap bank credit. But there are arguments that SOEs had other policy objectives to justify their better performance. Their performance quickly worsened, however, after 2008 and became closer to the level of the non-state sector.

---

2 *'Guanxi'* is a popular Chinese term referring to interpersonal or social relationships and connections (Calisle and Flynn 2005).

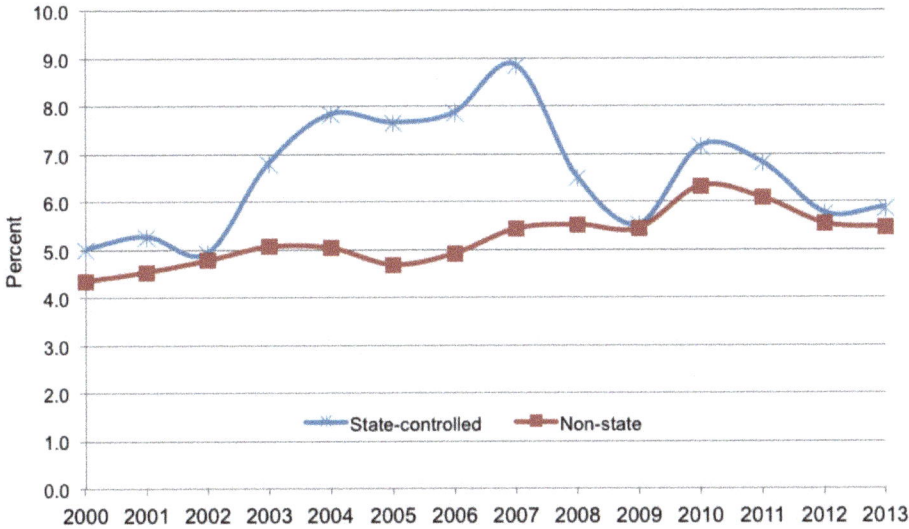

Figure 4.4 Profit Rate (Profits/Sales) of Industrial Enterprises, 2000–13
Sources: CEIC database; authors' estimates.

Figure 4.5 shows the performance of industrial enterprises in terms of returns on assets (ROA) during 2000–13. Before 2008, SOEs showed significant improvement in their ROA, which could be due to the reasons given above; however, the SOEs appeared to have consistently lower ROA than the non-state sector. There was a similar trend to that with the profit rate in that the SOEs' performance in terms of ROA worsened after 2008. The ROA gap between the SOEs and the non-state sector became larger. Baston (2014) suggested that the trend of worsening performance of the SOEs after 2008 indicates the structural problems of the SOE sector, with loss-making SOEs, despite the fact that deepening SOE reform had helped boost the performance of many SOEs through corporatisation and improved corporate governance. This suggests state control of assets would be reduced by restructuring inefficient SOEs and allowing more participation by private enterprises.

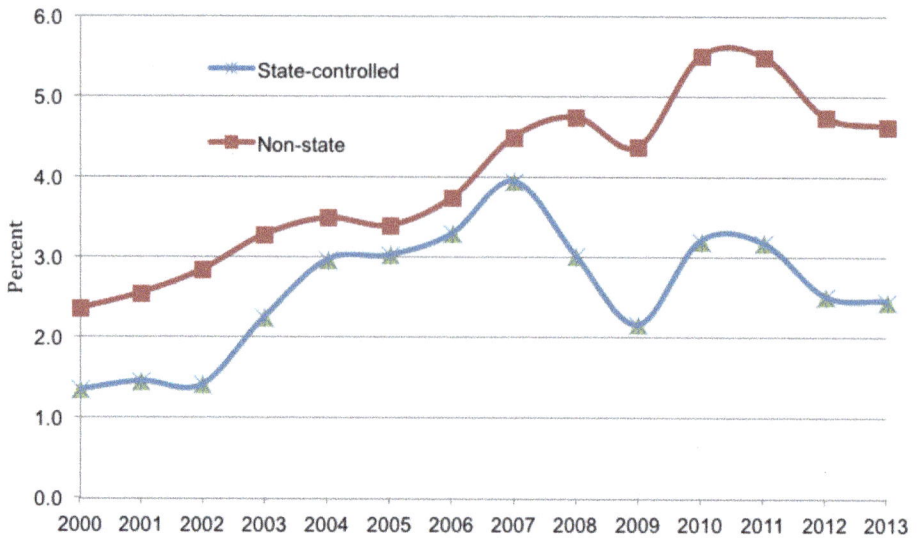

Figure 4.5 Returns on Assets of Industrial Enterprises, 2000–13 (per cent)

Sources: CEIC database; authors' estimates.

Changes in resource control and productivity performance

Further assessment of the efficiency of the state control of resources could be seen in the TFP performance in relation to financial performance. Figure 4.6 shows there is a positive association between TFP and profitability indicators, as commonly expected in the literature on firm performance (Zhang et al. 2002). In addition, SOE reform has had positive impacts on the SOEs' performance in terms of both productivity and profitability. As shown in Figure 4.6, in contrast with the period 1988–98, accelerated SOE restructuring appears to promote the annual profit rate of the state sector in the period 1998–2007. At the same time, SOEs' average TFP growth rate had a sharp increase from nearly zero per cent to more than 4 per cent.

Based on the estimation of labour productivity and growth accounting simulations, Brandt and Zhu (2010) provided some evidence of the impacts of state control of resources on the productivity performance of SOEs compared with non-SOEs, as shown in Table 4.4. In the period 1988–98, the labour productivity of non-SOEs was nearly double that of SOEs (6.17 per cent versus 3.46 per cent). The TFP growth of the non-SOEs had a greater impact on the growth of the TFP of two sectors. Notably, the data show that capital distortions played a more important role in promoting the productivity of SOEs, while they had a much smaller effect on promoting the productivity of non-SOEs.

In contrast, an increase in investment had little effect on the labour productivity of both sectors. Therefore, capital control was a significant factor after TFP for the labour productivity performance of SOEs.

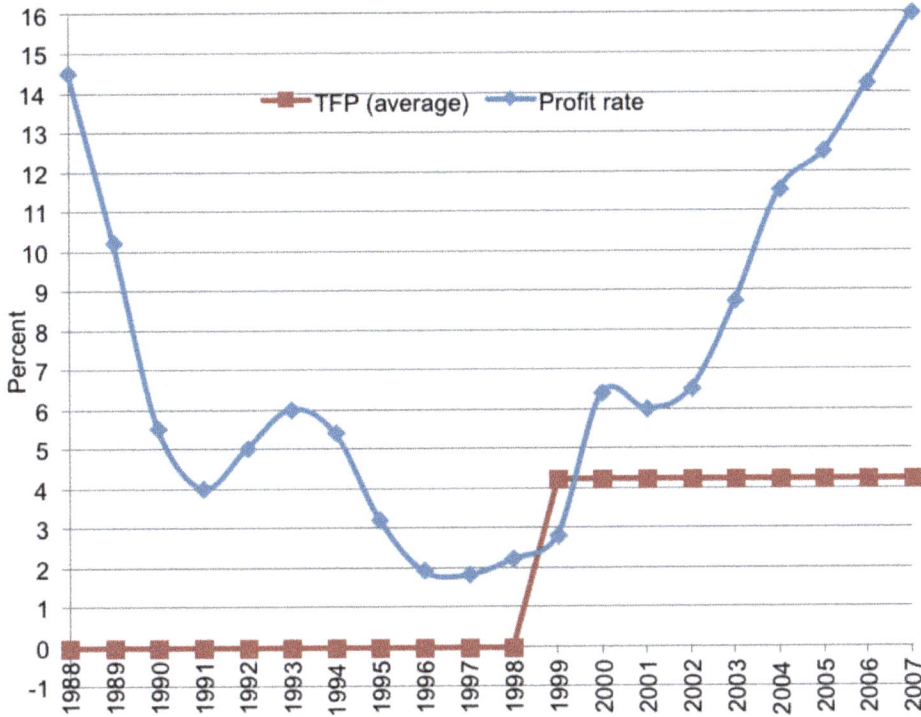

Figure 4.6 Profit Rate and TFP Growth Rate of the State Sector, 1988–98 and 1998–2007 (per cent)

Sources: Song (2014); Brandt and Zhu (2010).

Note: TFP growth rate is the average growth rate estimated by Brandt and Zhu (2010) for two periods: 1988–98 and 1998–2007. The profit rate of the whole state sector for each year is estimated by Song (2014).

During the period 1998–2007, SOEs had substantially higher labour productivity growth than non-SOEs. This could be due to the deepening of SOE reform that makes SOEs larger with more access to credit. In this period, the TFP growth of non-SOEs and SOEs had a quite similar effect on the labour productivity of other sectors. Again, investment had less impact on the labour productivity growth of non-SOEs than SOEs. It appears that, compared with the 1988–98 period, the SOEs' TFP performance improved significantly and was the main contributor to labour productivity growth, rather than investment. Most importantly, capital market distortions had a significant negative impact on the labour productivity growth of non-SOEs. In contrast, SOEs clearly benefited from capital market distortions. Therefore, in line with the development of factor markets, the state control of resources had significantly negative effects on the performance of non-SOEs, and private enterprises in particular.

Table 4.4 Reforms Related to Resource Control and Labour Productivity Growth (counterfactual simulations) (per cent)

Item	1988–98		1998–2007	
	Non-SOEs	**SOEs**	**Non-SOEs**	**SOEs**
Benchmark model	6.17	3.46	8.48	11.15
No TFP growth in non-state sector[a]	2.00	−0.71	1.87	4.54
No TFP growth in state sector[a]	5.52	2.82	4.95	7.62
No capital market distortions[a]	6.10	−0.34	9.01	9.03
No increase in investment rates since 1988 or 1998[a]	6.00	3.29	7.91	10.58

Source: Brandt and Zhu (2010).

Note: [a] refers to counterfactual situations, which are assumed to show what the labour productivity growth of each sector would be in comparison with the benchmark model.

Overall, the examination of the financial and productivity performance of the SOE and non-state sectors has shown that the state's control of resources, in terms of interventions in the factor markets, had negative impacts on the performance of private enterprises, despite their better performance compared with SOEs. This means that SOE restructuring and the change in focus of state resource control have promoted the performance of the state sector, but at the expense of efficiency losses of private enterprises in the non-state sector.

Concluding remarks

We have used the framework of entrepreneurship development to analyse the pattern and impact of change in the state's control of resources on the emergence and evolution as well as outcomes of private entrepreneurship in China during market transition over the past 30 years.

The examination of SOE reform and change in the state's control of resources has shown that private entrepreneurship has emerged and developed robustly in the context of China's market reform. Apart from improving the environment for private entrepreneurship, the change in the ways the Government controls key productive resources has had significant impacts on the performance of private enterprises. In the most recent period, when the product markets have been liberalised, state interventions in factor markets have had more negative impacts on the performance of the private sector. Given a larger share and better performance of private enterprises, reducing the state's control of key resources would promote productivity and economic growth in the future.

References

Ahmad, N. and Hoffman, A. (2008), *A framework for addressing and measuring entrepreneurship*, OECD Statistics Working Papers 2008/02, Paris: OECD Publishing. Available from <http://dx.doi.org/10.1787/243160627270>.

Arrow, K. (2001), 'The role of time', in L. R. Klein and M. Pomer (eds), *The New Russia: Transition Gone Awry*, pp. 85–91, Stanford, Calif.: Stanford University Press.

Bai, C. E., Lu, J. and Tao, Z. (2006), 'Property rights protection and access to bank loans: evidence from private enterprises in China', *Economics of Transition* 14(4): 611–28.

Baston, A. 2014, *Fixing China's state sector*, Paulson Policy Memorandum, The Paulson Institute, Chicago. Available from <http://www.paulsoninstitute.org/media/.../fixingchina_sstatesector_english.pdf>.

Baumol, W. J. (1990), 'Entrepreneurship: productive, unproductive and destructive', *Journal of Political Economy* 98(5): 893–921.

Blanchard, O. J. and Giavazzi, F. (2006), *Rebalancing growth in China: a three-handed approach*, January 2006, Discussion Paper DP5403, Center for Economic Policy Research, Washington, DC.

Bonin, J. P. and Huang, Y. (2002), 'China's opening up of the banking system: implication for domestic banks', in L. Song (ed.), *Dilemmas of China's Growth in the Twenty-First Century*, pp. 55–72, Canberra: Asia Pacific Press.

Bouckaert, B. R. (2007), 'Bureaupreneurs in China: we did it our way', *European Journal of Law and Economics* 23(2): 169–95.

Brandt, L. and Zhu, X. (2010), *Accounting for China's growth*, Working Paper Series IZA DP No. 4764, Institute for the Study of Labor, Bonn. Available from <ftp.iza.org/dp4764.pdf>.

Brandt, L., Tombe, T. and Zhu, X. (2013), 'Factor market distortions across time, space and sectors in China', *Review of Economic Dynamics* 16(1): 39–58.

Carlisle, S. and Flynn, D., (2005), 'Small business survival in China: *Guanxi*, legitimacy, and social capital', *Journal of Developmental Entrepreneurship*, 10(1): 79-96.

Carree, M. A. and Thurik, A. R. (2003), 'The impact of entrepreneurship on economic growth', in Z. J. Acs and D. B. Audretsch (eds), *Handbook of Entrepreneurship Research*, UK: Kluwer Academic Publishers.

Chang, C. and Wang, Y. (1994), 'The nature of the township-village enterprises', *Journal of Comparative Economics* 19: 434–52.

Chen, C. (2009), 'Inflow of foreign direct investment', in R. Garnaut, L. Song, and W. T. Woo (eds), *China's New Place in a World in Crisis: Economic Geopolitical and Environmental Dimensions*, pp. 325-47, Canberra: ANU E Press.

Choi, E. K. and Zhou, K. X. (2001), 'Entrepreneurs and politics in the Chinese transitional economy: political connections and rent-seeking', *The China Review* 1(1): 111–35.

Estrin, S., Meyer, K. E. and Bytchkova, M. (2008), 'Entrepreneurship in transition economies', in A. Basu, M. C. Casson, N. Wadeson and B. Yeung (eds), *The Oxford Handbook of Entrepreneurship*, pp. 679–723, New York: Oxford University Press.

Faccio, M. (2006), 'Politically connected firms', *American Economic Review* 96(1): 369–86.

Firth, M., Lin, C., Liu, P. and Wong, S. M. L. (2009), 'Inside the black box: bank credit allocation in China's private sector', *Journal of Banking & Finance* 33: 1144–55.

Garnaut, R., Song, L. and Yao, Y. (2006), 'Impact and significance of state-owned enterprise restructuring in China', *The China Journal* 55: 35–63.

Garnaut, R., Song, L., Yang, Y. and Wang, X. (2001), *Private Enterprise in China*, Canberra: Asia Pacific Press.

Gries, S. and Naudé, W. (2008), *Entrepreneurship and structural economic transformation*, UNU-WIDER Research Paper No. 2008/62, United Nations University/World Institute for Development Economics Research. Available from <http://www.wider.unu.edu/publications/working-papers/research-papers/2008/en_GB/rp2008-62/>.

Huang, Y. (2008), *Capitalism with Chinese Characteristics: Entrepreneurship and the State*, New York: Cambridge University Press.

Huang, Y. and Wang, B. (2010), 'Rebalancing China's economic structure', in R. Garnaut, J. Golley and L. Song (eds), *China: The Next Twenty Years of Reform and Development*, pp. 293–318, Canberra: ANU E Press.

Jefferson, G. H. and Rawski, T. G. (1995), 'How industrial reform worked in China: the role of innovation, competition, and property rights', in *Proceedings of the World Bank Annual Conference on Development Economics 1994* Washington, DC: The World Bank.

Karlsson, C., Friis, C. and Paulsson, T. (2004), *Relating entrepreneurship to economic growth*, CESIS Electronic Working Paper Series No. 13, Centre of Excellence for Science and Innovation Studies, Stockholm. Available from <http://ideas.repec.org/p/hhs/cesisp/0013.html>.

Khan, M. H. (2004), State failure in developing countries and institutional reform strategies, Paper presented at the Annual World Bank Conference on Development Economics—Europe 2003, Oslo, 24–26 June 2002. <http://eprints.soas.ac.uk/3683/1/State_Failure.pdf>.

Kirzner, I. M. (1998), *How Markets Work: Disequilibrium, Entrepreneurship and Discovery*, Sydney: Centre for Independent Studies.

Kolodko, G. W. (2000), 'Transition to a market and entrepreneurship: the systemic factors and policy options', *Communist and Post-Communist Studies* 33(2): 271–93.

Liao, D. and Sohmen, P. (2001), 'The development of modern entrepreneurship in China', *Stanford Journal of East Asian Affairs* 1: 27–33.

Lin, J. Y., Cai, F. and Li, Z. (1996), 'The lessons of China's transition to a market economy', *Cato Journal* 16(2): 201–31.

Lu, D. (1994), *Entrepreneurship in Suppressed Markets: Private-Sector Experience in China*, New York: Garland Publishing.

Lu, D. (2000), 'Industrial policy and resource allocation: implications on China's participation in globalisation', *China Economic Review* (11): 342–60.

Murrel, O. and Wang, Y. J. (1993), 'When privatization should be delayed: the effect of communist legacies on organizational and institutional reforms', *Journal of Comparative Economics* 17(2): 385–406.

Naudé, W. (2010), 'Entrepreneurship, developing countries, and development economics: new approaches and insights', *Small Business Economics* 34: 1–12.

Naughton, B. (1995), *Growing Out of the Plan: Chinese Economic Reform, 1978–1993*, Cambridge: Cambridge University Press.

Naughton, B. (2007), *The Chinese Economy: Transition and Growth*, Cambridge, Mass.: MIT Press.

Naughton, B. (2010), 'China's distinctive system: can it be a model for others?', *Journal of Contemporary China* 19(65): 437–60.

Qian, Y. and Wu, J. (2000), *China's transition to a market economy: how far across the river?*, CEDPR Working Paper No. 69, Center for Research on Economic Development and Policy Reform, Stanford University. Available from <http://siepr.stanford.edu/publicationsprofile/1503>.

Riedel, J., Jin, J. and Gao, J. (2007), *How China Grows: Investment, Finance, and Reform*, Princeton, NJ: Princeton University Press.

Schumpeter, J. A. (1934), *The Theory of Economic Development*, Cambridge, Mass.: Harvard University Press.

Shen, Y., Shen, M., Xu, Z. and Bai, Y. (2009), 'Bank size and small- and medium-sized enterprise (SME) lending: evidence from China', *World Development* 37(4): 800–11.

Sobel, R. S. (2008), 'Testing Baumol: institutional quality and the productivity of entrepreneurship', *Journal of Business Venturing* 23: 641–55.

Song, L. (2005), 'Interest rate liberalisation in China and the implications for non-state banking', in Y. Huang, A. Saich and E. Steinfeld (eds), *Financial Sector Reform in China*, pp. 111–30, Cambridge, Mass.: Harvard University Asia Centre.

Song, L. (2014), 'State and non-state enterprises in China's economic transition', in G. C. Chow and D. H. Perkins (eds), *Routledge Handbook of the Chinese Economy*, pp. 182–207, London and New York: Routledge.

Tanas, J. K. and Audretsch, D. B. (2011), 'Entrepreneurship in transitional economy', *International Entrepreneurship and Management Journal* 7: 431–42.

Tsai, K. S. (2007), *Capitalism without Democracy: The Private Sector in Contemporary China*, Ithaca, NY: Cornell University Press.

World Bank (1992), *China—Country Economic Memorandum: Reform and the Role of the Plan in the 1990s*, Washington, DC: The World Bank. Available from <http://documents.worldbank.org/curated/en/1992/06/736717/china-country-economic-memorandum-reform-role-plan-1990s>.

World Bank (2001), *World Development Report 2002: Building Institution for Markets*, New York: Oxford University Press.

World Bank and Development Research Center of the State Council, the People's Republic of China (DRC) (2013), *China 2030*, Washington, DC: The World Bank.

Wu, J. (2009), 'Market socialism and Chinese economic reform', in J. Kornai and Y. Qian (eds), *Market and Socialism: In the Light of the Experiences of China and Vietnam*, New York: Palgrave Macmillan.

Wu, J. and Cheng, M. L. (2011), 'The impact of managerial political connections and quality on government subsidies: evidence from Chinese listed firms', *Chinese Management Studies* 5(2): 207–26.

Xiao, G., Yang, X. and Janus, A. (2009), 'State-owned enterprises in China: reform dynamics and impacts', in R. Garnaut, L. Song and W. T. Woo (eds), China's New Place in a World in Crisis: Economic Geopolitical and Environmental Dimensions, pp. 155–78, Canberra: ANU E Press.

Yang, K. (2012), 'The dependency of private entrepreneurs on China's state', *Strategic Change* 21: 107–17.

Young, A. (2000), 'The razor's edge: distortions and incremental reform in the People's Republic of China', *The Quarterly Journal of Economics* CXV(4): 1091–135.

Zhang, A., Zhang, Y. and Zhao, R. (2002), 'Profitability and productivity of Chinese industrial firms: measurement and ownership implications', *China Economic Review* 13: 65–88.

Zhang, C. (2002), The interaction of the state and the market in a developing transition country: the experience of China, Paper presented at International Seminar on Promoting Growth and Welfare: Structural Changes and the Role of Institutions in Asia, Brazil.

Zhang, D. and Freestone, O. (2013), 'China's unfinished state-owned enterprise reforms', *Economic Roundup Issue 2*, The Treasury, Government of Australia, Canberra. Available from <http://www.treasury.gov.au/ PublicationsAndMedia/Publications/2013/Economic-Roundup-Issue-2/ Economic-Roundup/Chinas-unfinished-SOE-reforms>.

Zhang, X. and Tan, K. Y. (2007), 'Incremental reform and distortions in China's product and factor markets', *The World Bank Economic Review* 21(2): 279–99.

Zhang, Y., Wang, X. and Chen, K. (2012), *Growth and distributive effects of public infrastructure investments in China*, Working Paper 2012-07, Partner for Economic Policy Network. Available from <http://www.gdn.int/admin/ uploads/editor/files/.../YuMeiZhang_Paper.pdf>.

Zheng, J., Bigsten, A. and Hu, A. (2009), 'Can China's growth be sustained? A productivity perspective', *World Development* 37(4): 874–88.

Zhou, W. (2009), 'Bank financing in China's private sector: the payoffs of political capital', *World Development* 37(4): 787–99.

5. China's High Rates of Investment and Path Towards Internal Rebalancing

Owen Freestone and Dougal Horton[1]

Introduction

China's investment share of GDP remains at an unusually high rate, even when compared with other East Asian economies at a similar stage of development. This chapter documents the likely causes of China's high rates of investment and how the authorities' planned market-oriented reforms might play a role in reducing investment and boosting household consumption in the future. Using more-advanced Asian economies' experiences as a guide, our analysis suggests that a 10 percentage point reduction in China's investment share of GDP (and a commensurate rise in household consumption) could take place over a 10-year period, and could in theory occur without any major disruptions to economic growth and capital accumulation. Having established the plausibility of this scenario, we introduce this shock into a global computable general equilibrium (CGE) model with China's economy represented along with an offsetting rise in productivity, imagining that the Chinese authorities' planned reforms are successful in boosting the efficiency of capital across the economy. We do this simply to demonstrate the effects of such a development. We find that this shock leads to a shift in household spending towards services and away from manufactured goods, and a small decrease in exports while at the same time a small increase in imports, which reduces China's trade surplus, consistent with the shift from investment towards consumption.

This chapter is divided into two sections. The first section familiarises readers with the evolution of China's macro-economy, shows how its structure has changed through time compared with other economies at similar stages of their development, and discusses some of the reasons put forward for China's very high rates of investment.

1 The authors are, or were, from the International Economy Division of the Australian Treasury. The CGE modelling used in this chapter was developed by Liangyue Cao, Qun Shi, Cedric Hodges and Wallace Stark from the Macroeconomic Modelling and Policy Division. This chapter has benefited from comments and suggestions provided by Sam Hill, Bonnie Li, Mark Frost and Richard Wood. The views in this chapter are those of the authors and not necessarily those of the Australian Treasury.

Building on the findings of the first section, the second section explores the scenario of a gradual 10 percentage point reduction in China's investment share of GDP over a 10-year period. Having established the overall reasonableness of such a transition, results of a similar shock in a version[2] of the Global Trade and Environment Model (GTEM) (Pant 2007) are discussed, including how the authorities' planned productivity-boosting reforms might help offset the impact of lower investment on China's real GDP.

China's economic and industrial transformation since 1978

Overview of China's rise

Supported by vast labour endowments and the rapid accumulation of capital goods, the structural reform and opening-up processes have steered China's transition from an agrarian economy to one led by modern industry and services.

Similar to other East Asian economies before it, China has exploited to great effect the advantages of 'backwardness'. As a late developer, China has been able to import and quickly adapt the technologies and production techniques of advanced economies, without bearing the delays and costs involved in research and development.

Consequently, China's share of world output doubled in just over a decade from the beginning of reform in 1978. Over the past three decades, China's share of world output has increased eightfold and on most estimates it could overtake the United States as the world's largest economy by 2020.

This remarkable transformation has, however, coincided with substantial structural imbalances, and economic and social challenges. Chinese growth is heavily reliant on unsustainably high investment rates, encouraged by distortionary policies that divert resources away from households to the corporate sector to encourage the accumulation of physical capital stock.[3] These settings have led to over-leveraging and inefficient investment in some sectors, putting financial stability and future growth at risk. It has also come with high environmental costs, which may limit the rate of future industrial expansion, at least in some regions of China.

---

2   This is a version of GTEM with some modifications made by the Australian Treasury.
3   Hereinafter, the term 'capital stock' will refer to 'physical capital stock' unless otherwise stated.

Over the next decade, the key challenge facing the Chinese authorities will be to support the economy's transition towards a new pattern of growth. Only through shifting towards an economy driven by private, rather than state, investment decisions will China be able to make continued productivity gains and progress towards the higher-income East Asian economies. With China's demographics expected to become an increasing drag on growth in coming decades, continued productivity gains will be all the more crucial.

Of course, China is not the first economy to face such challenges. This section examines China's current economic structure, comparing China with other East Asian economies as they transitioned along their own development paths.[4] We also include the United States as a benchmark in our chart analysis, to show how China's transition compares with another economy that was large enough to affect the overall global economy during its development.

Falling household consumption share of GDP

The rapid expansion of China's productive capacity—including through massive investment in infrastructure—has supported (and been supported by) the migration of hundreds of millions of rural workers to higher-paying jobs in the urban manufacturing sector. These higher wages have flowed to the broader economy, underwriting a sustained increase in average household incomes and consumption. Since 1978, wages have increased at an average annual rate of 14 per cent, and household consumption by 15 per cent. Nonetheless, investment has grown at a much faster rate, pushing down the household consumption share of GDP to a historically low 35 per cent (Figure 5.1).

As indicated in Figure 5.1, the household consumption share of GDP typically declines in the first stages of economic development as the economy moves from a subsistence-like state in which most output is consumed. As the economy develops, investment accelerates. Surplus labour ensures that, although household incomes grow, the share of national income held by the household sector remains relatively low. As a result, investment grows faster relative to household consumption so that the consumption share of GDP

---

4   There are three main inputs into the production process: physical capital (factories, manufacturing equipment); human capital (the skills, knowledge and experience of the workforce); and natural capital (the stock of natural resources). The efficiency with which these inputs are used to produce an economy's output can indicate the level of economic development. In practice, however, calculating the productivity of capital can be difficult, primarily due to the difficulty in estimating the contribution from both human and natural capital. Instead, this chapter uses real GDP per capita (adjusted for purchasing power parity) to measure the level of development. GDP per capita is readily available for most economies and is an indicator of the relative productivity with which different economies use their resources.

falls. For example, the household consumption share of the Korean economy experienced a sharp fall, from more than 80 per cent in the early 1960s (Korea's 'take-off' point) to 54 per cent in 2012.

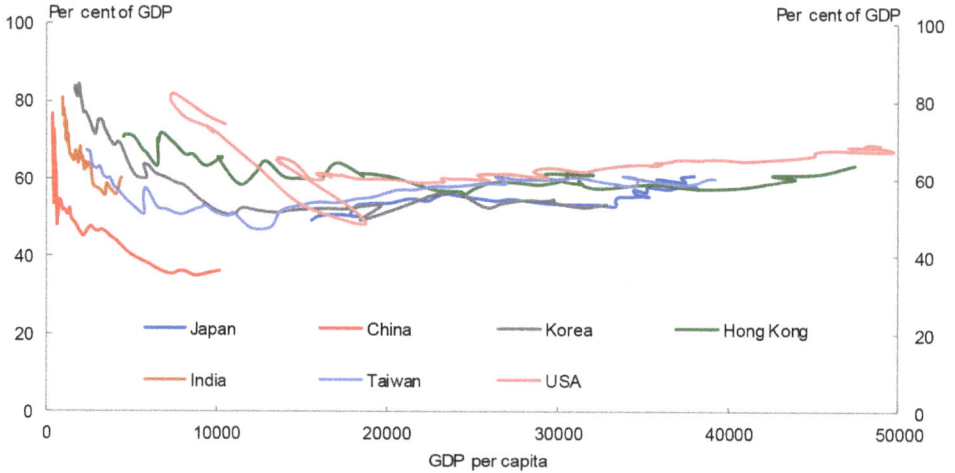

Figure 5.1 Household Consumption

Sources: World Bank (2012); CEIC Asia; US Bureau of Economic Analysis; Maddison (2010); and Australian Treasury.

Note: GDP per capita adjusted for purchasing power parity (PPP) (2011 prices).

Figure 5.1 also shows, however, that the household consumption share of Chinese GDP has fallen further and faster than that of its East Asian peers. In Korea, the share of GDP accounted for by household consumption reached a low of around 50 per cent in 1988 when at a similar stage of development as China is at today.

The low and declining share of Chinese household consumption over the past three decades has been predominantly driven by the household sector's declining share of national income (Aziz and Cui 2007). This decline has occurred across all main household income sources—wages, property income and government transfers—and reflects the traditional heavy bias in China's economic model in favour of the corporate sector. Features of this model include a very limited social safety net (especially for migrant workers), artificially low prices on factor inputs and so-called 'financial repression' (limited savings vehicles for households as an alternative to the state-regulated low returns on bank deposits and the implicit transfer of those funds to the corporate sector through a subsidised cost of capital).[5] Along with low wages stemming from surplus labour, these features have meant that the share of national income held by households remains relatively low, having fallen steadily since the mid 1990s. At the same time, these features have encouraged high rates of household saving, reinforcing China's low share of household consumption in GDP.

Industrialisation and export-led growth

Following in the footsteps of many other East Asian economies, China's rapid economic growth and rise in living standards since the modern reform period began have been driven by the accumulation of capital goods and the state-supported development of an internationally competitive manufacturing sector. As Rodrick (2013) notes, manufacturing industries can propel an economy forward, even in the presence of bad governance, bad policies and a disadvantageous context—not to say that China has been hampered by these factors.

As with other East Asian economies, China's export sector had a central role in underpinning China's rise. This partly reflects the positive spillover effects typically associated with export-led growth, especially in the transmission of new technologies and business practices to other sectors of the Chinese economy, which supported substantial economy-wide productivity gains. Equally, the large-scale migration of surplus rural labour to urban areas gave manufacturers access to a deep pool of low-cost labour, reinforcing the logic of this model of growth.

Over the 1970s, the manufacturing sector rose quickly as a share of the Chinese economy as easy gains were made through capital accumulation, technology transfer and the utilisation of cheap surplus labour. Between 1978 and 1980 manufacturing accounted for around 40 per cent of Chinese output. As incomes have risen and China has slowly moved towards a consumer and services-based economy, this share has eased to around 30 per cent today, comparable with Taiwan and Korea at similar stages of development.

Over the past two decades, this investment in productive capacity and other capital goods has contributed almost half of China's economic growth. Investment (gross fixed capital formation) averaged approximately 30 per cent of GDP in the 1980s, before steadily increasing to reach 47 per cent in 2012.

---

5 Aziz and Cui (2007) found that financial repression was a major reason for the low and declining household wage and investment income shares of national income. Borrowing constraints limiting firms' access to bank financing for working capital acted as a tax on labour input, discouraging the use of labour.

As shown in Figure 5.2, a sharp rise in the investment-to-GDP ratio is characteristic of a developing economy, reflecting the high returns on new capital during the earlier stages of development. At 47 per cent, however, the investment share of Chinese GDP is well above the peaks experienced in other East Asian economies. For example, the investment-to-GDP ratio in Japan peaked at 36 per cent in 1973 and in South Korea at 39 per cent in 1991.

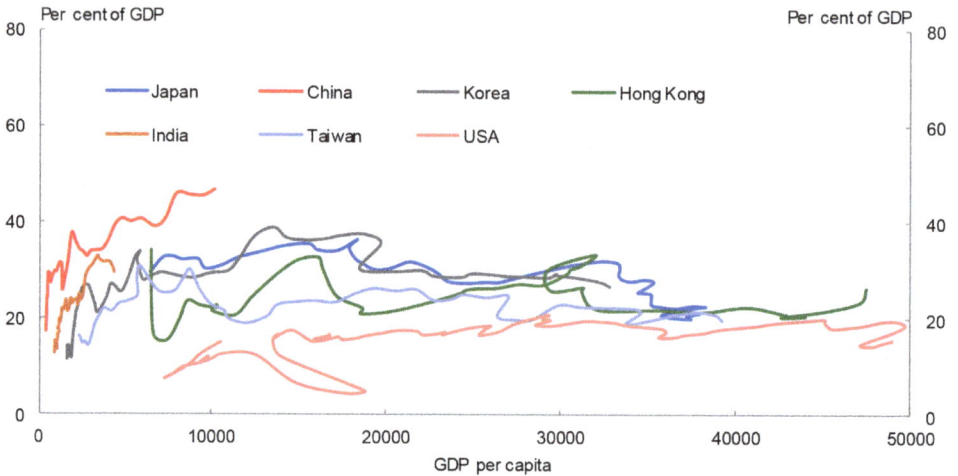

Figure 5.2 Investment

Sources: World Bank; CEIC Asia; US Bureau of Economic Analysis; Maddison (2010); and Australian Treasury.

Notes: GDP per capita adjusted for purchasing power parity (2011 prices). 'Investment' is defined as gross fixed capital formation.

China's capital stock is estimated to have grown at an average annual rate of 10 per cent in real terms over the past 30 years (Berlemann and Wesselhoft 2012). Despite this expansion, China's capital stock per worker remains a small fraction of that of advanced economies (Figure 5.3). Based on estimates from Berlemann and Wesselhoft (2012), China's capital stock per worker is only 5 per cent of that of the United States (in real terms at market exchange rates). Even after adjusting for differences in purchasing power, this figure is only 13 per cent. In comparison, Korea's capital stock per worker (in PPP terms) was around 30 per cent of the United States' in 1988 when at a similar stage of development to China today.[6]

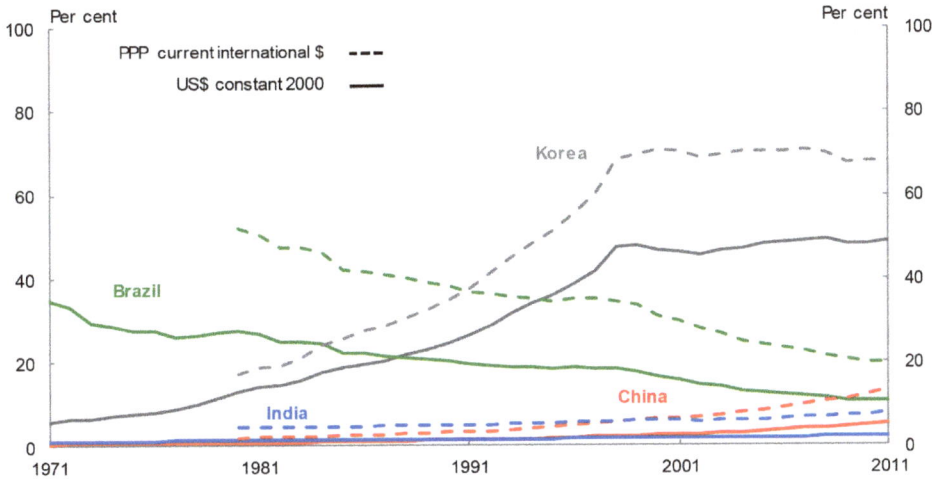

Figure 5.3 Physical Capital Stock Per Worker as Percentage of the United States

Sources: World Bank; Berlemann and Wesselhoft (2012); The Conference Board Total Economy Database™; and Australian Treasury.

Notes: GDP per capita adjusted for purchasing power parity (2011 prices). 'Worker' is defined as those persons who are employed as defined in The Conference Board Total Economy Database™.

State incentives support high national saving and investment

China's high investment rate has been supported by an even higher rate of domestic saving, which is elevated by international standards and has grown considerably since the modern reform period commenced. The national saving rate rose from around the 30 per cent range in the early 1980s to a peak of 53 per cent in 2008, before easing to 51 per cent in 2012. China's saving rate has consistently surpassed its investment rate for most of that period (Figure 5.4), and far exceeds that of its East Asian peers (Figure 5.5).

---

6   An issue worth noting when comparing capital stock per worker between economies at equivalent stages of development is that capital stock per worker is itself a measure of economic development; however, the efficiency with which physical capital is used by the workforce—that is, the productivity of the capital stock—would have implications for differences in capital stock per worker, and can be affected by the quality and quantity of an economy's stock of human and natural capital, and broader access to production technologies. Moreover, data for GDP are typically more reliable than those for capital stock, with capital stock data quite sensitive to depreciation rate assumptions. Therefore, we have used GDP per capita to measure stage of development. See Footnote 4 for further discussion regarding our choice of GDP per capita as the indicator of stage of development.

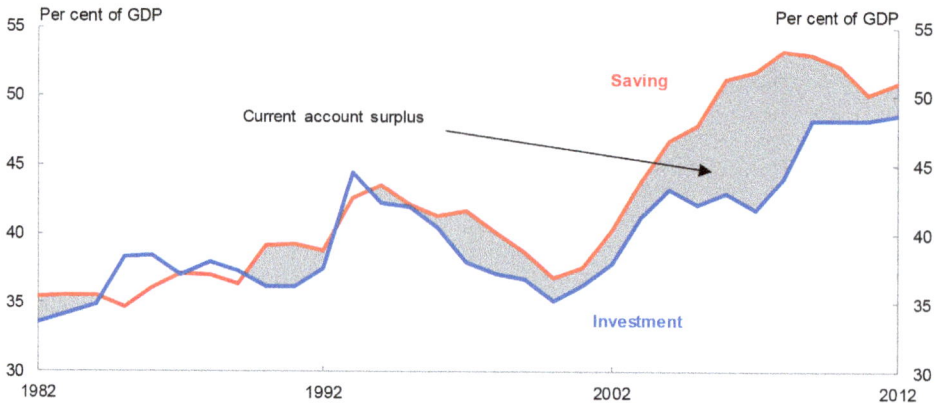

Figure 5.4 China's Saving and Investment Rates

Sources: IMF October 2013 WEO; CEIC China; and Australian Treasury.

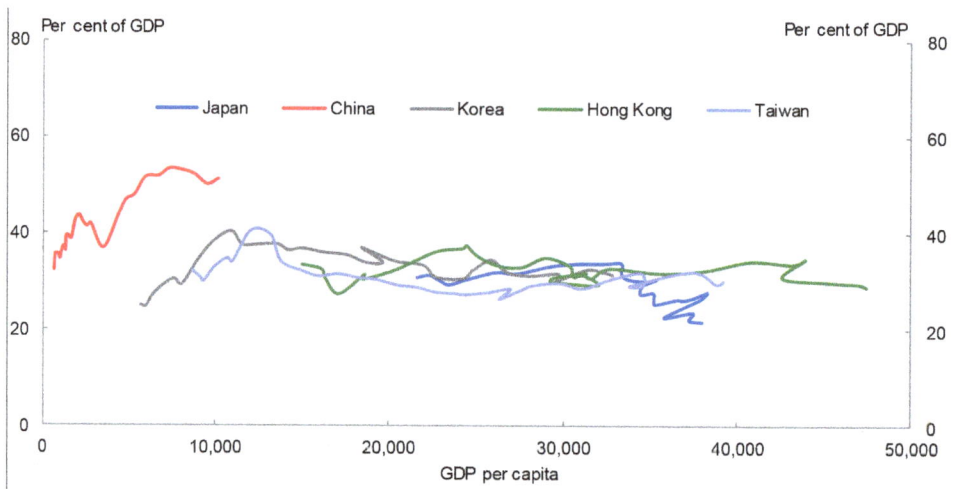

Figure 5.5 Saving

Source: IMF October 2013 WEO; Maddison (2010); and Australian Treasury.

Note: GDP per capita adjusted for purchasing power parity (2011 prices).

The household sector has accounted for around half of China's national saving since 1992. This has been driven over the past 30 years by a large and growing working-age population with a greater capacity to save compared with their young and elderly dependants (Kong et al. 2012). Incomplete domestic financial markets and limited access to foreign financial markets also encourage higher saving rates, as does the paucity of social services such as education, health care and social insurance.

Corporate saving, however, has also made a large contribution to the increase in national saving over this period, accounting for around 43 per cent of the increase. In particular, a lax dividend policy has allowed state-owned enterprises (SOEs) to retain and then reinvest most of their profits, rather than distribute to households via dividend payouts to the state. Financial underdevelopment has also made it difficult for the private sector, especially small businesses, to access intermediated financing, inducing higher saving rates in that sector.

The build-up in corporate saving has also been supported by favourable government policies designed to boost the development of the industrial sector—a key component of China's development model. For instance, domestic costs of key factor inputs such as land, water, energy and fuel have historically been relatively low by international standards, partly reflecting government policies that have regulated below-market prices (World Bank 2012).[7]

Most importantly, government policy settings have ensured the Chinese household and private sectors effectively subsidise the channelling of China's vast stock of savings into corporate investment at below-market prices. Market signals have only a limited role in China's underdeveloped and largely state-controlled banking system, which is characterised by the use of quantitative controls to manage the supply and allocation of credit and the regulation of benchmark deposit and lending interest rates (although the floor on the lending rate was removed for most bank loans in 2013). This regulated system both guarantees Chinese banks a minimum interest rate margin and allows banks to provide cheap loans to the corporate sector, especially SOEs.

After adjusting for inflation, returns on bank deposits have been negative for prolonged periods, with the real one-year benchmark deposit rate averaging −0.3 per cent over the past decade. The real one-year benchmark lending rate has averaged just 2.9 per cent over the same period.

Aided by relatively tight capital controls, these policy settings have secured a cheap and stable domestic funding source for China's large corporations and SOEs since the early 2000s, promoting high rates of economic growth through capital accumulation.[8]

---

7   The total value of China's factor market distortions could total almost 10 per cent of GDP (Ahuja et al. 2012).
8   Other factors have also contributed. Private home ownership, permitted from the late 1990s, has led to a surge in property investment. Moreover, central authorities implicitly encourage local government officials to generate high investment rates with an incentive structure that rewards rapid economic growth.

The relatively healthy headline rate of return on capital remains a powerful incentive for investment in China. Putting government subsidies to one side, the return on capital is generally an indicator of the productivity (or efficiency) of investment. The higher the return, the greater is the demand for new capital goods, consistent with the profitable opportunities for further investment.

Figure 5.6 shows two estimates for historical returns in China, suggesting a decline of approximately 10 percentage points since the early 1990s. Despite this moderation, the return on capital remains high in China relative to other East Asian economies. HSBC estimates that the return on capital in Singapore, Korea and Hong Kong could be less than 6 per cent, in part reflecting their much more advanced stages of development.

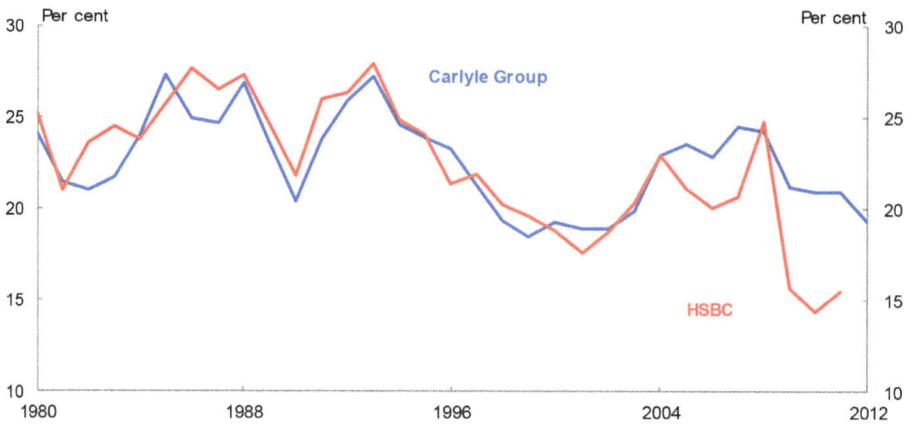

Figure 5.6 Return on Capital

Sources: HSBC Global Research (2013); Carlyle Group (2013).

A declining rate of return is consistent with a rising capital-to-output ratio, indicating an increase in the amount of capital required to generate one unit of output. As indicated in Figure 5.7, although China's capital-to-output ratio is rising, it remains low relative to more advanced economies.

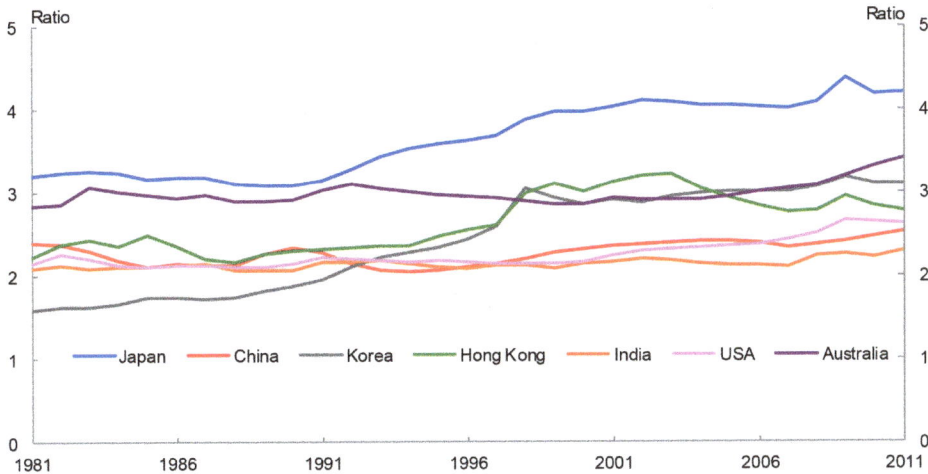

Figure 5.7 Capital-to-Output Ratio

Source: World Bank; Berlemann and Wesselhoft (2012); and Australian Treasury.

Note: Capital and output adjusted for purchasing power parity (2011 prices).

To some extent, declining returns and a rising capital-to-output ratio are natural outcomes as an economy modernises. As an economy shifts away from labour-intensive agriculture towards more capital-intensive modern industries, capital requirements per unit of output naturally increase. It is also consistent with rising labour costs associated with diminishing surplus labour. Moreover, the most recent decline in returns in China could be partly explained by the burst of investment related to the Global Financial Crisis (GFC) in longer-dated infrastructure projects, which tend to weigh on returns in the short term. Over the longer term, these projects can increase the overall efficiency and productive capacity of the economy, generating significant returns and an ongoing rise in living standards (although, some of the most poorly targeted investment during the GFC may never yield an economic return).

China is still in the catch-up phase of capital formation, as indicated by a low capital stock per worker (see Figure 5.3). Driven by the urbanisation process, demand for infrastructure remains substantial, particularly in urban housing, transport, water and energy, and education and health services. And as factor costs rise, China will need to shift up the value chain to remain globally competitive, requiring further upgrading of China's manufacturing and broader productive capabilities (Coates et al. 2012). As such, the relatively high returns available to investors will remain an incentive for continued investment in China, albeit to a lesser extent than in the past.

Diminishing returns to investment

Using the headline return as a measure of the efficiency of investment, however, assumes that inputs are priced according to market forces. The relatively high returns still available in China are probably distorted by the below-market pricing of factor inputs and other policies favouring the corporate sector, thus concealing the growing inefficiency of investment in some sectors of the Chinese economy.

For example, Lee et al. (2013) found that investment in inland provinces is progressively becoming less efficient. Reflecting this, private consumption in these regions only benefited in the short run through the direct effect of higher wages and other income paid out during the investment phase. In the longer run, the impact on private consumption was found to be small, as the poor quality of the project meant the capital stock was not sustainably increased by the investment.

Moreover, despite higher investment and rapid credit expansion, Chinese economic growth is easing, in part indicating diminishing returns to physical capital accumulation and the misallocation of resources (Nabar and N'Diaye 2013).

The decline in the return on capital and growing evidence of capital misallocation have contributed to concerns that China has invested in substantial capacity far ahead of demand, and that the productivity of investment is falling too quickly. According to this argument, although new investment generates an initial burst of economic growth, much of it is in unproductive or underutilised projects, and is unlikely to make a further contribution to GDP (unless this spare capacity becomes utilised in the future). In effect, this represents a reduction in the efficiency of capital. This can be seen, for example, in the build-up of overcapacity in parts of China's industrial sector, such as steel and shipbuilding, and in underused motorways. With sustained urbanisation and economic growth, however, it is important to remember that initially underutilised infrastructure can become economically useful over time.

China's falling capacity utilisation rate could provide evidence of overcapacity and a decline in the efficiency of investment. In November 2013, the National Development and Reform Commission reported that China's industrial capacity utilisation rate fell to 78 per cent in the first half of 2013, the lowest rate since the last quarter of 2009.[9] Some Chinese industries are more affected by overcapacity than others, particularly those related to the construction sector. For example, as of the end of 2012 the capacity utilisation rate for the shipbuilding industry was 75 per cent, and in the iron and steel industry the rate was only 72 per cent.

---

9   The IMF estimates that China's capacity utilisation rate declined from just less than 80 per cent before the GFC to 60 per cent in 2012 (IMF 2012).

The limited role of market signals in China's state-controlled banking system and low cost of capital have been key drivers of these developments. While the banking sector remains immensely profitable, the suppression of market forces has hampered the development of an efficient commercially oriented banking system with sufficient risk-management capabilities.[10] This strategy has encouraged over-leveraging[11] and, by diverting financial resources away from the more dynamic private sector to less-efficient SOEs, has contributed to the misallocation of capital.

How might China's transition take shape?

China's economic transition—towards household consumption, services and the more efficient use of factors of production—will, at least to some extent, occur even without substantial new economic reforms. The economic pressures from an exhaustion of surplus labour and the associated wage increases will boost the household sector's share of national income, and reduce the incentive for the corporate sector to invest (Huang et al. 2013). And, as noted by Garnaut et al. (2013) in the 2013 edition of the *China Update*, labour-market shifts have already been driving structural change in China since the mid 2000s.

This does not, however, discount the importance of government policy, as argued above. The combined effect of a regulated cost of capital (and other key inputs), a financial system consisting mainly of state-owned banks, a tightly controlled capital account and a system of government that has incentivised provincial leaders to prioritise economic growth above all else has undoubtedly contributed to some overinvestment. And with increasing evidence of poor investments and a falling efficiency of capital, Chinese authorities have come to accept that a new wave of market-oriented reforms is needed to maintain strong economic growth and reinforce the economy's transition towards a more services and consumer-based economy.

The market-oriented reform ambitions outlined at the Chinese Communist Party's Third Plenum in November 2013 provide the latest indication of the authorities' recognition of the need for fresh economic and structural reforms. At its core, this agenda recognises that China's continued economic development will require a more efficient allocation of resources, especially capital. Only through more market-based methods of allocating capital and other factors of production will China be able to achieve its objective of strong and sustained economic growth, and higher incomes and private consumption.

---

10 The development of China's shadow banking industry has occurred partly as a way of circumventing the tightly regulated conventional banking system.

11 China's total debt-to-GDP ratio (including household, corporate and all levels of government debt) is estimated at more than 200 per cent—high for an emerging economy.

Following the example set by other East Asian economies since the 1970s, China's transition will be characterised by a falling investment share of GDP. In China, this is expected to occur as state-led investment progressively gives way to greater private-led economic activity, supported by ongoing market-oriented reforms. As wages rise, the economy's resources will shift more towards the production of goods and services for domestic household consumption. Labour scarcity and the accompanying rise in wages will continue to drive Chinese manufacturing further up the production value chain towards more technologically sophisticated goods with a higher valued-added contribution from domestic sources, including from the services sector (Garnaut et al. 2013).

While there is clearly still far to go, a range of indicators suggests this transition is already under way. The household consumption and investment-to-GDP ratios appear to be stabilising after their natural transition paths were disrupted by the burst of GFC-related investment stimulus measures (see Figures 5.1 and 5.2). Last year, the services sector accounted for 46 per cent of Chinese GDP—larger than the share from the industrial sector (44 per cent). This was the first time since at least 1952 that the services sector has accounted for the single largest share of the Chinese economy. China's national saving rate has declined from a high of 53 per cent in 2008 to 51 per cent in 2012, and the current account surplus has narrowed from 10 per cent of GDP in 2007 to 2.3 per cent in 2012 (albeit driven in part by a surge in imports of raw materials and other inputs into China's GFC investment spree).

This section examines the potential transition path China might take in the coming decade. It will not attempt to add to the literature on the necessary reforms or prospects for implementation. Rather, we assume that over the next decade, through a combination of natural forces and appropriate economic reforms, China will shift further towards a more market-based economy. In our scenario, these reforms contribute to a gradual decline in China's investment-to-GDP ratio, in part through a reduction in the implicit investment subsidy that is currently provided by the household sector to the corporate sector discussed above.

Also, we do not initially attempt to estimate the 'reform dividend'—that is, the boost in private investment by non-SOEs that might result from better access to capital and a generally more conducive operating environment for private enterprise. Instead, in the final subsection of the chapter, we explore the idea of an offsetting (in terms of the net effect on real GDP) increase in capital efficiency, which is probably a more widely accepted way of thinking about China's reform dividend.

Declining investment-to-GDP ratio

Lee et al. (2012) used dynamic panel data models for 36 economies from 1955 to 2009 to relate the investment-to-GDP ratio to a broad range of explanatory variables to find the optimal rate of investment. Overinvestment in China was estimated at approximately 10 per cent of GDP. The cost of financing this overinvestment was found to be predominantly borne by households and small-to-medium-sized enterprises through a hidden transfer of resources, estimated at an average of 4 per cent of GDP per year. It was concluded that a 10 percentage point decline in the investment share of the Chinese economy over time would bring investment to levels consistent with fundamentals.

While this estimate is subject to much uncertainty, we proceed to use a 10 percentage point fall in investment as a share of GDP (defined as gross fixed capital formation as a share of GDP) as the basis for the following scenario.

Our analysis also assumes that this decline would take place progressively over the next decade, although we accept that nominating such a precise transition period is somewhat arbitrary.[12] For reference, our 10-year scenario represents a faster transition than in the 'upside reform scenario' detailed in Nabar and N'Diaye (2013), in which financial sector and resource pricing reforms gradually slow capital accumulation and eliminate excess investment by 2030. In their scenario, the gradual increase in investment from firms in non-manufacturing sectors—lured by prospects of future profits, particularly services—does not fully offset the decline in manufacturing investment, so the share of investment in GDP declines from more than 45 per cent in 2012 to around 35 per cent in 2030.

Our scenario of a 10 percentage point fall over a 10-year period is broadly consistent with the experiences of other East Asian economies as they developed and returns to capital fell (Figure 5.8). The key difference is that the investment share of the Chinese economy appears to have peaked at an earlier stage of China's development. In Korea, investment peaked at 39 per cent of GDP in 1991 at GDP per capita of $13 600 (PPP, 2011 prices). By 2001 it had fallen 10 percentage points to 29 per cent. In Japan, investment peaked at 36 per cent of GDP in 1973 at GDP per capita of $18 300. Over the following 10 years the

---

12 We begin our transition in 2013 mainly because it is simple, with 2012 the final year for which comprehensive annual data for China are available at the time of writing.

ratio fell to 28 per cent.[13] In the case of China, our scenario assumes that the investment share of the economy peaked in 2012 at around 47 per cent, at GDP per capita of $10 200.[14]

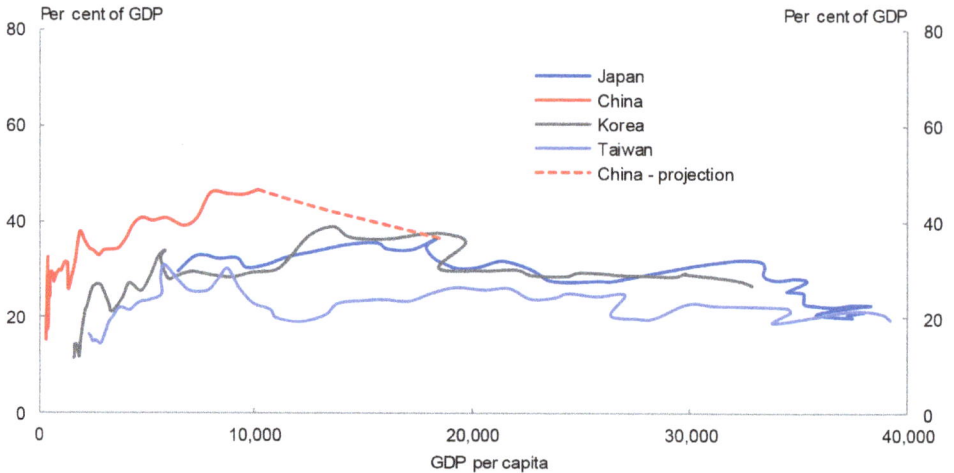

Figure 5.8 Projected Path of Investment-to-GDP Ratio

Sources: World Bank; CEIC Asia; Maddison (2010); and Australian Treasury.

Notes: GDP per capita adjusted for purchasing power parity (2011 prices). Investment defined as gross fixed capital formation.

A greater role for household consumption

In estimating how a 10 percentage point decline might be transmitted through China's economy, our analysis depends on a number of basic, but defensible, assumptions.

The share of GDP accounted for by government consumption, change in inventories and net exports is assumed to remain constant over the 10-year period.[15] Government consumption as a share of GDP has been very stable since 1952 (the beginning of the National Bureau of Statistics data set), averaging 13 per cent. This ratio is therefore set at 13.5 per cent over the decade from 2013, which is the average of the 10-year period from 2003. The change in

---

13 The declining trend in Japan's investment-to-GDP ratio was temporarily disrupted by the late 1980s investment boom, increasing to 32 per cent by 1990. The ratio fell again, however, during the 2000s to reach 25 per cent in 2000 and 21.2 per cent by 2012.

14 As explained previously, 2012 is the final year for which complete national accounts data were available when this chapter was being prepared.

15 The net exports assumption runs contrary to the conventional wisdom that China's trade surplus would narrow as a result of internal rebalancing. Some of our general equilibrium results below also cast doubt on this conventional wisdom.

the inventories-to-GDP ratio is set at 2.4 per cent—also the 10-year average from 2003. Net exports-to-GDP has been set at 2.5 per cent, compared with 2.7 per cent in 2012.

The household consumption share of GDP is then simply calculated as the residual of the sum of government consumption, gross fixed capital formation, change in inventories and net exports. Therefore, a 10 percentage point decrease in the investment-to-GDP ratio over the 10-year projection period results in the household consumption-to-GDP ratio growing from around 35 per cent in 2013 to 45 per cent by 2022.

This is at the upper end of the shifts towards household consumption in other East Asian economies as their very high rates of investment growth began to ease (Figure 5.9). Notably, this is a little faster than the increases seen in Japan and Korea, where household consumption as a share of GDP rose around 5 percentage points in the decade after peak investment.

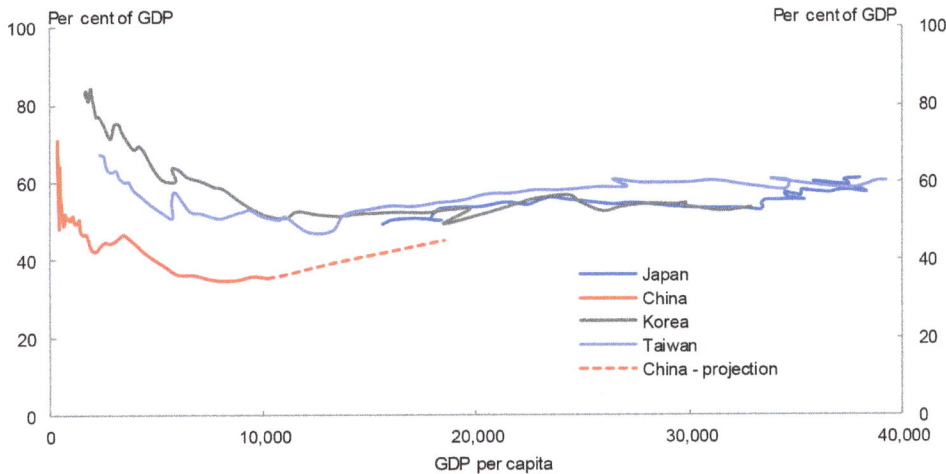

Figure 5.9 Projected Path of Household Consumption-to-GDP Ratio

Sources: World Bank; CEIC Asia; Maddison (2010); and Australian Treasury.

Note: GDP per capita adjusted for purchasing power parity (2011 prices).

In China, as the migration of labour from rural to urban areas runs its course, and as consumers demand more labour-intensive services, household incomes—and with this household consumption—will increase as a share of GDP. This process will be reinforced by market-oriented reforms that gradually reduce the hidden transfer of resources from households to the corporate sector.

Chinese policy is already turning towards measures that will support higher household consumption. These include the staged appreciation of the renminbi—which will increase Chinese consumers' purchasing power and promote greater domestic demand—financial market liberalisation and the development of alternatives to bank deposits with higher returns, hefty increases to minimum wages, and improvements to the social safety net to include items such as basic medical and unemployment insurance.

Implications for growth in GDP and the capital stock

An examination of the implied nominal growth rates over the 10-year projection period suggests these projected shifts in the shares of investment and household consumption do not have to lead to significant disruptions to economic growth and capital accumulation.[16] Rather, while this scenario implies a gradual easing in GDP growth rates, it arguably nudges the Chinese economy towards a more sustainable growth path.

This scenario will allow nominal GDP growth to slow from 10 to 8 per cent over the 10-year period.[17] Relative to average annual growth rates in the 10-year period immediately preceding our projection period, annual growth in household consumption expenditure will slow to 11 per cent, while growth in investment will slow to 5 per cent (Figure 5.10). The share of growth accounted for by household consumption will rise to 57 per cent and investment will decline to 24 per cent (Figure 5.11).

This scenario is also consistent with robust, but slower, growth in China's capital stock over the 10-year projection period. We have increased the 2011 capital stock estimate from Berlemann and Wesselhoft (2012) by our estimates for annual gross fixed capital formation (in US$ constant 2000 prices). The annual depreciation rate is set at 4.5 per cent over the projection period, broadly consistent with Berlemann and Wesselhofts' estimate for 2011.[18]

---

16 The nominal GDP (production) result for 2013 has been expanded out to 2018 using implied growth rates from IMF WEO October 2013 projections of nominal GDP levels. From 2019 onwards, nominal GDP projections have been extended by using the Australian Treasury's real GDP growth projections and assuming constant growth of 2.5 per cent in the GDP deflator—down from the IMF's forecast of 2.6 per cent in 2018.

17 While we have focused on nominal GDP growth rates, our basic assumption for growth in the GDP deflator implies a slowing in annual growth of real GDP to around 6 per cent by the end of the projection period.

18 Berlemann and Wesselhoft (2012) applied the same time-varying depreciation rate across all countries in their sample. Between 2000 and 2011, the depreciation rate grew within a range of approximately 4 to 4.5 per cent. This is arguably too low for a rapidly developing economy such as China; however, for consistency purposes we have chosen to use a depreciation rate of 4.5 per cent.

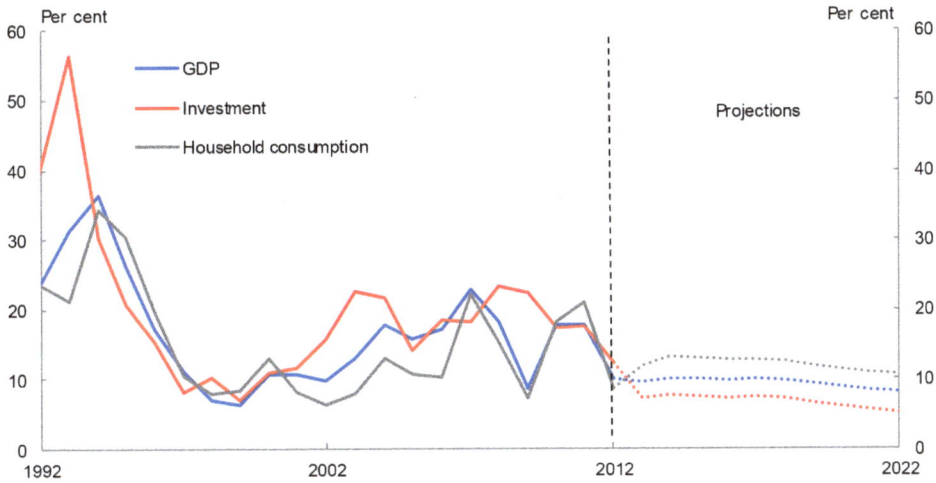

Figure 5.10 Growth in Nominal GDP, Household Consumption and Investment

Sources: CEIC China; IMF WEO October 2013; and Australian Treasury.

Notes: GDP (expenditure) breakdown for 2013 not available at time of publishing, hence projections for investment and consumption commence after 2012. GDP growth for 2013 is actual.

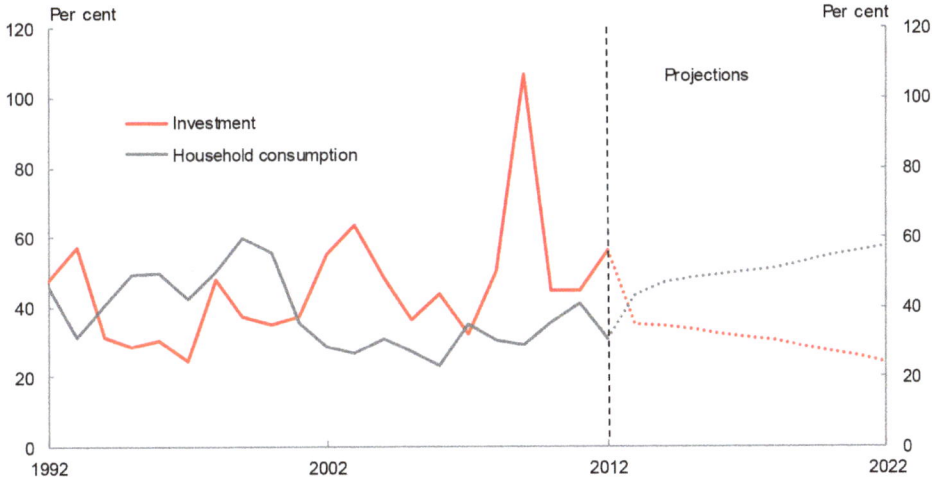

Figure 5.11 Share of Nominal GDP Growth

Sources: CEIC China; IMF WEO October 2013; and Australian Treasury.

Note: GDP (expenditure) breakdown for 2013 not available at time of publishing, hence projections for investment and consumption commence after 2012.

Under this scenario, real annual growth in capital stock will fall to around 7 per cent over the projection period (Figure 5.12). This is consistent with the experience of Korea, according to the results of Berlemann and Wesselhoft (2012). In the 10-year period from 1991, when the investment share of the Korean economy peaked, real annual growth in Korean capital stock fell from

14 to 6 per cent. China's capital stock per worker (in this case, measured as working-age population) will also continue to increase, although annual growth rates will decline to around 7 per cent over the projection period (Figure 5.13).

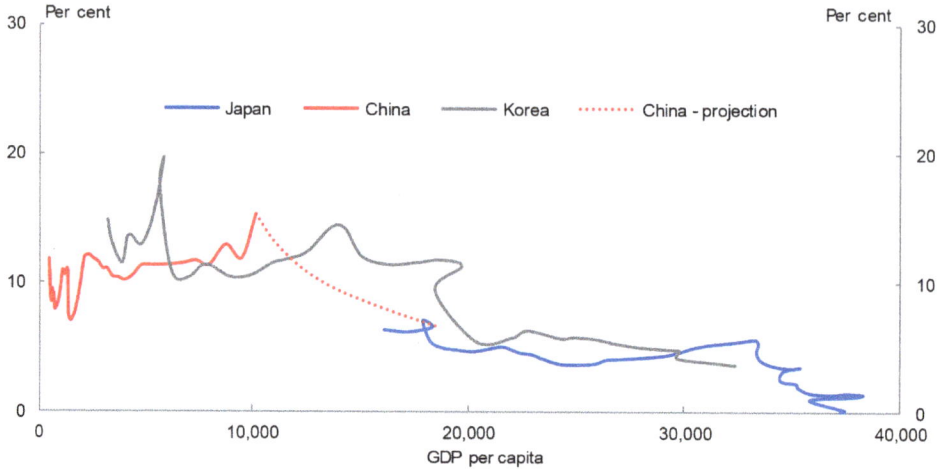

Figure 5.12 Annual Growth in Total Capital Stock

Sources: CEIC China database; IMF WEO October 2013; Berlemann and Wesselhoft (2012); Maddison (2010); and Australian Treasury.

Note: Capital stock is measured in US$ constant 2000 prices.

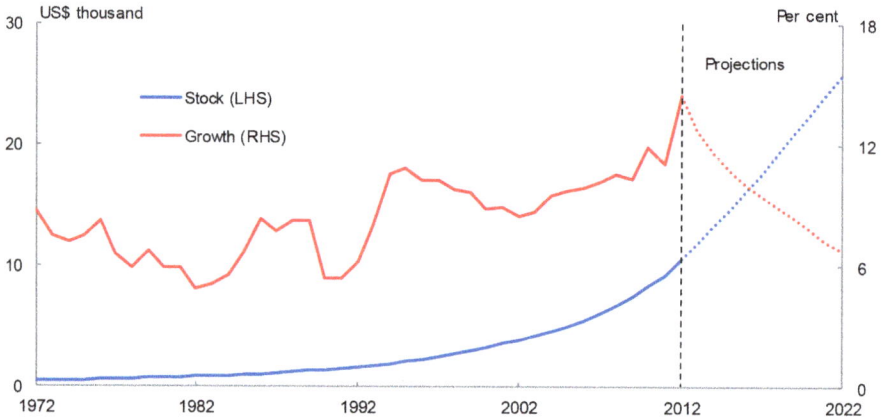

Figure 5.13 Capital Stock Per Worker

Sources: CEIC China database; IMF WEO October 2013; Berlemann and Wesselhoft (2012); and Australian Treasury.

Notes: Capital stock is measured in US$ constant 2000 prices. Due to data availability, data on working-age population (historical and projections) have been used as proxies for employed workers.

With China still in the catch-up phase of capital formation, solid growth in China's capital stock will be supported by the urbanisation process. The United Nations estimates that China's urbanisation ratio will reach 61 per cent by 2020, up almost 10 percentage points from 2012. This means more than 100 million extra urban residents with demands for housing, utility and transport infrastructure, and education and health services. Moreover, higher capital stock per worker will be essential to ensure that ongoing productivity gains go some way to offset the impacts of the decline in China's working-age population.

This suggests the focus on Chinese investment should not be on how excessive it might be, but should address the structural and policy issues in the Chinese economy that negatively affect the allocation and efficiency of investment. Were China to successfully implement the planned market-oriented reforms, private sources of investment could provide a significant offset to reductions in state-led investment, implying that our scenario may understate future growth in China's capital stock per worker.

It is unlikely that actual outcomes would be as smooth as we have assumed. Nonetheless, this analysis indicates that a fall in the investment-to-GDP ratio of 10 percentage points over the next decade need not be overly disruptive to the Chinese economy, in terms of the effects on China's economic growth and rate of capital accumulation. Moreover, this kind of adjustment would not be out of step with the experience of other East Asian economies at similar stages of development, although the sheer size of China's economy and its systemic importance to the global economy—even early in its development—may limit the usefulness of such historical comparisons.

CGE modelling results of a fall in the investment share of GDP

While our high-level analysis illustrates how a downward adjustment to China's investment share of GDP might take place, a CGE model can shed further light on the channels through which this adjustment would occur, including the impact on China's industry structure and composition of household spending. Given the key purpose of China's planned economic reforms is to improve the economy's productivity, we also explore scenarios in which these reforms boost various productivities and offset the effect on real GDP of lower investment.

To explore these scenarios, we use the version of GTEM mentioned earlier and run a negative 1 percentage point shock on China's investment share of GDP as well as a positive 1 percentage point shock on China's private consumption share of GDP incrementally over a 10-year period, consistent with the above analysis. By the tenth year, the shocks lead to a roughly 10 percentage point reduction in the private saving rate, a 10 percentage point rise in household consumption and a 10 percentage point reduction in investment (all as a percentage of GDP).

Consistent with our discussion above, the shock on investment could be seen as the result of removing the subsidies for corporate saving and investment, or more broadly, a rise in the cost of investment by the corporate sector. On the other hand, the shock on private consumption could be seen as encompassing wider social reforms that lead to a reduction of the current high rates of precautionary saving by Chinese households.

Compared with the baseline, reducing China's investment share of GDP by 10 percentage points leads to around 2.7 per cent reduction in real GDP, and reduces the size of the capital stock by around 11 per cent.

While the shock represents a significant rebalancing from investment to consumption as a share of GDP, the impact on China's external account is modest. In the absence of productivity improvement from the baseline, China's trade surplus as a share of GDP is around 0.4 percentage points larger because of the shock, while the exchange rate is around 0.5 half a percentage points lower, reflecting a relatively larger reduction in imports than exports.

To better separate the impact of rebalancing on the structure of China's economy from the obvious negative effect on output of lower investment, we implement an offsetting increase in productivity. Again, the kind of offsetting rise in productivity can be viewed as a 'reform dividend' that could accrue to the Chinese economy if the kind of package of reforms announced at the Third Plenum was successfully implemented.

In introducing an offsetting productivity shock, we explore three different channels: input-neutral efficiency; labour efficiency; and capital efficiency. Each of these channels has different effects on the economy, but the last channel— via capital efficiency—arguably lines up best with people's understanding of what China's reform agenda is trying to achieve.

Given China's existing capital stock by industry, there would need to be an approximate 1.6 per cent increase per year in the efficiency of capital to offset the effect of lower investment on real GDP over a 10-year period.

The rebalance from investment to consumption (while holding real GDP constant) leads to a shift in household spending towards services, compared with the baseline (Figure 5.14). Conversely, the shares of household spending on manufactured and rural goods fall. In effect, the boost in consumption reinforces the underlying trend towards services consumption that was already gradually occurring in the baseline in line with growing household incomes.

The rebalance while holding real GDP constant also sees a reduction in China's trade surplus, consistent with the fall in China's saving and the increase in domestic consumption. The shift from investment to consumption also has important effects on intermediate demand at the industry level, particularly the capital-producing industries. For example, the intermediate usage by the capital goods sector falls by around 27 per cent for each commodity by the end of the 10-year period.

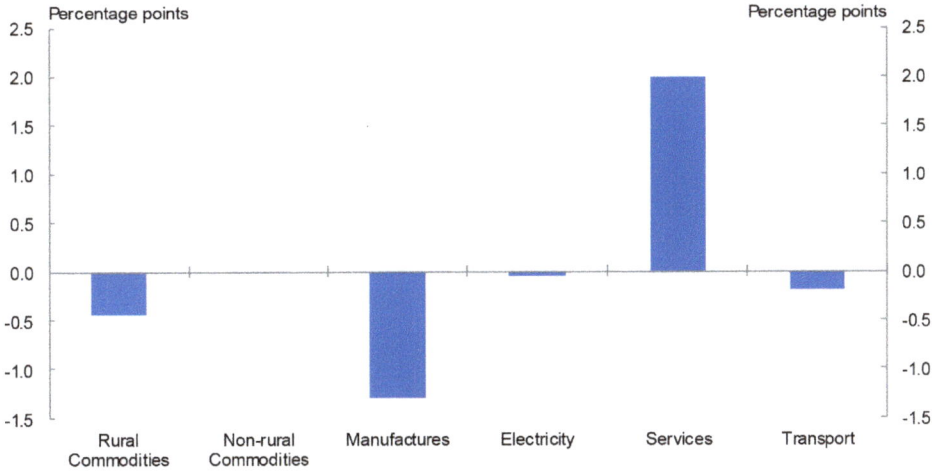

Figure 5.14 Change in Components of Household Consumption (Share of Total)
Source: Results from GTEM simulations.

Conclusion

While there is much debate about the causes and extent of overinvestment in China, we have argued that government policies have indeed contributed to an important degree of excessive investment in recent years. We have also argued that a moderate decline (in the order of 10 percentage points) from the current high rates would not be out of step with the experience of other East Asian economies at similar stages of development, and would be consistent with the market-oriented reforms outlined by the authorities at November 2013's Third Plenum.

While the exact magnitude and timing of any decline in investment rates are highly uncertain, our analysis suggests a 10 percentage point reduction over a 10-year period would be achievable without a destabilising effect on growth and capital accumulation. Moreover, the authorities' reform program—if implemented successfully—would probably provide a boost to productivity across the economy over time, helping to offset some of the reduction in real GDP growth that would otherwise result from lower growth in investment.

Finally, the results from the general equilibrium model suggest the effect of rebalancing from investment to private consumption—even when real GDP is fixed through an offsetting productivity boost—would lead to reduced demand for the output of capital-producing industries and will see consumers shift their spending towards services and away from manufactured goods.

References

Ahuja, A., Chalk, N., Nabar, M., N'Diaye, P. and Porter, N. (2012), *An end to China's imbalances?* IMF Working Paper No. 12/100, April.

Aiyar, S., Duval, R., Puy, D., Wu, Y. and Zhang, L. (2013), *Growth slowdowns and the middle-income trap*, IMF Working Paper No. 13/71, March.

Anand, R., Cheng, K., Rehman, S. and Zhang, L. (2014), *Potential growth in emerging Asia*, IMF Working Paper No. 14/2, January.

Au-Yeung, W., Kouparitsas, M., Luu, N. and Sharma, D. (2013), *Long-term international GDP projections*, Australian Treasury Working Paper 2013-02 (January 2014 update).

Aziz, J. and Cui, L. (2007), *Explaining China's low consumption: the neglected role of household income*, IMF Working Paper No. 07/181, July.

Berlemann, M. and Wesselhoft, J.-E. (2012), *Estimating aggregate capital stocks using the perpetual inventory method—new empirical evidence for 103 countries*, Working Paper Series No. 125, October, Department of Economics, Helmut Schmidt University, Hamburg.

Cai F., X. Peng and G. Gou (2013), 'The new normal of Chinese development', in R. Garnaut, F. Cai and L. Song (eds), *China: A New Model for Growth and Development*, pp. 35–54, Canberra: ANU E Press.

Carlyle Group (2013), *Recalibrating growth and return expectations in China*, June, The Carlyle Group.

Coates, B., Horton, D. and McNamee, L. (2012), 'China: prospects for export-driven growth', *Treasury Economic Roundup* (4), Canberra.

Dollar, D. (2013), *China's rebalancing: lessons from East Asian economic history*, October, Working Paper Series, John L. Thornton China Center.

Garnaut, R., F. Cai. and Song, L. (2013), 'China's new strategy for long-term growth and development: imperatives and implications', in R. Garnaut, F. Cai and L. Song (eds), *China: A New Model for Growth and Development*, pp. 1–16, Canberra: ANU E Press.

Hongkong and Shanghai Banking Corporation (HSBC) Global Research (2013), *China inside out, return on capital: perception vs reality*, April, The Hongkong and Shanghai Banking Corporation Limited.

Hubbard, P., Hurley, S. and Sharma, D. (2012), 'The familiar pattern of Chinese consumption growth', *Treasury Economic Roundup* (4), Canberra.

International Monetary Fund (IMF) (2012), *China: 2012 Article IV Consultation, Staff Report*, Country Report No. 12/195, July, International Monetary Fund.

Kong, V., McKissack, A. and Zhang, D. (2012), 'China in a new period of transition', *Treasury Economic Roundup* (4), Canberra.

Lee, I.-H., Syed, M. and Xueyan, L. (2012), *Is China over-investing and does it matter*, IMF Working Paper No. 12/277, November.

Lee, I.-H., Syed, M. and Xueyan, L. (2013), *China's path to consumer-based growth: reorienting investment and enhancing efficiency*, IMF Working Paper No. 13/83, March.

McKay, H. and Song, L. (2013), 'Chinese industrialisation: path dependence and the transition to a new model', in R. Garnaut, F. Cai and L. Song (eds), *China: A New Model for Growth and Development*, pp. 75–96, Canberra: ANU E Press.

Nabar, M. and N'Diaye, P. (2013), *Enhancing China's medium-term growth prospects: the path to a high-income economy*, IMF Working Paper No. 13/204, October.

Pant, H. (2007), *GTEM: global trade and environment model*, ABARE Technical Report, Australian Bureau of Agricultural and Resource Economics. Available from <http://www.daff.gov.au/abares/pages/models.aspx>.

Rodrik, D. (2013), *The past, present, and future of economic growth*, Working Paper 1, June, Global Citizen Foundation.

Szirmai, A. (2008), *Explaining success and failure in development*, Working Paper Series #2008-013, February, United Nations University, Unu-Merit.

Tyers, R. (2013), *Looking inward for transformative growth in China*, Centre for Applied Macroeconomic Analysis Working Paper No. 48/2013, August.

Tyers, R., Zhang, Y. and Cheong, T.-S. (2013), 'China's saving and global economic performance', in R. Garnaut, F. Cai and L. Song (eds), *China: A New Model for Growth and Development*, pp. 97–124, Canberra: ANU E Press.

World Bank (2012), *China 2030: Building a Modern, Harmonious and Creative High-Income Society*, The World Bank and the Development Research Centre of the State Council, People's Republic of China.

Zhang, J. and Zhu, T. (2013), Re-estimating China's underestimated consumption, 7 September 2013. Available from <http://ssrn.com/abstract=2330698>.

6. The Middle-Income Trap and China's Growth Prospects

Yingjie Feng and Yang Yao

Introduction

China reached the upper-middle income level in 2012 by the World Bank's criterion. There has been increasing debate about whether China's growth will be sustainable in the future. Will China follow the countries—notably, some in Latin America—that have fallen into the so-called 'middle-income trap': a situation in which a country's catch-up process stops once its per capita income reaches the middle-income level?

While the term 'middle-income trap' has been widely used, there is no precise definition of what it really means, and the understanding of the characteristics of the trap is also inadequate. This chapter is aimed at providing a general description of the middle-income trap and, drawing on the comparison between China and those successful economies in history, discusses China's prospects of avoiding the trap.

Section two provides a brief introduction to various approaches to defining the middle-income trap, and, using a case of success, Korea, as a benchmark, we show that both the relative-income criterion and the absolute-income criterion suggest the existence of this trap. Section three turns to the characteristics that distinguish those 'successful' economies from the 'failed' ones. It first provides a framework for analysis that synthesises the neoclassical economic growth model, the endogenous growth model, the structural change model and the political economy model. It then compares the successful and failed economies on several key growth drivers identified by the framework. It finds that among various economic, social and political indicators, investment, education, demographic structure, the manufacturing sector and income distribution are the most relevant to the middle-income trap. Drawing on these observations, section four compares China's characteristics with those of successful countries in history. By and large, China is quite similar to these countries in many aspects, providing a positive outlook for China's future growth, but some of China's distinctions, including its exceptionally high saving and investment rates and rising income inequality, pose some potential risks to the sustainability of its economic growth. We conclude in section five.

What is the middle-income trap?

The notion of the middle-income trap was proposed in a World Bank report, *An East Asian Renaissance: Ideas for Economic Growth* (Gill and Kharas 2008), and in Kharas and Kohli (2011). In these and other works the authors describe the middle-income trap as a situation in which 'countries that avoid the poverty trap and grow to middle-income levels subsequently stagnate and fail to grow to advanced-country levels' (Kharas and Kohli 2011, p. 281). A precise definition of the trap, however, is not as straightforward as it seems at first glance. We have to set an appropriate criterion for identifying the failed countries which accord with the above description, but there is always some arbitrariness behind a criterion.

In general, three approaches are used in recent discussions. First, some literature relates the middle-income trap to growth slowdowns (for example, Eichengreen et al. 2013). The middle-income trap can be redefined as a phenomenon in which fast-growing economies slowed significantly before their per capita GDP reached the high-income level. Eichengreen et al. (2013) find that while there was considerable dispersion in per capita income at which slowdowns occurred, two ranges are more common: one in the range of $10 000–11 000 and the other $15 000–16 000 (2005 purchasing power parity [PPP] dollars). The growth slowdown is, however, not equivalent to the original meaning of the middle-income trap. Slowdowns could be a natural outcome of growth itself, as predicted by classic growth theory. They can also happen for cyclical reasons. What really matters is the *stage at which* the growth slowdown occurs. Thus, the key to tackling this problem is a definition of income levels, which forms the foundation of the next two approaches.

The second approach classifies countries by their *absolute per capita income* and investigates their long-term transition between different income groups. The World Bank's income classification system is the most widely used to accomplish such a task. Per capita gross national income (GNI) is considered the best single indicator of a country's economic capacity. The Bank explains that $480, $1940 and $6000 (at 1987 price levels) were established as the original thresholds for lower-middle income, upper-middle income and high income respectively, and the Bank updates these thresholds annually according to the international inflation rate. In other words, the *real* income levels defined by this method remain constant over time.

Using this criterion, we describe the income transition of 104 countries (the largest set of countries with available data) between 1970 and 2010 in Figure 6.1. The horizontal axis represents real per capita GNI (in log terms) in 1970 and the vertical axis in 2010, respectively. The three horizontal lines indicate the three income thresholds described above, and so do the three vertical lines. Thus, the quadrant is divided into 16 parts, each of which represents a type of income transition. For example, China lies in the sub-area in which the first column overlaps with the third row (count from the origin), indicating that China moved from the low-income group in 1970 to the upper-middle income group in 2010. The figure shows that most countries realised growth in an absolute sense, although only 13 countries declined during this period. In comparison with the large group of countries stuck at the middle-income level, however, only 16 middle-income countries in 1970 entered the high-income group by 2010.

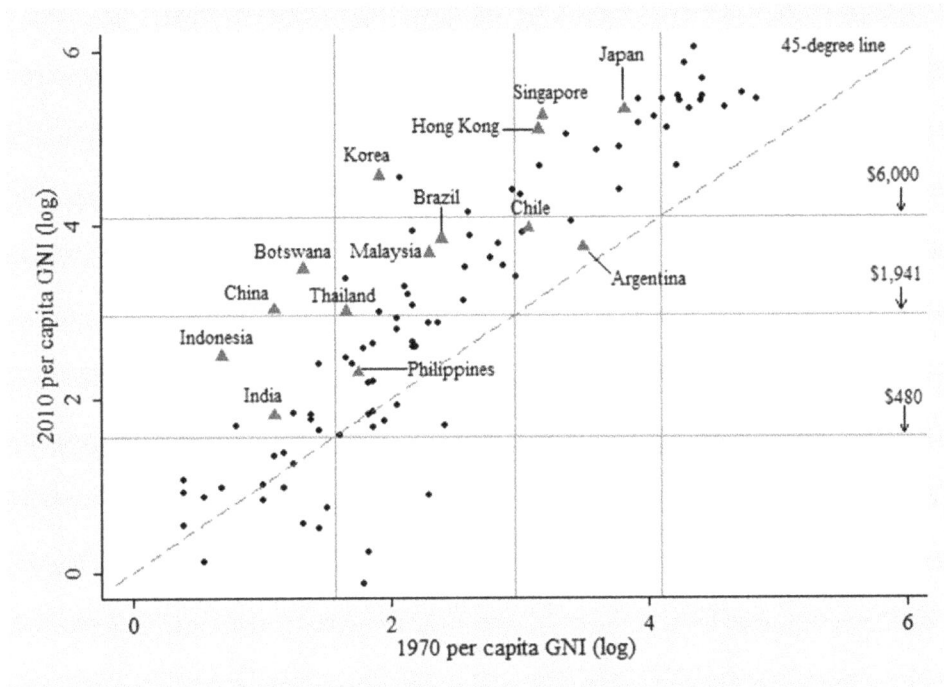

Figure 6.1 (Absolute) Income Transition in the World, 1970–2010
Source: World Bank (2013).

Despite the convenience offered by the absolute criterion, one may be concerned that this approach fails to reflect whether a less-developed country has caught up with more developed countries. A *relative-income* classification system provides a remedy in this sense. We define a country's relative income as the ratio of its absolute per capita income to that of the United States; however, a key difficulty arises when we consider how to establish the thresholds for middle-income and high-income groups. In order to reduce the arbitrariness as much as possible, we attempt to find a benchmark country which is generally believed to have successfully caught up with developed countries from a lower-income stage, and make our thresholds consistent with the relative income level of this benchmark at each stage. Korea, a case of success, may serve this purpose. The Korean economy took off in the early 1960s when its per capita income was 7 per cent of the American level. It then rose to 44 per cent of the American level in the mid 1990s when the World Bank accepted Korea as a high-income country. We then set these two levels of relative income as the thresholds for the middle-income and high-income groups, respectively. This approach tells us whether a country ever achieved Korea's initial relative income and whether it finally reached Korea's relative income in the mid 1990s. In short, it shows whether a country has succeeded in raising its relative income as well as Korea has achieved.

Figure 6.2 presents the income transition in the world between 1960 and 2010 using the above relative criterion. The results can be explained in the same way as those of Figure 6.1. The only difference here is that we turn to using relative instead of absolute income. Among the 88 low-income or middle-income countries in 1960, only 23 raised their relative income by at least 10 percentage points, and only 12 crossed the threshold for high-income countries. In contrast, more than half failed to narrow their income gap relative to the United States.

Despite the differences, the absolute-income criterion and the relative-income criterion draw some robust conclusions. First, the middle-income trap does exist. Most of the middle-income countries of 1960 or 1970 have failed to escape from this group. The exceptions are few. Japan, the 'Four Little Dragons' of East Asia and a few southern European countries are cases of success, while Brazil, Argentina, the Philippines and Malaysia are cases of failure.

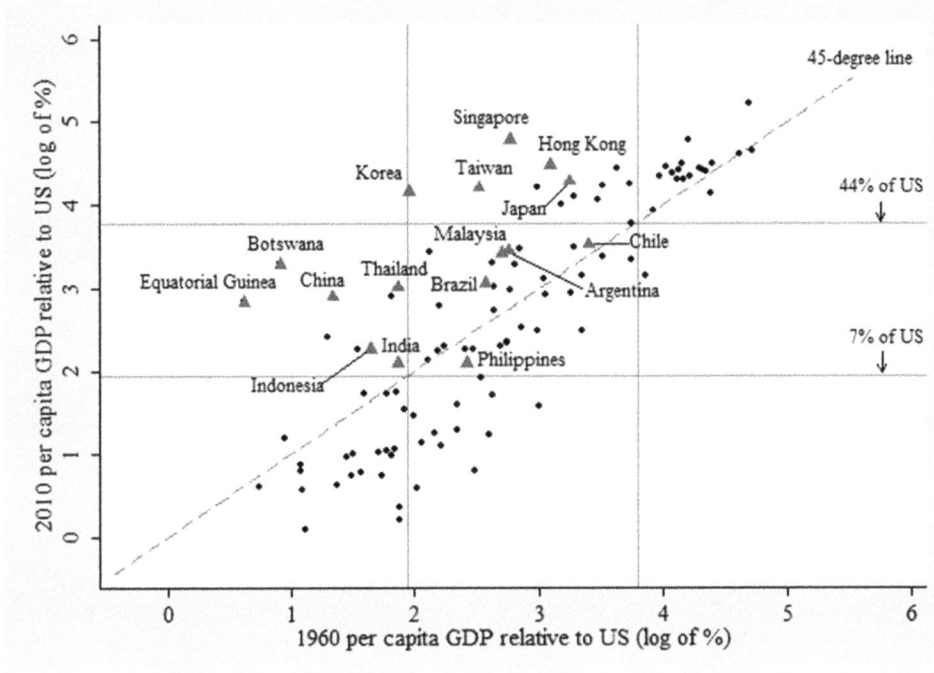

Figure 6.2 (Relative) Income Transition in the World, 1960–2010
Source: Penn World Table (*PWT 8.0*).

What characteristics distinguish 'successes' from 'failures'?

Since the middle-income trap does exist for whichever criterion we use, the next question is what characteristics distinguish those successful countries from the failed ones. In this section, we compare a series of economic, social and political indicators between the two groups of countries, and summarise their key differences.

Before we start the comparison, we provide a framework synthesising the neoclassical growth model, the endogenous growth model, the structural change model and the political economy model. In the standard Solow–Swan model, capital accumulation is the key driver of economic growth before a country reaches its steady state of growth. So the first set of indicators we use for our comparison includes consumption, savings and investment. Then, according to the endogenous growth model, human capital accumulation and technological change are two key drivers of economic growth. The second set of indicators we include for our comparison comprises education, health conditions and demography in a country/region. Unlike other similar studies, we put more emphasis on the role of structural change in defining a country's path to economic prosperity. It has already been established by theory and empirical work that structural change in a country takes the following trajectories: the share of agricultural employment (output) in total employment (national GDP) declines over time; the share of service employment (output) in total employment (national GDP) increases over time; and the share of manufacturing employment (output) in total employment (national GDP) follows an inverted U-shaped curve—increases first and then declines after a certain point. The most interesting pattern is the inverted U-shaped curve of the manufacturing sector. If a country reaches the turning point too early, or if its employment share does not increase to a certain level, that country may not be able to complete its industrialisation process and therefore may more easily fall into the middle-income trap. Related to this, we also look at a country's export structure. There has been a long debate on whether the export-led growth model helps a developing country to successfully catch up with advanced countries. We look not only at how much a country exports, but also what a country exports. In particular, we compare a country's manufacturing exports with its primary goods exports. Finally, we also consider some of the implications of the political economy model. In particular, we want to see if democracy is necessary and if corruption and political instability are detrimental for a country to leap over the middle-income trap. We also look at how income inequality differs between the successful and the failed economies. Our approach is empirical. We want to look at as many indicators as possible to identify the necessary conditions for a country to avoid the middle-income trap.

Two points are worth mentioning. First, to improve the comparability between the two groups, our comparison starts in the year when a country reached the middle-income level instead of a specific calendar year. We determine this starting point for each country according to its absolute income level. Since the data for GNI per capita provided by the World Bank are usually missing for observations in early years, we use data of GDP per capita from the Penn World Table (*PWT 8.0*) instead. To make it consistent with our definition in section two, we still use Korea as a benchmark, and choose $2000 (2005 PPP dollars) as the threshold.[1] Korea reached this level of income when it was classified as a middle-income country according to the World Bank criterion. Thus, a number of countries with high initial levels after World War II (mainly the highly developed economies in Europe and North America) are excluded from our analysis.

---

1   We also check the robustness by changing this threshold to $1500 or $2500, but the result does not differ much.

Second, we need to determine an appropriate length of time for comparison—that is, a 'normal' number of years a country spends in the middle-income category. Once we determine this number, we also set a threshold for failure. In other words, the failed countries usually spent significantly more years at the middle-income stage than this number.[2] Once again, we use typical successful countries as a benchmark. With just a few exceptions, most successful economies spent less than 30 years in the middle-income stage. For example, Korea, Taiwan and Japan stayed in the middle-income stage for 24, 29 and 27 years, respectively.[3] Instead, typical failed economies usually stayed in this category for more than 30 years, and some of them have been trapped for 40 or 50 years. Thus, we set 30 years[4] after entry into the middle-income group as the comparable time span. Actually, following the above steps, a new 'axis of time' has been established, and then we calculate the *within-group* average of each indicator for the two groups in a specific year on this axis.

Investment and savings

Figure 6.3 compares the shares of saving and investment in GDP between the two groups. The saving rate of the failed group ('*stay in middle*') remains at a relatively stable level while that of the successful group ('*from middle to high*') rose significantly from 15 per cent—almost the same level as the failed group—to 35 per cent within the first two decades. High saving inevitably led to high investment. The investment rate of the successful group rose quickly above 40 per cent during the corresponding period. In comparison, the failed group experienced only a modest increase.

Interestingly, the figure also indicates that the investment ratio of the successes has been higher than that of the failures at the starting point, while their saving rates were still comparable then. The difference between saving and investment arises from the portion of net exports, as shown in Figure 6.4. The successful group initially had a higher ratio of (merchandise) trade deficits, implying more capital inflows at their early stage of development.

---

2   In section one, we just generally discuss the long-term income transition after World War II instead of explicitly establishing such a threshold.
3   Using Korea as a benchmark, we set $15 000 as the threshold for high income.
4   Certainly, there is some arbitrariness when we use this number as the threshold for failure. We check robustness by changing it to 35 or 40 years. The result does not differ much.

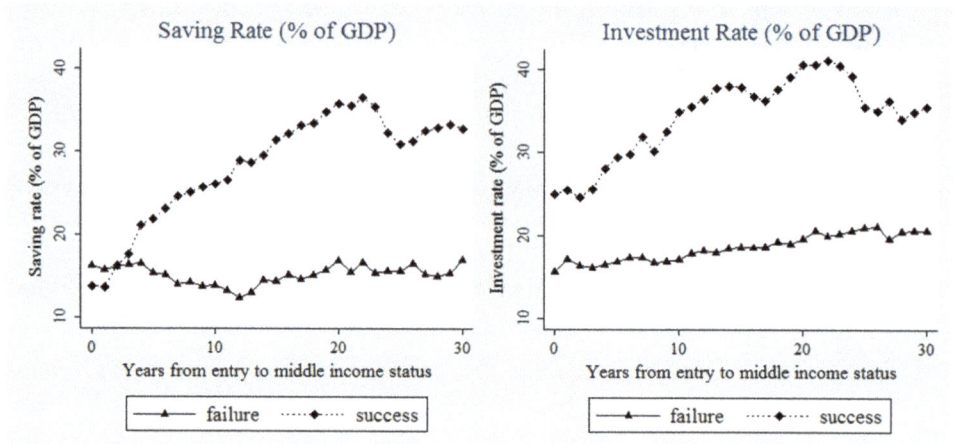

Figure 6.3 Savings and Investment
Source: Penn World Table (*PWT 8.0*).

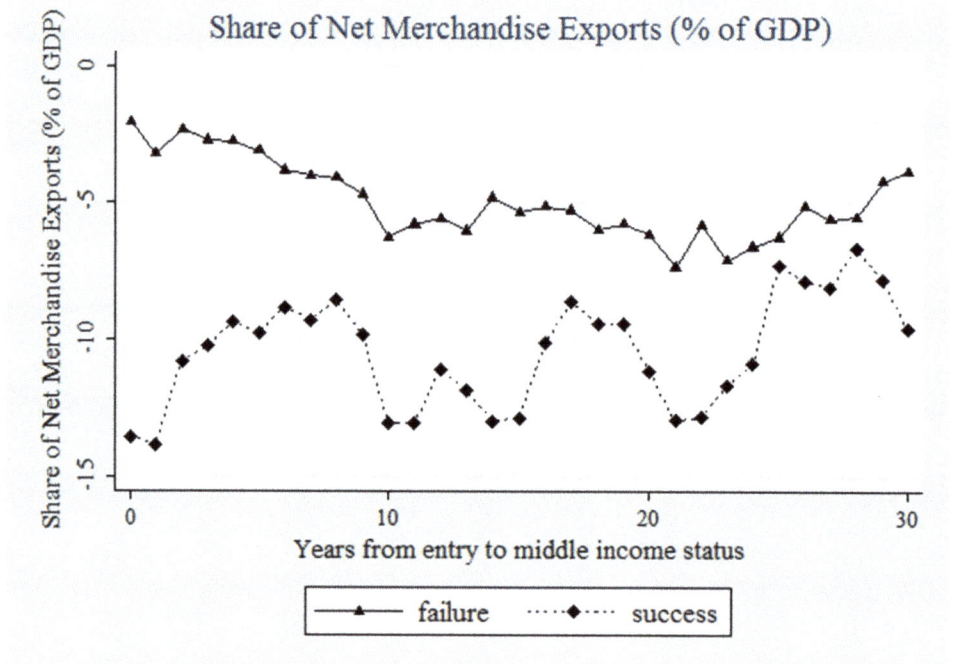

Figure 6.4 Net Merchandise Exports
Source: Penn World Table (*PWT 8.0*).

Manufacturing sector

Figure 6.5 presents the ratio of manufacturing value added to GDP in the two groups. A remarkable distinction arises: except for the early period, the manufacturing sector in the successful group had a much larger share than in the failed group. The general rule of structural change tells us that the development of the secondary sector should follow an inverted U-shaped curve. The successful group followed this rule. On average, its members reached the highest point of this curve in the twentieth year after they entered the middle-income stage; however, the path of the failed group fluctuated during the corresponding period. The trapped countries failed to complete their industrial transformation despite various supporting policies.

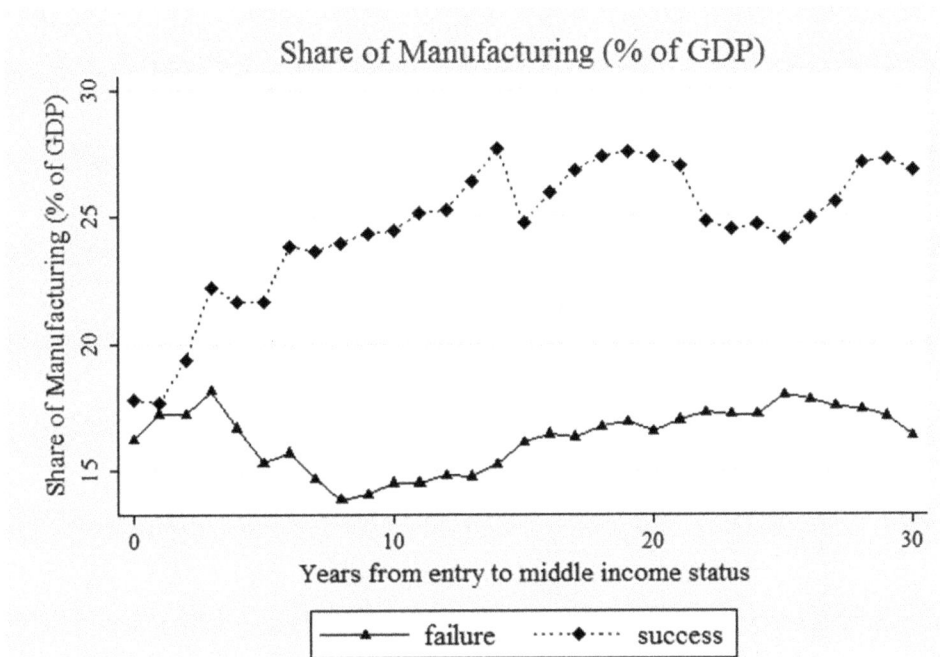

Figure 6.5 The Manufacturing Sector
Source: World Bank (2013).

Trade openness

Trade openness, defined as the ratio of total trade to GDP, is shown in Figure 6.6. It is surprising to find this share is much higher in the failed group than in the successful group, and this relationship emerged before they reached the middle-income level. The successful group has, however, experienced a significant rise in trade openness throughout their middle-income stage while the failed group stayed almost flat. Therefore, it seems that trade is a consequence, not a cause, of growth. Alternatively, it could be that the *level* of trade does not matter for growth in a middle-income country, but the *growth* of trade does.

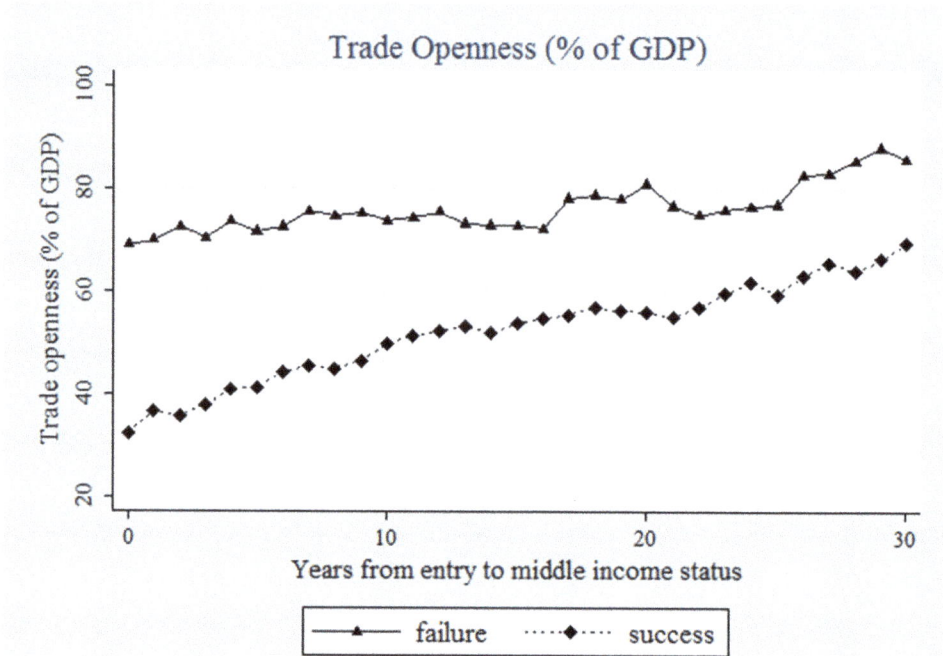

Figure 6.6 Trade Openness
Source: Penn World Table (*PWT 8.0*).

Trade patterns

Figure 6.7 shows how the trade patterns of the two groups changed over time. We calculate the Balassa index of revealed comparative advantage (RCA) for primary goods and manufactured goods. RCA is the proportion of a country's primary (manufactured) goods exports divided by the proportion of the world's primary (manufactured) goods exports. The result shows that the successful countries had a higher RCA for manufactured goods exports but a lower RCA for primary goods exports—that is, they were more specialised in exporting manufacturing goods. In contrast, the failed group was more specialised in exporting primary goods. More intriguingly, this distinction emerged before they attained middle-income status. This suggests that the difference in trade patterns between the two groups may not be an outcome of their divergence in economic growth in the middle-income stage, but was more likely to be a 'predetermined' condition arising from their previous development.

From Figures 6.6 and 6.7, we see that what a country exports is more important than whether it exports at all as far as economic growth is concerned. Exports of manufacturing help economic growth because the manufacturing sector has higher technological growth rates than primary goods sectors. In addition, the export of manufacturing goods has no limit while the export of primary goods is constrained by the stock of natural resources.

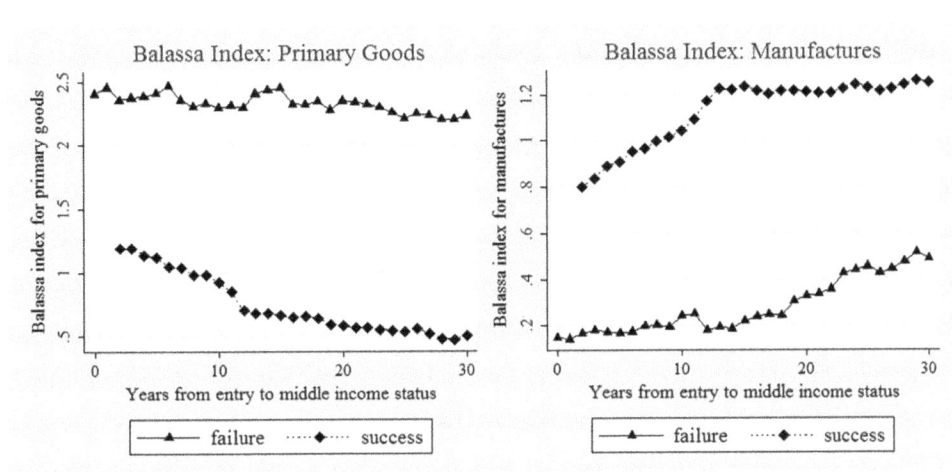

Figure 6.7 Trade Pattern: RCAs

Source: United Nations, Comtrade (<http://comtrade.un.org/>).

Note: The first two observations of the successful group have been dropped because the data are unavailable for most countries in this group.

Education

Figure 6.8 shows marked gaps in the level of education between the two groups. Two measures—average years of total schooling and average years of secondary schooling—are presented here. Both groups experienced a significant increase in the average schooling years, but the successful group had a higher level of education than the failed group, and this gap existed throughout the whole time span. In this sense, the level of education, which to a large extent represents the human capital accumulation of a country, is likely to be a driving force behind economic growth.

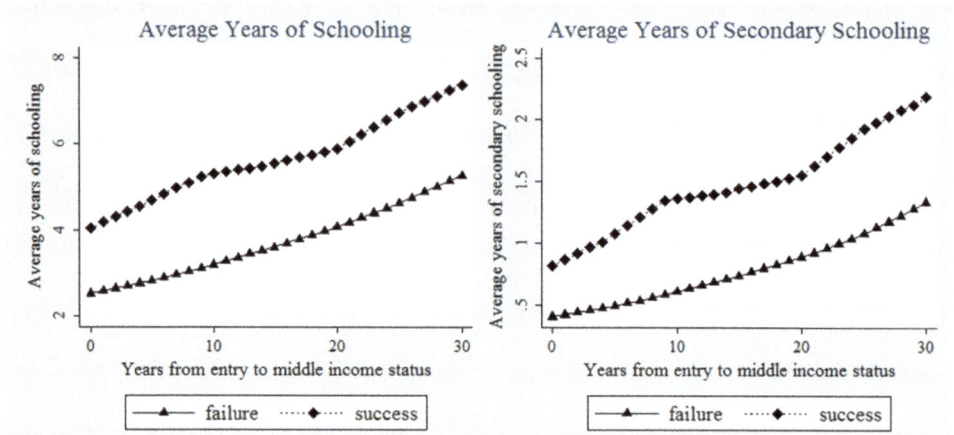

Figure 6.8 Average Years of Schooling: Total and Secondary

Source: BarrodLee Dataset v.1.3 (Barro and Lee 2010).

Demography and health

Figure 6.9 shows how the two groups of countries differ in demographic structure and life expectancy. The dependency ratio, defined as the ratio of dependents—people younger than 16 or older than 64—to the working-age population, declined in both groups; however, the decrease of the successful group was much sharper, and the gap between the two groups widened over time. On the other hand, both groups of countries raised the life expectancy of their population by about 10 years during the three decades; however, the level in the successful group was higher than in the failed group, and their gap remained about eight years throughout the whole period.

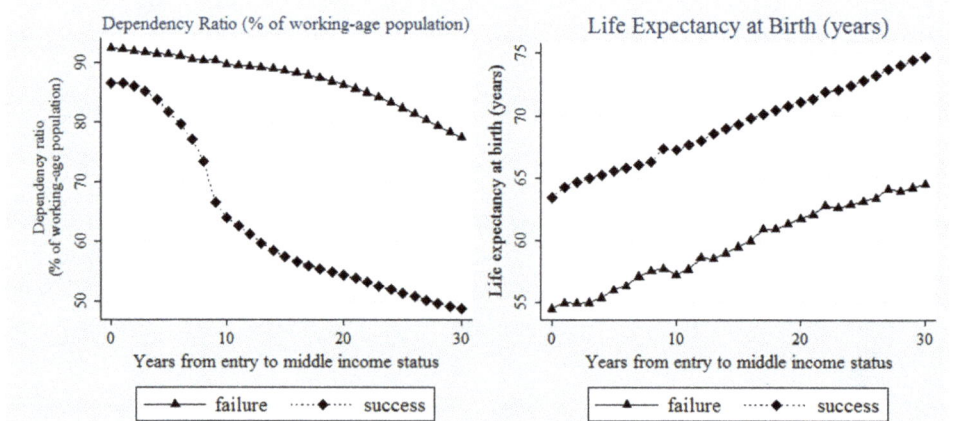

Figure 6.9 The Dependency Ratio and Life Expectancy

Source: World Bank (2013).

Income inequality

Income distribution is an important factor that may affect the process of economic development, though the relationship is quite controversial. Table 6.1 displays the average income Gini coefficients of the two groups. Since the data for Gini coefficients are unavailable for many years, we divide the whole period into three decades and calculate the average for each decade. Obviously, the failed group had a more unequal distribution of income throughout the 30 years, indicating that severe inequality may hinder a country moving out of the middle-income trap. This is consistent with the historical experience in some typical cases of failed countries, such as Brazil and the Philippines.

Table 6.1 Income Inequality

Group	Income Gini coefficient			
	First decade	Second decade	Third decade	30 years average
Failure	50.0	51.4	49.7	50.9
Success	35.4	35.2	35.6	35.4

Source: UNU–WIDER (2008).

Democracy and conflicts

Figure 6.10 (left-hand panel) compares the level of democracy between the two groups. We use the aggregate democracy index provided by *Polity IV* (Center for Systemic Peace 2012), which indicates to what extent a country's polity is democratic. Interestingly, there is no obvious distinction in this index between the two groups during the initial period. The divergence occurred at the later stage of development—that is, about 20 years after a country became a middle-income country. If we look at the democracy index of the two groups at the end of the 30-year span, the successful group did have a more democratic polity than the failed group. In this sense, democracy is more likely to be the outcome of economic growth than a necessary condition for it.

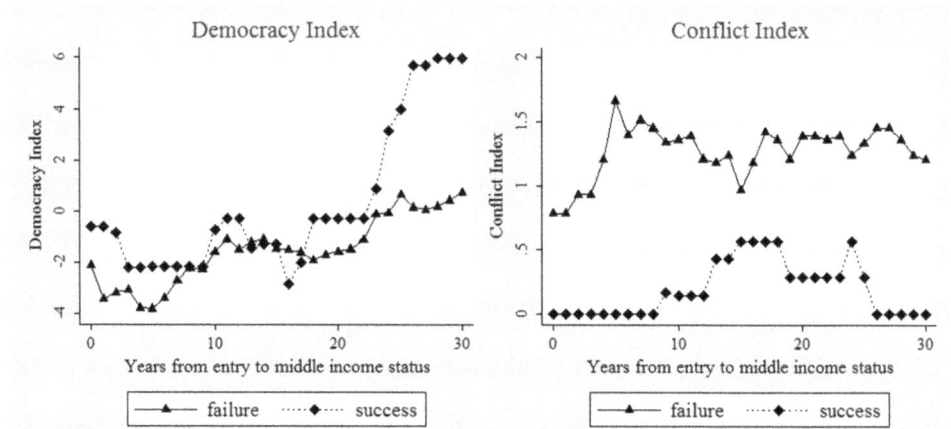

Figure 6.10 Democracy and Conflict

Sources: Center for Systemic Peace (2012); Marshall (2010).

Figure 6.10 (right-hand panel) compares conflicts in the two groups. The conflict index is obtained from the Major Episodes of Political Violence (MEPV) dataset and indicates how many domestic and international conflicts a country has in a specific year. Despite peaks in the middle of the time span, the successful group generally had fewer conflicts than the failed group throughout the 30-year span.

In summary, the successful economies are generally characterised by high saving rates, deeper industrialisation, high levels of education, more favourable demographic structures, a peaceful environment and more equal distribution of income. Most of these factors have long been established as key drivers of economic growth. The new finding is about industrialisation. We find strong evidence that deeper industrialisation in terms of both its duration and its share in the national economy helps a country to overcome the middle-income trap. Related with this finding, a country which is more specialised in exporting manufacturing products is more likely to overcome the middle-income trap than a country which is more specialised in exporting primary goods. These findings are pertinent to China, which we will turn to in the next section.

It is also worth mentioning that failed economies have failed for various reasons while the successful economies share strong commonalties, just as Tolstoy said in the opening of his novel *Anna Karenina*: 'Happy families are all alike; every unhappy family is unhappy in its own way.' A failed economy may share some of the success factors with the successful economies, but a key negative factor may put it in the middle-income trap. One of the examples is the Philippines. It was regarded as a star among developing countries in the early 1960s, which was why the Asian Development Bank (ADB) set up its headquarters in Manila.

In the early 1960s, the average Filipino enjoyed an income five times that of the average Chinese. Today, the fortunes of the two countries have been reversed: the average Chinese enjoys an income twice that of the average Filipino. It is widely recognised that the failure of the Philippines has been caused by its rigid social structure, which is still dominated by powerful families. Other countries may have failed for other reasons. The bottom line is, there are no universal causes for countries failing to escape the middle-income trap. For this reason, our approach to find the commonalties among the successful economies is better than regression-based analysis. Take the example of education. It is one of the commonalties among the successful economies; however, some of the failed economies also have relatively high levels of educational attainment among their population, yet one key failure may just hold them in the trap. As a result, a regression-based analysis would find that education is not a driver for a middle-income country to grow rapidly; but this may be caused only by a 'sticky' failure factor such as the rigid social structure in the Philippines.

Will China be able to avoid the trap?

In 2011, China's per capita GDP rose above $8000 (2005 PPP dollars). Korea reached the same level in 1987 and maintained an annual growth rate of 8.3 per cent in the next decade. It was also during that period that Korea crossed the World Bank's threshold for high-income countries. Will China be able to follow the development path of Korea and avoid the middle-income trap? In this section, we discuss how China is comparable with those successful economies described above, and the risks confronting China. A better understanding of these issues will provide us with a more reasonable sense of China's future growth.

Similarities

High saving and high investment

China has experienced a remarkable rise in saving and investment since the 1990s, as shown in Figure 6.11. This trend has been even sharper recently, which has raised serious concerns. This phenomenon should be viewed from two perspectives. On the one hand, as we have shown previously, a rising saving rate is among the most significant characteristics of successful economies in their rapid-growth stage. On average, their saving rate increased from 15 per cent at the starting point to a peak of 35 per cent at the end of the second decade. In this sense, China's performance in this field is similar to that of the successful economies in recent history. In addition, a rising saving rate is not a feature specific to the early period, but a long-term one. It existed almost throughout the entire middle-income stage in the successful economies. Because China is still far from the high-income threshold, its saving and investment rates will probably remain at relatively high levels for some time.

It is, however, worth noting that China's saving rate rose to 50 per cent by 2011—an amazing level even compared with the successful economies. For example, during the rapid-growth period, Korea's highest saving rate was around 40 per cent. A large set of literature has attempted to interpret this puzzle from various aspects, such as precautionary savings, rising housing prices and income distribution. A detailed discussion of this issue is beyond the scope of this chapter. Our comparison just reminds us to view the impact of China's high saving rates cautiously.

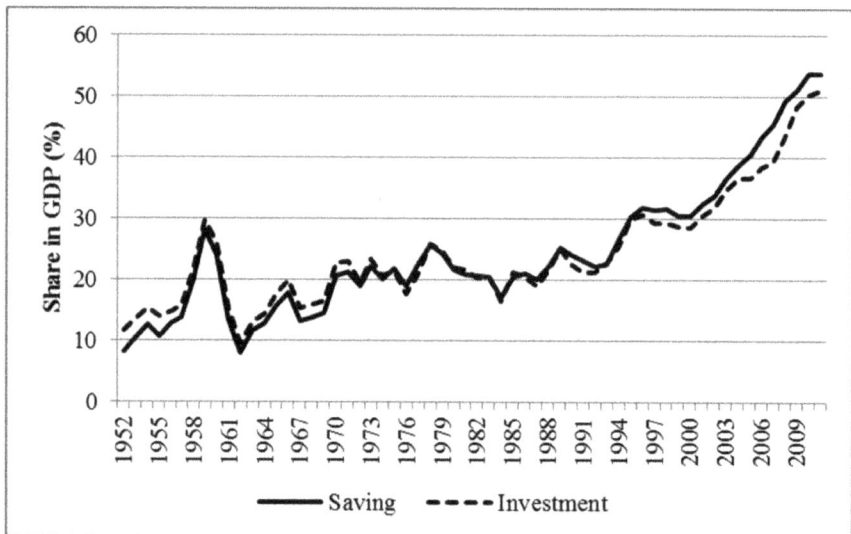

Figure 6.11 China: The Saving Rate and Investment Rate, 1952–2011
Source: Penn World Table (*PWT 8.0*).

Manufacturing-led growth

We have shown that the successful transition from an agriculture-based economy to a manufacture-led economy is of great importance for middle-income countries. As a legacy of its command economy, China has a high share of the manufacturing sector relative to its initial income level. Figures 6.12 and Figure 6.13 present the shares of the primary sector, secondary sector and tertiary sector in GDP and total employment. Except for the 1980s, the secondary sector maintained a stable share in GDP during the reform era. Its share in employment followed a different path. It stabilised around 23 per cent between 1986 and 2002, but has begun to rise since 2003, probably because China's accession to the World Trade Organisation (WTO) ignited a new wave of industrialisation in

China. No matter which measure we use, it is certain that the secondary sector plays a dominant role in China's economy, which is similar to the experience of successful economies at the same stage of development.

The performance of China's secondary sector during the transitional period also stands in marked contrast to some Latin American countries which have experienced 'de-industrialisation' in their transition era. Their industrial sectors established in the import-substitution era have suffered continuous decline since the 1980s. In this sense, China has managed its economic transition more smoothly and established a firm foundation for its fast growth.

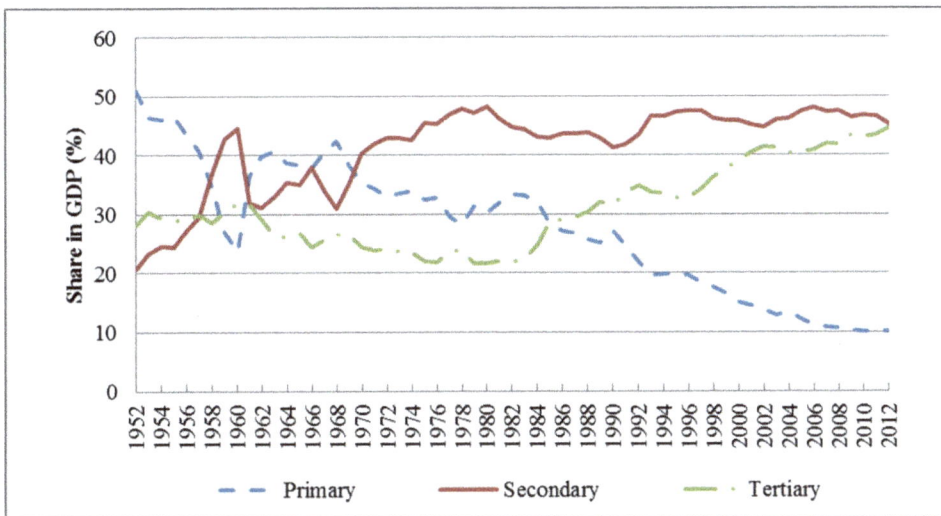

Figure 6.12 China: Shares of Three Sectors in GDP, 1952–2012
Source: National Bureau of Statistics at <http://www.stats.gov.cn>.

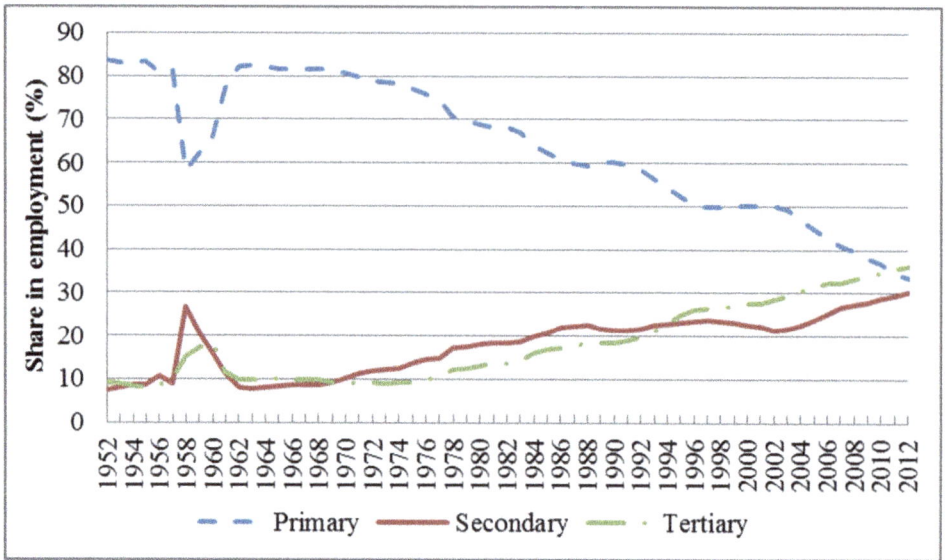

Figure 6.13 China: Shares of Three Sectors in Employment, 1952–2012

Source: National Bureau of Statistics at <http://www.stats.gov.cn>.

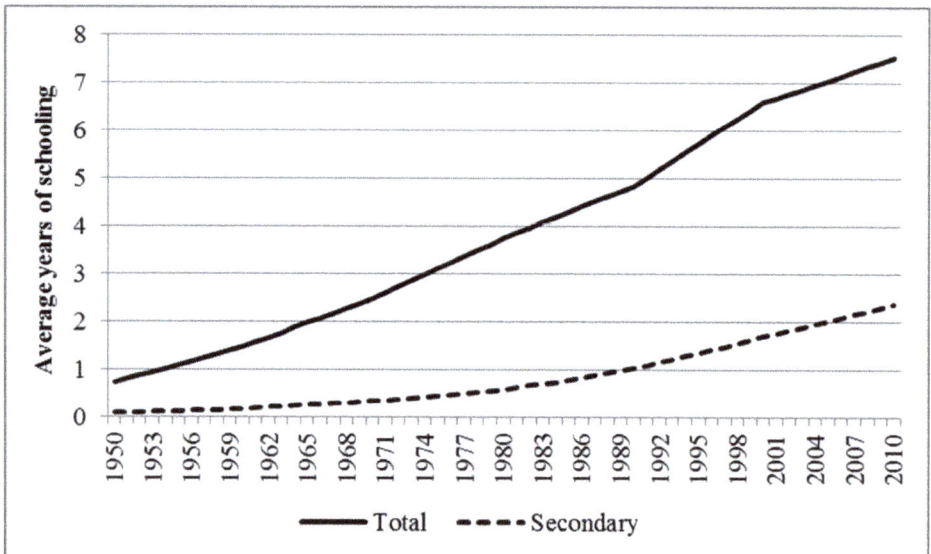

Figure 6.14 China: Average Years of Schooling, 1950–2010

Source: Barro–Lee Dataset v.1.3 (Barro and Lee 2010).

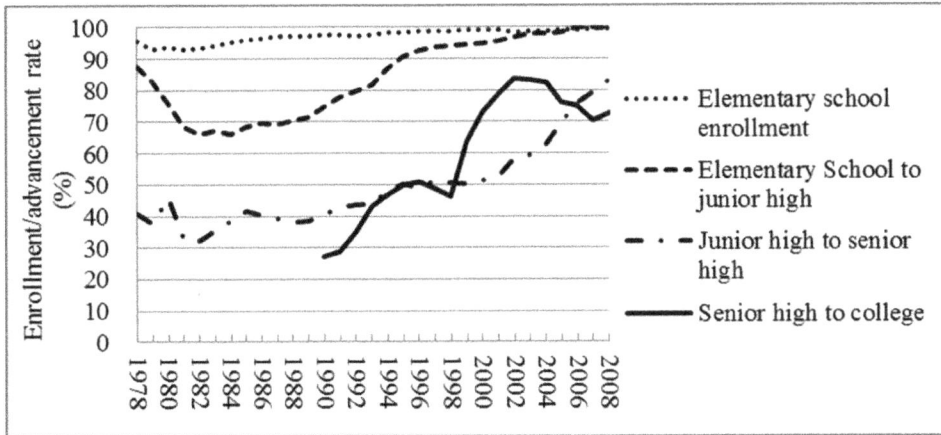

Figure 6.15 China: Enrolment Rates and Advancement Rates, 1978–2008
Source: NBS (2010).

Human capital formation

One of China's achievements by 1978 was a higher level of education, as shown in Figure 6.14. In 1982, the average years of total schooling in China reached four years—similar to the initial level of the successful country group. It continued to rise steadily afterwards, and achieved 7.54 years in 2010. As for the enrolment and advancement rates, China also did a good job (Figure 6.15). Despite some fluctuations, the general trend for these indicators was significant improvement. In 2008, most children advanced to junior high school, and 80 per cent of them also advanced to senior high school.

Demographic dividends

Similar to other successful economies in East Asia, China's dependency ratio has declined dramatically during the past four decades, as shown in Figure 6.16. The demographic dividend from this structural change in population is one of the most significant factors that accounts for China's past economic achievements. Recently, there has been considerable debate about whether this dividend has been exhausted. In fact, the one-child policy forced China to experience its demographic transition more rapidly than other countries in history. In 2011, China's dependency ratio fell to 36 per cent—almost the same level as today's Korea, but China's per capita GDP was just equal to 30 per cent of that of Korea. Thus, it is a reasonable concern that China will gradually lose its advantages in demography. We will, however, have to wait until 2030 for China's dependency ratio to rise above that of some major countries such as India. It is also worth noting that there is still a large rural population in China. At the macro level,

151

agriculture still employs 30 per cent of China's total labour force, although its share in national GDP is not much more than 10 per cent (see Figures 6.12 and 6.13). In light of China's incomplete structural change, labour movement from the countryside to the city will provide a powerful push for future economic growth.

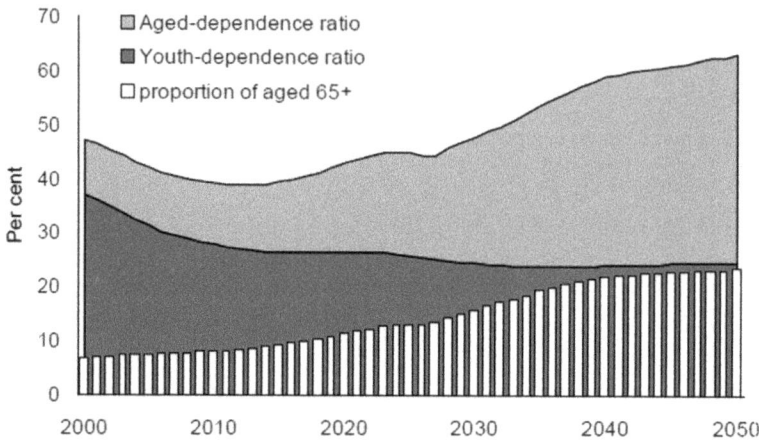

Figure 6.16 Demography in China
Source: Cai and Wang (2005).

Macro-economic stability

The failed economies are usually characterised by macro-economic instability, which is extremely detrimental to economic growth. Compared with other transitional economies, China's performance in this field is much better. Figure 6.17 presents China's inflation rate between 1978 and 2010. The highest peaks occurred in the late 1980s and between 1992 and 1995. The former was caused by price reform, and the latter reflected the investment frenzy after reform resumed in 1992; however, these high-inflation periods did not persist for long. After 1995, inflation became much milder, indicating more prudent economic management by the Government.

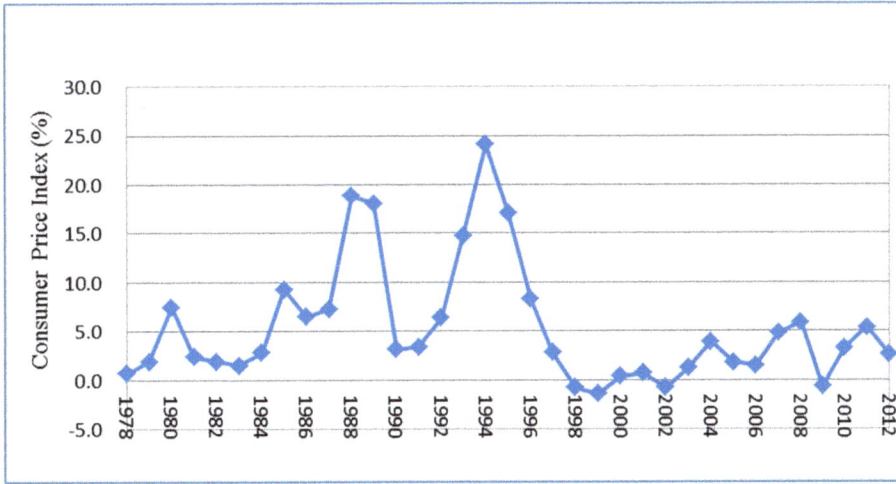

Figure 6.17 Inflation Rates, 1978–2012

Source: National Bureau of Statistics at <http://www.stats/gov/cn>.

Macro-economic stability is also reflected in the fiscal policy of China's Central Government. Figure 6.18 shows the Central Government's deficits and debts. The share of deficits in GDP remained at a relatively stable level over the observable period. The deficit–revenue ratio reached the peak, 45 per cent, in 2000, in response to the Asian financial crisis. Since then it has declined, except for 2008 and 2009, when the GFC resulted in another wave of stimulus policies, although it was much milder. In a word, China's government has been more successful over time in maintaining a stable macro-economic environment, which is crucial for sustainable growth.

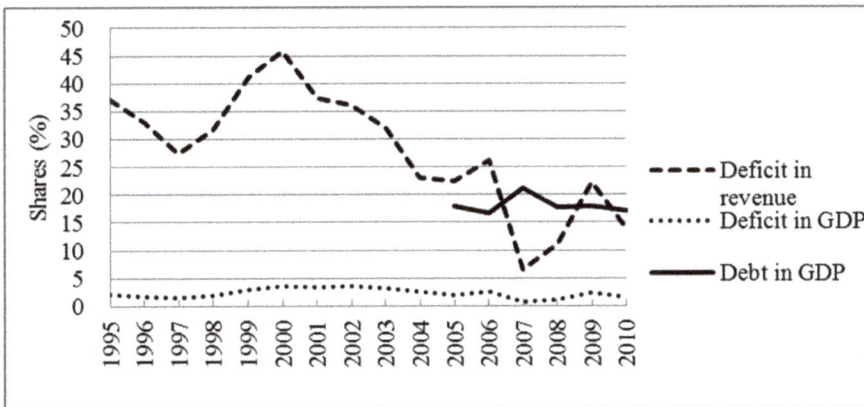

Figure 6.18 Central Government Deficits and Debts, 1995–2010

Source: NBS (various years).

The risk: rising inequality

The most remarkable distinction between China and the successful economies lies in its worsening income distribution. Figure 6.19 clearly presents such a trend. The Gini coefficient of income increased significantly in rural and urban areas as well across the whole country. For the whole country, the income Gini coefficient rose from less than 0.30 in the early 1980s to 0.45 in 2007. It continued to rise until 2010 when it began to decline slightly. Today, the income Gini coefficient is around 0.48 according to the official statistics and 0.50 according to independent studies. Despite considerable debate over the calculation of Gini coefficients, it is widely recognised that China has rising inequality and it has reached a relatively high level in recent years.

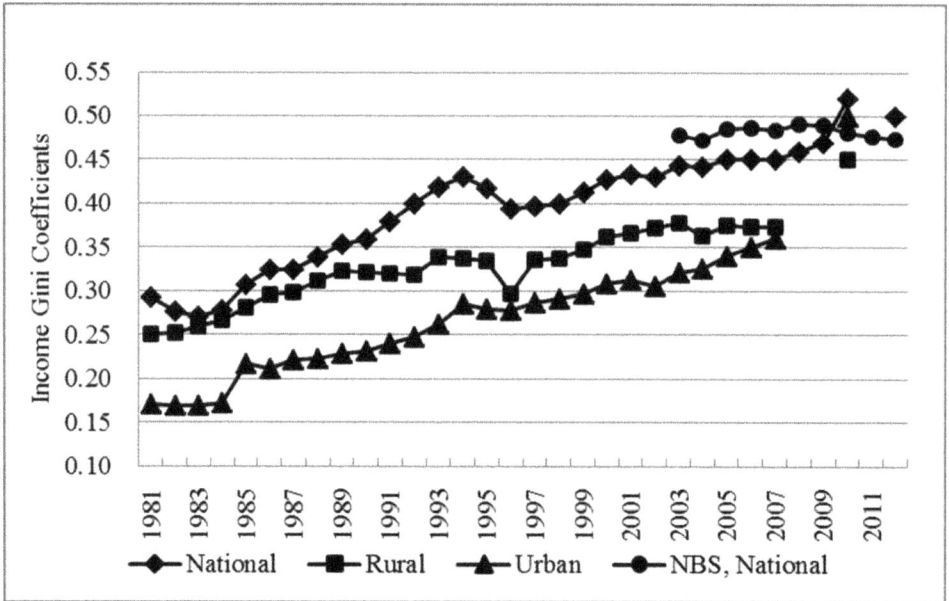

Figure 6.19 Income Gini Coefficients, 1981–2012
Sources: Cheng (2007); Li and Luo (2011); ISSS (2010, 2012); NBS (2013).

China's rising and high inequality stands in stark contrast with the equal distribution achieved by the successful economies in East Asia. For example, Korea limited its income Gini coefficients to around 0.30 throughout its rapid-growth period. While this difference may arise from some of China's specific historical and social features and should be interpreted with caution, it still rings an alarm bell for China's policymakers.

While inequality may delay a country's economic growth for various reasons, it is the education channel that may pose the most serious challenge for China. Although China produces seven million university graduates each year, the bulk of its floor workers, most of whom are migrants from the countryside, have low educational attainment. Evidence from the Chinese Family Panel Studies (CFPS), a national longitudinal survey conducted by Peking University, shows the average years of schooling of rural youth aged between 21 and 30 were barely more than seven years in 2010 (Yao forthcoming). That is, the majority of rural youth did not finish middle school before they entered the labour force. Their education is far from enough for China to successfully fulfil its ambition to transform into a knowledge-based economy. It will also hinder China avoiding the middle-income trap. For one thing, it is almost certain that with their current education, the migrant workers' income will never reach 45 per cent of the American level. Because migrant workers and farmers account for 60 per cent of China's labour force, this deficiency will inevitably hold China back from achieving high-income status.

Low educational attainments in the countryside are mostly related to the low income rural residents have to endure. The average rural resident earns less than one-third of the income enjoyed by the average urban resident. This gap is so large—the largest in the world—that many rural residents are discouraged to even try to jump over it. On the other hand, the current growth of wage rates in China has led to a paradoxical consequence: it discourages rural families from continuing their children's education. Many rural families take their children out of school and send them to cities to work for a salary of between RMB2000 and RMB3000 per month because this is a good income by their living standards. This will, however, have a greatly detrimental effect on these children's long-term income capabilities. If China were to be trapped in the middle-income group, it would be because the country has been defeated by its current success.

Conclusion

This chapter provides a comparative analysis of the middle-income trap and China's prospects for growth. The existence of the middle-income trap is confirmed by both the absolute-income and the relative-income criteria. Based on our definition using absolute income levels, we make a series of comparisons between the successful economies and the failed ones. Our descriptive analysis shows that the successes are generally characterised by high saving rates, robust manufacturing sectors, high levels of education, more advantageous demographic structures, a peaceful environment and more equal income distribution. China is quite similar to those successful economies in all of these aspects except for its rising inequality. Therefore, China still has great potential for growth, but some deliberate policies on income distribution are needed.

In particular, China should pay more attention to increasing the education levels of rural youth and providing adequate training to migrant workers. Currently, the provision of education is mostly a local affair. It is highly recommended that the Central Government takes over the mandate and fully funds 12-year education in the country. Improving human capital has many more longer-term benefits than investing in physical capital, as many empirical studies have indicated. China's Central Government should shift its spending from helping local governments finance their infrastructure building to directly financing local education.

References

Barro, R. and Lee, J.-W. (2010), *A new data set of educational attainment in the world, 1950–2010*, NBER Working Paper No. 15902, National Bureau of Economic Research, Cambridge, Mass.

Cai, F. and Wang, D. (2005), *Demographic transition: implications for growth*, Working Paper, Institute of Population and Labor, Chinese Academy of Social Sciences, Beijing.

Center for Systemic Peace (2012), *Polity IV Data Series*, version 2012, Polity IV Project, Center for Systemic Peace. Available from <http://www.systemicpeace.org/polity/polity4.htm>.

Cheng, Y. (2007), 'China's overall Gini coefficient and its decomposition by rural and urban areas since reform and opening', *Social Sciences in China* (4) [in Chinese]: 45–60.

Eichengreen, B., Park, D. and Shin, K. (2012), 'When fast-growing economies slow down: international evidence and implications for China', *Asian Economic Papers* 11(1): 42–87.

Eichengreen, B., Park, D. and Shin, K. (2013), *Growth slowdowns redux: new evidence on the middle-income trap*, NBER Working Paper No. 18673, National Bureau of Economic Research, Cambridge, Mass.

Feenstra, R. C., Inklaar, R. and Timmer, M. P. (2013), *The next generation of the Penn World Table*, NBER Working Paper No. 19255, National Bureau of Economic Research, Cambridge, Mass.

Felipe, J., Abdon, A. and Kumar, U. (2012), *Tracking the middle-income trap: what is it, who is it, and why?* Working Paper No. 715, Levy Economics Institute, Annandale-on-Hudson, NY.

Gill, I. and Kharas, H. (2008), *An East Asian Renaissance: Ideas for Economic Growth*, Washington, DC: The World Bank.

Institute of Social Science Survey (ISSS) (2010), *Chinese Family Panel Studies*, Beijing: Peking University. Available from <http://www.isss.edu.cn/cfps/EN/>.

Institute of Social Science Survey (ISSS) (2012), *Chinese Family Panel Studies*, Beijing: Peking University. Available from <http://www.isss.edu.cn/cfps/EN/>.

Kharas, H. and Kohli, H. (2011), 'What is the middle income trap, why do countries fall into it, and how can it be avoided?', *Global Journal of Emerging Market Economies* (3): 281–90.

Li, S. and Luo, C. (2011), 'How unequal is China?', *Economic Research Journal* (4): 68–79.

Marshall, M. (2010), *Major Episodes of Political Violence (MEPV) and Conflict Regions, 1946–2008*, July, Center for Systemic Peace. Available from <http://www.systemicpeace.org/inscr/MEPVcodebook2012.pdf>.

National Bureau of Statistics (NBS) (2010), *China Educational Statistical Yearbook 2009*, Beijing: Renmin Education Press.

National Bureau of Statistics (NBS) (2013), *China Statistical Yearbook*, Beijing: China Statistics Press.

National Bureau of Statistics (NBS) (various years), *China Statistical Yearbook*, Beijing: China Statistics Press.

United Nations University–World Institute for Development Economics Research (UNU–WIDER) (2008), *World Income Inequality Database*, Version 2.0c, May 2008. Available from <http://www.wider.unu.edu/research/Database/en_GB/database/>.

World Bank (2013), *World Development Indicators 2013*, Washington, DC: The World Bank. Available from <http://data.worldbank.org/data-catalog/world-development-indicators>.

Yao, Y. (forthcoming), 'The Chinese growth miracle', *Handbook of Economic Growth*.952-2012

7. Short-Run Effects of the Economic Reform Agenda[1]

Rod Tyers and Ying Zhang

Introduction

The 'East Asian' growth model has served both China and its trading partners well during the past three decades. It requires the transformation of lightly trained farmers into factory and service workers. The availability of these workers attracts capital from home and foreign savings to urban areas, raises the productivity of the transitioning workers and attracts further rural-to-urban migration. The snag is that the workers' are not sufficiently well trained to support heavy manufacturing or sophisticated services and so production is highly specialised in light manufactures. The transformation therefore requires considerable trade dependence. Moreover, in the East Asian experience, the resulting income growth has tended to outstrip perceived 'permanent incomes' (Modigliani and Cao 2004), so saving has been very high, causing current account surpluses. The domestic gains from the growth generated speak for themselves but trading partners have also gained, via both the product and the financial terms of trade (Tyers 2014b).

China's size and the slow growth of its trading partners now limit its capacity to continue to grow within this model so the inevitable turn inward is in progress. Thus far, the key elements in this transformation have been fiscal expansion and public investment, though provincial indebtedness will constrain these in future. China's government has therefore undertaken to identify reforms that will unleash further, necessarily inward, sources of growth. These include further reforms of industrial policy, trade policy, landownership laws, the one-child policy, fiscal federalism and taxation, financial market regulation, urbanisation (*hukou*) and capital account liberalisation under the general rubric of 'internationalisation' (State Council 2014). For most of these, change will be gradual and the short-run implications slight. For reforms to industrial policy and the capital account, however, short-run effects on overall economic performance are likely to be significant.

1   Funding for the research described in this chapter is from Australian Research Council Discovery Grant No. DP0879094. Thanks for useful discussions on the topic of this chapter are due to Jane Golley and Ligang Song.

The approach adopted centres on an economy-wide model that takes explicit account of oligopolistic behaviour in 17 industrial and service sectors. This model makes it possible to examine the interactions between industrial reform, regulatory policy and liberalisation of the capital account. The results suggest that industrial reform in heavy manufacturing and services has considerable potential, reducing costs and fostering growth in output, private consumption and modern-sector employment. The effects of capital and financial account liberalisation are less certain and could be negative depending on whether there is demand for foreign assets that has been constrained by outward capital controls.

The next section reviews China's ongoing transition, its causes and effects. In the third section, the special structure of the Chinese economy is detailed along with a discussion of the special sensitivity of its employment performance to real exchange rate changes. The fourth section describes the model used and the fifth offers estimates of the effects of further inward growth-generating industrial reforms. The sixth section draws out the implications of the relaxation of capital controls and the associated changes in external flows. Conclusions are offered in the final section.

China's transition: a motive for key reforms

Although China's rate of expansion during its three decades of reform has been spectacular, and in the past decade its economic size has approached and then surpassed Japan and soon the United States and the European Union. China's exports have grown especially rapidly since the turn of the century and now dominate world trade in light manufactures.[2] As of 2011 its unadjusted share of global GDP on a national accounts basis at current exchange rates was greater than Japan's and its shares of global exports, saving and investment were larger than those of the United States and close to those of the European Union (Table 7.1). Looking forward, notwithstanding China's modest per capita income, there is not the scope for the rest of the world to absorb export growth from China at historical rates. Moreover, there has been an accelerated

---

2 According to trade data from <http://data.worldbank.org>, Chinese manufactured exports now sum to more than one-third of the collective manufactured imports of the United States, the European Union and Japan, to which level growth has been extraordinary since 2001, when China's share was only 7 per cent.

rise in Chinese labour costs, foreshadowing a Lewis 'turning point',[3] which is associated with the depletion of mobile labour in rural areas and a nationwide demographic contraction stemming from China's one-child policy.

Table 7.1 Relative Economic Sizes of China and Other Large Regions, National Accounts at Current Exchange Rates, 2011

Percentage of world	China	US	EU (26)	Japan
GDP	11	22	26	9
Consumption, C	8	27	26	9
Investment, I	20	15	22	8
Government spending, G	7	20	30	10
Exports, X	17	17	25	7
Imports, M	15	21	23	8
Total domestic saving, S^D	19	13	20	9

Sources: The IMF *International Financial Statistics* database (IMF n.d.) is the major source but there is frequent resort to national statistical databases.

Superficially, it would seem that a switch from export-oriented to inward-focused growth is simply a matter of sustaining high investment and substituting consumption for exports. This has, however, been problematic because the growth to date has emphasised light manufacturing while China's growing middle class demands quality products and services that are as yet poorly represented in its production basket. To diversify China's output towards these products requires major reform of its heavy manufacturing and services sectors, and investment in associated human capital.[4] This requires the extension of industrial reforms into hitherto protected heavy manufacturing and service industries, where reductions in costs and prices could have major stimulatory effects on the economy as a whole.

A key element of the global imbalance to which China has contributed is associated with its high saving. It has tended to produce more than it has consumed as its rapid growth has run ahead of its citizens' permanent incomes. The effect of this has been to confer on the rest of the world gains via both the product and the financial terms of trade, but also losses due to wage rigidity and labour displacement as well as distributional stress and structural-adjustment costs (Tyers 2014b). A political backlash from the advanced economies has therefore also contributed to China's need for reforms that foster more inward-oriented

---

3   The timing of China's Lewis turning point is a subject of controversy, as suggested by the contrasts between the views expressed by Cai (2010), Garnaut (2010) and Golley and Meng (2011). There is, however, little doubt that the turning point is on its way, even if there is no agreement as to whether recent real wage rises suggest its presence.

4   For a discussion of the institutional and industrial reform agenda and its difficulty, see, for example, Riedel (2011) and Deer and Song (2012).

growth. The proposed financial reforms, combined with the internationalisation of the renminbi, are directed not only at improving the efficiency with which the large stock of savings is directed into investment, but also to the restoration of balance. For this reason, the pattern and trends in China's saving and in its current account are indicators of its transition and of the need for its reforms.

Saving

National saving includes that by households, corporations and government. Savings that exceed the value of domestic private and public investment ('excess savings') result in the net acquisition of foreign assets and they are measured by the current account surplus (Equation 7.1).

Equation 7.1

$$CA = S_{HH} + S_C + (T - G) - I = S_D - I = \Delta R - FI_{Inward} + FI_{Outward} = X - M + N$$

In Equation 7.1, S_{HH} is household saving, S_C is corporate saving, $(T - G)$ is government saving or the fiscal surplus, S_D is total domestic saving, I is investment (including public investment), ΔR is official foreign reserve accumulation, CA is the current account balance and N is net foreign factor income.[5] FI signifies foreign investment, inflows or outflows. In China's case these terms have traditionally been dominated by foreign direct investment (FDI) since cross-border portfolio investments have been restricted by its capital controls (Ma and McCauley 2007). Investment financing and the extent of imbalance therefore depend on household saving, corporate saving and government saving.

Household saving

China's households save between one-quarter and one-third of their disposable incomes. The pattern and time trend are analysed by Horioka and Wan (2007) and Horioka and Terada-Hagiwara (2012). They suggest China's saving is in a declining phase—a point with which Yang (2012) agrees, citing a range of mainly social and trade policy reforms that will see reduced incentives for household saving, many of which are stated priorities in the official reform

---

5   This identity is readily obtained by combining the expenditure identity, $Y = C + I + G + X - M$, with the disposal identity for GNP, $Y + N = C + T + S$, where $S = S_{HH} + S_C$.

agenda. Moreover, recent studies suggest that the household saving rate is falling faster than official statistics indicate (Ma and Yi 2010).[6] Thus, there is much to suggest a declining path for China's household saving rate.[7]

Corporate saving

National accounts 'flow of funds' data show corporate saving to have been fairly stable at about one-fifth of GDP through 2009. In the period since, and looking forward, changes in total corporate saving might be anticipated for three reasons. First, to the extent that slower global growth since the GFC and China's growth since 2011 has affected profitability in the state sector, corporate savings might be expected to have also declined in recent years. Second, ongoing industrial policy reforms, which have allowed substantial expansion in the share of private firms in the economy, are likely to have reduced oligopoly rents. Finally, financial development and the integration of formal and informal financial markets across the country have been proceeding apace, which can be expected to put downward pressure on the trend of corporate saving.

Government saving

Since the implementation of China's national tax law in 1994, an increasing share of economic activity has been taking place in the 'formal sector'. This has meant that Central Government tax revenue has grown at a rate that is notably faster than GDP.[8] Along with this, *Central* Government financial surpluses have expanded continuously. At the provincial level, however, borrowing from domestic commercial banks by SOEs and local governments has been extensive and deficits have expanded dramatically.[9] After 2007, the sum of provincial

---

6 If the weighted average of consumption-related retail and services sales growth is used to project the consumption share of GDP (Huang et al. 2013), the results suggest the consumption share of GDP *climbed* from 49 to 54 per cent during 2008–10, while China's National Bureau of Statistics (NBS) has it falling from 48 to 47 per cent. Huang et al. start with the official consumption share in 2000 and derive the GDP shares in remaining years using real GDP growth and their estimated consumption growth rates. Using similar data, Garner and Qiao (2013) suggest Chinese consumption expenditure is officially underestimated by US$1.6 trillion, also concluding that its GDP share is expanding.

7 Opposing voices include Wei and Zhang (2011) and Wen (2011). Wei and Zhang (2011) identify a link between saving and entrepreneurship effort on the one hand and China's increasingly inflated sex ratio on the other. The coincidence of son preference and sexual selection technology has seen a rise in the number of unmatched men and increasingly competitive behaviour by families with sons. Debate continues about the strength of this force for higher saving against those associated with policy reforms in the education, health and retirement insurance industries. Wen (2011), on the other hand, employs a model of rapid growth with constant proportional idiosyncratic risk, following Modigliani and Cao (2004), to conclude that saving will continue to rise with income per capita. The assumption of constant proportional risk is a strong one, however, in the face of social reforms to health and retirement systems.

8 According to China's *Statistical Yearbook* (NBS 2012), Central Government revenue has expanded its share of nominal GDP from 10 per cent in 1994 to 23 per cent in 2012.

9 See Zhang and Barnett (2014). This is notwithstanding the Central Government sharing national revenue with the provinces at a 50–50 rate in 2011.

deficits exceeded the central surplus, leading to a return to overall deficits with magnitudes expanding to unprecedented levels (Figure 7.1). Thus, government saving is also shifting in the negative direction in the post-GFC years and, as a consequence, there is diminishing scope for the further use of government spending to balance the economy.

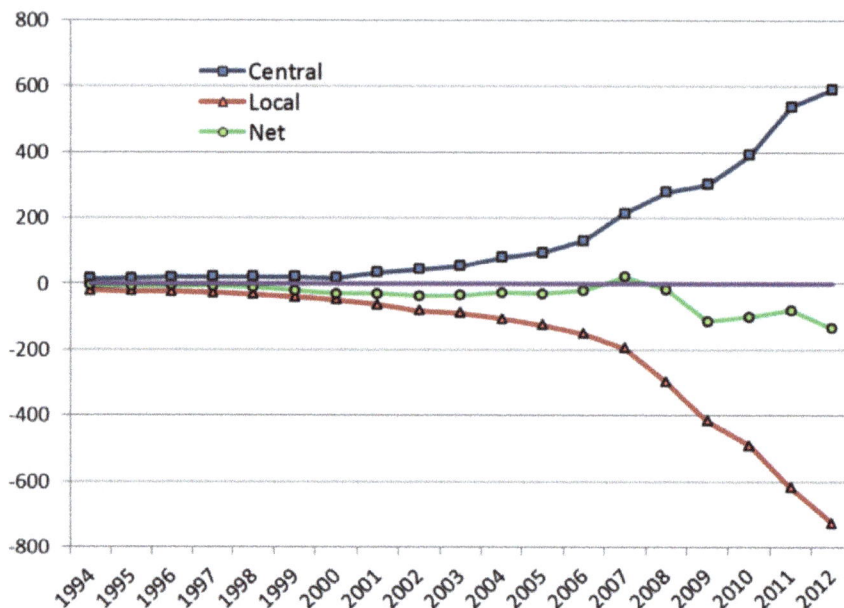

Figure 7.1 China's Governments' Net Surpluses (US$ billion)

Sources: Government debt and general government gross debt position: IMF Fiscal Monitor (2013); external debt outstanding: NBS (2012).

Current account balance

The above discussions lead us to expect a declining trend in China's total domestic saving rate even where this is not yet fully represented in the official statistics, which thus far show only a modest decline since 2010. Since then, however, total (private and public) investment has risen to nearly half of GDP.[10] The investment change has therefore been the primary driver of the declining trend in China's *official* current account surplus since 2010. Looking ahead, it is difficult to imagine a higher rate of both public and private investment without the prospect of increasingly wasteful projects (Singh et al. 2013). Declines in

---

10 In the medium term, at least, this has confirmed the prediction by Lee and McKibbin (2007) that investment would contribute substantially to China's 'rebalancing'.

household and corporate saving rates stemming from the combination of the proposed financial and industrial reforms are the least uncertain of the many likely consequences, suggesting further declines in the current account surplus.

Internationalisation and new roles for private financial flows

The reforms on international capital account will make private flows (the inward and outward private foreign investment terms in Equation 7.1) more influential. Eventually, it is expected that these will raise private holdings of foreign financial assets in both directions. This has not happened yet, however, as Figure 7.2 confirms. Since the GFC, gross flows on China's balance of payments have fallen relative to its GDP and the most recent trends continue to be negative. At the same time, official statistics suggest that at least three-quarters of the inflows and 90 per cent of the outflows are not in the FDI or portfolio investment categories, which include property investment. Since no long-term trends are yet evident in these shares, the traditional dominance of these flows by debt instruments can be expected to continue.

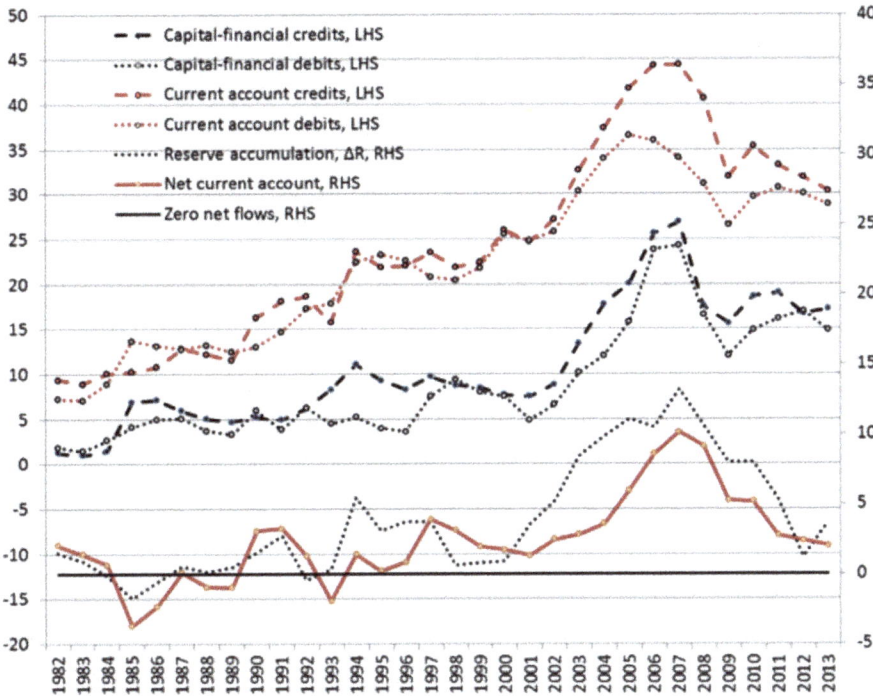

Figure 7.2 Gross and Net Flows on China's Balance of Payments (percentage of GDP)

Source: China SAFE, 'The Balance of Payments Table'. Available from <http://www.safe.gov.cn/>.

Yet expanded gross flows would seem inevitable. This raises the possibility that these flows could become unbalanced, favouring either inflows or outflows, due, for example, to pent-up demand for foreign assets that has been constrained by capital controls. The work of He and Luk (2013) does not foreshadow such unbalanced flows, nor does that of He et al. (2012), which envisions a trend towards trade balance, offset in the current account by higher yields on foreign (newly private) holdings. Indeed, reasons pent-up demand might not be a concern include that capital controls have been leaky enough for the wealthy to acquire the foreign assets they have wanted and that China's reserves are so large that they can be repatriated if private demand for foreign assets were to rise, so balance could be maintained for some years at levels desired by the Government. Moreover, with widespread expectation that Balassa–Samuelson appreciations will continue as China grows relative to the advanced economies, it is possible there will be aversion to foreign assets along the lines seen in Japan, where private portfolio holders tolerate very low rates of return on home assets. A trend decline in China's saving rates and the absence of pent-up demand are therefore the circumstances under which capital account liberalisation might be expected to proceed.

It remains possible, however, that liberalisation could see a surge in outflows reflecting yet unobserved pent-up demand. Indeed, this prospect has come sharply into focus recently as private financial flows out of China have accelerated with the winding down of unconventional monetary policy in the United States. The renminbi's appreciating trend has stalled and there is a temporary bolstering of Asian current accounts (Burns et al. 2014). The possibility of a substantial renminbi depreciation as a consequence is considered by Eichengreen (2014). The economic implications for China of these circumstances are therefore considered in section six.

Special sensitivity to the real exchange rate

The special sensitivity of China's economic performance to its real exchange rate stems from its economic structure, as summarised in Table 7.2. Note that: 1) the great majority of non-agricultural employment is in the export-oriented light manufacturing sector—indeed, employment in this sector exceeds that in agriculture; 2) this sector is relatively competitive—price mark-ups are low and therefore pure or economic profits make up only a small share of total revenue; and 3) the SOE-dominated energy, metals and services sectors are less labour intensive and at the same time they are oligopolistic, generating substantial rents that form a buffer against downturns. These facts clearly suggest that total labour demand in China's modern sector is comparatively sensitive to the relativities between home wages and export prices, and hence to its real exchange rate.

Table 7.2 Structure of the Chinese Economy[a]

Percentage	Value-added share of GDP	Share of total production employment	Share of total exports	Pure profit share of gross revenue
Agriculture	13	24	2	0
Petroleum, coal, metals	16	11	10	20
Light manufacturing	29	33	82	5
Services	42	32	6	20
Total	100	100	100	12

[a] Pure profits are calculated from national statistical estimates of accounting profits, deducting required returns to service industry-specific prime rates. Here they are presented gross of tax and corporate saving and as shares of total revenue.

Source: Model database (social accounting matrix) derived from Dimaranan and McDougall (2002) and an updating of the national data to 2005, as described in Tyers (2014a).

The key sensitivities explored here are between China's real exchange rate and pricing behaviour in its oligopolistic heavy manufacturing and services industries on the one hand, and the openness of its capital account on the other. As indicated in the previous section, financial and industrial reforms are likely to continue the trend towards declining private saving. This will reduce the leakage of income into foreign reserve accumulation. The result is that more Chinese expenditure falls on the home economy relative to the foreign economy, hence appreciating the real exchange rate. This has the effect of inducing either a home inflation or nominal appreciation of the renminbi. Either way, the trend will foster a shifting of economic activity from the export light manufacturing sector into heavy manufacturing and services.

The scale of this effect, however, will be sensitive to changes in oligopoly rents in a manner not commonly recognised. In essence, since the excess profits are achieved by supplying less output than would occur in competitive markets, they reduce productivity in the largely non-traded sectors of the economy. Again employing the abstraction that goods and services are either tradable or not, the effect of this productivity contraction on relative prices is illustrated in Figure 7.3. It raises the prices of non-traded goods relative to traded goods and hence China's real exchange rate. Further reforms to competition policy and regulatory practice that reduce these oligopoly rents would have the opposite effect and spur Chinese employment by sustaining the expansion in the labour-intensive and real exchange rate-sensitive light manufacturing sector.

To quantify the effects of these changes on the real exchange rate and hence on China's economic performance, a more complete model of the Chinese economy is now introduced.

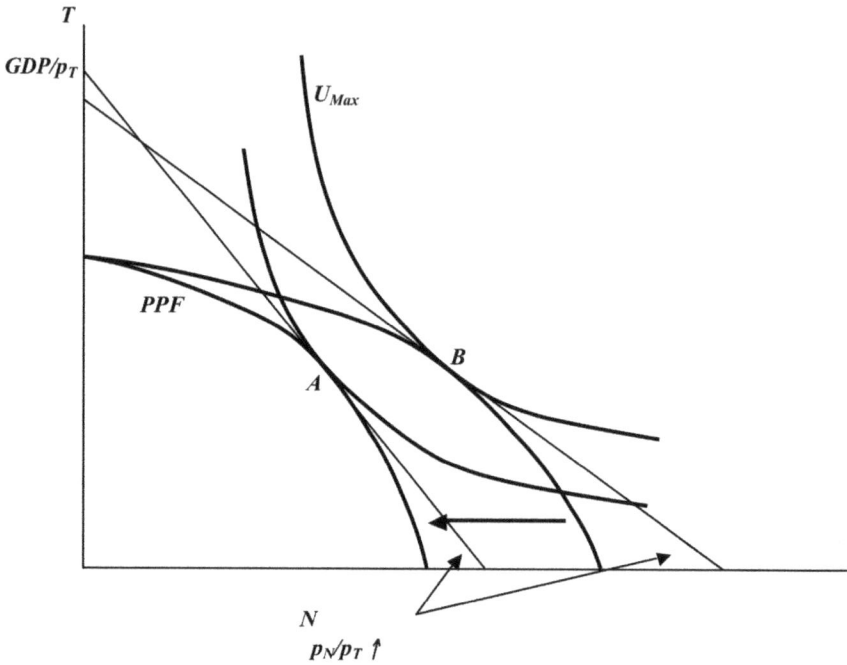

Figure 7.3 Service Oligopoly Rents and the Real Exchange Rate

An oligopoly model of the Chinese economy

We use a comparative static macro-economic model of the Chinese economy that embodies a multi-industry structure in which all industries are treated as oligopolies, with firms in each industry supplying differentiated products and interacting on prices.[11] Government expenditure creates demand for goods and services via nested constant elasticity of substitution (CES) preferences and government revenue stems from a tax system that includes both direct (income) taxes levied separately on labour and capital income and indirect taxes including those on consumption, imports and exports.[12] A capital goods sector is included, which translates investment expenditure into product and service demands, again using a nested CES preference structure. The level of

---

11 It is a distant descendant of that by Tyers (2005), though it is considerably generalised to include interaction on prices and short-run macro-economic behaviour.

12 Income taxes are approximated by flat rates deduced as the quotient of revenue and the tax base in each case.

total investment expenditure has Q-like behaviour, being influenced positively by expected home rates of return on installed capital (which drive the market values of firms' assets) and negatively by a financing rate obtainable from an open 'bond market' in which home and foreign bonds are differentiated to represent China's capital controls (the rates of which drive capital replacement costs).[13] Savings are sourced from the collective household at a constant rate and from corporations at industry-specific rates depending upon the magnitudes of pure (economic) profits earned. Foreign direct investment and official foreign reserve accumulation are both represented as per Equation 7.1 ($S_D - I = \Delta R - FI_{Inward} + FI_{Outward}$), to complete China's external financial accounts.

Model structure

The scope of the model is detailed in Table 7.3. Firms in all industries are oligopolistic in their product pricing behaviour, with the degree of price-setting collusion between them represented by conjectural variation parameters that are set to account for the level of regulatory surveillance. Each firm bears fixed capital and labour costs, enabling the representation of unrealised economies of scale. Home products in each industry are differentiated by variety, and output is Cobb-Douglas in variable factors and intermediate inputs. While firms are oligopolists in their product markets they have no oligopsony power as purchasers of primary factors or intermediate inputs.[14] The economy modelled is 'almost small', implying that it has no power to influence border prices of its imports but its exports are differentiated from competing products abroad and hence face finite elastic demand.[15] The consumer price index (CPI) is constructed as a composite Cobb-Douglas–CES index of post-consumption tax home product and post-tariff import prices, derived from the aggregate household's expenditure function. This formulation of the CPI aids in the analysis of welfare impacts. Because collective utility is also defined as a Cobb-Douglas combination of the volumes of consumption by generic product, proportional changes in overall economic welfare correspond with those in real gross national product (GNP).[16]

---

13 In the lengths of run considered there is no steady state that would equate expected net rates of return with current bond yields.

14 Imports in each industrial category are seen as homogeneous, differentiated from home products as a group, so that import varietal diversity never changes. Since all home varieties are exported there is no movement on the 'extensive margin' of the type that is evident in the models of non-homogeneous export industries by Melitz (2003) and Balistreri et al. (2007).

15 The effective numeraire is the import product bundle. Consumer and GDP price indices are constructed for real aggregations, following the practice in national modelling since Dixon et al. (1982) and Harris (1984).

16 When the utility function is Cobb–Douglas in consumption volumes, the expenditure function is Cobb–Douglas in prices. If the consumer price level, P^c, is defined as a Cobb–Douglas index of prices, the equivalent variation in income can be expressed in terms of the proportional change in this index. Thus, following any shock, the income equivalent of the resulting changes to income and prices is, approximately, the proportional change in real GNP.

Table 7.3 Model Scope

Regions	China
	Rest of world
Primary factors	Land
	Natural resources (minerals, energy deposits)
	Skilled (professional) labour
	Unskilled (production) labour
	Physical capital
Industries	Agriculture
	Metals, including steel, minerals and (non-coal) mining
	Coalmining and production
	Petroleum production and refining
	Processed agricultural products
	Electronic equipment
	Motor vehicles
	Chemical, rubber, plastic products
	Textiles
	Other manufactures
	Electricity supply and distribution
	Gas supply and distribution
	Telecommunications
	Insurance and finance
	Transport
	Construction
	Other services

Source: Aggregates of the 57-industry GTAP Version 6 database from Dimaranan and McDougall (2002).

The quantity of domestically owned physical capital is fixed in the short run, so that changes in the total capital stock affect the foreign ownership share and hence the level of income repatriated abroad. Long and short-run closures can be adopted but the analysis presented herein is focused on the short run: physical capital is fixed in supply and immobile between industries. Production labour is mobile between industries but at a fixed real (CPI-deflated) wage, so employment is endogenous, and the remaining factors, while also mobile between industries, are fixed in endowment and flexibly priced. There is no entry or exit of firms but the magnitudes of pure profits earned are endogenous. Consistent with China's fiscal conservatism, the base fiscal position is held constant so that changes in endogenous revenue lead to corresponding changes in government expenditure.

Macro-economic behaviour

As befits a comparative static analysis, the macro-economics embodied is elemental. The short-run closure fixes productive capital use in all industries but allows investment that would affect production in the future. Central is the open-economy capital market that is built around the market clearing identity—a version of Equation 7.1—in which inward and outward private financial flows are consolidated into 'net foreign saving': $S_{NF} = FI_{Inward} - FI_{Outward}$. Thus Equation 7.2.

Equation 7.2

$$I(r^{ce}, r) = S_D(Y_{DH}, \pi, G) + S_{NF}(r, r^*, \hat{e}_R^e) - \Delta R(r)$$

In Equation 7.2, r is the home real financing rate (bond yield), r^* is the real yield on bonds abroad (the two being differentiated and so offering different yields), $\hat{e}_R^e$ is the expected rate of appreciation of the real exchange rate and ΔR is the annual addition to official foreign reserves. Total domestic saving is the sum of saving by households, corporations and government: $S_D = S_H(Y_{DH}) + S_C(\pi) + (T - G)$, in which Y_{DH} is home household disposable income. The household saving rate is assumed fixed, so that $S_H = S_H Y_{DH}$. China's extraordinarily high level of corporate saving, S_C, is assumed to stem only from pure profits, π, with a distinct but fixed saving rate calibrated separately for each industry (Equation 7.3).

Equation 7.3

$$S_C = \sum_i S_{Ci} = \sum_i s_{Ci} \pi_i$$

The rate r^{ce} is the expected average net rate of return on installed capital, which takes the following form at the industry level (Equation 7.4).

Equation 7.4

$$r_i^{ce} = \frac{P_i^{Ye} MP_i^K}{P^K} - \delta_i$$

In Equation 7.4, P^K is the current price of capital goods, P^{Ye} is the product price level expected to prevail upon gestation and δ is the rate of depreciation. An average of the sector-specific rates, r_i^{ce}, is taken, which is weighted by value added in each industry to obtain the economy-wide level r^{ce}. Investment expenditure, I, is then determined by Equation 7.5.

Equation 7.5

$$I = P^K I_0 \left(\frac{r^{ce}}{r} \right)^{\varepsilon_V}$$

This relationship reflects the Q ratio in that r^{ce} determines the current value of firms' capital while r determines its current replacement cost.

In our comparative static analysis net foreign saving, S_{NF}, is motivated by changes in the level of an interest parity function that incorporates the difference between the home and foreign real bond yields and real exchange rate expectations. A linear relationship is used to allow for reversals of the direction of net flow in response to shocks (Equation 7.6).

Equation 7.6

$$S_{NF} = a_{SF} + b_{SF}\left(r - r^* + \hat{e}_R^e\right), \quad b_{SF} > 0.$$

With tight capital controls there is a low level of responsiveness, so b_{SF} is small (the supply of net foreign private saving is inelastic). Correspondingly, the combination of China's high saving rate with outward capital controls necessitates that the surplus of saving over investment, which has ranged up to one-tenth of GDP, be directed abroad by the People's Bank of China (PBC) as official foreign reserves. This behaviour depends on a relationship that is linear, for the same reason as in Equation 7.6 (Equation 7.7).

Equation 7.7

$$\Delta R = a_{DR} - b_{DR}r$$

In Equation 7.7, under capital controls, the movement of reserves is much more elastic to the home real interest rate than that of private financial capital, so that $b_{DR} > b_{SF}$. The effect of this is to stabilise the home real rate in response to shocks, which cause, instead, elastic movements in the rate of reserve accumulation.[17] The liberalisation of China's capital and financial accounts is then readily represented as a lessening of the gap between the parameters b_{DR} and b_{SF}.

---

17 It is argued elsewhere (Tyers and Zhang 2011, for example) that, under China's capital controls and given the high saving rate, the PBC had little residual discretion over annual increments to reserves. This is because there was no incentive for China's commercial banks to do other than relinquish unused foreign currency to the PBC. The scale of reserve accumulations was therefore not an instrument in the PBC's monetary policy. Equation 7.7 is intended merely as a reduced-form description of this process.

The capital market clearing identity (Equation 7.2) then determines the home real interest rate and the magnitude of the external financial deficit ($\Delta R - S_{NF} = S_D - I$)). This is equal in magnitude to the current account surplus, $X - M + N(r, r^*)$, in which N is net factor income from abroad.[18] The model is essentially Walrasian in that shocks originating in saving and investment, and hence in external flows, cause home (relative to foreign) product prices (and hence the *real* exchange rate) to adjust sufficiently to clear home markets and preserve the balance of payments.

Short-run effects in a real model

In the short run, nominal wage rigidity is important and this is not readily represented in real models such as this one. We can contrast two extreme monetary targeting regimes: the fixed nominal exchange rate and the float with a GDP price deflator target. With the fixed exchange rate regime, any change in the real exchange rate takes the form of a corresponding change in the domestic price level. If the nominal exchange rate, E, is defined as the number of units of foreign exchange obtained for a unit of the domestic currency, the real exchange rate, e_R, can be defined correspondingly as the rate of exchange between the home product bundle and corresponding bundles produced abroad. It follows that the real exchange rate can be approximated as the common currency ratio of the GDP prices of the two countries, P^Y and P_F^Y / E (Equation 7.8).

Equation 7.8

$$e_R = \frac{P^Y}{P_F^Y / E} = E\frac{P^Y}{P_F^Y}$$

And so, when E is targeted and there is no indirect effect on the foreign currency price level in the rest of the world, a real appreciation must take the form of an inflation: $e^R \uparrow = \bar{E}\, P^Y \uparrow / \bar{P}_F^Y$.

If we then assume that our short run is sufficiently tight to render the nominal wage of production workers rigid then the short-run real wage movement mirrors the real appreciation: $\bar{W}/(P^Y \uparrow) = w \downarrow$, so that $\hat{w} = -\hat{e}_R$. By contrast, a flexible exchange rate regime with a price-level target would see no change in the price level or real wage but a nominal appreciation of magnitude equal to the proportional change in the real exchange rate.

---

18 As modelled, N comprises a fixed net private inflow of income from assets abroad and fixed aid to the Government, less endogenous repatriated earnings from foreign-owned physical capital in China.

The liberalisation of capital controls requires increased nominal exchange rate flexibility, as the 'impossible trinity' dictates. While we always retain the real exchange rate as endogenous, both closures linking it to the price level and real wage rate are used in our experiments.

Oligopoly in supply

Firms in each industry supply differentiated products. They carry product variety-specific fixed costs and interact on prices. Cobb-Douglas production drives variable costs so that average variable costs are constant if factor and intermediate product prices do not change but average total cost declines with output. Firms charge a mark-up over average variable cost, which they choose strategically. Their capacity to push their price beyond their average variable costs without being undercut by existing competitors then determines the level of any pure profits and, in the long run, the potential for entry by new firms.

Thus, each firm in industry i is regarded as producing a unique variety of its product and it faces a downward-sloping demand curve with elasticity $\varepsilon_i (< 0)$. The optimal mark-up is then Equation 7.9.

Equation 7.9

$$m_i = \frac{p_i}{v_i} = \frac{1}{1 + \dfrac{1}{\varepsilon_i}} \qquad \forall i$$

In Equation 7.9, p_i is the firm's product price, V_i is its average variable cost and ε_i is the elasticity of demand it faces. Individual firms choose their optimal price on observation of the elasticity of demand they face and this depends on the price-setting behaviour of other firms, which we represent via a conjectural variations parameter. In industry i this is defined as the influence of any individual firm, k, on the price of firm j: $\mu_i = \partial p_{ij}/\partial p_{ik}$. These parameters are exogenous, reflecting industry-specific free-rider behaviour and the power of price surveillance by regulatory agencies. The Nash equilibrium case is a non-collusive differentiated Bertrand oligopoly in which each firm chooses its price, taking the prices of all other firms as given. In this case the conjectural variations parameter, μ, is zero. When firms behave as a perfect cartel, it has the value unity. This parameter enters the analysis through the varietal demand elasticity.

Critical to the implications of imperfect competition in the model is that the product of each industry has exposure to five different sources of demand. The elasticity of demand faced by firms in industry i, ε_i, is therefore dependent on the elasticities of demand in these five markets, as well as the shares of the home product in each. They are final demand (F), investment demand (V), intermediate demand (I), export demand (X) and government demand (G). For industry i, the elasticity that applies to Equation 7.9 is a composite of the elasticities of all five sources of demand (Equation 7.10).[19]

Equation 7.10

$$\varepsilon_i = s_i^F \varepsilon_i^F + s_i^V \varepsilon_i^V + s_i^I \varepsilon_i^I + s_i^X \varepsilon_i^X + s_i^G \varepsilon_i^G \qquad \forall i$$

In Equation 7.10, s_i^j denotes the volume share of the home product in market i for each source of demand j. These share parameters are fully endogenous in the model.

Thus, the strategic behaviour of firms, and hence the economic cost of oligopolies, is affected by collusive behaviour on the one hand and the composition of the demands faced by firms on the other, both of which act through the average elasticity of varietal demand. The collusive behaviour enters through conjectural variation parameters and composition through the demand shares, s_i^j. Each component demand elasticity depends on elasticities of substitution between firm varieties and between home and imported varieties, as well as on the conjectural variations parameters. The relationships are complex and differ as to source of demand.[20] Critically, export demand is more elastic than the others and final demand is more elastic than intermediate, government and investment demand. Thus, when shocks alter the distribution of the demand facing firms, the average elasticity faced is altered and so firms change their mark-ups.

To study the effects of price-cap regulation on oligopoly pricing, a Ramsey mark-up, m_i^R is formulated, as Equation 7.11.

Equation 7.11

$$m_i^R = \frac{afc_i + v_i}{v_i}$$

---

19 The expressions for these elasticities are messy and voluminous. They are derived in the technical appendix.

20 The relationships between the component demand elasticities facing firms and their underlying parameters are detailed in an appendix available from the authors.

In Equation 7.11, afc_i is average fixed cost and V_i is average variable cost in industry i. Compromise mark-ups can be simulated by altering the parameter φ_i in an equation for the 'chosen' mark-up: $m_i^C = (\varphi_i - 1)m_i^R + (2 - \varphi_i)m_i \quad \forall i$. Thus, when $\varphi_i = 1$, $m_i^C = m_i$, thus maximising oligopoly profits, and when $\varphi_i = 2$, $m_i^C = m_i^R$, eliminating pure economic profits altogether.

The database and its representation of China's economic structure

The flow data for the current model originate from the GTAP Version 6 global database for 2001.[21] It combines detailed bilateral trade, transport and protection data characterising economic linkages among regions, together with individual-country national accounts, government accounts, balance-of-payments data and input–output tables that enable the quantification of intersectoral flows within and between regions. Factor shares and input–output coefficients from these 2001 data are combined with Chinese national accounts and balance-of-payments data for 2005, inflating the database to that year and readjusting it for balance. Key structural elements are evident from Table 7.2, which shows that China's measured GDP is dominated by light manufacturing and services. The major contributors to exports are also those that export the largest shares of their output. The traded industries in general and the exporting light manufacturing industries in particular are intensive in production labour. This is most notably true of processed agricultural products and textiles.

Calibration of pure profits and oligopoly parameters

The flows represented in the database do not reveal details of intra-sectoral industrial structure. To represent oligopolistic behaviour, additional information is required on effective firm numbers, pure profits, fixed costs and minimum efficient scale for each industry. With the support of China's official statistics, these variables are calibrated in the following manner. First, pure profits are required as a share of total revenue in each industry. This is needed to finalise the flow database by splitting capital payments between market and over-market returns.[22] It is also a starting point for calibrating industry competitive structure. Second, rough estimates are required of strategically interacting

---

21 Documentation on the GTAP 6 Data package may be viewed at: <http://www.gtap.agecon.purdue.edu/databases/>.

22 Pure profit shares of total revenue in 2005 were high in 'metals and minerals', 'petroleum and energy', 'telecommunications', 'insurance and finance', and 'transport'. Data on accounting profits in the last three sectors are comparatively weak and the estimates are partly judgmental, accounting for such determinants as low borrowing rates for these SOE-dominated sectors and hence low capital service costs. See the appendices to Tyers and Lu (2008).

firm numbers in each industry and their corresponding conjectural variations parameters. Again, official statistics provide firm numbers and sizes and the proportions that are private and state owned.[23]

Third, to complete the formulation of industry demand elasticities, values of elasticities of substitution between home product varieties on the one hand, and between generic home and foreign products on the other, are required for each industry. These are initially drawn from the estimation literature.[24] Preliminary industry demand elasticities are then calculated for each source of demand (final, intermediate, investment, government and export). Initial shares of the demand facing each industry are then drawn from the database to enable the calculation of weighted average demand elasticities for each industry. Preliminary mark-up ratios are deduced from these via Equation 7.9. The initial equilibrium industry shares, elasticities and mark-up ratios for each industry are given in Table 7.4.[25] This completes the initial demand-side calibration. Work on the supply side begins with the application of mark-up ratios to deduce the initial level of average variable cost in each industry. Then the proportion of pure profits in total revenue is deducted from the mark-up to arrive at fixed-cost revenue shares.[26] Total recurrent fixed cost in each industry then follows. At this point these results are reviewed and, where conflicting information is available on fixed-cost shares of total turnover, the calibration is recommenced with new initial elasticities.[27]

---

23 *Effective* firm numbers are smaller than totals since a few large firms in each sector frequently dominate pricing. For oligopolistic sectors in China, these tend to be SOEs.

24 Summaries of this literature are offered by Dimaranan and McDougall (2002) and at <http://www.gtap.purdue.edu/databases/>.

25 Note that the reason the elasticities appear large in magnitude at first glance is that they do not represent the slopes of industry demand curves for generic goods. Rather, they are the elasticities faced by suppliers of individual varieties and are made larger by inter-varietal substitution.

26 Fixed costs take the form of both physical and human capital costs using the rule of thumb (based on estimates by Harris and Cox 1983) that physical capital has a fixed cost share of 5/6.

27 The actual calibration process is yet more complex than this because the elasticities of intermediate demand depend on intermediate cost shares, which depend on the variable cost share. It is therefore necessary to calibrate iteratively for consistency of elasticities and shares.

Table 7.4 Initial Demand Shares, Elasticities and Mark-Ups[a]

	Demand shares (%)					Demand elasticities					Average demand elasticity	Industry mark-up[b]
	Inter.[c]	Final	Export	Invest	Govt	Inter.[c]	Final	Export	Invest	Govt		
Agriculture	53	40	4	3	0	-10.2	-28.6	-40.1	-15.6	-16.0	-18.8	1.06
Metals, minerals	84	3	10	2	1	-2.9	-4.4	-8.9	-2.8	-2.8	-3.5	1.39
Coal	61	4	33	0	2	-3.6	-6.1	-11.2	-2.4	-2.5	-6.2	1.19
Petroleum	58	12	5	14	12	-2.1	-2.8	-6.2	-2.3	-2.1	-2.4	1.69
Processed agriculture	50	34	15	0	1	-12.0	-30.8	-26.8	-16.4	-17.0	-20.7	1.05
Electronics	24	4	65	6	0	-2.7	-6.4	-9.8	-2.9	-2.9	-7.5	1.15
Motor vehicles	46	8	15	29	1	-4.8	-10.0	-16.9	-3.4	-3.7	-6.6	1.18
Chemicals	77	6	17	0	0	-3.6	-6.3	-10.4	-2.5	-2.5	-4.9	1.26
Textiles	45	11	44	0	0	-6.5	-16.9	-25.7	-10.4	-10.2	-16.1	1.07
Other manufacturing	43	5	35	16	0	-2.6	-7.1	-9.5	-4.0	-4.0	-5.5	1.22
Electricity	84	13	1	1	1	-6.4	-12.3	-21.0	-7.5	-7.7	-7.3	1.16
Gas manufacturing and distillation	50	10	0	8	32	-4.9	-7.7	-13.4	-4.8	-4.9	-5.2	1.24
Telecommunications	42	24	1	5	27	-1.7	-1.4	-5.1	-1.5	-1.7	-1.7	2.45
Finance	57	29	2	3	8	-1.8	-2.6	-6.6	-2.2	-2.2	-2.2	1.86
Transport	53	18	8	7	14	-1.3	-1.6	-5.9	-1.6	-1.5	-1.8	2.26
Construction	4	2	0	86	8	-2.5	-5.1	-12.3	-4.4	-4.0	-4.3	1.30
Other services	46	21	4	4	25	-3.4	-8.6	-11.7	-3.1	-2.8	-4.7	1.27

[a] All these variables are endogenous in the model. Initial (base) values are provided here. In model simulations, because the elasticities are tied to database flows via mark-ups and hence pure profits, it is difficult to alter them without rebuilding the entire database. In short-run applications, where smaller elasticities are sensible, the export elasticities are shocked down within simulations. The short-run applications presented here have export elasticities shocked down by 70 per cent. For a discussion of elasticities and the length of run in comparative static analysis, see Cooper et al. (1985).

[b] Industry mark-ups are the ratio of producer prices and average variable costs.

[c] Inter. = intermediate.

Sources: Model database, derived from Dimaranan and McDougall (2002) and 2005 national statistics.

Importantly for the interpretation of later results, Table 7.4 also shows how different elasticities are across the five sources of demand. Export and final demand are the most elastic and intermediate demand the least.[28] Also from Table 7.4, it is evident that, where exports dominate demand, firms face larger elasticities and charge smaller mark-ups. Consistent with these observations, pure profit shares of total revenue tend to be small or even negative for export-oriented industries and very large for the SOE-dominated industries: petroleum, metals and minerals, telecommunications, finance and transport.

In model simulations, because the elasticities are tied to database flows via mark-ups and hence pure profits, it is difficult to alter them without rebuilding the entire database. In short-run applications, where smaller elasticities are sensible, the export elasticities are shocked down within simulations. The short-run applications presented here have export elasticities (in particular, the foreign elasticity of substitution between home and foreign products) shocked down by 70 per cent.[29] Oligopoly pricing is assumed to focus on a run longer than simulated, so these reductions in the external elasticities do not drive home pricing decisions. They represent only external adjustment at a length of run that is shorter than firms' planning horizons.

Further industrial reform and short-term growth

China's industrial reforms have contributed substantially to its overall economic growth in the past two decades, including its spectacular growth in non-agricultural employment. The extension of these reforms into industries that have tended to be dominated by SOEs and less accessible to FDI is part of the Government's official agenda (State Council 2014). Here two key elements of the industrial reform program are introduced: privatisation and competition policy. Privatisation, by itself, redirects income to households that might previously have gone directly to investment by a state-owned corporation. It is therefore modelled as a reduction in the corporate saving rate.[30] The other industrial reforms include oligopoly pricing surveillance and output price regulation, or price caps, both of which are now common in advanced economies, particularly

---

28 Export demand is found to be more elastic because of the larger number of substitutable product varieties available abroad while intermediate demand is relatively inelastic because of firms' reluctance to alter arrangements for intermediate input supply, which may depend on location or 'just in time' relationships. Harris and Cox (1983) address these issues empirically.

29 For a discussion of elasticities and the length of run in comparative static analysis, see Cooper et al. (1985). For the analytics of short-run changes to the responsiveness of export demand, see the accompanying appendix.

30 Direct productivity implications associated with take-over risk and access to FDI are ignored here, though they are considered in the long-run analysis by Tyers (2013).

in network services. Collectively, these reduce oligopoly prices, particularly of intermediate inputs, and therefore reduce costs throughout the economy while at the same time raising consumption expenditure as a proportion of GDP. In the experiments presented here these are packaged, modestly, to reflect the potential for reform in an individual year.

The package reduces the corporate saving rate by 10 per cent. This compares with a 70 per cent reduction that would bring the corporate saving level down to that prevailing in Taiwan and in many other advanced economies. The *level* of corporate saving is further reduced by additional reforms affecting the size of economic profits. The first of these is pricing surveillance, which is represented by a reduction in the conjectural variations parameters in all industries by 10 per cent (bearing in mind that, as per section four, values of zero indicate non-collusive oligopoly).[31] By making firms perceive more elastic demand, this reduces their profit-maximising mark-ups via Equation 7.9 in section four. Excess profits are further limited, directly, by imposing regulatory price caps that remove 10 per cent of the gap between the profit-maximising output price and average total cost in all industries (the parameter φ_i is raised by 10 per cent, as per the discussion of Equation 7.11 in section four).

The effects of this packaged shock are summarised in the first column of Table 7.5, which shows them to be substantial, indeed sufficient by themselves to sustain China's historically high growth for several years. The cost reductions that follow from reduced oligopoly rents, particularly in key sectors supplying widely used intermediate goods and services, foster expansions in output and employment throughout the economy. Moreover, they depreciate the real exchange rate, thus fostering long-run growth in exports.[32] Production is, on average, closer to minimum efficient scale and, even though oligopoly rents (pure profits) are reduced, average capital returns rise due to increased market rents on existing capital. The rise in these returns leads to increased investment expenditure that is financed by reduced net financial outflows in the form of reduced foreign reserve accumulation.

---

31 For the analytics of this, see the mathematical appendix.
32 In these short-run simulations, the export elasticities are smaller than those motivating firms' pricing behaviour (Table 7.4), so export growth is curtailed. It is nonetheless substantial in key sectors: mining, electronics, motor vehicles and other manufacturing, all of which enjoy export volume expansions of between 3 and 10 per cent.

Table 7.5 Short-Run Economic Effects of Further Industrial Reform[a]

	Short-run model simulations[b] with:	
	Capital controls and a fixed exchange rate[c]	A liberal capital account and floating exchange rate[d]
Percentage changes		
Real GNP[e]	5.5	6.7
Real GDP[f]	7.4	8.8
Real investment[g]	10.8	13.4
Real exchange rate	−2.2	−2.2
Production employment[h]	5.5	8.2
Average gross rate of return[i]	7.4	9.4
Production scale[j]	0.5	0.6
Pure profits/GDP[k]	−5.6	−4.4
Changes as percentage of initial GDP		
Investment expenditure, I/Y_0	2.6	3.5
Private financial flows, S_{NF}/Y_0	0.1	2.6
Reserve accumulation, $\Delta R/Y_0$	−2.3	−0.1
Current account, CA/Y_0	−2.2	−2.6

[a] These simulations use a short-run closure in which numbers of firms are fixed and pure profits endogenous, physical capital is fixed at the sectoral level with rates of return endogenous and the real wage of production workers is adjusted opposite to the change in the real exchange rate (consistent with a fixed nominal exchange rate) with all labour mobile between sectors. The fiscal closure has the government deficit exogenous while revenue and expenditure are endogenous. It is assumed that there is no change in expectations over the real exchange rate. There is no Ricardian equivalence, so the household and corporate saving rates are constant.

[b] A combination of reforms is introduced simultaneously: 1) progress on further privatisation is indicated by a 10 per cent reduction in the corporate saving rate; 2) oligopoly pricing is moderated via surveillance, which reduces the conjectural variations parameters in all industries by 10 per cent; and 3) excess profits are limited directly by imposing price caps that remove 10 per cent of the gap between output price and average total cost in all industries.

[c] This is using the standard model with capital controls represented by elasticities of S_{NF} and ΔR to the interest parity value of 0.2 and −10, respectively. The change in the real wage of production workers is equal to and opposite that of the real exchange rate, as discussed in the text.

[d] Here the model is modified to represent a liberalised capital account and floating exchange rate with a GDP price target. The elasticities of S_{NF} and ΔR to the interest parity value are 20 and −0.2, respectively, and the real wage of production workers is constant. Note, however, that these substantial parameter differences apply to marginal changes due to the fiscal policy shock only. The starting level of private inflow remains small and the rate of reserve accumulation is correspondingly large.

[e] To facilitate welfare interpretation, GNP is expressed relative to the consumer price index.

[f] As a measure of collective output volume, GDP is expressed relative to the GDP price.

[g] Measured relative to the home GDP price.

[h] This is the proportional change in the level of total production, or low-skill employment.

[i] The rate of return on physical capital is here gross of depreciation and inclusive of pure economic profits. The percentage change in the rate is shown, rather than the difference in percentage or basis points.

[j] This is the percentage change in the weighted average of the ratio of gross output to minimum efficient scale, measured across all industries.

[k] This is the percentage change in the sum of all pure or economic profits across industries as a proportion of current GDP.

Source: Simulations of the model described in the text.

As to industry-specific effects, mark-ups and pure profits decline in most industries, and particularly in those with high initial rents. There is also a redistribution of the production labour force out of agriculture, processed agricultural products and textiles and into industries that benefit most from cost reductions. These are the less labour-intensive industries and they include metals, motor vehicles, other manufactures, finance and transport. Real wages of production workers are modestly higher and those of skilled workers very substantially higher so the additional output is smaller in those industries with highest labour intensity. Even considering the higher unit factor rewards, most industries enjoy reductions in unit fixed costs as production runs expand. These include metals, petrochemicals, motor vehicles, other manufactures, transport and construction. Finally, the composition of exports changes with increased concentration in metals and motor vehicles and there is an expanded external role for the Chinese transport services industry.

In aggregate, then, even though this package of reforms allows the retention of some potentially distorting oligopolies, it raises modern sector employment and productivity while increasing the prominence of consumption expenditure and further reducing the external imbalance. Moreover, it moves the structure of the economy away from its prior dependence on inexpensive raw labour towards a more mature phase in which China's services industries are larger and more competitive and the composition of its trade is more similar to that of most industrialised economies.

Capital account liberalisation

In section two the empirical evidence to date is seen to suggest a trend decline in China's overall saving rate and it is noted that the studies available thus far do not suggest any significant pent-up demand for rebalancing of private portfolios in favour of foreign assets. This implies a smooth transition to balanced growth irrespective of the extent of capital account liberalisation. Here such a scenario is compared with one in which there is pent-up demand for foreign assets that causes an outward rebalancing following capital account liberalisation. Thus, the experiments presented consider modest declines in saving rates on the one hand and a structural shift that reflects the release of pent-up demand for foreign assets on the other. In each case the effects are evaluated assuming either a monetary defence of the nominal exchange rate or a float. The results are summarised in Table 7.6.

Table 7.6 Short-Run Effects of Capital Account Liberalisation[a]

	Capital account liberalisation in the presence of saving rate decline[b], with:		Capital account liberalisation in the presence of pent-up demand for foreign assets[c], with:	
	Defence of a fixed exchange rate[d]	A liberal capital account and floating exchange rate[e]	Defence of a fixed nominal exchange rate[d]	A liberal capital account and floating exchange rate[e]
Percentage changes				
Real GNP[f]	2.1	1.2	−1.7	−0.7
Real GDP[g]	2.4	1.4	−1.9	−0.7
Real investment[h]	2.1	1.0	−12.7	−11.5
Real exchange rate	1.7	2.0	−2.1	−2.4
Production employment[i]	2.7	0.6	−1.8	0.8
Average gross rate of return[j]	2.9	1.5	−3.5	−1.8
Production scale[k]	0.1	0.04	−0.1	−0.01
Pure profits/GDP[l]	1.1	0.3	−5.0	−3.9
Changes as percentage of initial GDP				
Investment expenditure, I/Y_0	1.2	0.9	−5.3	−5.0
Private financial flows, S_{NF}/Y_0	2.5	2.5	−19.5	−19.6
Reserve accumulation, $\Delta R/Y_0$	−0.9	−1.0	−16.2	−16.1
Current account, CA/Y_0	−3.3	−3.3	3.4	3.4

[a] These simulations use a short-run closure in which numbers of firms are fixed and pure profits endogenous, physical capital is fixed at the sectoral level with rates of return endogenous and the real wage of production workers is adjusted opposite the change in the real exchange rate (consistent with a fixed nominal exchange rate) with all labour mobile between sectors. The fiscal closure has the government deficit exogenous while revenue and expenditure are endogenous. It is assumed there is no change in expectations over the real exchange rate. There is no Ricardian equivalence, so the household and corporate saving rates are constant.

[b] The shock is a reduction by 10 per cent in both the household and the corporate saving rates.

[c] Here the shock is an arbitrary shift in the private net foreign inflow equation to the parameter a_{SF} (Equation 7.6) that creates a large net private financial outflow, in the presence of an enlarged elasticity of private flows to the interest parity term in Equation 7.6. There is no change to household or corporate saving rates.

[d] This assumes a liberalised capital account but a short-run monetary defence of the nominal exchange rate. The elasticities of S_{NF} and ΔR to the interest parity value are 50 and −10, respectively. The defence of the exchange rate requires a change in the real wage equal to that opposite to the change in the real exchange rate, as discussed in the text.

[e] Here the model is modified to represent a liberalised capital account and floating exchange rate with a GDP price target. The elasticities of S_{NF} and ΔR to the interest parity value are 50 and −10, respectively. The price-level target and sticky nominal wage ensure that the real wage of production workers is constant in this case.

[f] To facilitate welfare interpretation, GNP is expressed relative to the consumer price index.

[g] As a measure of collective output volume, GDP is expressed relative to the GDP price.

[h] Measured relative to the home GDP price.

[i] This is the proportional change in the level of total production, or low-skill employment.

[j] The rate of return on physical capital is here gross of depreciation and inclusive of pure economic profits. The percentage change in the rate is shown, rather than the difference in percentage or basis points.

[k] This is the percentage change in the weighted average of the ratio of gross output to minimum efficient scale, measured across all industries.

[l] This is the percentage change in the sum of all pure or economic profits across industries as a proportion of current GDP.

Source: Simulations of the model described in the text.

Consider first the effects of a smooth continuation of China's savings decline. This is represented by reducing the household and corporate saving rates by 10 per cent. This tightens the home financial market and, with liberalised capital and financial accounts, it draws in private foreign investment. The effects of this are partially offset by reduced reserve accumulation. Nonetheless, the private inflow is sufficient to cut the current account surplus by half. Combined with the boost to domestic consumption expenditure that accompanies reduced saving rates, this new inflow raises demand for home relative to foreign products and services and so appreciates the real exchange rate.

If monetary policy targets the nominal exchange rate, as in the first column of Table 7.6, this implies domestic inflation and, with nominal wage rigidity, there is a substantial boost to employment. Combined with new investment that is financed by the inflow and induced in part because greater employment raises capital returns, this leads to a substantial boost to real GDP growth. If the nominal exchange rate is allowed to appreciate the home inflation is avoided and much of the inducement to increase production employment disappears. Nonetheless, aggregate demand is still boosted by greater home consumption and the foreign private inflow, and there is therefore a modest rise in real GDP. In both cases the increases in production runs boost industrial efficiency. The increase in demand is, however, internal and hence it reduces perceived elasticities and raises mark-ups in key industries, thereby raising oligopoly rents. Overall, however, capital account liberalisation might be expected to have marginally positive effects under these circumstances.

Now consider the possibility that there is considerable home demand for foreign assets that is constrained by China's outward capital controls. To represent the effects of this following the liberalisation of the capital and financial accounts an arbitrary shift is introduced in the constant term of Equation 7.6, a_{SF} (which is initially negative), which reduces net private inflow at all levels of the home bond yield. As the third column of Table 7.6 indicates, this shift is sufficient in the experiment to cause a private outflow amounting to about one-fifth of GDP. Partially offset by a repatriation of foreign reserves, this shock also tightens the home financial market. This time, however, less investment is financed, it blows out the current account surplus and its effect on aggregate demand is therefore negative. The real exchange rate depreciates and, if monetary policy is directed to defend the nominal exchange rate, a deflation exacerbates a significant shedding of production employment and a contraction in real GDP.

If the nominal exchange rate is allowed to float downward the results are less dire, as indicated in the final column of Table 7.6. The private outflow still impairs investment financing and the current account still blows out but there is no deflation, and hence no contraction in employment, and the slide in GDP is much reduced. Clearly, this suggests that any commitment to capital and financial account liberalisation should accompany a preparedness to allow the nominal exchange rate to adjust, particularly downward, so as to avoid deflation. Interestingly, while the pent-up demand story is negative for China's growth, if the exchange rate is allowed to adjust to avoid deflation the costs are borne primarily by the wealthy. Oligopoly rents decline significantly as does the overall rate of return on capital, yet employment of production workers expands and real skilled wages rise, as do rents on land and natural resources. Thus, with flexible monetary policy, even a substantial outpouring of private flows need not impair China's short-term growth very much.

The only caveat to this conclusion is that the simulations ignore the possibility of a banking or wider financial crisis. Home yields rise by about 17 per cent, suggesting a collapse in asset values that could threaten major financial institutions. This would cause the temporary sequestration of existing physical capital and a potentially substantial loss of employment.

Conclusion

China's recent rapid growth and its current size limit its capacity to source further expansion from exports so the inevitable turn inward is in progress, as suggested by the declines in gross flows on its balance of payments relative to its GDP that have been persistent since the GFC. The large current account surpluses of the boom period are closing, thus far primarily due to fiscal expansion and some associated public investment. Unfortunately, this option is being closed off in the short run by the need for reform of fiscal federalism in China, to resolve growing provincial indebtedness. The key reforms with positive short-run implications focus on industrial policy and capital and financial account liberalisation under the general rubric of 'internationalisation'. The short-run effects of these policy shocks are examined using a 17-sector model of the Chinese economy that takes explicit account of oligopolistic behaviour and financial flows in the short run.

The results confirm that further fiscal expansions, even with large public investment components, will not contribute the major share of new growth, but industrial reform in heavy manufacturing and services would reduce costs and foster growth in output, private consumption and modern-sector employment. Moreover, the structural reforms would reduce external imbalance by curtailing corporate saving, cut distortionary oligopoly rents and increase production runs in previously inefficient industries, thus raising the productivity of existing physical capital and labour. At the same time, the anticipated trend towards reduced saving and increased private consumption would be rewarding under capital and financial account liberalisation since expanded home consumption demand would be supplemented by a greater inflow of private foreign investment, raising both employment and real GDP. Were pent-up demand for foreign assets to be revealed following further liberalisation, the resulting financial outflows would only be seriously damaging were monetary policy to attempt to defend the nominal exchange rate, or if declines in asset values were to precipitate a domestic financial crisis. Moreover, in the absence of financial disruption and with the cushioning effect of exchange rate flexibility, such temporary outflows are shown to be beneficial to Chinese employment and labour incomes, with temporary negative impacts falling on capita returns.

References

Balistreri, E. J., Hillberry, R. H. and Rutherford, T. J. (2007), Structural estimation and solution of international trade models with heterogeneous firms, Presented at the 10th Annual Conference on Global Economic Analysis, Purdue University, Lafayette, Ind., July.

Burns, A., Kida, M., Lim, J., Mohapatra, S. and Stocker, M. (2014), 'Unconventional monetary policy normalisation and emerging-market capital flows', *VOX*, 21 January.

Cai, F. (2010), 'Demographic transition, demographic dividend and Lewis turning point in China', *China Economic Journal* 3(2) (September): 107–19.

Cooper, R. J., McLaren, K. R. and Powell, A. A. (1985), 'Short-run macroeconomic closure in applied general equilibrium modelling: experience from ORANI and agenda for further research', in J. Whalley and J. Piggott (eds), *New Developments in Applied General Equilibrium*, pp. 411–40, Cambridge: Cambridge University Press.

Deer, L. and Song, L. (2012), 'China's approach to rebalancing: a conceptual and policy framework', *China & World Economy* 20(1): 1–26.

de Gregorio, J., Giovannini, A. and Wolf, H. (1994), 'International evidence on tradables and non-tradables inflation', *European Economic Review* 38: 1225–34.

Dimaranan, B. V. and McDougall, R. A. (2002), *Global trade, assistance and production: the GTAP 5 data base*, May, Center for Global Trade Analysis, Purdue University, Lafayette, Ind.

Dixon, P. B., Parmenter, B. R., Sutton, J. and Vincent, D. P. (1982), *ORANI, A Multi-Sectoral Model of the Australian Economy*, Amsterdam: North Holland.

Eichengreen, B. (2004), *Global imbalances and the lessons of Bretton Woods*, NBER Working Paper 10497, National Bureau of Economic Research, Cambridge, Mass.

Eichengreen, B. (2014), 'Yuan dive?', *Project Syndicate*, 12 March.

Fleming, J. M. (1962), *Domestic financial policies under fixed and floating exchange rates*, IMF Staff Papers 9, International Monetary Fund, Washington, DC.

Froot, K. A. and Rogoff, K. (1995), 'Perspectives on PPP and long run real exchange rates', in G. M. Grossman and K. Rogoff (eds), *Handbook of International Economics. Volume III*, Amsterdam: Elsevier.

Galstyan, V. and Lane, P. R. (forthcoming), 'The composition of government spending and the real exchange rate', *Journal of Money, Credit and Banking*.

Garnaut, R. (2010), 'Macroeconomic implications of the turning point', *China Economic Journal* 3(2): 181–90.

Garner, J. and Qiao, H. (2013), 'China—household consumption most likely US1.6 trillion larger than officially stated', *Asian Insight*, 28 February 2013, Morgan Stanley Research. Available from: <http://www.morganstanleychina.com/views/121217.html>.

Golley, J. and Meng, X. (2011), 'Has China run out of surplus labour?', *Chinese Economic Review* 22(4): 555–72.

Gunasekera, H. D. B. and Tyers, R. (1990), 'Imperfect competition and returns to scale in a newly industrialising economy: a general equilibrium analysis of Korean trade policy', *Journal of Development Economics* 34: 223–47.

Harris, R. G. (1984), 'Applied general equilibrium analysis of small open economies with scale economies and imperfect competition', *American Economic Review* 74: 1016–32.

Harris, R. G. and Cox, D. (1983), *Trade, Industrial Policy and Canadian Manufacturing*, Toronto: Ontario Economic Council.

He, D. and Luk, P. (2013), *A model of Chinese capital account liberalization*, Working Paper No. 12/2013, Hong Kong Institute for Monetary Research, Hong Kong.

He, D. and McCauley, R. N. (2013), *Transmitting global liquidity to East Asia: policy rates, bond yields, currencies and dollar credit*, Working Paper No. 15/2013, Hong Kong Institute for Monetary Research, Hong Kong; BIS Working Papers 431, October, Bank for International Settlements.

He, D., Cheung, L., Zhang, W. and Wu, T. (2012), 'How would capital account liberalization affect China's capital flows and *renminbi* real exchange rates?', *China and the World Economy* 20(6): 29–54.

Horioka, C. Y. and Terada-Hagiwara, A. (2012), 'The determinants and long term projections of saving rates in developing Asia', *Japan and the World Economy* 24: 128–37.

Horioka, C. Y. and Wan, J. (2007), 'The determinants of household saving in China: a dynamic panel analysis of provincial data', *Journal of Money, Credit and Banking* 39(8): 2077–96.

Huang, Y., Chang, J. and Yang, L. (2013), 'Consumption recovery and economic rebalancing in China', *Asian Economic Papers* 12(1): 47–67.

International Monetary Fund (IMF) (n.d.), International Financial Statistics, International Monetary Fund, Washington, DC. Available from <http://www.econdata.com/databases/imf-and-other-international/ifs>.

_____ (2013), *Fiscal Monitor: Fiscal Adjustment in an Uncertain World*, International Monetary Fund, Washington, DC, April. Available from <http://imf.org/external/pubs/ft/fm/2013/1/fmindex.htm>.

Kuijs, L. (2006), *How will China's saving–investment balance evolve?*, World Bank Policy Research Working Paper 3958, July, The World Bank, Beijing.

Lee, J. W. and McKibbin, W. J. (2007), *Domestic investment and external imbalances in East Asia*, CAMA Working Paper 4-2007, Centre for Applied Macroeconomics, The Australian National University, Canberra.

Lu, F., Song, G., Tang, J., Zhao, H. and Liu, L. (2008), 'Profitability of Chinese firms, 1978–2006', *China Economic Journal* 1(1).

Ma, G. and McCauley, R. N. (2007), 'How effective are China's capital controls?', in R. Garnaut and L. Song (eds), *China: Linking Markets for Growth*, pp. 267–89, Canberra: Asia-Pacific Press.

Ma, G. and Yi, W. (2010), 'China's high saving rate: myth and reality', *International Economics* 122: 5–40.

Melitz, M. J. (2003), 'The impact of trade on intra-industry reallocations and aggregate industry productivity', *Econometrica* 71(6): 1695–725.

Modigliani, F. and Cao, S. (2004), 'The Chinese saving puzzle and the life-cycle hypothesis', *Journal of Economic Literature* 42(1): 145–70.

Mundell, R. A. (1963), 'Capital mobility and stabilization policy under fixed and flexible exchange rates', *The Canadian Journal of Economics and Political Science* 29(4): 475–85.

National Bureau of Statistics (NBS) (2012), *China Statistical Yearbook 2012*, Beijing: China Statistics Press.

Riedel, J. (2011), *The slowing down of long term growth in Asia: natural causes, the middle income trap and politics*, School of Advanced International Studies, The Johns Hopkins University, Baltimore.

Singh, A., Nabar, M. and N'Daiye, P. M. (2013), *China's economy in transition: from external to internal rebalancing*, November, International Monetary Fund, Washington, DC.

Song, L., Yang, J. and Zhang, Y. (2011), 'State-owned enterprises' outward investment and the structural reform in China', *China and the World Economy* 19(4): 38–53.

State Council (2014), 'Decision of the Central Committee of the Communist Party of China on some major issues concerning comprehensively deepening the reform', State Council of the People's Republic of China, Beijing. Available from: <http://www.china.org.cn/china/third_plenary_session/2014-01/16/content_31212602_2.htm>.

Tyers, R. (2005), 'Trade reform and manufacturing pricing behaviour in four archetype Asia-Pacific economies', *Asian Economic Journal* 19(2): 181–203.

Tyers, R. (2014a), *Looking inward for transformative growth*, *China Economic Review*, forthcoming. Also available from CAMA Working Paper No. 48/2013, March, Centre for Applied Macroeconomic Analysis, The Australian National University, Canberra.

Tyers, R. (2014b), *International effects of China's rise and transition: neoclassical and Keynesian perspectives*, CAMA Working Paper No. 5-2014, July, Centre for Applied Macroeconomics, The Australian National University, Canberra.

Tyers, R. and Zhang, Y. (2011), 'Appreciating the *renminbi*', *The World Economy* 34(2): 265–97.

Tyers, R., Golley, J., Bu, Y. and Bain, I. (2008), 'China's economic growth and its real exchange rate', *China Economic Journal* 1(2): 123–45.

Wei, S.-J. and Zhang, X. (2011), 'The competitive saving motive: evidence from rising sex ratios and saving rates in China', *Journal of Political Economy* 199(3): 511–64.

Wen, Y. (2011), *Explaining China's trade imbalance puzzle*, Working Paper 2011-018A, August, Federal Reserve Bank of St Louis, Mo.

Yang, D. T. (2012), 'Aggregate savings and external imbalances in China', *Journal of Economic Perspectives* 26(4): 125–46.

Zhang, Y. S. and Barnett, S. (2014), *Fiscal vulnerabilities and risks from local government finance in China*, IMF Working Paper 14/4, January, International Monetary Fund, Washington, DC.

Part II: New Priority for Low-Carbon Growth and Climate Change Policy

8. Low-carbon Growth and its Implications for the Less-developed Regions[1]

Yongsheng Zhang

Introduction

With the Industrial Revolution, human society started a process of modern economic growth. Standards of living rose at an unprecedented pace in the countries in which was established. This growth paradigm was, however, built on high resource use, high carbon emissions and high levels of pollution. The paradigm has brought prosperity to the established industrialised countries, and motivated the rest of the world to achieve the same prosperity following the same pathway. The negative consequences associated with the old way of industrialisation include great damage to the environment, inevitably giving rise to various crises (Rockström et al. 2009).

The development paradigm of 'pollution first and clean-up later' established since the Industrial Revolution is no longer feasible.. A continuation of modern economic growth within that paradigm is inconsistent with the health of natural systems that are essential for the success of human society. The development paradigm must be fundamentally shifted to a new green development paradigm if climatic catastrophe is to be avoided. For all countries, including both developed and developing countries, green development is not a matter of 'whether', but 'how' to take it up. Latecomer countries to modern economic growth and poor regions can no longer achieve their economic development by taking the traditional development paradigm. Developed countries, too, are required to accelerate the shift towards green growth at a more advanced level of development.

It is therefore important to clarify from a theoretical point of view whether, as a new paradigm of development, green growth can help latecomer and poor countries or regions grow out of poverty. Various studies reach different conclusions (for example, UNEP 2011; King 2013; Dercon 2012). For green growth as a way to eradicate poverty, the narrative goes something like this: poor regions,

---

1 This chapter is based on a presentation the author gave in Guizhou Province, China, in 2013. Guizhou is one of the poorest provinces in China. The idea is being developed in a more rigorous analytical framework by the author.

and the majority of their populations, depend directly on natural resources. Their livelihoods are intricately linked with exploiting fragile environments and ecosystems (Barbier 2005). Therefore, transition to a green economy can contribute to the improvement of the environment and preservation of the ecosystems, through which poverty can be eradicated. A number of sectors with green economic potential are particularly important for the poor, such as agriculture, forestry, fisheries and water management. Investing in greening these sectors, including through scaling up microfinance, is likely to benefit the poor in terms of not only increasing jobs, but also securing livelihoods that are predominantly based on ecosystem services (UNEP 2011:19–20).

If, however, the implications of green growth for poverty reduction are limited to that sense, it may help impoverished areas rise out of poverty, but is unlikely to offer them abundant prosperity. Green growth represents a fundamental shift in the development rationale and paradigm. Such involves substantial changes in the structure of production, consumption, trade content, business models, conceptions of resources, and modes of urbanisation and living. These changes can overcome the traditional development constraints impeding poor regions from achieving economic prosperity, and open new opportunities. Accordingly, the implications of green growth for poverty reduction should be investigated in the context of the fundamental shift in the development paradigm.

This chapter investigates how green growth can become a new lever to accelerate development in poor areas. We first put the issue in the context of China, and then discuss its significance for the rest of the world. In the second section, we investigate some unique advantages poor regions have for promoting green growth under new conditions. The third section explores the implications of the green growth paradigm for poor areas. The following section focuses on the policy framework of how to make green growth a lever for new development. The final section concludes.

New advantages for poor regions in promoting green growth

Fundamental changes in historical conditions for development in poor regions

According to traditional development views, poor regions restrained by geographic remoteness, inaccessibility, small markets, and lack of resources, capital, talent and technology encounter a variety of development obstacles. Such a traditional concept of development no longer applies because of the substantial changes to two historical conditions, and the advantages and disadvantages of poor regions for development can even start to reverse to some extent.

First, the economic take-off in poor areas coincides with the fundamental changes of the development concept and paradigm worldwide. The reason developed countries and the coastal regions of China followed a path of high resource use, high carbon emissions, high levels of pollution and environmental degradation is largely because they knew no alternative path during the early stages of modern economic growth and did not have the concept of green growth in mind. Though the coastal regions of China followed the traditional path of industrialisation that had been taken by the developed countries, they suffered large environmental consequences. In contrast, poor regions, thanks to their unfortunate underdevelopment, avoided going down this traditional path and retained their beautiful natural and cultural characteristics. Today, with the rise of the green growth concept, these beautiful natural and human environments have become rare and valuable resources for economic development. Their advantages now stand out. It is possible for poor regions to take a new road by turning their vital natural and human resources into wealth.

Second, historic changes in global economic and technical conditions have created conditions for poor areas to follow a green path. All around the world, technical conditions and infrastructure linking poor areas with developed regions have undergone tremendous changes: broadband, information and communications technology (ICT), 'mega-data', freeways; high-speed railway; and advanced logistics systems. Small-scale, decentralised facilities based on renewable energy can provide electricity at costs that are as low as the large, centralised systems of the big cities. In China, more than 30 years of rapid development have hugely expanded domestic market size. China's coastal areas relied primarily on exports to Western markets as the mainland Chinese market was very small in the early years of reform and rapid growth. Now, developed areas in China can provide a sufficiently large market for poor regions to specialise in producing goods and services in which they have comparative advantage.

How changes to historical conditions have broken traditional development constraints

Changes in the two major historical conditions discussed above have removed or weakened many traditional development constraints in poor areas. Some disadvantages in poor areas have even reversed.

First, geographic remoteness in poor areas is no longer a prominent constraint on their development. Rapid development in broadband, ICT, freeways, high-speed railways, aviation, private vehicles and logistics systems have helped overcome the disadvantages of distance.

Second, the small local market in poor areas is no longer a problem. With the emergence of online shopping and convenient logistics systems, poor areas can be directly connected with advanced outside markets. In poor areas, people can also buy goods from around the world via e-commerce. Similarly, locally produced goods can easily be sold to the global market online.

Third, lack of capital is not a problem either. After 30 years of rapid development, China now generally has abundant capital. Additionally, as long as liberal financial policies are in place, microfinance is proving successful in very poor areas. Thus, capital is no longer a particular constraint. Resources are not allocated to where they are most needed due to the weaknesses in an inadequately reformed financial system and low capacity for innovation.

Fourth, human capital in poor areas is not really a big problem. New business models can, to some extent, solve this problem. For example, in franchise businesses, the franchisees don't have to be well educated. They just need to join a franchise network to access support. Thanks to ICT and mega-data, and rapid transport systems, massive use of distant talent is now possible. Professionals in Beijing, New York, London and other major cities are able to provide high-quality remote medical, educational and consulting services for any part of the world. In addition, a large number of rural migrant workers moving from poor areas to cities have been well trained through experience at work. They have important human capital for economic development in poor areas.

Finally, natural resources are not a particular problem. In the traditional development mode, tangible material resources like minerals and petroleum come to mind first and are important for development in poor areas. In the new model of green growth, poor areas have the most valuable natural environmental resources. As the traditional industrial model of 'pollution first and clean-up later' in developed areas is being left behind, the environmental advantages of poor areas rise even more prominently.

It is clear that, with new thinking and a new growth paradigm, many of the traditional restraints long hindering the development of poor areas have disappeared or have been greatly reduced. It is possible for poor areas to take a new green growth path. Moreover, unlike the developed economies the transition cost to green growth is relatively low in poor areas since they do not need to eliminate obsolete infrastructure and production capacity before switching to a green growth path.

It is therefore possible for poor regions to make the transition to green growth a lever to accelerate development. Poor regions can directly link to outside developed markets and convert their vital natural and human resources into wealth. Under a new development paradigm, some poor areas could jump into modern society within a relatively short period (World Bank and DRC 2012).

Green growth: new opportunities for poor regions

What opportunities can the green transition bring as a lever to poor regions? To recognise this, we need to understand the mechanism of economic development and know how it comes into play in the green growth paradigm.

Mechanisms of economic development

According to Yang (2003), the core of classical economics is development economics. According to Smith's theorem (1776), the division of labour is the source of economic growth; the division of labour is limited by the extent of the market; and the extent of the market depends on transport. Young (1928) further pointed out that not only does the division of labour depend on the extent of the market, but also the extent of the market depends on the division of labour. Transaction efficiency plays a decisive role in the evolution of the division of labour. Research on transaction costs offered a new perspective for understanding the division of labour (Coase 1937). Yang (2001) argued that the level of the division of labour increases with the increase of transaction efficiency, as does productivity. In particular, with an increase of transaction efficiency and the level of the division of labour, the possible ways for entrepreneurs to organise the division of labour will increasingly expand, thereby providing them with more room to make money.

Currently, one dramatic change is that transaction efficiency has increased significantly. First, information flows have become convenient. With the popularisation of ICT, mega-data, the Internet and smart phones, information flows quickly. Second, thanks to the rapid development and popularisation of high-speed transport systems, population mobility has become more convenient. Third, logistics systems have become fast. Fast, convenient and smart logistics systems have greatly enhanced transaction efficiency.

Enhanced transaction efficiency promotes the evolution of the division of labour and provides a driving force for economic growth. A larger change, however, is that economic development is transferring to the green growth paradigm. An essential change in the green growth paradigm is that the economy is being dematerialised and value added increasingly comes from information, knowledge, the environment and other intangible elements.[2] This contrasts with the traditional development paradigm, in which the focus is on material production and consumption. For example, as expenditure on online reading and recreation increases significantly, the corresponding services can be provided in a more dispersed, convenient and cheaper way. Services like massive online open courses (MOOC) and distance services for medical care, agriculture and production can be provided via ICT. From a Boeing 747 to an i-Phone, tangible materials take up an increasingly smaller proportion of value added, while information and technology account for an increasing proportion.

The downgrading of use and output of materials has significant implications. Since intangible products, like the environment and knowledge, are non-rival, they can be used and consumed innumerable times with almost zero marginal cost. This substantially enhances productivity in a fundamental sense. It leads to sustainable low material consumption, low-carbon emissions, and environmental protection, while the economy continues to grow. Meanwhile, as the production and consumption of dematerialised products do not particularly rely on the physical concentration of populations and goods, they in turn greatly enhance transaction efficiency and accelerate the evolution of the structure of the division of labour.

Opportunities created by green growth in poor regions

Since green growth is substantially different from traditional industrialisation established since the Industrial Revolution, many conventional development views formed under traditional industrialisation are no longer applicable. For poor regions, enormous new opportunities are emerging in green growth.

First, poor regions may undertake a different pattern of urbanisation to achieve economic prosperity. The conventional development notion treats economic development as a process of urbanisation in the form of massive population transfers from rural areas to big cities. Population concentration can greatly enhance transaction efficiency and minimise the cost of providing utilities and public services, generating the so-called agglomeration effect, economies of specialisation and economies of scale. Hence, the core value of urbanisation is to improve transaction efficiency and lower the cost of public services. Due to the rapid development of the Internet, ICT, transportation and logistics systems, however, transaction efficiency has been dramatically improved and public services can largely be provided online, so the physical

---

2   The dematerialisation is substantially different from the increase of the service sector's share occurring at an advanced stage of development. The change is irrelevant to development stages, but the value of intangible products and services should be fully recognised.

concentration of populations is much less important for economic development. Therefore, poor areas do not have to follow a conventional urbanisation pattern. This is especially the case since green growth in poor regions will be based substantially on their immovable natural ecology and rich local cultures and customs. Smaller towns and rural communities connected with ICT and fast transport may be an alternative path to take.

Second, with the change in the concept of resources, the advantages of poor regions are standing out, as a healthy ecological environment is an invaluable resource for green growth. The traditional industrialisation model relies on inputs of tangible material resources and neglects the value of intangible resources. Intangible resources, however, like the ecological environment and online social capital, can all be translated into wealth. For instance, expenditure on experiencing local culture has considerable value. In many poor areas, intangible local cultural and natural resources have been well conserved due to underdevelopment. Environmental resources—unlike coal and oil—are inexhaustible and non-rival, which means that, within carrying capacity, almost no marginal cost is incurred as more people enjoy the environmental services and more industries are based on it.

Third, the change in business mode brings about new opportunities for poor areas. E-commerce has stimulated enormous new business models. China's online shopping market has been growing rapidly. According to McKinsey and Company (2013), China's online shopping volume reached US$190 billion in 2012—almost equal to that of the United States. By 2020, the trading volume of online shopping in China will reach up to US$650 billion and surpass that of the United States, the United Kingdom, Japan, Germany and France combined. This has significant implications for economic development in poor areas. According to Smith's theorem, the division of labour is limited by the extent of the market. In the past, local markets in poor areas have been too small to support local economic development. Nowadays, with online trade, the market in poor areas has been dramatically expanded through direct links to advanced national and global markets. Moreover, consumers in poor areas can also conveniently buy goods from outside markets. The convenient transaction conditions lead to rapid expansion of market scale and provide necessary conditions for enlarging the production chain in poor areas.

Fourth, modern green agriculture in poor areas could be a high-value sector. Agriculture no longer equates with low productivity. In a traditional sense, economic development means to 'eliminate' farmers through industrialisation; however, great changes are currently occurring. Modern agriculture organised according to modern corporate systems based on a good ecological environment could be very profitable. Also, agricultural production organised according to the modern mode has become an industry integrating agriculture, processing and services. As transaction efficiency increases greatly, the market value of agricultural products produced in remote villages with healthy ecological environments could be significantly appreciated if sold in the high-end market.

Fifth, in the new development paradigm, farmers' labour activities might produce extra value added. For example, from the traditional perspective, farmers' work in paddy fields only produces rice. Nonetheless, the farmers' labour activities also produce scenery and experience that could be a big attraction to tourists. This is an example of how the resources that would previously have been neglected can be fully utilised in a new growth paradigm that is based more on non-material resources.

Sixth, the new patterns of economic development make it easier for poor areas to take a new industrialisation path. Unlike the traditional industrial mode of large-scale production, the third industrial revolution represented by three-dimensional manufacturing is a distributed and customised mode of production, in which more knowledge is compressed into less material resources. In China, some poor regions see the transfer old industries from the coastal areas as a big opportunity; however, this so-called opportunity is still on the traditional industrialisation path. Poor areas and countries should not depend on such industries and repeat the old model of 'pollution first and clean-up later'. They should go along a new manufacturing path by seizing the opportunity of the latest industrial revolution to outperform developed areas.

Seventh, it is possible for poor regions to overcome the barriers to development by taking advantage of ICT. For instance, the MOOC and online medical and educational services make it possible for poor regions to share the high-quality educational and medical services of the developed areas. The online provision of services goes beyond the limitations of time and space, and professionals do not have to travel to the poor regions in person to provide their services. Therefore, the lack of talent, education, medical care and so on in poor areas can be overcome in a different way by taking advantage of ICT.

Eighth, new energy resources have enormous potential in poor regions. This is particularly the case in China, since new energy resources including solar, wind and hydro-electric energy are richest in poor areas. In particular, the new distributed energy mode with feed-in-tariffs can provide a stable revenue source for individual farming households. With rapid development of new energy technologies, the cost of new energy resources is declining quickly. According to the *2011 Renewable Energy Report* of the United Nations (IPCC, 2011), new energy resources are expected to meet 80 per cent of global energy demands by 2050, and therefore are economically feasible.

Ninth, ecological and environmental protection in poor regions can become a new source of revenue. The following examples explain how. Some have argued that to shut down a polluting factory would decrease GDP; however, the output of a polluting factory may lead to greater losses for the surrounding area. Therefore, closing the factory or forcing it to clean up might actually improve output and the welfare of the whole society. Furthermore, environmental protection may enable the economy to jump to a more competitive structure for the division of labour. Take ecosystem services payments as an example. Ecological protection is of great value because it brings about: 1) increase in value of agricultural products, such as food, fibre and fuel; 2) ecological regulating services (such as pollinating crops, purifying water and stabilising climate); 3) cultural services (many industries can be developed based on a healthy ecological environment); and 4) ecological support services (Vincent 2012). For the ecological regulating services, if the upstream environment of a system is well protected, losses downstream will be greatly reduced, and its output will increase. The ecological services provided by the upstream environment cannot, however, be sold directly in the market, so provision of ecological services has little returns from the market. In this situation, it is difficult to have a 'win-win' outcome between the upstream and downstream, so the upstream adopts behaviour such as destroying forests to obtain short-term income. Consequently, ecological deterioration continues and a 'lose-lose' structure becomes reality. In this case, the Government must step in to identify the beneficiaries of ecological services in the downstream areas and charge them, and pay for upstream protection through transfer payments. This makes environmental services provision a self-interested behaviour and lead to a 'win-win' situation.

Tenth, regional cooperation to reduce carbon emissions can bring about considerable benefits for poor regions. Carbon emission entitlements are increasingly becoming a scarce resource. Once a country sets a goal for carbon emissions reduction, or an emissions cap, emissions entitlements become valuable. If carbon emission entitlements are allocated among all areas on a per capita principle, poor areas with low per capita emissions can benefit by selling carbon emission entitlements to developed areas, while taking a new low-carbon development path.

Finally, for poor areas, in addition to the revenues they can receive from ecological services, the most promising source of growth is to develop industries based on their high-quality environment. In a poor area, various services taking advantage of a healthy natural environment—such as an international convention centre, resorts, recreation, medical treatment, sports, health care, education, summer camps, music festivals, cultural creativity, and so on—can be developed in a relatively short period by taking advantage of ICT.

Mechanisms and policymaking for green growth

Challenges to the existing development model in China

Green growth poses quite a big challenge to China's long-established government-led development model. Green growth is largely decentralised and highly market-based, like the ICT industry or distributed renewable energy. The traditional Chinese growth model, however, especially the rapid development of some underdeveloped central and western regions in recent years, mostly depends on investment from the large enterprises owned by the Central Government. Though GDP in these poor areas has been quickly increased, it has resulted in enormous environmental damage, and ordinary people's incomes have not risen proportionately.

Over the past three decades, as a catch-up economy, China has been mainly copying the development path of Western countries. Green growth, however, must rely on innovation. When there's a target ahead, it is relatively easy for the Government to copy in decision-making. However, for green development, China has nothing to copy since green development is new in all countries. Only strongly innovative countries will become leaders in green growth.

How to achieve green growth in poor areas

The basic idea to make the green growth path a lever for promoting development in poor areas is to turn vital ecological qualities into wealth, by taking advantage of modern technologies and new business models. The following 'three pillars plus five policies' framework is particularly essential.

Pillar 1: Imposing a strict policy of environmental protection

The natural environment is a big assets for economic development in poor areas. The Government should implement the most stringent policies of environmental protection and emission mitigation. Strong government action on the environment is a requirement for the market to function well and for the improvement of the welfare of the whole society.

Pillar 2: Building up green infrastructure

The Government should vigorously build up green infrastructure in poor areas, which will create the conditions to convert the natural resources into wealth. Efforts should focus on the development of Internet access, ICT, fast transportation, logistics systems and renewable energy in poor regions.

Pillar 3: Establishing an effective mechanism to 'turn green into wealth'

In addition to the above conditions, the Government and the market must play their respective roles. Specifically, the Government can focus on the following five policies.

First, governments can use the new model to directly provide high-quality public goods and services to poor areas. For instance, by taking advantage of ICT, the Central Government can, at very low cost, easily provide poor areas with high-quality education, health care, manufacturing services, and access to online talent and other resources as public goods, so as to overcome the hurdles poor areas face in their development.

Second, the Government should introduce urban market forces into poor areas by deepening structural reforms. In particular, the Government should attract urban capital and talent to poor areas through land reform. Poor areas are unlikely to achieve economic take-off by relying on poorly educated local farmers. It is essential to completely lift the barriers separating urban and rural areas so as to facilitate the free flow of capital, talent and other resources from urban to rural areas. If rural land system can be reformed to allow urban residents to settle in rural areas, it would awaken the huge sleeping wealth in poor areas.

Third, strict environmental policies should be implemented on a market basis. This includes: 1) establishing and further improving ecosystem services payments; and 2) setting up a diversified system of emission reduction, including an emissions trading scheme.

Fourth, policies should be developed governing capacity-building and fostering green industries, including fiscal and tax reforms. At present, the deficiencies in fiscal and tax systems are an important factor preventing poor areas from taking the green growth path. Under such a system, local governments have a strong incentive to introduce high-pollution industrial projects with high output so as to quickly raise taxes and improve their capability for public service provision.

Finally, the Government should undertake some regional pilot projects for green growth. China has initiated a new round of comprehensive programs for deepening reform. Such institutional reforms will provide huge benefits for China's economic development. The eighteenth CPC National Congress proposed the concept of an ecological civilisation. China could set up a number of special ecological civilisation zones in which to experiment with some major relevant reforms.

Concluding remarks

To sum up, it is no longer feasible for poor regions to rise out of poverty and further achieve prosperity through the traditional development path that the industrialised countries took after the Industrial Revolution. All economies, including poor, rapidly developing and developed countries, need to take a new path of green growth. Green growth represents a development paradigm shift and could become a new lever to promote development in poor areas.

Poor areas possess unique advantages for green growth. Due to 'underdevelopment', most of these areas retain vital ecological and cultural advantages that become important, scarce resources for economic development. Especially with the support of the Internet, ICT, online shopping, and fast transport and logistics systems, this advantage becomes outstanding, and most of the traditional development constraints facing poor areas in the past are being overcome, and more and more opportunities are emerging.

Though this chapter focuses on the opportunities that green growth may bring for poor areas in the context of China, most of the ongoing changes under the new paradigm of green growth are universal. Its principle is applicable for economic development in the least-developed countries. Poor areas have their unique advantages to grow their economies in the green growth paradigm. If this exploration turns out to be successful in some areas, it would be a great contribution with global significance for other places in the world, including underdeveloped African countries. The paradigm the developed countries established from the Industrial Revolution can enable only a small portion of people on the planet to enjoy prosperity. The new path of green growth aims to bring about shared prosperity for the whole world.

References

Barbier, E.B. (2005), *Natural Resources and Economic Development*, Cambridge University Press, Cambridge.

Coase, R. (1937), 'The nature of the firm', *Economica* 4(16): 386–405.

Dercon, S. (2012), *Is green growth good for the poor?*, Policy Research Working Paper 6231, The World Bank, Washington, DC.

IPCC, 2011: IPCC Special Report on Renewable Energy Sources and Climate Change Mitigation. Prepared by Working Group III of the Intergovernmental Panel on Climate Change [O. Edenhofer, R. Pichs-Madruga, Y. Sokona, K. Seyboth, P. Matschoss, S. Kadner, T. Zwickel, P. Eickemeier, G. Hansen, S. Schlömer, C. von Stechow (eds)]. Cambridge University Press, Cambridge, United Kingdom and New York, NY, USA, 1075 pp.

King, M. (2013), *Green growth and poverty reduction: policy coherence for pro-poor growth*, OECD Working Papers No. 14, Paris: OECD Publishing. Available from <http://dx.doi.org/10.1787/5k3ttg45wb31-en>.

McKinsey & Company (2013), China's e-tail revolution: Online shopping as a catalyst for growth, March 2013. Available from <http://www.mckinsey.com/insights/asia-pacific/china_e-tailing>.

Rockström, J., Steffen, W., Noone, K., Persson, Å., Chapin, F. S., Lambin, E. F., Lenton, T. M., Scheffer, M. and Folke, C. (2009), 'A safe operating space for humanity', *Nature* 461: 472–75.

Smith, A. (1776), *An Inquiry into the Nature and Causes of the Wealth of Nations*, London: W. Strahan & T. Cadell.

United Nations Environment Program (UNEP) (2011), *Towards a Green Economy: Pathways to Sustainable Development and Poverty Eradication—A Synthesis for Policy Makers*, Washington, DC: UNEP. Available from <http://www.unep.org/greeneconomy>.

Vincent, J. R. (2012), *Ecosystem services and green growth*, Policy Research Working Paper 6233, The World Bank, Washington, DC.

World Bank and Development Research Center of the State Council (DRC) (2012), 'Seizing the opportunity of green development in China', in *China 2030*, Washington, DC: The World Bank.

Yang, X. (2001), *Economics: New Classical versus Neoclassical Frameworks*, New York: Blackwell.

Yang, X. (2003), Economic Development and the Division of Labor, New York, Blackwell.

Young, A. (1928), 'Increasing returns and economic progress', *The Economic Journal* 38: 527–542.

9. China's Climate and Energy Policy:

On Track to Low-carbon Growth?

Frank Jotzo and Fei Teng[1]

Introduction

China has become the world's largest emitter of greenhouse gases, and in many ways is the linchpin of global climate change policy. If China's coal use and carbon dioxide emissions keep growing alongside GDP then current global goals for limiting climate change will be out of reach. If, however, China manages to decouple its emissions trajectory from its economic growth then ambitious global emissions reductions scenarios remain feasible, and other industrialising countries may be inclined to emulate China's pathway.

For China's policymakers, climate policy goes hand in hand with other objectives, including reducing local air pollution, improving energy security and attaining a leadership position in advanced manufacturing technologies. The various targets to 2020 for emissions, energy use and energy technologies reflect this. China appears on track to achieving these, but action commensurate with strong global climate change mitigation during the following decade will require ongoing and strengthening policy effort.

China's climate change policy is intricately linked to two fundamental aspects of China's economic trajectory. First, macro-economic 'rebalancing', less rapid GDP growth and ongoing structural change in China's economy could facilitate a marked slowdown in the growth rate of energy demand, and hence carbon dioxide emissions.

Second, continuing the drive for market reform in China's economy, as the new leadership seems intent on, can help China achieve emissions reductions at lower economic cost. Putting a price on carbon emissions—by way of emissions trading or a carbon tax—can be more cost-effective than the command-and-control approach that has been dominant until now. To function well, however, this will require market reform in China's energy sector. Climate policy is thus part of the broader picture of economic and market reform in China.

---

1   Work for this chapter was in part supported by an Australian government grant under the Australia-China research program on climate change mitigation policy. Thanks to Shenghao Feng for research assistance.

It is now widely accepted that market mechanisms should play a key role in long-term climate policy in China, with seven regional emissions trading schemes a highly visible statement of policy intent.

In this chapter, we provide an update on China's emissions trends and its trajectory towards the 2020 emissions intensity target; an overview of China's moves to market-based climate change mitigation policies with a brief discussion of the seven emissions trading pilot schemes, most of which have recently come into operation; and a discussion of the need for reform in China's energy policy to make market instruments for climate change policy effective.

China's energy use and emissions: an update

China in international comparison

China overtook the United States as the largest emitter of carbon dioxide in 2006 (IEA 2013a). In 2011, China accounted for 21 per cent of global energy demand, 49 per cent of global coal use by energy content and 26 per cent of global energy-related carbon dioxide emissions (IEA 2013b; see Figure 9.1). China's per capita emissions have risen above the world average and are almost as high as those in the EU average, though still little higher than one-third of per capita emissions in the United States, Canada and Australia.

The primary reason for the rise in China's emissions has been China's very rapid economic growth, which has come with very rapid increases in energy use, and the bulk of the additional energy used is supplied from fossil fuels, in particular coal—the most carbon-intensive fuel.

China's challenge, and opportunity, in reining in emissions growth is the relatively high emissions intensity of its economy (Table 9.1). China's carbon dioxide output for every dollar of GDP, adjusted for purchasing power in 2011, was twice that of the United States and three times that of Europe. The ratios are 4.5:1 and about 7:1 when measuring GDP at exchange rates.[2]

The comparatively high emissions intensity of China's economy is primarily due to a comparatively high amount of energy used per unit of GDP, and also because of a relatively high amount of carbon dioxide per unit of energy used.

---

2 GDP at exchange rates is usually not a suitable measure for comparison across economies, but is relevant for the traded commodity sectors of the economy, including heavy industries, which are important in China's emissions profile.

The reasons for high energy intensity are found partly in China's economic structure, with a relatively high share of economic activity in heavy industries, supplying the rapid expansion of domestic infrastructure as well as exports, and partly in relatively low energy efficiency in many (though not all) industries and processes.

Both aspects provide great potential for improvement of China's energy intensity. China's infrastructure investment boom is slowing and the investment ratio in GDP is expected to fall, and it is likely the composition of China's exports will continue evolving to higher-value manufacturing.

Ongoing modernisation of industrial production facilities steadily improves the average technical energy efficiency of production in areas such as electricity generation (where new coal-fired power plants are typically of very high energy efficiency), steel production, chemical manufacturing and other industrial activities. There is also large scope for improvements in the energy efficiency of buildings and cars.

The relatively high emissions intensity of China's energy supply—around 20 per cent above US and global levels, and 36 per cent above average EU levels— is primarily due to the dominance of coal in China's energy supply. As discussed below, it is a Chinese policy objective to reduce the share of coal in the energy supply, with resulting reductions in the carbon intensity of the energy system.

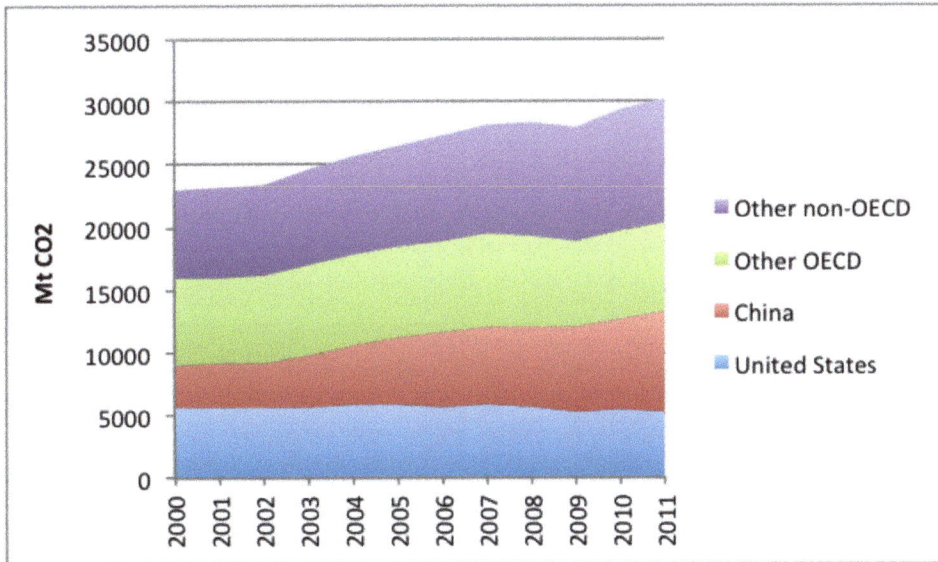

Figure 9.1 Global Carbon Dioxide Emissions

Source: IEA (2013a).

Note: Emissions of carbon dioxide from fossil fuel combustion.

Table 9.1 Emissions and Energy Intensity, Selected Countries and Regions, 2011

	Emissions per capita	Emissions intensity of the economy		Energy intensity of the economy		Emissions intensity of energy supply
	CO_2 emissions/ population (t CO_2 / capita)	CO_2 emissions/ GDP using purchasing power parity	CO_2 emissions/ GDP using exchange rates	Total primary energy supply/ GDP using purchasing power parity	Total primary energy supply/GDP using exchange rates	CO_2 emissions/ total primary energy supply (t CO_2/ terajoule)
		(t CO_2/US\$'000 [2005 prices])		(petajoules/US\$ billion [2005 prices])		
China	5.9	0.78	1.81	11.2	25.9	69.7
United States	16.9	0.40	0.40	6.9	6.9	57.6
European Union—27	7.0	0.25	0.24	4.9	4.7	51.2
OECD average	9.9	0.33	0.32	5.9	5.8	55.6
Non-OECD average	3.1	0.55	1.26	9.6	21.9	57.4
World	4.5	0.45	0.60	7.8	10.5	57.1

Source: IEA (2013a).

Trends in energy use, composition and carbon dioxide emissions

China's energy consumption grew by 8 per cent per year on average over the decade to 2011. Preliminary data for 2012 and 2013, however, indicate that growth in energy consumption is slowing, and that consumption of coal—the most carbon-intensive fuel—has been growing more slowly than energy consumption overall in the past two years (Table 9.2). As a result of slower GDP growth and also a greater rate of reduction in energy intensity of GDP, carbon dioxide emissions growth has slowed, although annual growth rates are still high compared with most other countries. The carbon intensity of energy supply has remained almost unchanged. According to our calculations, the emissions intensity of GDP fell by 3.9 per cent and 3.5 per cent during 2012 and 2013, respectively.

A caveat is in order on the data for 2012 and 2013. Our calculations in Table 9.2 rely on 2012 and 2013 growth rates for consumption of each fossil fuel, as reported in the *Statistical Communiqué of the People's Republic of China* (NBS various years), and data for earlier years as reported by the International Energy Agency (IEA 2013a). Emissions levels for 2012 and 2013 are inferred by grafting data for growth in energy use by fuel onto IEA data of carbon dioxide emission by fuel in 2011. The data in the *Statistical Communiqué* are often later revised in the *Statistical Yearbook*, which is considered a more authoritative data source.

No official Chinese data for carbon dioxide emissions levels are available, and internationally accepted data for emissions (for example, by the IEA) are available only to 2011. There has been, however, a recent official communication that emissions intensity fell by 10.7 per cent from 2010 to 2013, and energy intensity by 9 per cent. These official data for the period 2010–13 are reflected in Table 9.4; the data in Table 9.2 have the same underpinning features but do not match the official statement.

Looking at preliminary statistics for energy use by fuel reveals that the slowdown in emissions growth is mostly due to a deceleration in the growth of coal use. The annual average increase in coal use was around 8 per cent during the period 2005–11; according to preliminary data for 2012 and 2013, it slowed to around just 3 per cent per year during these past two years (Table 9.3). Coal accounted for 83 per cent of China's fossil fuel emissions during 2011, oil for 14 per cent and gas for 3 per cent (IEA 2013a).

The year 2012 was unusual in that there was an unusually large amount of hydroelectricity available due to heavy rains, and nuclear power plants came back online after temporary shutdown in the wake of the Fukushima nuclear accident in Japan. The fact that coal-use growth did not jump back to historical levels during 2013 indicates, however, that a more permanent effect might be at play.

A much discussed question is whether this slowdown in coal demand growth is a one-off or whether it is a permanent feature, which might lead to a stabilisation of absolute levels of coal used in the Chinese economy, and eventually a decline. This is discussed further below.

Table 9.2 Growth Rates in GDP, Energy Use, Carbon Dioxide Emissions and Intensities, China (per cent)

	Real GDP	Energy consumption	Carbon dioxide emissions	Emissions intensity of GDP	Energy intensity of GDP	Carbon intensity of energy
2005	10.4	10.6	11.7	1.2	0.1	1.0
2006	12.7	9.6	9.4	−2.9	−2.7	−0.1
2007	14.2	8.4	6.8	−6.5	−5.0	−1.5
2008	9.6	3.9	2.7	−6.3	−5.2	−1.1
2009	9.2	5.2	4.7	−4.1	−3.6	−0.5
2010	10.4	6.0	6.8	−3.3	−4.0	0.8
2011	9.3	7.0	9.7	0.3	−2.1	2.5
2012[a]	7.7	3.9	3.5	−3.9	−3.5	−0.3
2013[a]	7.7	3.7	4.0	−3.5	−3.7	0.3
2005−11 average	10.8	7.2	7.4	−3.1	−3.2	0.1
2012−13 average[a]	7.7	3.8	3.8	−3.7	−3.6	0.0

[a] Emissions and emissions intensity data for 2012 and 2013 are our approximations on the basis of data described below.

Sources: GDP and energy consumption for 2005–11 are from *China Energy Statistical Yearbook* (NBS 2011); growth rates for 2012 and 2013 are from *Statistical Communiqué of the People's Republic of China* (NBS various years), with data subject to revision; carbon dioxide emissions between 2005 and 2011 are from IEA (2013a); carbon dioxide emissions growth rates for 2012 and 2013 are inferred by applying the 2012 and 2013 growth rates for the use of coal, oil and gas (see Table 9.3) to the 2011 emissions data by fuel in IEA (2013a), and aggregating. See text for caveats.

Table 9.3 Growth Rates in Fossil Fuel Energy Use, China (per cent)

	Total energy consumption	Coal consumption	Oil consumption	Gas consumption
2005	10.6	10.6	2.1	20.6
2006	9.6	9.6	7.1	19.9
2007	8.4	7.9	6.3	19.9
2008	3.9	3.0	5.1	10.1
2009	5.2	9.2	7.1	9.1
2010	6.0	5.3	12.9	18.2
2011	7.0	9.7	2.7	12.0
2012	3.9	2.5	6.0	10.2
2013	3.7	3.7	3.4	13.0
2005−11 average	7.2	7.9	6.1	15.6
2012−13 average	3.8	3.1	4.7	11.6

Sources: Total energy consumption for 2005–11 are from *China Energy Statistical Yearbook* (NBS 2011); growth rates for 2012 and 2013 are from *Statistical Communiqué of the People's Republic of China* (NBS various years), with data subject to revision.

Emissions intensity targets

China has framed its aggregate goals for energy use and emissions in terms of the energy intensity and emissions intensity of the economy—that is, the amount of energy used and carbon dioxide emissions produced per unit of GDP.

China has a national target to reduce the emissions intensity of the economy (the ratio of carbon dioxide emissions to GDP) by 40 to 45 per cent from 2005 to 2020. The 45 per cent target will require an annual average reduction in emissions intensity of 3.9 per cent over that 15-year period. The target is expected to require significant efforts compared with a business-as-usual scenario (Stern and Jotzo 2010; McKibbin et al. 2011). There are also intensity targets in place for the five-year periods of the Eleventh and Twelfth Five-Year Plans (Table 9.4).

Emissions intensity targets are unusual in the international context, where most developed countries have adopted absolute emissions reductions targets. An emissions intensity target, however, is a relevant way of framing the policy goal. It addresses directly the key concern of climate change mitigation policy, which is to decarbonise economic activity, irrespective of the rate of economic growth. An emissions intensity target can also act as an automatic adjustment if GDP growth is volatile. It guards against overly large required emissions reduction efforts if GDP growth turns out to be very high, and ensures greater absolute emissions reductions than an absolute target if GDP growth is lower than expected (Jotzo and Pezzey 2007).

Both the energy intensity and the emissions intensity of the economy declined by 26 per cent from 2005 to 2013 (data and caveats as per Table 9.2), while carbon dioxide emissions per unit of energy (carbon intensity of energy) have remained stable. The reduction in energy intensity of the economy derives from two effects: first, improved energy efficiency—for example, through deployment of more energy-efficient power stations, industrial installations and cars; and second, as the result of changes in the composition of the economy, with lower energy-using sectors contributing a growing share of GDP.

Table 9.4 Emissions Intensity and Energy Intensity Targets and Performance (per cent)

	Emissions intensity change (ratio of carbon dioxide emissions to GDP)		Energy intensity change (ratio of total primary energy demand to GDP)		Carbon intensity change (ratio of emissions to energy demand)
	Target	Actual	Target	Actual	Actual
2005–10	n.a.	−21	−20	−19	−3
2010–13	n.a.	−10.7	n.a.	−9	−1.7
2010–15	−17	..	−16		..
2005–20	−40 to −45	..	n.a.	..	..

n.a. = not applicable

.. = not available

Sources: Actuals for 2005–10 from IEA (2013a) and for 2010–13 from Xinhua (2014); targets from Lewis (2011).

Outlook for emissions intensity

Given the rapid changes in the nature of China's economic growth and the dynamic policy environment, it is difficult to make predictions about the future trajectory of emissions intensity. However, some factors can be identified.

First, it may be that improvements in technical energy efficiency are becoming more difficult to achieve, as the low-hanging fruits such as replacing inefficient and outdated plants with new technology have been implemented.

Second, it is an open question as to what extent continued change in the composition of the economy can drive further reductions in energy intensity. It could be that structural change will become a more important driver of reductions in emissions intensity, and remain so for a long time. This question is crucial for China's longer-term emissions trajectory.

Third, reductions in the carbon intensity of its energy supply could play a greater role in future, especially if the rate of energy demand growth tails off. Together with increasing policy effort to dampen coal use, it is plausible that we will see a greater share of renewable energy sources such as wind and solar power as well as hydroelectricity, and also an increasing share of nuclear power in the overall energy mix.

A greater role for natural gas in the power system and industry—displacing coal, which is roughly twice as carbon intensive per unit of energy—may also assist. China does not, however, have large conventional gas deposits—it remains unclear to what extent shale gas can be exploited in China—and there are limits to reliance on large-scale importing of gas, which comes via pipeline from Russia or Central Asia, or by ship in the form of liquefied natural gas.

In the longer term, carbon capture and storage from fossil fuel-fired power stations and industrial installations are potentially an option to drastically reduce the carbon intensity of the energy system. The technology to date, however, is applied globally only in a small number of industrial installations and not in large-scale power stations. Just as importantly, applying carbon capture and storage is expected to remain costly.

What does China's 2020 emissions intensity target imply?

The 26 per cent decline in emissions intensity from 2005 to 2013 is broadly on the trajectory to achieve the target of a 40–45 per cent reduction from 2005 to 2020.

The dominant view in the expert community is that the 2020 target will be achieved. A survey of China-based experts (Jotzo et al. 2013) indicated strong confidence that the existing 2020 target will be achieved or surpassed. Of respondents, 87 per cent stated that they expect China will achieve or surpass its emissions intensity target; among them one-third believes the target will be surpassed.

What does the intensity target mean for absolute emissions levels? As long as GDP growth rates are above the targeted rates of decarbonisation then absolute emissions can continue to increase; however, a slowdown in economic growth rates would curtail the 'allowable' absolute amount of carbon dioxide emissions considerably.

The intensity target can be translated into absolute emissions levels by combining data for 2005–13 with an assumed rate of GDP growth from 2014 to 2020. The official target GDP growth rate for 2014 is 7.5 per cent. Huang et al. (2013) see China's growth potential for the current decade at 6–8 per cent per year. It follows that any disruptions to the growth experience could result in significantly lower GDP growth than the 7 per cent annual growth often used as a default assumption, though faster growth is of course also possible.

Assume, for illustration, annual average GDP growth for the remainder of the decade of 8 per cent per year as a 'high' case and 5 per cent as a 'low' case. The latter would be considered very low indeed, and in previous years such 'slow' growth scenarios have often been seen as unrealistic, however, signs are emerging that Chinese GDP growth is moderating, and that the Chinese Government may prioritise the quality of growth over maximising the rate of economic expansion.

If GDP were to grow at an average annual rate of 8 per cent between 2014 and 2020 then reducing emissions intensity by 45 per cent over the period 2005–20 implies that absolute emissions in China may increase by 29 per cent from 2013 levels to 2020 (Table 9.5).

In contrast, if GDP were to grow at an average rate of only 5 per cent per year during 2014–20, the same intensity target implies an increase in emissions of only 6 per cent over 2013 levels, or by 15 per cent for the less stringent emissions intensity target, over the remainder of the decade. Under such a low growth scenario, current trends in emissions would see the remaining 'headroom' for emissions growth well before 2020.

Table 9.5 'Allowable' Total Increases in Emissions between 2013 and 2020 for Different Scenarios of GDP Growth and Different Reductions in Emissions Intensity from 2005 to 2020

	40% reduction target	45% reduction target
5% GDP growth	15%	6%
8% GDP growth	40%	29%

Sources: GDP and energy consumption for 2005–11 are from *China Energy Statistical Yearbook* (NBS 2011); growth rates for 2012 and 2013 are from *Statistical Communiqué of the People's Republic of China* (NBS various years), with data subject to revision; carbon dioxide emissions between 2005 and 2011 are from IEA (2013a); carbon dioxide emissions growth rates for 2012 and 2013 are approximated by applying the 2012 and 2013 growth rates for the use of coal, oil and gas (see Table 9.3) to the 2011 emissions data by fuel in IEA (2013a), and aggregating.

Note: For the purposes of this calculation, 2013 carbon dioxide levels are 58 per cent above 2005 levels, and 2013 GDP levels are 116 per cent above 2005 levels.

Post-2020 trajectories and targets

China, along with all other major countries, is expected to submit a target for its emissions for the period 2020–25 or 2020–30, as part of the preparations for a new international climate change agreement aimed for at the UN climate conference at the end of 2015. Termed 'intended nationally determined contributions', these targets are not expected to be legally binding.

China has given no official indications of the nature and stringency of a post-2020 emissions target. There has been speculation that China might take on a target for absolute emissions levels rather than an intensity target. In a survey of experts (Jotzo et al. 2013), around 40 per cent of respondents expected an absolute target to be in place by 2025, and around 70 per cent by 2030. But it should be noted that such an absolute target might not be an absolute *reduction* target—it could provide a ceiling for China's emissions in the post-2020 period but still allow for moderate increases and then a peak and decline.

An increasing amount of quantitative analysis revolves around the question of when China's emissions will peak, and at what level.

As an illustration of the wide range of trajectories considered by analysts, see the three core scenarios produced by the IEA's *World Energy Outlook* (IEA 2013b) in Figure 9.2. Under the specific assumptions made by the IEA, continuation of current policies would see China's national emissions increasing until after the 2035 projection horizon; a scenario with new, additional policies would have emissions levels flattening out by 2030, at levels about 20 per cent below those in the 'current policy' scenario and about a quarter above current levels. A trajectory compatible with the globally shared ambition of limiting global warming to 2°—the so-called '450 scenario'—would see China's emissions falling drastically through the 2020s and beyond, to levels around half present levels by 2035.

Few analysts consider a scenario of early peaking in emissions followed by rapid reductions likely; however, as shown in technical analyses (for example, Jiang et al. 2013), China's carbon emissions could peak in the next decade, if options for energy efficiency and fuel switching are pursued across the economy and shifts occur in the patterns of production and consumption.

The peaking of China's emissions is also closely linked with the unknown future of China's economic growth. China's GDP growth in the past three decades has been about 10 per cent per year and the annual reduction rate of emissions intensity has been in the order of 4.5 per cent per year. Therefore, China's emissions have increased by about 5–5.5 per cent annually on average in past decades. If China can maintain this trend to reduce its emissions intensity, it can peak its emissions when the GDP growth rate falls from the current 8 per cent range to about 5 per cent per year.

So the fundamental question is twofold: when China's GDP growth rate will fall to a level equal to the rate of emissions intensity reduction; and whether there will be a more ambitious policy that can further improve the annual emissions intensity to achieve a peak in China's emissions at relatively high GDP growth rates.

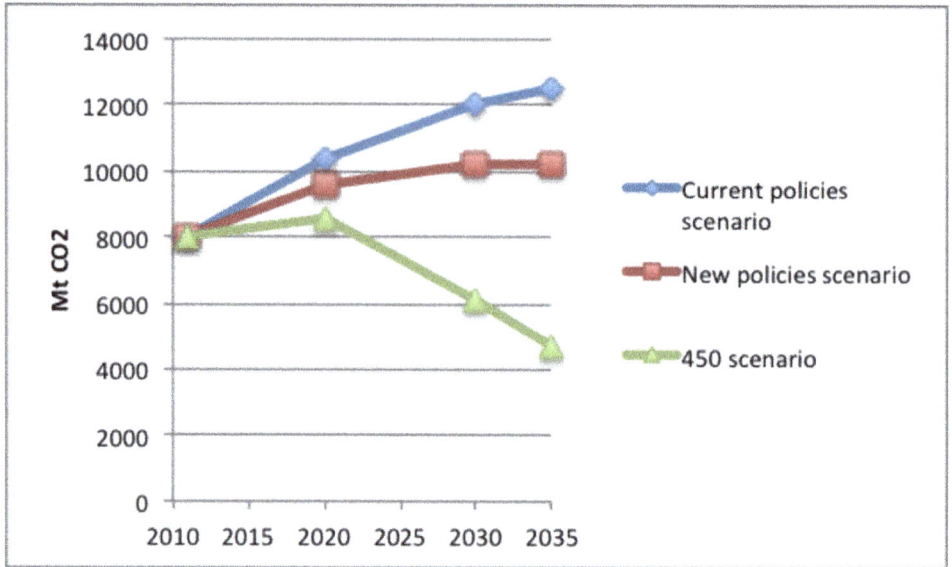

Figure 9.2 IEA Scenarios for China's Future National Emissions Levels
Source: IEA (2013b).

Challenges in China's energy sector

Current challenge in energy sectors

Adjusting the economic structure is necessary to develop China's economy since economic development is confronted with the prerequisite of energy constraints. The energy system in China faces many problems, among which are three prominent ones: the difficulties in the adjustment of energy structure, the dilemma of fossil fuel energy's growth, and pressure from the ever-increasing dependence on foreign energy.

Adjustment of energy structure

China is currently in the period of industrialisation with the total energy demand growing continuously. Although new and renewable energy sources have developed rapidly in recent years, the proportion in the total energy supply is still relatively low, and increases in renewable energy capacity have not been meeting the increases in demand.

Growth of the total amount of fossil fuel energy

Despite the rapid development of renewable energy and various energy-saving measures, rapid growth in energy demand leads to the growing consumption of coal, oil and other fossil fuel energies. While the growth rate is lower, the growth of fossil fuel energy has caused serious environmental problems, which have drawn more and more attention. The lingering thick smog and hazy weather in Beijing, Tianjin and Hebei provinces—namely, the problem of particulate matter (PM) 2.5 exceeding health standards—are mainly caused by coal combustion and vehicle exhaust emissions. Thus in order to solve environmental problems fundamentally, the structure of energy must be changed and the total amount of coal consumption must be controlled. Beijing, Tianjin and Hebei have now developed goals to control coal consumption.

Continuous rise of dependence on foreign energy

With growing energy demand, China's energy has increasingly depended on foreign sources. It is estimated that the proportion of imported oil will reach 70 per cent and natural gas 50 per cent by 2020, so dependence on overseas sources makes energy security an important focus of policy. Since the international environment is peaceful, energy supplies are unlikely to be interrupted; however, emergencies in some regions and geopolitical factors may cause a temporary shortage of supply and price fluctuations, which introduce risk to the stable operation of the economy.

Therefore, how to balance energy security, increase the supply of energy and solve the environmental problems are significant challenges for the energy system in China.

An energy strategy to manage demand

Ensuring energy supply has long been the main consideration in China's energy strategy. The level of supply accords with the demands of national economic and social development. Currently in China, however, especially in the context of climate change, reducing the consumption of fossil fuel energy is an important objective. The aim of China's energy strategy is not only to ensure supply, but also to adjust and guide demand, using policy to regulate and control requirements,.

China has proposed 'to promote the transformation of energy production and utilisation' in the Twelfth Five-Year Plan, which means improving energy efficiency, to plan energy production and to make the transition to renewable and clean energy.

The report of the Eighteenth CPC National Congress further highlighted this issue and altered the proposal from 'transformation of energy production and utilisation' to 'revolution of energy production and consumption'. There are two key changes. One is replacing 'utilisation' by 'consumption'. The emphasis on energy consumption reflects the desire to reduce unreasonable or adjustable energy demands. Replacing 'transformation' with 'revolution' means changing the energy system in a more intense and thorough way in order to adapt to the needs of economic and social development.

Phasing out coal

Fast-growing coal consumption in China has led to various problems. First, coal has been considered a domestic and safe recourse, but China has become a net coal importer since 2010, which poses an additional challenge to China's energy security concerns. Second, coalmining and consumption have added to acute local environmental issues. Substantial coalmining and consumption consume a large amount of water, and lead to slag penetration and deposition, resulting in the serious pollution of groundwater resources. In addition, coalmining can cause the collapse of surface areas that have been mined out underneath. Areas of subsidence in China have reached 10 000 sq km. Furthermore, the burning of coal is to a considerable degree responsible for conventional pollutants such as sulfur dioxide, nitrogen oxide and dust, including thick smog and haze such as that experienced in Beijing and Tianjin. Last but not least, coal combustion contributes a major share of China's carbon emissions.

Therefore, a cap on coal consumption is now widely seen as essential for China to address the combination of policy concerns. Although the policy road map to phase out coal is still not clear in China, the consensus is emerging from research communities that a coal cap is essential in the near term, driven above all by concerns about air quality.

Policy instruments and objectives

China's new leadership has reiterated the country's ambition to limit the growth in energy consumption and carbon dioxide emissions. President Xi Jinping remarked in a recent speech (The Economist 2013) that China's current growth pattern is 'unbalanced, uncoordinated and unsustainable', and China should pursue a new mode of growth to promote 'more efficient, equal and sustainable economic development'.

A host of regulatory interventions to improve energy efficiency and reduce the carbon intensity of China's energy system is already in place.

The new development is that market-based instruments for emissions control are likely to come into play, in the form of emissions trading pilot schemes and preparations for a national carbon emissions trading scheme, or possibly a carbon tax.

It is well-established that putting a price on emissions—by way of a carbon tax or emissions trading—is the most cost-effective policy approach to achieve broad-based emissions control. Direct regulation and subsidy approaches are suitable in specific instances, but are inferior if used as the sole policy instruments.

For carbon pricing to be effective, however, a number of prerequisites need to be in place. First among them is the operation of markets in relevant parts of the economy, allowing the price signal from a tax or emissions trading to determine incentives, and ultimately to influence the investment and consumption decisions of companies and individuals. In China, these prerequisites are not yet generally provided (Howes and Dobes 2010; Baron et al 2012).

Emissions trading pilot schemes

Seven pilot emissions trading schemes have been developed, with six operational at the time of writing in April 2014. In 2010 the seven pilot cities and provinces accounted for around 19 per cent of China's population, 33 per cent of its GDP, 20 per cent of its energy use and 16 per cent of its carbon dioxide emissions (Table 9.6).

The emissions trading pilot schemes cover only part of the total emissions in each city or province, but combined will be second in size only to the European emissions trading scheme, and much larger than the Australian and Californian schemes.

The pilots differ in important design features, reflecting diverse settings and priorities (Zhang et al. forthcoming; Qi and Wang 2013; Zhang 2013). They are set to provide a laboratory for gathering experience with different designs and implementation methods, and the effect of emissions pricing in different economic settings, encompassing fast-growing provinces heavily dependent on heavy industries, such as Hubei, through to advanced cities where services and high-value manufacturing dominate, such as Beijing, Shanghai and Shenzhen.

Table 9.6 Indicators for Pilot Provinces and Cities, 2010

	Population (million)	GDP (RMB billion)	GDP per capita (RMB '000)	Energy use (million t SCE)	Energy use per capita (t SCE/ capita)	Carbon dioxide emissions (million t)	Emissions per capita (t CO_2/ capita/ year)	Emissions intensity (kg CO_2/ RMB)
Shenzhen SEZ	10	903	87	49	4.7	n.a.	n.a.	n.a.
Beijing	20	1182	60	70	3.5	103	5.2	87
Tianjin	13	781	60	68	5.3	134	10.3	172
Shanghai	23	1556	68	112	4.9	211	9.2	136
Chongqing	29	616	21	79	2.7	125	4.3	203
Hubei	57	1250	22	151	2.6	320	5.6	256
Guangdong	104	4016	39	269	2.6	444	4.3	110
China	1341	31 234	23	3895	2.9	8146	6.1	261
Pilot schemes combined	256	10 303	40	798	3.5	1337	5.2	130

n.a. = not applicable

SCE = standard coal equivalent

Sources: *China Statistical Yearbook* (NBS various years); Guan et al. (2012) for emissions data (emissions data are not published as part of official Chinese statistics); authors' calculations.

A national emissions trading scheme?

China has stated its intention to establish a national emissions trading scheme in the future, as a central part of its climate change and energy strategy. This was first mentioned in the Twelfth Five-Year Plan (see Zhang et al. forthcoming for a chronology).

Originally, a national scheme was planned to start in 2015 or 2016. This timeline now appears unrealistic. In recent official communications no timeline has been given for the introduction of a national emissions trading scheme. The expert community, however, expects that a national scheme may be introduced by around 2020, coinciding with the Fourteenth Five-Year Plan and China's post-2020 emissions target period.

A blueprint for the design effort towards a national emissions trading scheme (NDRC 2013) identifies key areas for further analysis. This document foreshadows a scheme that might broadly resemble the approach taken in the EU emissions trading scheme, but might also take into account specific features of the Australian and Californian schemes, and making important modifications to cater to specific circumstances in China. The document emphasises the need for analysis and careful scheme design in the electricity sector, and as it applies to state-owned enterprises. It also raises practical issues of developing reliable company-level measurement, reporting and verification of emissions.

Policy objectives

The targets and steps for policy innovation need to be seen in the context of a broader vision of 'green growth', with emphasis on the quality of economic growth. This would see a reorientation of economic expansion to activities that place little stress on the natural environment—for example, advanced information networks and low-carbon transport systems, as well as health, education and other services—in preference to continued expansion of material-intensive growth structures (Zhang and Brandon 2012). The enveloping concept is that of 'ecological civilisation', embraced by the CCP at the Seventeenth National Congress, which has nature 'as part of our life rather than something we can exploit without restraint', and places emphasis on social justice and fairness in development (China Daily 2007).

China is still a long way from changing its growth model to a 'green' model, and resource-intensive, polluting and socially inequitable economic expansion can be expected to continue for a long time: 'brown' dominates 'green' growth and in most areas will continue to do so for some time.

There are important reasons why the Chinese leadership would pursue green objectives, and reflect them in policy. Local air pollution has long been a driver of programs to modernise industrial installations and reduce the burning of coal in and around cities. Recent extreme air pollution in Beijing and other cities served to further galvanise public discontent about the impacts on health and daily quality of life. Cutting pollution is now an urgent policy priority tied to maintaining social order.

Climate change also is recognised as a real and pressing concern in China, including for the risk of drier conditions in the northern parts of the country. This could exacerbate water shortages, with potentially destabilising effects on the economy and society, and require very large investments in infrastructure to pump water from the south of the country. China is large enough for its own greenhouse gas emissions trajectory to influence global climate change outcomes. Furthermore, China's actions on climate change are likely to influence other countries, thus amplifying the effect of Chinese policy decisions.

A further factor motivating change (Boyd 2012) is the desire for leadership in technology development and in rising manufacturing industries. Low-carbon policies are seen as a chance to foster innovation and for Chinese firms to gain dominance in emerging energy technologies, as has already happened in the manufacture of wind turbines and solar panels.

Energy security is another important policy objective pointing in the same direction. Policies to reduce energy consumption decrease reliance on imported energy including oil, and thus make the Chinese economy less vulnerable to international price shocks or geopolitical disruptions (Wu et al. 2012). China's rapid increase in coal use has also led to rapid increases in coal imports, which again can be seen to pose a risk to national energy security. Renewable energy sources (including hydro, wind and solar power), in contrast, do not depend on international trade. There is a clear synergy between the objectives to reduce emissions, air pollution and climate change and to improve energy security.

One view of the potential for change and the pace of China's modernisation holds that these new policy efforts have every chance of success, and indeed overachievement, as has been the case with the majority of market-based schemes of pollution control the world over (Daley et al 2011), and that China's economic structure can shift quickly towards 'cleaner', more high value-added industries and the services sector (Garnaut 2012).

Under these circumstances it may be possible for China to achieve faster rates of decarbonisation than targeted now. In the words of Ross Garnaut (2013), 'over-performance against the [2015 emissions intensity] pledge seems possible and strengthening of the pledges [is] feasible in the context of increased global effort'.

Whether relatively rapid transformation to a lower-carbon economy will occur depends on political will, institutional factors, economic developments and the effectiveness of policy instruments.

Conclusions

China continues to reduce the carbon emissions intensity of its economy as a result of improvements in energy efficiency and structural change in the economy. Preliminary data indicate that emissions growth slowed markedly during 2012 and 2013, mainly due to slower growth in energy demand and coal use. Further slowdown in the growth of coal use is on the cards, making it plausible that emissions growth will be much slower over the remainder of this decade than over the last decade. Continued change in the structure of the economy, along with sustained improvements in technical efficiency, are likely to reduce the growth in energy demand.

The impetus to clean up the energy sector derives not only from climate change objectives, but also increasingly from the desire to reduce urban air pollution. This means stemming the increase of coal use through continued improvements in energy efficiency and substitution in the energy mix, with a greater role for renewable and nuclear energy.

Policy efforts play an important role. The Chinese Government has stated its intention to place greater emphasis on market mechanisms, including in climate change policy. Pilot emissions trading schemes are under way, though the real test will be whether a national scheme of carbon pricing will be created—and, if so, whether it will be effective. For pricing mechanisms to work effectively in creating incentives to cut energy use and emissions in China's economy, China's energy markets will need to see market reform.

With growing policy interest in market reform across the board in China, the issues facing its broader economic policy reform are reflected in energy and environmental policies.

References

Baron, R., Aasrud, A., Sinton, J., Campbell, N., Jiang, K., & Zhuang, X. (2012), *Policy Options for Low-Carbon Power Generation in China: Designing an Emissions Trading System for China's Electricity Sector*, International Energy Agency, Paris.

Boyd, O. (2012), *China's energy reform and climate policy: the ideas motivating change*, CCEP Working Paper No. 1205, Centre for Climate Economics and Policy, Crawford School of Public Policy, The Australian National University, Canberra.

China Daily (2007), 'Ecological civilization', *China Daily*, 24 October: 10. Available from <http://www.chinadaily.com.cn/opinion/2007-10/24/content_6201964.htm>.

Daley, J., Edis, T., & Reichl, J. (2011) *Learning the hard way: Australian policies to reduce carbon emissions*, Grattan Institute, Melbourne.

Garnaut, R. (2012), 'The contemporary China resources boom', *Australian Journal of Agricultural and Resource Economics* 56(2): 222–43.

Garnaut, R. (2013), 'China's climate change mitigation in international context' in R. Garnaut, F. Cai and L. Song (eds), *China: A New Model for Growth and Development*, pp. 281–300, Canberra: ANU E Press.

Guan, D., Liu, Z., Geng, Y., Lindner, S. and Hubacek, K. (2012), 'The gigatonne gap in China's carbon dioxide inventories', *Nature Climate Change* 2: 672–5.

Howes, S. and Dobes, L. (2010), *Climate Change and Fiscal Policy: A Report for APEC*, Washington, DC: The World Bank.

Huang, Y., F. Cai., X. Peng. and Q. Gou (2013), 'The new normal of Chinese development', in R. Garnaut, F. Cai and L. Song (eds), *China: A New Model for Growth and Development*, Canberra: ANU E Press.

International Energy Agency (IEA) (2013a), CO_2 *Emissions Indicators 2013*, Paris: International Energy Agency.

International Energy Agency (IEA) (2013b), *World Energy Outlook 2013*, Paris: International Energy Agency.

Jiang, K., Zhuang, X., Miao, R. and He, C. (2013), 'China's role in attaining the global 2°C target', *Climate Policy* 13(sup01): 55–69.

Jotzo, F. and Pezzey, J. (2007), 'Optimal intensity targets for greenhouse gas emissions trading under uncertainty', *Environmental and Resource Economics* 38(2): 259–84.

Jotzo, F., de Boer, D. and Kater, H. (2013), *China carbon pricing survey 2013*, CCEP Working Paper No. 1305, Centre for Climate Economics and Policy, Crawford School of Public Policy, The Australian National University, Canberra.

Lewis, J. (2011), *Energy and Climate Goals of China's 12th Five-Year Plan*, Washington, DC: Pew Centre.

McKibbin, W. J., Morris, A. C. and Wilcoxen, P. J. (2011), 'Comparing climate commitments: a model-based analysis of the Copenhagen Accord', *Climate Change Economics* 2(2): 79–103.

National Bureau of Statistics (NBS) (2011), *China Energy Statistical Yearbook 2011*, Beijing: China Statistics Press.

National Bureau of Statistics (NBS) (various years), *China Statistical Yearbook*, Beijing: China Statistics Press.

National Bureau of Statistics (NBS) (various years), *Statistical Communiqué of the People's Republic of China*, Beijing: China Statistics Press.

National Development and Reform Commission (NDRC) (2013), *Market readiness proposal: establishing a national emissions trading scheme in China*, Prepared for Partnership for Market Readiness Program, The World Bank, Beijing.

Qi, S. and Wang, B. (2013), 'Fundamental issues and solutions in the design of China's ETS pilots: allowance allocation, price mechanism and state-owned key enterprises', *Chinese Journal of Population Resources and Environment* 11(1): 26–32.

Stern, D. I. and Jotzo, F. (2010), 'How ambitious are China and India's emissions intensity targets?', *Energy Policy* 38(11): 6776–83.

The Economist (2013), 'The party's new blueprint', *The Economist*, 16 November 2013. Available from <http://www.economist.com/blogs/analects/2013/11/reform-china>.

Wu, G., Liu, L.-C., Han, Z.-Y. and Wei, Y.-M. (2012), 'Climate protection and China's energy security: win-win or tradeoff?', *Applied Energy* 97: 157–63.

Xinhua (2014), 'China struggling to meet emission targets: minister', *Xinhua. net*, 21 April 2014. Available from <http://news.xinhuanet.com/english/china/2014-04/21/c_126416067.htm>.

Zhang, H. (2013), 'Design elements of emissions trading regulation in China's pilot programs: regulatory challenges and prospects', *Environmental and Planning Law Journal* 30(4): 342–56.

Zhang, Y. and Brandon, C. (2012), *Seizing the opportunity of green development in China*, Supporting report for World Bank, *China 2030: Building a Modern, Harmonious, and Creative High-Income Society*, Beijing: The World Bank.

Zhang, D., Karplus, V. J., Cassisa, C. and Zhang, X. (forthcoming), 'Emissions trading in China: progress and prospects', *Energy Policy*.

Part III: Financial System Reform

10. The Last Battles of China's Financial Reform

Yiping Huang, Ran Li and Bijun Wang

Introduction

China's financial reform began the moment its leaders decided to shift their policy focus from class struggle to economic development in December 1978. In 1998, Nick Lardy of the Brookings Institution published a book titled *China's Unfinished Economic Revolution*, in which he discussed changes in the financial sector during the reform period and outlined some necessary additional steps (Lardy 1998). More than 15 years later, the 'revolution' remains unfinished. Financial liberalisation is an important component of the comprehensive reform program approved by the Third Plenum of the Eighteenth Party Congress in November 2013.

China clearly lags behind many other emerging market economies in financial liberalisation. Many developing countries achieved market-based interest rates, floating exchange rates and capital account convertibility from the early 1980s. Chinese authorities started to accelerate the pace of reforms in these areas only recently. In the meantime, the Chinese economy recorded the most impressive growth performance during its reform period. This naturally begs the question of whether the conventional wisdom favouring rapid financial liberalisation is the right strategy or if the Chinese experience offers a pointer for other developing countries.

Financial reforms in China over the past decades exhibit a distinctive pattern of being strong on building an industry framework and growing transaction volume but weak on liberalising market mechanisms and improving corporate governance (Huang et al. 2013). On the one hand, China has already built a financial system with all types of financial institutions—from commercial banks to asset management companies, and from insurance agencies to regulatory bodies. The size of Chinese financial assets is also very large, even by international standards. Its bond market is already ranked third in the world in volume. The ratio of broad money supply M2 to GDP is close to 200 per cent— among the highest globally.

On the other hand, the Chinese financial system remains heavily repressed. According to one measure, for instance, financial repression in China is much more serious not only than the middle-income but also the low-income economies (Figure 10.1). The authorities maintain a broad set of restrictions on credit allocation and cross-border capital flows. They also regulate, directly or indirectly, interest rates and exchange rates. This leaves limited roles for the market system to play. In addition, many financial institutions still show very strong old-style state-owned enterprise (SOE) behaviour, although they are already listed on domestic and foreign stock markets.

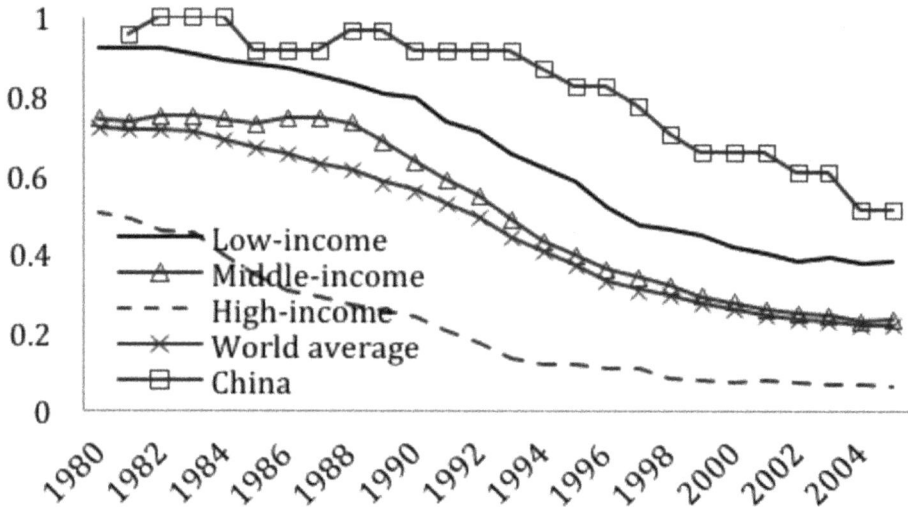

Figure 10.1 Financial Repression Indices for China and the World, 1980–2010
Source: Abiad et al. (2008); and authors' calculations.

Note that Figure 10.1 uses aggregate financial repression indices based on seven subcomponents, with higher values referring to a greater degree of repression. The central theme we attempt to explore in this chapter is how Chinese financial reforms might evolve in the coming years. Specifically, what kinds of changes, opportunities and risks might such reforms bring about? In order to offer insights on these important issues, we first analyse the rationale behind China's unique pattern of financial reform in the past. We then assess the achievements of and challenges caused by such a reform strategy. This helps us to understand why the authorities have now decided to accelerate financial reforms.

The comprehensive reform program contains reform measures in 11 areas, including opening to foreign and private financial institutions; developing multi-layered capital markets; building inclusive financial institutions; establishing market-based interest rates, exchange rates and risk-free yield curves; achieving capital account convertibility; and improving financial regulations. The central motivation of these reforms is to complete the transition to a market-based financial system. The key steps are interest rate liberalisation domestically and currency internationalisation externally.

The biggest uncertainty is whether financial liberalisation might be accompanied by increasing financial risk or even financial crisis. China is probably the only major emerging market economy that is not experiencing major financial disruption. Only time will tell whether this record can be kept for long. Regulators will face a series of tough decisions, such as allowing default of failing trust products—when doing so could increase financial instability, and not doing so would encourage moral hazard. This suggests that while the Government has now decided to take bold steps in liberalisation, actual implementation of such reform is likely to be cautious. But the change will eventually contribute to transformation of the Chinese growth model.

The Logic of China's financial reforms

Despite more than 30 years of successful reform, the Chinese economy still exhibits the typical features of repressive financial policies. First, the People's Bank of China (PBC) still sets the base interest rates for commercial banks and intervenes heavily in foreign exchange markets. Second, the state influences allocation of capital, with the majority of funds raised through direct and indirect financing channels still going to the SOEs. Third, the PBC frequently adjusts the required rate of return (RRR) for commercial banks, with the ratio exceeding 20 per cent in mid 2011. And, finally, the authorities maintain strict capital account controls, especially over portfolio investment, debt financing and foreign direct investment (FDI).

This, however, did not stop rapid financial development in China. The Chinese financial sector has grown from a mono-bank system 30 years ago to a very comprehensive system, with all types of institutions, clientele, markets and assets. China's broad money supply (M2) is already greater than that in the United States. Many of the Chinese commercial banks are already among the world's top 10 according to market capitalisation. The financial system, however, shows a strong bias towards the banking system. Total bank deposits already accounted for 190 per cent of GDP in mid 2011. Stock market capitalisation was 80 per cent of GDP, while bond market capitalisation was only half that.

Financial repression also did not prevent sound macro-economic performance in China. With the exception of several years during the past three decades, China's macro-economic conditions were stable, with consumer price index (CPI) inflation staying mostly around 3 per cent. GDP growth averaged 10 per cent a year during the reform period. China is the largest and most dynamic emerging market economy. It is also the second-largest economy in the world soon to overtake the US economy on a purchasing power parity (PPP) basis with significant influences on the income and welfare of people all around the world.

In this chapter, we review policy reforms and financial development in four broad areas: the banking sector; financial markets; the central bank and financial supervision; and exchange rates and external accounts. In general, China made significant progress in developing both the banking sector and the financial markets. Central banking and the capital account are the main areas lagging behind.

We can also classify changes in China's financial sector into four types. The first is construction of a financial framework. As China decided to move towards a market economy, development of a modern financial industry became necessary. For instance, the authorities took serious efforts to make the PBC a true central bank around the mid 1980s. They reconstructed the objectives of and tools for monetary policy. They also created lots of new financial institutions such as large and small banks, insurance companies and security firms. In the 1990s, the Government also developed the stock exchanges in Shanghai and Shenzhen and the interbank market. Clearly, when policymakers took these actions they had financial systems in advanced market economies in mind.

The second is promotion of quantitative financial development. Financial development can be defined according to both quantitative and qualitative measures. So, for instance, it can refer to growth of total outstanding loans and total banking assets. This may be reflected in rapidly growing numbers of financial institutions across the country. Meanwhile, it can also refer to the growing importance of capital markets in the country's total financing. China's financial development has been very rapid. While China's financial deepening, indicated by the rising proportion of M2 to GDP, is already well ahead of most developing and advanced economies, its financial intermediation still relies disproportionately on the banking sector.

The third is reform of financial institutions' governance structure and changing their behaviour. A typical example is ownership reform of the banking sector. Once a large and comprehensive banking industry was built in the mid 1990s, China faced serious financial risks because many banks did not allocate funds efficiently and control risk effectively. In part this was backward banking practice. But more importantly, it was related to the nature of public ownership of most banks. From the beginning of the twenty-first century, the authorities started to change the governance structure of the banks, through the introduction of foreign strategic investors and public listing on stock markets. Today, most major Chinese banks are listed on domestic or overseas stock markets, with relatively diversified ownership structures. Most financial institutions have also introduced independent directors, new accounting systems, risk-control mechanisms and information disclosure practices.

And the fourth is liberalisation of the financial industry and markets. Liberalisation here may refer to an increase in market competition, such as the introduction of private and foreign financial institutions. The proportion of the state-owned commercial banks (SOCBs) in the banking sector, for instance, declined from more than 80 per cent to close to 50 per cent during the reform period. It may also refer to the freeing up of prices in financial markets, such as interest rates, bond yields, stock prices and exchange rates. The Government has already lifted most of the restrictions on interest rates, although regulation of commercial banks' deposit and lending rates continues. And, finally, liberalisation could imply the lifting of controls over domestic markets and the capital account. From the early years of the reform period, the authorities opened up channels for cross-border capital flows in areas of inward direct investment.

Comparatively speaking, China made remarkable progress in putting into place the basic framework for the financial system and growing its financial assets. The Chinese financial system already resembles a modern financial sector in advanced economies, although important differences in quality remain. China still lags significantly in freeing up key financial market prices, especially interest rates and exchange rates. It also made important improvements in both the behaviour of financial institutions and the allocation of financial resources. Most commercial banks still behave more like SOEs than listed companies. A simple characterisation may be that the Chinese Government made serious efforts trying to build a modern financial sector but was not willing to give up all the controls.

So why did the financial reform show a unique pattern of being strong on framework and quantity but weak on price and quality?

We will try to explain the logic of China's financial reform, applying the framework identified by Huang (2010) in a series of recent studies: asymmetric liberalisation of product and factor markets. Huang noticed that during China's reform period, final product markets have been almost completely liberalised, with prices freely determined by demand and supply, but intermediate goods market distortions and factor market distortions remain widespread and serious. For instance, the Government still intervenes in the prices of important energy products, such as electricity, gas and oil. It also influences key interest rates and exchange rates. Some of these distortions are legacies of the central planning system, while others were introduced during the reform period.

Such distortions have a common feature: they repress factor prices and input costs and lower production costs. For instance, when international crude-oil prices were at their peak around US$150 per barrel, the domestic equivalent prices were only about US$80. Again, the real deposit rates in China were frequently in the negative territory during the reform period. Such distortions are like subsidies to producers, exporters and investors. They artificially raise profits of production, returns to investment and the competitiveness of Chinese exports. They help promote economic growth but, at the same time, cause serious internal and external imbalances.

Huang and his co-authors argue that the main rationale behind the asymmetric liberalisation approach is the Government's objective of achieving the fastest possible economic growth. In a typical market economy, the Government's main function should be to provide public goods and services, such as social and legal protection. In China, however, promoting economic growth is a top priority for the Government. Deng Xiaoping once said that development is a hard principle. Economists have since found that GDP growth was the single most important economic indicator determining local officials' chances of promotion. This is, perhaps, why mayors in China act more like corporate CEOs than heads of local governments. And the Chinese Government is sometimes described as being production or development oriented.

Therefore, asymmetric liberalisation is a rational choice by the Government given its policy objective. Free markets for products help overcome the inefficiency problem of the central planning system. At the same time, the Government retains distortions in factor markets, subsidising certain economic activities and allocating resources according to policy priorities. In fact, in the pre-reform period, China adopted a similar strategy to support growth. In the mid 1950s, the Government devised the so-called 'unified purchase and marketing system' for agricultural products. It bought the products from farmers and sold them to urban residents, both at below market prices. This enabled urban industry to generate extraordinary profits, which were reinvested. This was one of the ways of facilitating urban industrialisation.

The same logic is applicable to China's financial liberalisation. From the beginning of economic reform, Chinese policymakers recognised the importance of finance for growth. Therefore, the Government immediately got on with the task of building a modern financial system from scratch. It resulted in rapid growth of financial infrastructure, including the banking sector and capital markets, and financial assets, including loans, stocks, bonds and other financial products. Rapid financial development is consistent with the general style of market-oriented reform. Empirical examinations have confirmed the positive impact of financial development on economic growth during China's reform period.

Policymakers probably also understood the benefits of financial liberalisation, highlighted in analyses by McKinnon, Shaw and others (McKinnon 1973; Shaw 1973). Therefore, the Government continuously expanded the roles of market mechanisms in the financial system. It introduced joint-stock and foreign banks to promote competition. It also gradually allowed market-determined interbank rates and Treasury bond yields and increased the flexibility of exchange rates. It even slowly reduced restrictions on certain types of cross-border capital flows, especially inward FDI.

But liberalisation is not the whole story of Chinese financial reform. The Government continued to play an important role in the operation of the financial system, such as controlling interest rates and exchange rates, interventions in capital allocation and restrictions on cross-border capital flows.

So why did the Government choose financial repression instead of full liberalisation during the reform period? First, repressive financial policies were consistent with the general asymmetric liberalisation approach—supporting growth through repressed factor costs. Specifically, depressed interest rates and exchange rates were like subsidies to investors and exporters and, therefore, were favourable for boosting investment and exports. An undervalued currency, for instance, promoted exports and discouraged imports. This was particularly true during the years following the Asian financial crisis as the Government pursued both strong economic growth and large current account surpluses. Similarly, very low real interest rates encouraged investment, which at least in part contributed to the rising share of investment in GDP during the reform period.

Second, repressive financial policies ensured that sufficient resources were available for economic activities and, particularly, priority areas identified by the policy. Mandatory capital allocation became necessary when interest rates were kept below market levels due to excess demand for funds. More importantly, the Government often used the financial sector as an important means of supporting economic policy. During the Global Financial Crisis (GFC), for instance, the Government adopted a RMB4 trillion stimulus package to boost growth. At the same time it mobilised massive bank loans, which would not have been possible without a majority ownership in many financial institutions. Similarly, in the late 1990s, the Government also called upon the banks to support its 'go west' policy.

Third, repressive financial policies were necessary for the gradual and 'dual-track' reform approach. A key feature of the Chinese reform was to let economic activities grow outside the planning system, without hurting the planned economy initially. This meant the Government needed to continuously support the SOEs, even if they were not profitable. During the 1990s, many banks provided so-called 'stability loans' or policy loans to failing SOEs. Eventually, the Government had to abandon this practice due to the increasing financial burdens of the banking system; but the initial support, which was made possible under repressive policy, was critical for ensuring smooth progress of economic reforms.

And, finally, repressive financial policies might be critical for maintaining financial stability during the early stage of economic development. The general prediction that a fully liberalised financial system promotes efficiency and growth is dependent on a number of important assumptions, such as perfect competition and complete information. Without these, it would probably be easier for the Government to deal with problems of market failure and financial instability. China's own experiences provide some evidence of this argument. China would probably have suffered a major banking crisis during the Asian financial crisis and a recession during the GFC without majority state-ownership of the SOCBs and a still relatively tightly controlled capital account.

The case for acceleration of financial reforms

If financial policies worked so well in the past or, at least, if they did not prevent rapid economic growth in China, why should the Government accelerate reforms now? Here we provide three broad examples to explain why maintaining the status quo is no longer an option.

The first example is that the growth impact of repressive financial policies has changed from positive to negative. In an empirical examination of the Chinese case, Huang and Wang (2011) identified two theoretical effects of financial repression on economic growth: the 'McKinnon effect' and the 'Stiglitz effect'. The McKinnon effect refers to financial repression reducing economic efficiency and dampening financial deepening, and is thus negative for growth. The Stiglitz effect refers to financial repression helping financial intermediation and supporting financial stability, and is thus positive for growth. In the empirical analyses, Huang and Wang first constructed a composite financial repression index applying the principal component analysis method. The index shows steady decline during the first three decades of economic reform, confirming the trend of steady financial liberalisation.

Then they applied a typical growth equation, with the real GDP growth rate as the dependent variable, using a provincial panel dataset from China. In addition to financial repression (FREP), they also use investment rate (INV), trade openness (TRADE), size of the government (GOV) and the share of SOEs in the economy (SOE) as independent variables to explain growth performance. The basic estimation results reveal several important findings: between 1979 and 2008, financial repression had a positive impact on economic growth

(Table 10.1). The same conclusion holds for the period 1979–99. In Stiglitz's words, this is probably because, under imperfect competition and incomplete information, repressive financial policies actually enable the Government to better deal with market failure problems (Stiglitz 2000; Hellman et al. 1997).

When the empirical examination is focused only on the period 2000–08, however, the growth effect of financial repression turns out to be negative. This is probably because the McKinnon effect now outweighs the Stiglitz effect. If this finding is reliable then the conclusion is straightforward: while financial repression did not hurt growth in the 1980s and the 1990s, it is now reducing growth.

Table 10.1 Estimation Results of the Impact of Financial Repression on Growth in China

	Full Sample	1979–89	1990–99	2000–08
FREP	0.167***	0.787***	0.313***	−0.132***
	(0.041)	(0.132)	(0.073)	(0.037)
INV	0.133***	0.068	0.191***	0.100***
	(0.022)	(0.069)	(0.047)	(0.021)
TRADE	0.010	0.025	0.010	0.007
	(0.008)	(0.034)	(0.014)	(0.012)
EDU	2.361	1.934	0.561	0.438
	(0.539)	(6.445)	(0.627)	(0.745)
GOV	−0.189***	−0.225	−0.518***	−0.169**
	(0.055)	(0.141)	(0.191)	(0.083)
SOE	−0.039*	−0.048***	−0.119***	−0.039*
	(0.020)	(0.011)	(0.031)	(0.023)
Time trend	0.002***	0.008***	0.003***	0.002
	(0.0008)	(0.002)	(0.002)	(0.014)
Year-specific effect	YES	YES	YES	YES
Province-specific effect	YES	YES	YES	YES
Observations	750	275	250	225
R^2	0.179	0.138	0.326	0.187

* statistically significant at 10 per cent

** statistically significant at 5 per cent

*** statistically significant at 1 per cent

Source: Huang and Wang (2011).

Notes: Year-specific effect refers to certain years when there were special events such as the Asian financial crisis and the GFC. Numbers in parentheses beneath the coefficient estimates are related standard errors.

The second example is that repressive financial policies already contribute increasingly to macro-economic and financial risks. The first problem relates to the behaviour of the financial institutions. Many Chinese financial institutions have undertaken market-oriented reforms. Nevertheless, most of them still behave more like SOEs than market entities. For instance, the SOCBs went through a major transformation process during the past decade, including writing off non-performing loans, injection of public capital, introduction of foreign strategic investors and public listing. Despite adoption of a modern corporate structure, these SOCBs remain tightly controlled by the state. The senior executives of the banks, including their chairmen and presidents, are still appointed by the Chinese Communist Party (CCP). Important business and personnel decisions are still made by the party committees, not by boards of directors. A striking example is that when the financial institutions should have become cautious during the GFC, the Chinese banks all increased their lending aggressively to support the Government's policy. If the financial institutions continue to act on government instruction rather than market conditions then serious financial risks could emerge in the future.

The second problem is state intervention in capital allocation. For instance, bank lending still heavily favours the state sector. This has become an important constraint on the efficiency of capital allocation, as now the small and medium enterprises (SMEs) play a much greater role in driving Chinese growth. Since bank interest rates are generally depressed, there is a shortage of credit supply. For instance, the one-year base lending rate was 6.25 per cent in June 2011. At the same time, the lending rate in the curb market in Zhejiang province was at 24 per cent. SOEs now account for less than 30 per cent of industrial output, but they still take away more than half of the total loans. If we include borrowing by local government entities, the proportion might even be higher. The more dynamic SMEs, however, find it extremely difficult to obtain loans from the banks. In 2009, in Zhejiang province, where SME financing was better developed, only about 20 per cent of the SMEs obtained loans. Others had to meet their finance requirements through other channels, including borrowing from the curb market. This points to an important aspect of inefficiency in capital allocation.

The third problem includes the significantly distorted interest rates and exchange rates, which contribute to serious economic imbalances such as over-investment, under-consumption and large external account surpluses. Initially the Government utilised repressed interest rates and exchange rates to promote investment and exports. But now the investment share of GDP is already 48.5 per cent, while the current account surplus stayed at above 5 per cent of GDP in 2010. The real negative deposit rates encouraged speculative activities in asset markets in 2010. When the potential for stock and housing price increases diminished, investors rushed to speculate on products such as cotton, garlic, beans, apples and sugar. Prices of these products skyrocketed one after the other. Again, the undervalued currency has been the main cause of massive 'hot money' inflows. This added significant liquidity to the domestic system and at the same time undermined the independence of monetary policy. All these factors risk the stability of macro-economic conditions and the sustainability of economic growth.

The fourth problem is declining effectiveness of capital account controls, which caused volatile cross-border capital flows and weakened monetary policy independence. Empirical analyses in this study confirmed that it was becoming increasingly difficult for the Government to enforce the capital account control measures. The result was that short-term cross-border capital flows became much bigger and more volatile. This could threaten the stability of the financial system. According to the 'Mundell trilemma', a country can achieve only two of the following three international economic policy objectives: free flow of capital, stable exchange rate and independent monetary policy. Weakening capital restrictions reduce the PBC's ability to control domestic liquidity conditions and interest rates. In a normal year, the PBC sterilises only about 80 per cent of the injected RMB liquidity for foreign exchange market intervention. This contributes to increasing inflation pressure.

And the third example is that many of the policy restrictions are no longer sustainable. One good illustration is that, while the authorities still maintain relatively strict short-term cross-border capital flows, the so-called hot-money flow is already a major phenomenon whenever there is fluctuation in economic and financial activities. This probably means the effectiveness of capital account control is weakening over time. Another illustration is the rapidly growing shadow banking activities, such as trust products and entrusted loans (Figure 10.2). Shadow banking businesses are backdoor liberalisation of interest rates. As the market becomes impatient with strict interest rate regulations, it dis-intermediates the banks and develops large volumes of non-credit financial products. All this suggests that continuation of the status quo is no longer an option.

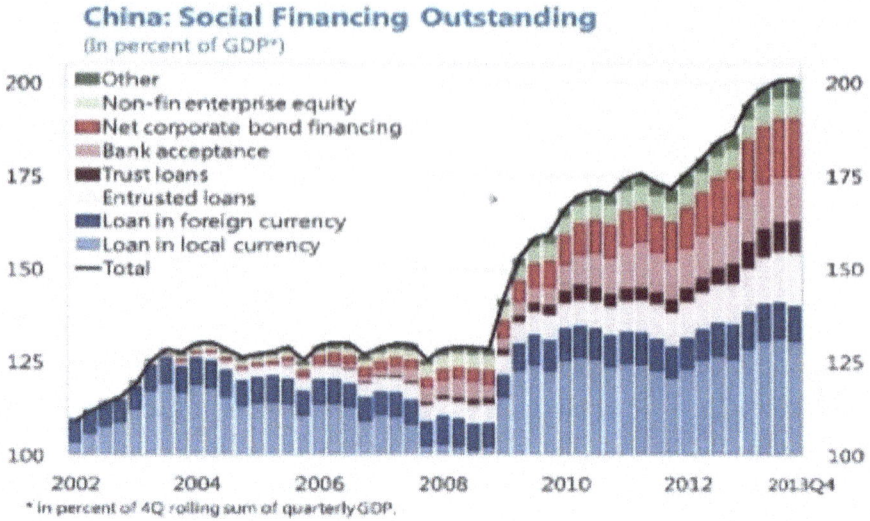

Figure 10.2 Total Social Financing in China
Source: IMF (2013).

What is likely to happen in the future?

There is another broad reason why financial liberalisation should accelerate now. In a recent study, Huang et al. (forthcoming) analysed the roles of financial liberalisation in economic growth at different stages of economic development. Applying a growth equation and 80-country dataset for 1980–2010, they found that the impact of financial repression on economic growth is insignificant in low-income economies, significantly negative in middle-income economies and significantly positive in high-income economies (Table 10.2).[1] These findings are similar to those of Huang and Wang (2011). In any case, today China is already a middle-income country, with per capita GDP of US$6700. Therefore, it should probably accelerate financial liberalisation even if just to continue rapid economic growth and avoid the middle-income trap.

---

1   The growth regression again uses real GDP growth as the dependent variable. The independent variables include financial repression (FREP), law and order (LAW), democracy (DEMC), initial level of income (LogGDPP), size of the government (GOVN), education (EDU), inflation (CPI), fertility rate (LogFERTI), life expectancy (LogEXPECT), investment rate (INVR) and trade openness (OPEN) (Huang et al. forthcoming).

Table 10.2 Growth Equation Estimation for 80 Countries, 1980–2010

	Low-income		Middle-income		High-income	
	(1)	(2)	(3)	(4)	(5)	(6)
FREP	-0.0302	0.0062	-0.0803***	-0.0789***	0.0394***	0.0390**
	(0.0379)	(0.0342)	(0.0203)	(0.0202)	(0.0148)	(0.0150)
LAW		0.0945***		0.0301**		0.0067
		(0.0219)		(0.0151)		(0.0161)
DEMC		0.0101		-0.0160		0.0044
		(0.0186)		(0.0121)		(0.0174)
LogGDPP	-0.0673***	-0.0812***	-0.1258***	-0.1293***	-0.1189***	-0.1224***
	(0.0193)	(0.0178)	(0.0143)	(0.0143)	(0.0163)	(0.0186)
GOVN	0.0828	-0.0618	-0.4517***	-0.4386***	-0.3984***	-0.3831***
	(0.1361)	(0.1233)	(0.0821)	(0.0816)	(0.1072)	(0.1126)
EDU	0.0130	0.0049	0.0165*	0.0150*	0.0199***	0.0193**
	(0.0099)	(0.0088)	(0.0085)	(0.0085)	(0.0073)	(0.0074)
CPI	-0.0338**	-0.0080	-0.0025**	-0.0026**	-0.0648	-0.0629
	(0.0158)	(0.0156)	(0.0010)	(0.0010)	(0.0733)	(0.0740)
LogFERTI	-0.0966**	-0.0478	0.0184	0.0257	-0.0391**	-0.0386**
	(0.0434)	(0.0428)	(0.0250)	(0.0251)	(0.0178)	(0.0183)
LogEXPECT	0.0359	-0.0469	-0.1445	-0.1827*	-0.0286	-0.0266
	(0.0732)	(0.0668)	(0.0935)	(0.0945)	(0.2367)	(0.2385)
INVR	0.1186	0.0997	0.1929***	0.2004***	0.2194***	0.2215***
	(0.0748)	(0.0670)	(0.0494)	(0.0492)	(0.0615)	(0.0640)
OPEN	0.0002	0.0010*	0.0005*	0.0006**	0.0010***	0.0010***
	(0.0006)	(0.0006)	(0.0003)	(0.0003)	(0.0002)	(0.0002)
Constant	0.4794	0.7533**	1.7030***	1.8743***	1.2671	1.2813
	(0.3390)	(0.3035)	(0.3865)	(0.3911)	(1.0771)	(1.0862)
Year effect	YES	YES	YES	YES	YES	YES
Country effect	YES	YES	YES	YES	YES	YES
R2	0.511	0.636	0.606	0.618	0.655	0.656
Observations	103	103	242	242	158	158
Countries	21	21	47	47	24	24
Hausman test	0.0000	0.0000	0.0000	0.0000	0.0000	0.0000

*** p < 0.01
** p < 0.05
* p < 0.1

Source: Huang et al. (forthcoming).

Notes: Standard errors in parentheses. We only report fixed-effect results here as the Hausman test indicates the fixed effect is more suitable.

So what will happen to financial reform in the coming years? The comprehensive reform program lists key changes in the following 11 areas:

- opening to foreign and private financial institutions
- promoting reform of policy for financial institutions
- developing multi-layered capital markets
- perfecting insurance and compensation systems
- developing inclusive financial activities
- encouraging financial innovation
- establishing market-based interest rates, exchange rates and yield curves
- achieving capital account convertibility
- improving financial regulation
- establishing a deposit insurance system
- strengthening financial infrastructure.

According to PBC Deputy Governor, Yi Gang, these reforms fall within three broad areas: reducing entry barriers, liberalising market forces and improving financial infrastructure.[2] These are the three critical pillars for building a market-based financial system—both improving efficiency and controlling risk. Alternatively, we may view this comprehensive reform program as two important tasks: interest rate liberalisation domestically, and currency internationalisation externally.

Interest rate liberalisation has been an ongoing process. In the early days of reform, the PBC set all types of interest rates for financial institutions to follow strictly. Over time, the PBC gradually relaxed its grip. Today, both money market and bond market rates are freely determined by demand and supply. Although the PBC still sets base deposit and lending rates, commercial banks enjoy certain degrees of flexibility. There is no longer a ceiling on lending rates, although there are still floors. The deposit rates are still regulated with more strict ceilings. The floors for lending rates and the ceiling for deposit rates ensure the minimum interest rate spread for the commercial banks. Many economists argue that the most critical step for interest rate liberalisation is to lift ceilings for deposit rates.

Lifting ceilings for deposit rates could symbolically be the last step of interest rate liberalisation. This step alone, however, requires a large number of prerequisite conditions to be met. For instance, effective reforms of commercial banks are necessary in order to avoid reckless competition for

---

2 Discussion by Yi Gang at the Twentieth Anniversary of the China Center for Economic Research at Peking University, Beijing, 19 April 2014.

deposits by significantly raising deposit rates without carefully considering financial consequences. Commercial bank reforms require at least two important steps: enforcement of market discipline through bankruptcy and default, and introduction of a deposit insurance system to control systemic risk. Similarly, soft budget constraints for some institutions such as the SOEs and the local government investment vehicles (LGIVs) need to be hardened. Otherwise these institutions may accept ridiculously high interest rates in order to crowd out more productive private enterprises.

In the meantime, if the PBC's base interest rate regulation is to go then it needs a new instrument for its monetary policy. One of the potential candidates is the Shanghai Interbank Offered Rate (Shibor). The PBC could influence levels of Shibor by increasing or decreasing liquidity in this market, just the way the US Federal Reserve affects the Federal funds rate through open market operation. Currently, however, Shibor is still way too volatile. The market needs to introduce many more institutional participants and to substantially increase liquidity. In addition, China needs a well-developed government bond market to generate an efficient yield curve, serving as the benchmark rates for the market.

One interesting question is often raised in discussion: would China's interest rate rise or fall after interest rate liberalisation? The answer is likely to be complicated. In the short run, interest rates in the formal sector, such as the commercial banks, could rise. The fact that there is a large non-formal credit market is strong evidence that the interest rate in the formal sector is too low. Excess demand is pushed to the informal markets, such as informal lending and shadow banking, where interest rates are unusually high. Interest rate liberalisation could lead to convergence in these two markets. In the long run, whether the interest rate in China would rise or fall is dependent on two factors: growth potential (slower growth means lower interest rates) and capital flows (outflow implies higher domestic interest rates).

The second key theme is internationalisation of the renminbi. The Government apparently stepped up efforts to promote international use of the renminbi after the GFC. This was partly because many saw the subprime crisis as foreshadowing a dimming future for the US dollar. More importantly, many also believed that an internationalised renminbi would bring tremendous benefits to the Chinese economy, such as greater exchange rate stability and lower balance-of-payments risk.

The PBC first formulated its strategy for internationalising the renminbi in 2006 when it proposed a dual-track strategy: promoting international use of the renminbi in trade and investment settlement, and liberalising the capital account. Many officials also argue that currency internationalisation could be used as an instrument to force domestic reforms. In the official document, however, the term internationalisation is never used. At the end of 1996, China realised current account convertibility. The comprehensive reform program approved recently specifically suggests achieving capital account convertibility as one of its key tasks.

The renminbi is, however, still a long way from becoming an international reserve currency. Many optimists tend to pay a lot of attention to China's already gigantic economy. The logic is simple: China is already a major world economy and, therefore, its currency should play some international role. A quick review of experiences of international currencies during the twentieth century suggests that the size of the economy may be an important favourable factor, but it is by no means a sufficient condition. We apply quantitative methods to identify determinants of international currencies' shares in global reserves and then use the results to predict the renminbi's potential share. We find that, if only GDP and trade weights are used then the renminbi's potential share could be as high as 10 per cent of global reserves at the end of 2011. If, however, policy and institutional factors such as capital account controls and economic freedom are considered, then the renminbi's potential share would only reach around 2 per cent (Figure 10.3). This suggests that the main obstacles to the renminbi becoming an international reserve currency are policy restrictions and institutional barriers.

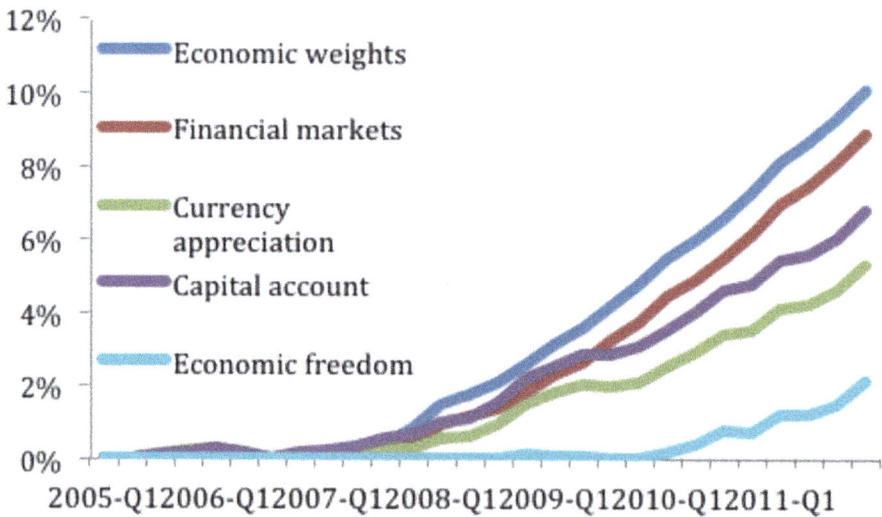

Figure 10.3 Predicted Shares of the Renminbi in Global Foreign Reserves
Source: Huang et al. (2014).

So what should China do to effectively internationalise the renminbi? It can certainly continue to push on the first track—that is, promoting use of the renminbi in international economic transactions, including establishment of more offshore markets, issuance of more RMB-denominated assets overseas and use of the renminbi for trade and investment settlement. China may also adopt two additional strategies for this purpose. One is to add the renminbi to the special drawing rights (SDR) basket of the International Monetary Fund (IMF), which should significantly raise the international profile of the currency and make internationalisation efforts a lot easier. And the other is to introduce a new mechanism for intra-regional crossholding of reserve currencies in Asia.

For the purpose of currency internationalisation, however, the broadly defined second of the two-track strategy is probably more critical as it creates the foundation of a global reserve currency. We identify reforms in the following three areas for this purpose.

The first is to support sustainable growth of the Chinese economy. While economic weights are not sufficient conditions for a global reserve currency, any hopes for the renminbi to become an international currency could collapse if the Chinese economy suddenly stagnates, as happened to the Japanese economy in the 1990s. An imminent challenge for the Chinese economy now is to change the growth model, which may be characterised as a combination of strong growth and serious imbalances. The key is to go further with economic reforms. The new Government's economic policy framework, popularly termed as 'Likonomics', contains three important pillars—that is, no more major stimulus, de-leveraging to control financial risks and structural reforms. Government officials and policy advisors are working on reform programs for a large number of areas, including the financial system, fiscal policy, land use, administrative controls, factor prices, income inequality and the household registration system. Successful transformation of the growth model depends on the following reforms: liberalisation of interest rates, exchange rates and the capital account; changing local governments' role from directly engaging in production and investment to public goods provision; and breaking the monopoly power of the state sector.

The second is to create an open, large, efficient and liquid financial market. To serve as an international reserve currency, the renminbi needs to be supported by a financial market that is easily accessible to non-residents. One major step is to liberalise the capital account. Capital account liberalisation has been an ongoing process, with the capital account control index declining from 100 per cent in 1977 to 53 per cent in 2011. The Government now plans to realise basic convertibility by 2015 and full convertibility by 2020. There is, however, a major debate about whether this might be too aggressive and could trigger a financial crisis. The answer to this caution should be to keep a close eye on both the necessary conditions and the sequencing of liberalisation.

Nevertheless, capital account liberalisation is also a necessary step for currency internationalisation; however, the financial markets need to be open, liquid and efficient, and equipped with well-developed hedge instruments.

The third is to improve the credibility of China's economic and political systems. The essence of an international reserve currency is that international investors have long-term confidence in it. To support such confidence, China needs to improve its economic, legal and political systems. This is particularly important, since all other existing international reserve currencies are from developed economies that have well-developed economic and political systems. We suggest three preliminary steps for China: 1) an independent monetary policymaking mechanism; 2) a sound legal system that protects property rights and enforces bankruptcy laws; and 3) a political system that is more transparent and better represented.

Even if all these efforts are successful, we think internationalisation of the renminbi will be a long-term process. We think the renminbi will not become a global reserve currency in the coming decade or any time soon after that. But the renminbi's international roles may be extended steadily, perhaps first in the neighbourhood, then in the region and finally globally.

Concluding remarks

China's financial liberalisation has been going on for more than three decades. Its financial policies, however, remain highly repressive. Previous studies have found these policies do not prevent rapid economic growth. On the contrary, they probably helped China's economic growth by effectively translating saving into investment and by supporting financial stability. But there are at least three reasons reforms should accelerate now: the negative impact of financial repression on economic growth; growing macro-economic and financial risks as a result of repressive financial policies; and the inherent unsustainability of policy restrictions at China's stage of development. Chinese leaders devised a comprehensive reform program for the financial sector, which includes specific measures in 11 areas. There are two very broad themes. In the near term, interest rate liberalisation should dominate, while over time, currency internationalisation, including capital account convertibility, should take over.

While we believe financial liberalisation is critical not only for China's transition towards a market economy but also for its sustainable economic growth, global experiences also suggest that the consequences of financial liberalisation are highly uncertain. We conclude discussions by addressing one big issue of financial liberalisation and financial risk or crisis.

We believe China's leaders are serious about financial liberalisation. The new leaders have repeatedly argued that it is time to tolerate slow growth in order to push ahead with tough reforms. The Government's official growth target has been lowered from 8 per cent to 7.5 per cent. The Government, however, remains extremely nervous whenever growth momentum slows, even if only marginally below the target. The same is reflected in the Government's reluctance to allow default in the financial market. The worry is that default of some financial products could lead to repricing of these assets and, therefore, hurt growth momentum by worsening terms of financing. Another worry is that default could lead to the beginning of a meltdown of the financial system. Without default, however, it will be impossible to enforce market discipline and to reduce moral hazard problems.

Will China be able to avoid a financial crisis and, therefore, become an exception in the emerging-market world? Our answer is that it is possible but depends on how China implements reforms. Financial liberalisation is tricky—it improves the efficiency of capital allocation but at the same time also raises financial volatility. The key to avoiding major financial problems in the wake of liberalisation is to emphasise the prerequisite conditions and reform sequencing. If the capital account is opened up before effective improvement of the commercial banks and other financial institutions, and before elimination of misalignment of interest rates, then financial crisis could be a certainty. Therefore, while financial liberalisation should accelerate, it is crucial to follow the proper procedure.

International investors routinely predict a meltdown of the Chinese economy or its financial system every six months. They often point to risks of the property markets, commercial banks, shadow banking businesses and local government investment vehicles. While there are real risks in these areas, we don't believe they could cause a meltdown in the near term. The truth is that most of the institutions involved are either state-owned or directly related to the state. Therefore, the risk of financial crisis in China today might be crystalised by a liquidity squeeze but is unlikely to be caused by insolvency. The Government still has a sound fiscal system to contain financial risks in individual areas; but this could also be a source of major concern, as the Central Government's credibility is overdrawn. If this is not stopped quickly, it could eventually amount to a big problem.

References

Abiad, A., Detragiache, E., & Tressel, T. (2008), *A New Database of Financial Reforms*, IMF, Washington, DC.

Hellmann, T., Murdock, K., & Stiglitz, J. (1997), 'Financial Restraint: Toward a New Paradigm', in M. Aoki, H.-K. Kim & M. Okuno-Fujuwara (eds.), *The Role of Government in East Asian Economic Development: Comparative Institutional Analysis*, Clarendon Press, Oxford.

Huang, Y. (2010), 'Dissecting the China puzzle: asymmetric liberalization and cost distortion', *Asian Economic Policy Review* 5(2): 281–95.

Huang, Y. Wang, X., Wang, B. and Lin, N. (2013), 'Financial reform in China: progress and challenges', in Y. C. Park and H. Patrick (eds), *How Finance is Shaping the Economies of China, Japan and Korea*, Columbia University Press, New York.

Huang, Y., Gou, Q., and Wang, X. (forthcoming), 'Financial liberalization and the middle-income trap: what can China learn from multi-country experience?', *China Economic Review*.

Huang, Y., Wang, D. and Fan, G. (2014), 'Paths to a reserve currency: Internationalization of renminbi and its implications', Paper presented at the concluding workshop on Currency Internationalization and Lessons for RMB, Asian Development Bank Institute, National School of Development, Peking University, Beijing, 28 March 2014.

Huang, Y., & Wang, X. (2011), 'Does Financial Repression Inhibit or Facilitate Economic Growth? a Case Study of Chinese Reform Experience, *Oxford Bulletin of Economics and Statistics,* 73(6): 833–55.

IMF, (2013). *People's Republic of China: 2013 Article IV Consultation*, Staff Report, IMF, Washington, DC.

Lardy, N. (1998), *China's Unfinished Economic Revolution*, The Brookings Institution Press, Washington, DC.

McKinnon, R. I. (1973), *Money and Capital in Economic Development*, The Brookings Institution Press, Washington, DC.

Shaw, A. S. (1973), *Financial Deepening in Economic Development*, Oxford University Press, New York.

Stiglitz, J. E. (2000), 'Capital Market Liberalization, Economic Growth and Instability', *World Development*, 28: 1075–1086.

11. Financial Reform in Australia and China

Alexander Ballantyne, Jonathan Hambur, Ivan Roberts and Michelle Wright[1]

Introduction

The financial architecture currently in place in the People's Republic of China shares some characteristics with Australia's financial system prior to deregulation in the late 1970s and early 1980s. In the late 1970s, Australia maintained a managed exchange rate regime, capital account transactions were subject to restrictions and the banking system was tightly regulated. Taken at face value, this is similar to China today, where portfolio capital flows are largely prohibited, the renminbi exchange rate continues to be managed and banking sector interest rates are only partially liberalised.

Naturally, there are important differences as well. Australia's weight in the global economy was smaller and its financial reforms occurred in the context of a much smaller and less integrated global financial system. While its capital account in the 1970s and early 1980s was more tightly restricted than other similar economies, Australia was somewhat more open to foreign portfolio investment than China is currently. China receives relatively larger direct investment flows today than Australia did prior to capital account liberalisation. In addition, parts of the Chinese financial system are now more developed than the Australian financial system was prior to financial deregulation.

Notwithstanding these differences, the Australian example serves to underscore both the potential importance of sequencing and the powerful catalytic effects of a decision to liberalise. The floating exchange rate is now widely recognised as having played a crucial role in helping to steer the economy through challenging periods (Beaumont and Cui 2007; Stevens 2013). Nevertheless, the full benefits of financial deregulation, the float and capital

1 The authors are from the International and Economic Research departments at the Reserve Bank of Australia. The discussion of financial reform in Australia in this chapter has benefited greatly from unpublished research by Lynne Cockerell. The authors would like to thank Chris Ryan, Alexandra Heath, James Holloway and Chris Becker for numerous helpful comments and suggestions. The views expressed in this chapter are the authors' own and do not necessarily reflect those of the Reserve Bank of Australia. The authors are solely responsible for any errors.

account liberalisation were not fully realised until economic agents had adapted, markets had developed and the credibility of Australia's economic policy framework and institutions had been established.

Although there had been efforts to deregulate the banking system in the 1970s, this process was not completed until after the float of the exchange rate and the liberalisation of the capital account. The combination of a newly liberalised financial sector and capital account exposed Australia's underdeveloped prudential regulation framework and banks' relative inexperience in the pricing of risk. This, in turn, led to an unsustainable boom in credit in the 1980s, followed by a sharp correction and significant effects on the real economy. Similarly, while foreign exchange markets had started to develop prior to the float, it was only after agents were subjected to greater exchange rate volatility and the discipline of a free market—underpinned by credible institutions and economic policies—that Australia's hedging and foreign exchange markets could fully develop.

China's own process of economic reform and opening began in the late 1970s. Its transition from a centrally planned economy began with the reform of agricultural and industrial product markets, and proceeded to the opening of external trade, the domestic corporate sector, and later the urban labour and property markets. Financial reform has occurred more slowly. In the late 1990s, the authorities began a process of gradually liberalising interest rates on loans that culminated in the removal of nearly all such restrictions in 2013. Deposit rates, however, have yet to be fully liberalised. Since 2005, China's renminbi–US dollar exchange rate has gradually become more flexible, although it continues to be managed closely by the authorities.

In recent years, the optimal sequencing of China's financial reform has been a subject of much discussion. The liberalisation of domestic interest rates, the exchange rate and the capital account have all been on the formal agenda of regulators since the early 2000s (PBC 2003; Zhou 2005) and were listed as national priorities in the Eleventh and Twelfth Five-Year Plans (Government of the People's Republic of China 2005, 2011) and the Third Plenum of the Chinese Communist Party in 2013 (CCP 2013). But within Chinese policy circles, the debate over China's future financial reforms has been polarised.

Some observers have advised China against prioritising the removal of capital controls on the basis that the domestic financial infrastructure and regulation framework are insufficiently developed to open the economy to short-term capital flows (Yu 2013). The deterioration in the quality of banking sector assets since China's policy stimulus during the GFC, rising corporate and local government debt and the expansion of off-balance sheet activities by banks are cited as reasons for delaying capital account convertibility. It is argued that domestic financial deregulation and increased exchange rate flexibility should happen first if the liberalisation of short-term capital flows is to occur in a non-destabilising manner (He 2013).

Others have called for the Chinese capital account to be liberalised within five to 10 years, on the grounds that China's large foreign exchange reserves, low foreign debt and the current absence of currency mismatches on the balance sheets of banks greatly lower the risk that speculative flows will create financial instability (PBC Department of Surveys and Statistics Task Force 2012a, 2012b). According to this argument, capital account liberalisation should proceed in conjunction with efforts to complete domestic interest rate deregulation and free floating of the exchange rate. Prioritising interest rate deregulation over capital account convertibility and currency flexibility is viewed as unnecessary: reform can be focused on one area until a certain stage of maturity is reached, and redirected towards another. The People's Bank of China (PBC) Department of Surveys and Statistics Task Force (2012b) contends that the historical experiences of Japan, South Korea, the United States, the United Kingdom and Germany do not support an interpretation that domestic financial deregulation must precede liberalisation of the capital account.

In general, the literature on the sequencing of financial reform tends to prioritise domestic financial reform and exchange rate flexibility ahead of capital account liberalisation. Based on numerous case studies, McKinnon (1982, 1991) argues that the development of domestic financial institutions, markets and instruments is a prerequisite for successfully liberalising the capital account, and that therefore capital account liberalisation should occur at a relatively late stage in the reform process. While stressing that a sound system of domestic financial regulation should be prioritised, Johnston (1998) notes that early capital account liberalisation can have an important catalytic role in broader economic reforms, and can help overcome entrenched vested interests that otherwise postpone necessary reforms. Ishii and Habermeier (2002) propose that, to avoid instability, longer-term capital flows—particularly foreign direct investment (FDI) flows—should be liberalised before short-term flows. Fry (1997) emphasises that the successful removal of interest rate ceilings requires certain preconditions to be met, including adequate prudential regulation and supervision of commercial banks.

This chapter contributes to discussions of financial liberalisation in comparative financial systems. It follows a substantial literature studying Australian financial deregulation (Battellino and McMillan 1989; Grenville 1991; Debelle and Plumb 2006; Battellino and Plumb 2011) and financial reform in China (McKinnon 1994; Lardy 1998; Prasad and Wei 2005; Prasad et al. 2005; Allen et al. 2012; Huang et al. 2013; Eichengreen et al. 2014). It should be emphasised, however, that this chapter does not interpret Australia's experience as a prescription for China. Indeed, it emphasises the differences in initial conditions and aspects of Australia's financial arrangements, which the 'sequencing' literature would consider, prior to reform, as suboptimal. The chapter also stresses the interdependence between financial reform and financial deepening.

The chapter proceeds as follows. The next section discusses Australia's historical experience with financial deregulation. We then consider China's financial reforms to date and itemise the restrictions that currently affect interest rates, the exchange rate and capital flows. We then outline differences and similarities in the Australian and Chinese experiences, before offering some concluding remarks.

Australia's experience with financial reform

Prior to the float of the Australian dollar in 1983, Australia made a gradual transition through a series of increasingly flexible exchange rate regimes. This transition was related closely to the development of Australian financial markets—including closer integration with global financial markets—which made it increasingly difficult for the authorities to manage the exchange rate and control domestic monetary conditions. The authorities responded to these challenges with a series of financial reforms throughout the 1970s and 1980s.

The 1950s and 1960s

Prior to the 1970s, Australia had a fixed exchange rate regime, which was underpinned by a system of capital controls and a highly regulated domestic banking sector. Although the domestic banking sector remained underdeveloped, the prevailing view of policymakers was that the fixed exchange rate had been beneficial. Australia's generally strong postwar economic performance provided little evidence against this view. And with global financial integration still in its infancy under the Bretton Woods system, there was relatively little pressure— for example, from waves of capital inflows and outflows—to deviate from the established framework.

The fixed exchange rate regime and system of capital controls

From 1931 until the early 1970s, Australia's currency was pegged to the British pound sterling. There were no significant exchange controls in place during most of the 1930s, but in subsequent years the fixed exchange rate was underpinned by a comprehensive system of exchange controls, which were first introduced as emergency measures during World War II (Phillips 1985; Laker 1988). Under this system, all foreign currency transactions were prohibited unless approved or specifically exempted by the Reserve Bank of Australia (RBA), and participation in the foreign exchange market was restricted to designated 'trading' banks, which acted as agents for the RBA.

In practice, however, foreign exchange transactions related to trade and most current receipts were generally approved by the RBA, as were private capital inflows and repatriations of capital by foreign investors. That is, while the system of exchange controls had the *potential* to be quite restrictive, it was *applied* in a more permissive manner. This relatively permissive approach to inflows (and outflows) of foreign capital was consistent with a broader recognition by policymakers of the important role played by foreign investment in Australia's economic development. In contrast, Australian investment abroad was heavily restricted, reflecting the authorities' preference for domestic savings to be channelled into domestic investment (Battellino 2007).

The asymmetric nature of Australia's system of exchange controls was reflected in the composition of Australia's capital flows. Australian investment abroad by the 'non-official' sector was virtually nonexistent during the 1950s and 1960s, averaging just 0.2 per cent of GDP throughout this period, compared with an average of around 2 per cent in the decade after the float and removal of capital controls in 1983. In contrast, foreign investment in Australia's non-official sector averaged around 2.5 per cent of GDP during the 1950s and 1960s and around 6 per cent of GDP in the decade after the float.[2]

To maintain the peg to the UK pound, these net inflows of foreign capital were offset, as required, by outflows of official capital in the form of foreign exchange reserve accumulation. This was reflected in fairly consistent net outflows of capital from the RBA in the 1950s and 1960s, and indeed until the mid 1970s (Figure 11.1).[3]

2   Unless otherwise stated, Australian historical data are sourced from the *Australian economic statistics—1949–1950 to 1996–1997*, which were originally published as Occasional Paper No. 8 and are now available from: <http://www.rba.gov.au/statistics/frequency/occ-paper-8.html>.
3   One notable exception was 1952–53, which coincided with the end of the Korean War and the related wool price boom and a large rise in net exports. For more information, see Atkin et al. (2014).

Per cent of GDP

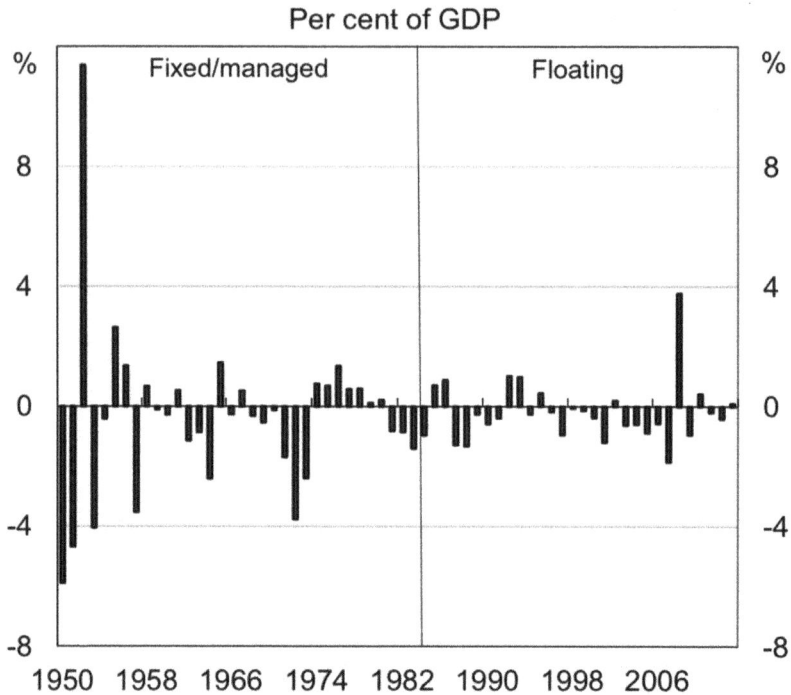

Figure 11.1 Net Capital Inflows to the RBA
Sources: Australian Bureau of Statistics (ABS); The Reserve Bank of Australia (RBA).

Domestic banking sector regulation

Australia also had a heavily regulated domestic banking sector, with quantitative and qualitative controls on bank lending, ceilings on banks' deposit and lending rates and reserve requirements all used.[4] These regulations, especially the reserve requirements, also served as the main tools for implementing monetary policy for much of the 1950s, 1960s and 1970s.

In addition to serving prudential and monetary policy purposes, these regulations also helped to maintain Australia's fixed exchange rate system by limiting capital inflows to the banking sector. For example, ceilings on deposit

---

4   For more detailed information on these regulations, see Grenville (1991) and Battellino and
    McMillan (1989).

rates limited the ability of domestic *trading banks* to attract overseas funding, while domestic *savings banks* were effectively unable to raise funds from overseas as they were not permitted to use wholesale funding.[5]

At the same time, however, heavy regulation of the banking sector impeded the sector's development. The ratio of bank assets to GDP stood at around 50 per cent in 1975, compared with around 200 per cent today. In comparison, the ratio of UK bank assets to GDP was higher in 1975, at around 100 per cent (Davies et al. 2010). Banks also had little experience in trading in foreign exchange markets, having been permitted to trade only as principals in the market from 1971—and then only in the context of a fixed exchange rate regime.[6]

The underdeveloped state of Australia's financial sector was an important consideration in the authorities' decision to retain a fixed exchange rate regime when the Bretton Woods system broke down in the early 1970s (Phillips 1984a). In contrast with most other present-day developed economies, which chose to adopt a more flexible exchange rate regime around this time, the Australian Government decided instead to simply replace the peg to the pound sterling with a peg to the US dollar (in recognition of the increased importance of the United States as a trading partner).

The 1970s

Maintaining the fixed exchange rate regime became more challenging in the late 1960s and early 1970s, as non-official capital inflows became larger and more varied in nature (Figure 11.2). In particular, the combination of larger capital flows, a growing non-bank financial sector and structural issues with the government debt market undermined the effectiveness of monetary policy (Grenville 1991). As a result, the authorities found it increasingly difficult to control domestic monetary conditions.

---

5 Broadly, savings banks lent to households and trading banks lent to businesses. While savings banks could accept deposits only from households and non-profit organisations, trading banks could raise wholesale deposits. Both were subject to a number of 'reserve requirements'; however, the requirements on savings banks were more stringent. For more information, see Battellino and McMillan (1989).
6 Before 1971, banks were only permitted to trade as agents of the RBA.

Non-official sector; per cent of GDP*

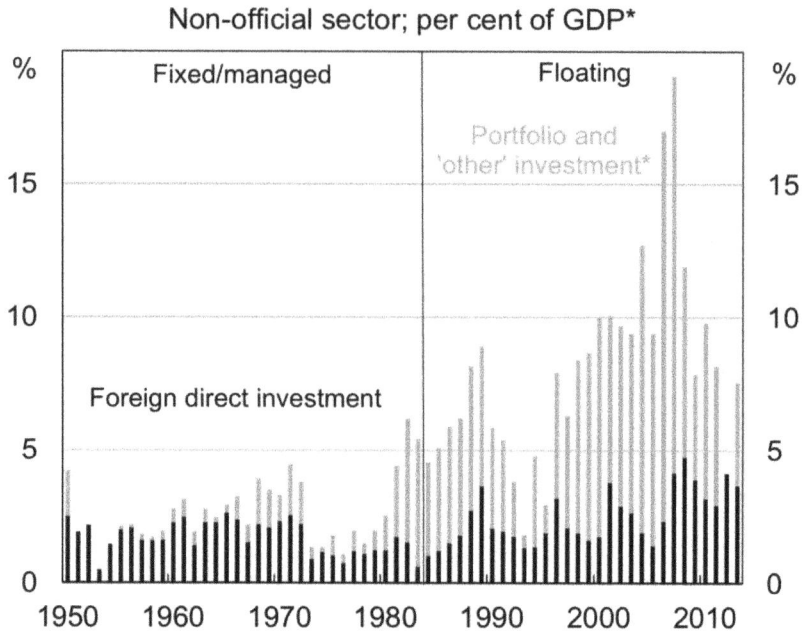

Figure 11.2 Australian Gross Capital Inflows

Sources: Australian Bureau of Statistics (ABS); The Reserve Bank of Australia (RBA).

Notes: Examples of 'other' investment flows are loans, deposits and accounts payable/receivable. Excludes financial derivatives where data are available.

The growth in the non-bank financial sector—which was fuelled partly by increased capital inflows—prompted the authorities to take initial steps towards banking sector deregulation. In many ways, this laid the groundwork for the eventual float of the exchange rate a decade later. Banking sector deregulation not only increased the challenges associated with capital flow management— arguably accelerating the transition from a fixed to a floating exchange rate regime—but it also facilitated domestic financial market development and innovation, laying the foundations for market participants to adapt to the new regime.

Capital flow management challenges

Australia experienced a period of noticeably larger capital inflows during the late 1960s and early 1970s—which coincided with a domestic mining boom— with gross capital inflows to the 'non-official' sector averaging almost 4 per cent of GDP in the five years to 1971–72, up from 2.5 per cent in the previous five years. Further, these flows increasingly arrived in the form of portfolio and 'other'—rather than direct—investment, which accounted for an average of 40 per cent of Australia's gross capital inflows in the five years to 1971–72, up from 20 per cent in the previous five years.[7] This shift in the composition of capital inflows was facilitated partly by an influx of international merchant banks into the Australian market, which increased domestic companies' awareness of, and access to, overseas capital (Australian Treasury 1999).[8]

These larger capital inflows made it increasingly difficult for the authorities to control domestic monetary conditions. Under the fixed exchange rate system, capital inflows added directly to domestic liquidity (and vice versa for capital outflows), as the RBA was obliged to meet all demand for Australian dollars at the official rate. While the authorities could (and did) attempt to sterilise the impact of the additional liquidity by changing reserve requirements on banks, this mechanism became less effective as banks lost market share to non-bank financial institutions. Authorities also could (and did) attempt to sterilise the additional liquidity via domestic market operations, but this often led to higher interest rates, which could then encourage further inflows. The effectiveness of open market operations as a liquidity management tool was further hampered by structural issues associated with the market for government securities.[9]

Early steps in the deregulation of the banking sector (discussed further below) compounded the effects of this additional liquidity on the domestic economy. In particular, the removal of quantitative controls on bank lending in 1971, and the removal of interest rate ceilings on large loans in early 1972, allowed banks to profitably lend these additional funds. Further, the removal of the ceiling on interest rates payable on certificates of deposit (CDs) in 1973 allowed banks to compete more effectively for these funds. These factors contributed to a large increase in the rate of growth in bank lending, which reached more than 30 per cent in year-ended terms in 1973 (Figure 11.3).

---

7   'Other' investment primarily consists of loans (including trade credit) and deposits.

8   Many of these merchant banks entered the Australian market with the intention of funding mining projects that, due to regulations, could not be funded by domestic banks.

9   These included procedural issues associated with the 'tap' system of primary issuance for government securities, as well as issues associated with banks' large 'captive' holdings of government securities. For more information, see Grenville (1991).

Annual*

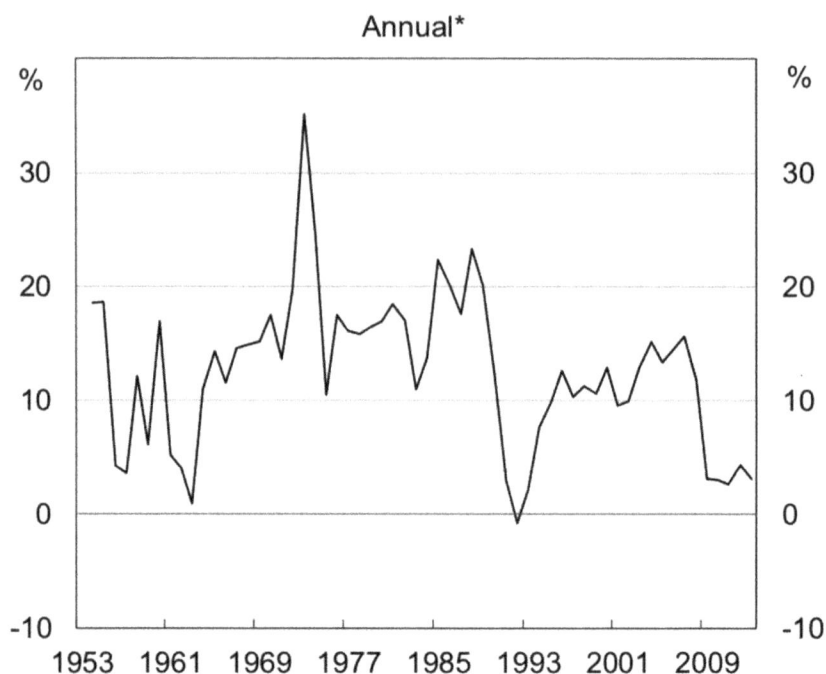

Figure 11.3 Australian Domestic Credit Growth

Source: The Reserve Bank of Australia (RBA).

Note: Series are break and seasonally adjusted where available.

The policy response

In response to these large portfolio inflows—and more specifically, to the effects of these flows on domestic liquidity and credit growth—the authorities revalued the Australian dollar by 7 per cent against the US dollar in late 1972. A number of 'supplementary' exchange controls were also introduced, including an embargo on loans from overseas with a maturity of less than two years and a variable deposit requirement (VDR) for overseas loans with a maturity greater than two years. The VDR was preferred over other forms of capital control as it was considered to be a more 'market-based' mechanism (Australian Treasury 1999).

The VDR initially required 25 per cent of overseas borrowings to be placed in an interest-free account at the RBA, which effectively acted as a tax. The measures were considered to be largely successful, contributing to a marked contraction in capital inflows, particularly portfolio inflows, and a sharp tightening in domestic monetary conditions (Australian Treasury 1999;

Debelle and Plumb 2006). Over the following decade, a number of changes were made to the VDR and the embargo in response to changes in the volume and composition of Australian capital flows.

Around the same time, authorities began to deregulate the banking sector. The move towards deregulation was prompted by a decline in the sector's market share, as banks found it increasingly difficult to compete with non-bank financial institutions (NBFIs). As NBFIs were not subject to the same stringent regulations as banks, they were able to compete more aggressively for funding and were able to provide loans to a broader range of borrowers (including riskier ones).

The growth of the NBFI sector diminished the effectiveness of monetary policy by lessening the economic impact of changes in bank reserve requirements, interest rate ceilings and credit directives.[10] While some policymakers favoured extending regulation to the NBFI sector, there was a growing consensus in favour of more market-oriented policies, rather than direct controls (Phillips 1984b). Consequently, the decision was made to remove some of the controls on banks' balance sheets and to attempt to transmit monetary policy through the general level of interest rates—which would in turn be influenced by the RBA's open market operations.[11]

The first major step in the deregulation of the banking sector was taken in 1973, when the interest rate ceiling on CDs was removed. This allowed trading banks to compete for funds and gave them control over a larger portion of their balance sheets.[12] In particular, it allowed them to manage their liabilities more actively, which has subsequently been cited as having played a crucial role in preparing banks for the larger capital flows that were ultimately associated with capital account liberalisation in the early 1980s (Battellino and McMillan 1989).

---

10 The effectiveness of monetary policy was further diminished by banks' increasing use of the bank bill market, which was off-balance sheet and was regulated less heavily (Grenville 1991).

11 This shift in the approach to monetary policy implementation was facilitated by a lower level of government debt—which had declined to 30 per cent of GDP by 1970, from 100 per cent in 1950—and the authorities' greater readiness to accept changes in interest rates (Grenville 1991).

12 Savings banks were still constrained by interest rate ceilings on housing loans and the prohibition on raising wholesale deposits. Consequently, their behaviour was largely unchanged in response to the removal of interest rate ceilings on CDs (Battellino and McMillan 1989).

The market response

Despite these policy changes, the Australian dollar's peg to the US dollar continued to be difficult to maintain. Following a number of upward revaluations in the early 1970s, the US dollar peg was replaced with a peg to a trade-weighted basket of currencies in 1974, at a rate that implied a 12 per cent devaluation against the US dollar (Figure 11.4).

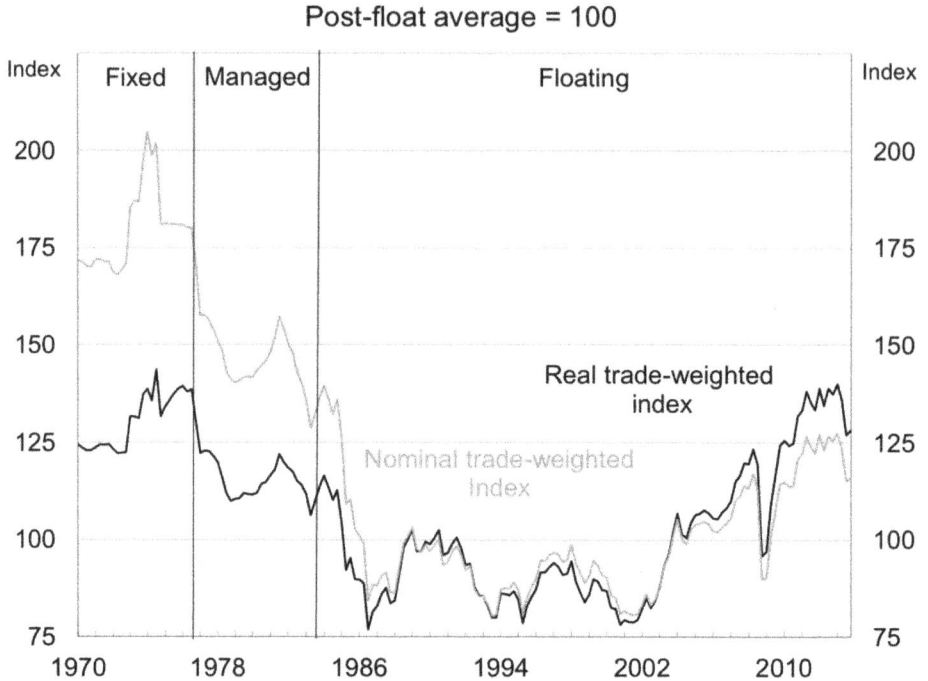

Figure 11.4 Australian Nominal and Real Exchange Rates

Sources: Australian Bureau of Statistics (ABS); The Reserve Bank of Australia (RBA); Thomson Reuters; WM/Reuters Service at <http://www.wmcompany.com/wmr/index.htm>.

In 1976, speculators forced a further large, discrete devaluation of the currency, leading to the adoption of a crawling peg (Laker 1988). The crawling peg was intended to prevent the build-up of appreciation or depreciation pressures (followed by large discrete adjustments). The value was to be set daily by joint decision of the RBA, Treasury and the Department of Prime Minister and Cabinet. While day-to-day changes in the value of the Australian dollar were initially small and infrequent, they became larger and more frequent over time. For example, in 1977 the value of the Trade Weighted Index (TWI) peg was adjusted on just 46 trading days, whereas in 1983 the TWI was adjusted on 121 trading days (prior to the eventual float of the currency on 12 December). Nevertheless, the magnitude of daily movements was still small compared with movements in floating currencies. Daily changes in the Australian dollar TWI rarely exceeded 0.2 per cent, whereas for the major currencies daily movements of more than 1 per cent were not uncommon (Laker 1988).

The large, discrete revaluations of the Australian dollar over the preceding few years—and then the introduction of an increasingly flexible peg to the TWI—meant the Australian dollar's bilateral exchange rate with the US dollar had become more variable. At the same time, firms were also increasing their use of foreign funding sources. As a result, firms were exposed to a greater degree of foreign currency risk than previously, providing them with stronger incentives to manage their foreign currency exposure actively.

In response, the private sector developed an unofficial foreign currency hedging market in an effort to supplement the relatively limited forward cover that was provided at the time by the RBA.[13] This market was an onshore non-deliverable forward (NDF) market: as the contracts were settled in Australian dollars, they did not violate the existing exchange controls. The onshore NDF market is now recognised as having been an important precursor to modern-day hedging markets, which have developed to play a crucial role in insulating Australian entities from foreign currency risk under the floating exchange rate regime.[14]

The 1980s

Although increased innovation and integration in financial markets were a natural consequence of deregulation, they also made Australia's system of exchange controls increasingly ineffective. For example, the NDF market provided a means by which participants could speculate on the exchange rate without the need for large upfront payments, while the gradual freeing up of restrictions on deposit rates (which ultimately included the removal of all ceilings on deposit rates by 1980) made it easier for banks to attract foreign funds (Battellino 2007).

The decreasing effectiveness of Australia's capital controls placed additional pressure on Australia's crawling peg. Large capital flows often occurred in anticipation of future change in the exchange rate, or in response to the RBA's attempts to tighten monetary policy. Under the managed exchange rate regime, these flows affected the money supply and contributed both to large misses

---

13 The RBA only provided forward cover for trade-related transactions, not for capital transactions. Further, from May 1974 this cover had to be obtained within seven days of the transaction. This was known as the 'seven-day rule'. It was introduced to prevent participants from taking out forward cover just before an expected revaluation (Manuell 1986:177; Debelle and Plumb 2006).

14 For more information on foreign currency hedging in Australia, see Becker and Fabbro (2006) and Rush et al. (2013).

of the monetary targets in the early 1980s and to volatility in short and long-term interest rates.[15] Consequently, by the late 1970s and early 1980s, Australia's relative exchange rate stability was being achieved at the cost of volatility in domestic financial conditions (Debelle and Plumb 2006).

While some measures were introduced in an attempt to counteract these capital flows, they ultimately proved ineffective.[16] On 9 December 1983, faced with the prospect of further large capital inflows, the authorities suspended banks' foreign currency trading to allow time to decide on a course of action. The decision was made to float the Australian dollar—effective from 12 December 1983. While some brief consideration appears to have been given to the alternative option of strengthening capital controls, such controls were considered costly, ineffective and inefficient (Laker 1988).

Although the decision to float the dollar and to liberalise the capital account was taken over the course of just one day, there had been growing acceptance—at least among some policymakers—of the potential merits of a more flexible exchange rate regime for some years. For example, in 1981 the Campbell Committee inquiry into the Australian financial system had recommended moving to a floating exchange rate regime, noting that exchange controls were costly and inefficient and were unlikely to be effective in regulating short-term capital flows (Laker 1988). Most capital controls were removed at the same time as the float, because they existed largely for the purpose of maintaining the fixed exchange rate. One key exception was a ban on foreign government and central bank purchases of Australian interest-bearing assets, which was maintained in an attempt to ensure that the Australian dollar would not become a reserve currency (Phillips 1985).

Deregulation of the banking sector was not complete at the time of the float. While interest rate ceilings had been removed for all deposits, ceilings on lending rates had been removed only for loans exceeding A$100 000. Moreover, the banking sector also remained subject to a number of balance sheet restrictions, with these restrictions—as well as the interest rate ceilings on small loans—remaining in place until the mid to late 1980s.[17]

---

15 The large misses of the monetary targets occurred despite introduction of the 'tender' system for primary issuance of government securities, which gave authorities more control over domestic liquidity. For more details, see Grenville (1991).

16 In particular, a number of measures were introduced to prevent participants from speculating on the next day's Australian dollar/US dollar mid-rate based on movements in major currencies during Australia's trading day. These included announcing the mid-rate in the afternoon, rather than in the morning, and occasionally making unexpected changes to the TWI peg (Debelle and Plumb 2006).

17 For a timeline of the changes to bank regulations, see Battellino and McMillan (1989).

The immediate effects of floating the Australian dollar and liberalising the capital account were largely as expected. In particular, capital outflows increased substantially as the relatively restrictive controls on overseas investment by Australian residents were removed (Figure 11.5). Capital inflows increased by even more, however, and net capital inflows settled at a level that was somewhat higher than they had been before the capital account was liberalised (Battellino and Plumb 2011).

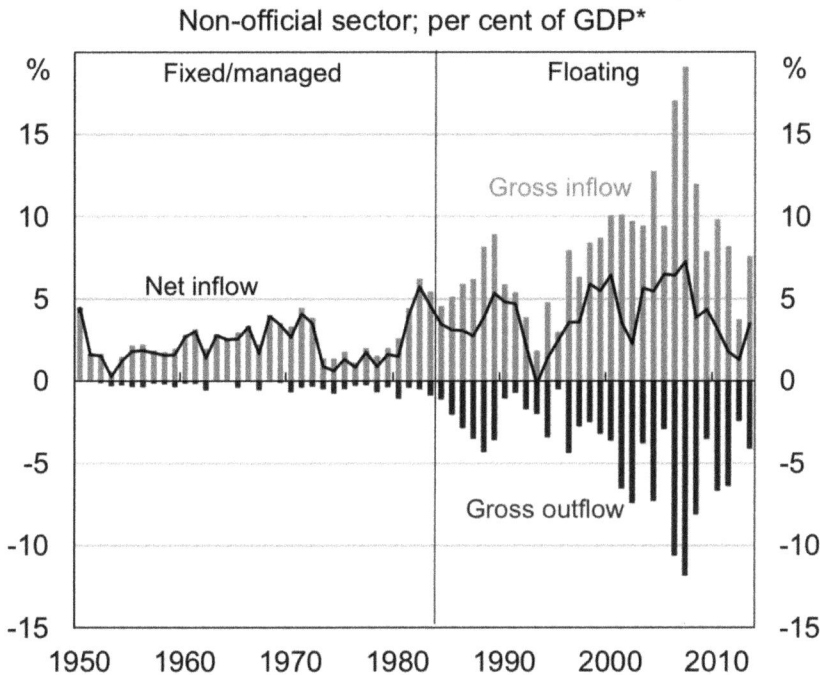

Non-official sector; per cent of GDP*

Figure 11.5 Australian Gross and Net Capital Flows
Sources: Australian Bureau of Statistics (ABS); The Reserve Bank of Australia (RBA);
Note: Excludes financial derivatives where data are available.

Meanwhile, the exchange rate naturally became more volatile after the float, interest rates became more stable and authorities were better able to control domestic financial conditions (Figure 11.6). This was reinforced by the adoption of an inflation target in the early 1990s, which was the culmination of an extended search for a credible nominal anchor and framework for monetary policy (Stevens et al. 2010).

Absolute monthly change; 6-month rolling average

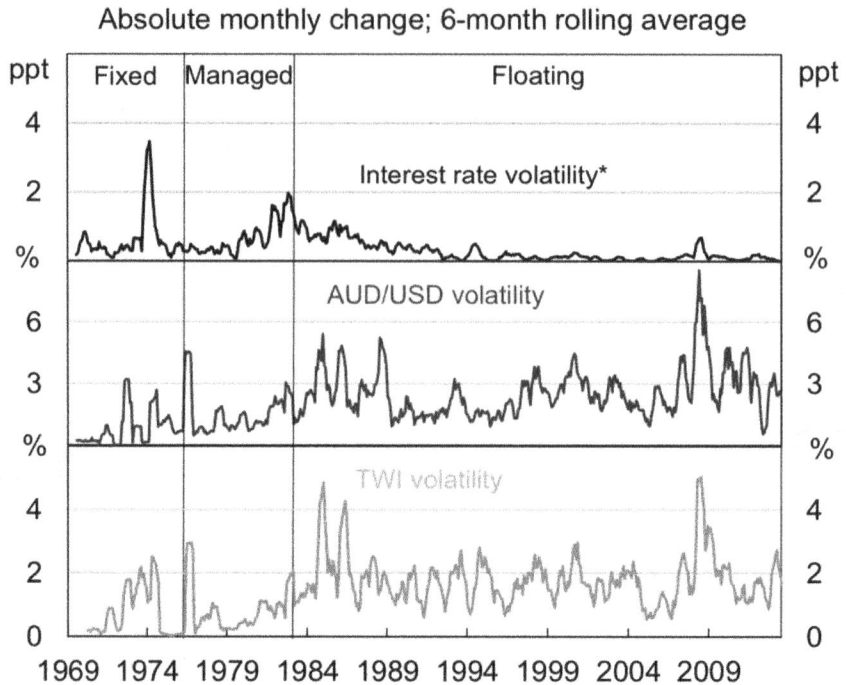

Figure 11.6 Australian Interest Rate and Exchange Rate Volatility

* 90-day bank bill

Sources: AFMA at <http://www.afma.com.au/home.html>; Bloomberg; Global Financial Data; Thomson Reuters.

Although the float itself was intended to be relatively 'clean', the RBA intervened frequently to influence the foreign exchange market throughout most of the 1980s. The RBA's intervention transactions during this so-called 'testing and smoothing' period tended to be small in size—but relatively frequent—and were designed both to increase the RBA's understanding of how the market operated and to dampen episodes of substantial volatility (Becker and Sinclair 2004; Newman et al. 2011). The focus on reducing volatility during these early years was motivated in large part by the fact that foreign exchange market participants still had relatively limited experience of managing their foreign currency exposure; however, as the foreign exchange market developed—and, in particular, as the supply of foreign exchange derivatives for hedging purposes increased—the RBA became less concerned about market participants' ability to hedge their exchange rate risk. As a consequence, intervention transactions became less frequent, but more targeted towards addressing episodes of market dysfunction. There were also some episodes where intervention was designed to affect the *level* of the exchange rate, rather than market dysfunction per se, but these were rare.

Developments since the float

The decision to introduce a floating exchange rate is now widely recognised as having brought substantial benefit to the Australian economy (Beaumont and Cui 2007; Lowe 2013; Stevens 2013). In addition to the advantages associated with monetary policy independence, exchange rate flexibility has played a crucial role in buffering the economy from external shocks, in particular—given Australia's status as a small, open commodity exporter—from terms-of-trade shocks. The exchange rate's role as a buffer was also exemplified during the Asian financial crisis in 1997–98, the tech boom and bust in the early 2000s, and again during the GFC in 2008–09. Sharp depreciations of the Australian dollar during each of these episodes served to offset part of the contractionary effects of these crises.

Nevertheless, there were challenges associated with Australia's adoption of a floating exchange rate, particularly in the early stages of the regime. Most notably, deficiencies in the prudential supervision framework and an underdeveloped foreign exchange hedging market meant that the transition was not smooth; however, both of these elements—which are now recognised as being crucial for minimising the financial instability risks that can be associated with a floating exchange rate and open capital account—have developed over time. In part, this has occurred in response to the incentives created by the floating exchange rate regime itself.

Banking supervision

At the time of the float, Australian banks and regulators were relatively inexperienced at assessing and pricing risk, notwithstanding some of the earlier steps taken towards financial deregulation in the 1970s. This reflected the fact that banking sector regulations had served to ration credit, so banks were accustomed to—and able to profit from—lending only to the most credit-worthy borrowers. Consequently, they had not developed the ability to assess and price risk for less credit-worthy borrowers (Thompson 1991; Lowe 2013).

When these regulations were removed, banks attempted to expand their market share by offering credit to higher-risk borrowers. This competition for market share intensified with the entry of foreign banks in the mid 1980s and was, at least in part, funded by increased capital inflows associated with the removal of capital controls. The combination of pent-up demand for credit, relatively underdeveloped risk-assessment frameworks (both for banks and for prudential supervisors), freer access to overseas capital and increased competition led to a boom in credit, and then to a bubble, and eventual bust, in commercial property prices in the late 1980s and large losses for banks (Figure 11.7). This episode led to an increase in the pace of reform to risk-management practices for banks and regulators and, later, a broader overhaul of the regulatory framework (Gizycki and Lowe 2000).

Per cent of nominal GDP*

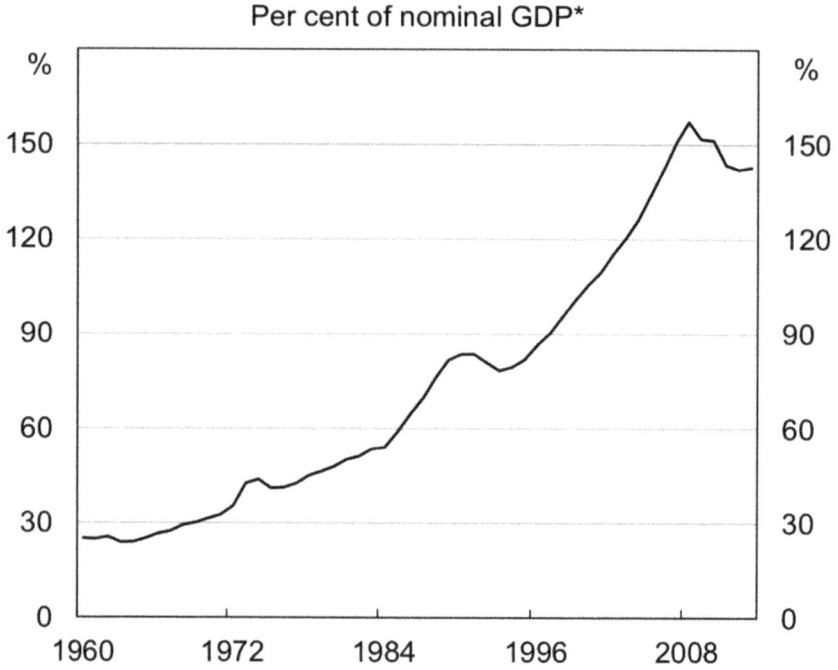

Figure 11.7 Australian Credit

Sources: Australian Bureau of Statistics (ABS); The Reserve Bank of Australia (RBA); Australian Prudential Regulation Authority (APRA) at <http://www.apra.gov.au/Pages/default.aspx>.

Note: Not adjusted for breaks.

Development of hedging markets

Market participants had developed a relatively small foreign exchange derivatives market before the float. Yet the float proved to be the catalyst for further development in Australia's (non-deliverable) hedging and (deliverable) foreign exchange markets, with these markets doubling and tripling in size, respectively, within a year (Phillips 1984a) (Figure 11.8).

Daily average; per cent of annual GDP*

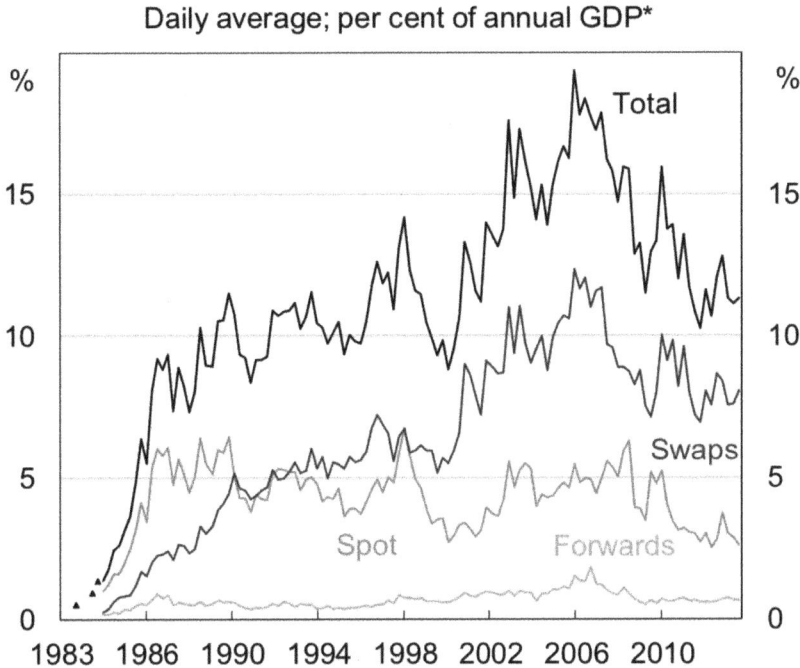

Figure 11.8 Foreign Exchange Turnover in the Australian Market

Sources: Phillips (1984a); The Reserve Bank of Australia (RBA).

Note: Excludes the non-deliverable 'hedge' market, which existed until the late 1980s.

Nevertheless, it took time for hedging practices to develop. While some entities had gained experience in managing their foreign currency exposure during the pre-float period, others were not sufficiently aware of the risks of such exposure in the early stages of the floating exchange rate regime. For example, in the mid 1980s a number of borrowers took out loans denominated in Swiss francs, without being adequately prepared for the potential exchange rate risk associated with this practice. When the Australian dollar depreciated sharply between 1985 and 1986, many were unprepared for the higher Australian dollar payments required to service the loans. While the scale of the borrowing and the associated losses were relatively small, the episode received a large amount of publicity. The high-profile nature of the episode, together with agents' growing experience with a relatively volatile floating exchange rate, may help to explain the relatively high level of hedging in the Australian economy today (Becker and Fabbro 2006; Battellino and Plumb 2011).

Finally, the market also needed to develop a deep and diverse pool of participants. In particular, the ability of Australian entities to hedge their foreign currency risk ultimately depends on foreigners being willing to hold Australian dollar exposure.[18] This demand for Australian dollar exposure depends on both the return and the perceived risk associated with the investment. Over time, the latter has been closely linked to investors' perceptions about the credibility of Australia's economic policy framework and institutions.

China's Financial System Reforms

Unlike Australia in the early 1980s, China's financial system reforms have occurred as part of a gradual, closely managed transition from a centrally planned economy towards a market-oriented economy. Prior to the period of 'reform and opening' initiated in December 1978, interest rates on loans and deposits were set directly by the Central Government; the interbank market, stock markets and bond markets did not exist; the renminbi was largely unconvertible for current and capital account transactions; and foreign investment was negligible. The decision to reform the financial system occurred at an early stage, and was consistent with a broader retreat from central planning towards a hybrid economic model characterised by a growing role for the market economy but continued high levels of government intervention.

Ambitious reforms to build a modern financial system and reduce the role of the state in the economy in the 1990s accelerated China's move towards deregulation; but rising banking sector fragility and the non-performing loan (NPL) crisis of the late 1990s—combined with the 1997–98 Asian financial crisis—highlighted the potential risks of moving quickly on financial reform, contributing to a very gradual pace of reform in the 2000s.

The expanding financial system

Initially, economic reforms focused on reducing price controls and creating market incentives in agriculture, and reducing barriers to entry in industries previously controlled by state-owned enterprises (SOEs). This resulted in rapid growth in productivity and output that was accompanied by an expansion of the financial system.

---

18 While there are some natural counterparties who wish to hedge Australian dollar exposures into foreign currencies, such as Kangaroo-bond issuers, these are not sufficient to meet the demand for the hedging of foreign currency exposures into Australian dollars. Consequently, foreign investors have tended to take a net long position in the Australian dollar (McCauley 2006).

Banking system and interest rate regulation in the 1980s

Banking deregulation in China followed a distinctly different path to that in Australia, in part because of the dominant role of SOEs and state-owned banks in the Chinese economy. In the pre-reform era, household savings were low and banks acted effectively as conduits for trade credit and working capital to SOEs, within limits set by a centrally determined credit plan. At the outset of reform, financial services were provided by three state-owned banks and a network of rural credit cooperatives (RCCs) that provided banking services in rural areas. Through the mid and late 1980s, the authorities approved the creation of numerous new national and regional bank and non-bank financial institutions, regulated by the PBC, which was designated as the central bank in 1983.[19] By the mid 1980s, a large number of non-bank financial intermediaries, including urban credit cooperatives and trust and investment companies, had emerged to supplement the SOE-oriented lending activities of banks and to meet the funding needs of the growing non-state sector (Lardy 1998:61–76).

At the start of reforms, the schedule of interest rates for deposits and loans of various tenors and types was set centrally by the Government. As the banking system expanded, however, the authorities began to experiment with increased interest rate flexibility. In 1983, the PBC was authorised by the State Council (China's cabinet) to vary interest rates by 20 per cent on either side of centrally determined benchmark rates.[20] Yet policymakers were initially reluctant to increase the floating range of interest rates, fearing it would harm the profitability of enterprises (Yi 2009).[21]

The authorities also experimented with floating deposit rates for RCCs, and trust and investment companies, but these pilot reforms were aborted when the resulting competition for deposits (particularly by the more poorly performing financial institutions) led to substantial movements of deposits across institutions and violations of interest rate ceilings on other products (PBC 2005). In 1987, the PBC permitted the large banks to increase lending rates for working capital loans by up to 20 per cent over the benchmark rate. In 1990 this flexibility was extended to lending rates for commercial banks and urban credit cooperatives, but problems that had been experienced in pilot efforts to float deposit rates led the authorities, in the same year, to prohibit increases in deposit rates above the benchmark for all financial institutions (PBC 2005).

---

19 The PBC coordinated with the State Planning Commission to develop the national credit plan. It was legally confirmed as the central bank in 1995.
20 This authorisation was given in State Council Document No. 100 (1983).
21 For this reason, the upward flexibility of lending rates was reduced to 10 per cent in 1996 (Yi 2009).

Capital controls and the exchange rate in the 1980s

Prior to economic reform, the Chinese Government had imposed a centralised foreign exchange system whereby detailed plans had to be submitted to the authorities for approval in advance of all trade-related or foreign investment-related foreign exchange transactions, foreign investment projects or external borrowing (Prasad and Wei 2005). All foreign exchange earnings had to be sold to the Government. This restrictive foreign exchange system had a parallel in restrictions on foreign trade: in the early years of reform, exports and imports were controlled by a complicated schedule of trading rights, import licences, quotas and tariffs (Lardy 2002: ch. 2).

The growth of the domestic financial system in the 1980s coincided with increasing openness to world trade, a dismantling of the pre-reform system of centrally planned exports and imports, and increased international flows of capital. To support inward direct investment, numerous 'special economic zones' featuring tax and other incentives to attract foreign investment were established. Regulations announced in 1980 retained centralised foreign exchange management (that is, requiring approval for individual current and capital account transactions), but resident entities and foreigners were allowed to retain or trade a portion of their foreign exchange.

The increased availability of foreign exchange onshore led to the creation of a market-based foreign exchange market (sanctioned by the Government) alongside the official market. A dual exchange rate system emerged, with only around 20 per cent of foreign exchange traded at the official rate (Yi 2008). From the mid to late 1980s, the official rate was devalued several times to bring it more in line with the market-determined rate, but the dual system prevailed until 1994.

Growth of financial markets and banking sector fragility in the 1990s

The period beginning in the mid 1990s and ending in the early 2000s saw an expansion of China's financial market infrastructure, but also risks to financial stability. Seeking to diversify funding for the corporate sector, the Government opened the Shanghai and Shenzhen stock exchanges in 1990 and 1991, respectively, and subsequently allowed the creation of numerous regional exchanges. These exchanges became a platform for various financial instruments including shares, government bonds and corporate bonds. Local currency bond repurchase agreements (repos) were first introduced in 1991 on a number of securities trading platforms, and in 1993 on the Shanghai Stock Exchange.

The development of capital market infrastructure centred on the stock exchanges resulted in leakages of bank funding, via securities companies and institutional investors, into the stock market. This aroused concern among policymakers about systemic risks stemming from rapid growth in asset prices. In response, in 1997–98 the Government created separate regulatory frameworks for the banking, trust, securities and insurance sectors, eliminated smaller securities markets and required all banks to migrate their business from the exchange markets to the interbank market, which had been expanding since the mid 1980s (Zheng 2007:52; Tan 2007:223–4). Between 1997 and 1999 interbank markets for bonds and repos were established, with floating interest rates for government bonds and policy financial bonds.[22]

Although the size of financial markets increased during the 1990s, they remained small compared with the formal banking system, whose fragility was underscored by the NPL crisis of the late 1990s. The crisis had its origins in the rising leverage of the SOEs. Growing competition from the private sector, and declining state support, led to more bank borrowing by unprofitable SOEs and a sharp rise in inter-enterprise liabilities—or 'triangular debt'—as firms incurred debts (often in the form of unpaid bills) to other firms. Some observers estimate that more than half of China's SOEs were insolvent by the mid 1990s (Lardy 1998:175).

Despite efforts to reform the SOEs through privatisation initiatives and to improve the asset-liability management of the banks (including imposing a 75 per cent maximum loan-to-deposit ratio), by 1997–98 the largest four banks' NPLs had risen to between one-quarter and one-third of total assets (Bonin and Huang 2001). Although China's strong capital controls allowed it to weather the 1997–98 Asian financial crisis, the concurrent NPL crisis heightened policymakers' concerns about domestic financial fragility. The Government responded swiftly, recapitalising the state-owned banks, introducing debt-for-equity swaps and creating four asset-management companies to purchase banks' NPLs at face value and begin the process of their disposal (PBC 2000:31–8). Subsequently, NPLs moderated steadily, but the fragility in the banking system that surfaced in the late 1990s contributed to subsequent gradualism in domestic financial reform.

---

22 Policy financial bonds are used as a source of funding by China's policy banks—namely, the China Development Bank, the Agricultural Development Bank of China and the Export–Import Bank of China.

Steps towards interest rate deregulation in the late 1990s – early 2000s

The 1990s saw incremental progress in deregulating bank lending and deposit rates. In 1993, the State Council issued a decision on financial system reforms that incorporated a strategy for interest rate liberalisation (PBC 2003:14). Following the deregulation of interbank lending and repo rates in the mid to late 1990s, the PBC resumed efforts to increase the flexibility of bank lending rates. The PBC's objective was to encourage banks to lend to small and medium enterprises, which tended to receive fewer loans than larger firms that were seen to be more credit-worthy (Yi 2009). In the late 1990s and early 2000s, interest rate ceilings for bank loans to small and medium-sized enterprises and foreign currency loans, and RCC lending rates were granted further flexibility (PBC 1999:22; 2000:26). In October 2004, ceilings on almost all lending rates were abolished while the floor was retained at 0.9 times the benchmark.

Efforts to reform deposit rates also resumed towards the end of the decade. In 1999 the PBC took tentative steps towards liberalising wholesale deposit rates by allowing banks flexibility to negotiate contract interest rates for large-scale commercial deposits with insurance companies (PBC 2003:15). Similar to the experience of the 1980s, broader reforms to deposit rates were delayed by concerns that upward flexibility would lead to unhealthy competition among banks that would diminish their margins. A small-scale trial to reduce ceilings on RCCs' deposit rates in 2002 failed to achieve the expected results, leading once again to such efforts being postponed (Guo 2013). But there was increasing recognition that the floors on deposit rates were redundant, and by October 2004 the floor on interest rates had been abolished for all deposits (Yi 2009). The 2004 reforms marked the start of a policy to manage only the floors of lending rates and the ceilings of deposit rates, effectively guaranteeing a minimum net interest margin for the banks.

The currency regime and capital controls in the 1990s

Moves to increase the flexibility of interest rates occurred alongside changes to exchange rate policy. In January 1994 the official and market-based exchange rates were unified at the prevailing market rate. This resulted in a large official devaluation of the renminbi (Figure 11.9). The exchange rate was initially allowed to follow a managed float, which resulted in gradual appreciation, but the authorities reimposed a peg to the US dollar during the Asian financial crisis, with this peg remaining in place until 2005.

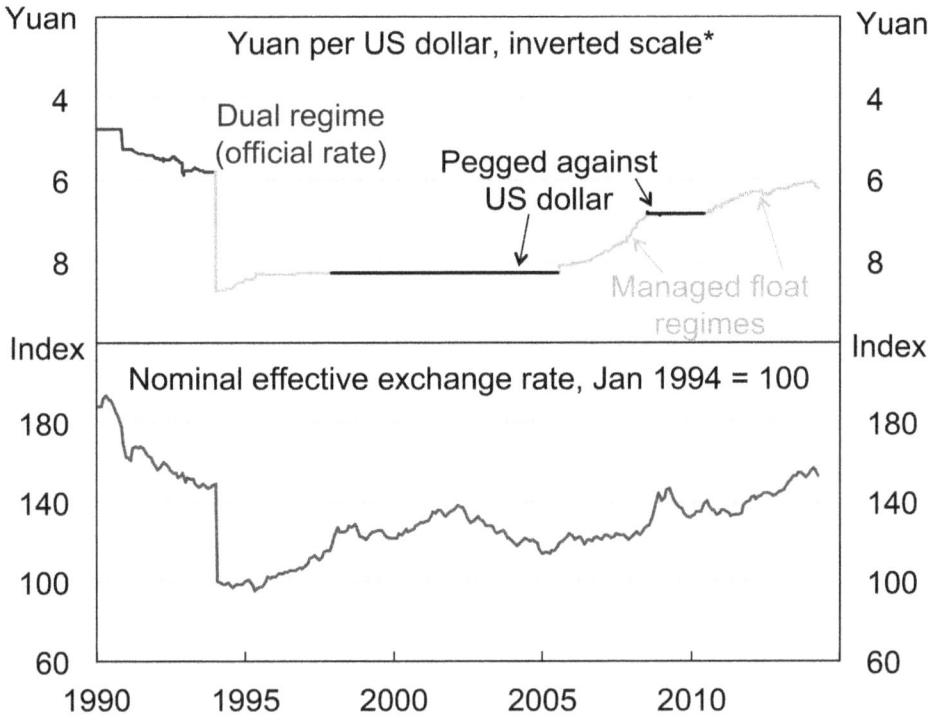

Figure 11.9 Chinese Renminbi

* Onshore exchange rates

Sources: Bank of International Settlement (BIS); Bloomberg; The Reserve Bank of Australia (RBA).

The 1994 exchange rate reform resulted in changes in the implementation of China's foreign exchange controls. The interbank China Foreign Exchange Trade System (CFETS) was established, initially with the PBC as the sole market maker and counterparty. Most enterprises were required to sell all foreign exchange earnings above certain limits to authorised banks, which would in turn convert these funds to renminbi on the CFETS. Importers seeking to purchase foreign exchange for trade settlement were required to submit import contracts and other documentation to authorised banks.

In 1996, China formally achieved convertibility on the current account, defined as trade in goods and services, net income from foreign investments and labour remittances. While current account transactions still required the submission of supporting documents and most foreign exchange earnings had to be sold to the banks, these transactions no longer required formal approval from the authorities. Capital account transactions, however, remained tightly controlled: all foreign exchange transactions affecting the foreign assets or liabilities of domestic residents either required official approval or were explicitly prohibited (Le 2007:114).

Similar to the Australian experience, in China, inward direct investment continued to be encouraged, and expanded significantly from the mid 1990s, albeit remaining subject to review by relevant authorities and subject to the Government's industrial policies. In contrast, portfolio flows such as transactions in capital market securities or money market instruments were generally prohibited without prior approval (Prasad and Wei 2005).

While the period between the early 1990s and the early 2000s saw modest changes in capital controls, it is likely that China's experience during the Asian financial crisis increased the Government's level of comfort with the prevailing arrangements (Yu 2013). Despite large currency depreciations among China's trading partners during the crisis, which led to a loss of competitiveness for Chinese exporters, policymakers resisted the temptation to engage in competitive devaluations and instead decided to peg the renminbi to the US dollar and accept export losses (Hu 2010). While China's trade performance during the crisis was poor, the strong capital controls in place provided substantial insulation from speculative capital flows. Following current account convertibility in 1996, policymakers initially planned to achieve capital account convertibility within five to 10 years (Huang et al. 2013:109), but the Asian financial crisis, and rising banking sector stress in the late 1990s, contributed to these plans being postponed.

China's evolving financial reform agenda

In the past decade, the overall framework of tight internal financial regulation, strong controls on portfolio capital flows and a steadily appreciating currency has remained in place, although there have been a number of significant changes. First, the regulatory framework has been strengthened, including through the creation of a separate banking regulator in 2003. Second, interest rates and the exchange rate have been given increased flexibility. Third, the emphasis of monetary policy has shifted. The PBC continues to guide individual banks' credit extension to priority sectors ('window guidance') and maintains informal loan quotas, but it has phased out mandatory credit ceilings, and has made more use of interest rate changes, required reserve ratio adjustments and open market operations. Fourth, further restrictions on capital flows have been removed, in particular those relating to inbound FDI in manufacturing. While control of portfolio flows has remained tight, since the late 2000s efforts by the authorities to promote the internationalisation of China's currency have seen growth in offshore renminbi deposits and an increase in avenues for cross-border flows.

Banking sector deregulation

According to Huang et al. (2013:97), between 1996 and 2007 around 120 types of interest rates underwent reform. In general, the approach to interest rate liberalisation followed the sequencing principles of 'foreign currency interest rates before local currency interest rates', 'loans before deposits', 'long-term wholesale interest rates before short-term retail interest rates' and 'rural areas before urban areas' (PBC 2000:26; 2005). In 2012, the PBC reduced the floor on lending rates and increased the flexibility of deposit rates slightly. In 2013 it abolished all restrictions on lending rates (except for rates on individual mortgages).[23]

Although lending rates are now largely liberalised, authorities have been reluctant to remove ceilings on regulated deposit rates. In late 2013, as a preliminary step towards deposit rate liberalisation, the PBC announced that banks would be given the flexibility to set negotiable rates on interbank CDs. In March 2014, the PBC's governor stated that deposit rates could be liberalised within one to two years (PBC 2014).

While policymakers have remained cautious about formally deregulating deposit rates, a significant de facto liberalisation of deposit rates has occurred in recent years. In response to the GFC of 2008–09, the authorities initiated a large-scale loosening of credit conditions to support growth (Figure 11.10). With banks restricted in lending by loan-to-deposit ratios and local governments restricted from borrowing directly on capital markets, the policy easing led to a rise in borrowing from corporate entities established by local governments, and significant intermediation of funds through NBFIs—particularly trust companies—working in cooperation with commercial banks. Banks were able to fund loans, off-balance sheet, to local governments, property developers and manufacturing firms by issuing 'wealth management products'—effectively term deposits with interest rates that were much higher than regulated deposit ceilings.

---

23 By this stage the floor on lending rates was not effectively binding: only 37 per cent of loans were extended at rates below or at the benchmark as of June 2013.

Annual flows; per cent of GDP

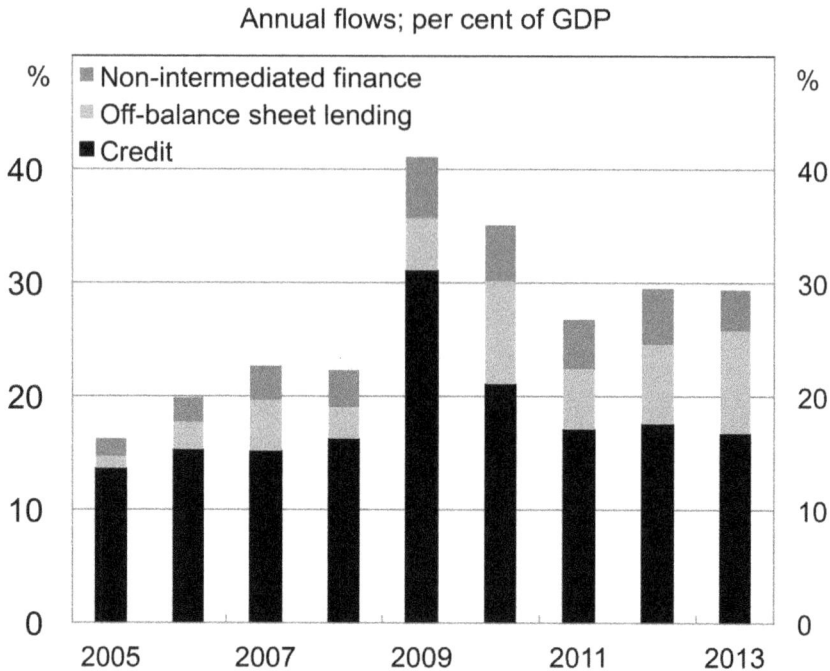

Figure 11.10 Chinese Total Social Financing

Sources: CEIC data at <http://dev.ceicdata.securities.com/about_ceic.html>; The Reserve Bank of Australia (RBA).

Capital controls

Since the early 2000s, capital controls have continued to be eased very gradually, although FDI in the services sectors (including financial services) continues to be limited and portfolio flows remain to a large extent forbidden. As a share of GDP, both gross and net flows have not increased dramatically compared with the 1990s, although they remain well above the level of the 1980s (Figure 11.11). Restrictions on foreign exchange purchases for foreign currency loans, foreign debts and pre-approved strategic foreign projects were removed in the early 2000s, and in 2002 a Qualified Foreign Institutional Investor (QFII) program allowed approved foreign investors to invest foreign currency in domestic shares. This scheme has been expanded and approved QFIIs can now invest foreign currency in equities, bonds, securities, funds, stock index futures and other financial instruments permitted by the securities regulator. The renminbi QFII (RQFII) scheme, initiated in late 2011, allows selected foreign financial institutions to invest renminbi obtained offshore in approved onshore assets. The Qualified Domestic Institutional Investor (QDII) scheme, initiated in 2006, allows authorised domestic institutions to invest funds raised onshore in selected offshore investments.

Non-reserve flows; per cent of GDP

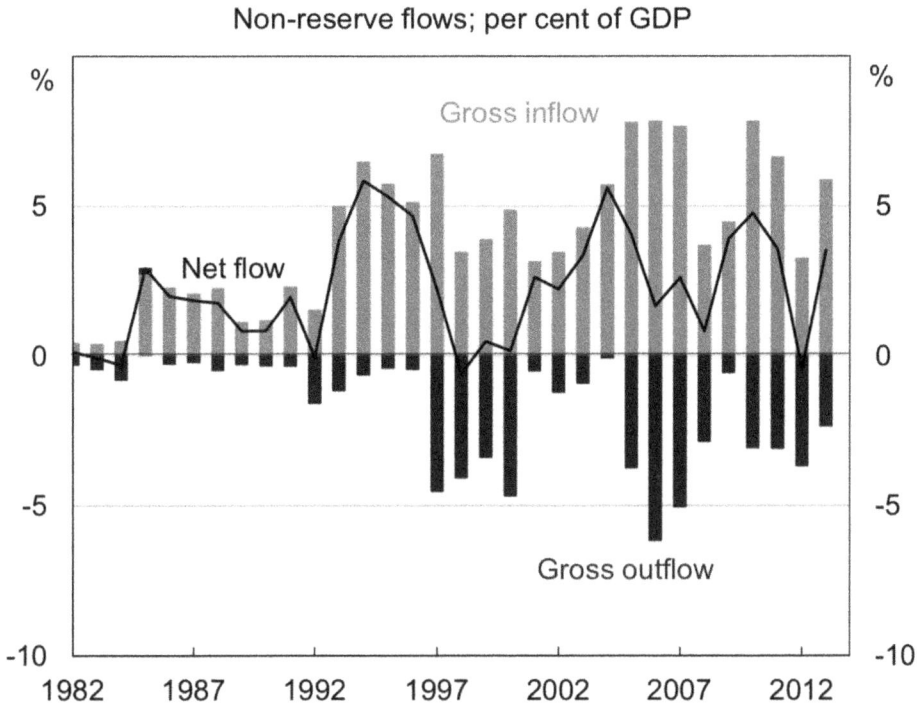

Figure 11.11 Chinese Gross and Net Capital Flows

Sources:CEIC data at <http://dev.ceicdata.securities.com/about_ceic.html>; The Reserve Bank of Australia (RBA).

Notwithstanding the expansion of these programs, FDI has continued to be the largest contributor to flows registered on the Chinese capital account in recent years, along with 'other' flows that appear to be mostly related to banks' and firms' short-term internal financing and trade credit (Figure 11.12). In 2013, total FDI (that is, the sum of inward and outward FDI) was worth approximately US$330 billion, or roughly 3.5 per cent of GDP. Cross-border portfolio investment schemes are relatively modest by comparison. PBC data indicate that the foreign liabilities of banks and other deposit-taking institutions (domestic-owned and foreign-owned) in China totalled approximately US$360 billion at the end of February 2013—much greater than the roughly US$76 billion of net foreign investment accounted for by the QFII and RQFII schemes. Even total foreign liabilities, however, represent only 1.4 per cent of the total liabilities of the banking system, implying that the Chinese banking system's current exposure to international markets is small.

Non-reserve flows; per cent of GDP

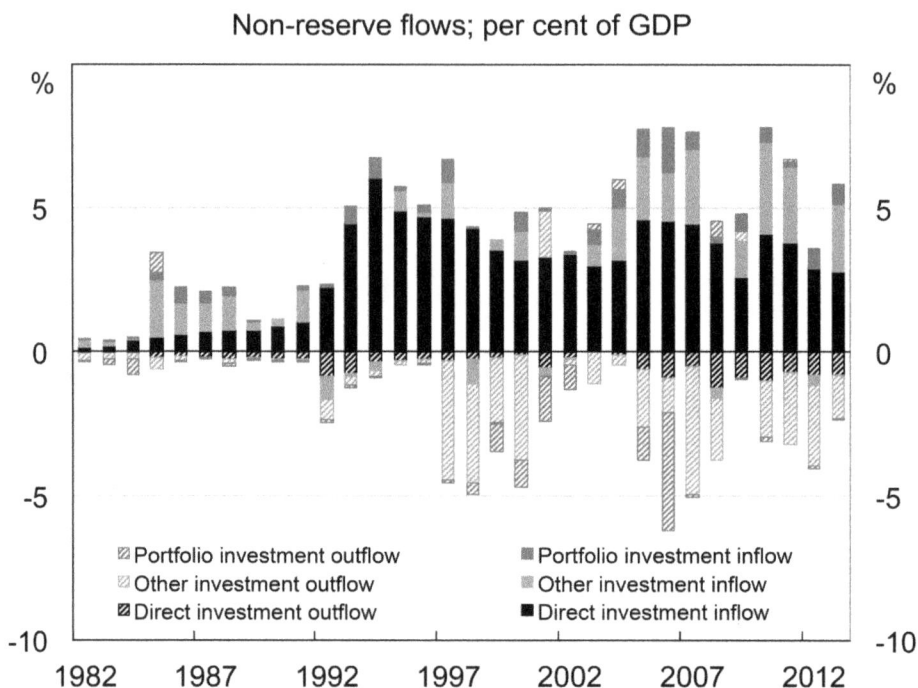

Figure 11.12 Chinese Gross Capital Flows

Sources: CEIC data at <http://dev.ceicdata.securities.com/about_ceic.html>; The Reserve Bank of Australia (RBA)

The exchange rate

Following its 're-pegging' during the Asian financial crisis, the US dollar/renminbi exchange rate was effectively fixed until July 2005, when the PBC announced that it would manage the renminbi in a 0.3 per cent band (later 0.5 per cent) against an undisclosed basket of currencies. This arrangement marked the beginning of a period of steady appreciation of the renminbi against the US dollar, aside from a two-year pause beginning in mid 2008 associated with the GFC. Appreciation pressures on the renminbi and the steady inflow of foreign currency due to the trade surplus (and, to an increasing extent, capital account inflows) following China's accession to the World Trade Organisation (WTO) in 2001 meant that the PBC needed to intervene in the spot foreign exchange market to maintain the trading band.[24] This has contributed to a quadrupling of China's foreign exchange reserves to US$3.8 trillion between 2005 and 2013.

---

24 The need to sterilise the domestic liquidity impact of these purchases of US dollars/sales of renminbi led to more intensive use of required reserve ratio adjustments in the second half of the 2000s (Ma et al. 2011).

Since mid 2005, the renminbi has appreciated by 33 per cent against the US dollar and by 42 per cent in real effective terms. In April 2012, the PBC widened the renminbi's daily trading band against the US dollar from +/–0.5 per cent to +/–1 per cent around its daily central parity rate ('fixing rate'), set by the PBC (via the CFETS) each trading day as part of its management of the renminbi against a basket of currencies.[25] From March 2014, the band was increased further to +/–2 per cent. Officially, the exchange rate is deemed to be freely floating within this trading band, with the PBC intervening to maintain the band. If movements of around 2 per cent per day relative to the previous trading day's spot rate were permitted, this would amount to a degree of exchange rate flexibility that is similar to most countries with floating exchange rates; however, as the band is defined relative to a reference rate set by the authorities each trading day, the central bank retains considerable control over the direction of movements in the exchange rate.

Steady development of the onshore foreign exchange market over the past decade has seen growing use of instruments to hedge foreign currency exposure. Prior to the mid 2000s, only spot foreign exchange transactions could occur on the CFETS. In 2005 foreign exchange (deliverable) forwards were introduced; foreign exchange swaps were introduced in 2006 (Xie 2009:476), and now record monthly turnover comparable with that of the spot market. However, the lack of volatility in the exchange rate, restrictions on the use of foreign currency in China and controlled access to offshore markets have limited the depth and liquidity of these hedging markets.

Official efforts have been made to 'internationalise' the currency in recent years, allowing a pool of renminbi to accumulate offshore where it is freely tradeable (subject to local regulations). This has facilitated the development of a range of offshore renminbi-denominated financial products, including foreign exchange products and hedging tools. The internationalisation process has the potential to bring significant benefits to Chinese firms. As international trade is increasingly denominated in renminbi, firms may be better able to reduce currency mismatches on their balance sheets, mitigating vulnerabilities that could arise as the exchange rate becomes more flexible. Another possible advantage is that as capital account liberalisation proceeds, the entry of non-residents to China's domestic financial markets will increase the depth of these markets, increasing the availability of counterparties for Chinese entities seeking to hedge their foreign currency liabilities (Lowe 2014).

---

25 Having effectively pegged the renminbi against the US dollar since 2008, in June 2010 the PBC announced that it would allow increased flexibility in the exchange rate, managing the renminbi against an unspecified basket of currencies.

Comparing financial reform in Australia and China

In some respects, China is now facing a similar set of policy challenges on its path towards financial liberalisation to those faced by Australia in the late 1970s and early 1980s. These include challenges currently posed by China's domestic financial system, including the rapid growth of financing channels outside a tightly regulated banking sector, and concerns about firms' ability to insure against increased exchange rate volatility. These challenges have led some observers (such as Yu 2013) to emphasise the risks of a rapid reduction in China's capital controls; however, the reforms currently under way in China are taking place in a very different domestic and global context to those which took place in Australia and, to an extent, these differences have been reflected in the contrasting approaches to reform taken in the two countries.

The context of reform

The global economy and financial system are much more interconnected today than they were 30 years ago. Australia's capital account and financial reform process began in the context of a breakdown in the Bretton Woods system and the very early stages of global financial integration. The combination of a fixed exchange rate regime, rising cross-border capital flows and the expansion of the NBFI sector made it increasingly challenging for the Australian authorities to control domestic monetary conditions.

Both China up to the late 1990s and Australia up to the float imposed asymmetric capital controls, with tighter restrictions on residents' investment abroad than on foreign investment in their domestic economies, and relatively relaxed policies towards FDI inflows in particular; however, Australia's capital account prior to 1983 was probably more open with respect to non-FDI inflows than China's is today (Figure 11.13).[26] The greater integration of the modern global financial system, larger global capital markets and a relatively low starting point in terms of non-FDI inflows all suggest that, in the event of capital account liberalisation, China will be exposed to a more substantial increase in capital flows than Australia faced in the early 1980s.

---

26 To some extent, the initial openness of Australia's capital account with respect to portfolio flows reflected the smaller role such flows had played in the global and Australian economies prior to the 1970s.

4-year average; share of total

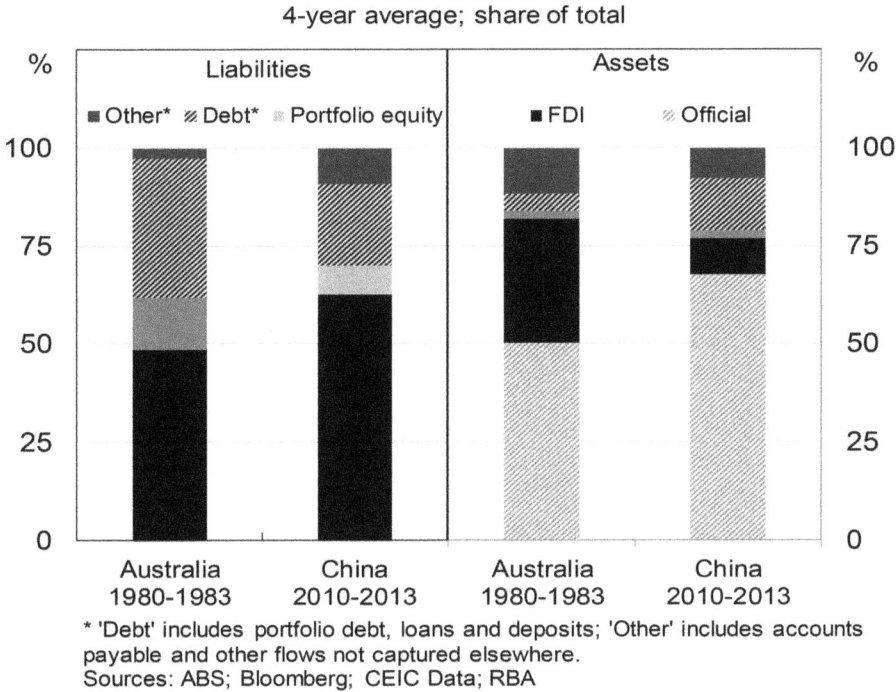

* 'Debt' includes portfolio debt, loans and deposits; 'Other' includes accounts
payable and other flows not captured elsewhere.
Sources: ABS; Bloomberg; CEIC Data; RBA

Figure 11.13 Australian and Chinese Gross External Positions

Sources: Australian Bureau of Statistics (ABS), Bloomberg, CEIC data at <http://dev.ceicdata.securities.com/about_ceic.html>; The Reserve Bank of Australia (RBA).

Notes: 'Debt' includes portfolio debt, loans and deposits; 'other' includes accounts payable and other flows not captured elsewhere.

The size and volatility of these flows may be amplified by China's already significant role in the global financial system—something Australian policymakers did not have to contend with in the early 1980s. At the time of the float, Australia was a relatively minor participant in global financial markets. Thus, there was little 'feedback' between financial developments in Australia and the global system. In contrast, the Chinese economy and financial sector are much larger than Australia's were at the time of liberalisation. In 1983, total assets of the Australian financial sector were 1.3 times the value of GDP, whereas in 2013, the value of the Chinese financial sector's total assets amounted to 2.7 times GDP. Scaled by the size of the Chinese economy, this implies that the liberalisation of China's capital account and financial sector is likely to be accompanied by a substantial increase in the size of inward and outward cross-border capital flows, and so will have significant spillover effects on global capital markets.

The size of China's economy and financial sector could provide some ballast against these flows, by providing China with more capacity to absorb speculative capital. In addition, China's large foreign exchange reserves, which were around 40 per cent of GDP in 2013, could provide a buffer against the impact of global capital flows (Australia's foreign exchange reserves were less than 5 per cent of GDP in 1983).

Notwithstanding these considerations, a more open capital account could still be a source of instability if the process is not carefully managed. For example, similar to Australia, in China, the recent rapid growth of the non-bank sector has posed challenges for the authorities in their control of aggregate financing flows. Such challenges are likely to be compounded by any surge in cross-border capital inflows and outflows.

The approach to liberalisation

The different starting points are partly reflected in the different roads to liberalisation taken by Australia and China. Australia's capital account and financial liberalisation were ultimately prompted by sizeable external pressures that were placed on the economy by the increasing integration of world financial flows, coupled with Australia's relatively open capital account and small (economic) size. The sequencing of reform in Australia prior to the float featured a series of currency regimes (a peg to the UK pound, a peg to the US dollar, a peg to a TWI and a crawling peg to a TWI), the removal of deposit rate ceilings prior to those for lending rates, and a gradual easing of financial sector and capital controls (albeit with the reimposition of some controls when the effects became severe). Contrary to the advice of one line of the academic literature on 'sequencing', at the time of the float the work of banking sector deregulation was only partly complete, and Australia lacked credible frameworks for macro-economic policy and prudential regulation.[27]

Nonetheless, Australia's approach to reform was not entirely 'reactive'. The Australian authorities had in most cases given advance thought to the need for reform and the manner of its implementation. Documents from the era, and the commissioning of the Campbell Committee inquiry into financial sector deregulation in the late 1970s, indicate that a considerable amount of planning went into reforming Australia's capital account and financial system (Cornish 2010: ch. 7). A characteristic of the Australian approach was, however, that the actual decisions to implement reform were often taken relatively quickly, and in response to external changes that exposed weakness in the existing system.

---

27 For example, while the RBA had powers to act if it appeared that deposits were in jeopardy, it was not given formal supervisory powers until 1989 (Thompson 1991).

The approach to financial reform taken by the People's Republic of China has, since the early 2000s (and implicitly since the mid 1990s), been characterised by a stated objective of eventual interest rate, exchange rate and capital account liberalisation. China's reform path first involved implementing partial reforms via pilot programs before expanding their scope and/or scale. The Australian authorities also used this approach to an extent—for example, removing interest rate ceilings for certificates of deposit prior to the removal of all deposit rate ceilings. In comparison, the Chinese approach to interest rate reform has emphasised tightly controlled pilots to increase the flexibility of various types of interest rates offered by different financial institutions, in some cases to specific classes of enterprises.

The difference in approach is especially noticeable in efforts to increase the flexibility of the exchange rate and open the capital account—for example, the staged widening of the renminbi's daily trading band against the US dollar since 2005, and staggered increases in quotas controlling the size of the QFII and RQFII programs. Domestic financial reforms have occurred in tandem with incremental efforts to improve currency flexibility, but to avoid destabilising outcomes, reforms to controls of portfolio flows have been particularly gradual.

Where risks have been encountered in China, as was the case with early efforts to increase the flexibility of deposit rates, the banking sector stress of the late 1990s and the threat posed to exchange rate stability by the Asian financial crisis, the Chinese authorities have usually responded by slowing the pace of deregulation. To some extent this has been facilitated by China's controls on portfolio capital flows, which have given policymakers an additional degree of flexibility in pursuing domestic financial reform by providing a buffer against external pressures.[28] In contrast, through the 1970s and early 1980s, Australian authorities were ultimately forced by the size of short-term speculative flows— and the resulting constraints on domestic monetary policy—to float the exchange rate.

Post-reform challenges

A feature of Australia's financial reform process was the interaction between financial sector development and capital account liberalisation. In particular, the Australian experience suggests there is the potential for positive feedback loops to develop once the process has begun (Lowe 2014). Two concrete examples of

---

28 While differences in political and administrative arrangements in the two countries are no doubt also important in explaining the differences in approach, such considerations are beyond the scope of this chapter.

this are prudential regulation and foreign exchange hedging markets, neither of which fully developed in Australia until some time after liberalisation had taken place.

The post-float boom and bust in credit and commercial property prices in Australia revealed the relative inexperience of financial institutions and regulators in forming risk assessments about borrowers. These skills were learned as a result of painful adjustment to the realities of the newly deregulated environment. The episode supports the arguments of Fry (1997), Johnston (1998) and Mishkin (2001) that, ideally, a good prudential supervision framework should be established before the financial sector and capital account are liberalised to mitigate risks to financial stability. It also highlights, however, the fact that it can be difficult to develop such a framework in the context of a highly regulated system that is not exposed to risk-taking behaviour (Lowe 2013).

In some respects, China's prudential framework could be considered more advanced than Australia's was before the float of the dollar. The late-1990s NPL crisis and subsequent recapitalisation of the banking system helped focus official attention on prudential regulation in the early 2000s. Significant progress has been made in introducing modern commercial banking practices to Chinese banks and the banking regulator has been active in strengthening banks' provision and capital buffers (Huang et al. 2013:132; Turner et al. 2012). The widespread perception that loans to SOEs have an implicit state guarantee—notwithstanding concerns about the quality of some of these assets—and the incomplete nature of interest rate deregulation may, however, still hinder the accurate pricing of risk by financial institutions. It may be hard for Chinese banks and regulators to develop risk-management capabilities fully prior to the transition to a system that lacks these guarantees and in which interest rates can move freely.

A similar example can be found in the development of hedging markets. For Australia, a deep and liquid foreign exchange derivatives market has, over time, proven crucial for allowing residents to access overseas funds while effectively managing their currency and interest rate exposure. Despite the development of an unofficial onshore foreign currency hedging market by the private sector prior to the float of the Australian dollar, the decision to reform the currency regime was the primary catalyst for the emergence of modern hedging markets and practices.

In China, the authorities have to date played a more direct role in fostering the development of hedging practices than Australia prior to the float. Reforms in the mid 2000s introduced foreign exchange derivatives and over-the-counter trading of the renminbi. More recently, the authorities' efforts to create offshore markets for the renminbi have accelerated the development of foreign exchange products, and helped lay the groundwork for an eventual loosening of capital controls. These offshore markets have the potential to increase the pool of future market participants by creating non-resident counterparties with renminbi exposures they may wish to hedge.

Recent moves by the PBC to bolster two-way volatility in the exchange rate could also lead participants to make greater use of onshore hedging markets. Naturally, the depth and liquidity of the market continue to be constrained by the managed exchange rate regime and capital controls, which restrict the interaction of onshore and offshore market participants—even more so than was the case for Australia prior to the float (Figure 11.14). The foundations that are already in place—including global and domestic market expertise and infrastructure, and the availability of a relatively broad range of potential hedging instruments—suggest, however, that China's hedging markets could develop quickly once the current restrictions are removed, as they did in Australia.

Ratio to gross quarterly trade and non-reserve capital flows

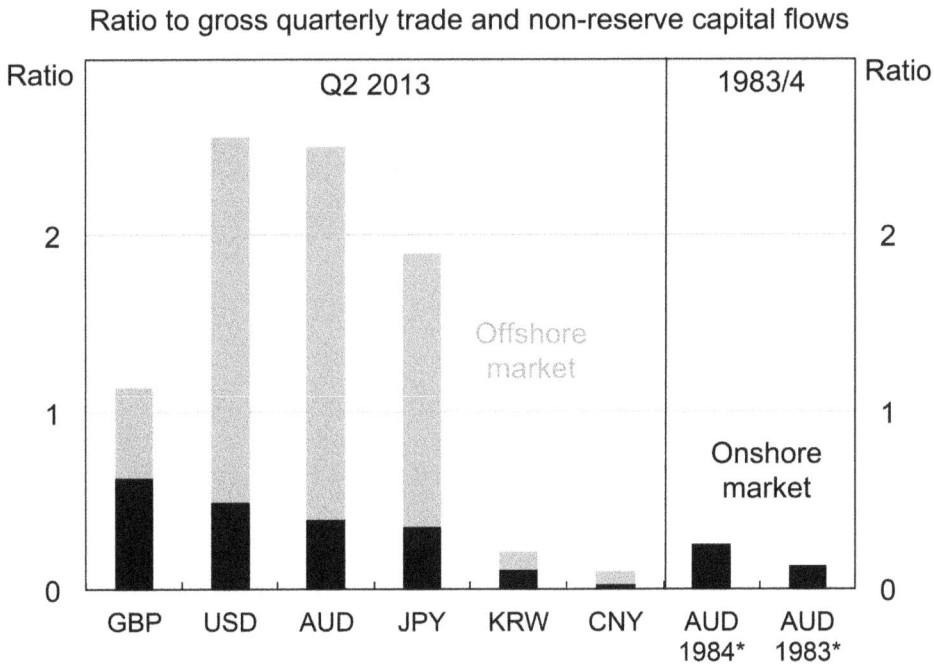

Figure 11.14 Average Daily Turnover in Selected Foreign Exchange Markets

* Post-float (1984) observation taken as at September; pre-float (1983) observation taken as at November.

Sources: Australian Bureau of Statistics (ABS); Bank of International Settlement (BIS); Phillips (1984a); CEIC data at <http://dev.ceicdata.securities.com/about_ceic.html>; The Reserve Bank of Australia (RBA).

Concluding remarks

China today faces markedly different domestic and global circumstances than Australia did in the late 1970s and early 1980s. The relevance of the Australian example for China is that it underscores the potential catalytic effects of a decision to liberalise financial development. Moreover, it suggests that the full benefits of a complete financial deregulation—encompassing deregulated interest rates, an open capital account and a floating exchange rate—may be felt only once the system has adapted to changed arrangements and the credibility of the post-reform policy framework and institutions has been established.

The specific sequencing of deregulation that occurred in Australia might not be optimal in a Chinese context. In several respects, China is now at a more advanced stage of reform than Australia was in the late 1970s, particularly with respect to the development of its financial system, including its hedging markets and prudential framework. Broadly speaking, the Australian experience has tended to support the conclusions of Johnston (1998) and Ishii and Habermeier (2002)—namely, that reform creates its own momentum. Domestic financial deregulation can create additional channels for capital flows, making capital controls less effective and creating pressure for their removal. By the same token, capital account liberalisation may increase the urgency of broader financial sector reforms to deal with the increased capital flows. Either way, the path to reform is not without its risks and the stakes are undoubtedly higher for China (and the world) today than they were for Australia in the early 1980s.

References

Allen, F., Qian, Q. J., Zhang, C. and Zhao, M. (2012), *China's financial system: opportunities and challenges*, NBER Working Paper No. 17828, National Bureau of Economic Research, Cambridge, Mass.

Atkin, T., Caputo, M., Robinson, T. and Wang, H. (2014), *Macroeconomic consequences of terms of trade episodes, past and present*, RBA Research Discussion Paper No. 2014-01, Reserve Bank of Australia, Sydney.

Australian Treasury (1999), 'Australia's experience with the variable deposit requirement', *Economic Roundup* (Winter): 45–56.

Battellino, R. (2007), Australia's experience with financial deregulation, Address to the China Australia Governance Program, Melbourne, 16 July 2007. Available from <http://www.rba.gov.au/speeches/2007/sp-dg-160707.html>.

Battellino, R. and McMillan, N. (1989), *Changes in the behaviour of banks and their implications for financial aggregates*, RBA Research Discussion Paper No. 8904, Reserve Bank of Australia, Sydney.

Battellino, R. and Plumb, M. (2011), 'A generation of an internationalised Australian dollar', in A. Filardo and J. Yetman (eds), *Currency internationalisation: lessons from the global financial crisis and prospects for the future in Asia and the Pacific*, BIS Papers No. 61, pp. 202–17, Bank for International Settlements, Basel.

Beaumont, C. and Cui, L. (2007), *Conquering fear of floating—Australia's successful adaptation to a flexible exchange rate*, IMF Policy Discussion Paper No. 07/2, International Monetary Fund, Washington, DC.

Becker, C. and Fabbro, D. (2006), *Limiting foreign exchange exposure through hedging: the Australian experience*, RBA Research Discussion Paper No. 2006-09, Reserve Bank of Australia, Sydney.

Becker, C. and Sinclair, M. (2004), *Profitability of Reserve Bank foreign exchange operations: twenty years after the float*, RBA Research Discussion Paper No. 2004-06, Reserve Bank of Australia, Sydney.

Bonin, J. P. and Huang, Y. (2001), 'Dealing with the bad loans of the Chinese banks', *Journal of Asian Economics* 12(2): 197–214.

Chinese Communist Party (CCP) (2013), *Decisions by the Central Committee of the Chinese Communist Party on Several Large Questions Concerning the Comprehensive Deepening of Reform*, Beijing: Readings on Party Construction Publishing House.

Cornish, S. (2010), *The Evolution of Central Banking in Australia*, Sydney: Reserve Bank of Australia.

Davies, R., Katinaite, K., Manning, M. and Richardson, P. (2010), 'Evolution of the UK banking system', *Bank of England Quarterly Bulletin* (December): 321–32.

Debelle, G. and Plumb, M. (2006), 'The evolution of exchange rate policy and capital controls in Australia', *Asian Economic Papers* 5(2): 7–29.

Eichengreen, B., Walsh, K. and Weir, G. (2014), *Internationalisation of the renminbi: pathways, implications and opportunities*, CIFR Research Report, March, Centre for International Finance and Regulation, Sydney. Available from <http://www.cifr.edu.au/assets/document/CIFR%20Internationalisation%20of%20the%20RMB%20Report%20Final%20web.pdf>.

Fry, M. J. (1997), 'In favour of financial liberalisation', *Economic Journal* 107 (May): 754–70.

Gizycki, M. and Lowe, P. (2000), 'The Australian financial system in the 1990s', in D. Gruen and S. Shrestha (eds), *The Australian Economy in the 1990s*, pp. 180–215, Sydney: Reserve Bank of Australia.

Government of the People's Republic of China (2005), *Summary of the Eleventh Five-Year Guideline for National Economic and Social Development*, Beijing. Available from <http://www.qibebt.cas.cn/kxcb/kpwz/nyzcgh/200906/P020090630584175269777.pdf>.

Government of the People's Republic of China (2011), *Summary of the Twelfth Five-Year Guideline for National Economic and Social Development*, Beijing. Available from <http://ghs.ndrc.gov.cn/ghwb/gjwngh/201109/P020110919590835399263.pdf>.

Grenville, S. (1991), 'The evolution of financial deregulation', in I. Macfarlane (ed.), *The Deregulation of Financial Intermediaries*, pp. 3–35, Sydney: Reserve Bank of Australia.

Guo, J. (2013), 'Interest rate marketisation and the interest rate pricing mechanism', *China Finance*, republished by Sina Finance. Available from <http://finance.sina.com.cn/money/bond/20131118/095417352836.shtml>.

He, F. (2013), 'Reform in a time of slowing growth', *China Finance*, republished by Sina Finance. Available from <http://finance.sina.com.cn/money/bank/bank_hydt/20130516/134615487270.shtml>.

Hu, X. (2010), A managed floating exchange rate regime is an established policy, Speech given by People's Bank of China Deputy Governor, Hu Xiaolian, 15 July. Available from <http://www.pbc.gov.cn/publish/english/956/2010/20100727144152118668062/20100727144152118668062_.html>.

Huang, Y., Wang, X., Wang, B. and Lin, N. (2013), 'Financial reform in China: progress and challenges', in Y. C. Park and H. Patrick (eds), *How Finance is Shaping the Economies of China, Japan, and Korea*, pp. 44–142, New York: Columbia University Press.

Ishii, S. and Habermeier, K. (2002), *Capital account liberalization and financial sector stability*, IMF Occasional Paper No. 232, International Monetary Fund, Washington, DC.

Johnston, B. (1998), *Sequencing capital account liberalization and financial reform*, IMF Paper on Policy Analysis and Assessment No. PPAA/98/8, International Monetary Fund, Washington, DC.

Laker, J. (1988), Exchange rate policy in Australia, Paper presented at the 17th South East Asia, New Zealand and Australia Central Banking Course, Sydney, 2 November.

Lardy, N. R. (1998), *China's Unfinished Economic Revolution*, Washington, DC: Brookings Institution Press.

Lardy, N. R. (2002), *Integrating China into the Global Economy*, Washington, DC: Brookings Institution Press.

Le, J. (2007), 'China's bond market', in S. N. Neftci and M. Y. Ménager-Xu (eds), *China's Financial Markets: An Insider's Guide to How the Markets Work*, pp. 137–70, New York: Elsevier.

Lowe, P. (2013), The journey of financial reform, Address to the Australian Chamber of Commerce in Shanghai, Shanghai, 24 April. Available from <http://www.rba.gov.au/speeches/2013/sp-dg-240413.html>.

Lowe, P. (2014), Some implications of the internationalisation of the renminbi, Opening remarks to the Centre for International Finance and Regulation Conference on the Internationalisation of the Renminbi, Sydney, 26 March. Available from <http://www.rba.gov.au/speeches/2014/sp-dg-260314.html>.

Ma, G., Yan, X. and Liu, X. (2011), *China's evolving reserve requirements*, BIS Working Paper No. 360, Bank for International Settlements, Basel.

McCauley, R. (2006), 'Internationalising a currency: the case of the Australian dollar', *BIS Quarterly Review* (December): 41–54.

McKinnon, R. (1982), 'The order of economic liberalization: lessons from Chile and Argentina', in *Carnegie-Rochester Conference Series on Public Policy. Volume 17*, pp. 159–86, Amsterdam: North-Holland.

McKinnon R. (1991), 'Financial control in the transition from classical socialism to a market economy', *Journal of Economic Perspectives* 5(4): 107–22.

McKinnon, R. (1994), 'Financial growth and macroeconomic stability in China, 1978–1992: implications for Russia and other transitional economies', *Journal of Comparative Economics* 18: 438–69.

Manuell, G. (1986), *Floating Down Under: Foreign Exchange in Australia*, Sydney: The Law Book Company Limited.

Mishkin, F. S. (2001), *Financial policies and the prevention of financial crises in emerging market countries*, NBER Working Paper No. 8087, National Bureau of Economic Research, Cambridge, Mass.

Newman, V., Potter, C. and Wright, M. (2011), 'Foreign exchange market intervention', *Reserve Bank of Australia Bulletin* (December): 67–76.

People's Bank of China (PBC) (1999), *Almanac of China's Finance and Banking 1999*, Beijing: People's China Publishing House.

People's Bank of China (PBC) (2000), *Almanac of China's Finance and Banking 2000*, Beijing: People's China Publishing House.

People's Bank of China (PBC) (2003), *2002 Monetary Policy Report*, Beijing: People's China Publishing House.

People's Bank of China (PBC) (2005), *Report on gradually pushing forward interest rate marketisation*, People's Bank of China, Beijing. Available from <http://www.pbc.gov.cn/publish/zhengcehuobisi/606/1276/12766/12766_.html>.

People's Bank of China (PBC) (2014), 'People's Bank of China Governor Zhou Xiaochuan responds to journalists' questions regarding "financial reform and development"', 26 March, People's Bank of China, Beijing. Available from <http://www.pbc.gov.cn/publish/goutongjiaoliu/524/2014/20140311120919964302085/20140311120919964302085_.html>.

People's Bank of China (PBC) Department of Surveys and Statistics Task Force (2012a), *The conditions for accelerating the opening of the capital account are basically mature*, People's Bank of China, Beijing. Available from <http://www.pbc.gov.cn/publish/diaochatongjisi/866/2012/20120523135503424585606/20120523135503424585606_.html>.

People's Bank of China (PBC) Department of Surveys and Statistics Task Force (2012b), *Push forward interest rate and exchange rate reform and capital account opening in harmony*, People's Bank of China, Beijing. Available from <http://economy.caijing.com.cn/2012-04-17/111815022.html>.

Phillips, M. J. (1984a), …Now for 1985, Address to the Australian Forex Association Second Annual Conference, Canberra, 10 November.

Phillips, M. J. (1984b), Financial reform—the Australian experience, Address to the Pacific Basin Financial Reform Conference, Federal Reserve Bank of San Francisco, San Francisco, 2–5 December.

Phillips, M. J. (1985), Policy on exchange rates and foreign exchange controls since the late 1960s, Address to the Australian Shippers' Council Shipper/ Exporter Workshops, April–May.

Prasad, W. E. and Wei, S.-J. (2005), *The Chinese approach to capital inflows: patterns and possible explanations*, IMF Working Paper No. WP/05/79, International Monetary Fund, Washington, DC.

Prasad, W. E., Rumbaugh, T. and Wang, Q. (2005), *Putting the cart before the horse? Capital account liberalization and exchange rate flexibility in China*, IMF Policy Discussion Paper No. PDP/05/1, International Monetary Fund, Washington, DC.

Rush, A., Sadeghian, D. and Wright, M. (2013), 'Foreign currency exposure and hedging in Australia', *Reserve Bank of Australia Bulletin* (December): 49–58.

Stevens, G. (2013), The Australian dollar: thirty years of floating, Speech to the Australian Business Economists' Annual Dinner, Sydney, 21 November. Available from <http://www.rba.gov.au/speeches/2013/sp-gov-211113.html>.

Stevens, G., Kent, C. and Cagliarini, A. (2010), 'Fifty years of monetary policy: what have we learned?', in C. Kent and M. Robson (eds), *Reserve Bank of Australia 50th Anniversary Symposium*, Sydney: Reserve Bank of Australia.

Tan, W. (2007), 'A history of China's stock markets', in S. N. Neftci and M. Y. Ménager-Xu (eds), *China's Financial Markets: An Insider's Guide to How the Markets Work*, pp. 215–36, New York: Elsevier.

Thompson, G. (1991), 'Prudential supervision', in I. Macfarlane (ed.), *The Deregulation of Financial Intermediaries*, pp. 115–42, Sydney: Reserve Bank of Australia.

Turner, G., Tan, N. and Sadeghian, D. (2012), 'The Chinese banking system', *Reserve Bank of Australia Bulletin* (September): 53–63.

Xie, D. (2009), 'China's money, bond and FX markets', in M. Zhu, J. Cai and M. Avery (eds), *China's Emerging Financial Markets: Challenges and Global Impact*, pp. 459–80, Singapore: Wiley.

Yi, G. (2008), 'Renminbi exchange rates and relevant institutional factors', *Cato Journal* 28(2): 187–96.

Yi, G. (2009), 'The thirty year course of interest rate marketisation in China's period of reform and opening', *Financial Research* 343(1): 1–14.

Yu, Y. (2013), The temptation of china's capital account, 27 March. Available from <http://www.project-syndicate.org/commentary/the-risks-of-easing-china-s-capital-controls-by-yu-yongding>.

Zheng, X. (2007), 'China's money markets', in S. N. Neftci and M. Y. Ménager-Xu (eds), *China's Financial Markets: An Insider's Guide to How the Markets Work*, pp. 41–86, New York: Elsevier.

Zhou, X. (2005), 'Thoughts on financial system reforms in the period of the eleventh five-year plan', *Study Times* 311, reprinted by Xinhua. Available from <http://news.xinhuanet.com/politics/2005-11/18/content_3798040.htm>.

Zhou, X. (2013), 'Comprehensive deepening of financial industry reform and opening: accelerating the improvement of the financial market system', in Chinese Communist Party, *Decisions by the Central Committee of the Chinese Communist Party on Several Questions Concerning the Comprehensive Deepening of Reform*, pp. 145–56, Beijing: Readings on Party Construction Publishing House.

12. Financial Openness of China and India

Implications for Capital Account Liberalisation

Guonan Ma and Robert N. McCauley[1]

Introduction

In recent years, policymakers in both China and India have announced their intention to further liberalise their still heavily managed capital accounts. The world has a huge stake in China and India integrating their finances into global markets without disruptive spillovers to the global financial markets (Hooley 2013). This is all the more true for China, which is larger and more willing to undertake incremental capital account liberalisation over the coming years.

The extent to which these economies have already become financially integrated with the rest of the world serves as a practical starting point for policymakers managing the task of further capital opening, by indicating potential challenges and attendant risks. A starting point of considerable integration would suggest that China and India have little to lose and much to gain if the opening serves to force the pace of domestic financial liberalisation. Little financial integration, however, would indicate greater risks and larger required adjustments in the domestic economy and markets in response to capital opening.

Much analysis of capital account openness uses the Chinn–Ito (2008) index, an interval, de jure measure derived from four on–off variables in the IMF's *Annual Report on Exchange Arrangements and Restrictions* (Figure 12.1, left-hand panel). For de facto openness, 'the most widely used measure' (IMF 2010:51) is the ratio of the sum of international assets and liabilities to GDP (Lane and Milesi-Ferretti 2003, 2007) (Figure 12.1, right-hand panel).

1   Guonan Ma is a visiting fellow at Bruegel and Robert McCauley is a senior adviser, Monetary and Economic Department, Bank for International Settlements (BIS). We wish to thank Claudio Borio for comments and Bat-el Berger and Tracy Chan for their excellent research assistance. This chapter is partially based on Ma and McCauley (2013). Views expressed are those of the authors and not necessarily those of the BIS.

Chinn-Ito indices of de jure openness[1]

International assets and liabilities[2]

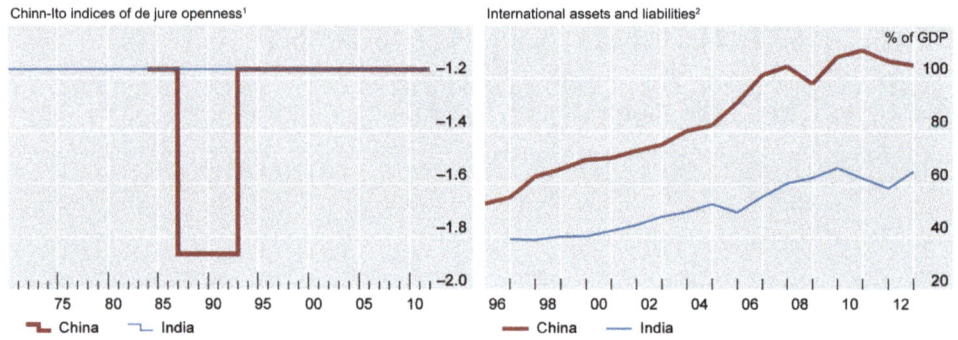

Figure 12.1 Capital Account Openness of China and India: De Jure and De Facto Measures

[1] It is based on the binary dummy variables that codify the tabulation of restrictions on cross-border financial transactions reported in the IMF's *Annual Report on Exchange Arrangements and Exchange Restrictions* (2010). For further details, see Chinn and Ito (2006).

[2] International investment position. Data for China before 2004 from Lane and Milesi-Ferretti (2007).

Sources: The IMF's *International Financial Statistics* (<http://www.econdata.com/databases/imf-and-other-international/ifs/>) and *World Economic Outlook* (<http://www.imf.org/external/pubs/ft/weo>).

We question whether these measures appropriately track the progress and relative position of China and India on the road to international financial integration.[2] We disagree with Chinn–Ito that China and India are both stalled on the road and agree with Lane and Milesi-Ferretti that both are often moving forward—that is, opening up. Admittedly, the process sometimes can be two steps forwards and one step back. Moreover, we question whether Chinn–Ito (tied) or Lane and Milesi-Ferretti (China ahead) have their relative position right, at least on average for the past decade.

We also question an emerging consensus regarding implications of capital opening for capital flows. Both He et al. (2012) and Bayoumi and Ohnesorge (2013) argue that when China fully opens up its capital account, there will be not only larger external positions, but also, on balance, larger net private assets. By contrast, Bayoumi and Ohnesorge (2013) expect India to experience little net private capital outflows. Neither study considers stocks of bank assets, which are inherently difficult to model. Our findings on the pricing of the three financial instruments onshore and offshore raise questions about this consensus, since relative prices would encourage bank inflows. In particular, our finding that in China money-market instruments are cheap onshore leaves us concerned that these baseline projections that neglect bank assets are missing the potential for huge short-term inflows.

---

2 See Lane and Schmuckler (2007); and Aizenman and Sengupta (2011).

We raise these questions based on an examination of three de facto price-based measures. For currency forwards, short-term interest rates and equity prices, we analyse average deviations from the law of one price. The basic idea is that, other things being equal and under normal market conditions, onshore and offshore prices of the same underlying financial instrument should be about the same, if capital is mobile. Also, we offer cross-country benchmarks as well as bilateral comparisons as a gauge of the remaining challenge of the capital account opening task. Finally, we look at the signs of these price gaps to see whether each financial instrument is priced more cheaply onshore or offshore, which can serve as signals of positive pressures from inward or outward private capital flows, respectively.

We advance four hypotheses, two in the time series (ts) and two in the cross-section (xs), and subject them to the evidence of the past decade: 2003–13.

- Hts1: Lane and Milesi-Ferretti are right: both China and India are opening.
- Hxs1: Chinn–Ito and Lane and Milesi-Ferretti are wrong: India is more open than China.
- Hts2: Both China *and* India remain some distance from financial openness.
- Hxs2: China faces net inflow pressures in the short term, while India may face more balanced outflows and inflows when opening up.

The chapter is organised as follows. Sections two to four present evidence on the three measures of onshore–offshore price gaps for foreign exchange forwards, money-market yields and stock-market prices. Section five draws on the evidence on price gaps to explore implications for China's capital opening, while the final section concludes.

Onshore and offshore foreign exchange forwards

We first contrast forward foreign exchange rates in Shanghai or Mumbai with those traded offshore in Hong Kong, Singapore or Tokyo. Capital mobility tends to equalise onshore and offshore forward rates. Thus, the currency with smaller differences in rates at home and abroad is more financially open. We define cross-border price gaps so that a positive value indicates that contracts are cheaper onshore. For currency forwards, a positive gap means that a dollar fetches more renminbi or rupee in Shanghai or Mumbai than offshore. For money markets, a positive gap means that prices are lower (yields higher) in Shanghai or Mumbai than offshore. For equities, a positive gap means shares are cheaper onshore.

As Liu and Otani (2005) argued, this measure benefits from using directly observed prices; but our comparison can only start when China inaugurated its onshore forward currency market in 2003. Since traders can access the domestic forward currency market only on the basis of 'real demand'—that is, underlying transactions backed by trade documents—domestic forward rates can differ from those in the offshore non-deliverable market, where allcomers can transact.[3]

We define the onshore–offshore forward currency gap as in Equation 12.1.

Equation 12.1

Forward currency gap$_t$ = $(F_t - NDF_t)/S_t$

In Equation 12.1, F_t is the onshore forward; NDF_t is the non-deliverable offshore forward; and S_t is the onshore spot exchange rate—all expressed as domestic currency per US dollar. A positive forward premium gap indicates the respective currency is cheaper—that is, priced for less appreciation or more depreciation—onshore than offshore. This in turn would be likely to attract more inflows than outflows when the capital account opens up.

Figure 12.2 strikes the eye with how both currencies became cheap offshore after the Lehman failure, both at the three-month (left-hand panel) and the 12-month (right-hand panel) tenor. It is also striking how expensive the longer forward of the renminbi used to be offshore, where speculators paid up in anticipation of its move from 8.2 to 6.1 per dollar. Also observe the sharp widening in the onshore/offshore foreign exchange forward gaps during the GFC, probably because of the market dislocations to be discussed below. Both the sign and the size of the forward gaps for the renminbi and rupee correlate substantially, possibly suggesting that some global factors such as the sentiment of global investors and market uncertainties may play a meaningful role in the evolution of the forward gaps.

Table 12.1 confirms that over the past decade, 2003–13, the average of the forward gap for the renminbi is clearly larger than that of the rupee. Hence the forward markets onshore and offshore have been more segmented for the renminbi than for the rupee, for both three-month and 12-month tenors, and for both the pre-crisis and the post-crisis periods. In this sense, India is financially more integrated with the global financial market than is China.

The dynamics of their forward premium gaps have, however, been quite different before and after the GFC. In particular, for both tenors, the onshore–offshore forward currency gaps of the renminbi have narrowed noticeably since

---

3 On NDFs, see Ma et al. (2004); Misra and Behera (2006); Ma and McCauley (2008a, 2008b); and McCauley et al. (2014).

the crisis, suggesting that China has become more open financially over recent years. Not so for India, which has witnessed wider forward premium gaps since the GFC. One possible reason could be the Chinese Government's promotion of external use of the renminbi, facilitating cross-border arbitrage. Another could relate to the emerging market sell-off in the wake of the expected US Federal Reserve's tapering signal mostly in the third quarter of 2013, which most hurt deficit emerging economies. Of course, one can ask why this last particular shock was so asymmetric and different for the renminbi and the rupee (Ma and McCauley 2013; McCauley et al. 2014).

Moreover, while the renminbi is priced more cheaply onshore than offshore in the foreign exchange forward markets in all cases, the Indian rupee forward is mostly more expensive onshore in most cases. This holds true for both the full sample and the pre and post-crisis periods. In other words, when the capital account opens up, the renminbi will most likely face appreciation and net private capital inflow pressures, while the rupee may endure some depreciation and net private outflow pressures. Even the adjustments can take place mainly through positioning rather than actual cross-border flows; expectations may bias broader gross private capital inflows in case of a cheaper currency in the onshore forward market.

On balance, trading of currency forwards suggests India has been more financially open than China over the past decade, more so for the pre-crisis period than the post-crisis period, though China is catching up faster and noticeably narrowing India's lead since the GFC. Upon capital opening, China may see stronger private capital inflow pressures than India does, other things being equal.

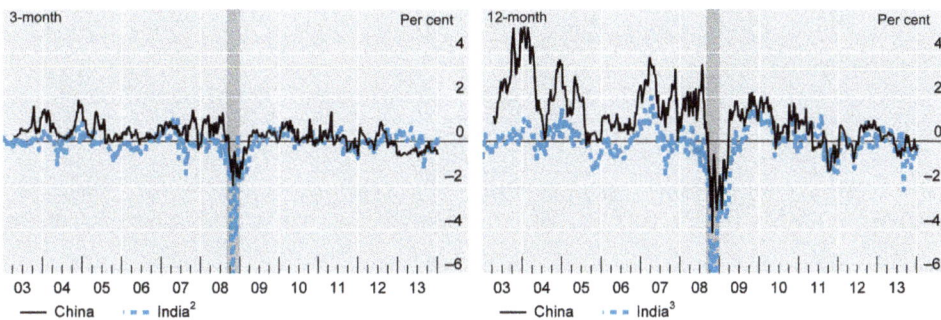

Figure 12.2 Onshore Foreign Exchange Forward Less Offshore Non-Deliverable Forwards (as percentage of spot rate)[1]

[1] Shaded area indicates the GFC period of September–December 2008.

[2] Minimum at −7.88 per cent on 24 October 2008.

[3] Minimum at −11.7 per cent on 24 October 2008.

Sources: Bloomberg; CEIC.

If currency forwards suggest that India has remained more open than China on average over the past decade, albeit with a shrinking lead, how far do they have to go in terms of capital account liberalisation? The euro/dollar trades, except in the most extreme markets, at the same rate in Frankfurt and in New York. Among currencies with a non-deliverable forward (NDF), the Korean won has the biggest and most integrated market. Post crisis, the rupee forward gap is between that of the won and a benchmark of six other NDF currencies for both tenors (Table 12.1). By contrast, the larger average absolute values for the renminbi are close to a benchmark of six other NDF currencies and point to weaker arbitrage and thus a longer way to go in capital opening.

Table 12.1 Onshore Less Offshore Foreign Exchange Forward Premiums (percentage of the spot)

	Three-month			12-month		
	Pre crisis	Post crisis	Full sample	Pre crisis	Post crisis	Full sample
Period average						
CNY[1]	0.5126	0.0494	0.2508	1.8510	0.3851	1.0518
INR	−0.0399	−0.0029	−0.0928	0.0297	−0.0745	−0.1601
KRW	−0.3007	−0.0287	−0.1726	−0.1263	−0.1015	−0.1334
Benchmark[1,2]	−0.1315	0.1019	−0.0369	−0.3403	0.2510	−0.0766
Average of absolute value						
CNY[1]	0.5303	0.3279	0.4489	1.8549	0.7464	1.3290
INR	0.2579	0.2849	0.3334	0.4476	0.6142	0.6511
KRW	0.4365	0.2056	0.3406	0.4676	0.2562	0.3865
Benchmark[1,2]	0.5828	0.3634	0.4628	1.1589	0.7246	0.8964

[1] Data start 7 April 2003 for renminbi, 7 January 2004 for Colombian peso, 12 January 2012 for Russian rouble.

[2] Benchmark averages Brazilian real, Colombian peso, Indonesian rupiah, Philippine peso, Russian rouble and Taiwanese dollar.

Sources: Bloomberg; Reuters.

Note: Daily data of forward premium gap are calculated as the difference between onshore forward and offshore non-deliverable forward as a percentage of spot price. Closing at Tokyo 8 pm for Asian currencies; at London 6 pm for Russian rouble; at New York 5 pm for Brazilian real and Colombian peso. The full sample period is between 6 January 2003 and 31 December 2013; the crisis period is between September and December 2008.

Onshore and offshore short-term interest rates

We next compare short-term yields onshore and offshore. Otani and Tiwari (1981) compared yen yields in Tokyo and offshore, and Frankel (1992) prescribed such comparisons to test for capital mobility. Prior to the expansion of the offshore renminbi market in 2010, we do not observe offshore yields for both currencies; rather we infer yields from NDFs, assuming they are priced off dollar Libor—a reasonable assumption before the GFC.[4]

Equation 12.2

$$NDF_t = S_t(1+i_t)/(1+r_t^{\$})$$

In Equation 12.2, i is the implied offshore interest rate on the home currency and $r_t^{\$}$ dollar Libor. Rearranging terms, we extract the implied offshore interest rate (Equation 12.3).

Equation 12.3

$$i_t = NDF_t^{*}(1+r_t^{\$})/S_t - 1$$

The onshore–offshore money yield gap is defined as (r_t-i_t), where r_t is the directly observed onshore three-month bank rate or a 12-month government bill rate. If (r_t-i_t) differs significantly from zero, the offshore market is segmented from the onshore. A positive money yield gap indicates that money-market instruments are priced cheaper (yield more) onshore than offshore. A smaller mean of the absolute yield gap points to greater financial openness.

Money-market yield gaps have narrowed somewhat for both economies in the 2000s (Figure 12.3). Ma et al. (2004) and Kohli (2011) found that this happened for the rupee in the early 2000s. The renminbi gap has narrowed since the GFC, but the rupee gap has widened instead. Again, we observe noted co-movements in the yield gaps of the renminbi and rupee, indicating possible important global drivers in addition to local impediments.

---

4   The GFC broke down covered interest parity (Baba and Packer 2009), observationally equivalent to pervasive capital controls. With a global 'dollar shortage' (McGuire and von Peter 2009), US dollar Libor cannot safely be inserted into Equation 12.3. Mancini and Ranaldo (2011) test interest rate parity without Libor. If dollar yields were equal onshore and offshore, and forwards were priced off interest differentials, our yield gaps would simply be transformations of the forward gaps above. But onshore dollar yields can and do deviate from offshore levels.

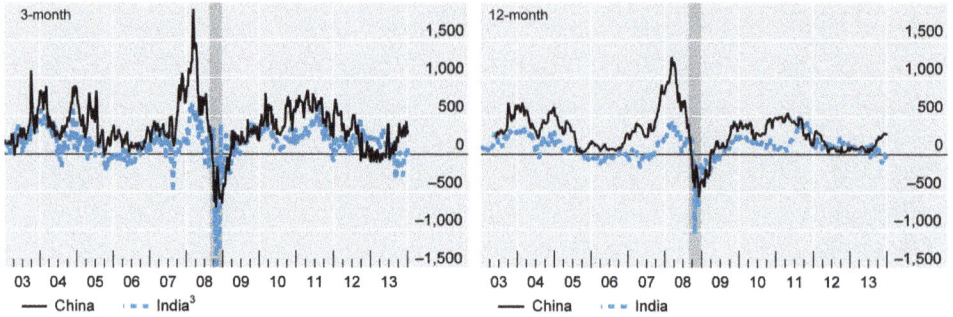

Figure 12.3 Onshore Money-Market Yield Less Offshore NDF-Implied Yield (in basis points)

Sources: Bloomberg; CEIC.

Notes: Weekly data. For China: three-month (12-month) NDF, three-month Chibor (one-year PBC bill auction yield before July 2008; secondary market yield thereafter), and three-month (12-month) Libor. For India: three-month (12-month) NDF, three-month Mumbai interbank offer rate (364-day Treasury Bill implicit yield), and three-month (12-month) Libor. Shaded area indicates the GFC period of September–December 2008. Minimum at −3310.89 bps on 24 October 2008.

In sum, most of the main findings for the foreign exchange forward gap also hold in the case of the money yield gap. Each and every pairwise comparison strongly suggests that over the past decade, cross-border arbitrage continued to have freer play in India to keep yields in line (Table 12.2). On balance, onshore and inferred offshore money rates, like trading of currency forwards, identify India as more financially open than China over the past decade, for the full sample, the pre-crisis period and the post-crisis period, though its lead has been narrowing. More interestingly, again, the post-crisis yield gap of the rupee has widened over the pre-crisis counterpart, while that of the renminbi has narrowed considerably and is rapidly converging with the rupee gap in the wake of the GFC. On this measure, China again is catching up in terms of financial openness.

One main difference between the currency forward and money-market instruments is that for both currencies, money-market instruments have been cheaper onshore than offshore, indicating potentially greater private capital inflows than outflows, at least under money-market instruments, once their capital accounts open further.

Again, the benchmark won suggests that both renminbi and rupee money remain some distance from high financial integration. In particular, onshore and offshore rupee yields remain further apart than their won counterparts even though the won gaps also widened after the crisis (and before the crisis relative to 2003–04) (Ma et al. 2004:90). If the rupee has a way to go, the renminbi has still further, but apparently the renminbi is catching up rapidly, while after the crisis, the rupee appears to have stepped back and is gradually losing its lead.

Table 12.2 Onshore Money-Market Yield Less Offshore NDF-Implied Yield (in basis point)

	Three-month			12-month		
	Pre crisis	Post crisis	Full sample	Pre crisis	Post crisis	Full sample
Period average						
CNY	436.8	316.1	354.7	381.1	208.2	280.1
INR	148.0	181.5	146.3	101.5	107.7	95.0
KRW	49.5	105.2	90.6	67.2	98.9	89.2
Average of absolute value						
CNY	437.0	345.3	392.7	381.1	235.4	308.9
INR	192.7	212.9	215.2	132.1	138.4	141.1
KRW	76.6	113.8	111.6	68.5	99.5	90.7

Sources: Bloomberg; CEIC.

Notes: Daily data. For China: three-month (12-month) NDF, three-month Chibor (one-year PBC bill auction yield before July 2008; secondary market yield thereafter), and three-month (12-month) Libor. For India: three-month (12-month) NDF, three-month Mibor (364-day Treasury Bill implicit yield), and three-month (12-month) Libor. For Korea: three-month (12-month) NDF, three-month certificate of deposit rate (one-year Treasury Bond yield in the secondary market), and three-month (12-month) Libor. The full sample period is between 27 May 2003 and 31 December 2013; the crisis period is between September and December 2008.

International integration of equity markets

The Chinese and Indian authorities have also run natural experiments by allowing firms to list their shares on exchanges both in Shanghai or Mumbai and in Hong Kong or New York. Onshore and offshore trades take place in different currencies, but a free flow of capital would ensure only minor differences in prices. Deviations from the law of one price point to markets segmented by official limits on foreign shareholdings in domestic markets. Following Levy-Yeyati et al. (2009), we analyse the difference between onshore and offshore share prices and the speed of their convergence.

We construct indices of shares that are cross-listed in Shanghai, Hong Kong and New York, on the one hand (Peng et al. 2008), and Mumbai and New York on the other. We weigh individual share price differentials by market capitalisations in Hong Kong and Mumbai. We define the price gap as the ratio of the offshore to onshore prices: a ratio greater than 100 indicates the share trades cheaper onshore than offshore. The closer this 'cross-market price premium' is to 100, the higher is the degree of onshore and offshore equity markets. Our Chinese index in Figure 12.4 resembles the commercial 'Hang Seng China AH [A: Shanghai; H: Hong Kong] Premium Index' (Ma and McCauley 2013).

A threshold observation is that the line for India lies above 100, while the lines for China lie below 100. Indian shares tend to be cheaper onshore. By contrast, Chinese shares trade at a premium in Shanghai over their prices in Hong Kong or New York. Chinese investors wish they could buy Chinese equities at Hong Kong or New York prices. Thus, the more expensive share prices in Shanghai would likely prompt more private outflows than inflows, once restrictions on the capital account are further removed. The opposite is true for India. Nevertheless, by late 2013, the Shanghai premium and Mumbai discount had largely vanished. Indeed, the Chinese equity market integration has come a long way and appeared to even have taken a small lead over India's by 2013.

Table 12.3 confirms that price differentials have tended to narrow since the GFC. Before the crisis, Indian shares in New York traded at a 30 per cent premium, while Chinese shares in Hong Kong traded at a discount of more than 45 per cent. After the crisis, the New York premium narrowed to less than 10 per cent for Indian companies and the Hong Kong discount to some 20 per cent for Chinese companies. So India managed to sustain the financial opening in the equity market, contrasting the back-stepping seen for the two fixed-income markets.

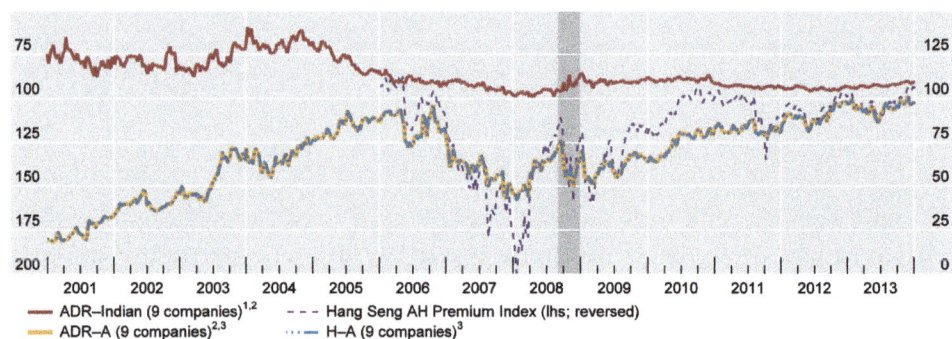

Figure 12.4 Ratios of Overseas Share Prices to Equivalent Local Share Prices (per cent, weekly average)

[1] Average of ICICI Bank, Wipro, Dr Reddy's Laboratories, HDFC Bank, Sterlite Industries (India) (until August 2013), Mahanagar Telephone Nigam, Tata Motors, Tata Communications and Infosys Technologies weighted by their domestic market capitalisation.

[2] Ratio of Asian closing to New York opening on the same day.

[3] Average of China Eastern Airlines, China Life Insurance, China Petroleum and Chemical, China Southern Airlines, Guangshen Railway, Huaneng Power International, Sinopec Shanghai Petrochemical, Aluminum Corporation of China and Petro China weighted by their Hong Kong market capitalisation. Shaded area indicates the Global Financial Crisis of September–December 2008.

Sources: Bloomberg; authors' calculations.

While for the full sample of 1999 and 2013, the Indian equity market is much more internationally integrated than that of China, it still has a long way to go when measured against the close alignment of prices of Chinese shares in Hong Kong and New York. Similarly, the Indian equity market has a way to go when compared with the sample 0.12 per cent mean difference between onshore and offshore share prices for a sample of emerging markets in Levy-Yeyati et al. (2009:441).

Table 12.3 Ratios of Overseas Share Prices to Local Share Prices and Convergence Speed

	H-A ratio 41 dual-listed companies	H-A ratio 9 triple-listed companies	ADR-A ratio 9 triple-listed companies	ADR-H ratio 9 triple-listed companies	ADR-India ratio 9 dual-listed companies
Period average (%)[1,2]					
Pre crisis	53.10	53.30	53.30	99.89	128.89
Post crisis	87.67	79.99	79.93	99.98	108.07
Full sample	64.91	62.29	62.25	99.91	121.64
Estimated half-life (days)[2,3]					
Pre crisis	255	125	111	1	35
Post crisis	109	213	162	1	13
Full sample	259	174	142	1	49

[1] Ratio of overseas share price to equivalent local share price for cross-listed companies; weighted average based on Hong Kong market capitalisation for China and at domestic capitalisation for India. See Figure 12.6 for further information.

[2] The full sample period is between 15 March 1999 and 31 December 2013; the crisis period is between September and December 2008.

[3] Based on estimation of Equation 12.4 in the text; see Annex 1 for details.

Sources: Bloomberg; authors' estimations.

Table 12.3 also reports estimates of the half-life of the convergence of onshore and offshore share prices to their centres of gravity for the periods before and after the crisis. This half-life is estimated from Equation 12.4 (Peng et al. 2008).

Equation 12.4

$$\Delta q_{i,t} = \alpha + \beta q_{i,t-1} + \Sigma \, \varphi_n \, \Delta q_{i,t-n} + \varepsilon_{i,t}$$

In Equation 12.4, $q_{i,t}$ is the logarithm of the overseas–local share price ratio for the cross-listed companies; Δ is the first difference operator. Since the estimated $\beta < 0$, the speed of convergence, or half-life of a shock, to the premium can be taken as $-\ln(2)/\ln(1 + \beta)$. Table 12.3 shows mixed results, though for both the Chinese and the Indian markets, the half-life fell in half of the cases after the GFC, indicating more integration (Ma and McCauley 2013). Again on this measure, the Chinese equity market on average remained three to five times more segmented than the Indian equity market. In contrast to the instantaneous arbitrage between New York and Hong Kong,[5] that between New York and Mumbai takes weeks and that between Hong Kong and Shanghai takes months.

Implications for capital account opening

In this section, we draw implications from our findings of price gaps for capital account opening, focusing on China's case. Studies of the likely profile of China's international assets and liabilities over the medium term given capital account opening highlight the scope for net private outflows of portfolio and direct investment. On direct investment, China's longstanding welcome for foreign companies contrasts with the quite recent adoption of the policy to encourage outward direct investment, particularly in commodity production. Limits on outward portfolio investment were eased just before the GFC and to this day the limits do not bind; but the upshot is that private portfolio claims on the rest of the world's stocks and bonds remain low, and the potential increase appears huge as the capital account opens up and the income level rises.

He et al. (2012) and Bayoumi and Ohnsorge (2013) present reasonable medium-term outlooks for a rise in net private external assets in the event of a full capital account liberalisation in China. Both project big increases in gross positions, assets and liabilities alike, and both predict private assets would increase more than liabilities. Thus, both foresee that China can be expected to experience net private capital outflows following thorough capital account liberalisation. Such net outflows would not necessarily put downward pressure on the renminbi's value if the current account remains in surplus, or if offset by a policy of a drawdown of the sizeable official reserves.

There are some differences between these exercises. He et al. (2012) examine both direct investment and portfolio stocks, and their result is driven by the legacy of asymmetric capital controls (with acquisition of external assets by private Chinese more tightly controlled, especially in direct investment), financial market development in China and higher growth there. They project a larger step-up in direct investment net assets of 10 per cent of GDP than that in net portfolio assets, of 8 per cent of GDP (Table 12.4). Bayoumi and Ornsorge (2013) analyse portfolio stocks only and find the increase in net private assets could result from an increase in gross portfolio assets of 10–25 per cent of GDP

---

5   Or a sample average of one to two days for emerging markets in Levy-Yeyati et al. (2009:444).

306

and gross liabilities of 2–10 per cent of GDP (Table 12.4). The resulting increase in net portfolio assets of 11–18 per cent of GDP exceeds the 8 per cent estimate of He et al. (2012).[6]

Table 12.4 Impact of Capital Account Liberalisation in China on Direct and Portfolio Investment (stock adjustment as percentage of GDP)

	Bayoumi & Ornsorge (2013)		He et al. (2012) I 2020	Memo: Actual 2010
		Adjusted for smaller domestic stocks		
FDI assets			21.6	5.3
FDI liabilities			11.2	25.1
Net FDI			10.4	−19.8
Portfolio assets	15.4–24.9	9.4–15.1	24.2	4.3
Portfolio liabilities	1.7–9.9	1.7–9.9	16.4	3.8
Net portfolio	10.7–8.1	4.1–8.2	7.7	0.6

Sources: Bayoumi and Ornsorge (2013:28); He et al. (2012:29).

Policymakers, however, have to be concerned about not only the medium-term resting place or steady state, but also the dynamic path, as well as the volatility realised along it. Both papers neglect the banking flows, which can be huge and volatile. This is understandable, since the cross-country pattern of external bank assets and liabilities is hard to account for in standard modelling exercises.

Moreover, these exercises based on stocks of financial assets and liabilities do not allow prices themselves to be a major driver of both portfolio and banking flows in the short term. Our evidence on the onshore/offshore price gaps may help shed light on possible short-term dynamics of capital flows upon full capital account liberalisation. In brief, we find that the inflow pressure in the money market is very strong in China, in sharp contrast with the medium-term prospect for portfolio and direct investment outflows.

6   If the domestic equity market is adjusted for untraded shares and the domestic bond market is adjusted for bank-held bonds then Bayoumi and Ornsorge (2013) put the stock adjustment at only 4–8 per cent of GDP. Any such projected net portfolio outflows or build-up in net private external assets could easily be accommodated by the official sector running down the large foreign exchange reserves resulting in a rebalancing between private and public portfolios. The privatisation of China's foreign assets should be seen as a natural consequence of allowing the private sector greater scope to buy foreign stocks and bonds (Ma and McCauley 2014).

In particular, we have shown that the binding capital controls allow differences in forward exchange rates onshore and offshore, and also in onshore and offshore short-term interest rates. These price gaps tend to favour net private capital inflows rather than outflows, since the price of the same financial instrucment is lower onshore than offshore.

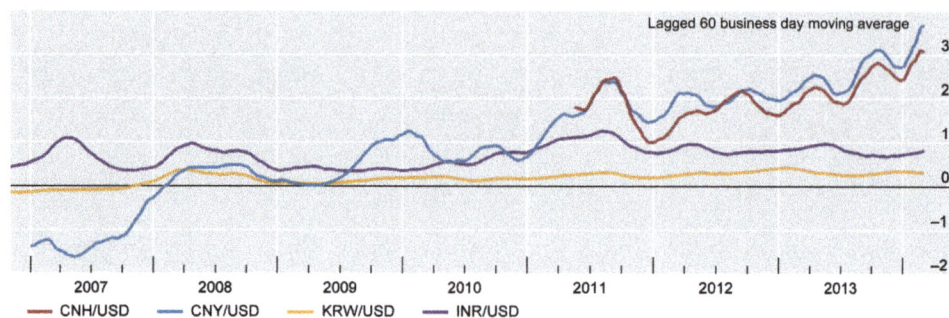

Figure 12.5 Sharpe Ratios

Source: Bloomberg and BIS staff calculations.

Note: Defined as the three-month interest rate differential (Shibor for renminbi, Mibor for rupee, 91-day certificate of deposit for won and Libor for dollar) divided by the implied volatility derived from three-month at-the-money exchange rate options for the relevant currency pair.

Moreover, the portfolio inflow pressure can be seen more clearly by consulting an ex ante measure of the risk-adjusted return on money-market carry trades. We take the short-term interest rate differential as a ratio of short-term volatility implied in currency options—a simple version of the Sharpe ratio. Figure 12.5 shows how attractive an open Chinese money market would be at recent levels of currency volatility. With three-month Shibor at 5 per cent and Libor at 0.25 per cent and the implied volatility of the renminbi at less than 2 per cent, non-residents would be strongly attracted to the Chinese money market.

Indeed, our simple Sharpe ratio for the renminbi averages 3.5 in recent months, compared to a range of 0.3 to 0.8 for other major emerging market currencies shown in Figure 12.5. Thus, the renminbi clearly represents an extremely attractive target among all the major emerging-market currencies for carry traders, suggesting substantial pressures from inward bank and bond flows into China, at least in the short term. Even the increase in implied volatility associated with the mild renminbi depreciation around the widening of the renminbi daily trading band in mid March 2014 left the carry-to-risk ratio very attractive (see below).[7]

---

7 Note that in contrast, although India's money-market rates at 8 per cent are much more attractive taken in isolation, when the volatility of the rupee/dollar rate is factored in, the carry is not so attractive.

We have illustrated the strong incentives for fixed income inflows at the three-month tenor, but the problem extends out the yield curve, albeit to a lesser extent. That is, the Chinese Government's yields exceed the US Government's yields all the way out to 10 years and beyond. Since the Chinese yield curve is on the flat side, the yield gap narrows with maturity.

Near-term developments will not necessarily lessen the attraction of the Chinese money market. While the normalisation of US dollar rates would tend to narrow the gap with Chinese yields, the liberalisation of interest rates in China is expected to widen it. He et al. (2014) use a variety of approaches to conclude that equilibrium yields in China could be 2.5–3 per cent higher from the current regulated level. Such a rise would take the Chinese yield curve to 5–6 per cent at the short end and 6–7 per cent at the long end. On the US side, Laskey and Whalen (2014) of the Congressional Budget Office project that the US Federal Reserve will take short-term rates up to 3.5 per cent later in this decade while 10-year Treasury yields will rise to 5 per cent. How precisely these two yield curves will relate to each other as normalisation and liberalisation play out is difficult to predict; but pressure from inward capital flows, especially at the short end, is a serious near-term prospect in light of a more liberal Chinese capital account. Thus, while domestic financial liberalisation is often considered a prerequisite for further external financial opening, it can add to its immediate challenges.

Our findings yield two useful insights for Chinese policymakers managing capital account liberalisation. First, the contrast between our short-term inflow pressures and the consensus medium-term outflow pressures could potentially imply volatility along the path towards full capital account openness. Policymakers need to carefully negotiate this risk-laden process. Ocampo and Erten (2014) suggest Chinese policymakers could first suspend the existing capital controls as a way to open up the capital account, without scrapping all the underlying institutional arrangements and control tools. At least, stronger and more transparent reporting and statistical systems could be put in place so that broad market positions and cross-border flows can be tracked in a timely and systematic fashion.

Second, a sustained increase in exchange rate variability ahead of substantial capital opening could serve to render the renminbi a less attractive carry-trade target. The PBC's widening of the permitted daily trading band from ±1 per cent to ±2 per cent in March 2014 clearly worked in this direction: the Sharpe ratio for the renminbi more than halved. More exchange rate risk would help tip the balance from short-term inflow pressure to medium-term outflow pressures.

Summary

In this conclusion, we recap the evidence bearing on our four hypotheses and draw implications.

First, both the Chinese and the Indian economies are opening up. Our price evidence clearly questions the relevance and usefulness of the Chinn–Ito indices of de jure controls. Advancing financial integration is allowing policymakers to gain both experience and confidence, facilitating rather than impeding an acceleration of desired capital account liberalisation.

Second, India is more open than China. Thus we challenge Chinn and Ito's index, which suggests that China and India restrict capital flows to a similar extent. And we question Lane and Milesi-Ferretti's ranking of China as the more open economy.[8] On balance, the capital opening task is bigger for China than for India.

Why has India been hitherto more financially open than China? The answer could lie in a mix of the need to fund current account deficits in India, the greater rigour with which the controls are enforced in China, the longstanding multinational operations of Indian private firms to arbitrage onshore and offshore markets (Subramanian 2009), and a larger footprint of global banks in the Indian domestic banking market. Future research could provide different explanations (Ma and McCauley 2013).

Whatever the cause of this longstanding difference, our evidence suggests China is rapidly eroding India's lead. As a policy intention, the paced internationalisation of the renminbi has no counterpart in India. By creating a pool of renminbi bank accounts and bonds outside the Chinese mainland and allowing for offshore delivery of the renminbi, this policy is also punching holes in the capital controls through which arbitrage transactions can pass. In fact, the renminbi internationalisation has been viewed by some as a part of the capital account liberalisation drive in China (Zhang 2014).

Third, an important conclusion of our study is, however, that on all three measures both the Chinese and the Indian economies have a way to go in terms of liberalising their capital accounts. Policy continues to segment onshore and offshore markets in both cases. More consistent opening movements lately in China may support its capital account liberalisation momentum.

---

8   We hope researchers will use these measures with greater care, even scepticism, and will look for new measures. The Chinn–Ito measure in particular is not clearly fit for the purpose to which it is often put. Moreover, there is little reason to think that 'the most finely gradated' (Quinn et al. 2011:492) measure of Schindler (2009) does not suffer from the same fundamental drawback. Looking at types of regulation does not reveal how restrictive they are, much less how restrictive they are in practice. De facto is the way to go.

Fourth, while the consensus medium-term prospect is for an increase in net private external assets for China, our findings of onshore/offshore price gaps across three important financial markets point to potential pressure from large inward capital flows in the event of full capital opening. In particular, the renminbi and money-market instruments have been priced lower onshore than offshore, while the premium of onshore share prices of Chinese companies had disappeared by 2013. Indeed, the renminbi was among the most attractive carry-trade targets until the volatility around the latest trading-band widening in March 2014. The full implications of this greater flexibility remain to be seen. The longer end of the renminbi yield curve could also attract substantial inflows with current and prospective yields. Therefore, our price gap evidence raises questions about the dynamics and volatility of net private capital flows during the process of a full Chinese capital account liberalisation.

Chinese policymakers need to take into account the risks of such dynamics and volatility on the journey to capital account liberalisation. The contrast between possible short-term net inflows and projected medium-term net capital outflows upon liberalisation may amplify the potential volatility.

Initially large inward portfolio and banking flows could interact in unpredictable ways with existing imbalances in the domestic financial system. Financial imbalances can build up over the longer financial cycles that are not simply operating at business-cycle frequency (Drehmann et al. 2012). In China, the government-sponsored investment and credit boom of 2008–09 (which responded to the fallout from the boom–bust cycle in US real estate) has lifted credit in China well above its trend deepening vis-a-vis GDP. Total credit to the non-financial private sector as a ratio to GDP, including the fast-expanding shadow banking, rose by more than 60 per cent in the wake of the GFC, from below 120 per cent in 2007 to above 180 per cent in 2013. This could be a sign of increased financial vulnerability (Drehmann et al. 2012).

Financial imbalances and vulnerability could trigger capital outflows in a more liberal environment. In response of liberalisation of bank flows in a situation in which dollar rates remain low, Chinese rates are tending higher and the exchange rate expectations show stability or an appreciation bias could be sizable. By the same token, a clear turn in the financial cycle in China, arguably in its late stages already, and the prospect of big credit losses in China, in combination with normalisation of US dollar rates, could risk a substantial private capital outflow from China. Such net private capital outflows would fundamentally differ from a desired and benign increase in the net Chinese private external claims on the rest of the world over the medium term.

Under the circumstances, policymakers need to be concerned not only about the immediate money-market yield differential and its relation to exchange rate volatility, but also about the hard-to-predict outcome of the surge of credit in China. These considerations do not argue against incremental capital opening but at a minimum they argue for keeping a strong measurement system in place so that the authorities do not find themselves flying blind.

References

Aizenman, J. and Sengupta, R. (2011), *The financial trilemma in China and a comparative analysis with India*, November, Mimeo.

Baba, N. and Packer, F. (2009), 'Interpreting deviations from covered interest parity during the financial market turmoil of 2007–08', *Journal of Banking and Finance* 33(11):1953–62.

Bayoumi, T. and Ohnsorge, F. (2013), *Do inflows or outflows dominate? Global implications of capital account liberalization in China*, IMF Working Paper No. WP/13/189, International Monetary Fund, Washington, DC.

Chinn, M. and Ito, H. (2006), 'What matters for financial development? Capital controls, institutions, and interactions', *Journal of Development Economics* 81(1).

Chinn, M. and Ito, H. (2008), 'A new measure of financial openness', *Journal of Comparative Policy Analysis* 10(3):309–22.

Drehmann, M., Borio, C. and Tsatsaronis, K. (2012), *Characterising the financial cycle: don't lose sight of the medium term!*, BIS Working Papers No. 380, June, Bank for International Settlements, Basel.

Frankel, J. (1992), 'Measuring international capital mobility: a review', *American Economic Review* 82:197–202.

He, D., Cheung, L., Zhang, W. and Wu, T. (2012), 'How would capital account liberalization affect China's capital flows and the renminbi real exchange rates?', *China and the World Economy* 20(6):29–54.

He, D., Wang, H. and Yu, X. (2014), *Interest rate determination in China: past, present, and future*, February, Mimeo.

Hooley, J. (2013), 'Bringing down the Great Wall? Global implications of capital account liberalisation in China', *Bank of England Quarterly Bulletin* 53(4):304–16.

International Monetary Fund (IMF) (2010), 'Measuring capital account restrictiveness: a survey of the literature', in *Annual Report on Exchange Arrangements and Exchange Restrictions*, pp. 48–51, Washington, DC: International Monetary Fund.

Kohli, R. (2011), *India's experience in navigating the trilemma: do capital controls help?*, Working Paper 257, Indian Council for Research on International Economic Relations, New Delhi.

Lane, P. and Milesi-Ferretti, G. (2003), 'International financial integration', *IMF Staff Papers* 50(Special Issue):82–113.

Lane, P. and Milesi-Ferretti, G. (2007), 'The external wealth of nations mark II: revised and extended estimates of foreign assets and liabilities, 1970–2004', *Journal of International Economics* 73(2):223–50.

Lane, P. and Schmuckler, S. (2007), 'International financial integration of China and India', in A. Winters and S. Yusuf (eds), *Dancing with Giants: China, India, and the Global Economy*, pp. 101–32, Singapore: The World Bank and Institute for Policy Studies.

Lasky, M. and Whalen, C. (2014), 'Economic growth is projected to be solid in the near term, but weakness in the labor market will probably persist', *Congressional Budget Office Blog*, 26 February.

Levy-Yeyati, E., Schmuckler, S. and Horen, N. (2009), 'International financial integration through the law of one price: the role of liquidity and capital controls', *Journal of Financial Intermediation* 18:432–63.

Liu, L.-G. and Otani, I. (2005), Capital controls and interest rate parity: evidence from China, 1999–2004, Presented to RIETI/BIS/BOC Conference on Globalization of Financial Services in China, March.

Ma, G. and McCauley, R. (2008a), 'Do China's capital controls still bind?', in B. Eichengreen, Y.-C. Park and C. Wyplosz (eds), *China, Asia, and the New World Economy*, pp. 312–40, Oxford: Oxford University Press.

Ma, G. and McCauley, R. (2008b), 'Efficacy of China's capital controls: evidence from price and flow data', *Pacific Economic Review* 13(1):104–23.

Ma, G. and McCauley, R. (2013), 'Is India or China financially more open?', *Journal of International Money and Finance* (39):6–27.

Ma, G. and McCauley, R. (2014), 'Global and euro imbalances: China and Germany', *China and World Economy* 22(1):1–29.

Ma, G., Ho, C. and McCauley, R. (2004), 'The markets for non-deliverable forwards in Asia', *BIS Quarterly Review* (June):81–94.

McCauley, R., Shu, C. and Ma, G. (2014), 'Non-deliverable forwards: 2013 and beyond', *BIS Quarterly Review* (March):75–88.

McGuire, P. and von Peter, G. (2009), 'The US dollar shortage in global banking', *BIS Quarterly Review* (March):47–63.

Mancini, T. and Ranaldo, A. (2011), *Limits to arbitrage during the crisis: funding liquidity constraints and covered interest parity*, Ms, Swiss National Bank.

Misra, S. and Behera, H. (2006), 'Non-deliverable foreign exchange forward market: an overview', *Reserve Bank of India Occasional Papers* 27(3):25–55.

Ocampo, J. and Erten, B. (2014), Latin America's lessons from capital account liberalisation, March, Paper submitted to Pardee Task Force on Regulating Global Capital Flows, Global Economic Governance Initiative, Boston University.

Otani, I. and Tiwari, S. (1981), 'Capital controls and interest rate parity: the Japanese experience, 1978–81', *IMF Staff Papers* 28(4):793–815.

Peng, W., Miao, H. and Chow, N. (2008), 'Price convergence between dual-listed A and H shares', in *Macroeconomic Linkages between Hong Kong and Mainland China*, H. Genberg and D. He (eds), pp. 295–315, Hong Kong: City University of Hong Kong.

Quinn, D., Schindler, M. and Toyoda, A. M. (2011), 'Assessing measures of financial openness and Integration', *IMF Economic Review* 59(3):488–522.

Reserve Bank of India (2006), *Report of the Committee on Fuller Capital Account Convertibility* [the Tarapore Report], July.

Schindler, M. (2009), 'Measuring financial integration: a new data set', *IMF Staff Papers* 56(1):222–38.

Subramanian, A. (2009), 'Discussion: resisting financial globalization in Asia', in *Financial Globalization and Emerging Market Economies. Proceedings of an International Symposium Organised by the Bank of Thailand, Bangkok, 7–8 November 2008*:223–6.

Zhang, M. (2014), *Whether China should accelerate capital account liberalisation now?*, Policy Discussion No. 2014.001, Chinese Academy of Social Science, Research Centre for International Finance.

13. Increasing the Resilience of China's Financial Sector and the Global Monetary System

Wing Thye Woo

Pursuing sustained modern economic growth

China entered the middle-income country category in 2006 according to Woo's (2012) Catch-Up Index (CUI), which is the ratio of a country's per capita GDP to US per capita GDP, with both measured in purchasing power parity (PPP) units. In Woo's classification, middle-income status begins with CUI at 20 per cent and high income begins at 55 per cent.

Continued fast progress by China to high-income status cannot be taken for granted. Four of the five largest economies in Latin American—Argentina, Brazil, Chile and Mexico—have been in the middle-income category since at least 1960. Furthermore, the secular decline in the CUI value of Venezuela, the fifth member, from its petroleum-induced high-income status, pushed Venezuela down into middle-income status in 1980. And Malaysia is a closer and more recent warning about the middle-income trap (Woo 2011). In Malaysia, after having been hailed in 1993 by the World Bank (1993) as an East Asian 'miracle' economy, catch-up growth stopped in 1995.

These large Latin American economies and Malaysia are no longer experiencing what Simon Kuznets (1971) called 'modern economic growth' (MEG). MEG is the type of economic growth that began in Western Europe in the late eighteenth century. It is distinguished from earlier types of growth by several qualities: a sustained high growth rate in per capita output, large shifts in the composition of output, increasing diversity in goods and services produced, and rapid institutional and ideological adjustments. Because the quintessential feature of MEG is continual change across many dimensions of society, the policy implication is that a country must change its economic policies after reaching each new stage of economic development in order to facilitate the continuation of growth.

Our research on economic growth in other countries has led us to the conclusion that China's successful economic transition from middle-income to high-income country cannot be achieved by the present dualistic policy regime of state-led industrialisation facilitated by state-directed allocation of capital, and enthusiastic private sector participation (mostly) in light industries and in the low and medium value-added portions of the service sector. The Soviet Union achieved middle-income status without private sector participation, but it ended in political and economic collapse in 1991. The achievement of middle-income status in Malaysia (with a Chinese-style policy regime of state–private dualism) has been followed by economic stagnation because of policy inaction caused by the government's short-sighted attitude of 'if it ain't broke, don't fix it'.

China has now reached the stage at which reform of its financial sector is among the urgently needed fundamental policy changes it must make in order to avoid falling into the middle-income trap. Continued inaction on comprehensive financial reform would spell the end of the latest of its attempts in the past 200 years to reach the productivity and living standards of the advanced economies.

The financial sector reform agenda

Most of the studies on the progress of financial development in China use an array of stock-flow ratios like the M2 to GDP ratio and the stock market capitalisation to GDP ratio. As the M2 to GDP ratio has increased from 124 per cent in 1998 to 188 per cent in 2010, and the capitalisation of the Shanghai and Shenzhen stock markets has climbed from an average of 30 per cent of GDP in 1997–2005 to 53 per cent in 2006–12, it is common for many China analysts to report steady progress in the country's financial development.

Two recent studies have, however, suggested that this steady upward march of the stock-flow ratios like M2–GDP hides some unfavourable trends in China's financial sector that could trigger a financial collapse (Liu and Qin (2014); Arcand (2014)).

Liu and Qin (2014) challenge the conventional view that there has been progress (albeit, insufficient) in China's financial development. They develop a price-based indicator instead of using the usual quantity-based indicator to measure the degree of structural friction in China's banking system. Their new indicator is called the 'shadow-minus-actual spread' (SAS) because this is the difference between the shadow interest rate and the actual interest rate.

To estimate the actual average interest rate (from the banking data on loans) and the shadow interest rate (from the composition of investment undertaken), Liu and Qin (2014) divide borrowers into two categories.

1. low-risk enterprises (LREs), which correspond with state-owned and shareholding enterprises (including shareholding and limited-liability enterprises, mostly state-controlled).

2. high-risk enterprises (HREs), which correspond with private, self-employed individuals, collective-owned (most of which are in fact private-owned township and village enterprises) and other categories of enterprises.[1]

Liu and Qin calculate the average return rate on bank loans, r, as Equation 13.1.

Equation 13.1

$$r = w_{LRE}r_{LRE} + w_{HRE}r_{HRE}$$

In Equation 13.1, w_{LRE} and w_{HRE} are the shares of the bank credit allocated to LREs and HREs respectively.

They calculate the shadow loan rate, r′, as the average cost of funding the *entire* investment through bank loans (Equation 13.2).

Equation 13.2

$$r' = v_{LRE}r_{LRE} + v_{HRE}r_{HRE}$$

In Equation 13.2, v_{LRE} and v_{HRE} denote the investment share of LRE and HRE respectively.

The difference between the shadow loan rate and the actual loan rate, the shadow-minus-actual spread (SAS), is hence given by Equation 13.3.

Equation 13.3

$$SAS = (r' - r) = (v_{HRE} - w_{HRE})(r_{HRE} - r_{LRE})$$

Equation 13.3 suggests to us that the key assumption behind the SAS is that the actual composition of investment reflected the socially optimal proportion of high-risk projects and low-risk projects. If the risk preference of the banking system were identical to the risk preference of society, then the proportion of bank loans extended to high-risk projects would equal the proportion of high-risk investments chosen by society.

Our interpretation is in line with Liu and Qin's (2014) argument that if the banks were to price the risks of enterprises correctly and allocate credit resources according to economic criteria, the shares that LREs and HREs received in bank

---

1 There are two key differences between an LRE and an HRE. First, the state-owned enterprises (SOEs) and state-controlled enterprises (SCEs) have lower default risk because these firms face soft-budget constraints—that is, when the SOEs and SCEs are faced with bankruptcy, the Government tends to rescue them (through channels like fiscal subsidies) (Woo 1999). Second, the productivity of an LRE is far below that of an HRE (Woo et al. 1994).

loans would roughly match their respective shares in investment spending—that is, v_{LRE} and w_{LRE} will have the same values, and SAS would equal zero. When, however, the banking system tilts the allocation of loans towards LREs, then $v_{LRE} < w_{LRE}$, which implies that $v_{HRE} > w_{HRE}$. Liu and Qing call this bias by the banks towards making loans to the LREs the structural friction in the banking system. They find the disturbing result that the spread between the shadow rate of return and the actual rate of return on bank loans has widened over time, from 1.02 percentage points in 2003 to 2.38 in 2005, to 3.25 in 2007 and then to 3.76 in 2010. They identify two factors in the cause of the increasing inefficiency:

1. the disproportionate amount of bank loans allocated to state-controlled companies, making $(v_{HRE} - w_{HRE})$ positive

2. the average productivity of the state-controlled companies being lower than the average productivity of domestic private companies, making $(r_{HRE} - r_{LRE})$ bigger.

Arcand (2014) also shares Liu and Qin's assessment that China's financial sector has become more dysfunctional over time. In an earlier analysis of cross-country data (Arcand et al. 2012), he found that an increase in a stock–flow ratio (for example, the M2–GDP ratio) when it is at a low value has a positive impact on economic growth, but there is a threshold value for the ratio beyond which an increase in the ratio will be harmful to economic growth. Specifically, this earlier study found that the marginal effect of financial development on economic growth becomes negative when credit to the private sector reaches 100 per cent of GDP.

In his more recent study, Arcand finds that this reversal from good effect to bad effect is generated in a simple model with endogenous default probability, credit rationing and bailout of state enterprises. The important point is that the presence of a bailout leads to a level of loans that is 'too large' with respect to the social optimum. When Arcand tests this model on Chinese data, he finds an empirical regularity that has hitherto gone unnoticed in the Chinese context: there is a large, negative and statistically significant impact from outstanding loans on the economic performance of provinces.

Financial reform is now clearly overdue. The most important requirement in the formulation of financial sector policy is recognition by the Chinese Government that the role of government in a middle-income country has to be substantially different from that of a government in a low-income country if dynamic catch-up growth is to continue. Specifically, the Chinese Government should now no longer focus primarily on raising funds cheaply to promote industrialisation because China is now a highly industrialised economy. The issue now is not the quantity but the quality of industrial expansion.

Furthermore, the fiscal position of the Chinese Government is now strong enough that it does not need to distort the financial sector in order to finance its support for industrialisation indirectly. Fiscal revenue has grown at an average 20 per cent per year since 2001, and fiscal revenue has climbed from 10.7 per cent of GDP in 1997 to more than 20 per cent of GDP in the past few years. The rapid appreciation of land prices has rendered the Government even more secure fiscally. The Government is now in a position to fund any promotion of industrialisation directly and so it should fund its industrialisation efforts directly and give up its direct intervention in the allocation of financial resources and to thereby reduce the economic cost of promoting industrialisation.

The time is right for a comprehensive reform of China's financial sector to help facilitate China's graduation from middle-income to high-income status. The four main sets of financial reforms that need to be undertaken are:

1. enlargement of the financial sector by diversifying the range of financial institutions and the range of financial assets, paying particular attention to the increase in equity issuance by private domestic firms

2. deregulation and modernisation of the banking sector

3. insertion of shock absorbers and circuit-breakers into the financial system to increase the resilience of the system against financial malfeasance and financial meltdowns, and to build up the financial firefighting capability of the regulatory agencies to minimise the costs of financial institution failure and to prevent financial contagion

4. updating the international dimensions of the financial sector consistently with the requirements of globalisation and China's emergence as a major economic power, and to enhance global monetary stability.

This chapter discusses the third and fourth of those sets of financial sector reform, focussing especially on steps that are necessary to avoid systemic financial collapse along the way to continuing modern economic growth.

Modernising the financial sector safely and bolstering financial firefighting capability

The discussion of how to avoid systemic financial crisis can usefully begin with analysis of the recent financial collapses in a number of advanced economies, and proceed to drawing lessons for China and other developing countries, which are seeking to reform their financial sectors to support MEG. Three excellent articles on this topic have appeared recently: Sachs (2014); Boone and Johnson (2014); and Honkapohja (2014).

Sachs (2014) examines the record financial malfeasance in the United States in the past 30 years and finds that one of the features of the 2008 GFC was the epidemic of lawlessness among America's major investment banks, commercial banks, hedge funds, financial conglomerates and stock exchanges, collectively known as Wall Street. Major Wall Street firms have been repeated law-breakers, and as a result have faced dozens of lawsuits and criminal actions regarding corporate practices at the core of their business. The startlingly common aspect of these legal actions is that, with few exceptions, senior Wall Street managers have not faced personal costs as a result of corporate malfeasance. When settlements are reached with the US Securities and Exchange Commission (the Federal financial market regulator) on cases of financial malfeasance, the defendant's firm typically pays a fine but has been allowed to 'neither admit nor deny wrongdoing' (a practice that has been, correctly, criticised by Federal Court judge Jed Rakoff as not serving the public interest). The fine is often a small fraction of the gains that accrued to the company as a result of its malfeasant behaviour. With no judgment of guilt or acknowledgment or denial of wrongdoing, no further action is taken against senior management (for example, a revocation of a manager's right to engage in banking).

It is useful to examine the Jeffrey Sachs paper in some detail because most of the weaknesses that gave rise to the widespread financial malfeasance that he identifies exist in all capitalist economies to similar degrees. Sachs (2014) argues that there are five main structural reasons for the intrinsic proclivity of US financial institutions to engage in overly risky transactions:

1. the CEOs are inadequately supervised

2. the firms are highly leveraged operations

3. the compensation scheme for CEOs are based on value of equity

4. the financial industry is under-regulated

5. the political power of Wall Street in Washington DC is large.

Large US companies have limited liability, are generally publicly owned and are characterised by highly dispersed shareholdings rather than ownership by a family or a small number of core investors. Because of the dispersed shareholding and limited liability, shareholders generally put little effort into monitoring corporate governance. The upshot is that CEOs have considerable authority with relatively low oversight from the board of directors, whose appointments are frequently made at the suggestion of management.

Banks tend to have an extremely high leverage ratio compared with non-financial corporations. A bank's job is to take on debt from depositors, other banks and the financial markets, to invest in assets. Using a simple numerical example, Sachs shows that high leverage increases the shareholder's appetite for risk beyond the social optimum if there is assymetry between the consequences of success and failure, with shareholders gaining a higher proportion of successes than of losses from failures. Leverage is encouraged by the presence of deposit insurance and by the implicit expectation of government bailouts of bank creditors in the event of a crisis. In the run-up to the GFC, US investment banks and European commercial banks had the highest leverage with a remarkable average of around 30 (total assets relative to equity). US commercial banks were less highly leveraged at around 10—still very high compared with non-financial companies.

In Sachs' view, a major factor in the soaring compensation of CEOs in the past three decades was the increasing use of equity-based compensation, especially in the form of stock options. He extends his simple numerical example on leverage to clarify how stock options increase the CEO's appetite for risk beyond that of the shareholders. The combination of highly leveraged firms and CEO pay packages laden with stock options is strong motivation for a CEO to treat his enterprise as an enormous gamble for riches.

The process of financial deregulation started in earnest in the early 1980s in the savings and loan (S&L) industry. Within a few years, the entire sector was bankrupt, in effect 'looted' by its CEOs (Akerlof and Romer 1993). Insolvent S&Ls took advantage of federal deposit insurance to attract new deposits, and then used deposit inflows to make payments of phantom profits and other insider payments to the owner-managers of the S&Ls. In the end, the Federal Government had to pay off the depositors, while many corrupt owners of bankrupt S&Ls walked away with fortunes.

The culmination and most important act of deregulation was the Gramm–Leach–Bliley Act of 1999, which repealed the 1933 Glass–Steagall Act, a major part of the Great Depression's financial reform that separated deposit-taking activities and investment banking activities. Glass–Steagall was repealed in 1999 with strong bipartisan support. The leading architect of the repeal, Treasury

Secretary Robert Rubin, immediately became chairman of Citigroup, a new financial conglomerate (formed in a US$140 billion mega-merger of Citicorp and Travelers Group—one of the largest mergers in history) made possible by the deregulation.

Sachs (2014) attributes the extremely low personal risk of any penalties for financial malfeasance that senior Wall Street managers face and the steady deregulation of the financial industry to the enormous political power of Wall Street in Washington. The money flows mainly in two forms: as campaign contributions and as lobbying outlays, much of which end up in political pockets indirectly through hiring politicians into lobbying firms (and law firms).

More controversially, Sachs hypotheses that there has been a change in the moral Zeitgeist in the United States that has increased the acceptability of self-serving or illegal behaviour. He makes the case that super-high managerial compensation is not the social norm in rich capitalist countries, by citing the case of a leading and highly successful Swedish CEO, Percy Barnevik, who engineered a retirement package typical of a US CEO. When news of the retirement package became commonly known several years later, the public outcry forced the retired CEO to recant the arrangement and step down from other public positions. In the United States, however, the social restraints on high compensation packages have diminished, thereby making it easier for US CEOs to take the opportunity to increase their own pay cheques.

Based on his overview of Wall Street lawlessness, Sachs (2014) suggests the following seven areas as needing the greatest attention in trying to promote financial sector development safely.

1. Limit the leverage of financial institutions because it promotes excessive risk-taking or outright looting.

2. Implement tougher scrutiny and regulatory limits on compensation packages of CEOs, as in the European Union. Shareholders should have an automatic vote on compensation packages, and the use of stock options should be limited to avoid excessive risk-taking.

3. Increase significantly the higher levels of marginal taxation, in part to tamp down the incentives for managerial abuse.

4. Legislate for CEOs and senior managers to face *personal* liability for major acts of malfeasance committed by their companies during their watch. Personal liability could include the loss of licence to practice, forced resignation from office, a ban on bonuses and personal liability for a portion of corporate fines and civil settlements in cases where CEO responsibility or negligence can be determined.

5. Bring criminal prosecutions against firms and individuals for large-scale financial malfeasance.

6. Bar Wall Street firms from lobbying activities and senior bank managers from making campaign contributions.

7. Undertake research on how to restore ethical norms on Wall Street.

Boone and Johnson (2014) investigate the roots of the systemic imprudence in the financial institutions of the developed countries. They show how prudent financial regulation, broadly defined, has proven difficult in wealthy nations. The economic incentives and political forces that promote undercapitalised financial institutions, over-leveraged production firms and unfinanced public entitlements have consistently and invariably won out over prudent management across Europe, the United States, Canada and Japan. This outcome has placed much of the wealthy world on a path lined with intermittent, but growing, financial crises. In particular, these countries are addicted to methods of economic management that are debt-financed (for example, recapitalising banks by issuing new government debt) because they have ageing populations, and future generations are not represented in the policymaking process.

Successive firm failures in financial crises are bailed out by the state, adding to deficits caused by ageing populations and limited political incentives to balance budgets. Rapid growth tends to obscure insolvencies. These difficulties usually surface only when growth turns down. Once large undercapitalised systems and structural budget deficits have developed, it is difficult to change course, leading to continued financial weakness and rising dangers. Inflation, financial repression and new crises follow from this systemic lack of prudence in wealthy nations.

While Boone and Johnson (2014) 'are skeptical that adequate changes can be achieved' in the developed economies 'without crisis', they see the possibility that rapidly growing economies (like China's) might be able to avoid the same outcome if they take the following three sets of actions now.

First, China must promote the safety of its financial institutions by:

1. enlisting the energy of creditors to monitor the financial institutions by passing strict no-bailout laws, which require creditor bail-in before public funds can be used

2. requiring financial institutions to have large buffers of equity and contingent capital

3. strengthening regulation by imposing multi-year restrictions on the participation of former financial regulators in private financial firms—that is, stopping revolving-door practices between the state and the private sector.

Second, China must promote stable public finance by:

1. enforcing balanced budget rules through constitutional amendment (this requirement keeps current spending in check but cannot prevent over-promises on pensions)

2. implementing means test requirements for pensions because this would reduce the size of the group lobbying for high pensions at the expense of future generations

3. increasing transparency in the financial implications of fiscal actions—for example, there should be a nonpartisan agency (like the US Congressional Budget Office) that makes projections on the budget

4. instituting regular auditor-general reports and prosecuting malfeasance.

Third, China must recognise that financial bubbles usually cannot continue for extended periods without the complicity of the central bank. The US Federal Reserve under Alan Greenspan encouraged bubbles by giving implicit bailout guarantees to systemically important financial institutions (for example, through the interventions on Long Term Capital Management and Bear Stearns). It is therefore important to create an independent 'financial stability oversight board' to look over the shoulders of the central bank and the other financial regulators. The existence of this independent financial sector overseer will increase the emergence of whistle-blowers whose timely warnings will help prevent financial collapses.

Honkapohja (2014) identifies the reasons for the financial crises in Finland, Norway and Sweden in the 1980s by reviewing the process of liberalisation in the Nordic countries in that decade. He arrives at four key conclusions after discussing the reasons Finland, Norway and Sweden drifted into financial and economic crises.

The first conclusion is that the Nordic countries paid too much attention to the 'how to' and too little attention to 'what is'. There was a lot of attention on what would be the optimum sequencing of policy actions to dispense with the system of financial market and capital account controls. There was insufficient attention to: 1) how the different markets and production sectors would adjust to the policy actions; and 2) what conditions the banks and other market institutions were in. It was thought that firms and households would know how to adjust to the new system and would do so in a flexible way. However, it turned out that both banks and their customers moved towards the new equilibrium too rapidly, causing a credit boom, an asset price bubble and, in the end, a banking crisis.

The Nordic countries did not realise clearly enough that liberalisation leads to increased risks and that behaviour needed to change in response. Prudential supervision did not have a significant role in the period of a controlled financial system, because the control mechanism by itself had substantially secured the stability of banks. How could the existing system of prudential supervision, which was not needed under the controlled system, have been counted on to start meeting its much heavier responsibilities right away upon financial deregulation?

It is important that all the parties involved understand the need to change ways of thinking and business practices. Traditional ways of thinking can become a trap. Market-based financial systems are inherently less controllable and thus market participants must prepare for new risks and uncertainties that were absent in a system of financial repression. Risk management and supervision become very important with financial deregulation.

Honkapohja's (2014) second conclusion was that strengthening the capital base of banks and reforming their supervisory systems are important requirements in advance of the major liberalisation steps.

The third conclusion was that the Nordic countries should have known that it would be difficult to maintain fixed exchange rates after they had moved to market-based financial systems and freed cross-border capital flows. The combination of free capital flows and a fixed exchange rate regime can generate immense speculative pressures, which make defence of the exchange rate costly.

The fourth conclusion is that it is important to try to time the main parts of the liberalisation so as to avoid a business-cycle upswing.

Honkapohja (2014) points out that the sheer size of China's economy makes its liberalisation process different from that of most countries. The reforms in China could have major spillover effects on other countries, and they might well take action in response to the Chinese reforms. China should therefore take into account in the planning of its financial deregulation the international repercussions of its financial sector reform and the possible foreign reactions to it.

To summarise, these three papers by Sachs (2014), Boone and Johnson (2014) and Honkapohja (2014) propose three sets of actions to modernise the financial sector safely and to bolster prudential oversight and financial firefighting capabilities. The first set seeks to reduce the incentives for and means of financial institutions and their managers engaging in excessive risk-taking by:

1. requiring the Government to prosecute financial institutions for financial malfeasance, and to make their managers bear personal liability for illegal acts by their firms

2. replacing bailouts of creditors and stockholders with bail-ins

3. increasing the buffer of capital requirements

4. reducing the leverage ratios of financial institutions, and the use of equity-based compensation for their managers.

The second set of reforms is to change the cosy, self-serving relationship between the financial industry and the political establishment by:

1. limiting the amount the financial industry can spend on political donations

2. stopping the revolving-door employment patterns between Wall Street and Pennsylvania Avenue by putting multi-year delays in moving from employment in one of these two places to employment in the other.

The third set of reforms is to strengthen the regulatory capability of the state financial agencies, and to limit the ability of the central bank and fiscal authorities to destabilise the macro-economy by:

1. establishing an independent systemic financial stability oversight board to audit the conduct of monetary policy by the central bank to: 1) end the practice of the 'Greenspan put' (policy to guarantee against stock market collapse) to protect the culprits of irrational exuberance; 2) prevent the bias towards the defence of an overvalued currency; 3) audit the work of the financial agencies in approving new financial instruments and in prosecution of financial fraud; and 4) monitor the readiness of the slew of federal financial agencies to handle the orderly restructuring of failed financial institutions and to prevent financial contagion within and across countries

2. passing a law to stop the bias towards debt-financed state spending by: 1) requiring the federal budget be balanced over the business cycle; and 2) establishing an independent fiscal mediation board to craft overall expenditure–revenue reconciliation.

Updating the international dimensions of financial policy

China is now the second-largest economy in the world and is projected to become the largest soon. China's growth has already brought a significant change in the international division of labour, as exemplified by the relative decline of the developed world's manufacturing sector. The changing balance in international economic power and the increased interdependence amongst nations should also bring about large shifts in the economic architecture of the world—for example, the emergence of new forms of Asian economic integration, amendments to the governance of international financial institutions like the International Monetary Fund and the World Bank—and new international initiatives on the regulation of capital flows, and financial sector supervision in order to strengthen the stability of the international monetary system.

To be in line with the large structural changes in the Chinese economy and to enhance the efficiency and stability of the new global economic order, it is necessary that China's exchange rate regime be changed to accommodate the structural changes and to promote global systemic resilience. Three analytically useful articles on this topic have became available recently: Wu et al. (2014); Pan et al. (2014); and Woo (2014).

Wu et al. (2014) identify the medium and long-term choices for the renminbi exchange rate regime. For the medium term, they recommend that China implements exchange rate management with the characteristics of 'basket, band and crawl' (BBC). Specifically, they suggest setting up a dynamic target zone for management of the effective exchange rate where the central parity rate (based on the Balassa–Samuelson hypothesis about relative labour productivity growth) maintains an annual 2 per cent appreciation in terms of the real effective exchange rate, with the width of the target zone set to allow +/–5 per cent fluctuation for the movements of the renminbi exchange rate around the central exchange rate. For the long term, they recommend China implements a monetary regime that combines a floating exchange rate system and generalised inflation targeting.

In line with China's growing impact on the world economy, it is natural for the renminbi (RMB) to become an international currency—a currency that is used to denominate the prices of goods and financial assets traded among foreign countries. Pan et al. (2014) believe that against the background of the centre of gravity of the global economy moving towards Asia and a multi-polar global economy being formed, there should be movement towards a multiple reserve currencies system that has an internal stabilising mechanism. RMB internationalisation is an integral component of this reform package. Wu et al. (2014) suggest that RMB internationalisation proceeds in two phases. In the early phase, the key task is to transform the Chinese economy and the financial system and foster international demand for the renminbi. In the later phase, the task is to open the capital account and increase substantially the supply of renminbi for global use.

Reform measures to promote financial openness include issuing licences to foreign financial institutions to conduct RMB-denominated business, and allowing mergers with and acquisition of branches from state-owned banks. It is desirable to pursue policies that favour capital outflow to provide incentives for large enterprises and financial institutions to go overseas.

To Woo (2014), the most important international aspects of China's financial reform are not whether or when the renminbi will be internationalised, or whether and when Shanghai should be allowed to become an international financial centre (IFC). He points out that once China's capital account is open like that of Taiwan, as it inevitably will be, the renminbi will automatically be internationalised like the Swedish krona and the Swiss franc, because foreigners could use it freely. Shanghai would automatically become an IFC like Stockholm and Geneva because foreign residents would be able to participate in China's stock and bond markets, and the Shanghai branches of foreign banks would be able to operate in any currency.

Woo (2014) identifies two fundamental international consequences of China's financial reform. First, the renminbi would become an international vehicle currency (IVC) like the US dollar and the euro—that is, it would join the small subset of internationalised currencies that other countries commonly use to denominate the prices of their traded goods and to denominate the international loans amongst themselves. Second, Shanghai would become a first-tier IFC (1-IFC) like the two present members, London and New York, in which the value of transactions in each is a quantum level higher than in the other IFCs like Frankfurt and Tokyo.

The Chinese Government should see the IVC and 1-IFC objectives as worth pursuing. These two developments would benefit China, for example through the creation of a new high value-added financial service industry, and the lowering of costs in international transactions. They would also bring large benefits to the world, increasing the supply of a basic global public good. The emergence of the renminbi as an IVC would help meet global demand for international reserves and for diversification of reserves. This would strengthen global financial stability by addressing an important systemic confidence problem.

In the present global monetary system in which the US dollar is the primary global reserve currency, there is a non-sustainable balance between the need for additional global liquidity to accommodate the growth of the international economy and the requirement for confidence in the US dollar as the global reserve currency. The larger the amount of US dollars held by non-US businesses and foreign governments, the greater is their concern about the ability of the US Government to maintain the purchasing power of the US dollar. (This present-day balance is not identical to the Triffin dilemma.)[2] The availability of the renminbi as another major store of value that is available for easy use as an international medium of exchange reduces global dependence on the ability

---

2 Triffin (1960) had expressed scepticism about the continued ability of the United States over time to swap gold for US dollars freely, as required by the Bretton Woods monetary system.

of a single central bank—the US Federal Reserve—to avoid mistakes in the conduct of monetary policy. It therefore increases international confidence in the resilience of the global monetary system.

Concluding remarks

Financial sector reform is of fundamental importance to the continuation of modern economic growth in China. It is important that China takes careful note of international experience with financial instability.

The fact that the developed economies have yet to produce a financial system that is absolutely safe to use should not be allowed to justify delaying the restructuring of China's financial industry. The key is to study foreign experiences carefully and to think critically about how the foreign lessons on building an efficient financial sector safely should be modified to take China's circumstances into account. This book contributes to that task. It is a lesson of experience that prudential measures should be taken both to prevent financial failures with effective monitoring and appropriate regulation, and also to facilitate the fighting of the financial fires that are still likely to ignite from time to time.

This concern for safety during financial transition is most strongly seen in the Chinese debate on whether, when and how the capital account should be opened. The concern is that capital account liberalisation could bring financial risks in two parts:

- excessive foreign capital inflows that cause asset bubbles and inflation
- an abrupt sudden reversal of the foreign capital flow that causes panic in domestic capital into joining the flight, and thus precipitate the collapse of the renminbi and financial system, and trigger a cessation of normal trade credit, and cause additional output decline.

These are valid concerns. However, the potential cost of financial openness has to be compared with the large benefits of financial openness. There is no way to eliminate the possibility of this disaster but actions can be taken to minimise the probability of it occurring (for example, requirements of large capital buffers and low leverage ratios), and actions to facilitate rapid control of the disaster and expeditious rebuilding afterwards.

The view that the capital account should not be opened until effective financial monitoring and prudential regulation systems are in place is untenable. The realities are that:

1. financial regulation is learned best in the classroom and in the marketplace. The recent establishment of the Shanghai Free Trade Zone (SFTZ) allows the emergence of an offshore international financial centre to give real-life training for China's financial regulators in recognising the signs of a developing financial storm and defusing the situation, and in handling efficiently the recapitalisation and reorganisation of failed financial institutions

2. a financial market is neither open permanently nor shut permanently. The degree of openness at any point in time is a policy choice at that time. A capital account once opened could always be partially closed temporarily without long-run adverse consequences if the closure is done for the right reasons—like stopping a financial panic.

When a financial disaster occurs, the most important action is to prevent oil from spreading. In a large financial crisis that is causing massive capital flight, the normal tools of management, like raising the interest rate to high levels and imposing macro-austerity, are usually ineffective.

Extraordinarily adverse financial market developments can be contained only with extraordinary state actions that break the general public's sense of panic about asset values and the economic future.

References

Akerlof, G. A. and Romer, P. M. (1993), 'Looting: the economic underworld of bankruptcy for profit', *Brookings Papers on Economic Activity* 24(2): 1–74.

Arcand, J.-L. (2014), 'Credit rationing, bank bailouts, and the deleterious impact of credit: evidence from China', in W. T. Woo, Y. Pan, J. D. Sachs and J. Qian (eds), *Financial Systems at the Crossroads: Lessons for China*, London: Imperial College Press & World Scientific Press.

Arcand, J.-L., Berkes, E. and Panizza, U. (2012), *Too much finance*, IMF Working Paper WP/12/161, International Monetary Fund, Washington, DC.

Boone, P. and Johnson, S. (2014), 'Systemic lack of prudence in wealthy nations: avoiding the dark side of financial development', in W. T. Woo, Y. Pan, J. D. Sachs and J. Qian (eds), *Financial Systems at the Crossroads: Lessons for China*, London: Imperial College Press & World Scientific Press.

Diaz-Alejandro, C. (1985), 'Good-bye financial repression, hello financial crash', *Journal of Development Economics* 19(1–2): 1–24.

Honkapohja, S. (2014), 'Lessons from the financial liberalization in the Nordic countries in the 1980s', in W. T. Woo, Y. Pan, J. D. Sachs and J. Qian (eds), *Financial Systems at the Crossroads: Lessons for China*, London: Imperial College Press & World Scientific Press.

Krugman, P. (2010a), 'Chinese New Year', *The New York Times*, 1 January 2010.

Krugman, P. (2010b), 'Taking on China', *The New York Times*, 15 March 2010.

Kuznet, S. (1971), Modern economic growth: findings and reflections, Lecture to the memory of Alfred Nobel, 11 December 1971. Available from <http://www.nobelprize.org/nobel_prizes/economic-sciences/laureates/1971/kuznetslecture.html>.

Liu, H. and Qin, T. (2014), 'The structural friction in China's banking system: causes, measurement and solutions', in W. T. Woo, Y. Pan, J. D. Sachs and J. Qian (eds), *Financial Systems at the Crossroads: Lessons for China*, London: Imperial College Press & World Scientific Press.

Liu, L.-Y. and Woo, W. T. (1994), 'Saving behavior under imperfect financial markets and the current account consequences', *Economic Journal* 104(424): 512–27.

Pan, Y., Xu, Y. and Wu, J. (2014), 'The internationalization of the renminbi in accordance with China's national interests and global responsibilities', in W. T. Woo, Y. Pan, J. D. Sachs and J. Qian (eds), *Financial Systems at the Crossroads: Lessons for China*, London: Imperial College Press & World Scientific Press.

Sachs, J. D. (2014), 'Wall Street lawlessness', in W. T. Woo, Y. Pan, J. D. Sachs and J. Qian (eds), *Financial Systems at the Crossroads: Lessons for China*, London: Imperial College Press & World Scientific Press.

The New York Times (2010a), 'Currency dispute likely to fray US–China ties', *The New York Times*, 4 February 2010.

The New York Times (2010b), 'Will China listen?', [Editorial], *The New York Times*, 17 March 2010.

Tobin, J. (1978), 'A proposal for international monetary reform', *Eastern Economic Journal* (July–October): 153–9.

Triffin, R. (1960), *Gold and the Dollar Crisis: The Future of Convertibility*, New Haven, Conn.: Yale University Press.

Wolf, M. (2010), 'China and Germany unite to impose global deflation', *The Financial Times*, 16 March 2010.

Woo, W. T. (1999), 'The real reasons for China's growth', *The China Journal*, Volume 49: 115–37.

Woo, W. T. (2008), 'Understanding the sources of friction in U.S.–China trade relations: the exchange rate debate diverts attention away from optimum adjustment', *Asian Economic Papers* 7(3): 65–99.

Woo, W. T. (2011), Understanding the middle-income trap in economic development: the case of Malaysia, Invited World Economy Lecture delivered at the University of Nottingham, Globalization and Economic Policy Conference, Globalization Trends and Cycles: The Asian Experiences, Semenyih, Selangor, Malaysia, 13 January 2011. Available from <http://www.nottingham.ac.uk/gep/documents/lectures/world-economy-asia-lectures/world-econ-asia-wing-thye-woo-2011.pdf>.

Woo, W. T. (2012), 'China meets the middle-income trap: the large potholes in the road to catching-up', *Journal of Chinese Economic and Business Studies* 10(4): 313–36.

Woo, W. T. (2014), *The future of the renminbi as an international currency and Shanghai as an international financial centre*, Working Paper, University of California at Davis.

Woo, W. T., Hai, W., Jin, Y. and Fan, G. (1994), 'How successful has Chinese enterprise reform been? Pitfalls in opposite biases and focus', *Journal of Comparative Economics* 18(3): 410–37.

Woo, W. T., Lu, M., Sachs, J. D. and Chen, Z. (eds) (2012), *A New Economic Growth Engine for China: Escaping the Middle-Income Trap by Not Doing More of the Same*, London: Imperial College Press & World Scientific Press.

World Bank (1993), *The East Asian Miracle: Economic Growth and Public Policy*, Washington, DC: The World Bank.

Wu, X., Pan, Y., Zhang, Z., Nie, J. and Zhou, S. (2014), 'The options for reforming the renminbi exchange rate regime', in W. T. Woo, Y. Pan, J. D. Sachs and J. Qian (eds), *Financial Systems at the Crossroads: Lessons for China*, London: Imperial College Press & World Scientific Press.

Part IV: Factor Market Reform

14. The Issue of Land in China's Urbanisation and Growth Model

Tao Ran

Introduction

Land reform is a key part of contemporary China's economic transition and development. The reform and opening-up process in China was initiated from rural land reform in the late 1970s and the early 1980s. With the introduction of the Household Responsibility System (HRS) in the early reform period, agriculture shifted from a collective-based farming system to a family-based one. This brought about robust growth in agricultural output and farmers' incomes throughout the first half of the 1980s. Rural land reform also laid a solid foundation for the rapid growth of township and village enterprises (TVEs). Without the success of rural land reform as the first push, one cannot even imagine the subsequent reforms in urban China that have generated the nearly double-digit growth rate of the past three decades. One also would not have thought China could shift from a closed planned economy to an increasingly open market economy.

Since the early 2000s, in particular after China's accession into the World Trade Organisation in 2001, China's economic growth has entered a new phase. There has been a consensus in Chinese academia and policy circles that industrialisation, urbanisation and globalisation have been the driving forces behind China's robust growth in this period. It was in this period that land-related issues became prominent as China experienced rapid urbanisation and industrialisation.

First, for industrialisation and urbanisation to occur, there needs to be conversion of agricultural land that allows the building of factories and urban housing and infrastructure. This involves the displacement of farmers from land around the cities in the process of urbanisation. Second, as industrialisation and urbanisation proceed, a set of institutions is needed to encourage farmers to move from rural to urban areas and from agriculture to manufacturing and service sectors. This requires a way to finance such migration and support the migrating farmers throughout what is inherently a risky process (Todaro 1969; Stark 1991). Land is an important element here since it is indispensible for providing decent and affordable housing for migrants so they can settle in cities on a permanent basis. Finally, since the process of industrialisation and urbanisation is a gradual and long one, the system must allow those who are left behind in the first wave of migration to be able to access resources so they can get themselves ready to move in either this or even the next generation (Johnston and Mellor 1961).

Precisely because there are inherent weaknesses in China's land system, land-related issues in China's rapid urbanisation have become increasingly acute in the past decade. Under the current land requisition system, rapid urbanisation has led to tens of millions of dispossessed farmers being left undercompensated. Under the current rural construction land management system, farmers are legally disallowed from developing their own land for non-agricultural purposes. This makes the provision of affordable housing with decent living conditions extremely difficult. The hundreds of millions of rural migrants have to live either in employer-provided dorms or in the 'urban villages' with poor planning and infrastructure. Unable to settle in cities on a permanent basis, the large numbers of migrants who are already earning most of their incomes in the cities and are unwilling to return to the countryside are still unwilling to give up their agricultural land. This, in turn, makes it difficult for those who are left behind in the countryside to expand their scale of agricultural production.

This chapter aims to analyse the main challenges in China's current land system and propose a reform package to address these challenges. The rest of the chapter proceeds as follows. In section two, we discuss the role of land as a key policy instrument employed by Chinese local governments in industrialisation and urban development. In section three, we discuss the distortions coming from China's current land management system. In section four, we introduce the current reform initiatives both at the central and at the local levels, and analyse why they are inadequate to improve land-use efficiency and to bring social justice to the countryside. In section five, we will propose an integrated reform package that includes land, *hukou* and fiscal reforms to help China complete its economic transition. Section six concludes.

Instrumental use of land in China's urbanisation and local development

Land became a key instrument in China's local economic development after the mid 1990s. This had to do with a major change in central–local relations—that is, the 1994 tax-sharing reform. The 1994 tax reform raised the Central Government's share of government revenues (World Bank 2002). Local governments, on the other hand, found their share shrinking in the late 1990s and early 2000s. A further hit to local public finance in the mid 1990s was large-scale restructuring and privatisation of local government-owned enterprises and TVEs that contributed a great deal to local revenues in the 1980s and the early 1990s. As industrial overcapacity emerged in manufacturing by the mid 1990s, it became clear that SOEs and TVEs, instead of being a tremendous asset, had become a liability for many local governments. To save them from endless drains on their finances, regional governments initiated the privatisation of small SOEs. When the new century dawned, the majority of SOEs and TVEs in the country had completed their transformation (Qian 2000).

As a result of these changes, local governments metamorphosed from asset owners to tax collectors. This redefinition of the state's role had powerful impacts on local governments' behaviour. As asset owners, local officials had strong incentives to support their own 'children' and ensure their profitability. Being tax collectors, however, they had to cater to all potential tax contributors. Alongside more efficient and profitable domestic private enterprises, foreign firms started to enter China en masse in the second half of the 1990s. Unlike SOEs and TVEs, these firms were mobile and were more responsive to local policy incentives. They would relocate to another jurisdiction if it offered more favourable tax deductions and better infrastructure. Local governments had to compete fiercely to grow their tax bases.

Fiscal centralisation and privatisation worked together to exacerbate the fiscal strain on local governments. As a result, local governments' resources could not keep up with their increasing fiscal obligations, including supporting retirees and laid-off workers from former SOEs and fulfilling various unfunded mandates from the centre (Tsui and Wang 2004). To make up for the revenue shortfalls, local governments gradually discovered the value of land. Cheap land now became a key instrument in regional competition for mobile tax bases. As the de facto owners of urban land, local governments could sell land-use rights to industrial investors for 50 years, businesses for 40 years and residential housing for 70 years. During the 2000s, land leasing fees grew rapidly and now constitute a large part of local fiscal revenues. What is more, when urban land was used up, local officials had the legal authority to convert farmland. Therefore, local revenues would grow with urbanisation. Since then, requisitioning farmland, leasing land and managing urban expansion have become the main business of China's local governments.

Local officials were particularly keen on attracting industrial land users for revenue reasons. In terms of taxes, manufacturing businesses mainly generate two kinds of revenue for local governments—that is, value-added taxes (VATs) and enterprise income taxes. Ultimately, only 25 per cent of VATs and 40 per cent of enterprise income taxes will stay locally; however, it has become common practice since the late 1990s for regional authorities to rebate all enterprise income taxes for the first three years and half in the next two years.

Moreover, in order for the enterprises to settle in their jurisdictions, localities must spend a large amount of financial resources on basic infrastructure, including land, roads, water and electricity. Nevertheless, because of fierce regional competition, local governments often had to offer manufacturing investors cheap land and sometimes they even leased land to industrial investors free of charge. The questions that naturally follow are why is manufacturing so desirable? How can local governments secure other financing to subsidise manufacturing in the short or even medium term? It turns out that local governments have developed a clever strategy to exploit this linkage and continue their development (Tao et al. 2009, 2010).

Figure 14.1 sketches a simplified analysis. All localities essentially deal with two kinds of businesses: manufacturers and service providers. As discussed above, manufacturing enterprises bring stable VATs and enterprise income taxes. What appeals to regional governments even more is their ability to spill over and foster service industries. Once factories start to operate, workers and managers living in the cities and towns have the financial means to improve their lives. Services and businesses such as shopping malls, restaurants, entertainment facilities, banks and real estate developers sprout up to cater to the growing needs of these people (Lin and Ho 2005; Tao et al. 2010).

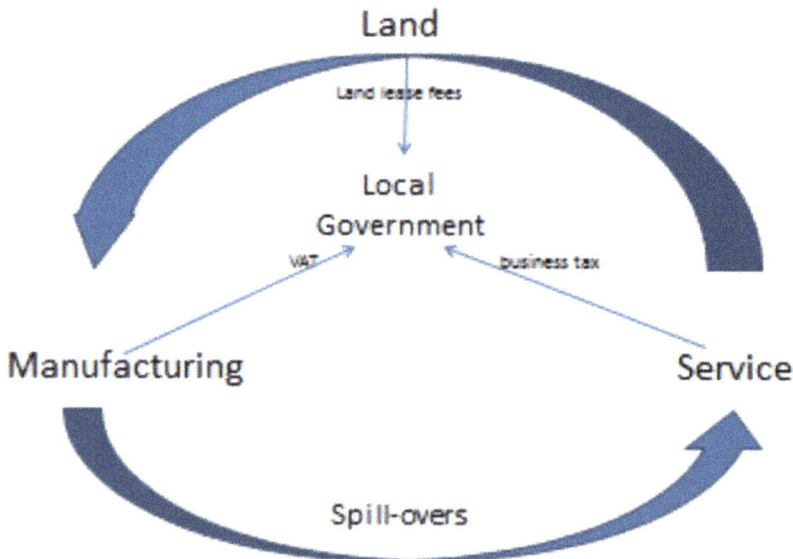

Figure 14.1 Local Government Development Strategy: Manufacturing, Services and Land

In recent years, we have conducted many interviews on local development practices and, almost without exception, local officials emphasised the importance in their decision-making of industrial spillovers from manufacturing to services. Therefore, from a revenue perspective, manufacturing not only generates VATs and enterprise income taxes directly, but also contributes to growing business tax—a tax assigned solely to local governments. Since manufacturing growth can stimulate local service sectors that generate handsome business taxes and land leasing fees, subsidising manufacturing land is worthwhile. In particular, significant profits can be generated by more competitive public auctions of commercial/residential land.

The past decade also witnessed a gradual geographical expansion of land developmentalism. Initially, in the late 1990s, large-scale industrial park and urban construction unfolded in coastal areas. Since the early and mid 2000s, inland areas have started to catch up in this industrialisation and urbanisation drive (Lin 2007). Inland localities did not join the regional manufacturing competition in the beginning due to relatively poor endowments such as infrastructure. As their infrastructure began to improve, inland regions were finally ready to compete for investment. Another equally important factor was the rural tax reform introduced between 2002 and 2006, which caused severe revenue shortfalls among inland governments. The rural tax reform deprived local governments in agriculture-based inland regions of the right to collect revenue from agriculture through formal taxes and informal charges. Unable to continue revenue collection from agriculture, local governments in inland China had to engage in fierce regional manufacturing competition in this period.

In hindsight, the emergence of land developmentalism was not an accident, but a natural outcome of China's unique land regulatory regime after fiscal recentralisation in the mid 1990s. Here China's land requisition system under which local governments have monopolistic control over land conversion from rural to urban use played a pivotal role. Local governments are de facto owners of all urban land in their jurisdictions. They can determine how land is used and collect revenue from leasing land-use rights on the market. Land in rural areas, on the other hand, is owned by rural collectives. Therefore, in each locality, there are two parallel land ownership regimes and only local governments have the power to cross this line and convert rural land to urban use. It is illegal and strictly forbidden for village collectives to directly lease land to urban users (Lin 2007; Zhu and Prosterman 2007; World Bank 2005; Lin and Ho 2005). This de facto regional monopoly of land supply allows local officials to discriminate against certain land users and leverage land for development. Local governments were found to strategically limit the amount of land for commercial and real estate businesses in their jurisdictions so prices would continue to rise

(Tao et al. 2010; Lin and Yi 2011; Wu 2010). Service businesses had no choice but to pay local governments high land-lease fees. Because limited land supply weakened competition, service providers passed the costs on to local residents.[1]

Under China's current development model, local governments rushed to build more and more industrial parks and development zones. By the end of 2003, the total number of industrial zones and parks had reached 3837. Among them, only 6 per cent (232) had received approval from the Central Government. Provincial governments approved 27 per cent of them (1019). Various city, county and township governments had taken their own initiative to get the majority of these zones (2586) up and running. By 2006, the figure jumped further, to 6015 (Zhai and Xiang 2007)—which was about two industrial parks per county on average. Developing and managing land have become a major business for local governments in many localities.

While comprehensive information about all industrial parks is rare, a government audit report offers a glimpse of the geographic distribution of the parks. In 2006, the Central Government was alarmed by the great-leap mentality among local officials and ordered the National Development and Reform Commission (NDRC), the Ministry of Land and Resources and the Ministry of Construction to launch a full investigation. Table 14.1 groups Chinese provinces into coastal and inland ones and summarises the number of development zones by the approving authority. Of 222 economic development zones, high-tech industrial parks, tariff-free zones and other types of zones approved directly by the State Council, two-thirds were located in coastal provinces. If we look at provincial government decisions, however, the regional imbalance is no longer prominent. Many inland provinces, such as Anhui, Jiangxi, Hubei and Hunan, were not far behind in setting up development zones. Even Gansu, a poor province in the remote western region, established 34 industrial zones, specialising in machinery, construction materials, food processing and chemicals. This audit did not cover development zones and industrial parks approved by municipal and county governments, but it is reasonable to assume the same pattern should hold. Overall, the rush to industrialise originated on the east coast but, by the mid 2000s, had become a national phenomenon and engulfed the whole of officialdom at the local level.

---

1 Both manufacturing and services create jobs and generate revenue, but they differ in one crucial industrial attribute: location specificity (Tao et al. 2010). Manufacturing enterprises mostly produce tradable goods for the domestic or international market. The tenuous attachment to specific locations enhances their mobility in response to production costs. If other regions provide better conditions, they may relocate their production facilities relatively easily. Service businesses, on the other hand, must establish contacts with local residents to deliver their products. This location rigidity gives local governments the upper hand in bargaining and creates a potential for backward linkage.

Table 14.1 Development Zones and Industrial Parks by Level of Approval and by Province

Approval authority	Coastal region	Number	Inland region	Number
State Council		147		75
Provincial governments		683		663
	Beijing	16	Shanxi	22
	Tianjin	25	Inner Mongolia	39
	Hebei	45	Jilin	35
	Shandong	155	Heilongjiang	29
	Liaoning	42	Anhui	85
	Jiangsu	109	Jiangxi	88
	Shanghai	26	Henan	23
	Zhejiang	103	Hubei	89
	Fujian	65	Hunan	73
	Guangdong	69	Chongqing	34
	Guangxi	23	Sichuan	38
	Hainan	5	Guizhou	13
			Yunnan	15
			Shaanxi	17
			Gansu	34
			Qinghai	3
			Ningxia	15
			Xinjiang	11

Source: NDRC et al. (2006).

After the audit, the Central Government decided to curb the overexcitement among local officials and consolidated development zones or ordered shutdowns in many places. Unable to set up more industrial parks without upper-level approval, most newly established industrial parks simply changed their names and became 'urban industrial functional zones' or 'urban industrial complexes' without any change in real functions. According to the author's observations, the number of industrial parks in operation after the mid 2000s actually increased with extension to areas further inland. This diffusion was further accelerated after the GFC, when the Chinese Government introduced its fiscal and financial stimulus package. As analysed earlier, to make the rapid industrialisation financially viable, rising real estate bubbles soon followed across the country, which gave many local governments in inland areas a fiscal illusion that they could borrow money for more industrial park building and pay it back using the fees through leasing residential and commercial land at higher prices. Manufacturing capacity built up quickly. To find markets for their products, enterprises had to be more aggressive on the international market, leading to ever-rising foreign exchange reserves.

Since the late 1990s, the fiscally strapped local governments in China have increasingly turned to land (Yang 2004). On the one hand, they lease land to manufacturing investors mostly by negotiation and at subsidised prices. Local governments usually incur a net loss in leasing land for manufacturing users. By providing land at negotiated and usually very low leasing prices, local governments strive to attract industrial investors through a 'site-clearing' style of packaged development. Usually at only nominal prices or even the so-called 'zero price', the prepared land was leased out for 50 years. Since local governments need to finance the land requisition costs (compensation to dispossessed farmers) and infrastructure preparation costs (costs of building roads and providing access to electricity, water, heating, and so on) ex ante, leasing out industrial land at low or even zero prices inevitably means local governments are incurring net losses in the process.

On the other hand, local governments lease most of the commercial and residential land by auction and public tender so as to earn as high extra-budget revenue as possible utilising their monopolistic position in urban land-leasing markets. In practice, almost every city has set up one or several industrial parks that supply cheap land to industrial users while most cities have also set up 'land reserve centres' that prepare land for residential and commercial use, and then auction it off to commercial and residential developers for profit. In many regions, the revenue from land leasing, especially the fees from commercial and residential land leasing, has become the single most important source of local extra-budget revenue. Studies consistently show that land transfer fees account for some 30–50 per cent of total sub-provincial government revenues, and in some developed regions, it amounts to 50–60 per cent of the total city revenue (World Bank 2005).

As Figure 14.2 shows, land-lease fees, as a part of local extra-budgetary income, were about 50 per cent of the formal budget at the provincial level. In some areas, the ratio was as high as 170 per cent. These revenues enabled regional governments to subsidise incentive packages, including cheap land and tax exemptions, to lure footloose manufacturing capital. In 2007 alone, local governments in China made 226 500 ha of land available for commercial and industrial use. Of this land, 115 300 ha (50.9 per cent of the total land leased— up 20.4 percentage points from 2006) were auctioned off. For the whole year, land sales generated close to RMB1 trillion (RMB913 billion for the January– November period), up from RMB767.7 billion in 2006 and only RMB49.2 billion in 2001. Simply put, local authorities have become hooked on land revenue as virtually a 'second budget' (Tao et al. 2010).

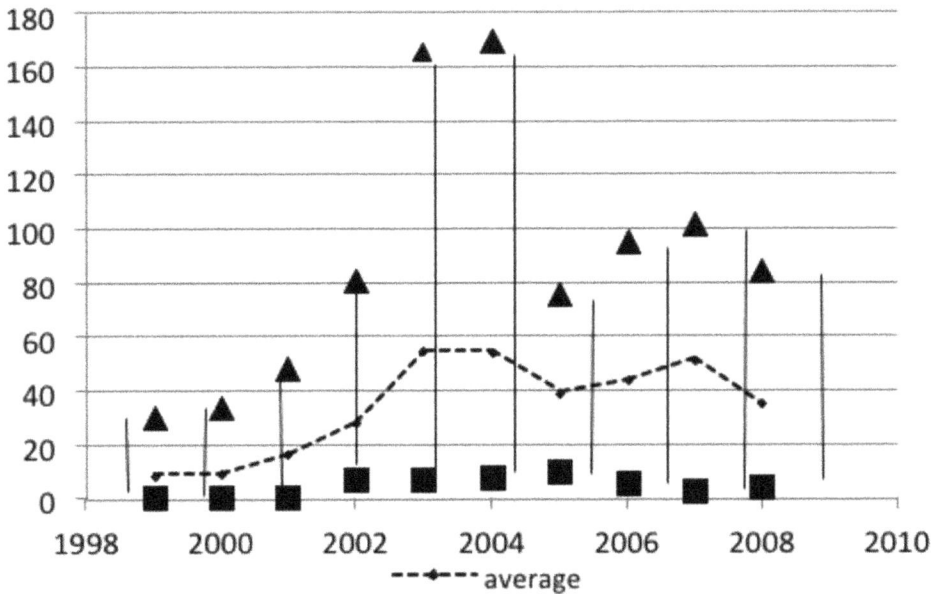

Figure 14.2 Land Lease Fees as a Ratio of Local Budgetary Revenues, 1999–2008

Sources: *China Statistical Yearbook* and *China Land and Resources Statistical Yearbook* (NBS various years).

Economic and social distortions resulting from China's land management system

Analysis of China's current economic growth model is useful in understanding the country's urbanisation model during the same period. It is also helpful to understand the economic and social distortions brought about by this urbanisation model. An instrumental use of cheap land in regional competition for manufacturing for investment has contributed to the investment-driven growth in the past decade. When land as a key production input is underpriced, the overall investment, especially the investment in the manufacturing sector, will be higher than the social optimum. This would lead to an over-industrialised economy as well as relatively low returns on industrial investment.

Imbalance between urbanisation of population and land

Land-use distortions have also led to an imbalance between China's urban spatial expansion and migration. As shown in Table 14.2, from 2001 to 2008, China's urban population grew at a rapid annual rate of 3.55 per cent, while the average annual growth rate of urban built areas was 6.2 per cent and the annual growth rate of urban construction land area was as high as 7.4 per cent. This means the urbanisation of the population has been much slower than the urbanisation of space.

Table 14.2 Comparison of Annual Growth Rates in Urban Populations and Urban Areas under Construction (per cent)

Year	Urban population	Urban built area	Area of urban construction land
2001–2005	4.13	7.70	7.50
2006–2008	2.57	3.73	7.23
2001–2008	3.55	6.20	7.40

Sources: Based on calculations from NBS (2008, 2009).

Notes: Data for urban construction land for Beijing and Shanghai in 2005 are missing. An average value based on data for 2004 and 2006 has been used.

Distortions in land-use structure

The imbalance in China's urban land-use structure is also serious. Currently, there are 240 000 sq km of construction land in rural and urban China, five-sixths of which is in the countryside owned by rural collectives and used by rural residents. Between 1990 and 2004, the area of urban land in China increased from 13 000 sq km to 39 140 sq km, or 155 sq m per capita (Tan and Li 2010).[2] In cities alone, the area of urban industrial land in 2004 had already reached 7900 sq km and by 2008 it was 9853 sq km, comprising a full 25 per cent of the total urban construction land, while ecological land made up only 10 per cent and residential land hovered around 31 per cent. The percentages of industrial land area in the more developed cities of Shanghai and Suzhou were as high as 25.77 per cent and 31.79 per cent respectively; however, the global standard for urban industrial land area is usually not more than 10–15 per cent (Huang 2007).

---

2 In 2004, China had a total village construction land area of 248 million mu. Based on the number of people engaged in agricultural work that year, the per capita area of village land was 217 sq m—45.3 per cent greater than the national limit of 150 sq m per person.

Table 14.3 Land-Use Ratios in Chinese Cities (2004–09)

Sq km/year	2004	2005	2006	2007	2008	2009
Urban construction land	30 781	29 638	31 766	33 923	36 711	38 727
Residential	9729	9297	9772	10 497	11 290	12 056
Public facilities	3772	3704	4229	4399	4678	4848
Industrial and warehousing	7900	7533	7998	8580	9265	9853
Transportation	1717	1448	1407	1498	1617	1673
Roads and squares	2989	2983	3378	3668	4031	4369
Municipal public services	1053	1069	1120	1164	1251	1300
Green space	2856	2911	3155	3404	3786	3868
Special use	766	694	708	713	794	760
Per cent/year	2004	2005	2006	2007	2008	2009
Urban construction land	100	100	100	100	100	100
Residential	31.6	31.4	30.8	30.9	30.8	31.1
Public facilities	12.3	12.5	13.3	13.0	12.7	12.5
Industrial	25.7	25.4	25.2	25.3	25.2	25.4
Transportation	5.6	4.9	4.4	4.4	4.4	4.3
Roads and squares	9.7	10.1	10.6	10.8	11.0	11.3
Municipal public services	3.4	3.6	3.5	3.4	3.4	3.4
Green space	9.3	9.8	9.9	10.0	10.3	10.0
Special use	2.5	2.3	2.2	2.1	2.2	2.0

Sources: China Statistical Yearbook for Urban and Rural Construction (NBS various years).

Note: The years 2009, 2008, 2007 and 2006 do not include data for Shanghai; 2005 does not include Shanghai or Beijing.

As shown in Table 14.3, the structure of land use in China's urban areas is highly distorted, with a high share of land going to industrial use, while a relatively low share of land is allocated for use by residential, transportation, green space and service sectors. This is because of the land-lease pricing strategies as discussed above. In 2006, the average price of land in major Chinese cities nationwide was RMB1544 per sq m, with commercial land valued at RMB2480/sq m, residential land at RMB1681/sq m and industrial land at RMB485/sq m. By 2010, the average price of land nationwide was RMB2882/ sq m, a RMB229 increase over the previous year. A breakdown of this number shows that the price of commercial land was the highest at RMB5185/sq m, followed by residential land at RMB4245/sq m, while the price for industrial land was RMB629/sq m (CASS, respective years).

Industrial land makes up 40–50 per cent of the total new leases every year. Table 14.4 shows that in 2003, 2005 and 2007, China provided 99 400, 90 500 and 135 600 ha of land for mining, industrial and storage use for each of the respective years, or 51.4 per cent, 54.7 per cent and 57.7 per cent of new urban land leases. Between 2003 and 2009, the area of industrial land leased out was 788 000 ha—51.3 per cent of the total land leased. The area of residential land and commercial land leased out was only 39 100 ha (25.4 per cent) and 198 000 ha (12.9 per cent) respectively. As a result, the price of industrial land rose very slowly over these three years, reaching RMB1.25 million, RMB1.38 million and RMB1.56 million per hectare for each respective year, while the price of commercial land rose from RMB3.55 million to RMB6.34 million and to RMB8.71 million per hectare, and the price of residential land was RMB5.98 million, RMB6.8 million and RMB11.31 million per hectare.[3]

Wasteful use of industrial land and the real estate bubble

The negative impacts of local government land-leasing strategies are obvious. Many cities have constructed 'garden-style factories' that use industrial land very inefficiently. Some industrial companies lease land at an extremely low price and use only part of it, leaving other areas undeveloped, or even carry out large-scale 'greenification' projects on the land.

In 2006, the Ministry of Land and Resources conducted a survey of 124 new industrial projects across 23 key cities around the country. The average land-leasing prices for eastern, central and western China were RMB183, RMB264 and RMB265 per sq m respectively, while the corresponding land requisition costs were RMB463, RMB325 and RMB268 per sq m respectively. That means a subsidy of RMB280, RMB61 and RMB3 per sq m respectively for eastern, central and western China.[4]

---

3 Overly high percentages of industrial land use and overly fast growth also exist in medium and small cities. For instance, the average annual increase in industrial land area for the city of Kunshan from 1990 to 2001 was 210.92 ha, which made up half of all the land area under construction and increased annually at a rate of 21.25 per cent. The average increase in industrial land per person was between 40 and 70 sq m for the cities of Kunshan, Wujiang, Zhangjiawan, Taicang, Yixing and Liyang. On the whole, China's per capita industrial land area has far exceeded the national standard of 15–25 sq m (Huang 2007).

4 Cited from Ministry of Land and Resources (2006).

Table 14.4 Total Land Area Transferred, Use Ratios and Prices (2003, 2005, 2007)

2003	No. of land transactions	Total land area (ha)	Percentage of area	Total transaction value (RMB billion)	Unit price (RMB million)
Total	207 387	193 603	100.0	542.13	2.80
Commercial	59 702	39 082	20.2	138.62	3.55
Industrial	58 827	99 435	51.4	124.73	1.25
Infrastructure	3628	5815	3.0	9.39	1.62
Public buildings	1864	2929	1.5	5.82	1.99
Residential	81 487	43 323	22.4	258.99	5.98
Transportation	581	600	0.3	1.07	1.79
Water services	128	800	0.4	0.28	0.35
Special use	1170	1618	0.8	3.22	1.99
2005	**No. of land transactions**	**Total land area (ha)**	**Percentage of area**	**Total transaction value (RMB billion)**	**Unit price (RMB million)**
Total	162 112	165 586	100.0	588.38	3.55
Commercial	34 386	23 268	14.1	147.41	6.34
Industrial	43 027	90 512	54.7	125.00	1.38
Infrastructure	2134	1994	1.2	10.67	5.35
Public buildings	1627	2436	1.5	5.86	2.41
Residential	80 285	43 675	26.4	296.93	6.80
Transportation	161	1246	0.8	1.51	1.21
Water services	311	268	0.2	0.22	0.82
Special use	181	2188	1.3	0.79	0.36
2007	**No. of land transactions**	**Total land area (ha)**	**Percentage of area**	**Total transaction value (RMB billion)**	**Unit price (RMB million)**
Total	160 404	234 961	100.0	1221.67	5.20
Commercial	25 737	26 975	11.5	234.95	8.71
Industrial	43 477	135 629	57.7	211.02	1.56
Infrastructure	1702	1454	0.6	4.83	3.32
Public buildings	1507	2121	0.9	12.01	5.66
Residential	87 393	66 575	28.3	753.09	11.31
Transportation	411	1414	0.6	4.89	3.46
Water services	127	606	0.3	65	1.07
Special use	50	188	0.1	24	1.29

Sources: *China National Resources Statistical Yearbook* (NBS various years).

As more and more regions engage in a race to the bottom style of competition for manufacturing investment, the area of industrial land grows rapidly. In 1996, the total area of independent industrial and mining land in China was 27 700 sq km. According to the 1997–2010 National Land Use Plan, between 1997 and 2010, the area of independent industrial and mining land could not exceed 33 000 sq km by 2010; however, by the end of 2005, the area had already reached 33 600 sq km. By the end of 2009, the area increased further, to 43 000 sq km—about 40 per cent of China's urban and industrial/mining land (Xinhua News Agency 2010). In other words, the area of independent industrial and mining land increased by about 15 000 sq km (9 million ha) and the average floor-area ratio was only 0.3–0.4—half of the National Government standards.

Contrary to these standards, in order to maximise profits from commercial and residential land, local governments usually undersupply such land and charge a very high land-leasing fee. For example, between 2003 and 2010, more than 15 million mu (100 000 ha) of industrial land (43 per cent of total land supply) was leased out with an average land price of RMB97 000/mu, while the area of residential land supplied was only 8.31 million mu (23.6 per cent of the total land supply), with an average land price of RMB560 000/mu (China's National Land Yearbook: NBS various years). The growing real estate bubble in China can also be largely attributed to the instrumental use of land by local governments—that is, oversupply of industrial land and undersupply of residential land. The depressed prices of production factors (including land and workers who lack labour protection or sufficient social insurance) and the relaxed enforcement of environmental protections in China's 'regional race-to-the-bottom' style of competition have resulted in excessive investment in manufacturing sectors and an excessive production capacity that cannot be absorbed by the domestic market. At the same time, the currently low level of compensation for expropriated land and insufficient levels of social insurance have made it difficult for the consumption levels of two major groups—that is, dispossessed farmers and migrant workers—to keep in step with the growth of the overall economy. This further exacerbates the problem of poor domestic demand in the course of China's economic growth.

The need to absorb this accumulated excessive production capacity, encouraged the Government to keep the value of the renminbi artificially low, ensuring excessive production capacity could thus be exported to the international market. Keeping the renminbi artificially low naturally resulted in a trade surplus. The renminbi's inability to appreciate as China's labour productivity grows naturally attracts speculators who believe the renminbi will eventually be forced to appreciate, resulting in a huge influx of hot money into China and therefore the country's ever-rising foreign reserve. In 1995, China had US$73.6 billion in foreign exchange reserves. By 2000, this had grown to

US$165.6 billion. By 2004, it quickly rose to US$609.9 billion. In 2006, China's foreign reserve was as high as US$1 trillion, and in April 2009 it exceeded US$2 trillion. This number exceeded US$3 trillion in March 2011. China's central bank was forced to release RMB24 trillion to sterilise the foreign reserve, leading to serious excessive liquidity in the economy.

Excessive liquidity naturally flooded into the undersupplied commercial and residential land market and the bubble in the real estate sector emerged. Prior to 2004, the growth of China's housing prices remained slow—below 5 per cent—but housing prices began to shoot up after early 2004, with an annual growth rate of nearly 10 per cent. In order to stabilise the market, the Central Government implemented regulatory policies that mostly focused on managing and standardising land supply. This happened because at the time it was believed that corruption in the land market fostered speculation and resulted in high prices; however, these land market control policies did not address the real problem and housing prices continued to grow at double digit rates. In May 2005, another round of housing price-control policies went into effect. In addition to providing public housing to middle and low-income households, there are articles to punish land speculators, and business tax was also used as a tool to control housing prices. While this did effect a slowing in housing price growth, the rate remained above 5 per cent. Realising that these policies would not control housing prices successfully, the Central Government started to take harsher measures, including forcibly regulating the lowest proportion of residential land and even the area of commercial housing. Tax revenue and interest rate controls were also put into place.[5] Starting from late 2006, as liquidity in the market continued to increase and the 'bidding, auctioning and public tender' policies for land leasing were widely implemented, land and housing prices soared further and new records for land-leasing prices were set every few days. None of the four consecutive interest rate increases by the central bank in 2007 was able to stem the rapid rise in housing prices. It was only in 2008, with the arrival of the GFC, that housing prices in China started to decrease. In the first quarter of 2009, housing prices dropped by 1.1 per cent.

---

5   Since 2003, the Chinese Government has put forward a myriad of control measures, including the '121 Document', the 'New and Old Eight Opinions', the 'Six Opinions' and the 'Fifteen Opinions' issued by the State Council, including the implementation of the 'three-step' approval process for controlling land as well as the push to build economised housing and low-rent housing, implementing financial and taxation rules such as eliminating low interest rate home loans, increasing down payments on new homes and levying transactional taxes on second-hand properties. Despite the implementation of these measures, housing prices continued to rise quickly and new highs continued to be set.

Investment platform boom and local debt accumulation after 2008

The central leadership is well aware of the potential problems associated with this development model and has attempted to steer the Chinese economy towards growth largely driven by domestic consumption. The reality is, however, more complicated. The old model has created its own vested interests and these actors—central and local, public and private—forged a strong growth coalition to perpetuate the existing path. The post-GFC episode illustrates this dynamic. In the aftermath of the GFC, Chinese exports dropped by more than 20 per cent in the second half of 2008 and early 2009. The Chinese Government's response was prompt and massive. It pledged RMB4 trillion in fiscal spending in two years as well as increasing bank credits by RMB9.6 trillion in 2009 and RMB7.95 trillion in 2010. The irony is that, instead of boosting consumption, the stimulus money reinforced the existing imbalance in the Chinese economy and further distorted land-use patterns in urbanisation. Flooded with cash, local governments initiated more ambitious industrial park construction and became more aggressive in attracting manufacturing businesses. Land leases for industrial purposes reached 0.14, 0.15 and 0.19 million ha in 2009, 2010 and 2011, respectively, which exceeded the pre-crisis level of 0.136 in 2007. Giant state-owned corporations, the other major beneficiaries of the stimulus, splurged on business expansion, including huge purchases of mines both domestically and in the global market. Both contributed to further build-ups in manufacturing in China. On the other hand, local governments' urbanisation schemes were kept buoyant by easy credit as well as speculative funds. Land-lease prices reached new highs as real estate developers chased the limited quantity of available land. The centrally controlled SOEs also invested heavily in the real estate sector and in many cases they overbid substantially, fuelling a real estate bubble. In many third or fourth-tier cities, housing prices more than doubled within one to two years. Local governments cashed in on land development, and lease fees doubled from RMB1.59 trillion in 2009 to RMB3.15 trillion in 2011. These revenues, combined with land-backed bank loans and bond sales, enabled local governments to launch massive urban infrastructure projects, such as railways, subways, roads and airports.

The GFC not only failed to shift China's primary driver of growth from investment to consumption, but also heightened the risk of a potential crash of the Chinese financial system due to overinvestment that built more overcapacity in manufacturing and industrial-related infrastructure. Worldwide recession and its associated protectionism have already put a damper on China's export growth, and rapid expansion in the future is unlikely. Massive investments in manufacturing and infrastructure really hinge on continual revenue flows from the housing and real estate sectors. Instead of becoming an alternative engine for Chinese growth, super-high property prices actually suck up the savings of the middle class and weaken their demand for other goods. Moreover, local governments' addiction to land revenue and intention of propping up the markets have invited rampant speculation and contributed to the build-up of a huge asset bubble. Like Japan and the United States in the past, in China, this game of musical chairs will have to end at some point. When the bubble bursts, local governments will lose the main source of income they have used to binge on industrial parks and infrastructure construction. The immediate shock to China's financial system will be devastating. Once land and housing values plummet, state banks will bear the brunt of easy credit and trillions of loans may turn into non-performing assets on their balance sheets.

Social impacts of China's land-based urbanisation

Economic imbalance aside, this developmentalism has also had a devastating impact on society. Over-leveraging land for development has caused social and political problems.

First, the rapid rise in housing prices and the formation of a real estate bubble over the past decade have made it impossible for the majority of rural migrant populations to afford commodity housing in cities. In fact, even the new entrants into the labour force with university degrees find that today's housing prices are far more than what they can afford. Clearly, this has become a major challenge for China to realise full urbanisation and urban–rural integration. In urban areas, residents are overburdened with skyrocketing housing prices. The red-hot housing market not only drained people's financial resources for consumption, but also carried the huge risk of a bubble (Su and Tao 2011).

Second, the great Chinese land grab has especially soured urban–rural relations. The need to generate revenue and subsidise manufacturing enterprises led to the twin problems of excessive requisition of farmland and under-compensation for landowners, resulting in millions of disgruntled farmers (Zhu and Prosterman 2007; Tao et al. 2010). Insufficient compensation for land requisition is now the primary reason for rural petitions and collective action by farmers against the state. A research report (China Land Problem Task Force 2007) estimates there were more than 40 million dispossessed farmers due to urban expansion and transportation projects. For a host of reasons but primarily because local governments tend to underpay, especially in light of soaring urban land prices, farmers losing their land are often dissatisfied with the amount of compensation. Moreover, under-compensated farmers who have lost their land easily become unemployed but generally have limited access to urban welfare benefits. A 17-province, 1962-farmer survey conducted in China in 2005 shows the number of land-related incidents increased more than 15 times during the past 10 years and appeared to be accelerating. In the first nine months of 2006, China reported a total of 17 900 cases of 'massive rural incidents', in which a total of 385 000 farmers protested against the Government. Approximately 70 per cent of these incidents were related to illegal land-taking. In some areas, land disputes have resulted in mass incidents and have greatly undermined social harmony.[6] And this is only the tip of the iceberg, as many Chinese peasants do not even protest when their land is taken away. The problem is so widespread that one commentator notes that an 'economic war is going on at the local level in China today especially on the fringes of expanding urban areas' (Subrahmanyan 2004).

Dualism in land management and rural collective land-use inefficiency

Under the current system, markets for urban and rural land have been artificially divided. A market-oriented reform for rural collective land is badly needed to improve both efficiency and equity in China's land use. The rising illegal use of land throughout the country and the spontaneous emergence of a rural construction land market in many localities indicate that the current land management system is no longer functioning under an increasingly market-oriented economy (Han 2003).

Special attention needs to be paid to China's rural residential land, which accounts for a majority of China's rural construction land. Under China's land management system, every rural household is eligible to apply for one, and only one, piece of residential land on which a house can be built for accommodation purposes.

Given the huge number of rural households (around 200 million) in China, residential land constitutes one of the most important land-use types in rural areas—next only to farmland. According to the first national land cadastral survey conducted in 1996, rural settlement occupied 164 558 ha of land, which was 6.21 times as high as urban settlements and which accounted for 68.4 per cent of all settlement and industrial/mining land (240 753 ha) (Lin and Ho 2005). More recent census data also showed that the total area of rural residential land reached 166 000 ha by the end of 2004—4.88 times the land taken up by urban construction uses (34 000 ha). This implies that per capita rural residential landholdings are 214 sq m—64 sq m higher than the standard defined by the National Village and Township Planning Standards.

---

6 According to statistical data from 2005, there were nearly 80 000 mass incidents nationwide, of which 30 per cent were to defend the rights of farmers, while 70 per cent of these cases were because of unfair compensation for land that had been reallocated. Of the more than 74 000 mass incidents examined on the CCTV program *Topics in Focus* in 2005, 15 312 were related to land disputes. Most of these were conflicts that arose because of the low price paid by local governments in reallocating the land. Later, land-related disputes rose to 60 per cent (Yu Jianrong 2006).

Unlike urban housing properties, however, rural residential properties, including the land and the housing unit, are still strictly regulated and cannot be traded freely on the market. It is alleged that the policy of allocating one piece of residential land for every rural household, but disallowing trading beyond the village, helps secure farmers' housing rights in an egalitarian way while at the same time protecting the country's limited arable land resources. Given the sheer size of rural residential land in China and the rural house-building craze in the reform era, both the Government and academia have continually expressed worries that rural residential land and its expansion 'may have contributed greatly to the loss of farmland in China' (Ho and Lin 2003). Since village housing accounted for about 5–6 per cent of the total area forfeited and the area lost to new housing was greatest in the central eastern provinces—traditionally a highly productive agricultural region (Sargeson 2002; Ash and Edmonds 1998)—these worries seem reasonable. As a result of policy tightening, rural residential land transactions beyond village boundaries have been completely prohibited since 1998. If any such transaction occurs, it would be illegal and thus no land and housing certificates would be issued.

The strict regulations on residential land use and transactions have met serious challenges in policy implementation. The main challenges come from the country's large-scale migration and rapid urban expansion, which generated land-use problems both in China's vast agriculture-based countryside and on the fringes of cities where urban expansion is fastest and where demand for residential land is intensive. In the agricultural areas far away from the city, such a challenge is mainly manifested in the fact that residential land continues to encroach on arable land while at the same time residential land-use efficiency remains low, since a large number of farmers leave their housing idle—that is, the phenomenon of 'hollow villages'. In suburban areas and even within cities, many 'suburban villages' and 'urban villages' have emerged and provide affordable housing for a great number of migrants.

Idle house sites and hollow villages in pure farming areas

Between 1996 and 2006, rural residential land accounted for 80 per cent of the 1 million mu (1/15 hectare) of newly occupied arable land due to rural construction. In the context of urbanisation, although an increasing number of farmers are earning higher incomes through off-farm employment, they are still unable to settle in cities on a permanent basis under China's household registration system (*hukou*). Since the rural population cannot be effectively reduced through permanent migration, and at the same time rural residential land cannot be traded freely beyond villages, local governments and rural community organisations have to allocate more land for residential housing construction when new families are formed in villages. This usually means occupation of existing farmland. At the same time, a significant share of existing rural residential properties are either underutilised or left totally idle as a large number of migrants go to cities. In many of the agricultural regions one can find hollow villages. Based on a survey of 119 villages, 59 townships and 30 counties across six provinces including Jilin, Hebei, Shaanxi, Sichuan, Jiangsu and Fujian in 2008, Wang et al. (2010) present the following interesting findings: first, for the surveyed 2230 rural families, 34 families (1.52 per cent) have no residential property, while 1965 families (88.1 per cent) own one residential property. Although government policy states that one and only one rural residential property can be allocated to each rural family, the survey shows that 231 families (10.36 per cent) possess two or more residential properties. Second, the average area of land occupied by residential property in rural China is 288 sq m per residential property.[7] Third, the higher the share of out-migration in a village, the more likely the village is to have a higher ratio of vacant residential properties. This relationship tends to be consistent with the general observations that people who leave their villages for urban jobs may leave their housing properties in the villages underused or even idle. Fourth, the average ratio of vacant residential properties was as high as 7.5 per cent for the six provinces. Among all of the 119 villages, there were 14 villages that had vacancy rates higher than 20 per cent, and seven villages with vacancy rates higher than 30 per cent. Finally, while there are significant shares of vacant housing in rural villages, new residential house-building continues to occupy arable land. Since 1978, on average, the share of residential housing built by occupying arable land has been more than 20 per cent of all the new residential building and this share was still as high as 23.4 per cent during the 1999–2008 period. In other words, on average, more than one-fifth of residential housing construction in rural China occupied arable land.

'Urban villages' and 'small-property-rights housing'

In contrast to hollow villages and inefficient residential land use in China's agricultural areas, many 'urban villages' and much 'small-property-rights housing' have emerged in China's suburban areas and even within cities. These are the locations where the value of rural collective land appreciates fastest due to booming demand for housing. Under current laws, only the state has the right to expropriate collectively owned rural land and then lease it to urban users.

---

7 Jilin Province had the largest area of residential land (511 sq m per residential property) on average, followed by Hebei Province (347 sq m per residential property). Jilin Province also experienced a steady increase in the average land area for rural residential property, with a more than 45 per cent increase from 1978 to 2008. As for the whole nation, the survey data revealed that the average size of the land taken for residential use had dropped slightly from the 1980s to the 1990s, but increased about 9 per cent afterwards despite the implementation of the so-called 'strictest' regulation for farmland protection in China.

Since expropriation of rural collective land by the state is often carried out with very low compensation, it is no surprise that farmers and village collectives on the urban fringe have strong incentives to engage in rent competition with the urban authorities, who monopolise urban land supplies (Zhu and Hu 2009). Informal land developments thrive on China's urban fringes, including the rapid development of a housing rental market targeting migrant farmers in urban villages and the fast growth of 'small-property-rights' housing.

Housing rental markets on urban fringes boomed largely due to the influx of a floating population of migrant workers. Limited by the *hukou* system, the floating populations have no access to public housing, nor are they eligible for the urban affordable housing programs that target urban permanent residents. Though in theory purchasing urban commercial housing is an option, rural migrants usually cannot afford the high prices. Moreover, without urban *hukou*, many in the floating population regard their presence in the cities as temporary; therefore they tend to minimise their living expenditure in cities, thus renting and sharing housing in the urban villages and suburban areas become their major housing choices. As a result, many suburban villages in China have become so-called 'migrant enclaves', or urban villages in which migrant workers from the countryside concentrate. It is estimated that at present around half of the 140–150 million migrant workers are living in around 50 000 urban and suburban villages in cities.

Under China's current land and *hukou* system, rapid migration inevitably leads to a large population of migrants living in 'urban villages'. The landlords of the urban villages (farmers who own the residential properties) can earn considerable income by renting out their houses. In this sense, the urban villages have played a significant role in China's urbanisation process. They not only provide affordable housing when urban governments fail to provide housing security for migrants, but also generate income for the landlords in urban villages whose arable land has already been requisitioned by local governments for urban expansion. This largely offsets the negative impacts of land requisition, which usually pays inadequate compensation. Therefore, one needs to recognise the important value of urban villages for two of the most vulnerable groups in China's urbanisation: the floating population and the dispossessed farmers. Certainly, the emergence of urban villages may have some negative consequences. Since local governments cannot obtain revenue from such land and housing development projects, they have no incentive to improve the infrastructure and public services in urban villages, thus environmental conditions in these localities are usually very poor and sometimes crime rates are also very high compared with other urban spaces under government control.

Precisely because urban villages provide dispossessed farmers with considerable income, urban redevelopment and renovation projects that target these urban villages are usually very difficult to implement. When the compensation to landlords in urban villages fails to reflect the opportunity costs of their rental income, strong opposition to local government moves to demolish and redevelop urban villages occurs. Unfortunately, as housing prices have skyrocketed in Chinese cities in recent years, many city governments and real estate developers now find demolishing urban villages an increasingly profitable business. Urban village demolition is being carried out in many cities across the country. Social unrest due to unfair compensation easily follows. The questions to ask, then, are: if urban villages are demolished, how can the dispossessed farmers (the landlords of urban villages who already lost their arable land) make a living since they can no longer receive the rental income to maintain their livelihood? Moreover, where can the large number of migrants find shelter if they are forced out of urban villages?

Besides urban villages, 'small-property-rights' housing is also booming in China's city fringes. Small-property-rights housing is the commodity housing developed either by village collectives or by farmers themselves for which ownership certificates are not issued by urban governments. These housing units may not be legally transacted on the market. Small-property-rights housing can refer either to the large-scale apartment buildings developed on rural land for sale or to the small-scale rural residential housing properties owned by individual rural households and then sold to people from outside villages. As a result of local governments' monopolisation of land supply in urban areas, land and housing prices have skyrocketed in the past decade. It is natural for the rural collectives and farmers to start commercial real estate development for profit on collectively owned land. Though there is no legal protection and the Government has issued many prohibitive policy documents, the growth of small-property-rights housing is just amazing. An estimate of the total construction area of small-property-rights housing suggests that by the end of 2007, it had reached 6.4 billion sq m, accounting for 17 per cent of the country's total urban housing stock (Wang and Tao, 2009)).

Land requisition and limited reform so far

Land requisition in China

Nowhere is the question of using public power to acquire land for private investment more prominent than in China, where, due to Chinese land laws, typically the only way land can become available for private investment is through a process of land requisition. Both the Chinese Constitution and the

1999 Land Administration Law (LAL) specify that the state, in the public interest, may lawfully requisition land owned by collectives, thus setting the stage for compulsory land acquisition.[8]

There is, however, no clear definition of 'public interest' in the law and in practice local governments acquire land from farmers and then either use it for infrastructure development and public projects such as public schools and hospitals or lease it to industrial and commercial/residential developers. According to the Land Administrative Law amended by 1998, 'all land used for urban development, as well as the land used for energy, transportation, water conservancy, mining and military projects outside the urban land use planning boundaries, if it needs to be taken from rural collectives, has to be acquired through the formal government land requisition process'. Moreover, decisions with regard to whether to acquire the land, how much land to acquire and the compensation and resettlement packages for land-taking are all to be made by the city and county governments unilaterally. Local governments only need to provide a Land Acquisition Notice and a Land Compensation Notice within 10 working days of the approval of a land-taking plan by upper-level governments—that is, either the provincial government or the Central Government, depending on the scale of land-taking (Ministry of Land and Resources 2001:Art. 3). The notice is a procedure to be fulfilled after the land-taking approval and after the compensation decisions have been made. Farmers whose land is to be acquired would only be informed about the decision and they would then be asked to register their names with the relevant government agency to deal with compensation and resettlement issues.

Land development in urbanisation is a complicated process because it requires first acquiring the land, then converting it to state ownership, resettling the displaced farmers and providing urban infrastructure before finally leasing the land to developers. It also involves the interactions of multiple players in land acquisition including individuals, corporations and governments. In China, the acquisition of new land for urban expansion is largely controlled by government officials through a process in which officials requisition land from nearby villages and pay compensation determined by the value of agricultural production, the value of land improvements and other factors as specified by law (Ho 2005; Ding 2007; Lichtenberg and Ding 2008). Under the current system, land acquisition is to be carried out without much, if any, participation of and negotiation with farmers. No land-taking contract needs to be signed with the rural collectives and

---

8   In 2004, Article 13 of the Chinese Constitution was amended to give constitutional protection to private property rights. It provides that '[t]he state may, for the public interest, expropriate or take over private property of citizens for public use, and pay compensation in accordance with the law'. This protection is echoed in Article 2 of the Land Administration Law, which was amended after the aforementioned constitutional amendment. The Chinese Constitution merely mentions compensation without any requirement that it be just.

its members whose land will be taken. The rural collectives and farmers affected by the land acquisition can only dispute the level and contents of compensation and resettlement packages, but not the land acquisition itself. According to the 1998 LAL and its 'Detailed Rules for Implementation' enacted in 1999, disputes about compensation and resettlement should not affect the land requisition process and the final decision about land compensation is to be made by county and city-level governments.[9] Chinese law provides only that the farmers affected are to be informed about land requisitioning and the compensation to be paid (LML 48). Thus, farmers are not involved in bargaining about the compensation amount and have no formal legal instrument for stopping land acquisition when they do not agree with the amount of compensation offered.[10]

Since the county and city-level governments are the same actors that implement land acquisition, it is difficult for them to make a fair arbitration when there are disputes about the compensation. Local courts also tend to ignore the lawsuits against local governments with regard to land requisition and the excuse is usually that the individual farmers are not the owners of the land.[11] Dispossessed farmers usually have to resort to petitions to the upper-level government or even engage in confrontational collective actions against local governments. In most cases, such protests are directed not against land grabbing but against the compensation farmers are to receive.

---

9 Under the 1986 Land Administrative Law, the state can acquire land for 'public interests' though there are no clear definitions of public interests. Article 13 of the 1986 LAL, however, stipulates that disputes about land use must be negotiated by the relevant parties and the final decision is to be made by the local governments at and above the county level; if any party involved is not satisfied with the Government's decision, it can file a lawsuit with the local court within 30 days of being informed of the Government's decision. Before the dispute is resolved, either by government decision or by the court, no party involved may change the status quo of land use. In other words, regulations from the 1980s stipulate that land users need to negotiate with rural collectives about the quantity of land to be acquired and the compensation and resettlement package, and sign land acquisition contracts.

10 Even the existing procedure is not well implemented, as recent research found only 20 per cent of the farmers whose land was acquired had received the required prior notice about compensation (Zhu et al. 2006). This shows that even if negotiations were required by law, many land developers would still be able to start construction without following procedure, whether it was a duty to provide information, as at present, or a duty to enter into negotiation, introduced in the future.

11 Initiating civil or administrative litigation against unlawful behaviour of land developers or local government has not been used much or with much success (van Rooij 2007). The nationwide data on legal redress for land-takings demonstrated that only 0.9 per cent of aggrieved farmers filed a lawsuit for more compensation (Zhu et al. 2006). Clearly, going to court has not been a preferred option for land-grab victims. The chances of winning a case against a local government or against land developers with good local connections are slim. Courts are paid and partly managed by their local governments and have tended not to bite the hand that feeds them. In addition, the context of judicial corruption and personal favours (*guanxi*) further denies poor peasants success in the courtroom. Courts, like lawyers, have refused to take on land cases, claiming they lack jurisdiction or that litigants do not have the right to stand (Phan 2005:18).

Even in the 2007 Property Rights Law, not much progress was made in protecting farmers from abusive land-taking. The law only stipulates that the 'government can acquire rural collective land for the purpose of public interests according to law and following the legal process', and still there is no clear definition of 'public interests'. As to the compensation and resettlement package, the law only vaguely stipulates 'compensation for the land itself; resettlement subsidies; and compensation for improvements to the land and for crops growing on the requisitioned land need to be paid in full. Social security payments should be arranged for the dispossessed farmers so that their livelihood [can] be maintained and their legal rights [can] be fully protected.'[12]

As securing cheap land for local governments to attract businesses became increasingly important after the mid 1990s, local officials had strong incentives to depress land compensation to farmers, which further pressured local officials into direct confrontation with farmers whose land was the target of forceful requisition. While this pressure applied to all municipal and county-level officials, the stress on township cadres was particularly acute. Sitting at the bottom of the local government hierarchy, they were responsible for almost all matters related to rural society. The municipal or county governments might set land development plans and propose terms for land requisition, but township officials were the ones who would carry out difficult negotiations with village collectives and were in charge of coercing defiant farmers to accept government-set terms. Having village cadres who shared their interests would not only lower the requisition costs, but also may determine whether or not the transaction could be accomplished at all. If the deal failed, their superiors would discount their leadership credentials, thus jeopardising their future career.

Therefore, township officials in localities that experienced a higher intensity of land requisition had stronger incentives to manipulate the rules to make sure that more cooperative cadres were elected. Drawing on two national surveys, recent research by Su et al. (2013) offers strong empirical evidence of the impacts of land-taking on Chinese Villagers' Committee (VC) elections. As shown in their analysis, there are no uniform rules in VC elections and villages have relied on different formulas to elect their leaders. Some rules are more transparent and democratic, but others leave a lot of grey areas that are open to manipulation. In villages with more intensive land requisition, electoral rules are more

---

12 The LML provides for a standard of compensation six to ten times the annual average output value of the three preceding years and a resettlement fee of four to six times average annual output. The law also provides absolute combined compensation maxima of no higher than 15 times annual output, or when approved by provincial authorities no higher than 30 times the annual output of the land compensated. The specific standards are determined at the provincial level. Both village committees and farmers are to be consulted about requisition compensation. Compensation payments must be made public, and the new law explicitly states that it is forbidden to embezzle or divert compensation funds (LML, ss. 47, 48, 49).

likely to be manipulated by their upper-level governments. For example, local government may intervene into the formation of election committees by appointing members of the committees, or they can intervene in the nomination of candidates so that they can pick their own favoured individuals.

Besides intervening in village elections to pick the 'right' cadres, local governments also have multiple other instruments to incentivise village officials to be on their side in the land acquisition process. Various economic incentives are used to induce cooperation from the village cadres. This can happen because the village collective is the basic socioeconomic organisation in rural areas, and its largest asset is the land collectively owned by its members. Even though China's laws recognise that both the collective and its members should be entitled to share compensation, there are no specific policy guidelines or regulations on how to divide the shares in different situations. In practice, among the three types of land compensation for acquisition—that is, compensation for the land itself, resettlement subsidies and compensation for improvements to the land and for crops growing on the requisitioned land—compensation for the land itself is usually paid to the village collective. Therefore, village cadres may benefit from land acquisition. In some localities such as Shanghai, rural collectives can share stock in the land they transfer for projects. In return, they receive annual cash payments equivalent to average profits from farming, which they can use. In other places such as Suzhou, local governments leave some non-agricultural land to the village collectives for non-agricultural development and thus the village cadres are able to obtain revenue simply by renting out the allocated land for non-agricultural purposes. Therefore, in the process of land acquisition, local cadres have strong incentives to cooperate with local governments or even the land users rather than the villagers, since the collective organisation and the cadres can benefit in terms of economic returns.

If local governments can influence village elections to elect cooperative village cadres and have multiple economic instruments to induce village cadre collaboration, it is very difficult for the land acquisition process to be transparent so farmers know very clearly when and how much of their land will be acquired and how much they will be compensated. Lack of transparency easily leads to corruption and a lack of legal channels for farmers to file appeals and protests against governments in compulsory land acquisition cases. The issues of accountability and transparency therefore figure prominently in land acquisition in which village cadres usually work together. Misappropriation of compensation funds for land and indulging in fraudulent means to acquire land from the farmers is inevitable (Ding 2007; Subrahmanyan 2004).

Limited reforms so far

For China's current development and urbanisation model to work, local governments must have access to a lot of cheap land to compete for the mobile manufacturing land users. Luckily, Chinese local governments are empowered by the present land requisition and leasing systems almost as the monopolistic player in land-taking, preparation and leasing processes.

An amendment to the Constitution in 2004 provides that the state may carry out land requisition to serve the public interest in accordance with the law and appropriate compensation will be made. The concept of 'public interest' has, however, not been clearly defined by relevant laws and regulations, such as the Constitution and the Land Management Law. In practice, not only does the land used for urban infrastructure construction need to be requisitioned from rural collectives, but also land for industrial, commercial and residential developments is prepared through government requisition. In the process, local governments generally have the power to decide the compensation standards. Concerning the compensation for land-taking, both the owners (rural collectives) and the users (individual rural households) of rural land are in a weak position.

For their own interests, local governments inevitably have strong incentives to set low compensation standards. Our fieldwork in recent years revealed that even in some developed areas dispossessed farmers received only very low cash compensation while at the same time there was no social security provided for them. Since a fair number of dispossessed farmers are poorly educated, they may easily become unemployed after land requisition. While some localities have started to implement a social security policy for dispossessed farmers (known as the 'land for social security' policy), its conditions are still set by the local government. Dispossessed farmers usually lack any negotiation power about the scope and the level of social security benefits. Some areas even use the 'land for social security' policy as a means to avoid short-term government fiscal obligations by promising dispossessed farmers certain social security benefits in the future. In this way, governments are able to obtain huge revenue by land leasing while at the same time delaying paying out social security benefits until a later date (Wang and Tao 2009).

Over the past 10 years, the majority of China's suburban areas have witnessed massive urban expansion, along with a fast-growing number of dispossessed farmers. In recent years, the scale of land requisition has reached approximately 3 million mu every year. If we assume per capita farmland is 1 mu in suburban China, this means that around three million farmers lose their land each year. By 2006, the total number of dispossessed farmers exceeded 40 million and this number will increase to 70 million in the next 10–15 years (Tianze Economic Research Institute 2007).

To address the challenges from excessive industrial land leasing and abusive land requisition practices by local governments, the State Council and the Ministry of Land and Resources in the past several years have issued a series of policies and regulations aimed at local governments. These include the elimination of industrial parks and strengthening land supervision as well as requiring local governments to lease land through more market-oriented approaches.[13] According to our fieldwork across the country, however, the central policies have rarely been implemented because of intense regional competition for manufacturing investment. The local strategy in response to the Central Government directive is what has been called 'designated bidding, auctioning and public tender'—that is, local governments usually set a series of conditions for participating companies to constrain competition in land leasing, so they can lease the land to a preselected industrial company. Therefore, enforcing a policy that requires the 'bidding, auction and public tender for industrial land leasing' is essentially ineffective. This is because this policy is unable to eliminate the root cause of intense regional competition for manufacturing investment.

The Central Government has also attempted to reform the land requisition system by raising compensation standards for land-taking and by limiting the scope of land requisition. The Central Government is now amending the Land Administration Law and has also issued the 'Measures for Public Notification of Land Requisition', so as to stop local governments from abusively taking farmland and infringing farmers' property rights. Due to fiscal pressure from the tax-sharing reform in 1994, however, local governments had no choice but to rely on the cheap transfer of industrial land to compete for manufacturing investment, while at the same time earning profits from leasing out commercial/residential land to support urban industrial park and infrastructure development. As long as local governments set the compensation criteria, it will be impossible to establish a good mechanism that can protect the property rights of dispossessed farmers. While short-term measures implemented by the Central Government to contain abusive land requisition and raise compensation for land-taking may help, the high monitoring costs and the unwillingness of local governments to cooperate will render such policies ineffective. Certainly, this does not imply that the Central Government should be responsible for setting compensation criteria

13 For example, requirements are specified in the Circular of the State Council on Intensifying Land Control (No. 31 [2006] of the State Council): 'industrial land shall be leased by means of public bidding, auction and public tender and by strictly following the procedures and methods prescribed in the Provisions on the Assignment of State-owned Lands by Means of Bidding, Auction and Public Tender and the Rules on the Assignment of State-owned Lands by Means of Public Bidding, Auction and Public Tender.' And, this 'is of great significance to strengthening macroeconomic control, strictly controlling land use and effectively controlling the total land; to bringing down the competition by lowering industrial land prices and overexpansion of industrial parks, and realizing value preservation and appreciation of state-owned assets; to establishing a functioning land market mechanism and to improving land use efficiency.'

for land requisitions at the local level. In a country as large as China, putting the land compensation setting power in the hands of the Central Government would not make much sense. A final solution to this problem requires a fundamental reform of the land management system.

The latest amendment of the Land Management Law (LML) serves as a good example of the limitations of reform so far. In 2009, the Ministry of Land and Resources came up with a highly controversial draft LML amendment. In the draft, the articles related to land requisition have been amended significantly. Compared with the existing LML, a new chapter on 'land expropriation and requisition' is added to standardise the scope and procedure of land requisition. The key idea is to restrict government power and narrow the scope of land requisition, as well as provide social security for dispossessed farmers.

Even though these changes demonstrate the Government's determination to improve the current land requisition system, the new draft LML still prescribes that 'within the urban construction area defined by the Land Master Plan, the state can requisition collective land for construction use according to the city planning', whether the land is used for public purposes (such as land for infrastructural development) or for non-public purposes (such as land for industrial, commercial and residential use). Only in areas beyond 'the urban construction area defined by the Land Master Plan' can rural collectives develop land for non-public purposes on their own.

Such a constraint on rural land development is inevitably problematic. First, it implies that the majority of rural land with high value for non-agricultural use will still need to go through the land requisition process even if the land is used for non-public purposes. In fact, this is in line with the interests of local government. If such a definition has not been made, local government will only be able to requisition the land that serves public interests such as land used for infrastructural development, public education and public health institutions. Then local governments will no longer be able to requisition land from farmers and lease it out for industrial, commercial and residential purposes.

Moreover, local governments may easily expand the 'urban construction area defined by the Land Master Plan' by adjusting land-use planning. This is evident in the implementation of the 1997–2010 Master Plan: the more economically developed one locality is, the more frequent are the planning adjustments. Although in principle the preparation, implementation and adjustment of the land-use planning need to go through a public hearing process, in reality there has been little public participation. If the aforementioned article of the LML amendment is adopted, it will be very difficult to placate farmers who live within the 'urban construction area defined by the Land Use Master Plan'. This, in turn, could lead to confrontations between local governments and farmers (Wang and Tao 2009).

Reducing the scope of land requisition and allowing rural collectives to develop land for industrial, commercial and residential uses on their own are two sides of one coin. If the rural collectives and farmers are allowed to develop rural land on their own, it would imply that such land development does not need to go through the process of state requisition preparation leasing. Therefore, progress in land requisition reform largely determines the progress in rural collective land reform.

For a long time, Chinese academia has been arguing for rural collectives and farmers to be granted the rights to develop collective land for non-public purposes. In 2007, China enacted a Property Law. The law has an element providing 'equal property rights protection for both the rural collective land and the state-owned land'; however, if no fundamental reform is carried out in China's land requisition system, it is extremely difficult to imagine that rural collective land can ever enjoy equal treatment in development. In this sense, land requisition system reform is a prerequisite for rural collective construction land reform.

Reducing the scope of government land requisition and allowing rural collectives to develop collective construction land on their own would not only contribute to limiting the development zone craze witnessed across the country and enhance land-use efficiency in China's urbanisation, but also help farmers on city fringes to share some benefits of urbanisation by engaging in land development. Our fieldwork in the past several years in the Yangtze River Delta, the Pearl River Delta, North China Plain and Chengdu–Chongqing area indicates, however, that the opposite is happening. Indeed, local governments in many localities, rather than limiting the scope of land requisition, have begun to demolish existing urban villages and requisition more land from urban suburbs so as to continue the distorted land-based urbanisation. Acquiring more land from urban villages to be leased to real estate developers not only generates substantial land revenue for city governments, but also helps to improve the physical image of the cities. Certainly, these requisition and demolition actions are often met with serious confrontation between farmers and the local government.

Towards a new model of urbanisation with coordinated reforms focusing on land

As detailed in the preceding sections, the complex challenges China faces in the course of urbanisation and economic development are closely related to China's land system. To address the distortions in urbanisation and help China to complete its great economic transformation, the Government must be resolved to carry out fundamental land reforms. Only by implementing real land reform and coordinating this with reforms to *hukou* and local public finance can the unsustainable model of urbanisation be rectified.

Reform of the land requisition system

A reform of the land requisition system needs to strictly define public versus non-public use of land. In other words, for land requisition to be considered legal, expropriated land must be designated for public use. In defining 'public', we believe that if a product manufactured on a piece of land is produced for market consumption then the land use itself should also be decided by the market. Only products that cannot be provided by the market, whether profitable or not, should be seen as public projects and land requisition applies.

Even for land requisition that targets public use, the Government should ensure that compensation is based on fair competition. No matter what the purpose of the project, citizens should not suffer loss from land requisition. Besides, compensation for land based on market values is an internationally recognised principle. At this point, it is worth looking at the methods the Beijing Municipal Government has used.

1. Provincial governments set minimum compensation criteria at the municipal and county levels for land expropriated within their jurisdictions. These criteria should not violate the 'law of one price', and should be based on the overall evaluation of local economic and social conditions such as land resources, production level, geographical condition and the supply–demand relationship, and so on.

2. Establish a negotiating mechanism between governments, developers, village collectives and local farmers.

3. Design a scientific land requisition system and a negotiation and arbitration mechanism in land requisition compensation, which are independent of the municipal or county government.

Reform of the collective construction land system

A decision by the Third Plenary Session of the Seventeenth Congress of the Chinese Communist Party (CCP) in 2007 stipulated that the scope of market transactions for collectively owned land should be gradually expanded. Based on the current revised draft of the Land Administration Law, however, lawmakers tend to constrain the location where farmers can obtain non-agricultural development rights on their own land. In another world, only farmers could develop on their own the land outside the defined scope of urban construction land. This regulation would, however, mean the vast majority of rural land with market value (within the defined scope of urban construction land) still needs to go through the land requisition/land preparation/land-leasing process and farmers could not develop it. This would also mean continued restrictions on commercial/residential development on collective land. The Chinese Government is apparently worried about losing control of construction land use; however, these policies have not been implemented well, as not only does 'small-property-rights housing' continue to flourish, the Government also has lost tax revenue that could have been collected if such properties had been legalised.

Granting development rights on collectively owned land not only would help to protect the interests of those with rights to the land, thus reducing social conflict, but would also be good for improved land-use efficiency. With regard to the widespread issue of small-property-rights housing, standardising and guiding the development of such properties in the amendment of the Land Administration Law would be preferable to an outright ban. As long as it is not against public interests and is in line with overall land use and urban planning, this land should be transferred to state-owned status and the development rights to most of the land should be given to the original property rights-holder. This would be the only way towards realising the law of one price between collectively owned and state-owned land. Under this model, both industrial and commercial developers could deal directly with village collectives or farmers, while the Government could be compensated by requiring developers to pay a standard transfer fee and/or charging a value-added tax on the land. In this way, while ensuring that a portion of the increased value of land goes to the Government, the village collectives and farmers, as holders of transferable land with a high potential for appreciation, could maintain the agricultural value of their land and a certain portion of the land value appreciation throughout this transition.

The implications of land reform would go far beyond simply providing reasonable compensation to dispossessed farmers. It would be essential to stabilise and even lower the high prices of residential land monopolised by local governments, and thereby control the corresponding skyrocketing housing prices. It would also be essential to stop local government from expropriating land at low prices and then building large-scale industrial parks. It would be essential for China to address the land-use distortions and the serious social conflicts due to abusive local land requisition. If these reforms can be implemented along with corresponding land-use planning adjustments, the issues of protection of farmland and excessive urban expansion would be addressed effectively. With the introduction of tax reforms, local government would also be compensated for the shortfall of land-leasing revenue.

Large-scale public housing versus market-based land reform for housing security

One key issue in China's urbanisation is to accommodate the huge migrant population in affordable housing. The Central Government is currently demanding that local governments increase the supply of public housing; however, due to the massive investment required, there is a serious lack of incentives for local governments. A more fundamental issue is whether any country could cover the floating population of 200 million people and their families with public housing and whether this is the best way to address the housing problems for the newly urbanised (Tao and Xu 2006, 2007).

In a global context, a healthy real estate development model is one in which public housing is targeted mainly at individuals at the lowest income levels who are not even able to afford market rental rates. The majority of people, whether through purchasing or renting, should be sheltered through market-provided housing. If the market price is so high that the Government has to provide a large proportion of mid to low-income households with public housing, reforms will be needed to address the prices.

The concept of 'affordable housing', in broad terms, can refer to housing provided by any entity for mid and low-income groups. This naturally includes public housing provided by local governments for low-income families who cannot afford to rent or purchase a home. This does not, however, necessarily mean that government needs to provide the housing directly, nor does it imply the creation of a welfare society in terms of housing. If the market can provide the majority of the population with housing that they can afford to rent or buy then housing affordability has been realised. As an example, in the Pearl River Delta region, where housing is relatively expensive, 40–50 per cent of the migrant population lives in dormitories, while the remaining floating population lives in rented housing within urban or suburban villages. While a majority of the rental housing is illegal small-property-rights housing without decent infrastructure or public services, it has provided migrant workers with a place to live with their families. In fact, experiences in Pearl River Delta cities such as Guangzhou, Shenzhen, Foshan and Dongguan show how local farmers and village collectives in suburban areas can proactively share the benefits of urbanisation and how they can provide affordable rental housing to migrants. In Shenzhen alone, half of the seven million migrants live in urban villages. In 2005, 327 000 people with local *hukou* lived permanently in these urban villages, while temporary residents totalled almost 4.7 million, or 14 times the number of permanent residents. According to the Shenzhen Municipal Housing Construction Plan 2006–2010, of the 250 million sq m of homes in the city, 120 million sq m belong to original village residents or village collectives. Of these, private homes concentrated in urban villages cover an area of 95 sq km (8 sq km within the special economic zone, or SEZ), with a total construction area of about 100 million sq m (20 million sq m within the SEZ).

In the course of China's urbanisation, the primary cause of the housing bubble is that local governments monopolise and undersupply land for residential use. Therefore, besides building some public housing or providing rent subsidies to low-income groups, allowing collectively owned construction land in suburban and urban villages to gradually enter the market is essential. Not only can local farmers build housing to share some of the land value appreciation in urbanisation, but also the hundreds of millions of migrants can be accommodated without much government expenditure.

Urban village redevelopment and coordinated land, *hukou* and fiscal reform

We propose that addressing the housing bubble and providing the migrant population with affordable housing in China can be achieved by innovative models of urban and suburban 'village' redevelopment. This will not only increase land-use efficiency, but also promote social equity.

The issue of redeveloping 'urban villages' deserves more elaboration here. At present, the common practice in most cities is to demolish these villages and lease the land out to commercial and residential developers after requisitioning the rural collective land as state-owned land. This not only leads to social conflicts in urban village redevelopment programs, but also drives away the migrant workers who find urban villages the only affordable housing sites in cities. Therefore, it is hardly a sustainable model of urban village redevelopment.

An alternative approach is to learn from the successful experiences of land value capture, land readjustment[14] and urban land consolidation[15] from the United States, Japan, South Korea and Taiwan. A land readjustment scheme is typically initiated by the municipal government designating an area that is about to be developed. A subdivision plan is developed for unified planning of the area. Provision of infrastructure and services is financed by the sale of some of the plots within the area, often for commercial activities. The original landowners are provided with plots within the reshaped area, which, although smaller, now have access to infrastructure and services.[16]

The redevelopment and renovation of China's urban villages can draw on these successful international land readjustment experiences and further innovate by taking into account China's specific conditions to provide affordable housing for migrants from the countryside. This can be done by requiring, through urban planning, the landowners of urban villages develop rental housing rather than commodity housing. The floor-area ratio can be lifted in these readjustment projects by the city planning authority. If such practices can be extended to a sufficient number of urban/suburban villages, the supply of rental housing would be adequate and rental prices can be kept reasonable even after urban village redevelopment. In this way, affordable housing can be provided for the huge floating population through market mechanisms rather than through direct government provision of public housing.

In fact, allowing farmers in urban and suburban 'villages' to build housing for non-local migrant populations—once proper planning, infrastructure and government taxation are in place—would not only imply a breakthrough in China's land reform, but also facilitate China's ongoing *hukou* reform. Once the issue of housing for migrants can be addressed effectively and public schools can be built for migrants' children in these redeveloped urban villages, an effective breakthrough in household registration reform would be realised.

---

14 'Land readjustment' refers to a situation when, after having expropriated and redeveloped an area of land, the Government takes a portion of the land for infrastructure use, another portion for public auction to cover the cost of land development, and the remaining portion (with a much higher plot ratio) mostly for returning to the original land rights-holders.

15 'Urban land consolidation' is a method by which, according to the development needs of a city, areas within urban planning zones, areas of urban–rural fringe zones or urban outskirts, sections of land that are irregular and poorly organised as well as areas that are overcrowded and not suitable for economic use are redeveloped under government order and reallocated to coordinate with public facilities, improving roads, parks, squares and rivers. Once it has been ensured that all plots of land are of a suitable size and square with a certain scale, they are reallocated to the land rights-holder. This guarantees that urban land is used more efficiently and economically, creating a clean and orderly urban environment.

16 A definition of the technique is provided by Archer (1987): 'Land readjustment is a technique whereby a group of neighboring landowners in an urban-fringe area are combined in a partnership for the unified planning, servicing and subdivision of their land with the project costs and benefits being shared between the landowners.'

The underlying economics can be illustrated by the following example. Assume an urban 'village' covers a land area of 100 units owned by 200 village households. During the course of redevelopment, local government first engages in direct negotiations with the village collective. After calculating the potential value added to the property after the redevelopment, the Government can requisition 45 units of land from the villagers. Of the 45 units taken by the Government, 30 can be used for infrastructure development in redevelopment while the remaining 15 units can be sold via public auction to cover the cost of infrastructure construction. Meanwhile, even though the original land rights-holders have given up 45 units, the remaining 55 units *may still have higher value with better infrastructure and higher floor-area ratios granted by the Government*. By extrapolating from this simple example, we can design a series of steps to implement coordinated reform in land, household registration and the local tax system.

First, in terms of the legal system and policy implementation, the land on which urban villages are built can be converted to state-owned land first; however, the Government will not grant land-use rights to a third party such as a real estate developer but to the original land rights-holder—that is, the urban villagers.

Second, in terms of development and financing, once the villagers are issued the certificates of state-owned land-use rights, they can work together to apply for a bank mortgage or bring in private funds to begin redevelopment on their own. With this funding, villagers can develop rental housing to accommodate migrants and other low and medium-income residents in cities.

Third, the land value appreciation in rural–urban land conversion can be largely attributed to the 'positive externality' generated by urban growth and infrastructure investment; there is therefore an economic rationale for the Government to take a certain share of land for free. The land can be used for infrastructure development and financing.

Fourth, the Government can in principle levy a tax on the rental income of urban villagers and, in the long run, a property tax on housing stock can be introduced to further consolidate local tax bases. Local government may use some of the tax revenue to pay for the education of migrants' children in newly built urban public schools.

In essence, the proposed reform allows rural communities in urban/suburban villages of migrant-receiving cities to take their non-farming land onto the urban housing market if these communities are willing to submit some of their land to local government for infrastructure development. One further condition is that for the first 10–15 years, they can only build properties used for rental purposes. After the transitional period, however, these houses would gain full rights and can be sold directly on the housing market.

This design has a number of advantages. Insulating rural construction land in the rental market initially provides a cushion for the existing housing market and prevents market panics and a crash of the housing bubble. On the other hand, eventually merging the two tracks in the future sends a credible signal to speculators that housing prices will not rise further; therefore, the Central Government can phase out its strict regulations on real estate markets installed since 2010 to curb the housing bubble. Both contribute to healthy growth of the housing market. Moreover, granting rural communities development rights (even though restricted during the transition) opens the legal channels for them to apply for bank loans for development. This can unleash a housing construction boom in urban villages and suburban areas, which provides a lift for construction-related industries with significant overcapacity. Finally, unlike the current housing bubble, this kind of real estate development is more socially beneficial and economically sustainable. Rural residents, particularly those living close to urban centres, benefit from this change directly. The growth in the rental property track also makes housing affordable for hundreds of millions of migrant workers, enabling them to settle in cities permanently. Urbanisation holds the potential of turning the Chinese economy away from an investment-driven model.

The key to the success of the proposed reform lies in the attitude of local governments. Their concern over revenue is legitimate and needs to be addressed in the reform package. Under the current system, local governments are burdened with too many spending responsibilities but do not have adequate revenue. After the reform, they will have limited power of land requisition and lose the sizeable land-lease fees and bank loans associated with that power. In the long run, property taxes should be levied so that local public finance can be supported by a stable source of income. Considering the strong resistance from the wealthy and the politically powerful in the trial cities, it is unrealistic to expect this new tax to take effect soon; however, the loss of revenue during the transitional period will be compensated by several sources.

First, the urban and suburban villages that are lured by the huge rents to join the proposed rental market track would be prepared to contribute some of their land for free to local governments in return for their newly gained land development rights for rental housing. The land readjustment technique proposed earlier is an effective way for government to capture the land value appreciation in urbanisation. Local governments would then be able to spare themselves having to pay for infrastructure improvement from their own budgets. In addition, the proposed rental income tax could be used to cover the education expenditures for migrants' children in urban public schools. Once China is able to accommodate hundreds of millions of migrants on a permanent basis, they would work, live and consume like urban residents—a further boost to domestic demand.

Second, for those rural communities that have already developed their land 'illegally' for urban usage, a gradual process of legalisation can be started if certain infrastructure and building standards are met and due taxes are paid. The land and house owners would be willing to pay local governments to gain full legal status.

Finally, another untapped source for local governments is underutilised industrial land. According to various reports, the floor-area ratio in China's industrial parks is only about 0.3–0.4, even in China's developed areas. Through reorganisation by negotiation, it is possible to double the land development intensity of industrial land use so that local governments can work with industrial land users to convert some industrial land to residential and commercial uses. Between 1997 and 2009, the area of industrial land increased by 15 000 sq km—that is, 22.5 million mu. This means if the floor-area ratio in China's industrial parks can be doubled to 0.6–0.8, at least 10 million mu of industrial land can be used for residential and commercial purposes. In fact, as cities expand, the location of much land in industrial parks becomes valuable for residential and commercial development. If this kind of land conversion can be gradually implemented with planning adjustment, at least 1 million mu of industrial land should be available for residential and commercial development each year. One way to make this happen is to allow industrial land users to redevelop their land for residential and commercial purposes, either by themselves or by working with real estate developers, on the condition they pay the difference between land-leasing prices for industrial purposes and for residential/commercial purposes. Assuming RMB750 000/mu for housing and commercial land (the 2008 price) and assuming local governments take only two-thirds of the revenue, local governments can collect RMB500 billion per year for the next 10 years. If we further assume that two-thirds of this converted land is used for housing, with a floor-area ratio of 1.5, about 600 million sq m of housing would be built each year. With a moderate price of RMB5000/sq m under the current tax system, local governments can raise RMB420 billion in real estate-related taxes. Therefore, even with some moderate assumptions, local governments can be largely compensated even if they gradually phase out land requisition for non-public uses. The key is to adjust the land-use structure of existing urban land by intensifying the use of industrial land and converting some underutilised industrial land to residential and commercial purposes.

If this can be done, local governments can use some of the revenue to pay for the debts incurred through local financial platforms. Their resistance to land requisition reform would be much weaker.

Conclusions

In China's lad reform, as in any reform, strategy matters. Gradualism can assist selection of the right sequencing so reforms make good economic sense and also can generate enough political support to overcome resistance. In our view, a reform package that centres on land and urbanisation provides the best chance of unleashing huge domestic demand and relieving the overcapacity problem in many industries in China.

China should focus on land reform because land has played an essential role in the making of China's growth model in the past 15 years, and it is also responsible for current woes in the economy. Even though China's land-based development model contributed to the dramatic rise of the Chinese economy, the negative consequences are also numerous and obvious.

Changing course is hard. The old model has created its own vested interests and these actors—central and local, public and private—have forged a strong growth coalition to perpetuate the existing path. In the aftermath of the GFC, the prompt and massive response from the Chinese Government reinforced the existing imbalance in the economy.

Despite tremendous inertia, some reform in land can no longer be postponed. A gradualist approach is proposed that aims to build a dual-track system. Under the current land regulatory regime, land ownership is separated into urban and rural, and only urban governments have the authority to take land from rural areas for urban development. This not only deprives rural residents of their development rights but also leads the Chinese economy down a quite destructive path. Total liberalisation, however, may result in a crash of the existing housing bubbles if large volumes of rural construction land are rushed onto the market. To alleviate this concern by local governments and urban homeowners, China may need to first set up a rental property market track targeting mainly the 200 million rural migrants who already choose to live and work in cities. This could be done by redeveloping urban/suburban villages so that local farmers in these villages can legally build rental housing for migrants. The land readjustment technique can be employed to ensure such land development conforms to urban planning and infrastructure development criteria. Government can also levy rental income tax and, in the long run, property tax so as to finance urban public services such as education for migrant children. To make up for the potential revenue shortfall due to this reform, local governments in China can also convert some industrial land for residential and commercial construction and levy a tax on land value appreciation from such conversion. This would not only alleviate the revenue concerns of local government, but also help to reduce the distortions in China's urban land-use structure.

At the current stage of development and transition, no reform in the Chinese economy is going to be easy. One certainly should not have any illusions about a quick fix. The proposed land reform package may, however, offer some hope of transitioning into a more healthy urbanisation model, boosting domestic consumption and alleviating the overcapacity problem in many industrial sectors. One particularly favourable factor of this reform is the new leadership's emphasis on a new urbanisation model by making real breakthroughs in reforms. What China needs now is a realistic road map for such reforms.

References

Archer, R. W. (1987), *Transferring the urban land pooling/readjustment technique to the developing countries of Asia*, HSD Working Paper No. 24, Human Settlements Development Programme, Asian Institute of Technology, Bangkok.

Ash, R. and Edmonds, R. L. (1998), 'China's land resources, environment and agricultural production', *The China Quarterly* (156): 840–52.

China Land Problem Task Force (2007), *Implementation and Protection of Land Property Rights in Urbanization*, Beijing: Unirule Economics Institute.

Ding, C. (2007), 'Policy and praxis of land acquisition in China', *Land Use Policy* 24: 1–13.

Ding, C. and Lichtenberg, E. (2011), 'Land and urban economic growth in China', *Journal of Regional Science* 51: 299–317.

Han, J. (2003), 'Change collective land ownership into shareholder ownership', *China Economic Times*, 11 November, [in Chinese].

Ho, P. (2005), *Institutions in Transition: Land Ownership, Property Rights and Social Conflict in China*, New York: Oxford University Press.

Ho, S. P. S. and Lin, G. C. S. (2003), 'Emerging land markets in rural and urban China: policies and practices', *The China Quarterly* 175: 681–707.

Huang, J., Tao, R., Xu, Z. and Liu, M. (2008), *Institutional Change and Sustainable Development: China's Agricultural and Rural Development for 30 Years*, 30 Years of China's Reform Series, Shanghai: People's Publishing House.

Huang, X. (2007), 'An in-depth analysis of current land issues', *Economic Perspective* (2).

Johnston, B. and Mellor, J. (1961), 'The role of agriculture in economic development', *American Economic Review* 51: 566–93.

Lichtenberg, E. and Ding, C. (2008), 'Assessing farmland protection policy in China', *Land Use Policy* 25: 59–68.

Lichtenberg, E. and Ding, C. (2009), 'Local officials as land developers: urban spatial expansion in China', *Journal of Urban Economics* 66: 57–64.

Lin, C. S. and Yi, F. (2011), 'Urbanization of capital or capitalization on urban land?', *Urban Geography* 32: 50–79.

Lin, G. C. S. (2007), 'Reproducing spaces of Chinese urbanisation: new city-based and land-centred urban transformation', *Urban Studies* 44: 1827–55.

Lin, G. C. S. and Ho, S. P. S. (2005), 'The state, land system, and land development processes in contemporary China', *Annals of the Association of American Geographers* 95(2): 411–36.

Lin, Y., F. Cai and Zhou, L. (1999), *China's Miracle: Development Strategy and Economic Reform*, Shanghai: People's Publishing House.

Ministry of Land and Resources (2001), *Regulations on Land Acquisition Notices*, Beijing: Ministry of Land and Resources.

Ministry of Land and Resources (2006), *Final Report from the Workshop on Industrial Land Price Evaluation and Analysis*, September, Beijing: Ministry of Land and Resources.

National Development and Reform Commission (NDRC), Ministry of Land and Resources and Ministry of Construction (2006), *An Audit Report of Development Zones in China*, Beijing: NDRC, Ministry of Land and Resources and Ministry of Construction.

Phan, P. N. (2005), 'Enriching the land or the political elite? Lessons from China on democratization of the urban renewal process', *Pacific Rim Law and Policy Journal* 14: 607–57.

Qian, Y. (2000), 'The process of China's market transition (1978–98): the evolutionary, historical, and comparative perspectives', *Journal of Institutional and Theoretical Economics* 156(1): 151–71.

Sargeson, S. (2002), 'Subduing "the rural house-building craze': attitudes towards housing construction and land use controls in four Zhejiang villages', *The China Quarterly* 172: 927–55.

Stark, O. (1991), *The Migration of Labour*, USA: Blackwell.

Tao, R. and Wang, H. (2009), 'On "Zhejiang model" of the transfer and trade of land development rights—system origin, mode of operation and its important meaning', *Management World* (September).

Tao, R. and Xu, Z. (2005), 'Urbanization, agricultural land system and social security for migrant workers: policy options from the perspective of a large developing country in transition', *Journal of Economic Research* (12): 45–56.

Tao, R. and Xu, Z. (2006), 'Groping for stones to cross river versus coordinated policy reforms? The case of two reforms in China', *Journal of Policy Reform* 9(3): 177–201.

Tao, R. and Xu, Z. (2007), 'Urbanization, rural land system and social security for migrant farmers in China', *Journal of Development Studies* 43(7): 1301–20.

Tao, R., Su, F., Liu, M. and Cao, G. (2010), '"Race to the bottom." Competition by negotiated land leasing: an institutional analysis and empirical evidence from Chinese cities', CEMA Working Papers, No. 294.

Tao, R., Lu, X., Su, F. and Wang, H. (2009), 'China's transition and development model under evolving regional competition patterns', *Journal of Economic Research* (7): 21–34.

Todaro, M. (1969), 'A model of labour, migration and urban unemployment in less developed countries', *American Economic Review* 59(1): 138–48.

Tsui, K. and Wang, Y. (2004), 'Between separate stoves and a single menu: fiscal decentralization in China', *China Quarterly* 177: 71–90.

van Rooij, B. (2007), 'The return of the landlord: Chinese land acquisition conflicts as illustrated by peri-urban Kunming', *Journal of Legal Pluralism* (55): 211–44.

Wang, H. and Tao, R. (2009), 'How to achieve systematic breakthrough in the land requisition system reform—proposal to "Land Management Law Amendment"', *Leader* (29).

Wang, H., Tao, R., Wang, L. and Su, F. (2010), 'Farmland preservation and land development rights trading in Zhejiang, China', *Habitat International* 34(2010): 454–63.

World Bank (2002), *China National Development and Sub-National Finance: A Review of Provincial Expenditures*, Washington, DC: The World Bank.

World Bank (2005), *China: Land Policy Reform for Sustainable Economic and Social Development*, Washington, DC: The World Bank.

Wu, W. (2010), 'Urban infrastructure financing and economic performance in China', *Urban Geography* 31: 648–67.

Xinhua News Agency (2010), 'Wasteful industrial land use in China is significant', *Xinhua News Agency*, 7 March. Available from <http://news.xinhuanet.com/legal/2010-03/07/content_13113869.htm>.

Zhai, N. and Xiang, G. (2007), 'An analysis of China's current land acquisition system and policy implications', *China Administration* 3, [in Chinese].

Zhu, K. and Prosterman, R. (2007), 'Securing land rights for Chinese farmers: a leap forward for stability and growth', *Cato Development Policy Analysis Series* (3).

Zhu, K., Prosterman, R., Jianping, Y., Ping, L., Riedinger, J. and Yiwen, O. (2006), 'The rural land question in China: analysis and recommendations based on a 17-province survey', *New York University Journal of International Law & Politics* 38: 761–839.

15. China's Labour Market Tensions and Future Urbanisation Challenges[1]

Xin Meng

Introduction

Over the past few years, China's per capita GDP growth has slowed significantly but real wages of migrant workers have continued to increase at more than 10 per cent per annum. Between 2012 and 2013, per capita real GDP increased by 7.7 per cent, while monthly real wages of migrant workers increased by 12.3 per cent, based on the latest Rural Urban Migration in China (RUMiC) survey data. Other small-scale surveys reveal a similar pattern. For example, the global investment research firm Gavekal Dragonomics reports almost exactly the same level of migrant wage growth for 2013 as the RUMiC survey (Miller and Gatley 2014).[2]

Many regard this real wage growth as a clear sign of an unskilled labour shortage emanating from reduced labour supply from the rural sector (the Lewis 'turning point'). But I have always insisted that the shortage of unskilled labour in cities is a consequence of institutional restrictions, explicit or implicit, on rural–urban migration. In this chapter, I use the latest household survey and aggregated data to discuss possible reasons for recent migrant wage increases. I also discuss how misreading China's urban labour supply 'shortage' as an absolute shortage, rather than a result of institutional restrictions, has led to specific policy directions that, together with the traditional rural–urban divide mentality and politicians' reluctance to accept large city slums, may generate potential challenges to China's future urbanisation and economic development.

---

1   I would like to thank Bob Gregory for his helpful comments and Sen Xue for his excellent research assistance.

2   The data sources, however, were not cited in the article.

Urbanisation strategy and industrial upgrading policy

China has always envisaged a different urbanisation path from the historical experience of the West. Ever since the start of economic reform, the Government has insisted that although farmers need to leave agriculture to seek other employment, they should not leave their hometown, and that Chinese urbanisation should be well planned and controlled to focus mainly on small-city expansion in order to avoid large-city problems—namely, slum development.

Economic reform started in the agricultural sector in 1978. Soon after, a sharp increase in agricultural productivity created a large surplus in agricultural labour. Where should these excess workers go? At the time rural–urban migration was forbidden. The only way out for surplus labour was to develop non-agricultural industries in their hometown. Consequently, during the 1980s and early 1990s government policy encouraged rural non-agricultural sector development. As a result, rural township and village enterprises (TVEs) flourished (Meng 2000). Between 1980 and 1995, the share of rural *hukou* labour force employed in the TVEs increased from 9.4 per cent to 26.3 per cent.

From the early 1990s, China's 'open-door policy' encouraged large inflows of foreign direct investment, which, in turn, increased the demand for unskilled labour in cities. In response, the Government gradually relaxed previously rigid rural–urban migration restrictions to allow rural people to work in cities; however, after two decades of allowing farmers to work in cities and gradually changing restrictions, migrant workers, as a general rule, are still not allowed to become city residents. Reasons for this restriction are the potential financial burdens and complications of changing the current public finance system to accommodate rural workers as city residents. Another reason is the deep-rooted idea that farmers may leave the agricultural sector but not their hometown, so as to avoid 'city disease'. Indeed, the newly published *National New Urbanisation Plan (2014–2020)* (State Council of China 2014) reflects this idea and emphasises the orderly building of small cities and towns to accommodate the future excess supply of agricultural workers.

Accompanying this new urbanisation strategy of building small cities and towns is the large-city 'industrial upgrading' policy. It is argued that if China wants to become an economic superpower its industrial structure should be dominated by capital-intensive high-technology industry, and future Chinese economic growth should be based on innovation and sophisticated technology but not cheap labour. The industrial upgrading policy assumes that China has run out of low-skilled labour and the time has come for China to move from being the world's factory with cheap labour to being the world's laboratory, employing more highly skilled workers. Since the GFC, many coastal cities have introduced industrial upgrading policies to actively push out low value-added firms and low-skilled labour.

These policies are having an increasingly significant impact on wages, labour supply and China's future urbanisation and economic development outcomes.

Changes in migrant wages

Facts

Since 2009, unskilled migrants' wages have increased at an above-average rate even though the real GDP growth rate has slowed. Figure 15.1 presents the growth rate of the real first month's pay for the first job for wage/salary-earning migrant workers—the most unskilled migrant workers—against average real per capita GDP growth. The figure clearly points to the fact that unskilled wage growth goes against the slowing trend of general economic growth.

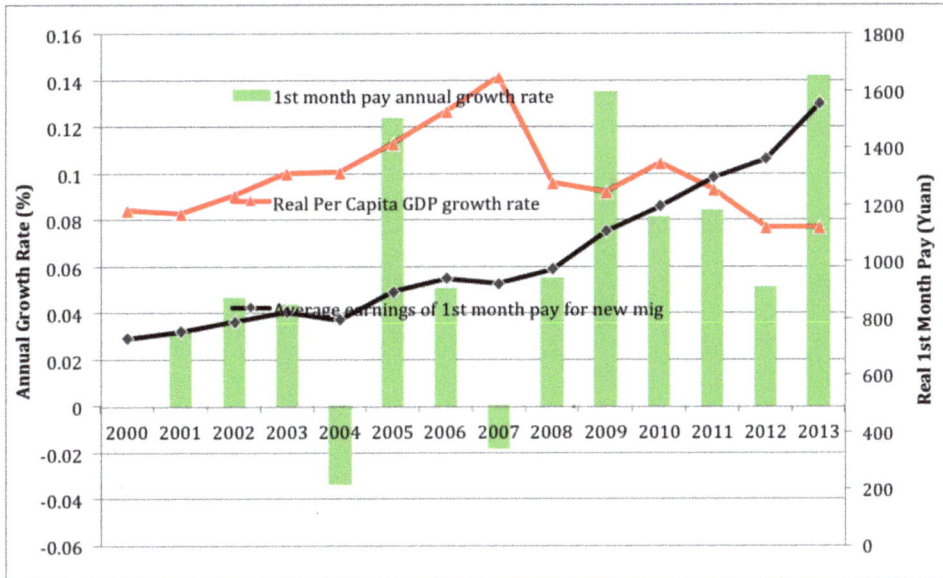

Figure 15.1 Per Capita GDP Growth and Migrant Wage Growth

Sources: Real GDP growth data are based on *China Statistical Yearbook*s (NBS various years). The real first-month earnings of migrants' first jobs are based on the RUMiC survey. Included in the sample are migrant workers who were sampled in each of the survey years (RUMiC New Sample). Consumer price indices used to calculate real earnings are province-specific annual CPI using year 2000 as the base (NBS various years).

The high rates of wage growth could be due to the changing composition of workers. If, from one year to another, the proportion of educated workers increased, for example, the wage increase may not reflect the increase in return to the same quality of workers. To eliminate this possibility, I estimate wage equations standardising for age, gender, marital status, education, year since first migration and city fixed effects. The coefficients on the year fixed effects can be used to indicate the annual wage growth, standardising for workers' quality. These coefficients are plotted together with the growth rate of unadjusted real first-month first-job pay for migrants in Figure 15.2. The standardised wage growth rate differs somewhat from the raw growth rate, but the trend is consistent in suggesting that recent wage growth is much higher than at the beginning of the decade.

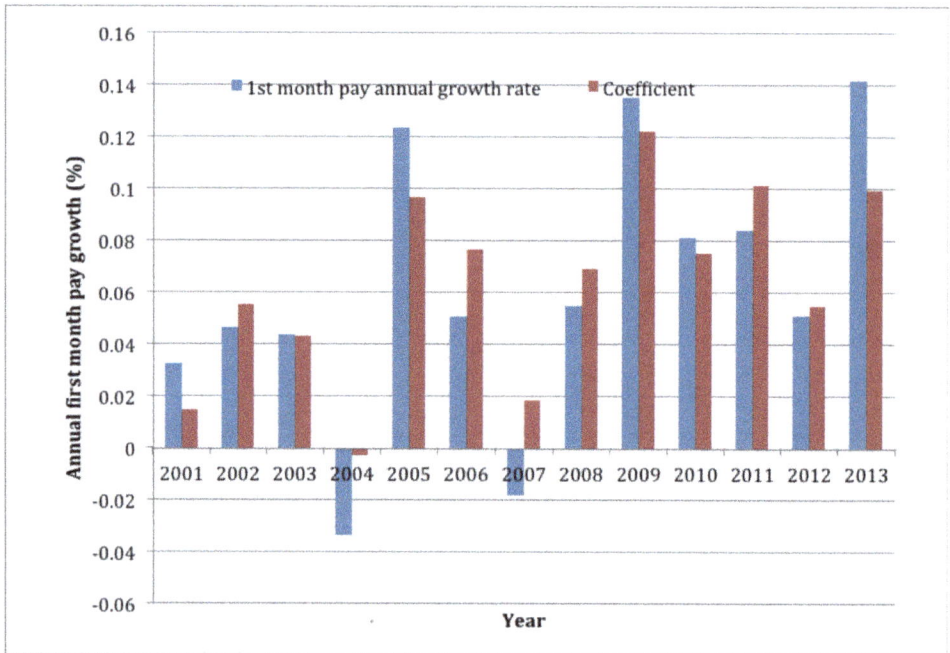

Figure 15.2 Comparison of Raw Wage Growth with Standardised Wage Growth

Sources: The real first-month earnings of migrants' first jobs are based on the RUMiC survey. Included in the sample are migrant workers who were sampled in each of the survey years (RUMiC New Sample). The adjusted wage growth rates are obtained from the author's estimations.

Reasons for real wage growth

The acceleration of real wage increases can be the result of: 1) labour shortages; and/or 2) direct government action on wages. I examine these potential causes in this subsection.

Labour shortage

Aggregated data published by the National Bureau of Statistics (NBS 2014) suggest that in 2013 China had 770 million workers. Of those, 72 per cent had rural *hukou*. Of the total 552 million with rural *hukou*, 283 million or 51 per cent remained employed in the agricultural sector. Of the 269 million classified in the non-agricultural sector, 166 million migrated to various levels of cities (including small county-level cities) to work (rural–urban migrants),[3] while the rest—103 million—worked in the non-agricultural sector in rural towns near their home village. Thus, unlike the common belief that there are 260 million rural–urban migrants working in Chinese cities, the actual number in 2013 was 166 million (see Table 15.1 for a detailed description). In other words, only 30 per cent of rural *hukou* workers migrated to county-level or larger cities in 2013, leaving 70 per cent of rural *hukou* workers employed outside those cities. This suggests there is considerable scope for future migration into cities if the institutional environment were to change and discrimination against these workers in cities were reduced.

Table 15.1 Labour Force Sector of Employment, 2013

	Frequency	% of rural *hukou* workers	% of total labour force
Total labour force	76 977		
Working in cities (both rural and urban *hukou*)	38 240		
Urban *hukou* workers	21 630		0.28
Rural *hukou* workers	55 347		0.72
Of which: working in various levels of city	16 610	0.30	0.22
working in rural non-agricultural sector	10 284	0.19	0.13
working in agriculture	28 453	0.51	0.37

Source: Author's interpretation from NBS (2014).

Household survey data tell a similar story. Using data from the Chinese Family Panel Studies (CFPS) conducted by Peking University in 2012 (ISSS 2012), I examine this issue again.[4] The survey comprises 14 630 rural *hukou* individuals aged sixteen to sixty-five who are currently working. Among them 22 per cent

---

3   Chinese cities have four different administrative levels, which also capture the size of the cities: 1) province-level municipalities including Beijing, Shanghai, Tianjin and Chongqing; 2) provincial capital cities; 3) prefecture-level cities; and 4) county-level cities.

4   Due to funding limitations, RUMiC Urban and Rural Household surveys were terminated in 2011. In addition, the RUMiC Rural Household Survey uses the same sample as the NBS survey. In case the sampling is biased, as many are currently arguing, it is important to use an independent survey with a different sampling frame to examine this issue.

migrated for work purposes (not living at home),[5] 28 per cent had a non-agricultural job at some time during the past year (but lived at home) and the remaining 50.3 per cent only had an agricultural job—again suggesting a large endowment of agricultural workers.

It is often argued, however, that this large supply of agricultural labour is not really employable in cities and therefore is not a labour supply that cities can easily tap. The evidence cited for this view is that these workers are on average older (see Figure 15.3a for the age distributions and Figure 15.3b for the actual numbers within each group) and therefore less educated. This description of remaining rural workers may to some extent be true but it misses two important points.

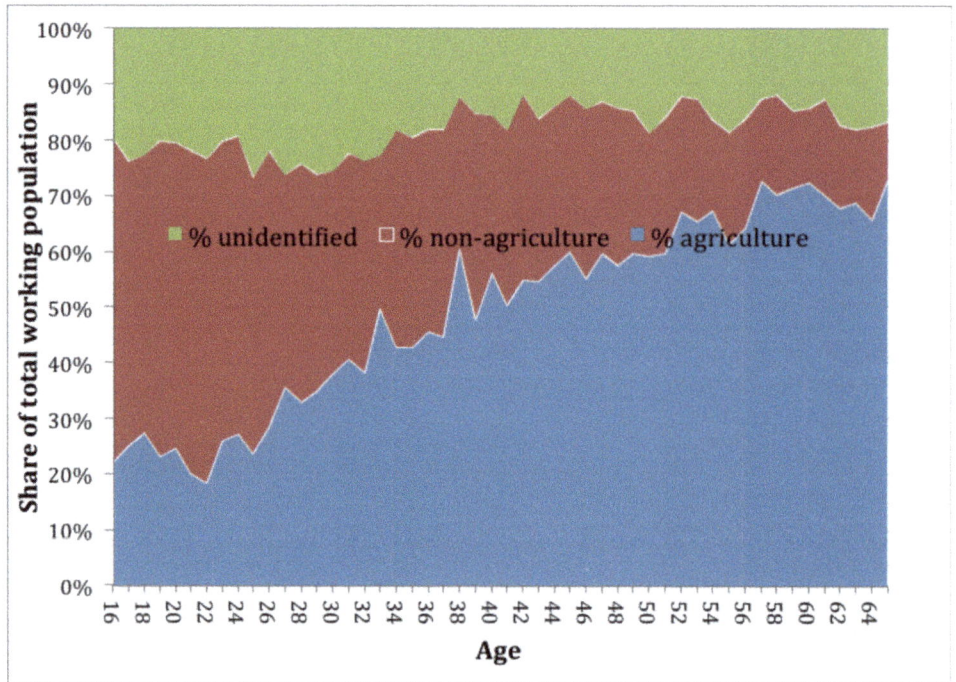

Figure 15.3a Age Distribution of Rural *Hukou* Workers by Sector of Employment, 2012

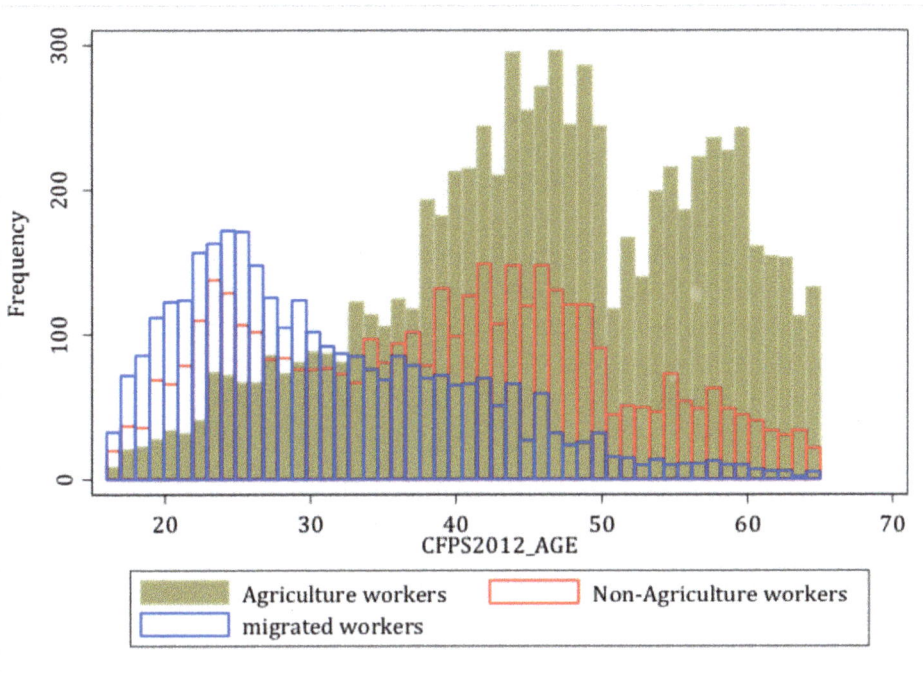

Figure 15.3b Number of Rural *Hukou* Workers as Migrants, Rural Non-Agricultural
Source: Author's calculations from CFPS (ISSS 2012).

First, when these workers were young a large proportion worked in cities. The data from the RUMiC Rural Household Survey indicate that 34 per cent of those who ever migrated have returned to rural villages (Meng 2013). Had there been no discriminatory policy hindering their ability to live in cities with their family they would probably have remained there and built up human capital by accumulating labour market experience. Hence, not only did the restrictions on migration lead directly to the labour shortages, but, if the policy were to change, the current group of migrants in cities would not need to return home as they age and this reduced turnover would significantly increase city labour supplies and the average skill level of migrant workers (Meng 2012).

Second, even if this group of workers not employed in cities is low skilled, they are China's resource endowment. As agricultural productivity increases, these people will need to find other ways to make a living. Thus, economic policies should encourage job creation that matches China's resource allocation. Sadly, currently policy is moving in the opposite direction. I will discuss this in the next section.

Both the NBS aggregated data for 2013 and the CFPS individual-level data suggest at least 50 per cent of the rural *hukou* labour force is still working in the agricultural sector, and another 20 per cent is working in the rural non-agricultural sector. Given the considerable increase in agricultural productivity over past years and the large productivity increases that are likely to come, there is and will increasingly be a significant excess supply of labour in rural areas. Recently, I visited a village in Hubei province during the planting season (a relatively busy season in agriculture) and witnessed a large proportion of individuals spending much of their day sitting around mahjong tables, and was told that such activity is common among adults in the region and beyond. If institutional restrictions and discrimination against migrant workers in the cities can be eliminated many of these idle rural workers who have stayed in rural areas for family reasons, such as looking after children or the elderly, would be able to migrate and stay in the urban labour market and improve labour supply conditions in cities (see Meng 2012).

City labour shortage and wage growth

There is no doubt, however, that employers in Chinese cities have been feeling the squeeze in the labour market for a few years and from their perspective many believe that labour shortages are increasing. Nevertheless, the issue is whether the significant increase in migrants' real wages in recent years indicates a significant tightening of labour market conditions. Table 15.2 presents three different measures of unemployment based on the RUMiC survey to directly measure unemployed resources. Admittedly, due to migrants having limited access to urban unemployment benefits, most migrants who remain in cities are employed and unemployment for migrant workers is generally low. Nevertheless comparisons across different years of unemployment rates can still shed light on whether during high wage-growth years labour market conditions in our survey cities are particularly tight.

The three unemployment measures are generated from the following questions: the first is constructed from a normal 'current labour force status' question; the second is based on whether the respondent worked at least one hour in the previous week; and the third uses a retrospective question on the number of times the respondent was unemployed in the past 12 months. I define a dummy variable equal to 1 if an individual was unemployed at least once in the past 12 months.[6]

Table 15.2 Different Measures of Unemployment Rates by Year (%)

	Unemployment measures		
	Are you currently employed?	Had a paid job last week?	Had at least one episode of unemployment in past 12 months?
	New sample		
2008	1.3	1.3	14.1
2009	1.1	2.1	14.5
2010	1.0	1.6	8.1
2011	0.8	2.2	9.8
2012	0.7	2.0	7.2
2013	0.9	2.2	12.0

Source: Author's calculations based on the survey data.

Table 15.2 shows that the unemployment rate based on the first measure has been very low and only increasing slightly in 2013.[7] The second and third measures of unemployment are somewhat higher and increasing over time for second and only since 2010 for third. In particular, if we examine the proportion of workers unemployed at least once during the past 12 months, the rate is between 7 and 14.5 per cent over this period. The highest unemployment period was during the GFC (2008 and 2009). After the GFC, however, although 2011 and 2013 saw the highest wage increases, the unemployment rates in these years were also the highest, at 9.8 per cent and 12 per cent, respectively.

---

6   The labour force status question asks all individuals to state their current labour force status from among the following 10 choices: 1) working; 2) retired and re-employed; 3) unemployed; 4) retired; 5) house workers; 6) family labour; 7) disabled; 8) at school; 9) waiting for a job; and 10) other. Individuals who are aged sixteen to sixty-five and not in categories 4, 5, 7, 8 and 10 above are defined as being in the labour force. For those who are in the labour force, the unemployed are defined as those who are in category 3 or 9. In addition, the employment module of the survey asks all those in the labour force two questions: 1) Did you work for at least one hour last week for income? 2) If you did not, why? The answer options for the second question are: 1) on vacation; 2) at school; and 3) unemployed. I define those who did not work for at least one hour for income due to unemployment.

7   Note that the total sample in the RUMiC survey includes individuals we followed over the years (labelled 'old-sample'), and those we drew randomly each year (labelled 'new-'sample). The latter sample is more representative for the year. See Meng (2013) for a detailed discussion of the representativeness of the RUMiC sample. Table 15.2 here reports only the measures from the new sample. Results from the total sample are consistent and are available by request from the author.

These results seem to suggest that there is no obvious reduction in unemployment to imply an increased labour shortage in cities and therefore increasing labour shortages may not be able to explain the particular pattern of wage increases over the past six years for rural–urban migrants.

A minimum wage effect?

China issued its first minimum wage regulation in 1993 and by July 1994 it became part of China's Labour Law. As living standards, prices and labour market conditions differ considerably across different regions, provincial and city governments are delegated to set their own minimum wages. The regulation specifies that local governments should do this in accordance with their own minimum living costs, productivity, unemployment, economic development and local average wages. The Minimum Wage Regulation was revised in 2004, and increased the penalty rate for violation from the original 20–100 per cent of the wage owed to 100–500 per cent of the wage owed.[8] According to the country's Twelfth Five-Year Plan, minimum wages are planned to increase by at least 13 per cent through 2015 (Lau and Narayanan 2014).

Among the 15 cities we surveyed, the minimum wage level over the past two decades has tripled (Figure 15.4). At the beginning of the period the minimum wage dispersion across different cities was fairly narrow and after 2005 the dispersion begins to widen, suggesting local government flexibility in setting minimum wages (Wang and Gunderson 2011).

During the past six years, many coastal cities have made the decision to upgrade their industrial structure from labour-intensive to technology and capital-intensive industries. One important policy tool used to achieve this is to significantly increase the minimum wage to make low-skilled labour-intensive firms, which are only marginally profitable, unviable in these cities.

In many developing countries, however, it is difficult to enforce minimum wage laws and, as a result, the minimum wage is often not binding. In the literature, economists often look into the distribution of wages to identify whether the minimum wage law is binding (see, for example, Brown 1999; Alatas and Cameron 2008).

---

8 The new regulation also specifies that subsidies and bonuses are not to be included in the calculation of wages (Frost 2002; Zhao and Zeng 2002; Wang and Gunderson 2011).

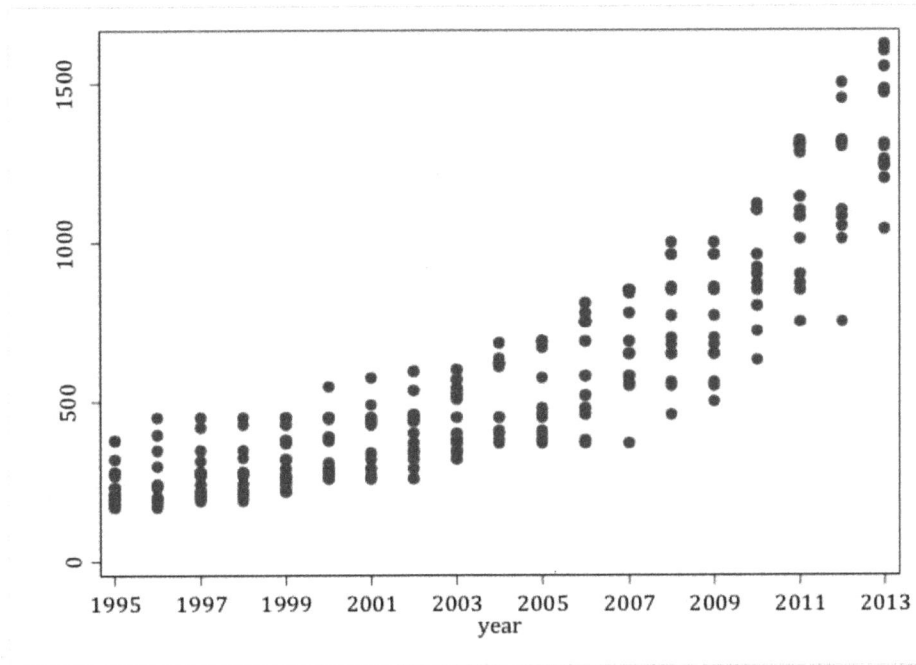

Figure 15.4 Fifteen-City Minimum Wage Changes
Source: Data collected from the official government web site for each of the 15 cities.

Figures 15.5a and 15.5b are presented to examine if the minimum wage law in China is binding. Because the minimum wage for different cities and years is set at a different level, I standardise monthly wages and the first month's pay for the first job using the following formula, which sets the minimum wage at zero for each distribution (Equation 15.1).

Equation 15.1

$$STANDARDIZED\,WAGE_{ijt} = \frac{Wage_{ijt} - Mini\_Wage_{jt}}{SD(Wage)_{jt}}$$

Figure 15.5a plots the minimum wage against the distribution of monthly wages while Figure 15.5b plots the minimum wage against the distribution of the first month's pay for the first job. The latter represents the most unskilled workers, and if the minimum wage is binding it should have the most effect on this group. Indeed, if we compare the two figures it is clear there is a large spike at the minimum wage for the individual's first month's pay from their first job, suggesting the minimum wage is binding for very low-skilled workers. Interestingly, when I separately plot the first month's pay for the first job by coastal and inland cities (Figure 15.6), it seems the spike is more obvious in coastal cities than in inland cities.

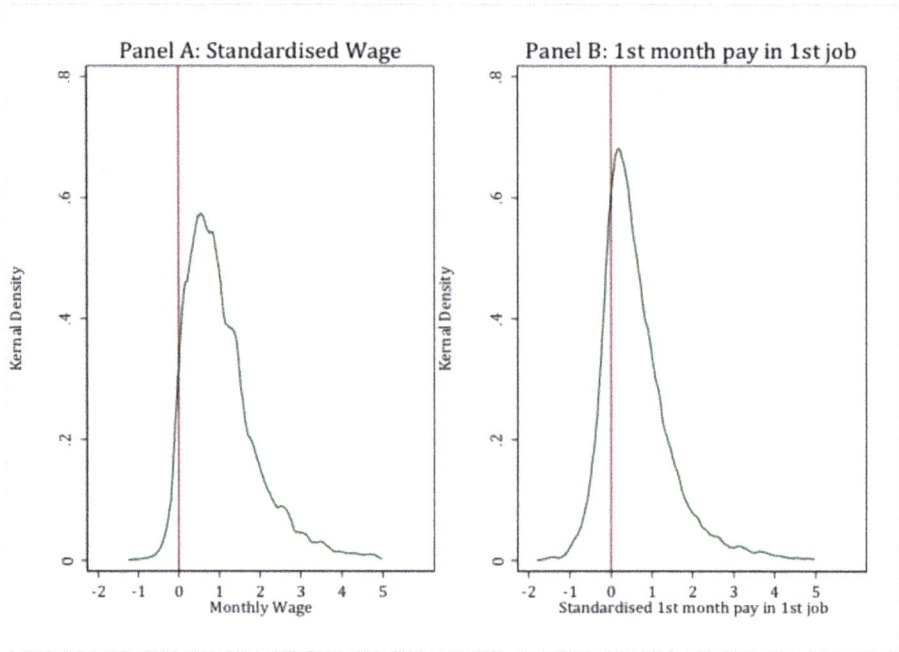

Figure 15.5 Wage Distribution against the Minimum Wage

Source: Author's calculations using RUMiC survey data, 2008–13.

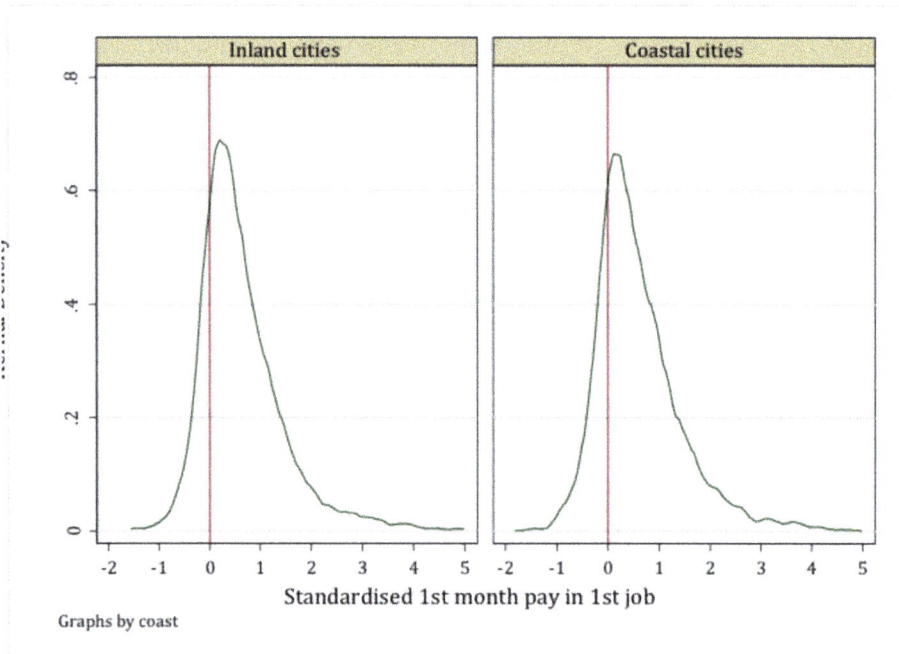

Figure 15.6 Standardised First Month's Pay by Region

Source: Author's calculations based on RUMiC survey data, 2008–13.

A recent study by the Standard Chartered Bank indicated that of 356 firms surveyed in the Pearl River Delta more than 60 per cent identified the minimum wage increase as one reason for continued wage growth in 2013; 10 per cent of these firms indicated that the minimum wage hike had a huge impact on wage levels and another 52 per cent answered that it had some impact and led to them increasing wages more than they initially planned (Lau and Narayanan 2014). This, from another angle, is indicative of a binding minimum wage. The question, however, is the size of the effect of the minimum wage increase and also if the effect is restricted to those earning just below and just above the minimum wage or whether the minimum wage increase has spillover effects further up the earnings distribution chain.

Using the latest RUMiC survey data, I examine these questions. Modifying Neumark et al. (2004) and Stewart (2012), I estimate Equations 15.2 and 15.3.

Equations 15.2 and 15.3

$$lw_{ijt} = \alpha + \beta_k lm_{jt} * \sum_{k=1}^{K} D_k(w_{ijt}, m_{jt}) + \sum_{k=1}^{K} \eta_k D_k(w_{ijt}, m_{jt})$$

$$+ \gamma X_{ijt} + \kappa CPI_{jt} + \delta_j + \theta_t + \sum_{j=1}^{15} \lambda_j T_j + \varepsilon_{ijt}$$

$$\frac{\Delta w_{ij}}{w_{ijt-1}} = \alpha' + \beta_k'(\frac{\Delta m}{m_{jt-1}}) * \sum_{k=1}^{K} D_k(w_{ijt}, m_{jt}) + \sum_{k=1}^{K} \eta_k' D_k(w_{ijt}, m_{jt})$$

$$+ \gamma' X_{ijt} + \kappa' \Delta CPI_{jt} + \delta_j' + \theta_t' + \sum_{j=1}^{15} \lambda_j T_j + e_{ijt}$$

Equation 15.2 uses repeated cross-section data to examine the effect of the current year minimum wage *level* on the *level* of earnings in the current year, while Equation 15.3 examines the effect of the *change* in the minimum wage over two years on the *change* in earnings.

In Equation 15.2, lw_{ijt} refers to the log of monthly earnings for individual i in city j at time t, *while* lm_{jt} is the log of the minimum wage for city j in time t.

$D(.)$ is a vector of seven dummy variables indicating individual i's position in the earnings distribution, relative to the minimum wage. Specifically, the earnings distribution is defined as (insert equation). The first dummy variable includes individuals whose earnings are below or equal to the minimum wage, which happens to coincide with the fifth percentile in the distribution. The second dummy variable equals 1 if the individual's earnings fall between just above the fifth and the tenth percentiles of the distribution. The third dummy covers the second decile. The next two dummies each capture two deciles, while the final dummy variable captures the three highest earnings deciles.

X_{ijt} is a vector of individual-level control variables, including age, its squared term, years of schooling, gender and year since the individual first came to a city. CPI is measured at the provincial level to capture price changes over time; δ_j is the city fixed effect; θ_t captures the year fixed effect; while T_j is a vector of city-specific time trends to eliminate city economic growth trends.

Equation 15.3 has the same specification, except that the dependent variable (monthly wages) and the main independent variable (city-level year-specific minimum wages) are the result of taking first differences.

The two equations capture the minimum wage impact on earnings of individuals at different positions on the wage distribution scale. Theoretically, one would expect that the effects are highest for those whose earnings are closer to the minimum wage, and gradually the effect dissipates as the distance between the minimum wage and individual earnings increases.

Equation 15.2 is estimated using the total sample of employed wage/salary earners. Equation 15.3 is estimated using a smaller sample of individuals for whom we have more than one year's information. Because minimum wages vary only across cities and over years, the standard errors in the regression are clustered at the city-year cell level. The selected results for Equation 15.2 are reported in Column 1 of Table 15.3. In general, the level effect is statistically significant for all groups, but it is strongest for the group which is just above the minimum wage. For individuals in this group, every 10 per cent increase in the minimum wage increases earnings by 9.8 per cent—almost a full spillover. The effect drops to around 5 per cent and stays that way for the next five deciles and then falls further to 3.9 per cent.

Table 15.3 Selected Results from Estimation of Equations 15.2 and 15.3

	Level effect		Change effect
	Full sample	Panel sample	Panel sample
Monthly wage < = minimum wage	0.403* (0.215)	0.407 (0.265)	0.024 (0.174)
Wage at fifth–tenth percentiles	0.977*** (0.288)	1.404*** (0.322)	0.579*** (0.194)
Wage at second decile	0.494** (0.211)	0.703*** (0.212)	0.392** (0.150)
Wage at third decile	0.480** (0.211)	0.671*** (0.205)	0.215 (0.187)
Wage at fourth–fifth deciles	0.500** (0.206)	0.671*** (0.193)	0.185 (0.151)
Wage at sixth–seventh deciles	0.483** (0.205)	0.685*** (0.191)	0.157 (0.188)
Wage > seventh decile	0.387* (0.204)	0.571*** (0.190)	0.135 (0.142)
Observations	28 930	11 306	11 306
R^2	0.861	0.788	0.168

Source: Author's own estimates.

As in any correlation analysis, the critical issue is causality—that is, do the minimum wage increases cause wages to increase or are minimum wage increases a response to increases in average wages? There is no perfect way to address this issue. In my estimation, I try to absorb potential endogenous effects by including city and year fixed effects as well as city-specific time trends. Nevertheless, inevitably, there will be remaining government intended policy changes (time-varying city effects) not controlled for. To further pin down the minimum wage causal effect, Equation 15.3 examines the impact of changes in the minimum wage on the changes in wages at different earnings deciles. These results are reported in Column 3 of Table 15.3. Taking changes (which require panel data) reduces our sample by half. To ascertain that the difference between the two estimations is not due to different samples, I estimated Equation 15.2 using the panel sample (see Column 2 of Table 15.3). The results show that the panel sample increases the estimated results on the minimum wage level effect, but it does not change the pattern of impact across different earnings deciles. The estimated results from Equation 15.3, however, show a significant reduction in the size of the impact. The intra-city changes in minimum wage affect just less than 60 per cent (58 per cent) of the changes in earnings for the fifth to the tenth percentile groups. Further up the earnings distribution ladder, the effect reduces to 38 per cent. And then from the third earnings decile onwards, the effect becomes smaller (between 20 per cent and 13 per cent) and is statistically insignificant.

These results (also presented in Figure 15.7) indicate that the minimum wage regulation has a strong impact on those at the minimum wage (the spike presented in Figure 15.5b) and just above. The effect dissipates somewhat for the level effect beyond the first two earnings deciles, but is still strong throughout the distribution. For the change effect, though, it becomes statistically insignificant after the twentieth percentile.

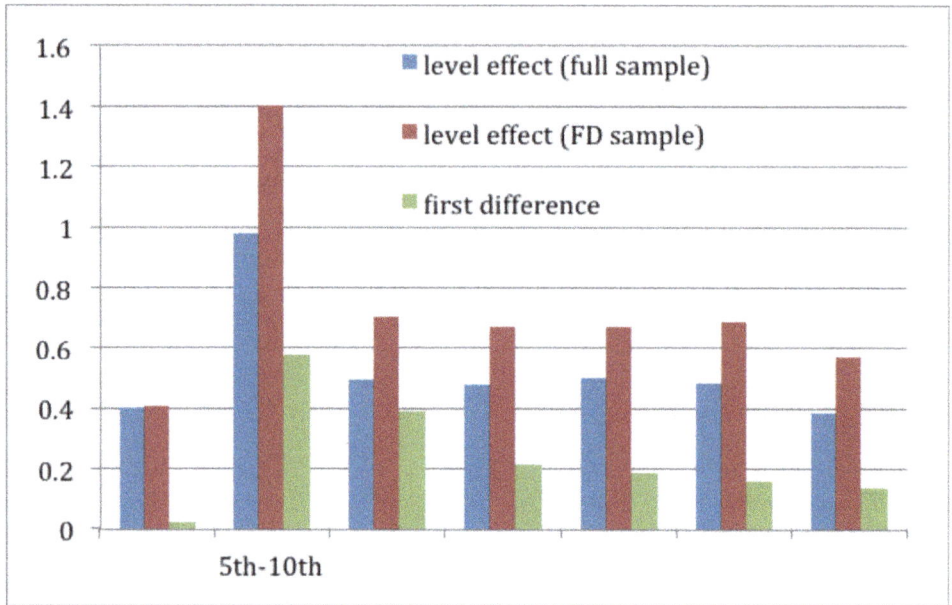

Figure 15.7 Estimated Minimum Wage Effects
Source: Author's estimation results (Table 15.3).

Agricultural subsidy and rural welfare provision

Other possible impacts on the increase in migrant wages are the changes in the agricultural subsidy and the increase in rural welfare provisions. These changes increase the opportunity cost of migration and migrant workers' reservation wages. They can act to slow the flow of rural workers to cities and put upward pressure on migrant wages in the city.

These changes in the agricultural subsidy and rural welfare provision over the past decade were in response to the increase in rural–urban income inequality. In 2004 China abolished the agricultural tax completely. In addition, the rural *hukou* population received increases in various agricultural subsidies. Based on an NBS report (2014), the total cost of subsidies to farm production amounted to more than RMB200 million in 2013, or equivalent to more than RMB360 per agricultural *hukou* worker. In addition, as part of the strategy of making rural areas richer and more livable, social welfare provisions, such as free education, pensions for the sixty-and-over age group and healthcare subsidies are gradually being put in place.

To sum up, many government policies—minimum wage increases, and increases in agricultural subsidies and rural welfare provision—are putting upward pressure on urban wage costs. The factors underlying the real wage increases for unskilled rural workers in cities are the result of many policies that effectively induced shortages of rural migrant labour.

New urbanisation strategy and its potential challenges

Over the past decades rural–urban migration restrictions have come under strong criticism, and reform of the system is inevitable. It is under this pressure that the *National New Urbanisation Plan (2014–2020)* was established (State Council of China 2014). The sad thing is that the original mentality that held that 'farmers should not live in cities' still plays an important role in designing the new urbanisation strategy of the orderly building of small cities and towns. The new idea is that 'farmers should not live in *large* cities'. This new urbanisation strategy may cast long shadows on China's future development path, just as the old rural–urban restrictions shaped China's current development path.

Migration restrictions, industrial upgrading and the change in industrial structure

China's rural–urban divide policy prohibited any rural–urban migration for 30 years starting from the early 1950s. Although economic growth over the past 30 years has led the Government to relax restrictions on rural–urban migration, workers born in rural areas are still treated differently in cities than their urban-born counterparts and rural workers are still regarded as temporary migrants. Because of this discriminatory policy, migrants could not permanently move to cities with their families. This has generated a special feature of rural–urban migration in China—that is, a very high turnover rate, as migrants who come to cities do not stay very long. If a normal working life is supposed to be 35 years, on average migrants stay in cities for less than 10 years, or less than one-third of their working life. When individuals are unable to bring their family with them, they inevitably need to go home to marry, when children are born and during the child-raising and schooling periods. Migrants also need to return home when parents are sick and need to be looked after. These life events should not substantially cut short people's working lives in a normal situation, but they do for migrant workers because they cannot live in the same place as their families. The higher turnover rate reduces the stock of migrant workers in the cities. This is probably the primary cause of China's current labour supply 'shortage' (see Meng 2012).

When the 'shortage' first became evident, the Government did not realise that it was a self-inflicted shortage and consequently did not move to systematically change restrictive migration policies. Instead, it was believed that China had come to the 'turning point' and it was time to upgrade industry and switch towards a high technology–high capital-intensive industrial structure and become a more service-driven economy. To do so, many cities, in particular coastal cities, used the minimum wage policy to actively push out low-tech industries.

This change is evident in the RUMiC data. Over the past six years there has been a significant switch in the industrial structure among RUMiC survey cities. Using the data from RUMiC censuses, conducted in 2007 (before the first wave of the survey) and in 2012,[9] I compare the change in industrial structure among the 15 cities. The first finding is that the total number of migrant workers in our survey cities reduced by 18 per cent. In addition, the proportion of migrants working in manufacturing and construction sectors reduced from 27 per cent to 15 per cent—a 12-percentage point reduction—while the share of those working in service/retail/wholesale trade increased by the same proportion. Figure 15.8 presents these changes for coastal and inland cities. It shows that the construction and manufacturing sectors reduced in both types of cities, but more so in coastal cities.

---

9   To establish a sampling frame for the RUMiC survey, the RUMiC team conducted a census within the randomly selected grids of each of the 15 survey cities. Within each grid, every workplace, including street vendors, was interviewed to inquire about the number of migrant workers employed in the factory/shop/construction site/restaurant/market or on the street (see <https://rse.anu.edu.au/rumici/> for a detailed discussion of the census procedure). We repeated this census procedure at the end of 2012 to make sure our sample continued to be representative.

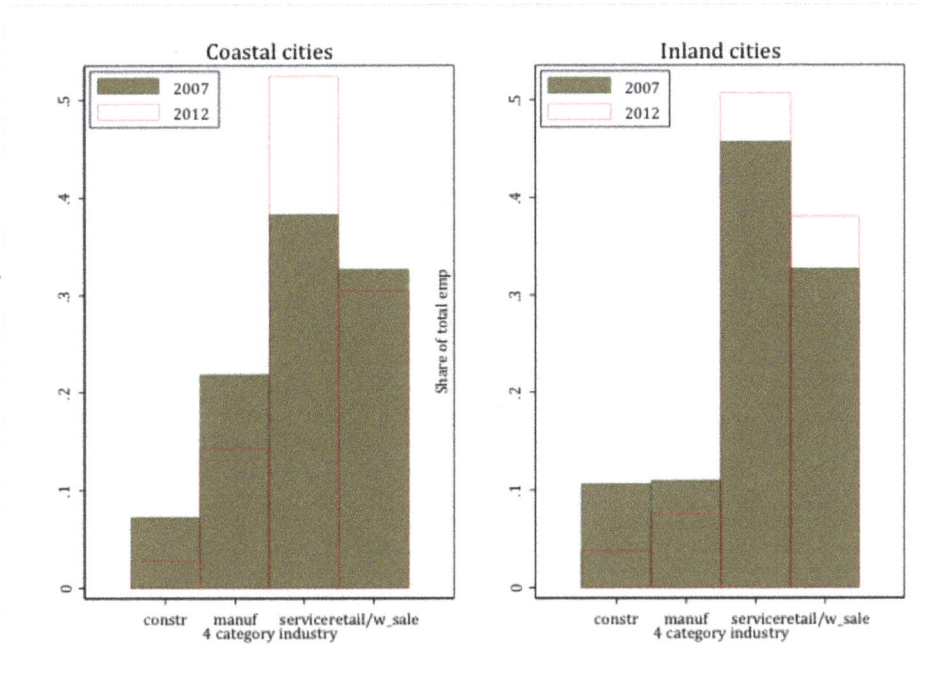

Figure 15.8 Industrial Structural Changes

Source: Author's calculations based on RUMiC survey data, 2008–13.

In addition to the significant reduction of manufacturing employment, we also observe a change in migrant occupations (Table 15.4). Due to differences in occupational coding, I present consistent coding for three survey years: 2008, 2009 and 2013. Over this period, the proportion of migrant workers working as private business owners, professionals and in other white-collar jobs increased from around 10 per cent to 20 per cent, while at the same time the proportion in production work reduced from 27 to 17 per cent. What is more important to note is that the average years of schooling for the private business owners and other white-collar workers are much higher than those for production workers. This change in the occupational distribution among migrant workers may imply an increasing demand for skilled workers rather than unskilled workers. This is consistent with the policy of industrial upgrading.

Table 15.4 Occupation Distribution (2008–13)

	Total sample			New sample		
Occupation distribution	2008	2009	2013	2008	2009	2013
Business owner or white-collar worker:	9.87	10.51	21.84	9.87	9.90	15.45
owner of private business	3.30	1.82	7.11	3.30	1.80	2.96
professional	0.79	0.61	1.96	0.79	0.37	1.42
manager, clerk or officeworker	5.79	8.08	12.77	5.79	7.74	11.07
Retail, wholesale trade	15.95	20.23	25.00	15.95	17.83	13.35
Service sector worker	33.42	35.39	23.21	33.42	38.16	33.00
Production workers	26.61	22.42	16.62	26.61	24.46	21.59
Self-employed	10.93	10.36	11.93	10.93	8.84	16.14
Others	3.21	1.09	1.39	3.21	0.80	0.47
Average education for each occupation:						
Business owner or white-collar worker	9.38	9.74	9.56	9.38	9.84	9.88
Retail, wholesale trade	8.85	8.78	8.44	8.85	9.08	8.96
Service sector worker	8.83	8.73	8.25	8.83	8.78	7.99
Production worker	8.76	8.78	8.60	8.76	8.72	8.34
Self-employed	8.03	8.08	8.28	8.03	8.26	8.08
Others	6.99	6.69	8.06	6.99	7.57	7.36

Source: RUMiC Survey.

There could be three reasons why we observe a reduction in total migrant numbers and a significant reduction in the proportion of migrant workers employed in construction and manufacturing. One possibility is that many of the city factories have been pushed outside our city boundaries. Initial survey boundaries were determined in 2007. To establish a complete sampling frame so that the survey can be representative within each surveyed city, the RUMiC team drove around each city boundary. The boundaries were drawn based on the rule that within 1 km of the boundary there should be no buildings or establishments that could hire migrant workers. We then divided the cities within our boundaries into grids and randomly selected grids in which to conduct the census. In 2009, due to the GFC, many factories were bankrupted and many were moved. To understand this effect, we redrew the boundaries. We found some effect of moving outside the boundary but it was quite small. The 2012 census was based on the new 2009 boundaries. It could be that as many cities have expanded, this boundary effect could be stronger.

The second possibility is that many manufacturing jobs have been pushed to smaller cities and towns, which the RUMiC survey does not cover. China has five tiers of cities: megacities (Beijing, Shanghai, Tianjin and Chongqing), provincial capital cities, prefecture-level cities, county-level cities and rural towns. Among the 15 cities included in our survey, nine belong to the first two tiers and the remainder belongs to the third tier. Based on the *China Statistical Yearbook* data (NBS various years), between 2008 and 2012, the manufacturing share of total non-agricultural employment at the aggregated level reduced from 27.6 per cent to 24.8 per cent—a 2.8 percentage point reduction—whereas the reduction of manufacturing share of the total urban non-agricultural employment was slightly less, at 2.3 percentage points. Because the first measure includes small towns while the second does not, this seems to suggest that even if there is movement of manufacturing factories to small towns, the effect cannot be large.[10]

The third possibility is that due to China's self-inflicted labour shortage in cities and the industrial upgrading policy, many labour-intensive manufacturing firms have moved to other countries where labour costs are much lower.

Given the nature of the available data it is not possible to precisely measure the size of these different effects although it is clear that manufacturing as a proportion of the Chinese economy and low-skilled employment has fallen over this period.

Potential challenges

Labour market myths due to industrial upgrading

As demand for low-skilled workers in medium and large cities falls as a result of industrial upgrading, the main question becomes whether this will bring China to a new equilibrium point with regard to migrant labour supply and demand. Two important issues come to mind: 1) is it true that China has run out of low-skilled labour and hence reducing demand for unskilled labour will resolve the 'shortage' problem; 2) if not, can unskilled workers who remain in the countryside be employed in cities where the industrial upgrading policy has significantly changed the type of workers needed?

My discussion in the 'Labour supply' subsection touched upon the first question. There I stressed that the institutional restrictions on migration and recent policy directions have contributed to the reduction in labour supply to cities. I also showed that more than 50 per cent of rural *hukou* workers are still mainly engaged in the agricultural sector. Does agricultural production require some 283 million workers? The short answer is no. Using RUMiC Rural Household Survey data, Kong et al. (2010) show that individuals mainly

---

10 The reason for the difference between the substantial reduction in manufacturing jobs in our survey cities and that observed from the aggregated data at this stage is unclear.

engaged in agricultural production on average worked 154 days a year in 2009. Using CFPS data, I calculate this figure again for full-time agricultural workers in 2012 and find that on average they were employed for 6.5 months in both busy and non-busy seasons, which amounts to 150 working days.[11] If we assume that a full-time worker should work 300 days a year then half of the 283 million workers who are currently fully engaged in agricultural work could be made more productive if they move out to become employed in the non-agricultural sector.

The above calculation is very conservative because it is likely the future will bring substantial increases in agricultural labour productivity. The village head in the village (Jiaoti) I recently visited in Hubei province told me the village is engaged in negotiation with a farming company that hires 14 people to plant 4000 mu[12] of farmland. Jiaoti village has around 1000 mu of farmland and the net income per mu is currently around RMB1300 per mu per year. The farming company has agreed to rent all the land from Jiaoti village at RMB1300 per mu per year. This seems to be a quite attractive deal for the village. If it is successful, almost all the workers from the village currently engaged in agricultural work (around 300) will be made redundant. According to the village head, many surrounding villages have successfully rented out their land. If the negotiation is successful in Jiaoti village, the remaining farm labourers will have nothing to do in the village.

Can these farmers be employed in cities? Perhaps not in the short to medium runs. Currently, the proportion of individuals aged sixteen to sixty-five not at school and not retired, but not at work, is around 29 per cent among the urban and 27 per cent among the rural *hukou* populations (ISSS 2012). Although the official unemployment rate is not high, the rate of the non-working population is high and may be a reflection of the high rate of discouraged workers. These circumstances would make it more difficult to absorb large numbers of surplus agricultural workers.

In addition, the skill level of the current agricultural workers may not suit the 'upgraded' city jobs. Panel A of Table 15.5 compares the distribution of education levels for those who are currently mainly engaged in agricultural work with those who are engaged in non-agricultural work or have migrated. Just a little more than 60 per cent of the former group has only primary school or below education whereas more than 65 per cent of the latter two groups has junior high school or above education. As indicated earlier, the current industrial upgrading movement in cities has already led to a change in industrial

---

11 Assuming two-thirds of their work period was during the busy season and one-third was during the normal season.
12 'Mu' is the land measurement unit used in China.

structure and an increase in demand for skilled workers. The continuation of this upgrading will worsen the employability of the remaining group of low-skilled agricultural workers.

Table 15.5 Education Distribution of Rural *Hukou* Workers in Different Sectors

	Total sample					
	Agricultural workers		Non-agricultural workers		Migrated workers	
	Frequency	%	Frequency	%	Frequency	%
Illiterate	2818	36.96	870	13.94	124	9.96
Primary school	2022	26.52	1345	21.55	291	23.37
Junior high	2163	28.37	2395	38.38	503	40.4
Senior high	553	7.25	1127	18.06	211	16.95
Three-year college	57	0.75	326	5.22	73	5.86
University	11	0.14	167	2.68	40	3.21
Masters	0	0.00	10	0.16	3	0.24
	Age 30–45					
	Agricultural workers		Non-agricultural workers		Migrated workers	
Illiterate	839	30.42	379	14.98	166	19.51
Primary school	883	32.02	640	25.30	260	30.55
Junior high	867	31.44	991	39.17	307	36.08
Senior high	141	5.11	330	13.04	75	8.81
Three-year college	26	0.94	128	5.06	27	3.17
University	2	0.07	57	2.25	15	1.76
Masters	0	0.00	5	0.20	1	0.12
	Age <30					
	Agricultural workers		Non-agricultural workers		Migrated workers	
Illiterate	106	15.59	53	2.82	54	4.92
Primary school	187	27.50	284	15.11	241	21.95
Junior high	301	44.26	785	41.78	503	45.81
Senior high	64	9.41	488	25.97	205	18.67
Three-year college	16	2.35	167	8.89	65	5.92
University	6	0.88	98	5.22	27	2.46
Masters	0	0.00	4	0.21	3	0.27

Source: Author's own calculations from CFPS (ISSS 2012).

One might argue that those who remain in the agricultural sector are less educated because they are older, and when older workers retire younger rural workers should better fit the demand for relatively high-skilled workers in cities.

But this may not be the case. I compare the education distribution for different age groups (Panels B and C of Table 15.5) for those working in agricultural and those working in non-agricultural sectors. For all age groups the agricultural workers are considerably less educated. So, it seems that the more educated rural *hukou* workers are more likely to be currently engaged in non-agricultural work or have migrated already and the less educated, be they old or young, have remained in agriculture. Thus, time and generational change will not quickly solve the problem. If the industrial upgrading policy continues, the situation will worsen for the less-educated group. In addition, rural education quality has always been poorer than that provided in cities, adding another obstacle to the demand for skilled rural labour.

In sum, the current industrial upgrading policy will not provide favourable labour market conditions for those currently engaged in agricultural work and who soon will be made redundant from the agricultural sector.

Small-city policy and its implications for China's future growth

Can the new urbanisation strategy be a solution? Will moving so many farmers to local towns create enough jobs for them?

In the *National New Urbanisation Plan (2014–2020)*, the words used to describe *hukou* permit access for megacities (five million people and above) are 'strictly restricted'; for large cities (three–five million) the term used is the very vague 'reasonably contained'; for cities with one–three million population, the document states that *hukou* restrictions can be relaxed slightly; for cities with 0.5 to one million population, *hukou* restrictions can be relaxed in an 'orderly' way; while for local towns there will be no restrictions. The intention seems to be to redirect current migrants to medium-sized cities and to reallocate many current farmers to small towns, but no concrete measures or indicative directions are given in the document. For example, it is unclear whether individuals and their families who are already working in megacities or large cities will be able to obtain *hukou* status there or will be redirected to medium or small cities.

The *National New Urbanisation Plan* documents at great length the *hukou* permit restrictions at different levels of cities, but very little is said about where the jobs will come from. In a normal urbanisation process, individuals choose to go to cities where they can survive or thrive, mainly through obtaining jobs, whereas the current plan uses permits for citizenship (*hukou*) to direct people where they can take their families to live with access to city privileges regardless of whether jobs are available. It is unclear whether the central planners are capable of designing such a large-scale social movement given the current less-planned nature of the Chinese economy.

There may be ways to redirect population movement towards medium-sized cities—for example, through building satellite cities near mega and large cities or by moving industries to medium and small cities. But all of these will involve some adjustment cost. Alternatively, using administrative tools, with which Chinese bureaucrats are familiar, may create more labour market tensions. The most important thing for policymakers is to understand the potential costs of each option. The new urbanisation document does not exhibit such understanding.

Moving farmers to local towns could be even more challenging. The main issue once again is when farmers are reallocated, where the jobs will come from. There are many anecdotes of such reallocation, most of which point to a deterioration of local communities and idleness of the workforce. Perhaps if farmers do not give up their rural land rights, having them live day-to-day in local towns will not be a huge problem for the time being, as rent from their land will support them. In the longer run, however, a large group of idle individuals of working age will be problematic. Thus, reallocation needs to be considered together with job opportunities.

In addition to the normal concerns of economic viability of small towns (too far away from the input and output markets, for example), the strategy of reallocating farmers to small towns may have long-term human capital accumulation implications. A recent paper has found that workers change occupation and industry less often in large cities than in small cities (Bleakley and Lin 2012). This is because there are just not enough firms in the same occupation or industry within small cities. As a result, individuals in less population-dense markets cannot be too specialised or they risk not being able to find another job once displaced. Consequently, encouraging the development of small towns in the long run may depress human capital investment.

Conclusions

Economic development paths in all countries are shaped by local institutional constraints. China's special rural–urban divide policies, which restrict rural labour supply to cities, have generated many past and future development challenges. In this chapter, I link a recent labour market phenomenon—namely, strong wage increases for migrant workers—to past and current institutional constraints and policy directions. I then discuss potential challenges for China's future development that will arise in response to the new urbanisation policy.

I reiterated in this chapter that China's urban labour shortage is a policy-induced phenomenon; however, previous misdiagnosis of the problem has led to special policy directions that in turn will generate future labour market friction and development challenges.

References

Alatas, V. and Cameron, L. A. (2008), 'The impact of minimum wages on employment in a low-income country: a quasi-natural experiment in Indonesia', *Industrial and Labor Relations Review* 61(2): 201–23.

Bleakley, H. and Lin, J. (2012), 'Thick-market effects and churning in the labor market: evidence from US cities', *Journal of Urban Economics* 72:87–103.

Brown, C. (1999), 'Minimum wages, employment, and the distribution of income', in O. Ashenfelter and D. Card (eds), *The Handbook of Labor Economics. Volume 3*, pp. 2101–63, Amsterdam: Elsevier.

Frost, S. (2002), 'Labour standards in China: the business and investment challenge', Presented to Association for Sustainable and Responsible Investment in Asia Conference: Labour Standards in China, The Business and Investment Challenge, United Nations University, Tokyo, 28–30 October.

Kong, S. T., Meng, X. and Zhang, D. (2010), 'The global financial crisis and rural–urban migration', in L. Song and W. T. Woo (eds), *China's New Place in a World in Crisis: Economic, Geopolitical and Environmental Dimensions*, Canberra: Asia Pacific Press.

Institute of Social Science Survey (ISSS) (2012), *Chinese Family Panel Studies*, Beijing: Peking University. Available from <http://www.isss.edu.cn/cfps/EN/>.

Lau, K. and Narayanan, C. (2014), 'China—375 clients talk wages in the PRD', in Standard Chartered Bank, *On the Ground*. Available from <https://research.standardchartered.com/configuration/ROW%20 Documents/China_%E2%80%93_375_clients_talk_wages_in_the_ PRD_18_03_14_02_00.pdf>.

Meng, X. (2000), *Labour Market Reform in China*, Cambridge: Cambridge University Press.

Meng, X. (2012), 'Labor market outcomes and reforms in China', *Journal of Economic Perspectives* 26(4): 75–102.

Meng, X. (2013), 'Rural–urban migration', in R. Garnaut, C. Fang and L. Song (eds), *China: A New Model for Growth and Development*, pp. 179–98, Canberra: ANU E Press.

Miller, T. and Gatley, T. (2014), 'Factory workers' fairytale', *China Update* (5 March), Hong Kong & Beijing: Gavekal Dragonomics.

Neumark, D., Schweitzer, M. and Wascher, W. (2004), 'Minimum wage effects throughout the wage distribution', *Journal of Human Resources* 39(2): 425–50.

National Bureau of Statistics (NBS) (2014), *2013 National Economic and Social Development Statistical Report*, Beijing: China Statistics Press.

National Bureau of Statistics (NBS) (various years), *China Statistical Yearbook*, Beijing: China Statistics Press.

State Council of China (2014), *National New Urbanisation Plan (2014–2020)*, Beijing: Xinhua News Agency. Available from <http://politics.people.com.cn/n/2014/0317/c1001-24649809.html>

Stewart, M. B. (2012), 'Wage inequality, minimum wage effects, and spillovers', *Oxford Economic Papers* 64: 616–34.

Wang, J. and Gunderson, M. (2011), 'Minimum wage impacts in China: estimates from a pre-specified research design, 2000–2007', *Contemporary Economic Policy* 29(3): 392–406.

Zhao, X. and Zeng, F. (2002), 'Labour interests have been infringed under minimum wage competition among the regions', *Southern Workers Daily*, 12 July 2002.

16. The Impact of FDI on China's Regional Economic Growth

Chunlai Chen

Introduction

Since late 1978, with the implementation of market-oriented economic reform, inward foreign direct investment (FDI) has been encouraged in China. As a consequence, foreign firms have been attracted by the huge domestic market and pool of relatively well-educated, low-cost labour, which has made China one of the most attractive destinations for FDI in the world. By the end of 2013, China had attracted a total of US$1.4 trillion in FDI inflows, making it the largest FDI recipient in the developing world.

What are the impacts of FDI on China's economic growth? It is expected that FDI brings into a host country a package of capital and firm-specific intangible assets and, as a result, it plays a positive role in the economic development process of a host country (Caves 1996; Dunning 1993; Markusen and Venables 1999; UNCTAD 1999, 2004). In the past three decades of remarkable economic growth, FDI has contributed greatly to China's economy in terms of capital formation, employment creation and export expansion (Chen 2011). The main interest in this chapter is to investigate and identify empirically how FDI has contributed to China's regional economic growth.

Using a panel dataset containing China's 30 provinces[1] over the period 1987–2010, this chapter estimates an augmented growth model in which direct effects (for example, raising output and productivity through capital augmentation and technological progress) and indirect effects (for example, improving productivity and efficiency through spillover effects on the local economy) of FDI on China's regional economic growth are analysed. The chapter first examines the impacts of FDI on China's regional economic growth by using the full sample of China's 30 provinces. Then the chapter examines how the local economic and technological conditions of host provinces influence the extent to which FDI contributes to local economic growth by subdividing China's 30 provinces into different province groups based on their economic and technological conditions.

---

1   Mainland China has 31 provinces. In this study, Tibet is excluded from the empirical regression analysis because of a lack of data on FDI inflows.

The chapter finds that FDI has contributed to China's economic growth directly through capital augmentation and technological progress and indirectly through knowledge spillovers on the local economy. The chapter also finds that the contribution of FDI to economic growth is influenced by local economic and technological conditions. FDI has a stronger impact on economic growth through capital augmentation and technological progress in the developed provinces than in the less-developed provinces. While FDI has a positive and significant impact on economic growth through knowledge spillovers in the developed provinces, the positive knowledge spillovers of FDI on economic growth are absent in the less-developed provinces.

This chapter makes three contributions to the literature on the impacts of FDI on China's economic growth. First, the empirical specifications used in this chapter not only include direct effects of FDI, but also enable us to examine the spillover effects of FDI on China's regional economic growth. Second, by subdividing provinces into different groups in the estimations we can examine empirically how provincial differences in economic and technological conditions affect the extent to which the spillover effects of FDI contribute to provincial economic growth. Third, this chapter extends the period of the panel dataset to 2010, which is the most recent period in existing studies.

The structure of the chapter is as follows. The next section discusses the theoretical explanations of how FDI contributes to developing host countries' economic growth and presents a brief literature review on how the economic and technological conditions of a recipient economy influence the extent to which FDI contributes to economic growth. The third section sets out the framework of analysis and specifies the empirical model. The fourth section describes the variables and the data. The fifth section presents the results from the regressions and explains the estimation results. The final section provides the conclusion and policy implications.

FDI and economic growth: theory and literature

The role of FDI in economic growth has different explanations under different growth models. In the neoclassical growth models, which emphasise technological progress, the long-run growth can only be achieved by technological progress that is considered to be exogenous. Therefore, FDI as a source of capital input would only affect output growth in the short run. In the long run, under the conventional assumption of diminishing returns to capital inputs with a given technology, FDI would have no permanent impact on output growth. FDI, however, brings into the host country a package of not only capital, but also technology, production knowhow and management skills (Caves 1996; Dunning 1977, 1993), which are exogenous to the developing countries. Therefore, under the interpretation of the neoclassical growth models, a positive relationship between FDI and long-run economic growth in developing countries should be expected. In the new growth models, which emphasise the role of science and technology, human capital and externalities in economic development, FDI is treated as one of the factor inputs along with labour and domestic capital and is expected to promote growth in the long run.

To understand how FDI contributes to developing countries' economic growth, it is necessary to compare the different roles of FDI and domestic investment in the economic growth process. Domestic investment is a necessary condition for production growth and technical progress, but it may not enable a developing economy to take advantage of advanced technologies available in the developed world. FDI is different from domestic investment in three important aspects although both can be treated as a basic physical input in the production process.

First, FDI accelerates the speed of adoption of general-purpose technologies in the host countries. The general-purpose technologies are technological inventions that affect the entire system in the global economy. The most recent examples of general-purpose technologies include the computer, Internet and mobile phone. Each general-purpose technology is capable of raising the aggregate productivity of labour and capital, but it takes a considerable amount of time for all countries, especially developing countries, to explore its potential. The developed countries tend to be frontrunners in the adoption of general-purpose technologies and their experiences can be diffused through the developing economies through FDI (Yao and Wei 2007).

Second, according to Dunning's 'ownership–location–internalisation' (OLI) explanation for FDI (Dunning 1977, 1993), for multinational enterprises (MNEs) to have a strong motive to undertake direct investment aboard, they must possess certain ownership advantages. It could be a product or production process, like a patent or blueprint. It could also be some specific intangible asset or capability, like technology and information; managerial, marketing and entrepreneurial skills; organisational systems; or access to intermediate or final goods markets. The ownership advantage confers some valuable market power or cost advantage on the firm sufficient to outweigh the disadvantages of doing business abroad. In addition, MNEs must have an advantage of internalising business activities, and at the same time, the foreign market must offer a location advantage that makes it profitable to produce the product in the foreign country rather than simply produce it at home and export it to the foreign market. Therefore, FDI is embedded with new technologies, knowhow, management skills and other intangible proprietary assets and information unavailable in the host countries. Such advanced technologies will be able to shift the host country's production frontier to a new level so that the same amount of material inputs can lead to a higher level of output.

Third, the ability of MNEs to combine the three advantages implies that they should be able to outperform indigenous firms in production. FDI may generate positive spillovers to host countries' economic growth through three channels. First, FDI can generate horizontal positive spillovers to domestic firms in improving productivity through demonstration effect and competition, which may improve host countries' total factor productivity (TFP). Second, FDI can generate vertical positive spillovers by strengthening domestic industrial linkages through the client and supplier networks, which will improve the productivity of domestic firms in the upstream and downstream industries. Third, FDI can generate positive spillovers through passing information to host countries about international markets, best business practice and the advancement of global technological innovation, thus facilitating host countries to adjust to the changes in the world economy, increasing the competitiveness of domestic firms in global markets. Therefore, through the knowledge spillovers such as learning by doing or learning by watching (demonstration effects), research and development (R&D), human resource movement, training courses, vertical industrial linkages, technical assistance and exposure to fierce competition, FDI can generate spillovers to improve the productivity and efficiency of local firms, thus shifting the production frontier of a host country.

The role of FDI in economic growth has been extensively studied in the literature. In the case of China, for example, Chen et al. (1995) find that FDI has been positively associated with economic growth and the increase of total fixed investment in China. Dees (1998) finds evidence supporting the view that FDI affects China's growth through the diffusion of knowledge and ideas. More recently, Vu et al. (2008), using sectoral FDI inflow data, evaluate the sector-specific impact of FDI on growth in China. The study finds that FDI has a statistically significant positive effect on economic growth, operating both directly and through its interaction with labour. The study also finds that the effects seem to be very different across economic sectors, with most of the beneficial impact concentrated in manufacturing industries. Tang et al. (2008) investigate the causal link between FDI, domestic investment and economic growth for the period 1988 to 2003. They find that FDI complements rather than crowding out domestic investment. As a result, FDI has not only assisted in overcoming shortage of capital, it has also stimulated economic growth through complementing domestic investment in China. Tuan et al. (2009) investigate the role inward FDI plays in the process of regional development and the channels through which economic growth would be affected by using city-level (cities in the Yangtze River Delta and the Pearl River Delta) panel dataset estimations for the period since China's economic opening and reform. While the study finds that FDI exerted spillover effects and affected TFP growth of the recipients, major technology and knowledge-related factors including R&D and human capital also played critical roles in TFP enhancement and regional growth. Whalley and Xin (2010) investigate the contribution of inward FDI to China's recent rapid economic growth using a two-stage growth accounting approach. After decomposing the Chinese economy into FDI and non-FDI sectors, the study's results indicate that China's foreign-invested enterprises may have contributed more than 40 per cent of China's economic growth in 2003 and 2004, and without this inward FDI, China's overall GDP growth rate could have been around 3.4 percentage points lower.

While empirical studies have found positive effects of inward FDI on host countries' economic growth, they also reveal that the strength of the positive effects of FDI on host countries' economic growth is dependent on the economic and technological conditions in host countries. For example, in an evaluation of the impact of FDI-induced technological change on growth in developing countries, Blomstrom et al. (1992) find that the positive and statistically significant impact of FDI is stronger the higher is the level of economic development in a host country. Borensztein et al. (1998) highlight the twin roles of the introduction of advanced technology and the degree of absorptive capability in the host country as determinants of economic growth. They find that FDI is more productive than domestic investment only when the host country has a minimum threshold stock of human capital. De Mello (1997) argues that an increase in the productivity of FDI can only be achieved if there is already a sufficiently high level of human capital in a recipient economy. In an investigation of the impact of FDI on local TFP, de Mello (1999) finds that FDI exerted a positive impact on TFP only for technological leaders, while a negative relationship arose between FDI and TFP for technological followers.

In the case of China, Wei (1996) finds statistical evidence that FDI is positively associated with cross-city differences in growth rates. In a study investigating provincial economic differences and the FDI–growth relationship in China, Buckley et al. (2002) find that the growth-promoting effects of FDI are evident in the developed rather than in the less-developed provinces and that the full benefits of FDI are realised when competition in local markets is at its strongest. Yao and Wei (2007) find that FDI has a positive and significant impact on China's economic growth both as a mover of production efficiency and as a shifter of the production frontier, and the positive impact of FDI on economic growth is larger in the east than in the central and western regions. Chen (2013), using a panel dataset containing 30 Chinese provinces over the period 1987–2005, finds that FDI has contributed to China's economic growth; however, the contribution is influenced by local economic and technological conditions. FDI has a stronger impact on economic growth through capital augmentation and technological progress in the eastern developed provinces than in the central and western, less-developed provinces. While FDI has a positive and significant impact on economic growth through knowledge spillovers in the eastern developed provinces, knowledge spillovers of FDI on economic growth are absent in the central and western, less-developed provinces.

The above findings provide empirical evidence and support that FDI brings into the host countries a package of resources that promotes economic growth. The findings also suggest that the way in which FDI affects economic growth depends on the economic and technological conditions in a host country. In other words, the economic and technological conditions of a recipient economy influence the extent to which FDI contributes to growth.

Systematic analysis on the mechanism through which FDI contributes to the economic growth process of a developing economy has not however, been well established and studied. In China, most previous studies only investigated the direct impact of FDI as a capital input to China's economic growth; the roles of FDI on economic growth from technological progress and spillover effects are overlooked. Although a few studies examined the spillover effects of FDI on economic growth, they failed to investigate the roles of FDI on economic growth through capital augmentation and technological progress. In addition, in the studies of the role of FDI on China's regional economic growth, most grouped the provinces and regions based on geographical location and administrative division, which overlooked the differences in economic and technological conditions between provinces. China is a large country with enormous contrasts in geographical and natural conditions between provinces, and also substantial differences in the degree of economic and technological development across provinces are manifested in per capita income, human capital, R&D capability and the level of infrastructure. These differences between provinces may influence the extent to which FDI contributes to local economic growth.

Therefore, in this chapter we would like to examine empirically the role of FDI on China's economic growth from three channels—capital augmentation, technological progress and spillover effects—with a particular emphasis on how the impact of FDI, especially the spillover effects of FDI, on economic growth are affected by regional differences in China at the provincial level.

Analytical framework and the empirical model

We estimate the impact of FDI on China's provincial economic growth by specifying an aggregate production function as follows (Equation 16.1).

Equation 16.1

$$Y_{it} = A_{it} L_{it}^{\beta_1} DK_{it}^{\beta_2} FK_{it}^{\beta_3}$$

In Equation 16.1, Y_{it} is the real gross domestic product (GDP) of province i in year t; A_{it} is the TFP level of province i in year t; L_{it} is the total labour input of province i in year t; DK_{it} is the domestic capital stock of province i in year t; and FK_{it} is the foreign capital stock of province i in year t.

In this specification, FDI is treated as a separate factor of capital input (FK) along with domestic capital input (DK) and labour input (L) in the aggregate production function.

Theoretically, because FDI brings into the host country a package of capital, technology, production knowhow, management skills, marketing skills and information, competition and so on (Caves 1996; Dunning 1993), it is expected that FDI can increase the host country's economic growth by a number of means.

First, the inflows of FDI will increase demand for labour and create employment in a host country, especially in developing countries. The increase in employment will contribute to an increase in total output, thus leading to a movement of output to a higher level along the existing production function. This positive effect of FDI on output growth is the contribution of FDI through employment creation, which can be expressed as $\partial Y / \partial L_{FK} > 0$, implying that the higher the employment created by FDI, the higher is the output growth of a host economy.

Second, the inflows of FDI increase a host country's fixed capital formation. Through capital augmentation in a recipient economy, FDI is expected to be growth enhancing by encouraging the incorporation of new inputs and technologies into the production function, thus shifting the production function of a host country. This positive shifting effect of FDI is the contribution of FDI as a capital input to output growth, which can be expressed as $\partial Y / \partial FK > 0$, implying that the higher the foreign capital input, the higher is the output growth of the host economy.

Third, FDI is believed to be a leading source of technology transfer and human capital augmentation in developing countries. Technological progress takes place through a process of capital deepening in the form of the introduction of new varieties of knowledge-based capital goods. It also proceeds via specific productivity-increasing labour training and skill acquisition promoted by MNEs. Therefore, FDI is expected to shift the production function of a host country over time as a result of technological progress. This positive shifting effect of FDI is the contribution of technology progress to output growth, which can be expressed as $\partial Y/\partial FK = f(t) > 0$, implying that the marginal product of foreign capital is an increasing function of time.

Fourth, through the knowledge spillovers such as learning by doing or learning by watching (demonstration effects), R&D, human resource movement, training courses, vertical industrial linkages, technical assistance and exposure to fierce competition, FDI is expected to increase the productivity and efficiency of the local firms of a host country. As a result, through knowledge spillovers, FDI can shift the production function of a host economy to a higher level. This positive shifting effect of FDI is the spillover effect on the local economy, which can be expressed as $\partial Y/\partial SFK > 0$, implying that the higher the presence of FDI, the higher are the spillover effects of FDI on local economic growth.

With the above propositions, the TFP, A_{it}, can be defined as Equation 16.2.

Equation 16.2

$$A_{it} = B_{it}e^{g(t,t*FK_{it},SFK_{it},Z)}$$

In Equation 16.2, A_{it} is the TFP level of province i in year t; B_{it} is the residual TFP level of province i in year t; t is a time trend, which captures the Hicks-neutral technological progress in province i in the absence of FDI or foreign technology; $t*FK_{it}$ captures the additional technological progress that is attributed only to FDI; SFK_{it} is the presence of FDI in province i in year t, which captures the spillover effects of FDI; Z is a set of other variables that can also improve productivity. One such variable is human capital (HK). It has been suggested in recent growth models as a determinant of growth (for example, Barro and Sala-i-Martin 1995; Levin and Raut 1997). In particular, these models predict a positive impact of human capital on economic growth.

Incorporating Equation 16.2 into the aggregate production function Equation 16.1, by taking the natural logarithm of the variables of labour (L), domestic capital (DK) and foreign capital (FK) in the production function, adding the variable of human capital (HK) to control the impact of human capital, and rearranging the items on the right-hand side, with the addition of a constant term (β_0) and an error term (ε_{it}), we obtain the empirical regression Equation 16.3.

Equation 16.3

$$LnY_{it} = \beta_0 + \beta_1 LnL_{it} + \beta_2 LnDK_{it} + \beta_3 LnFK_{it} + \beta_4 t + \beta_5 t*LnFK_{it} + \beta_6 SFK_{it-1} + \beta_7 HK_{it} + \varepsilon_{it}$$

In Equation 16.3, i (i = 1, 2, ..., 30) and t (t = 1987, ..., 2010) denote province i and year t; L and DK are labour and domestic capital stock;[2] FK is foreign capital stock, which captures the contribution of FDI to economic growth through capital augmentation; t is a time trend, which captures the Hicks-neutral technological progress in the absence of FDI or foreign technology; the interaction term t*LnFK captures the additional technological progress to economic growth that is attributed only to FDI; SFK is the presence of FDI (share of foreign capital stock to total capital stock), which captures the spillover effects of FDI to economic growth through improving the productivity and efficiency of the local economy; and HK is human capital.

This empirical model allows us to test the impact of FDI on China's provincial economic growth in three respects. First, we can test the direct contribution of FDI to provincial economic growth. If the coefficient β_3 is positive and statistically significant then FDI has directly contributed to provincial economic growth through capital input. Second, we can test the effect of technological progress of FDI on provincial economic growth. If the coefficient β_5 is positive and statistically significant then there is evidence that FDI has contributed to provincial economic growth through technological progress. Third, we can test the spillover effects of FDI on provincial economic growth. If the coefficient β_6 is positive and statistically significant then there is evidence that FDI has generated positive spillover effects—for example, diffusion of technology and management skills to the local economy, thus promoting provincial economic growth.

Equation 16.3 is the form of an augmented production function model that we will use to estimate the impact of FDI on China's provincial economic growth. The first part of the analysis is to examine the role of FDI on provincial economic growth through the three channels of capital augmentation, technological progress and spillover effects by using the full sample of China's 30 provinces. The second part of the analysis is to examine the impact of FDI on the economic growth of different provincial groups by using the sub-samples of province groups based on their economic and technological conditions in order to investigate whether local economic and technological conditions influence the extent to which FDI contributes to local economic growth. The following section will describe the variables and the data.

---

2   Official data for labour employed by FDI at the provincial level are not available. So, the total number of labour of each province is used in the regression.

Variable specification and the data

The data for provincial gross domestic product (Y) and provincial total capital stock are from Wu (2009).[3] Wu uses the conventional perpetual inventory method by employing the recently released national accounts figures to derive a capital stock series for China's 31 provinces and three economic sectors (that is, agriculture, manufacturing and services) for the period 1977–2010. This is one of the most comprehensive datasets of capital stock series for China's 31 provinces and three economic sectors.

The data for FDI stock (FK) are calculated in several steps. First, the US dollar value of annual FDI inflows is converted into renminbi value by using the annual average official exchange rate. Second, the renminbi value of annual FDI inflows is deflated into the real value at 1978 prices by using China's national consumer price index (CPI). Third, a 5 per cent depreciation rate is assumed for foreign capital (FDI). Finally, FDI stock is accumulated for each year end measured as billion renminbi at 1978 prices. The hypothesis is that provinces with a larger FDI stock will have higher expansion in production and higher technological progress over time, thus shifting the production frontier and accelerating provincial economic growth.

The domestic capital stock (DK) of each province is obtained by deducting the FDI stock (FK) from the total capital stock. Labour (L) is the total number of employed persons in each province measured as one million persons.

The presence of FDI is measured as the share of FDI stock in the total capital stock of a province (SFK) to capture the spillover effects of FDI on local economic growth. It is reasonable to assume that FDI inflows and spillover effects from FDI have a time lag, so the value of a one-year lag of SFK is used in the model. The use of the lagged value of SFK also can avoid the endogeneity problem in the regression. The hypothesis is that provinces with a higher share of FDI stock in total capital stock will have higher spillover effects from FDI to the local economy, thus increasing the productivity and efficiency of local firms and promoting provincial economic growth.

In this chapter human capital (HK) is measured as the ratio of the number of university students to the total population of each province. We expect the human capital to be positively related to the economic growth of the host province. The dependent and independent variables and the data sources are summarised in Table 16.1.

---

3 Data for 2007–10 are provided by Wu (2009).

Table 16.1 Variables of the Impact of FDI on China's Provincial Economic Growth

Variable name	Specification of variables	Sources
Dependent variable		
Y_{it}	Gross domestic product of province i in year t. Billion RMB at 1978 prices.	Wu (2009) and *China Statistical Yearbook* (NBS various years).
Independent variables		
L_{it}	Total number of employed persons of province i in year t. Million persons.	*China Statistical Yearbook* (NBS various years).
DK_{it}	Domestic capital stock of province i in year t. Billion RMB at 1978 prices.	Calculated from Wu (2009) and various issues of *China Statistical Yearbook* (NBS various years).
FK_{it}	FDI stock of province i in year t. Billion RMB at 1978 prices.	Calculated from various issues of *China Statistical Yearbook* (NBS various years) and the *Annual National Economic Report* (NBS various years) of each province.
SFK_{it-1}	Share of FDI stock in total capital stock of province i in year t–1. Per cent.	Same as above.
HK_{it}	Human capital of province i in year t measured as the ratio of the number of university students to total population. Per cent.	Same as above.

Source: Author's own description.

Regression results and explanations

The impact of FDI on economic growth: all provinces

The data used in the regression are a panel dataset at the provincial level, containing China's 30 provinces over the period 1987 to 2010.[4] We first conduct a Hausman test to choose between the random-effects model and the fixed-effects model for the regression. The Hausman test prefers the fixed-effects model. Therefore, we estimate Equation 16.3 under the fixed-effects model in order to eliminate the province-specific and time-invariant factors that may affect economic growth. For a robustness check, we also report the regression results under the random-effects model. The two models performed very well. All of the independent variables have the expected signs and are statistically significant at

---

4 Tibet is excluded from the sample because of a lack of data.

the 1 per cent level (except the variable of LnFK, which is statistically significant at the 10 per cent level in the fixed-effects model), and the models have high explanatory power. The regression results are reported in Table 16.2.

The regression results show that labour input (L) and domestic capital stock (DK) are positive and statistically significant at the 1 per cent level, indicating the significant contributions of labour and domestic capital inputs to provincial economic growth.

For the variables of our main interest—LnFK, t*LnFK and SFK—the coefficients are positive and statistically significant in both regressions. These results provide strong support for the propositions discussed in section three.

Table 16.2 Regression Results of Production Function of All Provinces, 1987–2010

Variables	Fixed-effects model	Random-effects model
Constant	0.8392 (5.94)***	−0.0386 (−0.36)
LnL	0.2665 (7.03)***	0.4600 (17.60)***
LnDK	0.3456 (15.75)***	0.4407 (20.13)***
LnFK	0.0098 (1.82)*	0.0235 (4.16)***
T	0.0539 (20.85)***	0.0376 (16.46)***
T*LnFK	0.0022 (6.59)***	0.0013 (3.74)***
SFK	0.0163 (9.01)***	0.0199 (10.31)***
HK	0.0574 (4.16)***	0.0974 (6.79)***
No. of observations	710	710
No. of groups	30	30
R^2 overall	0.90	0.96
	F-statistics = 11665***	Wald chi2 = 70050***

* Statistically significant at 0.10 level (two-tail test).

** Statistically significant at 0.05 level (two-tail test).

*** Statistically significant at 0.01 level (two-tail test).

Source: Author's own estimations.

Note: t-statistics are in parentheses.

First, the variable of foreign capital stock (LnFK) is positive and statistically significant at the 10 per cent level in the fixed-effects model and at the 1 per cent level in the random-effects model, which provides support that FDI as a factor of capital input directly contributes to provincial economic growth. The estimation results imply that provinces with higher FDI inflows will have higher economic growth contributed directly by the increase in foreign capital input.

Second, the interaction term of a time trend and the FDI stock (t*LnFK) is positive and statistically significant at the 1 per cent level in both regressions, which supports the proposition that FDI shifts the domestic production frontier through technological progress. The regression results show that over time, FDI helps the domestic economy to move continuously onto a higher steady-state technology. This change in the domestic production frontier caused by FDI is an additional enforcement of the Hicks-neutral technological progress represented by the coefficient on a time trend (t), which is positive and statistically significant at the 1 per cent level in both regressions.

Third, the variable of the spillover effects of FDI—the share of FDI stock in total capital stock (SFK)—is positive and statistically significant at the 1 per cent level in both regressions. This is consistent with the hypothesis that FDI has positive spillover effects on provincial economic growth through improving the productivity and efficiency of the local economy. Thus, the regression results have provided strong empirical evidence to support the hypothesis that FDI inflows into China together with a package of knowledge-based firm-specific assets have produced positive spillover effects on China's provincial economic growth. The estimation results imply that provinces with a higher share of FDI stock in total capital stock will have higher spillover effects from FDI to the local economy, thus improving the productivity and efficiency of the local economy and raising provincial economic growth.

Finally, the variable of human capital (HK) is positive and statistically significant at the 1 per cent level in both models, which provides empirical evidence that human capital contributes to economic growth.

The impact of FDI on economic growth: by region

China is a large country with enormous contrasts in geographical and natural conditions between provinces, and also substantial differences in the degree of economic and technological development in terms of per capita income, human capital and R&D capability, and the level of infrastructure across provinces. While an overall positive impact of FDI on economic growth is revealed in the above empirical analysis, the large disparity in economic and technological conditions across provinces could mean that the impact of FDI on economic growth is different between regions. To investigate the impact of regional differences on the role of FDI in economic growth, we subdivide the full sample of 30 provinces into three pairs of mutually exclusive groups based on their economic, technological and infrastructure conditions—namely: 1) the high and low economic development province groups; 2) the high and low human capital and R&D capability province groups; and 3) the high and low level of infrastructure province groups.

The economic development level is a comprehensive economic and social indicator of a province. A higher economic development level not only indicates good overall economic performance but also implies higher productivity associated with higher labour quality, higher research and innovation capability, advanced technology and better conditions of local infrastructure. In this chapter, we use per capita GDP as a proxy for the provincial economic development level. Provinces with per capita GDP above the national average are classified as the high-income provinces; otherwise they are classified as the low-income provinces. We expect that FDI will have a higher impact on economic growth in the high-income provinces than in the low-income provinces.

Studies of FDI and economic growth postulate a positive link between FDI and human capital and R&D capability, since the application of the advanced technology embodied in FDI requires a sufficient level of human capital and R&D capability in host countries. Therefore, the level of human capital and R&D capability not only indicates the ability of scientific and technological innovation and progress of an economy, but also reveals the absorptive capability of the host economy. We assume that economies with a higher level of human capital and R&D capability will find it much easier to absorb advanced technology and management skills from MNEs and will facilitate and enhance the diffusion of spillovers from FDI to the local economy, thus increasing economic growth. In this chapter human capital is measured as the ratio of the number of university students to the total population of each province, and the number of patent applications per 10 000 persons is used as a proxy for the level of R&D capability of host provinces. Provinces are classified as high human capital and R&D capability provinces if the ratio of the number of university students to the total population and the number of patent applications per 10 000 persons are above the national average; otherwise they are classified as low human capital and R&D capability provinces. We expect the impact of FDI, in particular the spillover effects of FDI, on economic growth will be stronger in the high human capital and R&D capability provinces than in the low human capital and R&D capability provinces.

The level of infrastructure in each province might be another important factor influencing the impact of FDI on local economic growth. We assume that better infrastructure not only is essential for FDI to be more productive but also can facilitate the diffusion of spillovers from FDI to the local economy. In this chapter two measures are used as the proxy of the level of infrastructure of a host province. One is the intensity of transport infrastructure and another is the level of telecommunications. The measure of the intensity of transport infrastructure is the ratio of the sum of the length of highways, railways and interior transport waterways divided by the size of the corresponding host province. The unit of the intensity of transport infrastructure is kilometres per 100 sq km of the host province's land area. The measure of the level of telecommunications is the number of telephone sets per 100 persons in each province. Provinces are classified as high-level infrastructure provinces if the intensity of transport infrastructure and the number of telephone sets per 100 persons are above the national average; otherwise they are classified as low-level infrastructure provinces. We expect that provinces with a high level of infrastructure will facilitate the diffusion of spillovers from FDI to the local economy.

For simplicity, we call the provinces with high per capita GDP, high-level human capital and R&D capability, and high-level infrastructure the developed province groups, while the provinces with low per capita GDP, low-level human capital and R&D capability, and low-level infrastructure the less-developed province groups. Table 16.3 presents the average value of the basic economic development indicators discussed above. From the table we can see there are large differences between the developed provinces and the less-developed provinces in terms of per capita GDP, human capital and R&D capability, and infrastructure conditions. These provincial differences are expected to play important roles in influencing the impact of FDI on provincial economic growth.

Table 16.3 Basic Economic Development Indicators by Province Groups (year 2010)

Basic economic development indicators	National average	Average of the developed province groups	Average of the less-developed province groups
Per capita GDP (RMB/person) (2000 = 100)	26 525	41 873	19 172
Human capital (university students/population) (%)	1.72	2.08	1.48
Level of R&D (patent applications/10 000 persons)	4.88	9.90	1.54
Transportation intensity index (km per 100 sq km)	93	141	69
Level of telecommunications (phone sets/100 persons)	89	113	77

Sources: Calculated from *China Statistical Yearbook* (NBS various years).

We also use Equation 16.3 to conduct the empirical analysis. To eliminate the province-specific and time-invariant factors that may affect economic growth, we run the regressions under a fixed-effects model with panel data. The fixed-effects regression results for the three pairs of province groups are reported in Table 16.4.

The regression results reveal a number of interesting findings. First, the variable of LnFK is positive and statistically significant at the 1 and 5 per cent levels in all regressions, which signifies the significant contribution of FDI to economic growth through capital augmentation.

Second, the variable of t*LnFK is positive and statistically significant at the 1 and 5 per cent levels in all regressions. This implies that FDI shifts the domestic production frontier through technological progress over time.

Third, the variable of SFK is positive and statistically significant at the 1 per cent level for the developed province groups, but is negative for the less-developed province groups. This implies that local economic and technological conditions affect the diffusion of knowledge spillovers from FDI to the local economy. This finding is consistent with those of Borensztein et al. (1998), de Mello (1997, 1999) and Tuan et al. (2009).

Table 16.4 Regression Results of Production Function by Province Groups, 1987–2010 (fixed-effects model)

Variables	Per capita GDP		HK and R&D capability		Level of infrastructure	
	High	Low	High	Low	High	Low
Constant	1.0845 (4.32)***	1.2635 (7.00)***	1.4476 (6.21)***	1.0038 (5.69)***	2.0092 (8.67)***	1.0837 (5.82)***
LnL	0.3352 (5.52)***	0.1286 (2.36)**	0.3787 (7.03)***	−0.0345 (−0.62)	0.2515 (4.70)***	0.0460 (0.82)
LnDK	0.2996 (7.39)***	0.3095 (9.56)***	0.2056 (5.58)***	0.4863 (15.80)***	0.1422 (3.91)***	0.4250 (13.70)***
LnFK	0.0321 (2.40)**	0.0215 (3.57)***	0.0284 (2.47)**	0.0371 (6.06)***	0.0469 (4.06)***	0.0329 (5.33)***
T	0.0548 (11.53)***	0.0574 (16.47)***	0.0518 (11.29)***	0.0395 (11.64)***	0.0613 (13.73)***	0.0462 (13.47)***
T*LnFK	0.0027 (3.46)***	0.0020 (4.52)***	0.0051 (6.43)***	0.0010 (2.23)**	0.0052 (6.74)***	0.0015 (3.15)***
SFK	0.0131 (4.53)***	−0.0081 (−1.42)	0.0145 (5.74)***	−0.0014 (−0.24)	0.0097 (4.00)***	−0.0165 (−3.12)***
HK	0.0367 (1.70)*	0.0751 (4.10)***	0.0357 (1.91)**	0.0948 (4.82)***	0.0196 (1.08)	0.0726 (3.71)**
No. of observations	264	446	278	432	230	480
No. of groups	11	19	12	18	10	20
R^2 overall	0.91	0.84	0.89	0.82	0.82	0.84
F-statistics	3474***	10100***	4304***	10078***	4320***	9769***

* Statistically significant at 0.10 level (two-tail test).
** Statistically significant at 0.05 level (two-tail test).
*** Statistically significant at 0.01 level (two-tail test).
High—for developed province groups.
Low—for less-developed province groups.
Source: Author's own estimations.
Note: t-statistics are in parentheses.

Fourth, the regression results provide strong empirical evidence that FDI not only directly contributes to economic growth through capital augmentation and technological progress, but also indirectly contributes to economic growth through knowledge spillovers on the local economy in the developed provinces. While the regression results also suggest that FDI can contribute to economic growth through capital augmentation and technological progress in the less-developed provinces, FDI may not improve the productivity and efficiency of the local economy through knowledge spillovers in the less-developed provinces. This finding has important policy implications for regional economic development.

Fifth, comparing the province groups with high per capita GDP and high-level infrastructure with the province groups with low per capita GDP and low-level infrastructure, although FDI has a positive and statistically significant impact on economic growth through capital augmentation and technological progress in all groups, the regression results do show that the coefficients of the variables of LnFK and t*LnFK are higher in the province groups with high per capita GDP and high-level infrastructure than those with low per capita GDP and low-level infrastructure respectively. This implies that FDI has a larger impact on shifting the local production frontier to accelerate economic growth in the developed provinces than in the less-developed provinces.

Finally, there is significant difference between the developed province groups and the less-developed province groups in the values of estimated labour (L) and domestic capital (DK) elasticities. At the national level, there is no significant difference between labour elasticity and domestic capital elasticity. In the developed province groups, variables of both labour and domestic capital are positive and statistically significant; however, labour elasticity is around two to three times domestic capital elasticity, implying that the marginal product of labour is not only much higher than that of the marginal product of domestic capital in the developed province groups but also substantially more than that in the rest of the country. This also suggests that labour may be a constraint on economic growth in the developed provinces. In contrast, in the less-developed province groups, the variable of domestic capital is positive and statistically significant but the variable of labour is statistically insignificant. This implies that the marginal product of domestic capital is much higher than that of labour due to the relative abundance of labour supply and scarcity of capital in the less-developed provinces.

Referring to the differences in economic and technological conditions between the developed province groups and the less-developed province groups and the regression results, we may argue that, given the level of FDI stock, provinces with a higher level of economic development (per capita GDP), higher level of human capital and R&D capability and higher level of infrastructure will facilitate and enhance the role of FDI to local economic growth through capital augmentation, technological progress and spillover effects. Thus, this chapter also provides empirical evidence to suggest that local economic and technology conditions, especially local absorptive capability, play important roles in determining the impact of FDI on economic growth and in influencing the diffusion of knowledge spillovers from FDI to the local economy.

Conclusion

The main purpose of this chapter is to investigate empirically the contribution of FDI to China's economic growth through the channels of capital augmentation, technological progress and spillover effects, with a particular emphasis on how the role of FDI on economic growth is affected by regional differences in China at the provincial level. Based on theoretical foundations, an augmented empirical growth model is specified, and a panel dataset containing China's 30 provinces over the period from 1987 to 2010 is used under the panel regression models. The chapter has provided the following main findings.

First, the regression results of all provinces provide strong evidence that FDI contributes to China's economic growth both directly through capital augmentation and technological progress and indirectly through spillover effects on the local economy. This implies that provinces with higher FDI inflows, higher foreign capital stock and a higher share of FDI stock in total capital stock have higher economic growth contributed directly by the increase in foreign capital input associated with technological progress and indirectly by the diffusion of knowledge spillovers from FDI to the local economy.

Second, the impact of FDI on economic growth is different between province groups with different economic and technological conditions. The regression results show that the contributions of FDI to economic growth are higher in the developed provinces than those in the less-developed provinces. In the developed provinces, FDI not only directly contributes to economic growth through capital augmentation and technological progress but also indirectly contributes to economic growth through spillover effects. In contrast, in the less-developed provinces, FDI is found to contribute to economic growth through capital augmentation but is not found to improve the productivity and efficiency of the local economy due to the lack of knowledge spillovers. Referring to the difference in economic and technological conditions between the developed and less-developed province groups and the regression results, this finding provides empirical evidence to suggest that local economic and technological conditions, especially local absorptive capability, do matter in influencing the diffusion of knowledge spillovers from FDI to the local economy.

Third, the provincial difference in the role of FDI on economic growth deserves attention for both policymaking and academic research. The real problem is not that FDI causes the widening gap between the developed provinces and the less-developed provinces, but that FDI has played a much larger and more significant role in the former than in the latter. As a result, policy should be designed to encourage FDI flows into the less-developed provinces. To achieve the full potential of FDI, conditions have to be created, such as investment in education and infrastructure; but other policies such as inter-regional migration and cross-regional investments are also important in reducing regional disparity in income and production.

Finally, the chapter finds that although the empirical regression results show a positive and statistically significant impact of FDI on economic growth, the magnitude of the contribution from the technological progress and spillover effects of FDI to China's economic growth was still very small. This implies that China still has a lot of benefits to gain from FDI. Therefore, apart from improving local economic and technological conditions to attract more FDI inflows, China should encourage contact, information exchange, production and technological cooperation, joint R&D activities, industrial linkages and competition between domestic firms and FDI firms, in order to enhance and accelerate the technological progress and the diffusion of positive spillovers from FDI to China's economy.

References

Barro, R. and Sala-i-Martin, X. (1995), *Economic Growth*, New York: McGraw-Hill.

Blomstrom, M., Lipsey, R. and Zejan, M. (1992), *What explains developing country growth*, NBER Working Paper No. 4132, National Bureau of Economic Research, Cambridge, Mass. Available from <http://www.nber.org/papers/w4132.pdf>.

Borensztein, E., Gregorio, J. and Lee, J. (1998), 'How does foreign direct investment affect growth', *Journal of International Economics* 45:115–35.

Buckley, P., Clegg, J., Wang, C. and Cross, A. (2002), 'FDI, regional differences and economic growth: panel data evidence from China', *Transnational Corporations* 2(1):1–28.

Caves, R. (1996), *Multinational Enterprise and Economic Analysis*, 2nd edn, Cambridge: Cambridge University Press.

Chen, C. (2011), *Foreign Direct Investment in China: Location Determinants, Investor Differences and Economic Impacts*, Cheltenham, UK, and Northampton, Mass.: Edward Elgar.

Chen, C. (2013), 'FDI and Economic Growth', in Y. Wu (ed.), *Regional Development and Economic Growth in China*, Series on Economic Development and Growth No. 7, pp. 117–40, Singapore: World Scientific.

Chen, C., Chang, L. and Zhang, Y. (1995), 'The role of foreign direct investment in China's post-1978 economic development', *World Development* 23(4):691–703.

Dees, S. (1998), 'Foreign direct investment in China: determinants and effects', *Economics of Planning* 31(2):175–94.

de Mello, L. (1997), 'Foreign direct investment in developing countries and growth: a selective survey', *The Journal of Development Studies* 34(1):1–34.

de Mello, L. (1999), 'Foreign direct investment-led growth: evidence from time series and panel data', *Oxford Economic Papers* 51(1):133–51.

Dunning, J. (1977), 'Trade, location of economic activity and the multinational enterprise: a search for an eclectic approach', in B. Ohlin, P. Hesselborn and P. Wijkman (eds), *The International Allocation of Economic Activity*, pp. 395–418, London: Macmillan.

Dunning, J. (1993), *Multinational Enterprises and the Global Economy*, Wokingham, UK: Addison-Wesley.

Levin, A. and Raut, L. (1997), 'Complementarities between exports and human capital in economic growth: evidence from the semi-industrialized countries', *Economic Development and Cultural Change* 46(1):155–74.

Markusen, J. and Venables, A. (1999), 'Foreign direct investment as a catalyst for industrial development', *European Economic Review* 43(2):335–56.

National Bureau of Statistics of China (NBS) of each province (various years), *Annual National Economic Report of each province*, online sources.

National Bureau of Statistics of China (NBS) (various years), *China Statistical Yearbook*, Beijing: China Statistics Press.

Tang, S., Selvanathan, E. and Selvanathan, S. (2008), 'Foreign direct investment, domestic investment and economic growth in China: a time series analysis', *World Economy* 31(10):1292–309.

Tuan, C., Ng, L. and Zhao, B. (2009), 'China's post-economic reform growth: the role of FDI and productivity progress', *Journal of Asian Economics* 20(3):280–93.

United Nations Conference on Trade and Development (UNCTAD) (1999), *World Investment Report 1999: Foreign Direct Investment and the Challenge of Development*, New York and Geneva: United Nations Publication.

United Nations Conference on Trade and Development (UNCTAD) (2004), *World Investment Report 2004: The Shift Towards Services*, New York and Geneva: United Nations Publication.

Vu, T., Gangnes, B. and Noy, I. (2008), 'Is foreign direct investment good for growth? Evidence from sectoral analysis of China and Vietnam', *Journal of the Asia Pacific Economy* 13(4):542–62.

Wei, S. (1996), 'Foreign direct investment in China: sources and consequences', in T. Ito and A. Krueger (eds), *Financial Deregulation and Integration in East Asia*, NBER-EASE Vol. 5, pp. 77–105, Chicago: University of Chicago Press.

Whalley, J. and Xin, X. (2010), 'China's FDI and non-FDI economies and the sustainability of future high Chinese growth', *China Economic Review* 21(1):123–35.

Wu, Y. (2009), *China's capital stock series by region and sector*, Discussion Paper No. 09.02, Business School, University of Western Australia, Perth. Available from <http://www.business.uwa.edu.au/__data/assets/pdf_file/0009/260487/09_02_Wu.pdf>.

Yao, S. and Wei, K. (2007), 'Economic growth in the presence of FDI: the perspective of newly industrialising economies', *Journal of Comparative Economics* 35(1):211–34.

Part V: Productivity, Patent Institution and Investment Law

17. Accounting for the Sources of Growth in Chinese Industry, 1980–2010[1]

Harry X. Wu

Introduction

Although China's reform has been unquestionably market-oriented in general, it has not yet reduced the role of the Government in business. In fact, the resurgence of consolidated and enlarged state-owned enterprises (SOEs) in so-called 'strategic industries' and the increasing government interventions in resource allocation since the mid 2000s, especially following the GFC in 2008, have remained at the centre of policy debate concerning further and deeper structural reforms. What has been missing in the debate, however, is the productivity performance of industries or sectors with different degrees of state involvement and interference. By abandoning the command economy and encouraging activities to reap China's comparative advantage, the Chinese Government has (so far) successfully solved the growth problem, but it remains unclear whether strong state interventions have also solved the inefficiency problem and hence have been able to promote genuine productivity growth.

Despite numerous empirical studies attempting to account for the sources of growth in the Chinese economy, there has been no consensus among scholars on China's post-reform productivity performance. Empirical studies have shown that the estimated contribution of total factor productivity (TFP) to China's GDP growth in the post-reform period (though not with an identical duration) ranges from negative to as high as more than 50 per cent (see reviews in Wu 2011; Wu 2014a). We may argue that since almost all of these studies adopted the same neoclassical growth accounting framework, the contradictory estimates of China's TFP growth clearly and logically suggest that there are serious problems with data and measurement. Indeed, I have shown that using exactly the same

1   Reported in this chapter are the interim results of the author's ongoing China Industrial Productivity (CIP) and China KLEMS Database projects. The CIP/China KLEMS project aims to construct input and output data for standard growth and productivity analysis. Support from RIETI, IER of Hitotsubashi University, the Japanese National Science Foundation (JSPS 24330076) and The Conference Board (TCB) China Center is gratefully acknowledged. Part of the work presented in this chapter has benefited from comments and suggestions at the first and second World KLEMS conferences at Harvard University. The author is responsible for any error or omission.

input and output data, the different choices of output measures, investment deflators, as well as factor income shares, can result in very different estimates of the TFP growth for the aggregate economy (Wu 2014a).

Nevertheless, to address the productivity problem and to relate it to the policy debate over future reform, we need to examine the industry-level rather than the aggregate-level TFP performance of the Chinese economy. This is because we are interested in the role of the Government, which may be captured, though indirectly, by the productivity performance of state-monopolised or influenced industries. After all, government interventions are often made through industry-specific policies and related institutional arrangements. Our newly constructed industry-level data for the period 1980–2010 serve this purpose.

The rest of the chapter will be organised as follows. In section two, I conceptually discuss the role of the Government in the Chinese economy to support my datum handling for industry grouping later. In the subsequent section, I discuss the methodological issues that are considered for economy-wide coherence in input, output and the costs of factor and intermediate inputs, as well as the inter-industry cumulative effect of productivity changes. In section four, following the earlier conceptual discussion and the feature of the Domar aggregation approach, I introduce the industry grouping as well as the data used. Finally, I present and discuss the results in section five and conclude this study in section six.

Considering the role of the Government

My main objective here is to examine whether government involvement has affected the productivity performance of the Chinese economy. This is challenging because policy or institutional factors are not an inherent part of the standard theory of production function; however, government policy is industry-specific and industries are connected through vertical input–output links. Therefore, to explore the role of the Government, I first distinguish industries with different types of government interventions and then explore their productivity implications and how the aggregate industrial economy is affected.

Despite a significant decline of the state sector over the reform period, governments at all levels have maintained strong intervention in the allocation of resources to support the so-called strategic industries, of which the majority are either owned or heavily influenced by the state. One important change with reform, however, is that government intervention is no longer all embracing, as it was in the central planning era, which completely ignored the market. It has become industry-specific through subsidisation, administrative interference or both. Subsidisation aims to reduce producers' costs of inputs including energy, land, environment, labour and capital (see Huang and Tao 2010). In contrast, administrative interference aims to serve the state's interests and state 'strategic plans' by controlling or influencing output prices or various aspects of business operations from managerial personnel to the choice of technology.

I argue that whether or to what extent governments use administrative interference or subsidies depends on the distance of an industry from final demand, especially the international market. Local governments use subsidisation mainly to promote export-oriented industries that produce semifinished and finished goods. These industries are mainly labour intensive and therefore crucial for China to reap its demographic dividend in a timely fashion. Since these industries face international competition, direct administrative interference is counterproductive; however, the Central Government or higher-level authorities tend to become directly involved in upstream industries because they are considered strategically important to sustain the growth of downstream industries. Administrative measures such as managerial and price controls are used to ensure that upstream industries can provide sufficient and cheap supplies to downstream industries. Nevertheless, subsidisation could also be used to support upstream industries whenever administrative interference is not cost-effective.

Considering the behaviour of enterprises in such a policy environment and the implications for efficiency improvement and productivity growth, we may suppose that industries that are mainly supported by input subsidies could be more efficient and productive than those that are subject to administrative interference. We argue that when subsidies do not come with administrative interference in business decisions, enterprises may still behave like true market competitors although their competitiveness is arbitrarily enhanced by the cheaper cost of some factors influenced by the Government.[2]

In contrast, the upstream industries are far from the end market. They are traditionally dominated by SOEs and do not conform to China's comparative advantage. Their assumed 'strategic importance', however, gives them strong bargaining power in negotiating for government support and in return they have to accept controls by the authorities. This distorts their behaviour and is a disincentive in their efforts towards efficiency improvement.

---

2   This is conditional on whether they can repeatedly negotiate for benefits regardless of their true performance. Here we assume this is not the case.

The nature of government interventions is cross-subsidisation; however, the key to sustain this 'cross-subsidisation game' is that the income of the downstream industries must be able to grow faster and relatively more efficiently than the rise of the cost due to all kinds of subsidies, to either the upstream or the downstream industries.

Measuring total factor productivity

In this study, we estimate China's industrial TFP growth with the Jorgensonian growth accounting approach in which primary and intermediate inputs are weighted in their nominal costs, coherently linked to factor income accounts in the national input–output framework. This approach is theoretically underpinned by the seminal contribution of Jorgenson and Griliches (1967). It is put in a more general input–output framework in Jorgenson et al. (1987) and further developed in Jorgenson et al. (2005).[3] It begins with consideration of the production possibility frontier where industry gross output is a function of capital, labour, intermediate inputs and technology indexed by time. Each industry, indexed by j, can produce a set of products and purchases a number of distinct intermediate capital and labour inputs to produce its output. The production function is given by Equation 17.1.

Equation 17.1

$$Y_j = f_j(K_j, L_j, M_j, T)$$

In Equation 17.1, Y is output, K is an index of capital service flows, L is an index of labour service flows and X is an index of intermediate inputs, either purchased from domestic industries or imported.

Under the assumptions of competitive factor markets, full input utilisation and constant returns to scale, the growth of output can be expressed as the cost-weighted growth of inputs and technological change (A^Y), using the trans-log functional form (Equation 17.2).

Equation 17.2

$$\Delta \ln Y_{jt} = \bar{v}_{jt}^K \Delta \ln K_{jt} + \bar{v}_{jt}^L \Delta \ln L_{jt} + \bar{v}_{jt}^M \Delta \ln M_{jt} + \Delta \ln A_{jt}^Y$$

---

3 Also see application of the approach in O'Mahony and Timmer (2009).

In Equation 17.2, $\bar{v}_{jt}^K = \dfrac{P_{jt}^K K_{jt}}{P_{jt}^Y Y_{jt}}$, $\bar{v}_{jt}^L = \dfrac{P_{jt}^L L_{jt}}{P_{jt}^Y Y_{jt}}$ and $\Delta \ln X_{jt} = \sum_m \bar{w}_{m,jt}^M \Delta \ln M_{m,jt}$ are weights in normal costs for respective input, and $\bar{v}_{jt}^K + \bar{v}_{jt}^L + \bar{v}_{jt}^M = 1$. Each input as expressed in the right-hand side of Equation 17.2 indicates the proportion of output growth accounted for by the growth of intermediate materials, capital services, labour services and technology or TFP, respectively.

One of the advantages of this approach is that it can better account for services provided by different types of labour due to different demographic, educational and industrial attributes. This has relaxed the usual strong assumption that treats numbers employed or hours worked as a homogenous measure of labour input. We define total labour input as a Törnqvist quantity index of individual labour types as follows (Equation 17.3).

Equation 17.3

$$\Delta \ln L_{jt} = \sum_h \bar{w}_{h,jt}^H \Delta \ln H_{h,jt}$$

In Equation 17.3, $\Delta \ln H_{h,jt}$ indicates the growth of hours worked by each labour type, h (with specific gender, age and education attainment), and their cost weights, $\bar{w}_{h,jt}^H$, given by the period average shares of each type in the value of labour compensation controlled by the labour income accounts as in the input–output accounts. This approach ensures that the effect of demographic change on the economy can be properly counted. The same user cost approach is also applied to K ($\Delta \ln K_{jt} = \sum_k \bar{w}_{k,jt}^K \Delta \ln K_{k,jt}$) and X ($\Delta \ln X_{jt} = \sum_m \bar{w}_{m,jt}^M \Delta \ln M_{m,jt}$) to fully account for different types of capital assets and intermediate inputs in production.

Next, we consider using the Domar aggregation approach to examine whether and to what extent the productivity performance of downstream industries has sustained the cross-subsidisation game and whether and to what extent the productivity performance of upstream industries has affected the cost of downstream industries through input–output linkages, hence influencing the productivity performance of the whole industry.

The Domar aggregation approach was first proposed by Domar (1961) and further elaborated by Hulten (1978). The idea is that for an industry-wide equivalent, we can postulate the existence of an industry-wide production possibility frontier (PPF) that relates available primary factor inputs to deliveries to the final demand. An aggregate productivity change is then defined as a shift of the aggregate PPF over time, or the rate of change in A—that is, TFP—

which can be measured as the difference between the rate of change in total final demand (*FD*) and the rate of change in the input of primary factors ($Z = L \times K$) and intermediate inputs from domestic sources (M_D) and abroad (imported) (M_M). The Domar aggregation is expressed in Equation 17.4.

Equation 17.4

$$\frac{d \ln A}{dt} = \sum_j \frac{P^j Q^j}{P \cdot FD} \cdot \frac{d \ln A^j}{dt}$$

In Equation 17.4,

$$\frac{d \ln A^j}{dt} = \frac{d \ln Q^j}{dt} - \frac{P^j_z Z^j}{P^j Q^j} \cdot \frac{d \ln Z^j}{dt} - \frac{P^j_{MD} M^j_D}{P^j Q^j} \cdot \frac{d \ln M^j_D}{dt} - \frac{P^j_{MM} M^j_M}{P^j Q^j} \cdot \frac{d \ln M^j_M}{dt} .$$

A direct consequence of this integration is that the weights do not sum to unity, implying that aggregate productivity growth amounts to more or less than the weighted average of industry-level productivity growth. This reflects the fact that productivity change in the production of *intermediate inputs* not only has an 'own' effect, but also leads to reduced or increased prices in downstream industries, and that effect accumulates through vertical links.

This Domar aggregation approach is distinguished from the traditionally used aggregation approach that is based on simple weighted averages of industry-level productivity growth, which does not account for the links between industries connected via flows of intermediate products. In the process of such integration, intra-industry deliveries are netted out to obtain productivity measures at a higher level of the economy. Conceptually, it treats every level of the aggregation as if it were a single unit of production with its specific technology and productivity pattern.

In the Domar aggregation, however, sectoral output coincides with final demand at the level of the entire economy. A consistent link is therefore established between industry-level and aggregate observations on productivity growth. The weights used for the aggregation are given by each industry's gross output relative to economy-wide value added. The sum of these weights is not necessarily equal to unity. Productivity gains of the integrated economy may exceed the average productivity gains across industries because flows of intermediate inputs between industries contribute to aggregate productivity by allowing productivity gains in successive industries to augment one another. The same logic can explain productivity losses.

Data, industry grouping and periodisation

In this growth accounting exercise, I use a newly completed dataset for Chinese industry from a series of studies by my associates and me (see Wu 2008, 2014b; Wu and Yue 2012; Wu et al. 2014; Ito and Wu 2013; Wu and Ito 2014). The data are constructed in line with the principles for the production function analysis in the above-discussed Jorgenson–Griliches framework. It satisfies all the empirical requirements of Equations 17.2 to 17.4. It covers China's entire reform period, from 1980 to 2010, which also allows us an examination of the effect of the 2008 GFC and its aftermath.

To investigate the TFP performance of industries located in different positions in the production chain, which may be subject to different degrees of government intervention, we categorise 21 mining, manufacturing and utility industries into four groups. They are 'energy', 'commodities and primary input materials' (C&P), 'semifinished goods' and 'finished goods'.[4] According to their 'distance' from final demand, the 'energy' group stays on the top of the production chain, which is followed by the 'C&P' group, the 'semifinished goods' and finally the 'finished goods' groups. According to the technological nature of different groups, the 'finished goods' group is more labour intensive than the upstream groups, and hence more in line with China's comparative advantage. Therefore, it should be more productive than others.

This grouping aims to reflect the different methods and degrees of government intervention as hypothesised. The 'energy' group is monopolised by SOEs due to its strategic importance, and therefore receives more administrative interference or stronger state intervention. The 'C&P' group is the next most important group that is also heavily influenced, if not owned, by the Government. The 'semifinished goods' group is to some extent similar to the 'C&P' group, especially heavy machinery industry, which is also subject to varied state interference. Finally, the 'finished goods' group consists of mainly private enterprises including foreign-invested enterprises. Since the last two groups, especially the 'finished goods' group, are closer to the market, I suggest government intervention tends to be more indirect or less administrative, which leaves more room for enterprises to engage in market competition.

---

4 The 'energy' group includes coalmining, oil and gas extraction, petroleum refining, and utility supply; the 'commodities and primary input materials' group includes metal mining, nonmetallic mining, textiles, paper and printing, basic chemicals, building materials and primary metals; the 'semifinished goods' group includes metal products, machinery, electrical equipment, instruments, and office equipment; and the 'finished goods' group includes food, apparel, leather goods, electronic and telecommunications equipment, and transport equipment. I use quotation marks to indicate that this grouping is by no means a clear cut between groups, especially between the downstream groups. Besides, as in my earlier exercises (Wu 2013; Wu with Girardin 2013), I also exclude three industries in this grouping: tobacco, sawmill and wood products, and miscellaneous manufacturing.

To examine the impact of major policy regime shifts on Chinese industry we can also divide the entire period 1980–2010 into four sub-periods—namely, 1980–91, 1992–2001, 2002–07 and 2008–10. The first sub-period covers early industrial reforms, though nationwide industrial reform began in 1984 with the dual-track price reform. This period experienced various institutional shocks as well as the political turmoil of 1989. The second sub-period began with Deng Xiaoping's call for bolder reform and the official adoption of a 'socialist market economy', which kicked off serious reforms to the state sector. This was followed by China's post-World Trade Organisation (WTO) period during which there were, however, mixed changes. On one hand, WTO-induced wider opening to foreign trade and direct investment moved China further towards the market system; on the other hand, consolidated and enlarged state corporations made a resurgence and, meanwhile, growth-motivated local governments became more involved in local business. The last sub-period began with the GFC, during which the role of the state was further enhanced by its unprecedented fiscal injection.

Results and discussion

Descriptive observations

Before proceeding to more rigorous growth accounting analysis, an examination of the indicators presented in Tables 17.1 to 17.4 may help explore the underlying efficiency and productivity performances of Chinese industry and its major groups. Let us start with the indicators presented in Table 17.1. There are some observations that are worth noting. First, for industry as a whole over the entire period under examination, net investment, as reflected by the increase in net capital stock (net K), grew faster than gross value added (VA), suggesting that China's post-reform industrial growth was on average driven by investment. Before reaching a nearly 15 per cent annual growth rate post WTO accession (2002–07), industrial net investment maintained a steady rate of growth of about 10 per cent a year during the 1980s and 1990s. The next, perhaps unprecedented, investment drive due to the Government's fiscal injection was observed in the wake of the GFC, which resulted in net capital stock growth of nearly 19 per cent per annum in 2008–10.

Table 17.1 Annual Change of Gross Value Added, Hours Worked and Net Capital Stock by Industry Group in China, 1980–2010 (per cent per annum)

	Energy			C&P			Semifinished goods			Finished goods			Total industry		
	VA	Hours	Net K	VA	Hours	Net K	VA	Hours	Net K	VA	Hours	Net K	VA	Hours	Net K
1980–91	-2.2	4.2	10.7	6.1	4.1	10.5	11.7	3.1	6.8	13.4	2.9	27.3	5.9	3.5	10.4
1992–2001	6.6	-0.9	13.7	11.2	-2.1	8.1	13.2	-1.3	7.6	18.1	0.9	11.2	12.7	-1.0	10.3
2002–07	10.6	5.0	14.9	12.6	3.3	13.8	17.6	7.3	14.8	19.3	7.0	16.3	15.8	5.6	14.7
2008–10	3.6	1.5	14.5	9.5	1.6	20.4	19.3	4.2	26.0	14.8	3.2	19.5	13.8	2.8	18.8
1980–2010	3.8	2.3	12.9	9.4	1.6	11.3	14.1	2.5	10.5	16.3	3.1	18.7	10.9	2.3	12.0

Source: Author's calculation. See references in data section for more information.

Table 17.2 Structure of Chinese Industry in Value Added, Hours Worked and Net Capital Stock by Industry Group, Selected Benchmark Years (total industry = 1)

	Value added				Hours worked				Net capital stock			
	Energy	C&P	Semifinished goods	Finished goods	Energy	C&P	Semifinished goods	Finished goods	Energy	C&P	Semifinished goods	Finished goods
1980	0.228	0.423	0.226	0.123	0.087	0.392	0.247	0.274	0.276	0.405	0.247	0.072
1992	0.167	0.435	0.232	0.166	0.094	0.415	0.234	0.257	0.296	0.404	0.176	0.125
2002	0.227	0.346	0.215	0.212	0.096	0.367	0.229	0.309	0.380	0.324	0.140	0.155
2008	0.224	0.354	0.228	0.194	0.089	0.316	0.259	0.336	0.376	0.322	0.158	0.144
2010	0.207	0.334	0.255	0.205	0.087	0.313	0.262	0.339	0.352	0.331	0.167	0.150

Source: Author's calculation. See references in data section for more information.

If broken down by industry group, the 'finished goods' group experienced the most rapid growth in net investment over the entire period—18.7 per cent a year—followed by the 'energy', 'C&P' and 'semifinished' groups, respectively. If observed by sub-periods, the 'finished' group was well ahead of all others in China's post-WTO period and the 'energy' group took the lead during China's reform in the 1990s. Following the GFC in 2008, however, the growth in net investment of the 'semifinished goods' group reached 26 per cent a year—unprecedented by any standard.

Our second observation emphasises the relative annual growth rates between output and capital stock by sub-period, which may shed important light on the underlying inefficiency problem. For industry as a whole, the most 'efficient' sub-period appears to be the one beginning with Deng Xiaoping's trip to southern China in 1992 calling for bolder reforms, in which the industrial value added grew 24 per cent faster than that of industrial net investment. In the next most efficient period, however, following China's WTO entry, this favourable 'relative pace' between the two indicators declined substantially, to 8 per cent. On the opposite side, the initial reform period was the most 'inefficient', in which the annual growth of industrial value added was 43 per cent slower than that of industrial net investment. Such a mismatch was also evident following the GFC, when the former was significantly behind the latter by about 25 per cent.

At group level, using the same yardstick of 'relative pace' between output and net investment, the best performers appear to be the 'semifinished' and 'finished' groups over the 1990s and the post-WTO period. It should be noted that the record fiscal injection in response to the GFC forced the growth of net investment far ahead of the growth of value added in all groups, among which the state-monopolised 'energy' group appears to be most inefficient.

Third, we find that the performance of employment (measured by hours worked) was unstable over the entire period, reflecting the impact of rapid changes in both institutional and market conditions. On average, China maintained positive growth in employment over the period, by 2.3 per cent per annum; however, the total number of hours worked fluctuated highly from an absolute decline of −1 per cent per annum in 1992–2001 to annual growth of 5.6 per cent per annum in 2002–07. Such changes may reflect a significant improvement of serious labour redundancy and misallocation problems nurtured and developed under central planning. Indeed, healthy labour reallocation is reflected by the absolute decline in 1991–2001 across all groups except the 'finished goods' group that is more in line with China's comparative advantage. Another sign is the difference in the change of hours worked among industry groups following China's WTO entry, ranging from 3 per cent per annum in 'C&P' to more than 7 per cent per annum in 'semifinished' and 'finished'.

Table 17.2 shows the structure of gross value added, hours worked and net capital stock by industry group in selected benchmark years. As a consequence of different growth performances among groups over sub-periods, China's industrial structure has changed substantially. Here, let us focus on the structural change by more than 5 percentage points (ppts) in either direction. For the entire period, the structural change in capital stock was somewhat balanced between similar declines in 'C&P' (−7.4 ppts) and 'semifinished' (−8 ppts) and similar increases in 'energy' (+7.5 ppts) and 'finished' (+7.8 ppts). For sub-periods, the most significant structural changes in either direction took place in the period 1980–91, with 'semifinished' dropping by 7.2 ppts and 'finished' increasing by 5.2 ppts, and in the period 1992–2001, with 'energy' rising by 8.4 ppts and 'C&P' dropping by 7.4 ppts (all calculated based on Table 17.2).

On the other hand, the major structural changes in gross value added mainly took place in 'C&P' and 'finished', with a drop of 9 ppts in the former and a rise by 8.2 ppts in the latter for the entire period. For sub-periods, however, the major structural changes could be observed mainly in 'energy' by −6.1 ppts in 1980–91 and in 'C&P' by −8.9 ppts and in 'energy' by +6 ppts in 1992–2001. The major structural changes in hours worked, however, took place between the decline in 'C&P' and the rise in 'finished', reflecting the labour-intensive nature of the latter and perhaps continuous technological upgrading in the former.

To continue our exploration through descriptive observations, in Tables 17.3 and 17.4 we present labour productivity (Y/L), the capital–labour ratio (K/L) and capital–output ratio (K/Y) in both level and growth rate, respectively. Here, Y/L is calculated by value added per worker, standardised using constant numbers of hours worked per year (2400 hours) to control for homogeneity in physical intensity. The denominator in the capital deepening measure, K/L, follows the same approach for consistency. Besides, K/Y is the ratio of K/L to Y/L. Note that the quality of labour and capital has not yet been controlled at this stage (see TFP analysis later).

Based on the level indicators presented in Table 17.3, the most significant observation is that the labour productivity (Y/L) of 'semifinished' had surpassed the Y/L ratio of 'energy' and 'C&P' by 2002. Meanwhile, the Y/L ratio of 'finished' had almost reached the same level as 'C&P'. Such trends continued in the following decade, and by 2010, the Y/L ratio of 'semifinished' had not only remained highest among all groups, but also doubled the level of 'energy'. In the same period, the Y/L ratio of 'finished' had surpassed that of 'C&P' by about 15 per cent.

Table 17.3 Value Added Per Worker, Net Capital Per Worker and Capital–Output Ratio by Industry Group in China, Selected Benchmark Years (output and capital are in RMB 1990)

	Energy			C&P			Semifinished goods			Finished goods			Total industry		
	Y/L	K/L	K/Y	Y/L	K/L	K/Y	Y/L	K/L	K/Y	Y/L	K/L	K/Y	Y/L	K/L	K/Y
1980	18 258	20 379	1.12	4703	6503	1.38	2388	6576	2.75	1343	419	0.31	4384	6055	1.38
1992	10 253	44 558	4.35	7107	13 558	1.91	6852	10 706	1.56	4663	4765	1.02	6716	13 551	2.02
2002	20 933	168 048	8.03	22 949	35 805	1.56	26 011	24 088	0.93	22 146	12 993	0.59	23 209	38 738	1.67
2008	23 771	307 409	12.93	37 276	74 030	1.99	43 635	44 332	1.02	36 936	21 773	0.59	37 606	69 560	1.85
2010	27 603	390 057	14.13	43 844	101 430	2.31	59 300	61 312	1.03	49 902	29 351	0.59	48 537	91 518	1.89

Source: Author's calculation. See references in data section for more information.

Note: Labour is standardised based on the estimated total number of hours worked and assumed to be 2400 hours per worker per year.

Table 17.4 Annual Change of Labor Productivity, Capital Deepening and Capital–Output Ratio by Industry Group in China, 1980–2010 (per cent per annum)

	Energy			C&P			Semifinished goods			Finished goods			Total industry		
	Y/L	K/L	K/Y	Y/L	K/L	K/Y	Y/L	K/L	K/Y	Y/L	K/L	K/Y	Y/L	K/L	K/Y
1980–91	-6.1	6.3	13.2	2.0	6.2	4.1	8.3	3.8	-4.2	9.9	12.3	2.2	2.3	6.7	4.3
1992–2001	7.6	14.8	6.7	13.6	10.5	-2.8	14.4	8.0	-5.6	16.7	10.4	-5.4	13.8	11.4	-2.1
2002–07	5.4	9.5	3.9	9.0	10.2	1.1	8.1	6.6	-1.4	11.9	8.5	-3.1	9.7	8.6	-1.0
2008–10	2.0	12.7	10.5	7.8	18.5	9.9	10.4	22.7	11.2	13.9	16.5	2.3	10.7	15.6	4.4
1980–2010	1.4	10.3	8.8	7.7	9.6	1.7	10.5	7.5	-2.7	12.9	11.3	-1.4	8.3	9.5	1.0

Source: Author's calculation. See references in data section for more information.

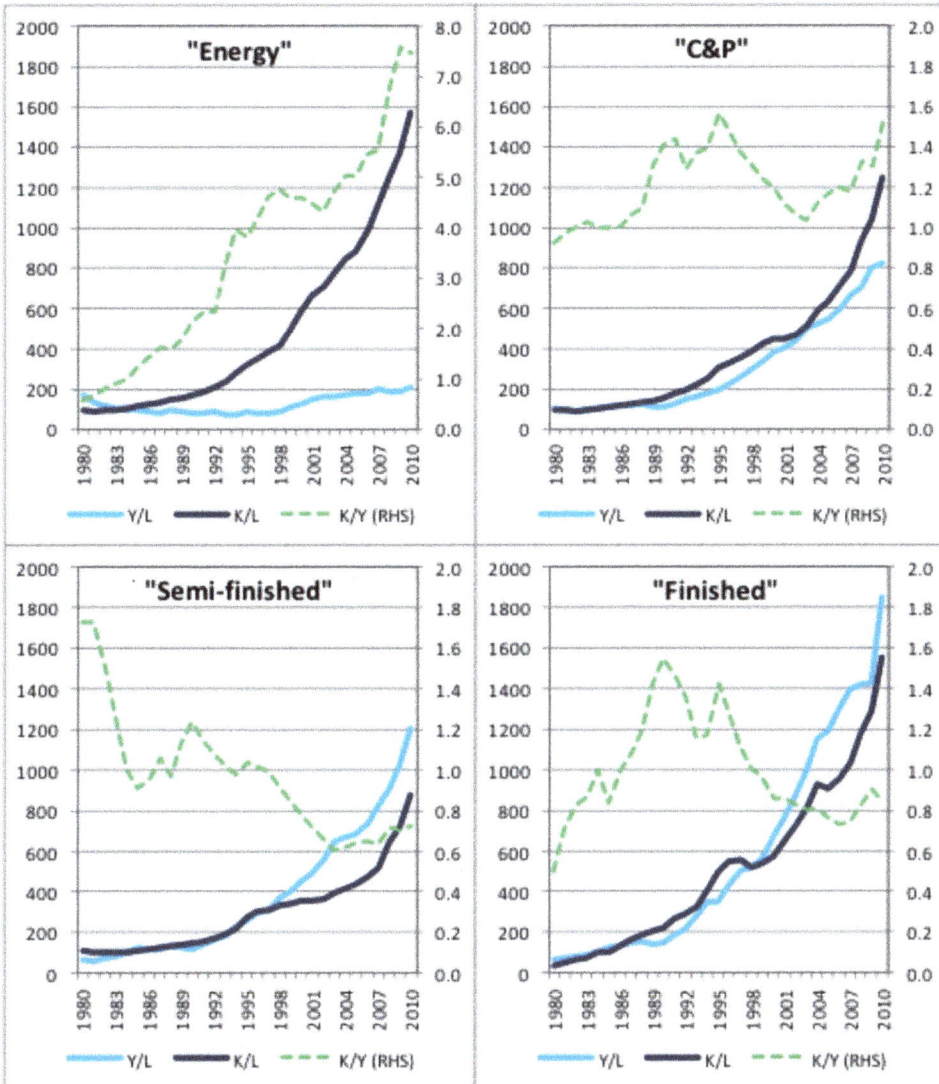

Figure 17.1 Indices of Labour Productivity, Capital Deepening and Capital–Output Ratio by Industry Group (1984 = 100)

Source: Author's calculation.

Notes: K/Y = (K/L)/(Y/L); 1984 = 1 (on the right-hand scale).

More importantly, alongside these changes, the capital–labour ratio (K/L) of 'semifinished' remained only about 15 per cent of the level of 'energy', and declined from about 80 to 60 per cent of the level of 'C&P'. The K/L ratio of 'finished goods' was the lowest of all groups and declined from 54 to 48 per cent of the K/L level of 'semifinished'. Consequently, the capital–output ratio (K/Y) of 'semifinished' and 'finished' stayed at a very low level of around 1 and 0.6, respectively, since 2002. Meanwhile, the K/Y ratio of 'energy' reached an

443

astonishingly high level of 14. The annual changes of these ratios over the entire period and its sub-periods are provided in Table 17.4. It shows that the 'finished goods' group, in which China has enjoyed strong comparative advantage and benefited from the demographic dividend, was the most dynamic group in both labour productivity and capital deepening. To help the examination in a continuous time frame, Figure 17.1 depicts the growth index of these ratios based on 1984, which was when the nationwide industrial reform began.

Total factor productivity performance

The growth of TFP for Chinese industry can be calculated in a growth accounting exercise based on Equations 17.2 to 17.4 with and without considering inter-industry connections. The estimation procedures are followed at two levels. The first level is the individual group level at which all industries within the group are treated as identical and in one unit. In other words, there is no intra-group relationship that is considered. The second level is China's total industry. At this level, two sets of TFP growth estimates are obtained using the Domar and non-Domar aggregations. The estimation of the Domar-weighted TFP growth for total industry considers a cumulative productivity effect from upstream to downstream industries, whereas the estimation of the traditional or non-Domar TFP growth treats all groups as identical in one enlarged economy-wide unit.

In Table 17.5, we show the growth of each input factor weighted by its nominal costs (with their sum equal to the national gross value of output in industry from the national accounts). The residual so derived is the estimated TFP growth rate for each group as well as for industry as a whole. It should be mentioned again that in this estimation, as given by Equation 17.3, both labour and capital are measured in their services rather than in physical units. This ensures that quality change in labour and capital is not inappropriately measured as TFP change.

Table 17.5 Accounting for the Sources of Gross Output Growth in Chinese Industry by Industry Group (per cent per annum)

	GO	L input	K input	M input	TFP	TFP (Domar)
1980–91						
Energy	0.9	0.4	3.5	1.9	−4.9	
C&P	7.9	0.4	2.4	5.9	−0.8	
Semifinished	13.6	0.3	1.5	9.7	2.0	
Finished	13.7	0.2	2.6	10.5	0.3	
Total (new)	8.6	0.3	2.4	6.7	−0.8	−2.0
1992–2001						
Energy	7.0	−0.1	3.4	4.7	−1.0	
C&P	11.0	−0.2	1.4	8.0	1.7	
Semifinished	13.6	0.0	1.2	10.4	2.0	
Finished	16.3	0.1	1.8	12.3	2.2	
Total (new)	12.7	0.0	1.8	9.4	1.5	5.0
2002–07						
Energy	15.0	0.3	3.2	11.7	−0.2	
C&P	15.2	0.1	2.1	12.3	0.8	
Semifinished	19.7	0.4	2.0	15.9	1.4	
Finished	22.0	0.4	2.0	18.2	1.4	
Total (new)	18.8	0.3	2.2	15.1	1.2	2.3
2008–10						
Energy	2.4	0.1	2.6	1.5	−1.7	
C&P	8.9	0.1	2.8	6.9	−0.8	
Semifinished	18.0	0.1	2.9	14.5	0.5	
Finished	14.0	0.2	2.3	11.4	0.2	
Total (new)	13.3	0.1	2.5	10.5	0.2	−2.3
1980–2010						
Energy	5.9	0.2	3.3	4.8	−2.4	
C&P	10.5	0.1	2.1	8.0	0.3	
Semifinished	15.3	0.2	1.6	11.6	1.8	
Finished	16.3	0.2	2.2	12.7	1.1	
Total (new)	12.5	0.2	2.2	9.7	0.5	1.1

Source: Author's estimation based on Equations 17.2–17.4.

Note: See text for Domar aggregation-derived TFP.

Let us first examine China's industrial TFP growth performance, assuming there are no intra-group and inter-group effects—that is, without using the Domar weights at any level of the aggregation. As Table 17.5 shows, for industry as a whole over the entire period 1980–2010, TFP performance is disappointing, growing by only 0.5 per cent per annum. At the group level, the best performer is the 'semifinished goods' group, followed by the 'finished goods' group, with annual TFP growth by 1.8 and 1.1 per cent, respectively. The 'C&P' group achieved annual TFP growth of just 0.3 per cent, while the 'energy' group suffered from a TFP decline by a shocking −2.4 per cent per annum.

Examining the performance over different sub-periods, for industry as a whole, the best period was 1992–2001, when the annual TFP growth rate reached 1.5 per cent. This result may reflect the Government's first efforts to adopt the ('socialist') market system and to implement de facto privatisation of some SOEs. Although the large and 'strategic' industries remained state-owned or controlled, the TFP effect of the reform appears to be rather encouraging. During this period the 'finished goods' group took the lead in TFP growth, by 2.2 per cent per annum, followed by the 'semifinished' group (2 per cent) and 'C&P' group (1.7 per cent). In fact, the 'semifinished goods' group maintained its TFP performance in the previous period, 1980–91, whereas the 'C&P' and 'finished goods' groups achieved a substantial improvement from their previous performance of −0.8 and 0.3 per cent annual TFP growth, respectively. Meanwhile, the 'energy' group experienced an annual TFP decline of −1 per cent, though much improved from its previous record of −4.9 per cent.

China's WTO entry was not, however, accompanied by a continuous TFP improvement as one may expect. The annual TFP growth for total industry fell to 1.2 per cent in 2002–07, although Chinese industry experienced its fastest output growth in history—that is, 18.8 per cent compared with 12.5 per cent in 1992–2001. Compared with the previous period, the annual TFP growth of the 'semifinished' and 'finished' groups slowed considerably, by about 30 per cent to 1.4 per cent, whereas the average TFP growth of the 'C&P' group slowed by about 50 per cent to 0.8 per cent. Meanwhile, the 'energy' group somewhat improved its performance though it remained in the negative zone. As we argued earlier, the declining productivity performance of this period could be caused by the resurgence of large state corporations and the greater involvement of local governments in resource allocation. Nevertheless, this trend was enhanced by the unprecedented fiscal injection in the wake of the GFC.

Figure 17.2 provides a 1984-based TFP index for the entire period for each industry group as well as for industry as a whole. It resembles the results of different periods in Table 17.5 in time-series and helps compare the current TFP level with that in the base year. It shows that by 2010 the 'energy' group's TFP level was 40 per cent below its base-year level; the 'C&P' group was 12 per cent above its base-year level, and the 'semifinished' and 'finished' goods groups were about 35 per cent of their original productivity level in 1984.

Our main concern is whether the state-dominated upstream industries have affected the productivity performance of Chinese industry as a whole. As argued, since upstream industries provide intermediate inputs to downstream industries, their productivity performance inevitably affects the TFP performance of downstream industries. This inter-industry effect on the annual TFP growth of industry as a whole can be examined by the Domar-aggregation approach as presented in the last column of Table 17.5, which is also indexed in Panel B of Figure 17.2.

If considering the inter-industry TFP effect, the entire period achieved annual TFP growth by 1.1 per cent (Table 17.5). The best TFP effect, transmitted from upstream to downstream industries, appears to be from the mid 1990s to the early 2000s, largely corresponding to the period 1992–2001. For this period, the Domar-weighted TFP grew by 5 per cent per annum compared with the non-Domar TFP growth of 1.5 per cent per annum. For the post-WTO period, 2002–07, however, the Domar-weighted TFP growth fell to 2.3 per cent per annum. During the period 2008–10, after the GFC, the 'energy' and 'C&P' groups became the major beneficiaries of the Government's unprecedented monetary injection to save the economy. TFP in this period, however, suffered an annual decline by −2.3 per cent.

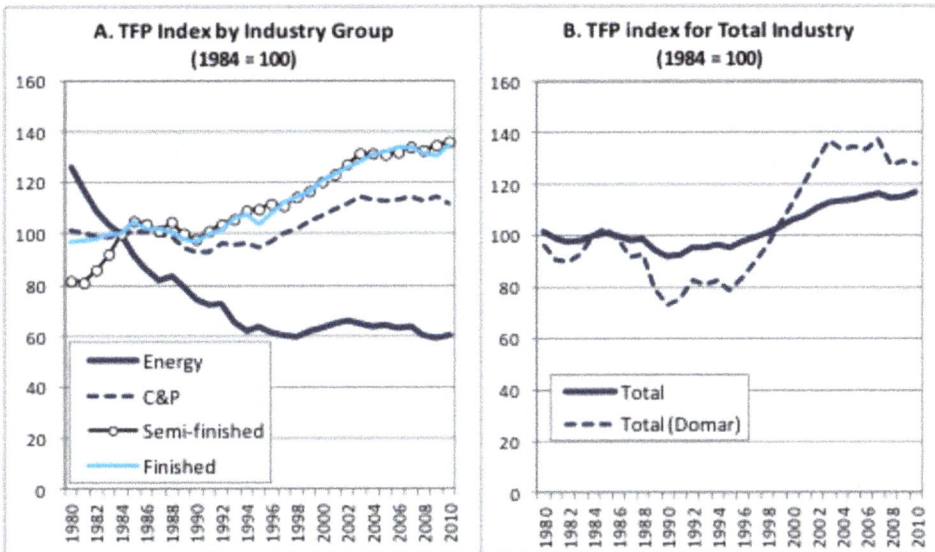

Figure 17.2 China's Industrial TFP Growth by Industry Group (1984 = 100)

Source: Constructed based on results in Table 17.5.

Examining the two panels of Figure 17.2, it is clear that the 'semifinished' and 'finished' goods groups were the ones that sustained positive, albeit still slow, TFP growth in Chinese industry for the entire period. The better productivity performance of these two groups ensured a continuous increase in government revenue and hence a continuous flow of public resources to support inefficient upstream industries, which were required to provide subsidised inputs to make downstream industries more competitive. Indeed, we find that both the 'semifinished' and the 'finished' groups have become more and more reliant on intermediate inputs (Table 17.5). Without question, our broad grouping may not reflect the complete story of each industry within the group, but it reflects the average performance of each group. Obviously, without the 'semifinished' and 'finished' goods groups, the cross-subsidisation game cannot exist.

Concluding remarks

This study applies the Jorgenson–Griliches framework in growth accounting to a newly constructed industry-level dataset for China to examine the sources of growth in Chinese industry 1980–2010. In data handling, the quality improvement of labour and capital has been taken into account. At industry level, instead of using simple quantity measures for primary inputs and imposing hypothetical income shares for them, this approach uses cost-weighted measures for all inputs that are controlled by the national accounts and the input–output table-based time-variant factor income shares. At the aggregate level, using the Domar aggregation approach, it also takes into account the cumulated productivity effect from the upstream to downstream industries.

Our preliminary results show that the TFP growth of China's industrial sector as a whole for the entire period is only 0.5 per cent per annum. If based on the Domar aggregation approach, the estimate can be raised to 1.1 per cent per annum. The best sub-period appears to be the one from 1991 to 2001, with annual TFP growth of 1.5 per cent, or 5 per cent based on the Domar aggregation approach. This is followed by the second-best sub-period, 2001–07, with TFP growth of 1.2 per cent per annum, or 2.3 per cent based on the Domar approach.

China's industrial TFP performance is not respectable if compared with international experience, especially East Asian experience. If controlling for the stage of development by per capita GDP US$2000 to US$6000 measured in purchasing power parity (PPP) at 1990 prices (TCB 2013; Wu 2014a), and taking into account the general tendency for that TFP growth in the industrial sector to be faster than that of the national economy (as most available TFP studies focus on national economy), China's annual TFP growth in industry would be 1.2 per cent (1992–2010)—much lower than Japan's 4.4–5.1 per cent for its national economy (1950–73), based on Maddison (1995) and Wolff (1996). Besides, South Korea's TFP growth in manufacturing could be 3 per cent per annum in 1966–90 if based on Young (1995). Taiwan's industrial TFP growth could be gauged at between 3 and 5 per cent per annum if based on Young (1995) and Kawai (1994).

Although semifinished and finished goods industries have maintained slow TFP growth in the past three decades, the persistent TFP decline in energy industries and deteriorating TFP performance in industries that produce input materials have clearly suggested that the cross-subsidisation between the upstream and downstream industries through government interventions is absolutely unhealthy and unsustainable. We also show that the downstream industries have been relying more and more on intermediate inputs. Therefore, the efficiency and productivity of the latter inevitably have a significant bearing on the cost of the former. This is a fundamental problem facing the Chinese economy that should be addressed seriously in the current policy debate.

References

Bosworth, B. and Collins, S. M. (2008), 'Accounting for growth: comparing China and India', *Journal of Economic Perspectives* 22(1): 45–66.

Domar, E. (1961), 'On the measurement of technological change', *Economic Journal* 71.

Huang, Y. and Tao, K. (2010), 'Factor market distortion and the current account surplus in China', *Asian Economic Papers* 9(3).

Hulten, C. (1978), 'Growth accounting with intermediate inputs', *Review of Economic Studies* 45.

Ito, K. and Wu, H. X. (2013), Construction of China's input–output table time series for 1981–2010: a supply–use table approach, Presented at the Second Asia KLEMS Conference, Bank of Korea, Seoul, 22–23 August 2013.

Jorgenson, D. W. and Griliches, Z. (1967), 'The explanation of productivity change', *Review of Economic Studies* 34(3): 249–83.

Jorgenson, D. W., Gollop, F. and Fraumeni, B. (1987), *Productivity and U.S. Economic Growth*, Cambridge, Mass.: Harvard University Press.

Jorgenson, D. W., Ho, M. S. and Stiroh, K. J. (2005), *Information Technology and the American Growth Resurgence*, Cambridge, Mass.: MIT Press.

Kawai, H. (1994), 'International comparative analysis of economic growth', *The Developing Economies* XXXII(4): 373–97.

Maddison, A. (1995), *Monitoring the World Economy, 1820–1992*, Paris: OECD Development Centre.

O'Mahony, M. and Timmer, M. P. (2009), 'Output, input and productivity measures at the industry level: the EU KLEMS database', *The Economic Journal* 119(June): F374–F403.

The Conference Board (TCB) (2013), *Total Economy Database*, New York: The Conference Board.

Wolff, E. N. (1996), 'The productivity slowdown: the culprit at last? Follow-up on Hulten and Wolff', *American Economic Review* 86(5): 1239–52.

Wu, H. X. (2008), Measuring capital input in Chinese industry and implications for China's industrial productivity performance, 1949–2005, Presented at the World Congress on National Accounts and Economic Performance Measures for Nations, Washington, DC.

Wu, H. X. (2013), Accounting for productivity growth in Chinese industry—towards the KLEMS approach, Presented at the Second Asia KLEMS Conference, Bank of Korea, Seoul, 22–23 August 2013.

Wu, H. X. (2014a), *China's growth and productivity performance debate revisited—accounting for China's sources of growth in 1949–2012*, Economics Working Papers EPWP1401, The Conference Board, New York.

Wu, H. X. (2014b), Constructing China's net capital stock and measuring capital service in China, Presented at CIP Special Project Meeting, IER, Hitotsubashi University, Tokyo, 20 March 2014.

Wu, H. X. and Ito, K. (2014), Reconstruction of China's national output and income accounts, producer price indices, and annual supply–use and input–output accounts, Presented at CIP Special Project Meeting, IER, Hitotsubashi University, Tokyo, 20 March 2014.

Wu, H. X. and Yue, X. (2012), *Accounting for labor input in Chinese industry, 1949–2009*, Discussion Paper Series 12-E-065, RIETI, Japan.

Wu, H. X., with Girardin, E. (2013), China's growth cycles: common features of GDP and coincident economic indicators, Presented at Ninth CERDI-IDREC International Conference on the Chinese Economy, University of Auvergne, Clermont-Ferrand, France, 24–25 October 2013.

Wu, H. X., Yue, X. and Zhang, G. G. (2014), Constructing employment and compensation matrices and measuring labor input in China, Presented at CIP Special Project Meeting, IER, Hitotsubashi University, Tokyo, 20 March 2014.

Wu, Y. (2011), "Total factor productivity growth in China: A review", *Journal of Chinese Economic and Business Studies* 9(2), 111-126.

Young, A. (1995), 'The tyranny of numbers: confronting the statistical realities of the East Asian growth experience', *Quarterly Journal of Economics* (August): 641–80.

18. Growth, Structural Change and Productivity Gaps in China's Industrial Sector

Yanrui Wu, Ning Ma and Xiumei Guo

China's high economic growth in recent decades has been associated with rapid industrialisation; however, there are considerable regional variations in industrial development in the country. Several authors have provided empirical evidence of possible regional convergence in recent decades (Wang and Szirmai 2013; Rizov and Zhang 2014; Lemoine et al. 2014). Wang and Szirmai (2013) considered provincial industrial labour productivity and found regional evidence of convergence in the 1980s and 2000s. Rizov and Zhang (2014) employed micro-level data to show that the density of economic activity, economic policy and structural factors have affected regional productivity levels and growth differentials. Lemoine et al. (2014) argued that China's interior regions are catching up with more developed coastal areas in terms of labour productivity levels and hence the country is becoming more integrated technologically. This study adds to the existing literature. Its objective is to present a shift-share analysis of productivity gaps in industrial sectors across Chinese regions. For this purpose, a review of China's industrial growth in recent years is presented first. Then an assessment of possible structural change in the industrial sector is provided. This is followed by the analysis of labour productivity gaps across regions. The main findings are summarised in the concluding section.

Industrial growth and analysis

Figure 18.1 shows the contributions of agriculture, industry and services to GDP growth over time. It is apparent that the industry has the largest share among the three sectors. This share has, however, shown a declining trend in recent years. This phenomenon may reflect the country's policy shift to promote consumption-driven economic growth. After three decades of high growth, the Chinese economy is now in the process of transformation from being labour intensive to innovation oriented, and from being overly dependent on investment to greater reliance on domestic demand. The industrial sector is changing in response to ongoing macro-economic adjustment. This section provides a brief review of recent trends and developments in the industrial sector.

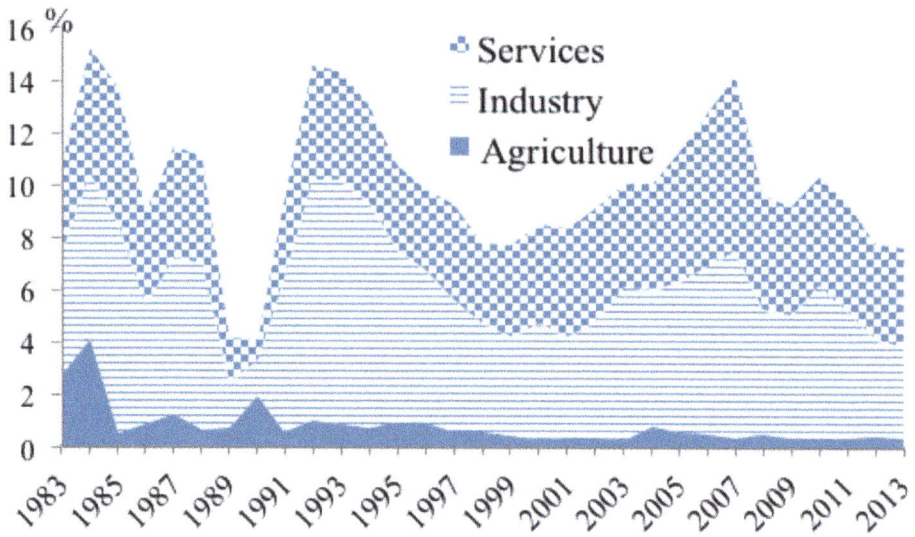

Figure 18.1 Contribution to Economic Growth by Sector, 1983–2013
Source: Authors' calculations using statistics from NBS (various years).

Table 18.1 presents the average growth rates of industrial output in selected subsectors in China. All subsectors experienced high growth during the period 1994–2010, which corresponds with the deepening of economic reforms after Deng Xiaoping's 1992 tour of southern China. Growth in the 2000s (with an average rate of 21.2 per cent during 2001–10) was much faster than that in the 1990s (with an average rate of 9.9 per cent during 1994–2000). This difference may be due to two factors. First, growth in the 1990s was interrupted by the 1997 Asian financial crisis. Second, China's accession into the World Trade Organisation (WTO) in 2001 stimulated the country's export sector. Industry groups with above average growth for the period 2001–10 include pharmaceuticals, non-metallic minerals, smelting and processing of ferrous and nonferrous metals, general and special-purpose machinery, transportation, electrical and telecommunications equipment, and instruments and meters. In particular, the six sectors at the bottom of the list in Table 18.1 exhibited the highest growth. These sectors mainly cover industries embodying relatively high technology (transport, electrical and communication equipment, and measuring instruments), which enjoyed an export boom after China became a WTO member in 2001.

Table 18.1 Average Growth Rates of Industrial Output by Sector (per cent)

Sectors	1994–00	2001–05	2006–10	2001–10
Food processing	4.1	19.9	20.1	20.0
Food manufacturing	0.8	20.8	20.8	20.8
Beverages	13.4	11.9	22.2	17.0
Tobacco	8.0	12.8	15.0	13.9
Textiles	2.6	19.7	15.2	17.4
Paper and paper products	6.8	22.5	19.1	20.8
Petroleum	2.6	12.4	8.9	10.6
Chemical products	9.7	19.1	21.7	20.4
Pharmaceuticals	5.0	24.2	20.7	22.4
Chemical fibres	8.8	15.0	12.6	13.8
Nonmetallic products	6.7	20.1	25.3	22.7
Ferrous metals	1.1	28.4	16.8	22.6
Nonferrous metals	9.0	24.3	21.9	23.1
Metal products	12.2	19.2	23.3	21.2
General purpose machinery	21.2	28.7	26.0	27.3
Special purpose machinery	10.4	22.8	27.1	25.0
Transport equipment	11.7	27.0	28.4	27.7
Electrical equipment	14.9	25.5	23.2	24.3
Communication equipment	28.7	38.1	18.8	28.4
Measuring instruments	20.3	31.1	19.3	25.2

Sources: Authors' calculations using data from *China Statistical Yearbook* (NBS various years) and *China Statistical Yearbook of Industrial Economy* (NBS various years).

At the regional level, China's regions experienced remarkable growth in industrial output 1994–2010 (Table 18.2).[1] Consistent with the growth trend at the sectoral level, regional growth in the 2000s was much faster than that in the 1990s. In addition, average growth in the coastal area (coded number 1 in Table 18.2) was much higher than that in the rest of the country. This trend was maintained in the early 2000s. In the second half of the 2000s, however, industrial growth in the non-coastal areas exceeded that in the coastal areas. Several policy changes might be responsible for the catch-up of the non-coastal areas. These include the implementation of the western development program in 1999, the north-east regional reinvigoration program in 2003 and the 'middle region rise' strategy in 2006. In Table 18.2, the middle, western and north-east regions are coded 2, 3 and 4, respectively. On average, the annual growth rate during 2006–10 was 17.6 per cent for the coastal group, 26.3 per cent for the middle regions and 21.1 per cent for both the western regions and the three north-eastern provinces.

---

1   Tibet is excluded due to missing data.

Table 18.2 Average Growth Rates of Industrial Output by Region (per cent)

Code	Region	1994–00	2001–05	2006–10	2001–10
1	Beijing	6.0	20.7	10.9	15.8
1	Tianjin	7.7	21.8	17.8	19.8
1	Hebei	8.7	22.6	19.3	20.9
1	Shanghai	6.5	21.2	13.7	17.4
1	Jiangsu	8.4	24.9	21.7	23.3
1	Zhejiang	10.8	27.1	16.0	21.5
1	Fujian	9.6	25.5	20.8	23.1
1	Shandong	10.9	28.5	20.0	24.2
1	Guangdong	10.7	25.6	18.2	21.9
2	Shanxi	8.2	19.0	17.7	18.4
2	Anhui	3.2	19.0	29.1	24.0
2	Jiangxi	3.2	21.4	31.8	26.6
2	Henan	10.5	20.7	24.3	22.5
2	Hubei	6.2	12.2	26.9	19.5
2	Hunan	3.9	19.9	28.0	24.0
3	Hainan	4.8	15.5	26.9	21.2
3	Inner Mongolia	4.2	29.4	26.6	28.0
3	Guangxi	3.4	17.4	25.4	21.4
3	Chongqing	11.6	22.0	26.6	24.3
3	Sichuan	−1.2	22.0	26.3	24.2
3	Guizhou	9.5	15.3	13.4	14.4
3	Yunnan	6.6	16.5	15.7	16.1
3	Shaanxi	6.7	18.3	23.1	20.7
3	Gansu	4.1	15.9	13.9	14.9
3	Qinghai	6.3	14.5	24.3	19.4
3	Ningxia	5.1	20.5	18.7	19.6
3	Xinjiang	9.4	13.4	18.0	15.7
4	Liaoning	1.8	17.9	23.6	20.8
4	Jilin	7.0	15.8	26.4	21.1
4	Heilongjiang	3.1	10.7	13.4	12.0

Sources: Authors' calculations using data from *China Statistical Yearbook* (NBS various years) and *China Statistical Yearbook of Industrial Economy* (NBS various years).

Industrial growth analysis

Numerous studies on industrial growth, structural change and productivity analysis have focused on Asian, European and North American regions. Esteban (2000) used the standard shift-share analysis to decompose regional productivity gaps relative to the European average into three components—industry mix, regional components and allocative components. Esteban's results reveal that inter-regional differences can be almost fully explained by region-specific productivity inequality. Thus, from a policy perspective, in order to close the gap between advanced and less-developed regions, economic policies should focus on factors affecting the productivity of backward regions. Somewhat similar to Esteban (2000), Fiaschi and Lavezzi (2007) examined sectoral contributions to aggregate growth in European regions during the period 1980–2002 by decomposing the average growth rate into two components—the productivity growth effect (PGE) and the share effect (SE). Their results illustrated that the contribution of PGE to overall growth is remarkably large relative to that of SE. The growth rate is therefore almost completely attributable to technological changes within sectors. The PGE mainly benefits from the increase in productivity in manufacturing, mining, agriculture and transportation, while the other market service sector suffers from a fall in productivity over the period. SE benefits from the contribution of the other market service and non-market service sectors but this benefit is almost offset by the negative contributions of the agricultural, manufacturing and mining sectors. Overall, other market service, manufacturing, non-market service, wholesale and retail, and transportation are the sectors with the greatest contributions to productivity growth.

Furthermore, Benito and Ezcurra (2005) applied non-parametric techniques to examine the evolution of the distribution of regional productivity in the European Union between 1977 and 1999. Their method involves the shift-share analysis. They argued that there are clear spatial links as neighbouring regions of the European Union are found to share a similar pattern of labour productivity. Moreover, regions with relatively low and medium labour productivity have a greater tendency towards geographical clustering than regions with high labour productivity. They also found that the industry mix contributed relatively little to regional dispersion in the European Union. The main factors determining regional inequality in productivity would be basically those that have a uniform effect on productivity in all sectors (Benito and Ezcurra 2005). The structural component appeared to have played a minor role in regional inequality during the period covered.

Kallioras and Petrakos (2010) calculated the coefficient of structural change (CSC) and the index of dissimilarity of industrial structures (IDIS) for regions within the EU new member states (EU NMS) during the period 1991–2000. Their results revealed that each EU NMS region experienced its own level of structural adjustment. While the majority of the regions of the more advanced EU NMS (including Slovenia, Hungary and Estonia) tend to show a low degree of structural change, most of the less-advanced regions (such as Bulgaria and Romania) show a high degree of change. In addition, the estimated IDIS values show that most of the Bulgarian and Romanian regions have increased their dissimilarity (Kallioras and Petrakos 2010). Almon and Tang (2011) used a decomposition technique to determine the contribution of each industry to economic growth in Canada and the United States. They found that the manufacturing sector was the main source of the post-2000 slowdown in labour productivity in Canada and it continued to contribute less to aggregate growth than in the United States. Their results indicated that the manufacturing sector in both Canada and the United States was adversely affected by structural change during the period 2000–08.

Timmer and Szirmai (2000) also investigated productivity growth by using shift-share analysis. They used four Asian countries as their case study and found that resource allocation did not make extra contributions to aggregate productivity growth, in addition to growth in individual sectors. They hence argued that manufacturing sector-wide effects on productivity growth are more important than industry-specific effects in rapidly growing developing countries. This argument is consistent with theories of conditional convergence, which stress the importance of economy-wide factors for growth. These factors include innovation, the provision of financial and business services, development of an extensive physical infrastructure and high investment ratios (Abramovitz 1989; Timmer and Szirmai 2000).

Studies of Chinese industries

The papers reviewed in the preceding section are mainly concerned with developed economies partly because of the abundance of data for these countries. Recently a number of scholars have also investigated industrial structural change in China. For example, O'Callaghan and Yue (2000) found that Chinese industrial sectors including freight transport, petroleum and natural gas production and other mining industries were responsible for more than 50 per cent of overall structural change between 1987 and 1995. Many scholars have also examined factors that affect industrial structure. For example, Chen and Wu (2003) focused on technology, innovations and foreign direct investment (FDI), while Li and Long (2001) focused on consumption structure. Wen (2004) examined industrial clustering and illustrated that Chinese manufacturing industries became increasingly geographically concentrated. Based on the analysis of a panel dataset of 32 industries in 29 regions, Bai et al. (2004) found that the geographic concentration of industrial production increased between 1984 and 1997. Fan and Scott (2003) provided evidence to support the existence of a positive relationship between industrial clustering and productivity growth. They also argued that China's economic reform has a positive impact on macroeconomic and local conditions under which industrial clustering can emerge.

China's robust economic performance is not only due to the accumulation of physical capital and conditional convergence, but also to the improvements in factor productivity through structural change (Xu and Voon 2003). Many discussions of China's industrial performance have focused on the differences in productivity between the coastal and inland regions. Using a balanced panel dataset covering more than 250 000 'above designated size' enterprises, Jefferson et al. (2008) found significant productivity variation among the firms across the regions between 1998 and 2005. The authors also provided evidence of partial catch-up, particularly for the central region. They argued that much of the catch-up reflects the relative backwardness of firms outside the coastal regions. Their results also showed that productivity growth in the inland regions remains the same as or lower than that of the coastal region, thereby barring the firms in central and western China from the opportunity of achieving productivity parity with their coastal counterparts. Moreover, they found that by 2005, the industrial productivity gap between China's central and coastal regions had narrowed substantially, while the productivity levels of the west and north-east, respectively, rose to 83 per cent and 85 per cent of that of the coast.

Dong et al. (2011) used panel data from 31 provinces spanning three decades and examined the relationship between economic growth and industrial structure. They concluded that short-run economic fluctuation could cause industrial structural imbalance while a long-run bi-directional causal relationship exists between industrial structural imbalance and economic fluctuation. Using regression analysis, they found that per capita GDP, domestic consumption, income inequality, labour force and capital stock are important determinants of China's industrial structure. Their empirical evidence confirms that a long-term relationship exists between industrial structure and economic growth, and that domestic consumption also significantly affects China's industrial structure.

Marti et al. (2011) investigated the effect of China's WTO membership on regional industrial productivity. They found that China's central zone recorded the largest increase in industrial productivity during the period 1995–2006; however, practically all regions have improved remarkably as a result of China becoming a member of the WTO. Overall growth in productivity has been driven by the enhancement of technology. Therefore, as illustrated by the results of technical efficiency estimates, more emphasis should be placed on using inputs more efficiently. Moreover, convergence results do not reveal great changes in the country as a whole post 2001. Existing regional differences in terms of industrial value added are, however, seen to have decreased slightly due to the western regions developing more rapidly (Marti et al. 2011).

Lin et al. (2011) provided evidence of positive correlation between industrial clustering and productivity. They argued the Government should continue to implement its industrial park policy and hence create agglomerations of high-technology firms with positive externalities that can enhance firm-level productivity. Small firms established in clustered regions could benefit more than large firms from the positive externalities of agglomeration. Such positive externalities are associated with information sharing, greater ease in finding professionals, the savings from lower transportation costs, and so on. Thus, the Government could more actively promote industrial zones for small firms in order to help them improve their productivity and development. In addition, foreign enterprises have the highest productivity, followed in turn by the private enterprises and state-owned enterprises (SOEs). Therefore, there is room for productivity improvement in private enterprises. Furthermore, the Government should continue the course of SOE restructuring to strengthen management and productive efficiency (Lin et al. 2011).

Furthermore, Wei (2000) argued that regional spillover effects may be sufficient to reduce inequality in the regions of China. The tests for inter-regional spillover effects indicate that output growth in the coastal zone spills over into the growth of the central and western zones and that the central zone's growth also affects the western zone's development (Zhang and Felmingham 2002). More recently, Peng and Hong (2013) explored productivity spillovers among linked sectors. They argued that productivity in a sector is determined not only by production factors such as labour and capital but also by spillovers from linked sectors. One of the spillovers—namely, the knowledge spillover among sectors—could lead to cost reduction. Peng and Hong adopted the concept of economic distance to measure intersectoral linkages. They concluded that economic distance plays a more important role than spatial distance in transmitting productivity spillover.

The above-surveyed studies have contributed to the understanding of industrial development, structural change and productivity growth in China; however, most of the studies have analysed data either for a limited time span or at a highly aggregated level. This study adds to the existing literature by exploring sectoral data within each region in China.

Structural change in the industrial sector

To analyse the pattern and changes of industrial structure in China's regions during 2000–10, the coefficient of structural change (CSC) is estimated. Havlik (1995) stated that the CSC correlates the shares (S) of each sector i (i = 1, 2... n) in region r between an initial year, t, and an end year, $t + k$. Symbolically, the CSC can be expressed as Equation 18.1.

Equation 18.1

$$CSC_{r,t\_t+k} = CORREL_{i=1}^{n}(S_{r,i,t}, S_{r,i,t+k})$$

In Equation 18.1, *CSC* takes values in the interval [0, 1]. Values close to zero indicate that significant structural changes have taken place during the period between *t* and *t* + *k*, whereas values close to 1 indicate that almost no structural change has taken place. The shares can be based on either output or employment across the regions.

The data used in this study are collected from China's official statistical resources, and the sample covers 2000–10, 20 manufacturing subsectors and 30 Chinese regions. According to Tables 18.3 and 18.4, some regions experienced more structural change while others demonstrated very little variation over time. At the national level, structural change was modest during 2000–10. Among the regions, Hunan and Hainan have the lowest CSC scores between 2000 and 2010, implying the most structural change recorded among the regions. Within the 10 best-performing regions, seven show more structural change in the second half of the decade (Table 18.3). Regions with the least change in their CSC scores include Fujian, Guangdong and Chongqing. Eight of the 10 regions with the least structural change between 2000 and 2010 have CSC scores above 0.90 (Table 18.4). Tables 18.3 and 18.4 also show that there is no clear distinction between the coastal and interior regions in terms of structural change. The results using employment shares are not reported and show similar patterns.

Table 18.3 Regions with More Structural Change

Regions	2000–05	2005–10	2000–10
National	0.91	0.96	0.86
Liaoning	0.92	0.72	0.54
Heilongjiang	0.88	0.82	0.57
Jiangsu	0.81	0.96	0.71
Anhui	0.84	0.92	0.69
Jiangxi	0.91	0.77	0.62
Shandong	0.91	0.87	0.68
Hunan	0.87	0.67	0.43
Guangxi	0.83	0.95	0.68
Hainan	0.70	0.49	0.34
Shaanxi	0.88	0.89	0.66

Sources: Authors' calculations using data from *China Statistical Yearbook* (NBS various years) and *China Statistical Yearbook of Industrial Economy* (NBS various years).

Table 18.4 Regions with Less Structural Change

Regions	2000–05	2005–10	2000–10
National	0.91	0.96	0.86
Hebei	0.93	0.98	0.90
Shanxi	0.95	0.97	0.92
Inner Mongolia	0.88	0.84	0.75
Jilin	0.97	0.99	0.94
Fujian	0.98	0.99	0.97
Guangdong	0.97	1.00	0.96
Chongqing	0.99	1.00	0.98
Yunnan	0.98	0.98	0.92
Qinghai	0.98	0.96	0.94
Xinjiang	0.96	0.87	0.76

Sources: Authors' calculations using data from *China Statistical Yearbook* (NBS various years) and *China Statistical Yearbook of Industrial Economy* (NBS various years).

A further assessment of the nature of the industrial structural patterns in China's regions can be conducted through the estimation of the index of dissimilarity of industrial structures (IDIS). The IDIS is defined as the sum of the square of the difference between the share (S) of sector $i(= 1, 2..., n)$ in region r and the share in a benchmark economy b in a given year, t (Kallioras and Petrakos 2010). In mathematical form this is Equation 18.2.

Equation 18.2

$$IDIS_{r\_b,t} = \sum_{i=1}^{n}(S_{r,i,t} - S_{b,i,t})^2$$

Here the average share of each sector across the region is used as the benchmark score. The IDIS takes values greater than (or equal to) zero. High values imply high levels of structural dissimilarity with the national average, whereas low values indicate low levels of structural dissimilarity. Increasing values of the IDIS indicate that the regions under consideration are becoming more dissimilar, whereas decreasing values imply that the corresponding regions are becoming more similar. In the cases of less-developed regions, increasing structural dissimilarity is an indication of a negative (defensive) structural change, whereas decreasing structural dissimilarity is an indication of a positive (offensive) structural change. Defensive structural changes can be noticed as impulsive reactions to the conditions and requirements of an emerging economic environment whereas, offensive structural changes can be seen as strategic choices (Kallioras and Petrakos 2010).

In general the estimated IDIS values in terms of industrial output for each region during 2000–10 are very low, ranging from the lowest of 0.002 to the highest of 0.223. These values indicate low levels of structural dissimilarity among the Chinese regions. Yunnan, Chongqing and Jilin recorded relatively high IDIS scores over time. Thus these regions have an industrial structure with high dissimilarity with the national average structure. To make interpretation easy, the average scores for 2000–04 and 2006–10 for each region are computed and compared. Three regions with the greatest increase in IDIS scores (defensive structural change) are Hebei, Shanghai and Guangdong, which all are coastal regions (Table 18.5). Seven regions—namely, Yunnan, Jilin, Qinghai, Tianjin, Inner Mongolia, Ningxia and Hainan—show decreased dissimilarity with the benchmark average structure. This implies that these regions experienced intra-industry types of economic integration and most likely undertook offensive structural changes between 2000 and 2010.

Table 18.5 Regions with the Most Structural Changes

Regions	2000–04	2006–10	Changes
	Defensive		
Hebei	0.051	0.083	0.032
Shanghai	0.029	0.060	0.031
Guangdong	0.090	0.110	0.021
	Offensive		
Yunnan	0.179	0.102	−0.077
Jilin	0.191	0.152	−0.039
Qinghai	0.147	0.111	−0.036
Tianjin	0.061	0.042	−0.018
Inner Mongolia	0.055	0.037	−0.018
Ningxia	0.069	0.051	−0.017
Hainan	0.071	0.055	−0.016

Sources: Authors' own estimates.

Understanding productivity gaps

Regional productivity performance has important implications for government policymaking at both the national and the regional levels in China. The reduction of income inequality and the improvement of social welfare in less-developed areas depend on improvements in productivity. Economic growth in China in recent decades has been outstanding compared with that of other countries. Key factors underlying this growth are the technological and institutional changes associated with economic reforms initiated in the 1980s. Productivity has also played an important role in effecting these changes.

As a result, efforts to evaluate China's economic growth have focused on the measurement of productivity in the Chinese economy. There is a large body of studies in this area (Wu 2011). Most authors provided estimates of total factor productivity (TFP) growth and its contribution to economic growth. This study differs from the existing ones by focusing on regional productivity gaps. For this purpose, labour productivity is decomposed into structural, regional and allocative components. The objective is to explore productivity inequality between regions and within zones (coastal, central and western). Labour productivity used in this study is calculated by dividing the industrial output by the number for workers in each sector within the regions.

Labour productivity (LP) at the national level has increased steadily since 2000 regardless of whether gross output or value added is employed in the estimation (Figure 18.2). Across the 20 subsectors covered by this study, however, labour productivity varies considerably. The leading sector is tobacco, followed by communication equipment, ferrous metals, transport equipment and nonferrous metals sectors. There is regional variation also in labour productivity.[2] In the early years of the sample period (2000–10), Shanghai led the regions with the highest labour productivity followed by Beijing, Tianjin, Guangdong and other coastal provinces. Xinjiang is the only western region where the labour productivity level was above the national average and compatible with the performance of the coastal regions (it was actually ranked number three, just behind Shanghai and Beijing in 2000). In 2005 Tianjin overtook Shanghai to become the leader in terms of labour productivity; however, in 2006, Hainan Island's labour productivity exceeded Tianjin's, and Hainan maintained its number one ranking at the end of the sample period (2010). By 2010, among the top 10 performing regions, seven were coastal provinces (Hainan, Tianjin, Shanghai, Beijing, Liaoning, Shandong and Hebei). Inner Mongolia is the only western region which made it into the top 10, and it benefited mainly from the resource boom in recent decades. Anhui as a central region was ranked number 10. Jilin is a north-eastern province and was in second position in terms of labour productivity performance. The worst-performing region is Ningxia, a western region, with estimated average labour productivity less than half Hainan's in 2010. In general, labour productivity in western regions (except Inner Mongolia and Xinjiang) was lower than the national average during the period 2000–10. Interestingly, the ranking of Guangdong dropped dramatically from number five in 2000 to number 28 in 2010 (just before Ningxia and Shanxi).

---

2 The estimated values by region, sector and year are not shown due to space constraints.

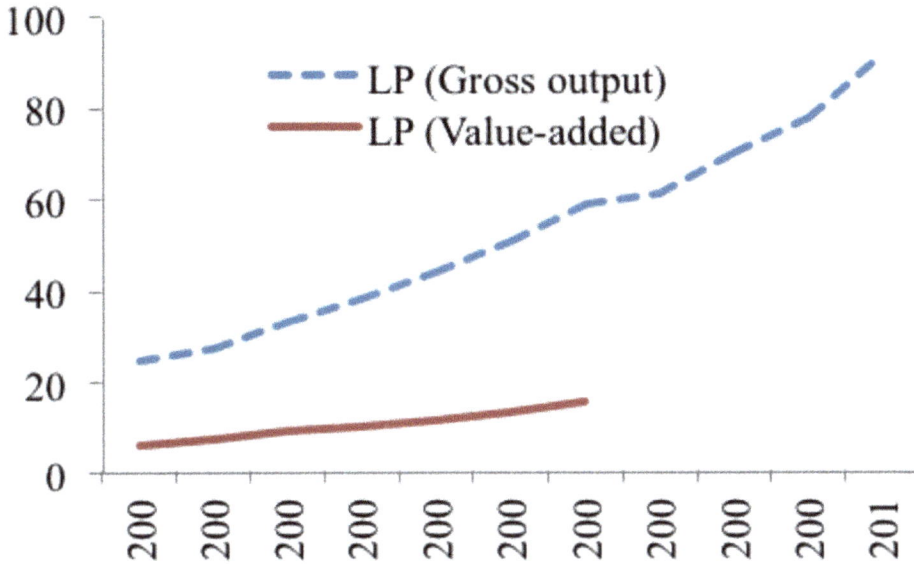

Figure 18.2 Average Labor Productivity in China's Industrial Sector, 2000–10

Source: Authors' calculations. To understand the above-discussed productivity differences, the shift-share analysis technique is adopted to decompose the productivity gap into several components. For this purpose, the aggregate labour productivity of a region, X_r, can be expressed as the weighted average of productivity across its sectors. Thus for region r, X_r can be written as Equation 18.3.

Equation 18.3

$$X_r = \frac{I_r}{L_r} = \sum_{i=1}^{n}(\frac{I_{ir}}{L_{ir}})(\frac{L_{ir}}{L_i})$$

In Equation 18.3 the subscripts i and r denote the ith industrial sector and the rth region respectively; I stands for the industrial value added and L for employment. Equation 18.3 states that regional productivity differences can be attributed to two factors. First, differences in labour productivity in the i sectors result in regional disparities in productivity. Therefore, even if there were no regional disparities in each individual sector, regions specialising in more productive sectors would achieve productivity higher than the national average. Second, there are differences in the regional characteristics that have the same influence on productivity in different sectors.

In order to evaluate the relevance of each of these two factors it is necessary to decompose the gap between regional productivity and the national average productivity. According to Esteban (2000), a useful technique for this exercise is the shift-share analysis, which originates from the field of labour economics, and was designed as a technique for analysing growth in regional employment (Benito and Ezcurra 2005). It can, however, be applied to the study of labour productivity as well. Following this approach, the productivity gap between a given region and the national average can be decomposed into three components—structural, regional and resource allocation factors.

Let $E_{i,r}$ be sector i's employment share in region r and E_i denote sector i's employment share at the national level. Therefore, $\Sigma E_{i,r} = 1$ for all regions, r and $\Sigma E_i = 1$. Assume X_i and $X_{i,r}$ represent labour productivity in sector i and labour productivity sector i in region r, respectively. The structural or industry-mix component, μ_r, of region r measures the effect on the productivity differential due to the difference between region r's industrial structure and the national average, assuming that sector productivity in each region is equal to the national average. The *structural component* can be written as Equation 18.4.

Equation 18.4

$$\mu_r = \sum_i (E_{i,r} - E_i)X_i$$

In Equation 18.4, μ_r has a positive value if the region is more specialised in sectors with high labour productivity at the national level and de-specialised in sectors with low labour productivity. μ_r reaches the maximum value if the region specialised in sectors with the highest productivity. Conversely, μ_r would plunge to the minimum if the region had specialised in sectors with the lowest productivity.

The regional or productivity differential component, π_r, is related to the impact of sector-by-sector productivity differences between regional and national average productivity, assuming the region's industrial structure is the same as the national average. The *regional component* can be written as Equation 18.5.

Equation 18.5

$$\pi_r = \sum_i E_i(X_{i,r} - X_i)$$

In Equation 18.5, π_r has a positive value if the region's sector productivity is above the national level.

The *allocative component*, θ_r, is defined as Equation 18.6.

Equation 18.6

$$\theta_r = \sum_i (E_{i,r} - E_i)(X_{i,r} - X_i)$$

In Equation 18.6, θ_r is positive if the region is specialised in sectors which have productivity above the national average. This component is the intersection of the structural and regional components, which may be used as an indicator of the efficiency in allocating resources among the sectors in each region. Given the definitions of the three components, the regional productivity gap can be expressed as Equation 18.7.

Equation 18.7

$$G_r = X_r - X = \mu_r + \pi_r + \theta_r$$

Equation 18.7 implies that the productivity gap between a region and the national average can be decomposed into three components.

To apply the above-discussed decomposition technique, the average productivity gaps of each region for the period 2000–10 are computed. A summary of the data is presented in Figures 18.3 and 18.4 in which the average gaps for the periods 2000–04 (the first half of the period) and 2006–10 (the second half) are presented. According to Figure 18.3, nine regions led by Shanghai and Tianjin recorded a positive average productivity gap during 2000–10. The positive gaps on average were much bigger in the second half of the period than in the first half. It is interesting to note that Inner Mongolia changed from a negative gap region to a significantly positive one, while Fijian changed from a positive gap province to a negative one. Furthermore, as expected, the majority of the regions with a positive gap are coastal regions.

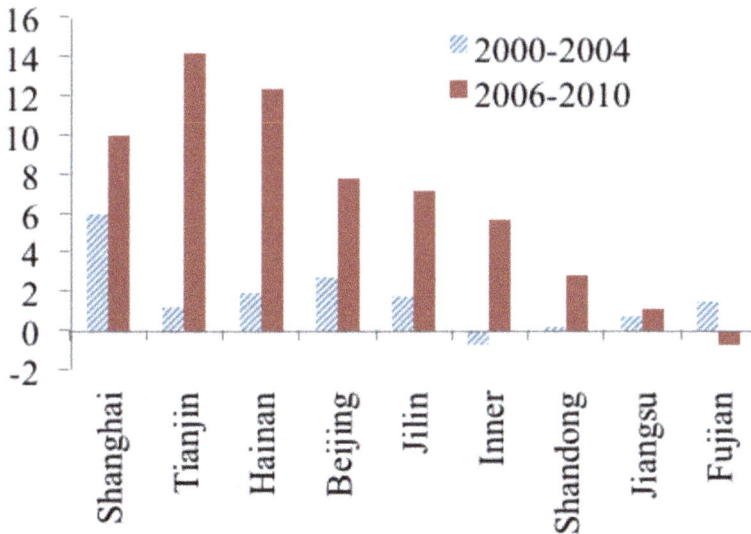

Figure 18.3 Regions with Positive Productivity Gaps

Source: Authors' calculations.

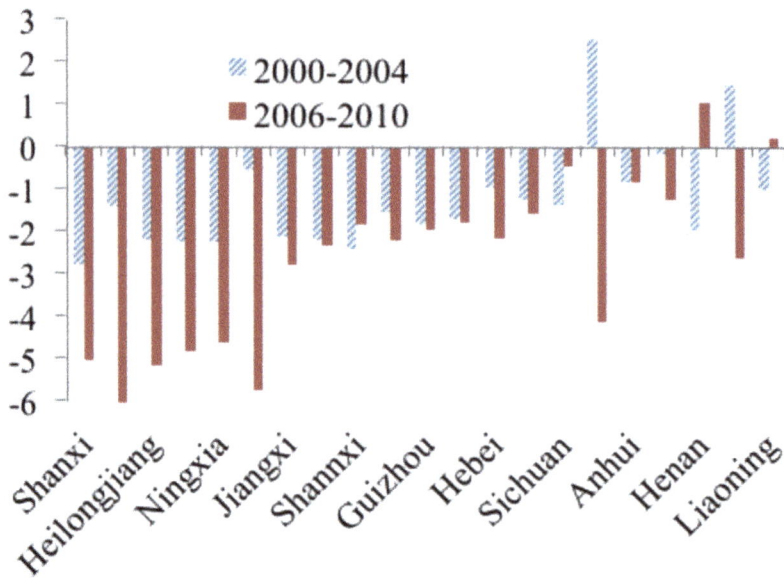

Figure 18.4 Regions with Negative Productivity Gaps
Source: Authors' calculations.

As for the 21 regions with an average negative productivity gap during 2000–10, the regions with the largest gaps are mainly western (Xinjiang, Gansu and Ningxia) and central (Shanxi, Heilongjiang and Jiangxi) regions. Zhejiang is an exception as it is one of the regions with the largest gaps while it is also a relatively developed coastal region (Figure 18.4). The gaps in the second half of the period tend to be bigger than those in the first half. Yunnan and Guangdong moved from a positive position to a negative one while Henan and Liaoning moved in the opposite direction.

The decomposition results show different patterns of productivity gaps among the nine regions with positive gaps. Only three regions (Tianjin, Beijing and Jilin) have achieved allocative efficiency. Shanghai, with the highest productivity gap, has not benefited from allocative efficiency. Hainan and Inner Mongolia also suffered from allocative inefficiency though their productivity is well above the national average. It is also found that Shandong, Jiangsu and Fujian are not specialising in sectors with high productivity.

In the literature on regional disparity, China is often divided into three zones—namely, the coastal: Beijing, Tianjin, Hebei, Liaoning, Shanghai, Jiangsu, Zhejiang, Fujian, Shandong and Guangdong; the central: Shanxi, Jilin, Heilongjiang, Anhui, Henan, Hubei, Hunan and Jiangxi; and the western: Inner Mongolia, Guangxi, Hainan, Chongqing, Sichuan, Guizhou, Yunnan, Shaanxi, Gansu, Qinghai, Ningxia and Xinjiang. It is thus useful to examine productivity gaps across the three zones. The estimated results show that while all three zones have had a remarkable growth in labour productivity during the past decade, the central zone's average productivity increased significantly from 2000 to 2005 and the coastal region's average productivity increased dramatically between 2006 and 2010. These increases were driven by good performance in some subsectors. For example, the productivity of the central zone in the smelting and processing of nonferrous metals, and the manufacture of ordinary machinery and transportation equipment, was above the national average in 2005. The productivity of the western zone in the industries of food processing, food manufacturing, beverage manufacturing, petroleum processing and cooking products was above the national average in 2010.

Table 18.6 presents the summary statistics of the productivity gap and its decomposition for the three zones. It is apparent that on average the coastal zone enjoys a small positive productivity gap while the central and western zones show negative gaps. All three zones seem to suffer from allocative inefficiency (negative allocative scores). The coastal zone has labour productivity above the national average while both the central and the western zones have productivity below the national average during 2000–10. Table 18.6 also demonstrates that the coastal zone is not necessarily specialising in sectors with high productivity. On the contrary, the central and western zones may actually specialise in high-productivity sectors according to the same table.

Table 18.6 Summary Statistics of Productivity Gaps by Zone

Zone	Gap	Structural	Regional	Allocative
Coastal	0.31	−0.54	1.22	−0.36
Central	−1.31	0.13	−1.34	−0.10
Western	−1.09	1.12	−1.85	−0.36

Source: Authors' calculations.

Further analysis of productivity gaps

In order to determine how much the productivity gap of each component is due to a regional effect or a zonal effect, Equation 18.7 is extended as Equation 18.8.

Equation 18.8

$$G_r = \mu_{I,r} + \mu_{E,r} + \pi_{I,r} + \pi_{E,r} + \theta_{I,r} + \theta_{E,r}$$

In Equation 18.8, each of the three productivity gap components (that is, the structural, regional and allocative components) can be expressed as the sum of an internal factor (indicated by the subscript I) and an external factor (indicated by the subscript E). The internal factor represents the difference between a particular region and the zone average, while the external factor reflects the difference between the average within the zone and the national mean. The decomposition technique in Equation 18.8 originates from the analysis of income inequality (Lerman 1999). The objective of this section is to examine the contribution of each of the components in Equation 18.8 to total inequality in China's regional productivity differentials. In practice, to accommodate the direct effect and possible indirect impact of each component on national or global (G) productivity gaps, the variance of the regional productivity gap (G_r) is considered and variance decomposition is then adopted.[3] Accordingly, the global productivity gap is decomposed into six components in a way similar to Equation 18.8; however, due to the use of variance and hence covariance, the contribution of an individual component could have a negative value if the corresponding covariance is negative. In this case, the component in question would exert an offsetting effect on the global productivity gap generated by other components.

As there are six components after decomposition, there are several ways to organise the results. The first set of results is presented in Figure 18.5. Panel 5a shows the percentage shares of the structural, regional and allocative components. It is apparent that the regional component made the dominant contribution to productivity gaps during 2000–10. In recent years this trend seems to have strengthened. It is also shown that the contribution of the structural component has been small and stable over time. In terms of the external (between zone and national means) and internal (between individual province and zone means) factors, their percentage contributing shares are very close, with the external factor share being slightly higher (51 versus 49 on average) (Panel 5b). This finding has important implications. For a long time, policymakers as well as researchers have been concerned mainly with disparity between the zones (coastal, central and western). Regional differences within the zones may be overlooked, and should be addressed.

---

3 For technical details, see Lerman (1999) and Benito and Ezcurra (2005).

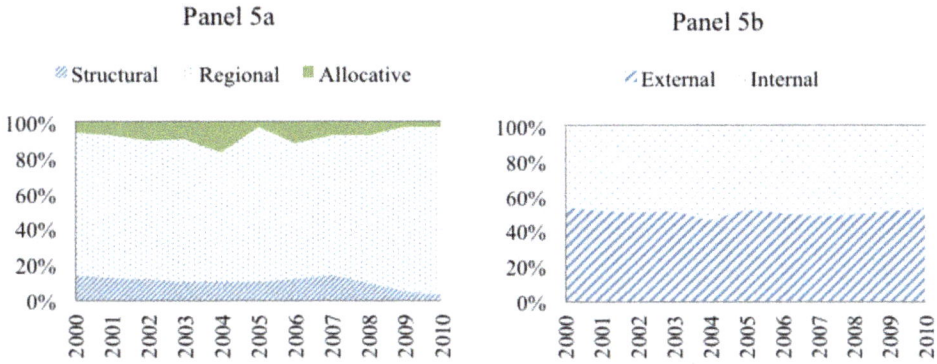

Figure 18.5 Productivity Gap Decomposition, 2000–10

Source: Authors' calculations.

Figure 18.6 shows the composition of the external and internal components. In both cases regional differences are the dominant contributor to productivity gaps. Panel 6a illustrates that the three components (structural, regional and allocative) are relatively stable over time. This is consistent with the observation in Panel 5b of Figure 18.5; however, although the internal factor (Panel 5b of Figure 18.5) may be stable, its three components have changed over time, according to Panel 6b of Figure 18.6. Within the zones, regional differences in productivity have increased during 2000–10, particularly in the second half, while the contribution of allocative efficiency and structural components to productivity gaps has declined slightly (Panel 6b).

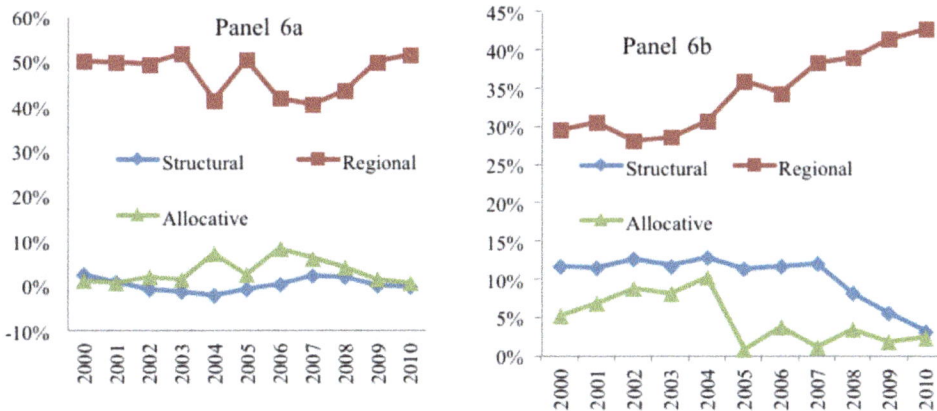

Figure 18.6 Decomposition of External (Panel 6a) and Internal (Panel 6b) Components

Source: Authors' calculations.

Among the three components, the role of the external and internal factors is not exactly the same. Figure 18.7 shows that the internal factor dominates the structural contribution to productivity gaps. For several years the contribution of the external factor is negative. For regional variation, its contribution is, however, dominated by the external factor and tends to be stable over time. As for allocative efficiency, it was initially dominated by the internal factor and in the second half of the period the external factor took over the dominant role (Figure 18.7).

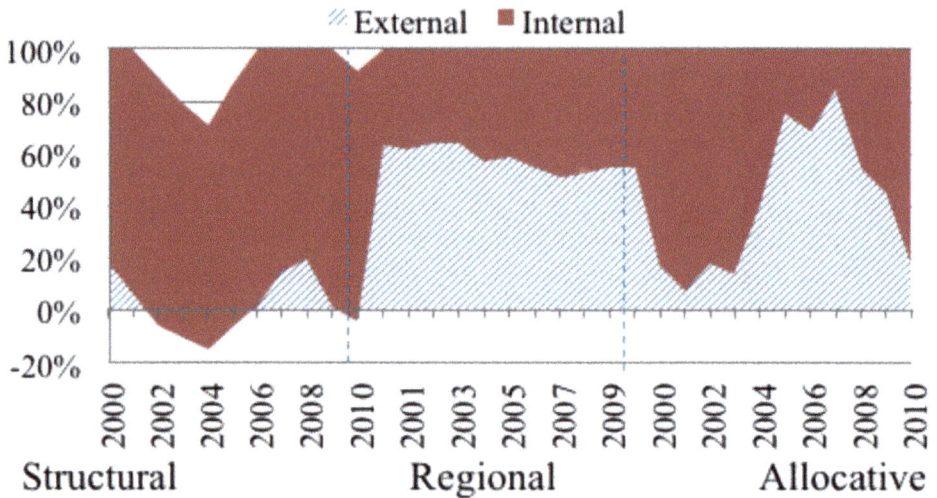

Figure 18.7 Decomposition of the Three Components
Source: Authors' calculations.

Conclusion

To sum up, using provincial sector-level data during 2000–10, this study examined several issues associated with growth, structural change and productivity gaps in the Chinese manufacturing sector. Overall the country's manufacturing output has been growing rapidly, with the coastal zone growing much faster than the central and western zones. The last two have, however, shown a catch-up in the second half of the period of 2000–10 due to various government policies supporting economic development in these areas. Furthermore, China's manufacturing industry has undergone a great degree of structural change, which also varies between regions. It seems that structural change has accelerated in recent years (in the second half of the 2000s covered by our sample). In addition, the findings in this study show that more coastal regions seem to undergo defensive structural change while offensive structural change is more likely to occur in the western regions. There are of course exceptions. Tianjin, for example, is a relatively developed region and it falls into the group with offensive structural change.

As for labour productivity performance across the regions, it is found that growth during 2000–10 was on average impressive. There is, however, considerable regional variation. About one-third of the country's 30 regions recorded a positive productivity gap (relative to the national average). Most of these regions are in the coastal area. Hainan, Jilin and Inner Mongolia are exceptions. Regions with relatively large negative productivity gaps are located mainly in western China. Zhejiang is an exception: it has the sixth-largest negative gap though it is a coastal province. In Yunnan and Guangdong, the productivity gap changed from a large positive one in the first half of the sample period to a large negative one in the second half of the period.

The results of decomposition analysis indicate that the regional component made the greatest contribution to the total productivity gap. This trend seems to have persisted in recent years. Productivity gaps are also attributable to differences within each of the three zones (coastal, central and western) and variation between each zone and the national average. These two seem to be equally responsible for the total productivity gap according to this study. Our estimates also show that disparity within the zones tends to have been worse in recent years while differences between each zone and the national average remain stable.

The findings in this study imply that it is necessary for the Government to formulate province-specific policies. For instance, regions in the central and western zones should focus more on productivity improvement while the coastal zone should focus on structural rationalisation and allocative efficiency. In addition, economic policies should address both inter-zone disparity and intra-zone inequality in productivity. Over the past decade, western region development, the rise of the middle regions and north-eastern reinvigoration programs made significant contributions to the reduction of inter-zone disparity. The central and local governments should also work together to deal with intra-zone productivity inequality.

References

Abramovitz, M. (1989), *Thinking about Growth and Other Essays on Economic Growth and Welfare*, Cambridge and New York: Cambridge University Press.

Almon, M. J. and Tang, J. (2011), 'Industrial structural change and the post-2000 output and productivity growth slowdown: a Canada–US comparison', *International Productivity Monitor* 22(1): 44–81.

Bai, C. E., Duan, Y., Tao, Z. and Tong, S. T. (2004), 'Local protectionism and regional specialization: evidence from China's industries', *Journal of International Economics* 63(2): 397–417.

Benito, J. M. and Ezcurra, R. (2005), 'Spatial disparities in productivity and industry mix: the case of the European regions', *European Urban and Regional Studies* 12(2): 177–94.

Chen, X. L. and Wu, X. (2003), 'Technological innovation: the basic cause of industrial structural evolution', *Lilun Yuekan* [*Theory Monthly*] 12(1): 84–5.

Dong, X., Song, S. and Zhu, H. (2011), 'Industrial structure and economic fluctuation—evidence from China', *The Social Science Journal* 48(3): 468–77.

Esteban, J. (2000), 'Regional convergence in Europe and the industry mix: a shift-share analysis', *Regional Science and Urban Economics* 3(3): 353–64.

Fan, C. and Scott, A. (2003), 'Industrial agglomeration and development: a survey of spatial economic issues in East Asia and a statistical analysis of Chinese regions', *Economic Geography* 79(3): 295–319.

Fiaschi, D. and Lavezzi, A. M. (2007), 'Productivity polarization and sectoral dynamics in European regions', *Journal of Macroeconomics* 29(3): 612–37.

Havlik, P. (1995), 'Trade reorientation and competitiveness in CEECs', in R. Dobrinsky and M. Landesman (eds), *Transforming Economies and European Integration*, 141–62, Aldershot, UK: Edward Elgar.

Jefferson, G. H., Rawski, T. G. and Zhang, Y. (2008), 'Productivity growth and convergence across China's industrial economy', *Journal of Chinese Economic and Business Studies* 6(2): 121–40.

Kallioras, D. and Petrakos, G. (2010), 'Industrial growth, economic integration and structural change: evidence from the EU new member-states regions', *The Annals of Regional Science* 45(3): 667–80.

Lemoine, F., Mayo, G., Poncet, S. and Ünal, D. (2014), *The geographic pattern of China's growth and convergence within industry*, Working Paper No. 2014-04, CEPII Research Center, Paris.

Lerman, R. I. (1999), 'How do income sources affect income inequality', in J. Silber (ed.), *Handbook of Income Inequality Measurement*, 341–62, Boston: Kluwer Academic.

Li, Z. and Long, F. (2001), *Study on Industrial Economy in China*. Chengdu: Southwest Financial University Press.

Lin, H. L, Li, H. Y. and Yang, C. H. (2011), 'Agglomeration and productivity: firm-level evidence from China's textile industry', *China Economic Review* 22 (3): 313–29.

Marti, L., Rosa, P. and Fernandez, J. I. (2011), 'Industrial productivity and convergence in Chinese regions: the effects of entering the World Trade Organisation', *Journal of Asian Economics* 22(2): 128–41.

National Bureau of Statistics (NBS) (various years), *China Statistical Yearbook*, Beijing: China Statistics Press.

National Bureau of Statistics (NBS) (various years), *China Statistical Yearbook of Industrial Economy*, Beijing: China Statistics Press.

O'Callaghan, B. A. and Yue, G. (2000), 'An analysis of structural change in China using biproportional methods', *Economic Systems Research* 12(1): 99–111.

Peng, L. and Hong, Y. (2013), 'Productivity spillovers among linked sectors', *China Economic Review* 25: 44–61.

Rizov, M. and Zhang, X. (2014), 'Regional disparities and productivity in China: evidence from manufacturing micro data', *Papers in Regional Sciences*.

Timmer, M. P. and Szirmai, A. (2000), 'Productivity growth in Asian manufacturing: the structural bonus hypothesis examined', *Structural Change and Economic Dynamics* 11: 371–92.

Wang, L. and Szirmai, A. (2013), 'The unexpected convergence of regional productivity in Chinese industry, 1978–2005', *Oxford Development Studies* 41(1): 29–53.

Wei, Y. H. (2000), *Regional Development in China: States, Globalization, and Inequality*, London: Routledge.

Wen, M. (2004), 'Relocation and agglomeration of Chinese Industry', *Journal of Development Economics* 73(1): 329–47.

Wu, Y. (2011), 'Total factor productivity growth in China: a review', *Journal of Chinese Economic and Business Studies* 9(2): 111–26.

Xu, X. and Voon, J. P. (2003), 'Regional integration in China: a statistical model', *Economic Letters* 79(1): 35–42.

Zhang, Q. and Felmingham, B. (2002), 'The role of FDI, exports and spillover effects in the regional development of China', *Journal of Development Studies* 38(4): 157–78.

19. The Importance, Development and Reform Challenges of China's Rail Sector

Robin Bordie, Stephen Wilson and Jane Kuang[1]

Introduction

China's rail sector is crucial to the nation and the economy. The first railway was built in China in 1876. Substantial growth occurred in the decades after the establishment of the People's Republic in 1949, and the railway system has become the dominant mode for both passenger and freight transport. Since the beginning of the new millennium, the rapidly increased energy requirements of industrialisation, rising incomes and the increased mobilisation accompanying urbanisation have increased the demands on China's rail system.

In the early to mid 1990s, institutions such as the World Bank, working with the Economic Research Centre (ERC) of the State Planning Commission (SPC), were concerned about the ability of the rail system to transport sufficient coal to meet China's growing demand: 'Since the mid-1980s, China's economic growth has been hampered by shortages of either coal, electricity, or both, due to a shortage of power-generating capacity and the inability to transport enough coal from where it is produced to where it is needed' (ERC 1995:xi). The authors noted that at that time, China was the only country in the world to produce or consume more than 1 billion tonnes of coal in a year—a milestone passed in 1990.[2] As it turned out, coal demand more than trebled from 1990 to 2010. In 1990, China's railways moved 2.6 billion passenger kilometres. This number had also more than trebled by 2010.

---

1 The authors acknowledge research support from their Rio Tinto colleagues Lara Dong, William Wang, Jane Li and Parth Goyal; and valued comments from Dr Wu Jianhong at Beijing Jiaotong University. Any errors are the responsibility of the authors.
2 Only the United States has passed the milestone of 1 billion t of coal production, in seven of the years since 1997, and is currently slightly below that level. The forecasters at the ERC expected this to double to 2 billion t a year by 2010.

No other rail system in the world is asked to move as many people and as great a quantity of goods over such large distances as is China's railway system. No other rail system in the world is as vital as China's to the reliability of national energy supply.

This chapter is written at a time of momentous institutional change for China's rail system, with the dissolution of the former Ministry of Railways (MOR) in 2013, and the establishment of the China Railways Corporation (CRC). The world's largest high-speed rail system is rapidly growing. As China rises through the current middle-income stage, and with the less-developed inland provinces aspiring to follow the development lead of coastal cities and provinces, the rail system will be asked to support even greater demands for the safe, efficient, fast and economical movement of people, energy and goods. The reform of the rail sector, in parallel with the growth and evolution of other parts of the economy, will bring new challenges for policymakers.

This chapter is organised in three main sections and a conclusion. The first section describes the historical context and current situation of the rail sector in China. The second section summarises conditions in 10 countries with significant rail sectors and some attributes that may be of interest for comparison with China's rail sector. The third section describes China's rail reforms and the challenges ahead.

Historical context and the current situation

Passenger transport

In 1949, China's railway system transported 103 million passengers, and by 2012 this number had increased by an average rate of 4.6 per cent to more than 1.5 billion (Figure 19.1). Consequently, the passenger transport volume has grown to more than 778 billion passenger kilometres—close to threefold on the 1990 figure of 260 billion passenger km (Figure 19.2).

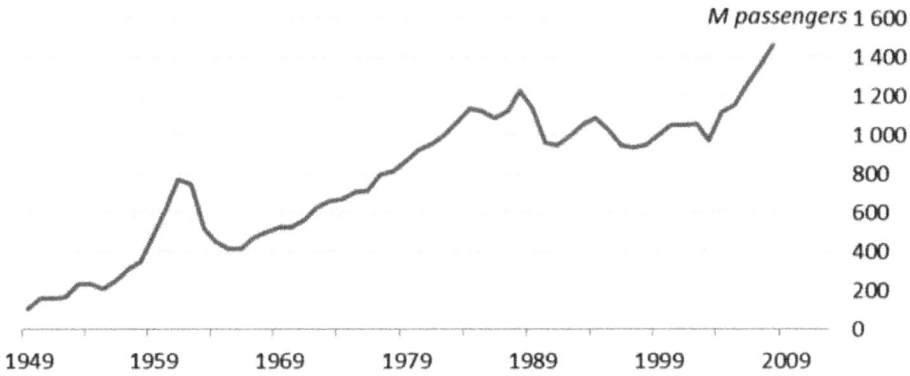

Figure 19.1 China's Railway Passenger Trips, 1949–2008
Source: NBS (2012).

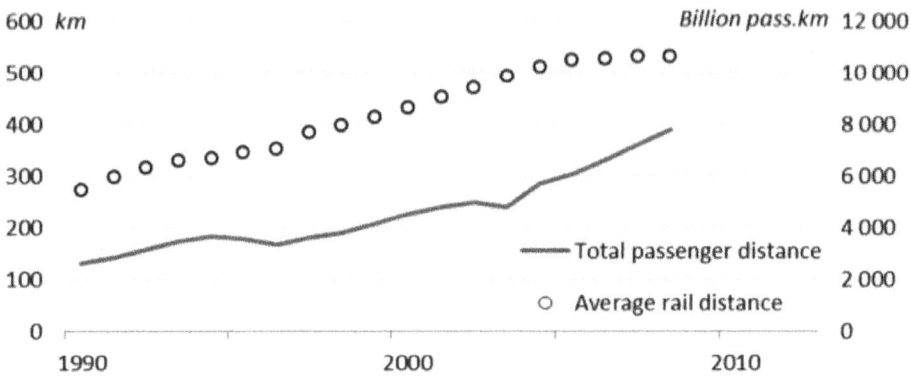

Figure 19.2 Total Passenger Distance Travelled, Average Trip Length, 1990–2008
Source: NBS (2012).

In 1990, 46 per cent of passengers were transported by railway. The proportion had declined to around 34 per cent by 2008 (Figure 19.3). During the same period road transport's share grew from 47 per cent to 54 per cent. Despite the decrease in share, rail remains a dominant and the most efficient passenger transport mode in China. The Spring Festival travel rush, 'Chun Yun', presents the biggest challenge in human history for large-scale annual return visits for people to be with family, generating extremely heavy traffic loads. The period usually begins 15 days before the Lunar New Year's Day and lasts for around 40 days. During the 2014 Spring Festival period, the daily rail passenger demand exceeded 6.5 million passengers and in total more than 266 million passengers travelled by rail during the 40-day period—an increase of 12 per cent on the previous year—and 10 million more passengers than expected.

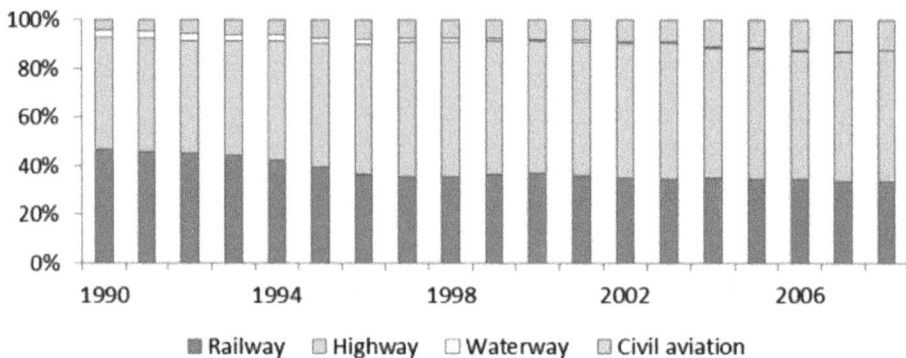

Figure 19.3 Passenger Transport Share by Mode, 1990–2008
Source: NBS (2012).

Freight transport

The railway system transported 4 billion tonnes (Bt) of goods in 2012 (Figure 19.4), compared with 1.5 Bt in 1990, and less than 2 Bt in 2000. At the same time, freight demand increased from less than 1.4 trillion tonne kilometres (t.km) in 2000 to almost 3 trillion t.km in 2012 (Figure 19.5). Despite the increase of rail freight in absolute terms, however, rail's dominance of the freight market has declined over time. Its share in national freight started to fall from more than 40 per cent in 1978 to just 10 per cent in 2012 (Figure 19.6). At the same time, rail's share of freight tonne kilometres, which was between 70 and 80 per cent in the two decades after 1949, declined to 50 per cent by 1980 and then to less than 20 per cent by 2012.

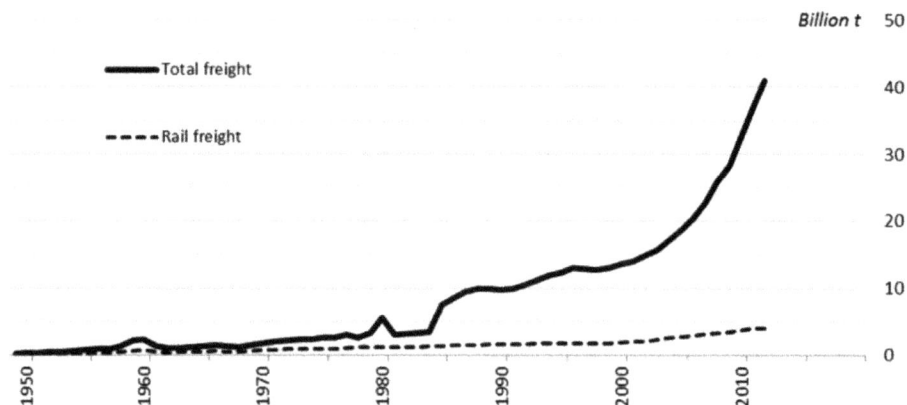

Figure 19.4 Rail Freight Transported
Source: NBS (2012).

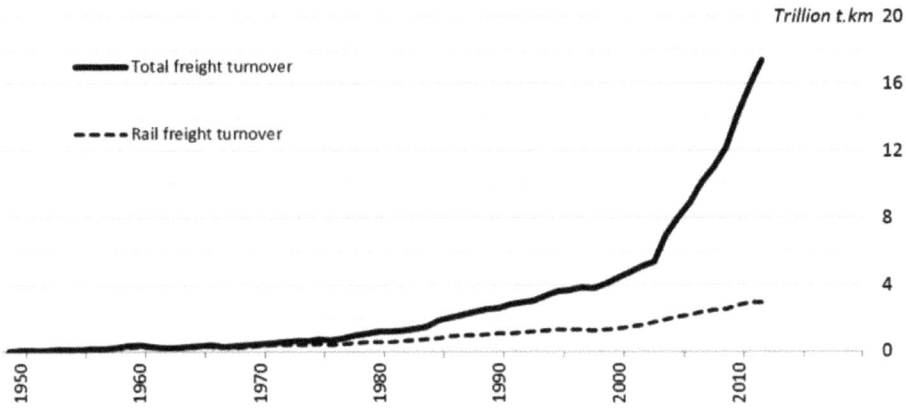

Figure 19.5 Freight Demand: Volume by distance
Source: NBS (2012).

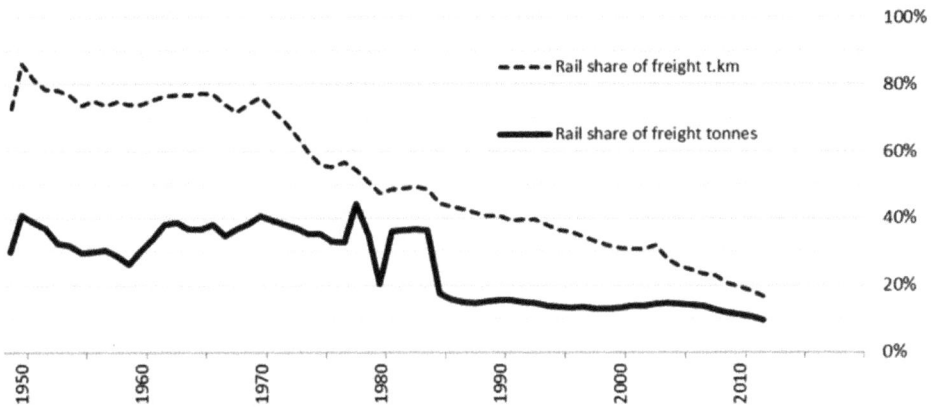

Figure 19.6 Rail Share of Freight and of Total Freight Distances
Source: Authors' calculations based on data from NBS (2012) shown in Figures 19.4 and 19.5.

There was increasing use of cars and trucks, especially for journeys of less than 200 km. Figure 19.7 shows the mean distance for rail freight increased from 400 to 500 km prior to 1980, and since 1990 has been 700 to 800 km. In comparison, the mean distance for non-rail freight was just 50 to 100 km prior to 1970, whereas today it is about 400 km. This is still only about half the distance of the mean rail freight transport haulage.

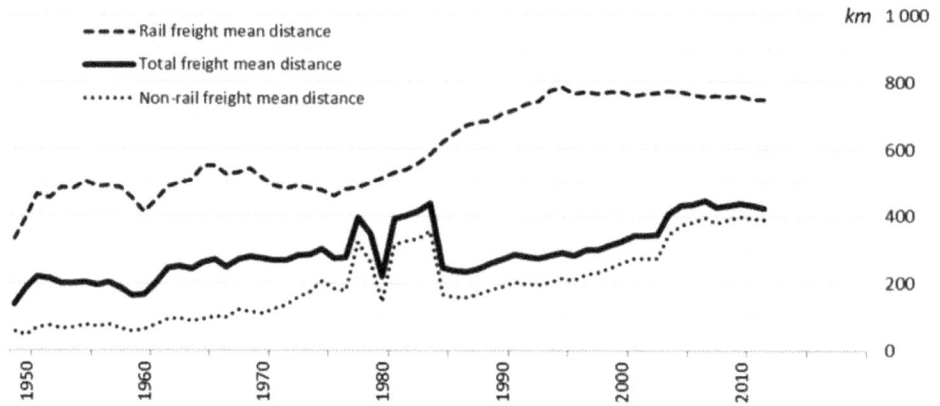

Figure 19.7 Mean Freight Distances

Source: Authors' calculations based on data from NBS (2012) shown in Figures 19.5 and 19.6.

A major factor contributing to this shift has been underinvestment in railway systems over the previous three decades or so, while highway construction has dominated the transport infrastructure investment of the past decade (Figure 19.8).

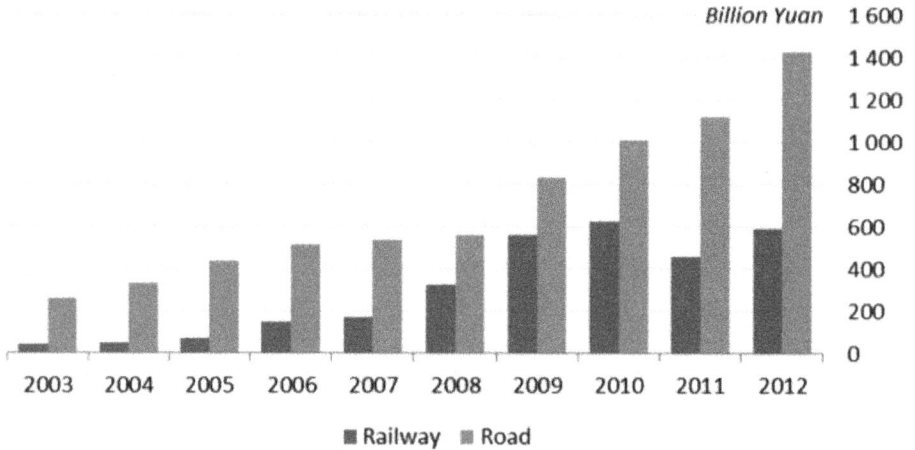

Figure 19.8 Comparison of Rail and Road Investment, 2003–12

Source: NBS (2012).

Figure 19.9 also shows that for the past three and a half decades, the operational length of railway has merely doubled, increasing from 52 000 km in 1978 to 98 000 km by 2012, whereas highway construction, starting from 100 km in 1988, has expanded exponentially. (China's first highway was built between Shanghai and Jiaxing, with a total length of 20 km.) In the two decades to 2012, the operational length of highways increased from almost nothing to equal the length of railways.

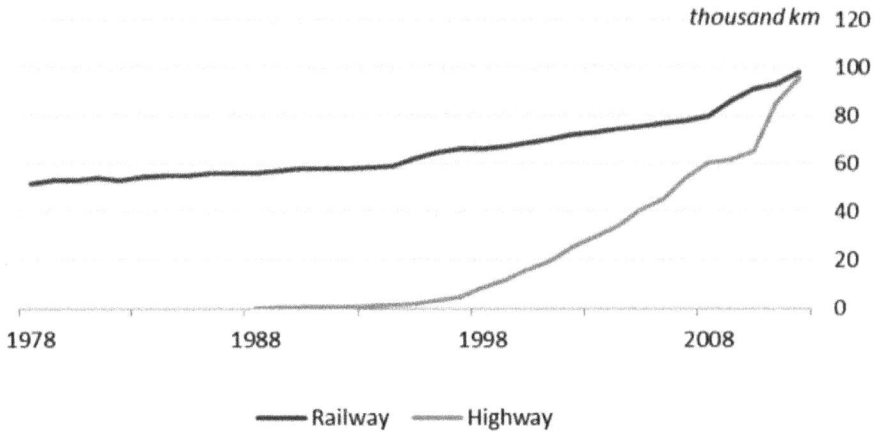

Figure 19.9 Railway and Highway Route Length Compared, 1978–2012
Source: NBS (2012).

The increase in road transport is driven by two main factors. First, China's financial institutions, especially commercial banks, are very willing to lend money for highway construction as they see these projects as low risk and able to generate stable returns via tolls. Second, local governments are very supportive of road development, because they consider these capital-intensive fixed-asset investment projects to be major drivers of local GDP: 'To become rich, construct a road first' has become a popular slogan in China in the past two decades. The available capital and local governments' policy incentives have enabled the massive expansion of China's highway development. In contrast, rail network development has been hindered, with limited availability of finance the major constraint to railway development. Rail financing is discussed further below.

Coal transport

Although rail is not the dominant freight transport mode, it is nonetheless crucial to China's bulk commodity transport, most importantly to coal—the primary energy source in China. Coal is by far the largest volume cargo type transported on China's railway system. At around 2.3 Bt per annum, coal represents more than half of total freight volume (Figure 19.10).

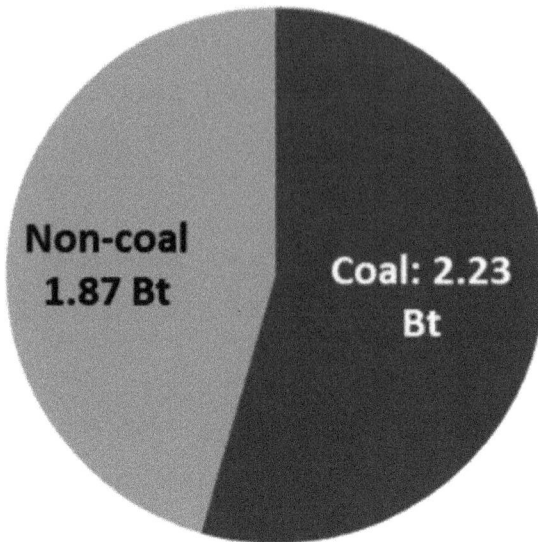

Figure 19.10 Coal and Non-Coal Rail Volumes, 2012
Source: NBS (2012).

The largest capacity coal rail line in the world is the DaQin line belonging to China Rail, transporting more than 400 million t (Mt) per year between Datong in Shanxi Province and the Qinhuangdao (QHD) port. Shenhua, the world's largest coal producer, with production in 2012 of more than 400 Mt and traded volume of more than 650 Mt, owns and operates more than 1500 km of railway line dedicated to coal transport. Shenhua's case is, however, an exception, as almost all other Chinese coalmines rely on the national railway system for transport, and are hence subject to the centralised capacity planning and 'wagon allocation' system. Of China's annual production of more than 3.5 Bt, about 2–2.5 Bt per year of coal is transported by rail, slightly more than the total production of key state-owned enterprises (SOEs) from 21 key provinces. Monthly quantities of coal moved by rail vary, driven by power-coal variability (Figure 19.11).

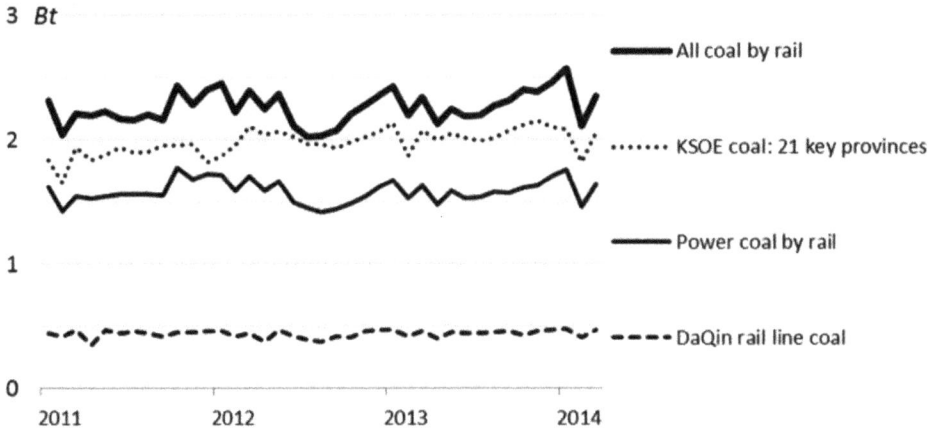

Figure 19.11 China's Monthly Coal Rail Transport Quantities at Annual Rates, January 2011 – March 2014

KSOE = key state-owned enterprises

Sources: NBS (2012); Fenwei/Shanxi Coal (2014).

More than 80 per cent of China's coal is extracted from mines located in the northern and western parts of the country, well away from China's industrial centres along the eastern and southern coasts. The geographical disparity requires large volumes of coal to be transported from inland to the coast over great distances. The major routes are rail to northern ports, QHD and other ports on the rim of the Bohai Sea, and then shipping via coastal freighters to southern ports. There is some southbound rail capacity, but on a per kilometre basis, shipping is considerably cheaper than rail for bulk commodities such as coal. The average coal haul has increased to more than 650 km, reflecting the fact that new mines tend to be located ever further inland and mines closer to the coast tend to be older and subject to closure due to resource depletion, higher costs or safety issues.

The resource-rich regions are usually less economically developed than coastal cities, so consumption in these areas is generally lower. Rail wagons full of coal bound for coastal southern China usually return empty. Lack of 'backhaul' cargoes adversely affects the cost and economic efficiency of the rail system.

Although coal is deemed the commodity of greatest economic importance, its transport is also affected by seasonal variations and other factors—for example, passenger transport priorities—creating pressure in the rail system. Furthermore, wagon dispatch, which is the primary mechanism for allocating scarce capacity in China's rail system, is highly centralised. The rail capacity deficit has not only exacerbated the railway congestion problem, but also made rail capacity allocation for coal a rent-capture opportunity for railway bureaus.

Ministry of Railways and the China Railway Corporation

The rail sector is the last of China's large network or infrastructure industries previously organised as government ministries to be reformed. Other network and infrastructure sectors in China that have already been reformed include telecommunications, airlines, power and water, gas and highways. The telecommunications sector operates on a commercial basis, with several leading companies. The airline sector operates on a commercial basis with numerous companies operating domestic and international services. The national highway system continues to be developed, with the extensive (practically universal) use of toll roads. The gas sector is undergoing reform of pricing and network access arrangements as it grows and develops. The former Ministry of Electric Power and Water Resources was restructured, including the separation of generation from transmission and the creation of major generation companies. Electricity prices remain regulated.

Prior to 2013, the Ministry of Railways (MOR) was wholly responsible for the national railway system of both passenger and cargo transport, reporting to the National Development and Reform Commission (NDRC). There were 16 railway bureaus and five railway companies under the MOR, which employed about two million people.

The MOR was both the industry regulator and the operator of almost the entire rail network; it worked with the NDRC on tariff-setting and had the authority to approve the construction of new railway lines shorter than 300 km. Lines longer than 300 km required approval from the State Council.

Of China's 100 000 km of railway network, more than 80 per cent was owned and operated by the MOR. Only a small proportion is controlled by local authorities, constructed under the sponsorship of local governments serving local needs and providing interconnections with the national railway system.

Reform of the rail sector has proved to be very challenging, as it needs to balance national security, economic efficiency, primary energy transport, social stability and many other factors. Apart from this, the natural monopoly characteristics of the rail sector created vested interests in the very large 'benefit and profit chain', further hindering efforts at reform. Of the three previous major economic reform efforts in China's history—in 1986, 2000 and 2008—all failed to deliver railway reform, or simply left it for a later time.

That time arrived in early 2013, triggered by a major accident on one of the busiest sections of the new high-speed rail system, the rail sector's debt crisis and the revelation of corruption within the MOR. China Railway Corporation

(CRC) was established on 14 March 2013 to replace the MOR, reporting to the Ministry of Transport. In the same year, Liu Zhijun, the former Minister of Rail, received a suspended death sentence in the High Court for abuse of power and taking bribes totalling more than $10 million in exchange for national railway contracts. The creation of the CRC is the first step towards operation on a commercial basis. After the next section on international comparisons, the final section discusses further China's railway reforms.

Selected international comparisons with China's rail sector

China is the fourth-largest country in the world by land area, the most populous and the second-largest economy by GDP. China currently ranks third in the world for rail track length. No country is directly comparable with China, and no country's rail sector is directly comparable with China's rail sector. Nevertheless, there are comparable countries for particular characteristics of China and its rail sector.

This section provides 10 international comparators for the Chinese railway sector. These include

- nine of the top 10 countries by rail track length, plus Japan, which ranks eleventh
- eight of the 10 largest economies in the world by GDP at purchasing power parity (PPP), plus Canada and Australia—two resource-rich countries with substantial bulk commodity rail systems
- the seven largest countries by land area, plus Japan, Germany, France and the United Kingdom
- five of the 10 most populous countries in the world, plus Germany, France, the United Kingdom, Canada and Australia.

The selected countries' attributes and points of interest for comparison with China are as follows.

- **The United States** is the world's largest economy, already developed but comparable in scale with China. The US rail system has almost three times the track length of China. Private monopoly rail systems are used for long-distance coal haulage.
- **India** has a similar population size to China; it is also an emerging market, using a state-owned rail system for domestic coal movements. The Indian rail system's track length is shorter than China's.

- **Russia** has the largest land area of any country in the world, is a former centrally planned socialist economy, has long rail-haul distances, a rail system with very similar track length to China's, is a neighbouring country and an export supplier to the international coal market.

- **Brazil** is a large country, with the fifth-largest land area, the fifth-largest population, an emerging market with the seventh-largest economy in the world and with a bulk rail system—notably, for iron ore—with the tenth-largest rail track length of any country in the world.

- **Canada** has the second-largest land area in the world, a small population and a medium-sized developed economy. Canada has the fifth-longest rail system in the world and some similarities to Australia. Canada does move coal on rails and may have lessons for China.

- **Australia** has substantial coal and iron ore resources, which are relatively close to the coast, but still require rail systems several hundred kilometres long for their efficient delivery to export ports. Coal in New South Wales and Queensland on the east coast is delivered to port via multi-user rail systems. In New South Wales, coal from the Hunter Valley also shares the rails with small passenger trains, impacting efficiency. Iron ore in the Pilbara region of Western Australia is delivered to ports via highly efficient private proprietary dedicated bulk rail systems.

- **Japan** is seen as a leader, particularly for its high-speed passenger system, which China is emulating with China Railway High-speed (CRH). Japan's coal is all imported and used in coastal power plants and steel mills, so Japan does not have China's enormous coal rail transport challenges.

- **Germany** is generally considered to be a model of industrial efficiency. Germany moves a lot of coal by river barge, and has an extensive rail system, with the world's sixth-longest track length. Germany's rail system is far more dense than Japan's in terms of track length per square kilometre.

- **France** is also seen as a leader in high-speed passenger rail, with the TGV system, but with the dominance of nuclear power is not a major coal consumer.

- **The United Kingdom** was the global pioneer in commercialising railways in the nineteenth century. Since then, the United Kingdom has tried almost all rail sector models, from private to nationalised, back to private and now a hybrid of state and private ownership. While mostly about passenger rail, the United Kingdom's recent experience demonstrates the complexity of rail sector reform and regulation.

Table 19.1 summarises key characteristics of China and the 10 selected comparator countries.

Table 19.1 Summary Overview of the Rail Sector of China and 10 International Comparators

Country	Land area (million sq km)	Population (millions)	First rail (year)	Track length ('000 km)	Current rail companies (No.)	Ownership (type)
China	9.60 No. 4	1349 No. 1	1876 No. 10	98* No. 2	2	State*
United States	9.83 No. 3	317 No. 3	1828 No. 2	228 No. 1	Many	Private
India	3.29 No. 7	1220 No. 2	1853 No. 7	64 No. 4	1	State
Russia	17.1 No. 1	142 No. 9	1837 No. 6	84 No. 3	1	State
Brazil	8.51 No. 5	201 No. 5	1854 No. 8	30 No. 10	12	Private
Canada	9.98 No. 2	35 No. 37	1836 No. 5	52 No. 5	Many	Private
Australia	7.74 No. 6	22 No. 55	1831 No. 3	38 No. 7	Several	Mixed
Germany	0.357 No. 63	81 No. 16	1831 No. 3	33 No. 6	Many	Mixed
Japan	0.378 No. 62	127 No. 10	1872 No. 9	20 No. 10	Many	Mixed
France	0.644 No. 43	66 No. 21	1832 No. 4	30 No. 8	1	State
United Kingdom	0.244 No. 80	63 No. 22	1807 No. 1	16 No. 11	Many	Mixed

* Two 'private' coal rail lines are owned and operated by Shenhua, which is also a state-owned enterprise.

Source: World Bank (2013).

Note: By 2012, China ranked second after the United States—total operational rail track length had reached 98 000 km.

Table 19.2 provides further detail on the ownership, industry structure, key companies, legislation, and the form of economic regulation and identity of the independent regulator, if there is one, for China and the 10 comparator countries.

Table 19.2 Railway Industry Structures and their Interactions with Ownership, Regulation and Competition

	China	United States	India	Russia	Brazil
Sector structure	Vertical integration	Tenant operators	Vertical integration	Vertical integration	Tenant operators
Ownership of railways	Public	Private companies	Public	Public	Private companies
Main company	China Railways Corporation	8 major private companies	Indian Railways	JSC RZD	8 major companies after privatisation in 1998
Other companies	Shenhua: two coal rail lines	338 Class I, 16 Class II, + others	None	None	4
Number of companies	2 + 16 subsidiary bureaus and 5 companies	~ 630	1	1	12
Key legislation	Railway Law (1991)	Staggers Rail Act (1980)	The Railways Act (1989)	Federal Law on Railway Transport in the Russian Federation (2003)	n.a.
Structural separation/ regulation	Yes. 2013 corporatisation	Light. Trackage rights exist (Amtrak)	None	Light. 2003 restructuring	Management by companies; trackage rights exist
Economic regulator	NDRC as notionally independent rail freight tariff and passenger fare regulator	US Department of Transportation and the Surface Transportation Board	None: direct control of the ministry	MOT and MEDT; Federal Antimonopoly Service and Federal Service for Tariffs	Agência Nacional de Transportes Terrestres (ANTT)
Form of economic regulation	Price regulation: end charges to users	Price freedom and closures of loss-making lines	Price regulation: end charges to users	Price regulation. Passenger service: end charges to users Freight service: tariff cap	Price regulation
Competition*	Intermodal only	Intermodal and limited intra-modal	Intermodal only	Intermodal only	Intermodal and limited intra-modal

Canada	Australia	Germany	Japan	France	United Kingdom
Tenant operators	Competitive access	Competitive access	Tenant operators	Vertical integration	Competitive access
Private companies	Mixed	Mixed	Mixed. Japan National Railways privatised in 1987	Public	Private companies
CN and CP	5 major companies (1 federal and 4 state-owned companies)	1 major private company	Japan Railways (7 subsidiaries)	SNCF (6 subsidiaries)	3 major companies
50+ regional and short-line carriers	18	160 big freight/ passenger companies + others	16 major private companies; 6 semi-major private companies; 83 others	4	26 train operating companies 7 freight operating companies
~ 82	23	~ 1500	~ 112	5	36
Canadian Transportation Act (1996)	Australian National Railways Commission Act (1983)	General Railway Act (2005)	Railway Business Act (1986)	Regulation of Railway Transport (2009)	The Railways Act (2005)
Light regulation	Light regulation	Light regulation	Restructuring in 1990s	Light regulation	Heavy regulation: total separation after restructuring in 1994
Canadian Transportation Agency (CTA)	State-specific independent regulators for essential services including railways	German Federal Railway Authority (Eisenbahn-Bundesamt, EBA and Bundesländer)	No independent regulator; direct control of Railways Bureau, Ministry of Land, Infrastructure, Transport and Tourism	Regulatory Authority for Railway Activities	Office of Rail Regulation (ORR)
Revenue cap	Third-party access to national and east coast multi-user systems. Dedicated private bulk systems in Western Australia	Price regulation: terms of user access	Yardstick competition	Price regulation	Fixed track access charges + regulated track and station access charge
Intermodal and limited intra-modal	Intermodal and intra-modal	Intermodal and intra-modal	Intermodal and some intra-modal	Intermodal only	Intermodal and intra-modal

MOT = Ministry of Transport

MEDT = Ministry of Economic Development and Trade

* Intermodal competition is assumed to be present everywhere.

491

The 1980s generally saw a steady loss of market share for railways globally—outcompeted by various alternative modes of transportation. As car ownership rose with disposable incomes, the convenience of private road transport took market share from passenger rail services over shorter distances, while the speed of air travel saw it take market share over longer distances. National rail companies incurred heavy losses, which were financed by public subsidies in many countries. In the freight sector, loading and unloading efficiencies and door-to-door service enabled trucking to take market share from rail. These intermodal competitive pressures created an imperative for revival of the 'productivity and profitability' of the respective rail companies through a process of reform and restructuring.

The next sections discuss the differences and similarities of China's railway sector in comparison with other international economies, and its areas of uniqueness.

China's profile in the global rail industry

China today has the second-largest railway network in the world, behind only the United States, having overtaken Russia in 2009. In terms of passenger transport, China has a high population density in settled areas and about 160 cities of more than one million people. A growing inclination to travel, and the construction of the world's largest high-speed rail network, is driving the largest-scale and most intense intercity rail passenger flows in the world.

With regards to freight transport, China's economy relies heavily on high volume, long-distance movements of coal, metal ores, iron and steel and other bulk products. In particular, movement of coal by rail is crucial to the economy, as coal generates about three-quarters of China's electricity and provides about two-thirds of its primary energy.

Considering passenger and freight traffic together, China's railway system is one of the busiest in the world, with the highest traffic density (million traffic units per route kilometres) in 2011 (Figure 19.12). Railway systems in the United States, Canada, Australia and Brazil are dominated by freight movement with very minimal passenger traffic.

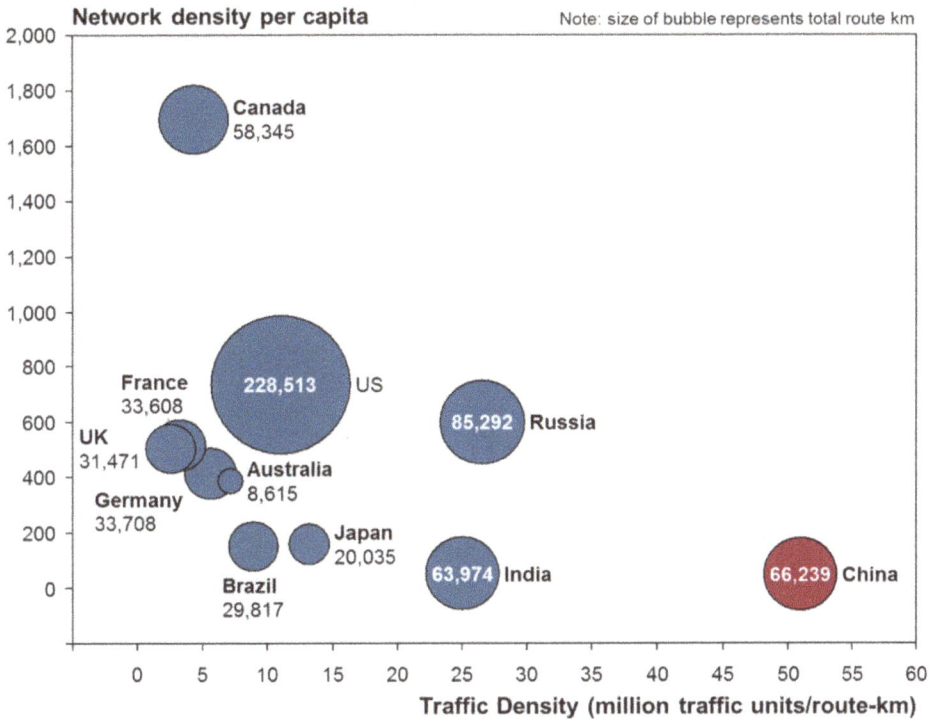

Figure 19.12 Global Comparison of Rail Systems

Source: Authors' analysis using data from The World Bank database.

Even though China has seen a rapid increase in the size of its rail system, its network density per capita (measured as route kilometres per million people) is one of the lowest in the world—similar to India's. China's rail infrastructure is so heavily used that in 2011 it carried 27 per cent of the world's rail traffic on around 7 per cent of the world's rail network.

Railway regulation in global context

This section identifies similarities and differences in the regulatory and institutional structures of 11 countries that collectively carry 90 per cent of the total long-distance rail traffic in the world—that is, excluding urban mass transit systems.[3]

Apart from India, all the other countries have a comparable transport ministry at the central government level that aims to promote the public interest across all modes of transport. The transport ministry in all these countries has

---

3   Authors' estimates. China also has and is extending large mass transit systems, but they are beyond the scope of this chapter.

a public policy agenda to integrate the national railways with other modes of transportation. Before March 2013, China had the independent MOR, which was responsible for developing and administering policies for the railway sector as well as owning and operating the rail system. The dissolution of China's MOR has ensured that the role of policymaking and regulation is now separated from asset ownership and service delivery. This is a significant landmark in the history of China's railways, as the separation is likely to facilitate more efficient forms of organisation for the service providers.

All comparator countries have undergone some form of structural reforms in their railway sectors. The railways in the United States and Canada began with private investment in the late 1800s. After a short period of nationalisation, both economies today have completely privatised railway systems.

The 1990s saw the introduction of competitive access in Japan and Australia, as they moved towards partial privatisation of their national railways. During the same period, rail industries in Germany and the United Kingdom introduced various models of vertical separation through privatisation by separating the roles of infrastructure management from service delivery. Structured rail reforms in Russia and Brazil introduced privatisation to the national railways during the early years of the twenty-first century. China and India, unlike other countries, have so far refrained from major reforms to their railway sectors—the reasons for which are well documented. In recent years, China has allowed a number of dedicated coal freight lines. Sometimes called 'private rail lines' in China, as they are not wholly owned by the former MOR or its successor, the CRC, these are more correctly referred to as 'jointly owned rail lines'. Shenhua holds the controlling interest and operation rights, while CRC and other local companies hold the remaining interest.

All countries except India and France now have a defined corporate structure distinct from government. While distinctions across ownership exist (state versus private), corporate structure allows for competition and productivity gains. In the case of China, the recently established state-owned CRC is responsible for operating commuter and freight transport via subsidiary companies. The national rail operator in France, SNCF, while not a corporation, is a state-owned railway company that operates under its own legislation. In India, the Ministry of Railways continues to single-handedly operate the state-owned monopoly, Indian Railways. Institutional governance and regulatory regimes for the rail industries of the 11 countries are depicted in the matrix below (Figure 19.13).

Framework for analysis of ownership structures and regulatory approaches

Historically, rail transportation in many countries has been perceived to be a public good or a form of social service, irrespective of its complexity and profitability. Rail networks tended to be viewed as having strong natural monopoly characteristics. State ownership is a common remedy to the natural monopoly problem, but other models are possible. In this chapter, we adopt a two-axis categorisation, providing a matrix framework for the various models of organisational structures and regulation of railways around the world (Figure 19.13).

On one axis we consider the *ownership* of the rail sector, distinguishing state-owned from privately owned rail systems, and acknowledging that in some countries there is a mix of the two, whether from one region of the country to another, for different systems (for example, freight and passenger), different parts of the sector (for example, the tracks 'below rail' and the rolling stock 'above rail'), or through partial floats of shares in companies.

On the other axis we consider the *regulation* of the industry. We note that models exist where there is either no formal regulation (of private rail companies) or no notion of a separation between the ownership of rail assets and their regulation—for example, where a self-regulating government ministry owns the assets. So, the regulation axis includes the concept of regulatory *separation* between the ownership of the rail sector assets and their regulation, distinguishing no separation, from light regulation and heavy regulation.

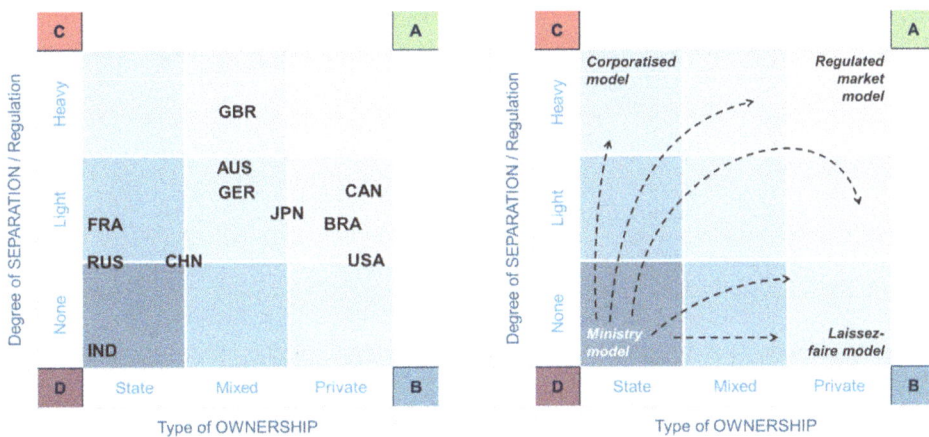

Figure 19.13 Rail Sector Models for 10 Comparator Countries and Possible Pathways for China

This framework provides a three-by-three matrix for comparing rail sector models between comparator countries, and how they have changed since their networks were first built. The four corners of the matrix define four distinct models: the ministry model with state ownership and no separate, independent economic regulatory function; the corporatised model with state ownership but a separate economic regulatory function; the fully laissez-faire model with full private ownership and no economic regulatory oversight; and the regulated market model with full private ownership and an independent regulator endeavouring to ensure competitive or 'market' conditions prevail.

China, Russia and France have all moved away from the full ministry model, and among the comparator countries, only India remains in this part of the matrix. It is notable that among the 10 comparator countries, none of them occupies any of the other three corners of the matrix. The tendency is towards private or mixed state and private ownership, and towards light regulation.

There are no examples of a heavily regulated state-owned corporate rail sector. No examples of a regulated market model are found, due to the practical difficulties, even with independent regulatory oversight, of overcoming the natural monopoly characteristics of railways to create market competition. There is no full laissez-faire model in the rail sector (it could be argued that the pioneering entrepreneurs of railways in Britain operated under that model in the nineteenth century). The closest example is the United States, where private rail operators are lightly regulated and in the freight sector in particular are able to adjust prices to capture rent from coal producers.

Based on this analysis and the international experience of ownership and regulatory models, the dotted lines showing possible pathways for the future reform of China's rail sector all stop short of reaching the three corners of the matrix as reform 'destinations'.

China's rail reforms and the challenges ahead

Overview

On 14 March 2014, the Chinese Government began dismantling the MOR, folding its administrative functions into the Ministry of Transport and creating the CRC to carry out the former ministry's commercial functions. These changes were the latest phase of a reform process begun to repair the damage caused by a ten-year commitment to expand and upgrade China's rail system.

In 2003 the MOR began a massive program of network expansion, including the construction of thousands of kilometres of high-speed rail track, to upgrade the country's passenger and freight transport systems. Figure 19.14 shows the 2020 network plan.

Years of aggressive rail construction led to an accumulation of some RMB2.8 trillion (US$459 billion) in debt by the end of 2012 (Yan 2013). At the same time, the rail system was facing competition from the parallel build-out of the country's highway system (Figure 19.9), enabling the development of regional short and long-distance trucking fleets. Debt repayment obligations, low rail freight tariffs and insufficiently diversified passenger ticket pricing constrained system profitability well beyond the servicing capability of ordinary cash receipts, further compounding the problem.

The break-up of the old railway ministry is only the first milestone in the ongoing process of rail reform. Beyond sector restructuring, other aspects of the reform program include piloting a market-based ticket pricing system, a greater diversification of freight tariffs and the creation of a railway development fund to rationalise the financing of further rail expansion.

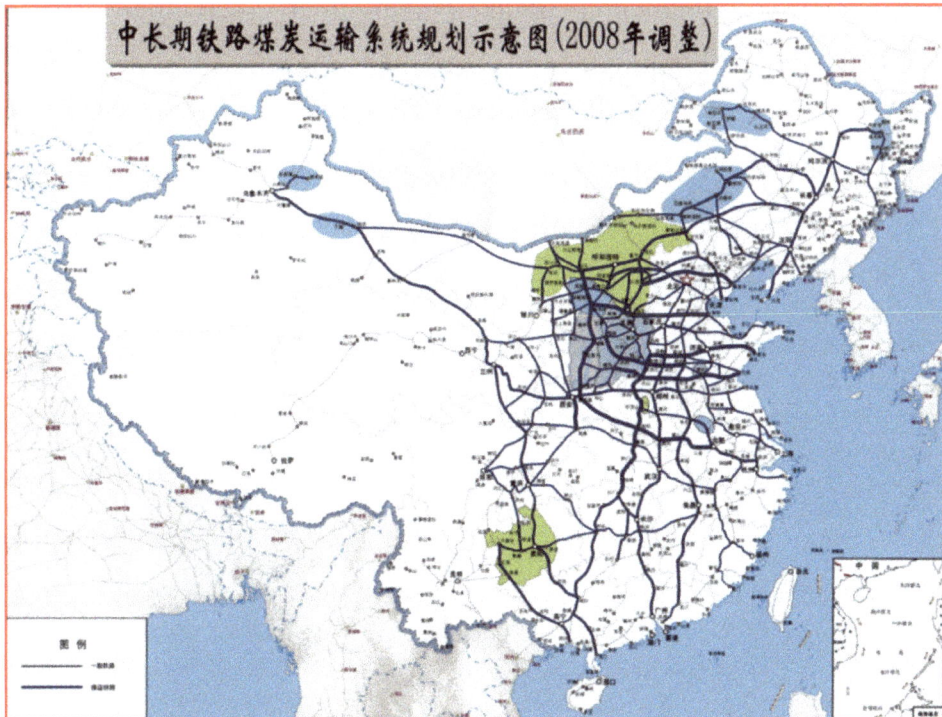

Figure 19.14 China's 2020 Rail Network Plan
Source: MOR (2008).

Constrained profitability

China's rail system revenues are a function of passenger ticket and freight receipts, plus income from other diversified businesses. Although passenger and freight revenues grew steadily over the past 10 years, total profitability was poor due to a low average ticket price, an increasing debt-servicing burden and rising freight transport costs that offset improvements in the revenue stream.

The rail system has traditionally been operated as a public good, with a mandate to make sure the system is available to all income brackets and freight products. With particular regard to passenger fares, the rail system has been the primary form of long-distance transport for the low-income population and effort has been made to keep fares low. Hence passenger services have tended to be priced below their full economic cost.

At the same time, China's rail system remains one of the most densely trafficked in the world, with demand outstripping supply on many routes both for passengers and freight (Scales et al. 2011). The twin concerns of affordability and density mean that the rail system has not needed flexible pricing strategies, with the Government instead implementing a system of rail priorities that favours passengers during important holidays and coal and agricultural products at other times of the year. Further, until rail expansion began in 2003, regulated tariffs and ticket prices plus the railway construction surcharges provided adequate system revenue. It is only with the line expansions of the past decade that debt has begun to accumulate. Furthermore, with the completion of around 120 000 km of track by 2020, the system managers will move from rationing capacity to selling it.

Finally, it must be noted that the complexity of application procedures for rail freight access, combined with long waiting times for wagons, and local issues associated with the loading and unloading of cargo have exerted a cumulative efficiency tax on revenues. Rent-seeking behaviour—sometimes legitimate and sometimes not—exerts a further cost for users and encourages the use of alternative transport methods such as trucking and, where available, inland waterway transport.

Debt accumulation

It should not be surprising that a rail capacity build-out of the scale in China over the past 11 years should be accompanied by a massive increase in debt. With the exception of the Government's RMB40 billion investment in the state-funded Qinghai–Tibet railway line, most railway construction since 1949 was funded by the MOR through a combination of fiscal funding, loans and bonds. Fiscal funding and construction surcharges accounted for some 70 per cent of total railway funding in 2004, dropping to 10 per cent by 2010 when loans and bonds provided some 60 per cent of funding requirements. Between 2005 and 2011, the railway sector accumulated about RMB500 billion in debt a year, much of which was funded by a combination of loans, bonds and even short-term financing (Wu 2011). The RMB4.5 trillion in accumulated railway assets at the end of 2012 was equivalent to about 9 per cent of total GDP in that year. This left the rail system with RMB2.9 trillion in total debt—a debt-to-asset ratio of 62 per cent, and long-term debt making up 76 per cent of total liabilities.

The seriousness of the problem surfaced in the wake of the 2011 Wenzhou high-speed rail accident in Zhejiang Province, which killed 40 people and injured 192. The ensuing government investigation revealed shortcomings in both construction quality and financing arrangements on one of the most highly trafficked high-speed lines in the country. When the official report revealed the size of both debt and system operating losses, the State Council undertook measures to provide emergency loans and issue multi-sectoral government-backed bonds, as well as additional temporary subsidies to stabilise the railway system's financial situation while longer-term reforms were worked out.

Reform and restructuring

The Wenzhou accident investigation highlighted a fundamental structural problem within the railway ministry. Administrative, operational and commercial mandates were combined within one entity, with the day-to-day business of running the railway often confused by government administrative and regulatory functions. The dismissal and subsequent imprisonment of former railway minister Liu Zhijun in February 2011 also revealed that the apparent conflict of interest had provided a fertile breeding ground for corrupt activity.

At the March 2013 National People's Congress session it was announced that the State Council had decided to resolve this conflict by dissolving the MOR and moving policy and planning functions to the Ministry of Transport and Communications, and rail administration to the newly formed State Railway Administration (SRA). Meanwhile, all commercial and operational functions were folded into the newly formed China Railway Corporation (CRC), with the previous railway minister, Sheng Guangzu, appointed as its head.

In the context of the announcement, the Government also revealed that while the CRC would function as a commercial entity, it would report directly to the State Council. Furthermore, it would continue to fulfil the social obligation of the old ministry by implementing a government-backed rail-subsidy mechanism to ensure the continued discounting of fares for students and disabled passengers and freight rates for agricultural products. The CRC is also responsible for funding railway research and the operation of the Qinghai–Tibet line on behalf of the Government. The 18 regional rail bureaus and associated employment of roughly two million workers have been folded under the CRC's mandate.

The CRC's primary functions are passenger and freight transport, and the management and maintenance of the national rail network. The CRC also has responsibility for developing and implementing plans for sustainable railway construction investment funded from both public and private sources. Finally, the CRC has been given final accountability for rail safety.

The SRA is responsible for formulating railway technical standards, providing oversight of rail safety and service quality, and ensuring quality standards are met.

Rail construction, private investment and reform

One of the key questions for the newly formed CRC is how it will be able to finance planned rail construction targets. Given its status as a government office, the old MOR had little difficulty obtaining bank financing, but it is so far not clear how easy it will be for the CRC to obtain funds for planned projects. While Sheng Guangzu stated in 2013 that the Government would continue to offer financing for projects deemed necessary for social reasons, commercial projects would need to rely at least in part on private sector investment.

A diversified financing scheme was proposed several years ago as a potential solution to this problem and is being revisited now. Under such an arrangement, state-level players will continue to be responsible for main lines while private and foreign investment will be encouraged for feeder lines, with local governments taking the lead in land acquisition and resettlement. Given high entry costs and low returns, there has been little private sector interest so far, with the exception of a limited number of dedicated line projects.

A State Council document issued on 19 August 2013 intended to accelerate reform of railway investment and financing. The document revealed that private investors would be allowed to own and operate railway networks and services. In addition, it called for the establishment of a railway development fund to be financed by the Central Government. The document also called for the development of stations and land along railway lines as a means of improving investment revenue and stressed the need for market-based reform of freight tariffs while it supported a subsidy scheme for rail fares.

The reason for weak private sector interest is tied to subsidised constraints around passenger fares and freight charges. As Hu Shuli, editor of *Caixin*, argued in a recent editorial:

[P]rivate investors will only enter the market when competition is introduced into rail network construction and train services, and when a mechanism is in place to adjust fares based on market conditions. In fact reform of the railway system shares something in common with reforms of other strategic industries such as electricity, telecoms, civil aviation and oil, which are mainly led by state enterprises. Reform in all of these sectors is a two-step process: first, separate government functions from enterprise management; second break up the monopoly by introducing competition. (Hu 2013)

Debt management

A consensus has arisen that the Government should develop a plan to relieve the CRC of the debt inherited from the MOR. Statistics from the National Audit Office indicate that the CRC carried RMB2.9 trillion in debt by June 2013, most of it inherited from the MOR. Most experts believe that a dividing line should be drawn between old and new rail debts, with the CRC responsible only for the debt it incurs. Wang Mengshu of Beijing Jiaotong University argues that the state should write off part of the CRC's total debt as non-performing bank loans, since a considerable portion of them were provided in the national interest (Qi and Yang 2014). Other proposals go further, urging that the MOR's old debt be separated from the CRC's portfolio and managed by a state-run asset-management entity similar to the State Asset Supervision and Administration Commission (SASAC) set up by the State Council to manage SOE debts.

Beyond the question of how to dispose of the MOR's old debts is the question of how the CRC should most effectively manage its own obligations. On the one hand, an increase in freight and passenger tariffs would be helpful, but on the other, the CRC is prevented from sharply increasing rates by its social obligation to keep the rail system affordable. Furthermore, the rail system has already lost market share to inter-regional trucking and bus fleets, which take advantage of China's new highway system to competitively move long-distance freight. Raising freight and passenger tariffs too much too quickly would undermine the system's competitiveness, causing further damage to its financial position.

According to Sheng Guangzu, the rail network's share of total freight volumes shrank from about 48 per cent in 1980 to 17 per cent in 2012. In contrast, road freight's market share rose to 35 per cent from only 6.4 per cent over the same period. Rail still captures the largest volume of raw material bulk transport but the trucking fleet is better able to efficiently ship components and finished goods, especially over shorter distances.

Rail tariff reform

Notwithstanding the above concerns, an increase in rail freight tariffs is seen as the most direct means of reducing system debts. A joint project between Beijing Jiaotong University and the World Bank in 2013 indicated that the CRC would be able to pay off its debt within 10 years with an average freight rate of 13 cents/t/km, assuming average annual growth in railway freight and passenger volumes remained above 5 per cent.

In early 2013 the NDRC approved an increase in rail tariffs by an average of 1.5 c/t. After the rail reforms were announced in late March, the CRC itself began to push for further reform of rail and passenger tariffs. Tariffs were raised on 14 February 2014 from the previous system-wide average of 12 c/t/km to 15 c/t/km. Besides helping to pay down debt, the increase in freight tariffs is expected to increase returns to potential private investors. A second step, to introduce a dynamic pricing system to better capture revenues on peak demand, is under consideration, though the details have yet to be fully worked out.

Some experts remain worried that the increase in rates will seriously damage rail freight's competitiveness, especially over short distances. Zhao Jian of Beijing Jiaotong University estimates that rail freight has lost its price competitiveness over distances of less than 1000 km. Sun Zhang, a professor at the institute of railways and urban mass transit at Tongji University in Shanghai, argues that freight tariff increases should be selective and applied to routes dominated by bulk goods such as coal.

Rail service reforms

A further dimension to system competitiveness is the issue of service quality and efficiency. Even though rail freight charges may be on average lower than trucking charges at distances of more than 500 km, the time required to apply and receive approval for rail freight access and then load and unload the goods may double the time it takes for a shipment to go through. In contrast, truck freight pick-ups can be arranged at only a short interval in advance and delivery can be made straight to the client, rather than having to be unloaded at the destination station and reloaded to make the final trip to the consumption point.

The CRC is moving to address these issues, announcing in June 2013 the launch of measures such as an express train service and door-to-door delivery. It is also looking at ways to simplify the application process with the introduction of an online booking system and telephone hotlines.

Conclusion

The CRC is facing a series of conflicting challenges. It must pay down debt while continuing to pursue an aggressive build-out of track, particularly high-speed track for dedicated passenger services. Private investment is encouraged by revenue growth, but social obligations and related subsidies must be maintained. It must raise freight rates, while remaining competitive with trucking fleets and other alternative modes of transportation offering more flexible and door-to-door service. Service efficiency and quality must improve while the system remains the lowest cost and most environmentally sustainable transport option over long distances. The experience of other national rail systems suggests that, while there may be no perfect solution, gradual implementation of tariff reforms and efficiency improvements are essential to stabilising system economics.

Further restructuring of the rail sector is likely in coming years. Multiple options for further reform are under active debate and include: 1) preservation of the CRC's current near-monopoly to maximise system efficiency; 2) breaking the CRC up into regional enterprises to increase competition and pricing efficiency, perhaps via benchmark or yardstick regulation; and 3) separating passenger transport into a separate business distinct from freight transport to facilitate passenger subsidies while increasing the commercial competitiveness of freight. Though it is not yet clear which option will be selected, sector structure will be critical in determining the development path of the railway system and will drive other reforms such as pricing the degree of competitive and economic regulatory pressure.

China is in the early stages of the reform process of its rail sector. In no country in the world is the rail system as vital as it is in China to the movement of people, goods and energy. There is a variety of models around the world for the ownership, management and economic regulation of passenger and freight railways. As the review in this chapter shows, across China and 10 other major countries representing some 90 per cent of the world's rail transport, no two countries are exactly alike with respect to ownership and regulatory arrangements. The industry structure and regulation in each country reflect history, the stage of development and the general approach to public policy.

No one model of economic regulation of railways is perfect. International experience indicates that the introduction of 'perfect competition' is impossible in the rail sector. Care is needed in drawing analogies with other large, formerly state-owned sectors. For example, China's coal sector has been recently reformed such that prices are today largely determined by dynamic market forces. But although coal is transported via rail and road networks, and is supplied to a network-connected industry (electricity), coal is not itself a network industry, nor does it have natural monopoly characteristics. China's power sector, in contrast, was restructured a decade ago, but the Central Government nevertheless continues to set wholesale and retail electricity tariffs rather than use market competition to determine prices. The power system is a closer analogy to the rail system than is the coal sector. Like rail, power is a network industry with natural monopoly characteristics, at least in transmission and distribution. Like railways, the power system has stringent technical requirements for its safe and reliable operation. Like railways, the power system can also be considered to have strong public good characteristics, as the economic cost of a single widespread supply disruption or service interruption event tends to be orders of magnitude larger than the economic gains from continuous efficiency improvements.

China is likely to continue to set prices for both passenger and freight transport in the rail sector through a regulatory process that takes into account wider economic and social considerations.

References

Amos, P and Bullock, R (2011), *Governance and structure of the railway industry: three pillars*, China Transport Topics No. 2, December, The World Bank, Beijing.

Bullock, R, Salzberg, A and Jin, Y (2012), *High-speed rail—the first three years: taking the pulse of China's emerging program*, February, China Transport Topics No. 4, The World Bank, Beijing.

China Coal Transport and Sale Society (CCTSS) (2014), Database 2014, Beijing: China Coal Transport and Sale Society. Available from <http://www.cctd.com.cn>.

Economic Research Centre (ERC) (1995), *China Investment Strategies for China's Coal and Electricity Delivery System*, Beijing: The World Bank.

Fenwei/Shanxi Coal (2014), *China Coal Weekly*, Newsletter and database, Shanxi: Fenwei Energy Consulting Company Limited. Available from <http://www.sxcoal.com>.

Hu, S. (2013), 'Spur competition and ease back on controls to keep rail reform on track', *South China Morning Post*, Insight and Opinion, 19 September, provided by Caixin Media, [also published in Chinese in *Century Weekly*].

Ministry of Railways (2008), Map. Available from <http://bbs.railcn.net>.

Ministry of Transport (2008a), *Long-Term Railway Development Plan*, Beijing: Ministry of Transport.

Ministry of Transport (2008b), *Mid-Term Railway Development Plan*, Beijing: Ministry of Transport.

Muzutani, F. and Nakamura, K. (2004), *The Japanese Experience with Railway Restructuring*, Cambridge, Mass.: National Bureau of Economic Research.

National Bureau of Statistics (NBS) (2012), *China Statistical Yearbook*, Beijing: China Statistics Press.

Organisation for Economic Cooperation and Development (OECD) (1997), *Railways: Structure, Regulation and Competition Policy*, Policy Roundtables, Paris: OECD.

Organisation for Economic Cooperation and Development (OECD) (2005), *Structural Reform in the Rail*, Policy Roundtables, Paris: OECD.

Organisation for Economic Cooperation and Development (OECD) (2013), *Recent Development in Rail Transportation Services*, Policy Roundtables, Paris: OECD.

Qi, Z. and J. Yang (2014), 'China implements radical railway reform', *International Railway Journal*.

Scales, J., Olivier, G. and Amos, P. (2011), *Railway price regulation in China: time for a rethink?*, China Transport Topics No. 1, December, The World Bank, Beijing.

Scales, J., Sondhi, J., and Amos, P. (2012), *Fast and focused—building China's railways*, China Transport Topics No. 3, February, The World Bank, Beijing.

Stanley, T. and Ritacca, R. (2013), *All Aboard: High-Speed Rail Network Connecting China*, China 360, KPMG Global China Practice.

Wang, P., Yang, N. and Quintero, J. (2012), *China: the environmental challenge of railway development*, China Transport Topics No. 6, June, The World Bank, Beijing.

Williams, R., Grieg, D. and Wallis, I. (n.d.), *Results of railway privatization in Australia and New Zealand*, Transport Papers, The World Bank, Washington, DC.

World Bank (2013), *Database 2013*, Washington, DC: The World Bank. Available from <http://data.worldbank.org/>.

Wu, J. (2011), *China's Railway Debt Crisis Accelerates Reform*, Beijing: Beijing Jiaotong University.

Yan, P. (2013), *The Challenges and Opportunities of China Railway's Marketization*, New York: Dragon Gate Investment Partners.

20. Patent Institution, Innovation and Economic Growth in China

Haiyang Zhang

Introduction

The patent institution is regarded as an effective way to stimulate innovation, facilitate technological dissemination, promote trade and enhance competitiveness (Idris 2003). However, by granting exclusive property rights, the patent institution creates a monopoly which in itself results in the loss of social welfare by impeding the use and development of the patented technologies by others (Drahos 1995, 1999). Therefore, the overall role of the patent institution in promoting economic development, especially for developing countries characterised by a generally low technology level, is rather ambiguous, and depends on facts that vary from case to case.

Economic reform and development in China have been accompanied by the evolution of the Chinese patent institution. Moreover, China now is in a critical transition period from a manufacturing-centric to an innovation-based economy. The patent institution is seen as playing an increasingly important role in China's technological and economic development. This chapter provides some insights into whether and how the Chinese patent institution has stimulated research and development, influenced technology transfer from advanced economies and promoted economic growth in China.

Section two reviews the basic economic theories behind the patent institution, followed by the arguments for and against it in section three. The fourth section introduces the development of China's patent institution, while section five discusses what we can learn from past studies of the roles of the patent institution in China's economic development. Section six concludes by summarising policy suggestions for designing and improving the patent institution for China.

The core economic theories behind the patent institution

Like knowledge or information, a new invention costs human and financial resources to create. However, it has characteristics of a public good: non-rival and non-excludable in consumption. The non-rival character of knowledge implies that the amount of knowledge available to any user does not decrease when others use it, while the non-excludable character of knowledge is in the sense that once it is produced, others cannot be stopped from benefiting from it, and as a result everyone can freely use it unless the state creates a legal exclusive right. Although an invention sometimes can be excludable by keeping it secret, such as the recipe of Coca Cola, there is a risk that such secrets may be easily discovered by reverse engineering or through other means.

A patent for an invention is a property right granted by a government to the patent owner or owners to exclusively make, use and sell that invention for a certain period, and as an exchange condition, it is required to disclose the invention to the public. Thus, acquiring a patent for a particular creation of knowledge is an example of making a non-rival good excludable. By granting the exclusive right on a patented invention, the patentee(s) can charge a higher price or enjoy a lower marginal cost while excluding others from doing so.

Since newly invented knowledge has the characteristics of non-excludability and non-rivalry, the provision of such goods will be below the socially desired level due to the free-rider problem. That is, unless there are some incentives granted by the government, entrepreneurs who expect profit from research and development (R&D) may not be willing to take on the risks and costs of such activities since any rewards from doing so may dissipate due to imitation. In such a context, it is traditionally argued that perfect competition in the market of knowledge-based products does not allow innovators to recover their innovation costs such as R&D investment (Arrow 1962). It is called innovation market failure—summarised in Martin and Scott (2000) and Colombo and Delmastro (2002)—which mainly refers to the phenomenon of underinvestment in innovation from the social standpoint. The patent institution is a social institution intended to alleviate the negative impact of innovation market failure by granting patent owners exclusive rights to make, use and sell their inventions for a certain period.

The exclusive rights given by the Chinese Patent Law may, however, cause monopolies, which are another sort of market failure. Basic economics indicates that a monopoly harms social welfare at least from the static point of view. Although not all patents can cause a monopoly, the market power associated with patents can impose social costs even as it encourages invention and commercialisation. Accordingly, societies limit the power of patent grants not only in duration and scope, but also in disclosure requirements. Some scholars argue that there is no general market failure for innovations as, in most industries, the cost of invention is low: or just being first in the market confers a durable competitive advantage (Moir 2008; Posner 2012). Therefore, the core economics of patents, also applied to some other intellectual property rights, is that it is an institution facing the inherent trade-off between encouraging innovation and suffering the consequences of potential monopoly.

Arguments for and against the patent institution

As modern economic growth depends more and more heavily on technological progress, the role of the patent institution attracts more and more attention and debate. Arguments for and against patents continue. At the time when the patent institution was being established, those who were in favour of it believed it could stimulate inventions and creations (Smith 1776; Bentham 1839), whereas some thought the patent institution was unnecessary because inventions were based on the inspiration of inventors and had little to do with incentives, and even when some inventions were induced by profit incentives, the profits obtained through selling first in the market were large enough to compensate for invention costs (Taussig 1915; Pigou 1920).

Today, it is commonly recognised that the patent is a necessary and valid policy instrument to overcome market failure caused by the non-rival and non-excludable features of knowledge, and to encourage investment in R&D and thus promote the production of knowledge and innovations. Debate is more heated about the optimal design of the patent institution: whether the patent institution has led to an excessive monopoly distortion due to excessively long and wide patent protection, and hence a slowdown in the pace of technological progress (Boldrin and Levine 2002; Heller and Eisenberg 1998; Merges and Nelson 1994).

This debate has been intensified and complicated by the current context of economic globalisation. The Agreement on Trade-Related Aspects of Intellectual Property Rights (TRIPS) was reached during the Uruguay Round (1986–94) of negotiations on the reform of the world trading system, with a view to reducing or eliminating tensions due to cross-country differences in the treatment of intellectual property rights (IPRs). The TRIPS Agreement imposes on all member economies 'minimum' standards for the protection of intellectual property. For example, the term of patent protection is at least 20 years counted from the filing date, and the patentable subject matter covers almost all fields of technology including pharmaceuticals, agriculture, chemicals, food and microorganisms, where most developing countries used to provide no or little patent protection. Although the countries on the United Nation's list of least-developed countries may delay implementation of action of TRIPS in respect of pharmaceutical products until 1 January 2016, extended by the Doha Declaration, the standard on intellectual property (IP) protection required by TRIPS is still rather high for most developing countries.

In such a context, some argue strongly that IPRs including patents are necessary to stimulate economic growth, which, in turn, contributes to poverty reduction. By stimulating invention and the development of new technologies, patents will increase agricultural and industrial production, promote domestic and foreign investment in technology R&D, facilitate technology transfer and improve the availability of medicines necessary to combat disease. Others argue the opposite: that patents do little to stimulate invention in developing countries, because the necessary human and technical capacities are often absent. Patents are ineffective at stimulating research to benefit poor people because they will not be able to afford to buy the newly developed products at high prices. Patents limit the option of technological learning through imitation and allow foreign firms to drive out domestic competition by obtaining patent protection and to service the market through imports rather than domestic manufacture. Moreover, they increase the costs of essential medicines and agricultural inputs, affecting poor people and farmers particularly badly (UK Commission on IPR 2002).

Thus, the relationship between patents and economic development is complex. Moreover, there seems to be a gap between the economic research and patent institution design, especially in the case of China, which might have been caused by a lack of communication between economic researchers and the patent community, whose members are mainly scientists, engineers and legal professionals.

The patent institution in China

China promulgated its first modern Chinese Patent Law on 12 March 1984, which came into effect on 1 April 1985. Until now, the law has been amended three times. The first revision, undertaken in 1992, extended the patent length from 15 to 20 years for invention patents and from five to 10 years for patents of utility model and industrial design;[1] expanded patent protection scope to include pharmaceuticals, food and drinks, and chemical products; and adopted some other measures to strengthen patent protection.

The second revision, which was completed in September 2000, eliminated the provisions under the old law that prevented state-owned enterprises from trading their patents in technology markets, introduced new provisions designed to make it more rewarding for employees to innovate, and amended some provisions that were not in line with the TRIPS Agreement, such as extending patent protection to offering for sale patented products. Since these two revisions, the Chinese Patent Law has been pretty much in line with the international standard.

In 2008, the Chinese Patent Law was revised for the third time. The main points of the third revision include: enhancing the threshold of patentability by changing the criteria of novelty from relative novelty to absolute novelty—one of the three factors (novelty, inventiveness and industrial applicability) of patentability in China; providing regulations on the protection of genetic resources; improving industrial design systems; improving the confidentiality examination system for applications to a foreign country; invalidating the designation of foreign-related patent agencies; increasing the responsibility of the State Intellectual Property Office (SIPO) for the distribution of patent information; endowing right holders of industrial design with the right to offer to sell, introducing pre-litigation preservation measures, and including the cost to the right holder incurred for stopping the infringing act to the calculation of damage compensation; codifying the prior art defence; allowing parallel imports; providing exceptions for drug and medical apparatus experimentation; and improving the compulsory licence system.

As we can see from the past three revisions, the Chinese Patent Law has been further strengthened step by step in a pro-patent direction. Moreover, since the mid 2000s, the Chinese Government has launched a coordinated phalanx of laws, policies and initiatives—all aimed at aggressively increasing China's capacity for

---

1   According to the Chinese Patent Law, there are three types of patents: invention, utility-model and design patents. 'Invention' in the Chinese Patent Law means any new technical solution relating to a product, a process or improvement thereof. 'Utility model' in the Chinese Patent Law means any new technical solution relating to the shape, the structure or their combination in a product, which is fit for practical use. 'Design' in the Chinese Patent Law means any new design of the shape, the pattern or their combination of the colour with shape or pattern, of a product, which creates an aesthetic feeling and is fit for industrial application. In most countries, however, patents refer only to the invention patents in the sense of the Chinese Patent Law. For example, the United States does not have a utility-model system, and its utility patents are virtually equivalent to invention patents in the Chinese Patent Law. Some other countries do not treat utility models and designs as patents but rather as independent types of intellectual property rights. According to the Chinese Patent Law, only invention patent applications are required for substantive examination, while utility models and designs only require preliminary examination.

innovation. In 2006, the Government announced its 15-year 'Medium-to-Long-Term Plan for Scientific and Technological Development' (hereinafter the 15-Year Plan). The 15-Year Plan included policies and standards aimed at increasing indigenous IP development before 2020, including a series of quantitative targets for development. Another key aspect of the plan was the development of 16 mega-projects focusing on key technological fields. The 15-Year Plan has since been supplemented with other policy statements and objectives—all recognising the importance of establishing and expanding the community of stakeholders in a strong IP regime. Such policy statements encourage IP transfer and alliances among companies, universities and research institutes, in order to catch up with and leapfrog into positions of leadership in several technological areas such as clean energy, electric vehicles and computing technology.

In June 2008, the Outline of the National Intellectual Property Strategy (hereinafter the 2008 Strategy) was promulgated for the purpose of improving China's capacity to create, utilise, protect and administer intellectual property, making China an innovative country and attaining the goal of building a moderately prosperous society in all respects. The 2008 Strategy emphasised the importance of creating and utilising intellectual property. More concretely, the 2008 strategy sought to make IP creation and use ubiquitous in the research and innovation activities of companies and government bodies. For example, the strategy encouraged companies to incorporate IP into their technical standards and encouraged universities to commercialise their IP.

In the more recent National Patent Development Strategy of 2010, the Government was even more assertive about benchmarks for future performance. A few of the highlights include:

- by 2015, the number of patent filings will reach two million, which will quadruple the number filed in 2010
- by 2015, China will rank in the top two countries for the number of invention patents granted to domestic applicants
- by 2020, a quadrupling of the number of invention patents per capita and the quantity of Chinese-origin patent applications filed abroad.

In order to achieve these objectives, the Chinese Central Government, local governments, as well as universities and companies have promulgated generous incentives for the creation of IP. In universities, academic staff who do so are more likely to win tenure and promotion. Workers and students who file patents not only are entitled to prizes, but also are more likely to earn a *hukou* (residence permit) to live in a desirable city. For some patents, the Government pays cash bonuses; for others, it covers the substantial cost of filing. Corporate income tax can be cut from 25 per cent to 15 per cent for firms which file many patents. They are also more likely to win lucrative government contracts.

Many companies therefore offer incentives to their employees to come up with patentable ideas. Huawei, a telecommunications equipment manufacturer that seeks both government contracts and global recognition, pays patent-related bonuses of RMB10 000–100 000 ($1500–15 000) for inventions and creations. In addition to the above incentives, many local governments offer subsidies for the cost of filing a patent, and some provide better housing as an incentive.

Under such measures, the number of patent applications and grants has increased rapidly. Figure 20.1 shows the number of annual patent applications and grants increasing from 1985 to 2012; both patent applications and grants increased more rapidly since 2000, with an average rate of increase of more than 25 per cent. In 2011, China received 526 412 applications for (invention) patents, for the first time overtaking the United States to become the largest recipient of patent applications in the world.

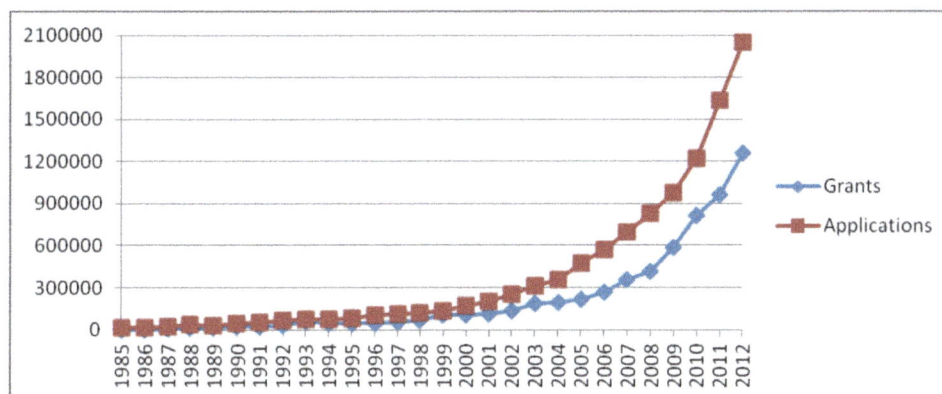

Figure 20.1 Annual Number of Patent Applications Filed and Granted at the Chinese Patent Office, 1985–2012

We can, however, see some different growth patterns if we distinguish the patent applications and grants by their types (invention, utility model and design). Figures 20.2 and 20.3 compare the patterns of three types of patents in application and grant. In Figure 20.2, we see that the three types of patent applications have been growing almost together. However, in Figure 20.3 the number of invention patents granted has been growing much more slowly than their applications in Figure 20.2, indicating a higher percentage of invention patent applications were rejected. Therefore, it is more appropriate to use the number of patent grants than patent applications to describe innovation output.

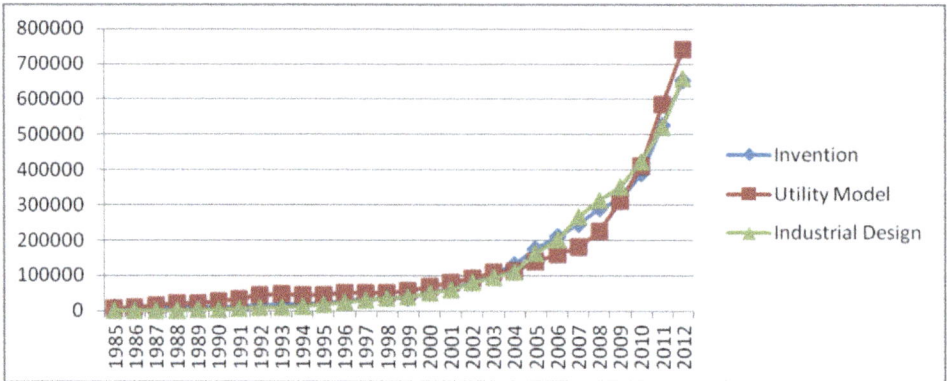

Figure 20.2 Three Types of Patent Application in China, 1985–2012

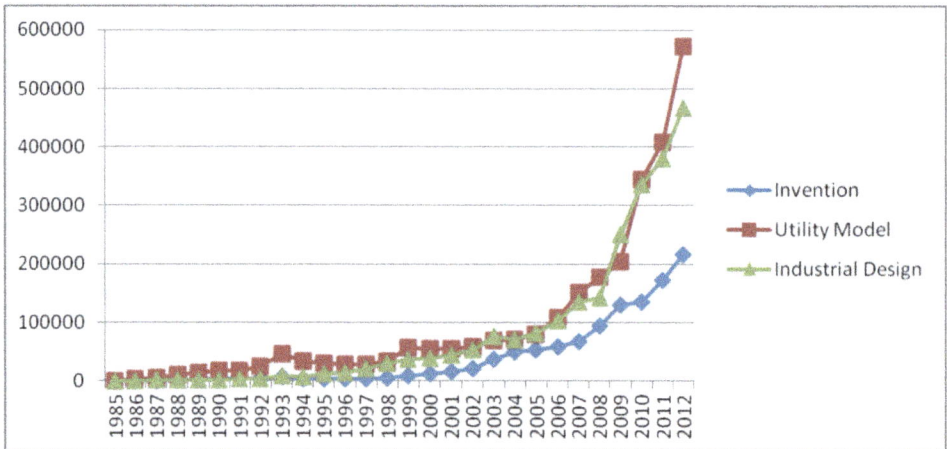

Figure 20.3 Three Types of Patent Grant in China, 1985–2012

If we compare the patents granted according to their types and origins in Figures 20.4, 20.5 and 20.6, we find that foreigners are more interested in obtaining invention patents than the other two types of patents in China. We also notice that in Figure 20.4, after the GFC in 2008, there was a clear drop in patent grants to foreigners. These comparisons carry two important messages: first, foreigners attach greater importance to invention patents in China than the other two types of patents. Second, foreign patent applicants seem more likely to be affected by the world economic situation than China's domestic patent applicants.

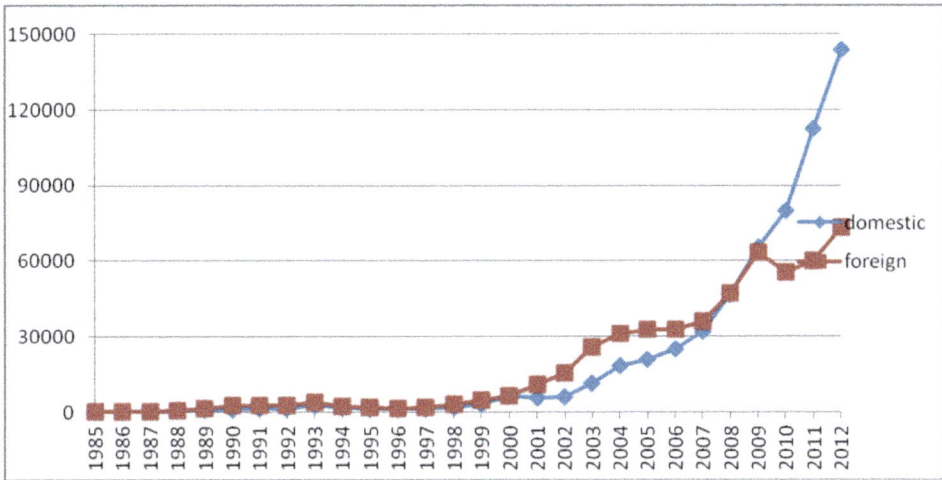

Figure 20.4 Invention Patents Granted Annually to Domestic and Foreign Entities, 1985–2012

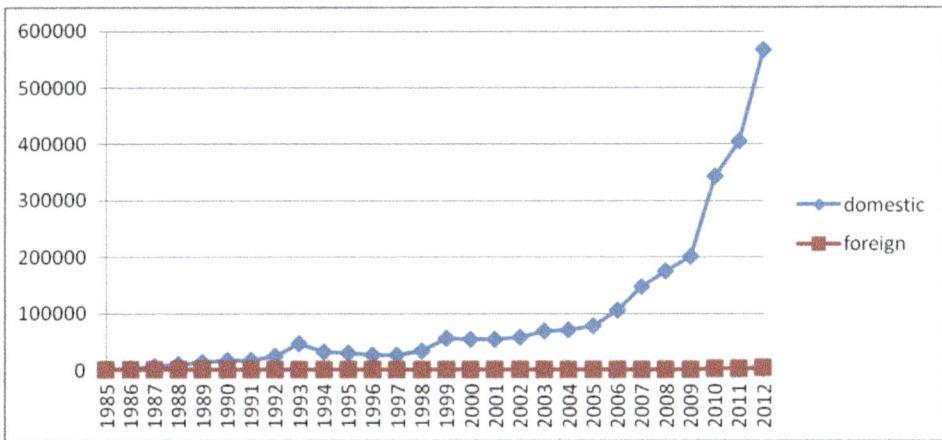

Figure 20.5 Utility Model Patents Granted Annually to Domestic and Foreign Entities, 1985–2012

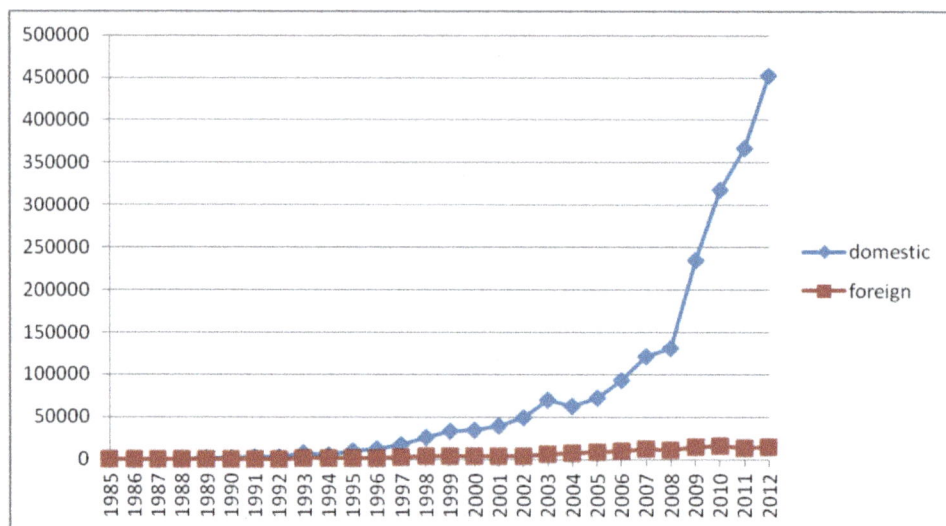

Figure 20.6 Industrial Design Patents Granted Annually to Domestic and Foreign Entities, 1985–2012

At the international level, China has also increased its international patent applications under the Patent Cooperation Treaty (PCT) in recent years, especially since the mid 2000s. Figure 20.7 shows the trend of PCT applications for the top-five origins—namely the United States, Japan, Germany, China and Republic of Korea—from 1990 to 2012. According to recently released data from the World Intellectual Property Organisation (WIPO), China has surpassed Germany and ranked third in the world in the number of PCT applications by the end of 2013.

An interesting question is whether the rapid increase of patenting activities by Chinese entities in China and abroad truly reflects the country's innovation capabilities. The answer is not clear. On the one hand, patent statistics do have some advantages as a measure of innovation especially in the lack of good measures of technological change. Patent statistics are available, by definition related to inventiveness, and based on what appears to be an objective and only slowly changing standard. As noticed by Griliches (1990), in spite of many difficulties and reservations, patent data remain a unique resource for the study of innovation and technical change in both micro and macro-economic activities.

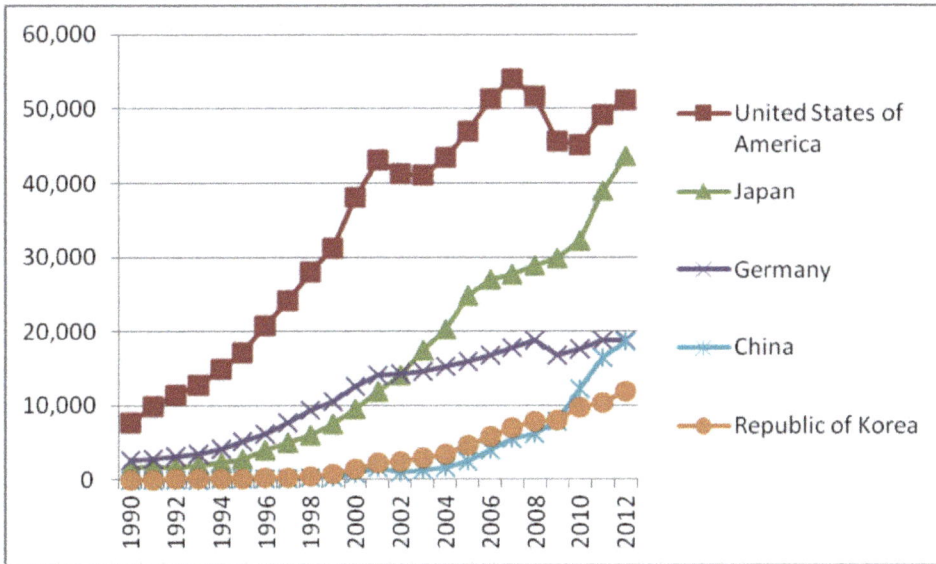

Figure 20.7 Trend in PCT Applications for the Top-Five Origins, 1990–2012

On the other hand, there is reason to question whether the number of patent applications or grants is a good indicator of innovation. While, by definition, patents (invention) need to be novel, inventive in technology and useful in industrial application, innovation is not limited to patented technology. Many patents have never been used in industry, and some are only invented to obtain government subsidies or intimidate competitors. Innovation refers to the introduction or application of new ideas, things or methods, whereas patents (or invention) refer more directly to the creation of them. Therefore, if a patent (or an invention) is not put into use, it can hardly be called an innovation. According to Xu and Gao (2002), the patent commercialisation rate was around 10 per cent in 2000, which was far below the level of developed countries— between roughly 60 per cent and 80 per cent.

Second, patents vary greatly in technical and economic significance. Even in the same industry or technology subclass, patents differ greatly in value. Therefore, simple comparisons of numbers of patents do not convey much useful information related to innovation. Moreover, patent statistics are classified according to the International Patent Classification (IPC), which is based on technological categories and cannot be directly translated into industrial sectors. Although some economists (Evenson and Putnam 1988; Schmoch et al. 2003) have tried to merge patent classes with economically relevant industries or product groupings, there remain some inherent ambiguities and difficulties— for example, some patents may belong to several industries depending on their usage.

Last but not least, in recent years various government subsidies and incentives have attracted a rapid increase in patent applications in China. As noticed by Wild (2011) and Liang (2012), the combination of subsidised patent application processes plus major tax savings creates a large incentive for Chinese companies to apply for patents, but may not result in uniformly high patent quality. There are better and more ingenious ways to increase and improve innovation than setting arbitrary benchmarks for patent filings and offering tax breaks, money and in-kind rewards that outweigh the costs of filing patents. Such incentives have induced a flood of 'junk' patents. Patents may lose any relation to true innovation. Rather than equate patents with novel and useful inventions, companies and individuals will instead perceive patents as a tax break, or some other short-term financial benefit. This wastes a huge amount of social resources, including examination and administration.

What can we learn from the literature on optimising the patent institution in economic development?

Optimal design of the patent institution

The core issue in designing the patent institution is how to balance private incentives and public interests.

To tackle the trade-off between providing incentives and causing potential monopoly inherent in the patent institution, many economists try to fit the patent system with a measurable design of optimal patent length (life) and breadth (scope). Nordhaus (1969) and Scherer (1972) initiate an analysis of the optimal patent life by modelling the trade-off inherent in the patent institution—an institution that creates static losses by granting innovators temporary monopoly power in order to realise social gains by inducing greater innovative effort. According to their argument, it is better to restrict patent life in order to reduce the associated deadweight loss because usually the longer the duration of patent protection, the stronger the incentive for innovation, but also the greater the monopoly power.

Theoretically, differentiated patent protection terms are better than a unified statutory patent life for all types of technologies. In reality, however, it is impractical for any government to determine which inventions should be given longer or shorter patent life due to asymmetry of information and inherent uncertainty of invention. Thus, in the real world, patent length is almost statutorily the same: usually 20 years from the filing date for invention patents and 10 years for utility models and industrial designs, as regulated by the TRIPS Agreement. Although it is difficult to differentiate statutory patent life individually, an annual patent maintenance fee system was created to let patent owners themselves decide whether they would like to pay the annual patent fees in order to keep their patents valid. The annual patent fee system thus plays an important role in balancing the trade-off between private and public interests in patented technologies.

Since it is technically and practically difficult to allow different statutory patent lengths across technologies and in reality governments usually fix a finite statutory patent duration and use an annual fee system to avoid excessive monopoly power, more follow-on research is concentrated on the optimal design of patent breadth (scope). The breadth of a patent refers to the patent scope in the sense of patent law; it is determined by claims made in an application and accorded by patent examiners to a patentee, defining the boundaries between what is protected and what is not. As most technologies are based on previous innovations, patent breadth becomes extremely important in balancing the incentives for the first-generation and follow-on innovations.

There are two main opposing camps on how to balance the incentives for first-generation inventors of initial technologies and second-generation innovators of applied R&D. Scotchmer (1991), Chang (1995), Green and Scotchmer (1995) and Matutes et al. (1996) argue that first-generation inventors of initial technologies should be given strong forward protection so as to overcome the inter-temporal externality that arises when second-generation improvements can be obtained by outsiders. Broad forward protection can, however, stifle second-generation products, affect the accessibility of patented knowledge embedded in the initial inventions, and thus slow the rate of innovation, as emphasised by Merges and Nelson (1994) and Heller and Eisenberg (1998).

Clearly, there are no simple conclusions about the optimal patent breadth. It is not necessarily optimal to protect the first innovation so broadly that every second-generation product infringes, nor so narrowly that a new product never infringes. In reality, an applicant usually wants to claim as much as possible, and then a patent office must decide what claims are allowable. While decisions regarding what to allow are constrained by a number of legal principles, and by the invention itself, in many cases a patent office has considerable room for discretion. Within that discretionary zone, the office must decide which claims should be admitted and which pruned or rejected.

According to the TRIPS Agreement, with some very limited exceptions, 'patents shall be available for any inventions, whether products or processes, in all fields of technology, provided that they are new, involve an inventive step and are capable of industrial application' (Clause 1 of Article 27, the TRIPS

Agreement, 1994). Under this general requirement, however, a national patent law can be flexible in recognising what inventions can satisfy its standards for novelty, non-obviousness (an inventive step) and industrial applicability. For example, some inventions related to software or business methods are recognised as patents by the US Patent and Trademark Office (USPTO), but they may be turned down by the Chinese Patent Office, as Chinese patent examiners may interpret such inventions as lacking an inventive step according to the Chinese Patent Law. Thus, we can see that patent breadth or scope is closely related to patentability requirements. Therefore, patentability requirements are an important and operational instrument for optimal patent design at a national level; however, there is a tendency to harmonise the substantive patent laws at an international level, which will further limit the discretionary power in patent examination in each nation.

One general conclusion we can draw is that China should make its own patent institution according to its technological and economic strengths so as to address the trade-off between promoting the diffusion of knowledge and rewarding innovators. Sakakibara and Lee (2001) find that before 1988 Japan traditionally had a narrower patent scope than the United States since Japan had a comparative advantage in applied R&D. Unfortunately, in the formation and revision of the Chinese Patent Law, economists have rarely provided advice on the design and improvement of the Chinese patent institution. Most of the early Chinese patent founders learned their patent knowledge in the 1970s and 1980s abroad, where they were taught about the positive aspects of patents in promoting invention and creation, but little was emphasised about the potential negative side of patents for the monopoly they could cause. Moreover, there seems to be a gap between the theoretical optimal patent design and real-world patent policymaking, which might have been caused particularly by a lack of communication between economic researchers and the patent community, whose members are mainly engineers and legal professionals; but it might also be due to the inability of economists to make their messages operational.

The patent institution, international trade and technology transfer

Another important role of the patent institution in the context of economic globalisation is to facilitate technology transfer. As Hayami and Godo (2005:349) assert, '[e]ffective borrowing of technologies developed in advanced economies is the key for late starters of industrialization to catch up with early starters'. Therefore, it is interesting to explore the impacts of an increasingly pro-patent policy on China's international trade and technology transfer.

Basically, the protection strength of patents or other IPRs affects international trade flows. If a nation strengthens its patent law, it could experience higher or lower imports as foreign firms may face increasing net demand for their products due to strengthened patent protection, but they may also choose to reduce their sales in this nation's market because of their greater market power in an imitation-safe environment. Maskus and Penubarti (1995) find that strengthening patent protection has a positive impact on bilateral manufacturing imports into large developing economies, but a negative impact on small ones. Further, Fink and Primo Braga (1999) provide new evidence regarding the effects of patent protection on international trade. They confirm a positive link between patent protection and trade flows for the aggregate of non-fuel trade, but do not find a significant positive relationship between patent protection and high-technology trade flows.

Maskus (1997) summarises the predicted relationship between patent protection, FDI and technology transfer. First, FDI and technology transfer are relatively insensitive to international differences in patent protection in sectors that have old products and standardised, labour-intensive technologies because FDI is influenced more by factor costs, market size, trade costs and other location advantages than by patent policies in this setting. Second, other things being equal, FDI that represents complex but easily copied technologies is likely to increase as patent protection is strengthened. Third, to the extent that stronger patents reduce licensing costs, FDI could be displaced over time by efficient licensing. Finally, whatever the mode, the likelihood of the most advanced technologies to be transferred increases with the strength of patents.

Empirical studies provide mixed messages about the effects of patents on technology diffusion. In some models, technology is transferred through imitation by firms in developing countries. When the global patent system is strengthened by the adoption of minimum standards set in the TRIPS Agreement, imitation becomes more difficult as foreign patents are enforced. The rate of imitation declines, but contrary to what might be expected, this decline slows the global rate of innovation also: if innovative firms expect slower loss of their technological advantages, they can earn higher profits per innovation, reducing the need to engage in R&D (Helpman 1993; Glass and Saggi 2002). This result is, however, sensitive to model assumptions and may not hold up to alternative specifications. Indeed, Lai (1998) found that product innovation and technology diffusion are strengthened under stronger patent protection if production is transferred through FDI, rather than through imitation. This result points clearly to the need for developing economies to remove impediments to inward FDI as they strengthen their patent institutions.

Hall (2011) finds that stronger patent protection encourages FDI and technology transfer to mid-level developing countries, but that there is little clear evidence that stronger patent protection encourages indigenous innovation in least-developed countries. These conclusions seem consistent with the idea that a certain level of absorptive capacity is necessary to make use of and learn from imported technology, but that if a country has the absorptive capacity, it is more likely to receive the technology if the foreign firm from which it comes feels that its ownership rights are protected. It should be noted, however, that although IP protection is clearly considered a favourable factor for foreign investment and technology transfer, factors such as the size of the recipient economy, its expected growth and the availability of qualified personnel are all important to attract FDI and foreign technology.

China has been pushed to establish and strengthen its patent institution since the 1980s. Patent and other IP protection has been on the top of the negotiation list of developed countries doing business with China. In the late 1980s and early 1990s, the United States and some other developed countries claimed they lost billions of dollars of revenue annually due to rampant piracy and counterfeiting in China. The US Government threatened China repeatedly with economic sanctions, trade wars and non-renewal of most-favoured-nation status to protect their business. As China tried to join the World Trade Organisation (WTO), it had to meet the international minimum standards on IP protection under the TRIPS Agreement by substantially revising its IP-related laws and regulations.

Meanwhile, China gradually realised the importance of IP in stimulating innovation and facilitating trade. Weak IP enforcement is regularly cited as a major problem for companies operating in China and as a barrier that restricts the types of activities companies are willing to undertake. Strong IP protection plays a much larger role in signalling to potential investors that a particular country recognises and protects the rights of foreign firms to make strategic business decisions with few government impediments. Because IP protection has taken on increasing importance to multinational enterprises, the adoption of stronger IP regimes has become a primary device that the Chinese Government has used to indicate a shift towards a more business-friendly environment. Until now, there have been more and more foreign multinational R&D centres established in China. From 2000 to 2010, the number of foreign-invested R&D centres increased from less than 200 to more than 1300.[2] Due to both 'external pushes' and 'internal pulls', China has strengthened patent and other IP protection.

---

2   Please refer to The Business Times (2011).

Hu and Jefferson (2009) and Zhang (2010) confirmed that R&D intensification in China is one of the primary driving forces of China's patent boom. They also find that the impact of FDI on patenting is large, but slightly less important than R&D in explaining the patent explosion. In addition, the pro-patent amendments to the Chinese Patent Law in 2000, China's entry to the WTO and the deepening of enterprise reform all partially explain the patent boom. Using data from 1995 to 2000, Cheung and Lin (2004) find that provinces with more FDI have more domestic patent applications. They attribute this to a form of spillover from foreign investment—namely, a demonstration effect on domestic enterprises.

The patent institution and economic growth

A good understanding of the two previous issues is helpful in understanding the connection between the patent institution and economic growth. The growing consensus is that strong IP regimes in developing countries could have a long-term beneficial effect on their economic growth. This favourable effect is dependent, however, on other important factors, such as improving human capital, particularly in technical skills, expanding technical infrastructure, developing efficient managerial techniques, investing in R&D, increasing the openness and transparency of the domestic market, and encouraging international trade and investment from abroad. While sufficiently strong IP protection is helpful for promoting FDI and other forms of technology transfer, it is absolutely critical for encouraging investment in R&D. Thus, economic development cannot be disconnected from technology transfers and the protection of patents. Strong patent protections are seen to encourage economic development by: 1) promoting domestic innovation by protecting the development of nascent technology; 2) preventing brain drain by ensuring innovators are rewarded for their effort; and 3) fostering technology transfers, such as FDI, licensing and imports.

A few studies have investigated the impact of IP protection on cross-country economic growth. Gould and Gruben (1996) estimate a growth model on a cross-section of up to 95 countries with data averaged over the period 1960–88, including an index measuring patent protection strength created by Rapp and Rozek (1990) in their regression. They find that IP protection can have a slightly larger impact on growth in open economies. Therefore, trade liberalisation in combination with stronger patent protection enhances growth because it improves the competitive nature of markets and increases access to foreign technologies.

Thompson and Rushing (1996) employ a switching regression model to examine whether increased patent protection is more beneficial once a country has reached a particular level of development, as measured by initial

GDP per capita. Their results indicate a break in the data, at an initial level of US$3400 (1980 prices). For countries below this no relationship between patent protection and growth is found; above it, there is a positive and significant relationship. Thompson and Rushing (1999) extend this model and once again suggest that patent protection has a positive and significant impact upon TFP only for the most advanced countries, with insignificant coefficients found for the full sample and the sample of developing countries.

Park and Ginarte (1997) create an index of patent rights for 110 countries for the period 1960–90. The index is used to examine what factors or characteristics of economies determine how strongly patent rights will be protected. The evidence indicates that more developed economies tend to provide stronger protection; but the underlying factors that influence patent protection levels are the country's level of R&D activity, the market environment and international integration, which are correlated with its level of development. The R&D activity influences patent protection levels after a nation's research sector reaches a critical size. An implication is that to raise patent protection levels in weakly protecting countries, it is important to foster a significant research base in those countries and thereby create incentives for protecting patent rights.

Maskus and McDaniel (1999) investigate empirically how the Japanese patent institution has affected postwar growth in Japanese total factor productivity (TFP). The postwar Japanese patent institution before 1988 was recognised as a mechanism for promoting technological catch-up and diffusion through incremental innovation. Given certain patent procedures, such as pre-grant disclosure, single-claim requirement, first-to-file and lengthy pending periods, the Japanese patent institution has enabled a channel of technology transfer through the application process. Maskus and McDaniel (1999) find that technology diffusion through utility-model applications had a positive impact on Japan's postwar productivity growth.

There have been few empirical papers dealing with the impact of patents on economic growth in China. Zhao and Liu (2011) find that China's domestic patents had a positive impact on China's TFP from 1988 to 2009, and the impact of invention patents on TFP is much larger than utility-model patents and design patents in 1999–2009. However, before 1999, invention patents seemed to have had little impact on TFP. After 1999, the technological progress reflected by the increase of invention patents in China seemed to play an increasingly important role in economic growth.

Conclusions and implications

The above overview of the patent institution from past economic studies of patents has underlined a series of practical issues that deserve policymakers' attention in China and also in developing countries.

First, patent protection is a double-edged sword, with both a positive and a negative side. Patents are usually effective in stimulating inventions, encouraging disclosure of new technologies and facilitating market transactions for new technologies. On the other side, they can also generate costs to society partially due to the potential monopoly and barriers to free use of the patented technologies. Competitive rents, in the absence of patent protection, might compensate innovators in certain circumstances. For instance, first-mover advantages arising from seizing the market are important and the cost of imitation is high; patents may not be necessary to encourage such innovation. An optimal patent institution should establish a good balance.

Second, patentability requirements, such as novelty, non-obviousness and industrial applicability, are important instruments to avoid the granting of unqualified patents that increase the social cost of the patent institution. Moreover, strict application of such principles in patent examination is also an effective measure to prevent broad patent protection scope that could deter further innovation and improvement.

Third, in the current globalisation context, such as TRIPS and other international patent agreements, a nation often has limited leverage in making its own patent law and policy—for instance, the statutory patent life should be at least 20 years and patent protection should cover almost all technologies, which may not be in the interests of most developing countries. It is important for developing countries to realise this point and cooperate with each other to seek their interests in international negotiations on IP and patent protection.

Fourth, empirical studies seem to support the theoretical importance of the patent institution in promoting trade, attracting FDI and facilitating technology transfer. However, the net impact on technology transfer to developing countries under the current international patent framework is still ambiguous. It seems stronger patents encourage technology transfer only to mid-level developing countries, but they have little effect on technology transfer to the lowest-income countries.

Last but not least, cross-country analyses seem to show that IP or patent protection has a positive and significant contribution to the economic growth in high-income countries, while for low-income and middle-income countries, the net impact is ambiguous.

The relationship between patents and economic development in developing countries is more complex than that observed in developed countries. In the short term, developing countries may be disadvantaged in filing competitive patents; and developed countries may take advantage of the international harmonised patent institution to secure their innovation and market power in developing countries. In the long term, it depends on developing countries' domestic enterprises whether they can learn fast and compete with multinational companies under a framework that favours of stronger technological innovators.

References

Arrow, K. (1962), 'Economic welfare and the allocation of resources for invention', in *The Rate and Direction of Inventive Activity: Economic and Social Factors*, pp. 609–26, Cambridge, Mass.: National Bureau of Economic Research.

Bentham, J. (1839), *The Works of Jeremy Bentham*, J. Bowring ed., *The Online Library of Liberty*. Available from <http://oll.libertyfund.org/title/1922>.

Boldrin, M. and Levine, D. (2002), 'The case against intellectual property', *American Economic Review* 92(2):209–12.

Chang, H. (1995), 'Patent scope, antitrust policy, and cumulative innovation', *The RAND Journal of Economics* 26(1):34–57.

Cheung, K.-Y. and Lin, P. (2004), 'Spillover effects of FDI on innovation in China: evidence from provincial data', *China Economic Review* 15(1):25–44.

Colombo, M. G. and Delmastro, M. (2002), 'How effective are technology incubators? Evidence from Italy', *Research Policy* 31:1103–22.

Drahos, P. (1995), 'Information feudalism in the information society', *The Information Society* 11:209–22.

Drahos, P. (ed.) (1999), *Intellectual Property*, Aldershot, UK: Ashgate.

Evenson, R. and Putnam, J. (1988), *The Yale–Canada patent flow concordance*, Economic Growth Centre Working Paper, Yale University, New Haven, Conn.

Fink, C. and Primo Braga, C. A. (1999), *How stronger protection of intellectual property rights affects international trade flows*, Working Paper No. 2051, The World Bank, Washington, DC.

Glass, A. J. and Saggi, K. (2002), 'Intellectual property rights and foreign direct investment', *Journal of International Economics* 56(2):387–410.

Gould, D. M. and Gruben, W. C. (1996), 'The role of intellectual property rights in economic growth', *Journal of Economic Development* 48:323–50.

Green, J. and Scotchmer, S. (1995), 'On the division of profits in sequential innovation', *The RAND Journal of Economics* 26(1):20–33.

Griliches, Z. (1990), 'Patent statistics as economic indicators: a survey', *Journal of Economic Literature* 28(4):1661–707.

Hall, B. H. (2011), 'The internationalization of R&D', in A. Sydor (ed.), *Global Value Chains: Impacts and Implications*, pp. 179–210, Ottawa: Foreign Affairs and International Trade Canada, Government of Canada.

Hayami, Y. and Godo, Y. (2005), *Development Economics: From the Poverty to the Wealth of Nations*, New York: Oxford University Press.

Heller, M. and Eisenberg, R. (1998), 'Can patents deter innovation? The anticommons in biomedical research', *Science* 280:698–701.

Helpman, E. (1993), 'Innovation, imitation, and intellectual property rights', *Econometrica* 61(6):1247–80.

Hu, A. G. and Jefferson, G. H. 2009, 'A great wall of patents: what is behind China's recent patent explosion', *Journal of Development Economics* 90:57–68.

Hulme, E. W. (1896), 'The history of the patent institution under the prerogative and at common law', *Law Quarterly Review* 46:141–54.

Idris, K. (2003), *Intellectual Property—A Powerful Tool for Economic Growth*, Geneva: World Intellectual Property Organisation.

Lai, E. L. (1998), 'International intellectual property rights protection and the rate of product innovation', *Journal of Development Economics* 55(1):133–53.

Liang, M. (2012), 'Chinese patent quality: running the numbers and possible remedies', *The John Marshall Review of Intellectual Property Law* 11:478–512.

Maddison, A. (1999), 'Poor until 1820', *Wall Street Journal* [Europe], 11 January 1999.

Martin, S. and Scott, J. T. (2000), 'The nature of innovation market failure and the design of public support for private innovation', *Research Policy* 29(4–5):437–47.

Maskus, K. E. (1997), The role of intellectual property rights in encouraging foreign direct investment and technology transfer, Prepared for the Public–Private Initiatives after TRIPS: Designing a Global Agenda Conference, Brussels.

Maskus, K. E. and McDaniel, C. (1999), 'Impact of the Japanese patent system on productivity growth', *Japan and the World Economy* 11(4):11 557–74.

Maskus, K. E. and Penubarti, M. (1995), 'How trade-related are intellectual property rights?', *Journal of International Economics* 39:227–48.

Matutes, C., Regibeau, P. and Rockett, K. (1996), 'Optimal patent design and the diffusion of innovations', *The RAND Journal of Economics* 27(1):60–83.

Merges, R. and Nelson, R. (1994), 'On limiting or encouraging rivalry in technical progress: the effect of patent scope decisions', *Journal of Economic Behaviour and Organization* 25:1–24.

Moir, H. V. J. (2008), *What are the costs and benefits of patent systems?*, Centre for Governance of Knowledge and Development Working Paper, The Australian National University, Canberra.

Naik, G. (2010), 'China surpasses Japan in R&D as powers shift', *The Wall Street Journal*. Available from <http://online.wsj.com/article/SB100014240527487 0373420457601971391768354.html>.

Nordhaus, W. (1969), *Invention, Growth and Welfare: A Theoretical Treatment of Technological Change*, Cambridge, Mass.: MIT Press.

Park, W. G. and Ginarte, J. C. (1997), 'Determinants of patent rights: a cross-national study', *Research Policy* 26:283–301.

Pigou, A. C. (1920), *The Economics of Welfare*, 4th edn, *The Online Library of Liberty*. Available from <http://oll.libertyfund.org/Ebooks/Pigou_0316. pdf>.

Posner, R. (2012), 'Why there are too many patents in America', *The Atlantic*, 12 July 2012. Available from <http:/www.theatlantic.com/business/ archive/2012/07/why-there-are-too-many-patents-in-america/259725/>.

Rapp, R. T. and Rozek, R. P. (1990), 'Benefits and costs of intellectual property protection in developing countries', *Journal of World Trade* 24(5):75–102.

Sakakibara, M. and Lee, B. (2001), 'Do stronger patents induce more innovation? Evidence from the 1988 Japanese patent law reforms', *The RAND Journal of Economics* 32(1):77–100.

Scherer, F. M. 1972, 'Nordhaus' theory of optimal patent life: a geometric reinterpretation', *American Economic Review* 62(3):422–7.

Schmoch, U., Laville, F., Patel, P. and Frietsch, R. (2003), *Linking technology areas to industrial sectors: final report to the European Commission, DG Research.* Available from <ftp://ftp.cordis.europa.eu/pub/indicators/docs/ind_report_isi_ost_spru.pdf>.

Scotchmer, S. (1991), 'Standing on the shoulders of giants: cumulative research and the patent law', *Journal of Economic Perspective* 5(1):29–41.

Smith, A. (1776), *Wealth of Nations*, London: W. Strahan & T. Cadell.

Taussig, F. W. (1915), *Inventors and money makers.* Available from <http://www.unz.org/Pub/TaussigFW-1915>.

The Business Times (2011), 'World to gain from an innovative China', *The Business Times*, 11 July 2011. Available from <http://www.businesschina.org.sg/en.php/resources/news/317/1>.

Thompson, M. and Rushing, F. (1996), 'An empirical analysis of the impact of patent protection on economic growth', *Journal of Economic Development* 21(2):61–79.

Thompson, M. and Rushing, F. (1999), 'An empirical analysis of the impact of patent protection on economic growth: an extension', *Journal of Economic Development* 24(1):67–76.

United Kingdom Commission on Intellectual Property Rights (UK Commission on IPR) (2002), *Integrating Intellectual Property Rights and Development Policy.* Available from <http://www.iprcommission.org/graphic/documents/final_report.htm>.

Wild, J. (2011), 'Quality is China's biggest patent challenge—updated', *IAM Magazine.* Available from <http://www.iam-magazine.com/blog/Detail.aspx?g=e81c5421-bccc-4eb5-9895-f347443cf73e>.

Xu, W. and Gao, Y. (2002), 'Venture investment system and counter measures in the process of hi-tech achievements' transformation', *Journal of Technology College Education* 21(4).

Zhang, H. (2010), 'What is behind the recent surge in patenting in China?', *International Journal of Business and Management* 5(10):83–91.

Zhao, Y. and Liu, S. (2011), *Effect of China's domestic patents on total factor productivity: 1988–2009.* Available from <ftp://ftp.zew.de/pub/zew-docs/veranstaltungen/innovationpatenting2011/papers/Liu.pdf>.

21. Foreign Investment Laws and Policies in China

Historical views and current issues

Xiang Gao and Huiqin Jiang

Introduction

The Chinese Government has welcomed and encouraged foreign investment since the reform and opening-up began in 1978. There was a lift in the importance of inward direct foreign investment (DFI) in 1984 with deepening of urban reform, and again from 1992 with stronger commitment to developing an internationally oriented market economy. Foreign investment has played a significant role in China's economic growth and also to its overall social development. Foreign investment laws in China have been gradually improved along with the progressively deeper reform which has provided a legal environment that is better able to attract foreign investment. The development of foreign investment in China is closely related to and results from changes in foreign investment laws and policies. The amount of realised foreign capital coming into China since 1983 illustrates this correlation (Figure 21.1). Before 1992, the amount of realised foreign capital in China was small. After 1992 the amount increased significantly, as the Chinese Government accelerated movement to a market economy and sought to provide an efficient legal environment for foreign investment. Since then, the amount of realised foreign capital coming into China has increased substantially.

This chapter provides a comprehensive overview of China's foreign investment laws and policies, in three sections. The first section briefly introduces the basic framework of China's foreign investment laws and policies. The second reviews the historical developments of China's foreign investment laws and policies, providing a context for the past few decades. The third discusses the current issues China's foreign investment laws and policies are facing.

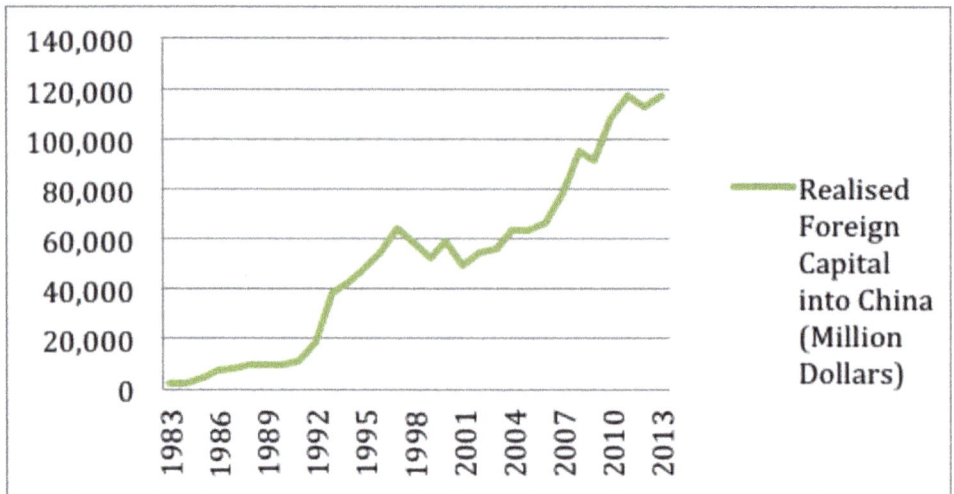

Figure 21.1 Realised Foreign Capital Coming into China, 1983–2013

Sources: NBS (2013); MOFCOM (2014).

Basic framework of China's foreign investment laws and policies

Within China's centrally planned economy before reform and opening-up, the number of foreign investments was small, and there was no body of laws or policy on foreign investment.[1] The framework of China's foreign investment laws and policies has been gradually built since 1978.

---

1 For example, Provisions on the Establishment of Schools by Charitable Donations by Overseas Chinese (promulgated on 2 August 1957; expired); Consolidated Industrial and Commercial Tax Regulations of the People's Republic of China [Draft] (promulgated on 14 September 1958; expired).

Legislation

The first foreign investment law in China was the Law of the People's Republic of China on Chinese-Foreign Equity Joint Ventures (hereinafter 'Law of Equity Joint Ventures') promulgated in 1979.[2] Since then, the Chinese Government sequentially promulgated the Law of the People's Republic of China on Foreign-Capital Enterprises (hereinafter 'Law of Foreign-Capital Enterprises'), in 1986,[3] and the Law of the People's Republic of China on Chinese-Foreign Contractual Joint Ventures (hereinafter 'Law of Contractual Joint Ventures'), in 1988.[4] These three laws are collectively referred to as the 'Three Investment Laws' regulating foreign investment in China. To ensure the implementation of the Three Investment Laws, the State Council promulgated three regulations or rules: Regulations for the Implementation of the Law of the People's Republic of China on Chinese-Foreign Equity Joint Ventures (hereinafter 'Regulations of Equity Joint Ventures') in 1983,[5] Rules for the Implementation of the Law of the People's Republic of China on Foreign-Capital Enterprises (hereinafter 'Rules of Foreign-Capital Enterprises') in 1990,[6] and Rules for the Implementation of the Law of the People's Republic of China on Chinese-foreign Contractual Joint Ventures (herein after 'Rules of Contractual Joint Ventures') in 1995[7] (collectively referred to as the 'Regulations of the Three Investment Laws'). The Three Investment Laws and the Regulations of the Three Investment Laws constitute the basic framework of Chinese foreign investment laws.

Article 18 of the Company Law of the People's Republic of China (1993)[8] (hereinafter '1993 Company Law ') stipulated that it 'shall apply to limited liability companies with foreign investment. Where laws concerning Chinese-foreign equity joint ventures, Chinese-foreign contractual joint ventures and foreign-funded enterprises provide otherwise, such provision shall prevail.' This article specified the basic principle that foreign-invested companies must follow: there are special laws beyond the general laws applied to domestic

---

2   Law of the People's Republic of China on Chinese-Foreign Equity Joint Ventures (promulgated on 8 July 1979; amended on 4 April 1990 and 15 March 2001).

3   Law of the People's Republic of China on Foreign-Capital Enterprises (promulgated on 12 April 1986; amended on 31 October 2000).

4   Law of the People's Republic of China on Chinese-Foreign Contractual Joint Ventures (promulgated on 13 April 1988; amended on 31 October 2000).

5   Regulations for the Implementation of the Law of the People's Republic of China on Chinese-Foreign Equity Joint Ventures (promulgated 20 September 1983; revised on 15 January 1986, 21 December 1987, 22 July 2001 and 19 February 2014).

6   Rules for the Implementation of the Law of the People's Republic of China on Foreign-Capital Enterprises (promulgated on 21 December 1990; revised on 12 April 2001 and 19 February 2014).

7   Rules for the Implementation of the Law of the People's Republic of China on Chinese-Foreign Contractual Joint Ventures (promulgated on 4 September 1995, revised on 19 February 2014).

8   Company Law of the People's Republic of China (promulgated on 29 December 1993; amended on 25 December 1999 and 28 August 2004; revised on 27 October 2005; and amended on 28 December 2013).

companies. This principle still stands. The 1993 Company Law was amended in 1999 and again in 2004, but Article 18 stood untouched. The 2005 Revision of the Company Law (hereinafter '2005 Company Law) revised Article 18 by including the foreign-investment companies, both limited liability companies and corporation owned by shareholders. Article 218 prescribed that the 2005 Company Law 'shall be applicable to foreign-invested companies with limited liability and such companies limited by shares; and where laws on foreign investments provide otherwise, the provisions there shall be applicable'. Article 218 of the 2005 Company Law remained the same after its 2013 amendment.

In addition, China has also developed a large number of implementation regulations on foreign investment.[9] These regulations, together with the Three Investment Laws, the Regulations of the Three Investment Laws and, most recently, the 2005 Company Law (2013 amendment), provide a relatively complete legal environment for foreign investment practice in China.

Guiding catalogues

The Three Investment Laws and Regulations of the Three Investment Laws provide guidance on the areas and industries in which foreigners may invest.[10] In 1995, in order to provide further guidance for foreign investment and to ensure foreign investments are consistent with China's national economic and social development plans, the State Council and its responsible departments promulgated the Interim Provisions on Guiding Foreign Investment Direction (hereinafter 'Interim Provisions on Guiding Direction'). These provisions— for the first time—outlined in law 'encouraged, restricted and prohibited' industries for foreign investment (see Chinese Investment and Development

---

9   For example, Measures for Strategic Investment by Foreign Investors upon Listed Companies (promulgated on 31 December 2005); Measures for the Administration of Foreign-Capital Lease Industry (promulgated on 3 February 2005); Provisions on Mergers and Acquisitions of Domestic Enterprises by Foreign Investors (promulgated on 8 August 2006).

10 Article 3 of the Regulations of Equity Joint Ventures (promulgated 20 September 1983; revised on 15 January 1986, 21 December 1987, 22 July 2001 and 19 February 2014) stipulates that the main industries in which Chinese-foreign equity joint ventures are permitted to be established are energy development, machine manufacturing, electronics and computer industries, light industry, agriculture, tourism and service trades. Article 3 of the Law of Foreign-Capital Enterprises (promulgated on 12 April 1986; amended on 31 October 2000) stipulates, in principle, that foreign-capital enterprises shall be established to help the development of China's national economy, shall use advanced technology and equipment or market all or most of their products outside China. In addition, it also authorises the State Council to make regulations regarding this direction. Therefore, according to this authorisation, Articles 4 and 5 of the Rules of Foreign-Capital Enterprises (promulgated on 21 December 1990; revised on 12 April 2001 and 19 February 2014) outline industries that are prohibited and restricted. The prohibited industries are the press, publishing, broadcasting, television, movies, and so on; and the restricted industries are public utilities, communications and transportation, trust investment, and so on. Article 4 of the Law of Contractual Joint Ventures stipulates, in principle, that the establishment of productive contractual joint ventures that are export-oriented or technologically advanced is encouraged.

1995(7):52). The interim provisions provided that a 'Guiding Catalogue for Foreign Investment Industries' (hereinafter 'Guiding Catalogue') would be used to review and approve foreign investment applications.[11]

On 11 February 2002, the State Council promulgated the Provisions on Guiding Foreign Investment Direction (hereinafter 'Provisions on Guiding Direction'), which went into effect on 1 April 2002; the Interim Provisions on Guiding Direction ceased to be effective on the same day.[12] The Provisions on Guiding Direction provide that the Guiding Catalogue and the Catalogue of Priority Industries for Foreign Investment in the Central-Western Region (hereinafter 'Central-Western Region Catalogue') are to serve as the basic policies for reviewing, evaluating and approving foreign investment projects and enterprises.[13]

The Guiding Catalogue is a nationwide directory for foreign investments. It sets up three categories of industries—encouraged, restricted and prohibited. Those not included in the catalogue fall into a default fourth category: 'permitted' industries,[14] which allow foreign investors to participate according to the principles of the market economy. The Guiding Catalogue, since its publication in 1995, has been revised five times, in 1997, 2002, 2004, 2007 and most recently in 2011.

The Central-Western Region Catalogue was first published in 2000 for the implementation of the 'Western Region Development Strategy' of the State Council. It was meant to improve the quality of the overall economic development of central and western regions. The industries listed in this catalogue are those that are seen to have significant advantages in each province in terms of environment, natural resources, human resources, production, technology, markets, and so on, and that may enjoy preferential policies as industries that are encouraged for foreign-investment.[15] The Central-Western Region Catalogue has been revised three times—in 2004, 2008 and most recently in 2013.

Policies

The Twelfth Five-Year Plan 2011-15 regulates matters relating to foreign investment in China. It reiterates that China will continue to advance and deepen its opening-up policy, and affirms the strategic objectives of 'bringing in' and 'going out'. Part XII of the Twelfth Five-Year Plan points out that:

---

11 Interim Provisions on Guiding Foreign Investment Direction (promulgated on 20 June 1995; expired), Art. 3.2.

12 Provisions on Guiding Foreign Investment Direction (promulgated on 11 February 2002), Art. 17.

13 Ibid., Art. 3.2.

14 Ibid., Art. 4; Interim Provisions on Guiding Direction (promulgated on 20 June 1995; expired), Art. 4.

15 See Provisions on Guiding Direction (promulgated on 11 February 2002), Art. 11.

'[I]n order to sit well with the new situation of China's opening up—to equally steer imports, exports, and inbound and outbound investments—the Chinese Government must actively employ a more proactive opening up strategy, constantly explore new areas and places to open up, expand and deepen the convergence of interests for all parties, improve the mechanism to better adapt to the development of an open economy, and effectively prevent risks, so as to promote development, reform and innovation by opening up.'[16]

The Decision concerning Deepening Reforms at the third Plenum of the 18th Party congress in 2013 provides additional guidance on matters of foreign investment. It indicates that China will further promote economic reform and opening-up, reduce the limitations on foreign investment in China, promote the unification of laws regarding foreign and domestic investors, expand the opening-up of financial sectors and interior borders, accelerate the negotiation and signature of free-trade agreements and the construction of free-trade zones. These principles send a positive signal to foreign investors aiming to invest in China.

Historical development of China's foreign investment laws and policies

Geographical areas expanded

The geographical areas permitting foreign investment have been expanded progressively (see State Council 2006; State Council Information Office 2008). After 1979, China first established four special economic zones: Shenzhen, Zhuhai, Shantou and Xiamen. In 1984, China further allowed foreign investment in 14 coastal cities. Also in 1984, China established the first group of 14 national economic and technological development zones. Then in 1988, the Chinese Government approved Shandong Peninsula and Liaodong Peninsula as coastal economic development zones and approved the establishment of Hainan Special Economic Zone. In 1990, the Chinese Government opened Shanghai's Pudong District to foreign investors. In 1992, it further opened five riverside cities, four provincial capital cities in border and coastal regions and 11 inland provincial capital cities, expanding the open areas from coastal to inland provinces. Since accession to the World Trade Organisation (WTO) in 2001, China has further expanded areas in which foreign investment is allowed; now the areas are 'broadened from limited areas to all-around areas; from a trial opening

---

16 See <http://www.gov.cn/2011lh/content_1825838_13.htm>.

led by government policies, into a foreseeable opening on a legal basis; from a self-unilateral opening into a mutual opening up among WTO members' (State Council Information Office 2008).

Investment field broadened

1) Guiding Catalogue

There were three categories outlined in the Guiding Catalogue in 1995: encouraged (A), restricted (B) and prohibited. No preferential policies are referred to in this catalogue, but relevant preferential treatments are still given in accordance with the previously promulgated and implemented laws and regulations.[17] By comparing industries under each category with the amendments thereafter, it is clear that the authorities have gradually reduced restrictions on foreign investment.

The Guiding Catalogue published in 1997 added 15 industries to the 'encouraged' category (see Table 21.1). In 2002, in order to fulfil its WTO commitments, the Chinese Government for the second time revised the Guiding Catalogue. Seventy-five industries were added to the 'encouraged' category and 36 industries were removed from the 'restricted' category. There were two significant changes in this revision. First, an appendix was introduced to specify the organisational forms and equity ratios. Second, the division of the 'restricted' category into two types, A and B was abolished. In 2004, the catalogue was amended for the third time. Some industries were removed from the 'encouraged' list, including scrap-steel processing and aluminium production with a capacity of 300 000 t and over per annum. In 2007, the catalogue was amended for the fourth time. There was further opening-up in the services sectors, encouragement of foreign investment enterprises in the recycling and renewable energy industries and environmental protection, and the promotion of comprehensive utilisation of resources. In addition, the separate appendix to the Guiding Catalogue was integrated into each specific industry. By 2011, 10 years after China's accession to the WTO, the catalogue was amended for the fifth time to further expand the opening-up process. For example, financial leases and medical institutions were moved from the 'restricted' into the 'encouraged' category; 11 areas that had been subject to equity ratio limitations for foreign investment were removed.[18]

---

17 For example, product-for-export enterprises and technologically advanced enterprises could receive a reduction of or exemption from the site-use fees (except for those located in busy urban sectors of large cities) and enterprise income tax, and could receive a conditional refund of the total amount of enterprise income tax. Provisions of the State Council for the Encouragement of Foreign Investment (promulgated on 11 October 1986), Art. 4, 8–10.

18 See 'Interpretation of the Latest Catalogue for the Guidance of Foreign Investment Industries by the Development and Reform Commission and Other Departments' (<http://news.xinhuanet.com/fortune/2011-12/29/c_111334458.htm>).

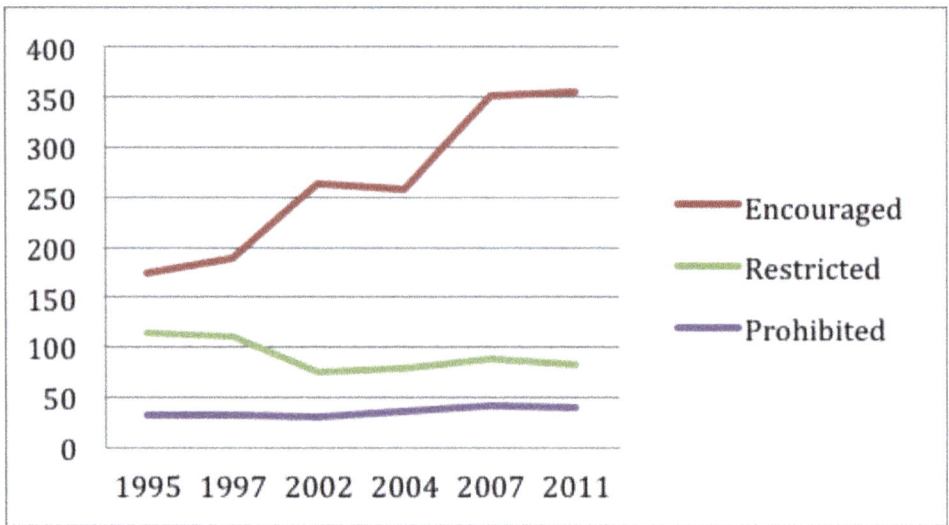

Figure 21.2 Numbers of Industries in Each Version of the Guiding Catalogue

Note: The authors analysed the data according to each version of the Guiding Catalogue since 1995. For more details, see Table 21.1.

Table 21.1 and Figure 21.2 compare the changes to industries with the previous Guiding Catalogue in the encouraged, restricted and prohibited categories. The comparison demonstrates that restricted industries are tending to be reduced and encouraged industries tending to increase. This suggests a trend towards encouraging foreign investment in China.

Table 21.1 Numbers of Industries in Each Version of the Guiding Catalogue

Version	Total	Encouraged	Restricted (A)	Restricted (B)	Subtotal of Restricted	Prohibited
1995	317	172	38	76	114	31
1997	329	187	25	86	111	31
2002	366	262	-		75	29
2004	370	257	-		78	35
2007	478	351	-		87	40
2011	476	354	-		83	39

Sources: Guiding Catalogues, published in 1995, 1997, 2002, 2004, 2007 and 2011.

2) Central-Western Region Catalogue

In June 2000, in order to implement the Western Development Strategy, the Chinese Government released the Central-Western Region Catalogue. This catalogue, together with the Guiding Catalogue, has since become the guide for directing and approving foreign investment projects and foreign invested enterprises. The industries in the Central-Western Region Catalogue are chosen according to the peculiarities of each province; some of the industries also include restrictions on management or equity share ratios.

The Central-Western Region Catalogue is organised by region. In the catalogue published in 2000, the 'Central-Western region' refers to the following provinces and areas: Shanxi, Inner Mongolia Autonomous Region, Jilin, Heilongjiang, Anhui, Jiangxi, Henan, Hubei, Hunan, Guangxi Zhuang Autonomous Region, Chongqing Municipality, Sichuan, Guizhou, Yunnan, Tibet Autonomous Region, Shaanxi, Gansu, Ningxia Autonomous Region, Qinghai, and Xinjiang Uygur Autonomous Region. In 2005, the State Council released Opinions of the General Office of the State Council on Promoting the Opening-Up of the Old Industrial Base in Northeast China, which stipulated that by the end of the transitional period of China's entry into the WTO, Liaoning Province would be added into the Central-Western Region Catalogue, rather than listing it under the Catalogue of Priority Industries for Foreign Investment in Liaoning Province. In 2009, the State Council released Several Opinions of the State Council on Promoting the Construction and Development of the Hainan International Tourism Island, which further broadened the Central-Western region by adding Hainan Province. Therefore, there are 22 regions in the current Central-Western Region Catalogue published in 2013.

Each amendment to the Central-Western Region Catalogue is accompanied by the addition of a certain number of industries; some of the newly added industries are even available for the entire Central-Western region. One key feature of the amendments is that the number of encouraged industries has increased. For example, in the Central-Western Region Catalogue published in 2000, there were only 256 industries; however, the number went up to 268 in 2005, then to 412 in 2008. The number is now 500—almost double the number in 2000. Another key feature of the amendments is that the 'encouraged' category has broadened gradually, with some of the newly added industries available for the entire region. For example, according to the Central-Western Region Catalogue published in 2004, road transportation of passengers, and construction and business operation of urban gas supply, heat supply, water supply and drainage systems were added to the original list. According to the 2008 catalogue, value-added telecommunication[19] was added. According to the 2013 catalogue, nursing homes were added. In addition, wholly foreign-owned investments are encouraged in medical institutions in all of the 22 Central-

---

19 Subject to China's WTO commitments.

Western regions in the 2013 catalogue, compared with seven regions and limited forms of Chinese-foreign equity joint ventures and Chinese-foreign contractual joint ventures in 2008.[20]

Organisational forms increased

The types of business that foreign investors could invest in have gradually expanded in successive laws and regulations. Currently, the types of business permitted include but are not limited to: Chinese-foreign equity joint ventures; foreign-capital enterprises; Chinese-foreign contractual joint ventures; branches of foreign companies; companies limited by shares with foreign investment; investment companies by foreign investment; and foreign-funded partnership enterprises. In addition, foreign investors may invest in China by way of mergers and acquisitions.

Three types of business are listed in the Three Investment Laws and the Regulations of the Three Investment Laws: Chinese-foreign equity joint ventures; foreign-capital enterprises; and Chinese-foreign contractual joint ventures. Chinese-foreign equity joint ventures are limited-liability companies incorporated in China by foreign joint ventures (such as foreign companies, enterprises, other economic organisations or individuals) and Chinese joint ventures (such as Chinese companies, enterprises or other economic organisations), according to relevant Chinese laws.[21] Foreign-capital enterprises are limited-liability companies or other forms established in China exclusively by foreign investors (such as foreign enterprises, other foreign economic organisations and individuals), according to relevant Chinese laws.[22] Chinese-foreign contractual joint ventures are limited-liability companies or other forms established in China jointly by foreign parties (such as foreign enterprises and other economic organisations or individuals) and Chinese parties (such as Chinese enterprises or other economic organisations) and operated under their joint-venture contracts, according to relevant Chinese laws.[23] These three types of business are different from each other in organisational form, legal status, distribution of profits and loss, and operation and management model, (see Table 21.2).

---

20 The authors analysed the data according to each version of the Central-Western Region Catalogue since 2000.

21 Law of Equity Joint Ventures (promulgated on 8 July 1979; amended on 4 April 1990 and 15 March 2001), Art. 1, 4.1.

22 Law of Foreign-Capital Enterprises (promulgated on 12 April 1986; amended on 31 October 2000), Art. 1–2; Rules of Foreign-Capital Enterprises (promulgated on 21 December 1990; revised on 12 April 2001 and 19 February 2014), Art. 18.

23 Law of Contractual Joint Ventures (promulgated on 13 April 1988; amended on 31 October 2000), Art. 1–2; Rules of Contractual Joint Ventures (promulgated on 4 September 1995, revised on 19 February 2014), Art. 14.

Table 21.2 Comparison of Three Types of Foreign Investment Vehicles

	Chinese-foreign equity joint ventures	Chinese-foreign contractual joint ventures	Foreign-capital enterprises
Key regulations	Law of Equity Joint Ventures; Regulations of Equity Joint Ventures	Law of Contractual Joint Ventures; Rules of Contractual Joint Ventures	Law of Foreign-Capital Enterprises; Rules of Foreign-Capital Enterprises
Contributor(s)	Foreign companies, enterprises, other economic organisations or individuals, together with Chinese companies, enterprises or other economic organisations	Foreign enterprises and other economic organisations or individuals, together with Chinese enterprises or other economic organisations	Foreign enterprises, other foreign economic organisations and individuals
Proportion of foreign investor's investment	Not less than 25 per cent of its registered capital	According to the joint-venture contract	100 per cent
Transfer of rights	Consent of the other party; the other party has a pre-emptive right if transferred to a third party	Written consent of the other party	—
Distribution of profits, risks and losses	In proportion to their contributions to the registered capital	According to the joint-venture contract	—
Organisational form(s)	Limited-liability company	Limited-liability company or other forms	Limited-liability company or other forms (if approved)
Legal status	Legal persons	Legal persons if meet relevant conditions	Legal persons if meet relevant conditions
Nationalisation or requisition of assets	Nationalisation: no◻ Requisition: no, subject to special circumstances and compensation	—	Nationalisation: no Requisition: no, subject to special circumstances and compensation
Examination and approval authorities	State's competent department in charge of foreign economic relations and trade	Department in charge of foreign economic relations and trade under the State Council or department or local government authorised by the State Council	Department under the State Council in charge of foreign economic relations and trade, or an institution authorised by the State Council
Review period (from the application received date)	Within three months	Within 45 days	Within 90 days
Operation and management	Board of directors	Board of directors or a joint managerial institution	In accordance with the approved article of association
Duration of entity	Through agreement by the parties (with approval); could be extended	Through agreement by the parties (with approval); could be extended	Foreign investor's report (with approval); could be extended

Sources: Law of Equity Joint Ventures 2001; Regulations of Equity Joint Ventures 2014; Law of Contractual Joint Ventures 2000; Rules of Contractual Joint Ventures 2014; Law of Foreign-Capital Enterprises 2000; Rules of Foreign-Capital Enterprises 2014.

As early as the 1993 Company Law, the Chinese Government had allowed foreign companies to establish a branch in China. A branch is not a legal person, but a division of a foreign company (which is a company registered and incorporated outside China in accordance with foreign laws).[24]

In 1995, the Ministry of Foreign Trade and Economic Cooperation (MOFTEC)[25] issued the Provisional Regulations of the Ministry of Foreign Trade and Economic Cooperation on Certain Issues Concerning the Establishment of Companies Limited by Shares with Foreign Investment, which allowed foreign investment to take the form of companies limited by shares. These are companies established in China by foreign and Chinese shareholders in accordance with these provisional regulations, and which bear their liabilities with their total assets. The capital stock of such companies is made up of equal value shares by all the shareholders, and the foreign shareholders may purchase and hold more than 25 per cent of the company's total registered capital, which is raised by means of promotion or public offer.[26] Following the implementation of these provisional regulations, the Ministry of Commerce (MOFCOM) promulgated more notices or circulars in order to regulate matters such as the approval of such companies' establishment or alteration, the applications to issue A shares and B shares, and so on.[27]

In 1995, MOFTEC also promulgated the Interim Provisions concerning the Establishment of Investment Companies by Foreign Investment, which allowed foreign investors to establish investment companies. Investment companies by foreign investment are limited-liability companies established exclusively by foreign investors or jointly by foreign and Chinese investors, for the purpose of direct investment. The registered capital of such companies should exceed RMB30 million.[28] In 2003, MOFCOM promulgated the Provisions on the

---

24 Company Law (promulgated on 29 December 1993; amended on 25 December 1999 and 28 August 2004; revised on 27 October 2005; and amended on 28 December 2013), Art. 199, 203.

25 The Ministry of Foreign Trade and Economic Cooperation was merged into the Ministry of Commerce in 2003.

26 Provisional Regulations of the Ministry of Foreign Trade and Economic Cooperation on Certain Issues concerning the Establishment of Companies Limited by Shares with Foreign Investment (promulgated on 10 January 1995), Art. 2, 5, 7.

27 Circular of the General Office of Ministry of Foreign Trade and Economic Cooperation on Relevant Issues of Joint Stock Companies with Foreign Investment (promulgated on 17 May 2001); Notice of the Ministry of Commerce on the Relevant Issues concerning the Conversion of Unlisted Foreign Capital Shares of Foreign-Funded Joint Stock Limited Companies into Tradable B-Shares (promulgated on 30 July 2008); Notice of the Ministry of Commerce on the Decentralisation of Approval on the Alteration of Foreign-Funded Joint-Stock Companies and Enterprises (promulgated on 5 August 2008).

28 Interim Provisions Concerning the Establishment of Investment Companies by Foreign Investors (promulgated on 4 April 1995), Art. 1, 3.

Establishment of Investment Companies by Foreign Investors,[29] which replaced the previously issued series of interpretations, notices and supplementary provisions concerning investment companies by foreign investment.[30]

In 2009, the State Council promulgated the Measures for the Administration on the Establishment of Partnership Business by Foreign Enterprises or Individuals in China, which allow foreign investors (with foreign companies and foreign individuals included) to join established Chinese partnerships, or to jointly set up partnerships with other foreign investors, Chinese companies or Chinese individuals in China.[31] In 2010, the State Administration for Industry and Commerce (SAIC) issued the Administrative Provisions on the Registration of Foreign-Funded Partnership Enterprises, amended in 2014, which regulates the establishment, modification and cancellation of foreign-funded partnerships.

In addition to the establishment of these forms of foreign investment, the Chinese Government also allowed foreign investors to invest in China by way of business restructuring, mergers and acquisitions. In 1998, the State Economic and Trade Commission (SETC) issued the Interim Provisions on State-Owned Enterprises' Utilising of Foreign Investment for Reshuffling, which allows state-owned enterprises (SOEs) to utilise foreign direct investment to acquire other domestic enterprises, to complement self-owned floating assets and to reimburse enterprise debts.[32] In 2002, the China Securities Regulatory Commission, Ministry of Finance (MOF) and SETC jointly released Issues Related to Transferring State-Owned Shares and Institutional Shares of Listed Corporations to Foreign Investors (expired), which allows the transfer of state-owned shares and institutional shares of listed companies to foreign investors, subject to the requirements of the Guiding Catalogue.[33] In the same year, SETC, MOF, SAIC and the State Administration of Foreign Exchange jointly issued the Interim Provisions on Introducing Foreign Investment to Reorganise State-Owned Enterprises, which allows the introduction of foreign investment to 'reorganise state-owned enterprises and corporate enterprises with state-owned equities (financial enterprises and listed corporations are excluded) or turn them

29 Provisions on the Establishment of Investment Companies by Foreign Investors (promulgated on 10 June 2003; revised on 13 February 2004 and 17 November 2004). This regulation had been revised twice. Supplementary Provisions to the Provisions on the Establishment of Investment Companies by Foreign Investors (promulgated on 26 May 2006) were issued.
30 For example, Supplementary Provisions on the Interim Provisions Concerning the Establishment of Investment Companies by Foreign Investors (promulgated on 24 August 1999, expired); Second Supplementary Provisions on the Interim Provisions Concerning the Establishment of Investment Companies by Foreign Investors (promulgated on 31 May 2001, expired).
31 Measures for the Administration on the Establishment of Partnership Business by Foreign Enterprises or Individuals in China (promulgated on 25 November 2009), Art. 1–2, 12.
32 Interim Provisions on State-Owned Enterprises' Utilising Foreign Investment for Reshuffling 1998 (promulgated on 14 September 1998), Art. 2.
33 Issues Related to Transferring State-Owned Shares and Institutional Shares of Listed Corporations to Foreign Investors 2002 (promulgated on 1 November 2002; expired), Art. 2.

into corporations with foreign investment'.[34] Specifically, foreign investment could be introduced to reorganise SOEs into foreign-invested enterprises by transferring equity to foreign investors, increasing shares, and selling all or major assets of the SOE to foreign investors.[35]

In 2003, MOFTEC and four other ministries issued the Interim Provisions on Mergers and Acquisitions of Domestic Enterprises by Foreign Investors, which were revised by the MOFCOM in 2006 by issuing the Provisions on Mergers and Acquisitions of Domestic Enterprises by Foreign Investors (hereinafter 'Provisions on M&A by Foreign Investors').[36] In 2009, in order to ensure the Interim Provisions on Mergers and Acquisitions of Domestic Enterprises by Foreign Investors sat well with the Anti-Monopoly Law of the People's Republic of China and the Provisions of the State Council on Standards for Declaration of Concentration of Business Operators, the Provisions on M&A by Foreign Investors were amended by MOFCOM.

Approval process improved

The Three Investment Laws are essential in regulating the review of foreign investment in China. Before these laws, local approval measures were the main source of regulations, but they were scattered and inconsistent.[37] After the introduction of the Three Investment Laws, foreign investment review processes in China have been unified and standardised.

The review and approval of foreign investment in China can be classified into two categories: approval before establishment and approval after establishment. Approval before establishment mainly refers to the article of association and/or agreement approval by MOFCOM, the provincial commerce department and local departments authorised by the State Council. Approval after establishment refers to the approval of such matters as major or substantial changes, equity transfer contracts and corporate liquidation.

---

34 Provisions on Introducing Foreign Investment to Reorganise State-Owned Enterprises (promulgated on 8 November 2002), Art. 2.

35 Ibid, Art. 3.

36 Provisions on Mergers and Acquisitions of Domestic Enterprises by Foreign Investors (promulgated on 8 August 2006; revised on 22 June 2009).

37 For example, Implementing Measures for the Regulations of Shanghai Municipality on Discussion and Examination and Approval Procedures of the Establishment of Chinese-Foreign Equity Joint Ventures and Foreign Enterprises (promulgated on 1 July 1984; expired).

According to the Three Investment Laws, review and approval of foreign investment in China is the responsibility of MOFCOM, the provincial commerce departments and the local authorities authorised by the State Council.[38] In recent years, MOFCOM has issued a series of regulations to gradually decentralise and allow lower-level departments to make decisions on foreign investment.[39] Now it reviews and approves only some foreign investment applications. The latest decentralisation was in 2010, referred to as the Notice of the Ministry of Commerce on Decentralising the Examination and Approval Power for Foreign Investment. According to the notice, the approval authorities are diversified according to the categories in the Guiding Catalogue and the value of investment capital involved.[40]

Super-national treatment phased out

In the early years of economic reform and opening-up, in order to attract foreign investment, the Chinese Government gave foreign-invested entities specified super-national treatments regarding taxation and land use. After 1994, the Chinese Government began unifying the taxation system regarding domestic-invested and foreign-invested entities. By enriching implementation regulations and rules,[41] the Government gradually unified different taxation categories: value-added tax, consumption tax, business tax, and urban and township land-use tax. On 1 December 2010, the super-national treatment for foreign investment, in terms of preferential taxation treatment ended with the unification of the urban maintenance and construction taxes and educational surcharges.

---

38 See Law of Foreign-Capital Enterprises (promulgated on 12 April 1986; amended on 31 October 2000), Art. 6; Law of Contractual Joint Ventures (promulgated on 13 April 1988; amended on 31 October 2000), Art. 5; Law of Equity Joint Ventures (promulgated on 8 July 1979; amended on 4 April 1990 and 15 March 2001), Art. 3.

39 For example, Notice of the Ministry of Commerce on the Decentralisation of Approval on the Alteration of Foreign-Funded Joint-Stock Companies and Enterprises (promulgated on 5 August 2008); Notice of the Ministry of Commerce on Further Simplifying and Regulating the Foreign Investment Administrative Licensing Issues (promulgated on 26 August 2008); Notice of the Ministry of Commerce on Decentralising the Examination and Approval Power for Foreign Investment (promulgated on 10 June 2010).

40 Notice of the Ministry of Commerce on Decentralising the Examination and Approval Power for Foreign Investment (promulgated on 10 June 2010), Art. 1–6.

41 The main unification of the taxation regime happened between 2006 and 2010. For example: 1) Decision of the Standing Committee of the National People's Congress concerning the Application of Interim Regulations on Such Taxes as Value-Added Tax, Consumption Tax and Business Tax to Enterprises with Foreign Investment and Foreign Enterprises (promulgated on 29 December 1993); 2) Enterprise Income Tax Law of the People's Republic of China (promulgated on 16 March 2007); 3) Notice of the State Council on Extending the Urban Maintenance and Construction Tax and Educational Surcharges from Chinese to Foreign-Funded Enterprises and Citizens (promulgated on 18 October 2010).

Sub-national treatment reduced

Before China's accession to the WTO, the Chinese Government also applied some sub-national treatments to foreign-invested entities, alongside major super-national treatments. For example, higher requirements on capital and local content were imposed on foreign-invested entities. The former required that the capital of foreign investment by shares should be higher than the required amount specified in the Company Law;[42] and the latter required the foreign-invested entities to give first priority to purchasing material (such as required raw and processed material, fuel, parts and auxiliary equipment) in China.[43] After China's accession to the WTO, the aforementioned provisions were gradually eliminated in order to fulfil China's WTO commitments.

Further reform: China (Shanghai) Pilot Free Trade Zone

After China fully opened economically, it began to explore new ways of deepening the market economy. After the setting up of the Shanghai Waigaoqiao Free Trade Zone in 1990, the State Council approved the establishment of some types of special Customs-supervised bonded zones, such as bonded areas,[44]

---

42 Article 7 of the Provisional Regulations of the Ministry of Foreign Trade and Economic Cooperation on Certain Issues concerning the Establishment of Companies Limited by Shares with Foreign Investment (promulgated on 10 January 1995) stipulates that '[r]egistered capital of a company shall be the total capital stock recorded with registering departments. The registered capital of a company shall be at least RMB30 million.' According to Article 78.2 of the Company Law 1993, however, '[t]he minimum amount of registered capital of a joint stock company limited shall be RMB10 million. Requirements for the minimum amount of the registered capital of a joint stock company limited to be higher than the above amount are provided for in separate laws or administrative decrees.' After the amendment of the Company Law 2005 in 2013, the registered capital for stock companies limited by shares was cancelled.

43 For example, Law of Foreign-Capital Enterprises (promulgated on 12 April 1986; amended on 31 October 2000), Art. 15; Law of Equity Joint Ventures (promulgated on 8 July 1979; amended on 4 April 1990 and 15 March 2001), Art. 9.2; Law of Contractual Joint Ventures (promulgated on 13 April 1988; amended on 31 October 2000), Art. 9.2.

44 A bonded area refers to special areas in China under the control of the Customs authorities, which are established upon approval by the State Council. The area is isolated, according to the supervision requirements of Customs, from other areas in the territory of the People's Republic of China. See Procedures on Customs Control over Bonded Areas (promulgated on 1 August 1997), Art. 2–3.

export processing zones,[45] bonded logistics centres,[46] bonded logistics parks,[47] bonded port areas[48] and comprehensive bonded zones.[49] On 29 September 2013, the China (Shanghai) Pilot Free Trade Zone (PFTZ) came into operation, which marked a milestone in China's economic reform.[50]

PFTZ aims to accumulate experience in the next two to three years in boosting China's reform and opening-up within new legal structures compatible with international trade and investment standards. Pilot programs will be launched in this zone to transform the functions of government, the opening-up of financial services, the reform of the approval process, and the operation of foreign investment review systems. The aims of the PFTZ can be specified in more detail as follows.

---

45 An export processing zone is a certain area as approved by Customs within the territory of China in which to undertake export processing, which is under close supervision by Customs. See Interim Measures for the Administration of Processing Trade in Export Processing Zones (promulgated on 22 November 2005), Art. 2–3; Interim Measures of the General Administration of Customs of the People's Republic of China for the Supervision over Export Processing Zones (promulgated on 24 May 2000; revised on 2 September 2003), Art. 3–4.

46 Bonded logistics centres could be classified into bonded logistics centres (type A) and bonded logistics centres (type B). The former are places under Customs surveillance as approved by the General Administration of Customs, which are operated by legal enterprises within the territory of China to undertake business operations of bonded warehousing logistics. The latter refers to places under concentrated surveillance as approved by the General Administration of Customs, which are operated by a Chinese domestic enterprise with legal status and where many enterprises enter to undertake the business operations of bonded logistics warehousing. See Interim Measures for the Administration of Bonded Logistics Centres (Type A) by the General Administration of Customs of the People's Republic of China (promulgated on 23 June 2005), Art. 2; Interim Measures for the Administration of Bonded Logistics Centres (Type B) by the Customs of the People's Republic of China (promulgated on 23 June 2005), Art. 2.

47 A bonded logistics park is a special zone under Customs supervision, which is established within the planning areas of a bonded zone or a special port section adjacent to the bonded zone for the development of modern international logistics upon the approval of the State Council. See the People's Republic of China Customs Bonded Logistics Park Management Measures (promulgated on 28 November 2005), Art. 2.

48 A bonded port area is an area under special Customs supervision, which has the functions of a port for logistics, processing and so on, and is established within the port areas opened to the outside by the state and specific areas adjacent upon approval by the State Council. Such areas are isolated from other areas within the Customs territory of the People's Republic of China by checkpoints, fences, video surveillance systems and other facilities that meet the requirements for Customs supervision. See Interim Measures of the Customs of the People's Republic of China for the Administration of Bonded Port Areas (promulgated on 3 September 2007; amended on 15 March 2010), Art. 2, 4.

49 Currently, there is no specific regulation on comprehensive bonded zones. According to the State Council's announcements on the establishment of the Tianjin Binhai Comprehensive Bonded Zones, Beijing Tianzhu Comprehensive Bonded Zones and Haikou Comprehensive Bonded Zones, the functions, tax policies and foreign exchange policies of such zones are subject to the State Council's reply on the establishment of the Yangshan Bonded Port Area. See the State Council's Reply on the Establishment of Tianjin Binhai Comprehensive Bonded Zones (issued on 10 March 2008); the State Council's Reply on the Establishment of Beijing Tianzhu Comprehensive Bonded Zones (issued on 23 July 2008); and the State Council's Reply on the Establishment of Haikou Comprehensive Bonded Zones (issued on 22 December 2008).

50 Pilot Free Trade Zone (<http://www.shftz.gov.cn/WebViewPublic/NewsPaper.aspx?new=1>).

1. To explore protocols of cooperation, leading to a one-stop service, integrated review and approval, and efficient operation, and to perfect an information disclosure system with the participation of foreign investors and compatible with international rules.

2. To broaden the opening-up of the service sectors. Special measures will be imposed on 18 service sectors, such as finance, transportation, commerce and trade, professional, cultural and public services. Special measures refer to the suspension or cancellation of restrictions such as requirements concerning the qualification of investors, limitations on foreign participation, restrictions concerning business scope, and so on.

3. To implement a pre-entry national treatment to foreign investors and a 'Negative List' mechanism within PFTZ. For areas that are not in the negative list, foreign and domestic investors will receive the same treatment, by following filing procedures instead of approval requirements (with the exception of areas specifically defined by the State Council), and the Shanghai Municipal People's Government will be in charge of the project filing procedures.

4. To develop shipping-related industries such as shipping finance, international shipping, international ship management, and international ship brokerage, to simplify the application process permitting international shipping and to create a more efficient ship registration system.

5. To enhance the development of financial services by allowing certain foreign-invested financial institutions to incorporate foreign-invested and Chinese-foreign equity joint-venture banks in PFTZ; gradually permitting foreign-incorporated entities to participate in commodity futures trading; supporting equity escrow institutions to establish comprehensive financial platforms in the zone, and encouraging the RMB reinsurance business.

6. To strengthen protection by enhancing the regulatory system, and by terminating or modifying current laws and regulations.

7. To implement preferable policies on income tax, pilot policies of export tax refund for qualified financial leasing businesses and consumption taxes, so as to promote investment.[51]

---

51 Framework Plan for the China (Shanghai) Pilot Free Trade Zone [中国（上海）自由贸易试验区总体方案] (<http://www.shftz.gov.cn/WebViewPublic/item_page.aspx?newsid=635158957941988294&coltype=8>).

Foreign investment laws and policies in China: current issues

The laws and regulations regarding foreign investments in China have been gradually improved, and national treatment of foreign investors is increasing in prevalence. Notwithstanding all the accomplishments, certain issues remain to be resolved.

Cumbersome and inconsistent legislation

Foreign investment in China is regulated by the Three Investment Laws and the Regulations of the Three Investment Laws, together with the Company Law and hundreds of administrative regulations. The Three Investment Laws each cover one type of foreign investment entity, making the legal system very complicated. The complexity is demonstrated in the following ways (Qiu 2013). First, the separate settings of the Three Investment Laws are a waste of legislative resources, as more than half of the regulations are similar to one another and therefore could be combined. In addition, the regulations lack coordination, meaning different types of foreign-invested entities are treated differently (for example, there are different approval periods, and different rules regarding the board of directors). Second, the Three Investment Laws are not sophisticated enough to include many essential provisions, leading to unnecessary delegated agencies and delegated regulations and complexity of regulations, thus making it difficult to thoroughly understand the content of China's foreign investment laws. Third, the numerous local rules trump higher legal authorities, making it essential to understand the local regulations in addition to the statutes and administrative regulations when investing in China. And fourth, certain provisions in the Three Investment Laws are in conflict with the Company Law.

Ambiguous approval criteria

The criteria that can be used to block a foreign investment are ambiguous.[52] Operationally, it is impossible for foreign investors to predict the results of their proposals under China's foreign investment approval system, which puts them in a difficult situation. For example, Article 9 of the Rules of Contractual Joint Ventures (2014) stipulates that:

---

52 It is, however, normal practice for the criteria to approve foreign investment to be vague. For example, in Australia's *Foreign Acquisitions and Takeovers Act 1975*, 'national interest' is adopted as a criterion; in the United States' *Foreign Investment and National Security Act* of 2007, 'national security' is followed in the review process; and in Canada's *Investment Canada Act 1985*, 'national security' is used as a criterion.

Under any of the following circumstances, approval will not be granted to an applicant for establishment of a contractual joint venture: (1) Harming state sovereignty or social public interests; (2) Endangering state safety; (3) Causing pollution to the environment; (4) Other circumstances which violate the law, administrative regulations or state industrial policies.

Article 4 of the Regulations of Equity Joint Ventures (2014) similarly stipulates that:

Applications to establish joint ventures shall not be granted approval if the project involves any of the following conditions: (1) detriment to China's sovereignty; (2) violation of the Chinese law; (3) nonconformity with the requirements of the development of China's national economy; (4) environmental pollution; (5) obvious inequity in the agreements, contracts and articles of association signed impairing the rights and interests of one party.

Article 5 of the Rules of Foreign-Capital Enterprises (2014) also stipulates that:

No application for the establishment of a foreign-capital enterprise shall be approved if the proposed enterprise is under any of the following circumstances: (1) injuring China's sovereignty or social and public interests; (2) endangering China's national security; (3) in violation of Chinese laws and regulations; (4) not in keeping with the requirements of China's national economic development; (5) may result in environmental pollution.

Restricted investment industries

Even though the industries opened to foreign investment have been greatly broadened, some industries are still restricted, or even prohibited from foreign investment. According to the latest Guiding Catalogue published in 2011, 83 industries under the restricted category allow foreign investment, subject to certain conditions. For example, foreign investors can invest in the area of exploration and mining of special and scarce coals, but in these activities the Chinese party shall hold the majority of shares. Foreign investors can invest in the development of real estate, but such investment should take the form of equity joint ventures or contractual joint ventures. These conditions have limited the ability of foreign investors control to the invested entity. Thirty nine areas are still prohibited from foreign investors.

Undefined compensation standards in requisition

In the case of requisition of foreign-invested entities, the compensation standard is ambiguous. For example, Article 2.3 of the Law of Equity Joint Ventures (2001) prescribes that '[t]he State shall not nationalize or requisition any equity joint venture. Under special circumstances, when public interests require, equity joint ventures may be requisitioned by following legal procedures and appropriate compensation shall be made.' Similarly, Article 5 of the Law of Foreign-Capital Enterprises (2000) prescribes that '[t]he State does not nationalise or requisition any enterprise with foreign capital. However, under special circumstances when public interests require, enterprises with foreign capital may be requisitioned through legal procedures and appropriate compensation shall be made.' It is clear that Chinese-foreign equity joint ventures and foreign-capital enterprises in China are principally beyond the scope of requisition by the Chinese Government. In some special circumstances, however, when required by the public interest, requisition could be applied, subject to legal procedures and appropriate compensation. The problem is that the standard of appropriate compensation in China is not specified.

Conclusion

Since 1978, economic reform has transformed China from a centrally planned closed system to an open and modern market economy. Chinese foreign investment laws and policies have also gone through steady improvements—from nothing to something, from good to better. Overtime, Chinese foreign investment laws and policies promote an increase in the areas, industries forms in which foreign investment is permitted, and approval processes have been improved towards prevalence of national treatment. Major decisions regarding the reform and opening-up, especially China's decision to establish a socialist market economy and to join the WTO, have played significant roles in the development of China's foreign investment legislation.

China's foreign investment laws now comprise the Three Investment Laws as the basic laws, the Company Law as the general law, supplemented by hundreds of administrative and local regulations. Reform is still needed on coordinating and reducing complexity of foreign investment laws and regulations, reducing ambiguity of foreign investment approval criteria, eliminating restrictions on investment in some industries, and defining compensation standards in the case of requisition. Thus, China still has some distance to travel in order to make its foreign investment laws becoming an integral part of the system of rules of law, which China is endeavouring to establish.

References

Chinese Investment and Development (1995), 'A major initiative to further opening up: a reply on the Interim Provisions on Guiding Foreign Investment Direction by Senior Officials of National Planning Commission', *Chinese Investment and Development* 7: 52.

Ministry of Commerce (MOFCOM) (2014), Regular press conference, 16 January 2014. Available from <http://www.mofcom.gov.cn/article/difang/henan/201401/20140100462805.shtml>.

National Bureau of Statistics (NBS) (2013), National data, Beijing: NBS. Available from <http://data.stats.gov.cn/workspace/index?m=hgnd>

Qiu, R. (2013), 'Conflicts and coordination in China's foreign investment laws.' Available from <http://www.civillaw.com.cn/article/default.asp?id=57721>.

State Council (2006), *Eleventh Plan for Economic and Social Development of the National Economic and Technological Development Zone 2006*, Beijing: State Council.

State Council Information Office (2008), *Thirty Years of Reform and Opening Up: Major Achievements of Foreign Direct Investment in China*, Beijing: State Council Information Office. Available from <http://www.scio.gov.cn/zt2008/gg30/03/200812/t250340.htm>.

Appendix Table 21.1 Realised Foreign Capital into China, 1983–2013

Year	Realised foreign capital into China ($ million)	Year	Realised foreign capital into China ($ million)	Year	Realised foreign capital into China ($ million)
1983	2 260	1994	43 213	2005	63 805
1984	2 870	1995	48 133	2006	67 076
1985	4 760	1996	54 805	2007	78 339
1986	7 628	1997	64 408	2008	95 253
1987	8 452	1998	58 557	2009	91 804
1988	10 226	1999	52 659	2010	108 821
1989	10 060	2000	59 356	2011	117 698
1990	10 289	2001	49 672	2012	113 294
1991	11 554	2002	55 011	2013	117 586
1992	19 203	2003	56 140		
1993	38 960	2004	64 072		

Sources: NBS (2013); MOFCOM (2014).

Index

absorptive capability 411, 420, 424, 522

advanced economies 3, 5, 12, 21, 23, 108, 112, 116, 161, 166, 179, 180, 234, 235, 316, 320, 507, 520, 524

agglomeration 198, 460

Agreement on Trade-Related Aspects of Intellectual Property Rights (TRIPS) 509, 510, 511, 519, 521, 522, 525

agricultural
    collectives 78, 79
    employment 20, 138, 152, 166, 182, 344n.2, 380, 383, 384, 399–401, 402
    land 91, 335, 336, 337, 351, 352, 353, 354, 361, 362, 366, 367, 400
    output 57, 84, 335
    production 79, 176, 182, 199, 200, 201, 236, 252, 336, 357, 399, 400, 498, 499, 510
    productivity 199, 380, 385, 386, 400
    subsidies 394–5
    see also non-agricultural

Agricultural Bank of China 82

Agricultural Development Bank of China 273n.22

agriculture 20, 57, 78, 82, 88, 117, 148, 167, 170, 178, 194, 198, 199, 270, 335, 339, 353, 354, 380, 386, 416, 453, 457, 509, 534n.10

Anhui 340, 341, 456, 461, 464, 468, 539

appreciation 20, 123, 166, 167, 171, 173, 184, 262, 274, 276, 280, 281, 298, 299, 311, 319, 327, 348, 354, 362n.13, 366, 368, 370, 371, 374

Argentina 28, 136, 315

Asia 14, 107, 166, 247, 300, 304, 326, 327, 456, 458

Asian Development Bank (ADB) 146

Asian financial crisis 4, 8, 63, 84, 153, 237, 238, 239, 267, 270, 273, 274, 276, 280, 285, 454

asymmetric liberalisation, *see* liberalisation—asymmetric

Australia 208, 221, 223, 251–88, 487, 488, 489, 491, 492, 494, 549n.52
    see also Reserve Bank of Australia

Australian dollar 254, 259, 260, 262, 263, 264, 265, 267, 269, 270, 286

Austria 60

'backwardness' 108, 234, 340n.1, 457, 459

balance of payments 165, 173, 176, 185, 245

Balassa index 142

Balassa–Samuelson 166, 327

bankruptcy 85, 245, 248, 317n.1, 321, 398

bank 234, 240, 251–88, 301, 310, 320, 321, 323–6, 329, 338
    assets 234, 257, 296, 307
    balance sheets 252, 253, 261, 277
    bonds 307n.6, 308
    Chinese 115, 234, 240, 279, 286, 548
    commercial 17, 82, 89, 90, 95, 163, 172n.17, 231, 233, 235, 244–5, 249, 253, 271, 277, 286, 320, 321, 483
    crisis 185, 238, 270, 272–3, 324
    deposits 90, 110, 115, 124, 233, 256, 274
    deregulation 252, 258, 259, 261, 264, 271, 274, 277, 284, 319
    flows 19, 307, 308, 311
    foreign 89, 237, 259, 267, 328
    inflows 296
    interbank market 234, 237, 270, 273, 274, 275, 277, 302
    loans 58, 62, 95, 96, 111n.5, 115, 237–8, 240, 256, 257n.5, 259, 271, 274, 277, 316, 317–18, 350–1, 370–1, 500, 501
    reform 17, 18, 82, 234
    regulation 251, 256, 261, 267–8, 271, 276, 281, 282, 286
    sector 18, 57, 119, 234, 235, 236, 252, 253, 285, 319

www.ingramcontent.com/pod-product-compliance
Lightning Source LLC
Chambersburg PA
CBHW041429270326
41932CB00033B/3405